THE SCIENCE FICTIONARY

THE SCIENCE FICTIONARY

An A-Z Guide to the World of
SF Authors, Films, & TV Shows

ED NAHA

SEAVIEW BOOKS

NEW YORK

for my family

Library of Congress Cataloging in Publication Data

Naha, Ed.
    The science fictionary.

    1. Science fiction—Dictionaries.   I. Title.
P96.S34N3   1980   809.3'.003   80–5195
ISBN 0-87223-619-6

Designed by Tere LoPrete

CONTENTS

ACKNOWLEDGMENTS

The author would like to thank, in amazingly random order, the following people for their help, pity, and coffee: Joyce Frommer, Diana Price, Anne Kostick, Connie Ennis, Robin Snelson, Robert Mecoy, Barbara Krasnoff, Bob Woods (thanx for the tauntaun), Craig Miller of Lucasfilm, Mary Dykema of Morale Inc., Larry Steinfeld of AIP, Scott Yoselow of AFD, Mick Garris of Avco Embassy, Gene Roddenberry, Susan Sackett, Maggie Geoghegan of Paramount, Steven Spielberg, Gail Siemers, Karen Renfroe, Robert Sheckley, Fred Pohl, George Pal, Harlan Ellison, George Lucas, Gary Kurtz, Brian Poole of 20th, absolutely nobody at Warners, Frank Petraglia and Phil Castanza at Disney, Vic Ghidalia at ABC-TV, Forrest J. Ackerman, Jane Covner at New World, Roger Corman, Pat Hill, Alex Gordon, Bert I. Gordon, Bill Van Assen, Ray Bradbury, Jeff Sillifant, Harry Orwell, Roscoe Pound, Susan Adamo, Robert Martin, Laura O'Brien, and select members of the House of Pain.

PREFACE

Science fiction is a tricky subject to play around with. Really. At its best, science fiction can be invigorating, instructive, entertaining, and thought-provoking. At its worst, however, it can induce more groans-per-minute than the most ineptly plotted gothic novel or spaghetti Western.

Science fiction fans are a rather erratic cadre to contend with as well, encompassing as they do every facet of society, from far-thinking futurists and intellectually starved closet-philosophers to out-and-out nerds.

Keeping all this tantalizing ambiguity in mind, prepare yourself for *The Science Fictionary.*

It is a book about science fiction in three of its most popular forms: literature, cinema, and television. It doesn't pretend to be the definitive work on the genre as an art form, the Rosetta stone of heavy thinking and lofty ideals. Rather, it is a fun yet detailed reference book—a guide to some of the best (and worst) films, television presentations, authors, and publications ever to arise from the realm of science fiction.

Some people will find all of their favorite sf people present and accounted for and will walk happily away from this tome whistling the theme song from *Star Trek.* Others will not find their fave raves herewith and will return to their local book shops with phasers set on "maim." As I mentioned before, science fictiondom is fraught with ofttimes exciting eclecticism.

Within *The Science Fictionary*'s simple, alphabetized format, you can discover the cast and credits of *2001: A Space Odyssey,* the year that *Captain Video* first zoomed across television screens, the name of Isaac Asimov's first sf story, and how many Oscars *Star Wars* won.

What you won't find are the answers to the dozens of subjective questions that plague the genre today:

Who is the real father of science fiction, Verne or Wells?

Which was better, *Star Trek* or *Space: 1999*?

Was Edgar Rice Burroughs's work science fiction or science fantasy?

Is Harlan Ellison still angry?

Alas, this book doesn't deal in opinions. For the most part, it deals with facts. And there is a very logical reason for this seemingly narrow-minded editorial point of view. If you ask six sf fans what science fiction is, chances are good to excellent that you will get at least seven answers. *Webster's Third New International Dictionary* defines the genre as "fiction dealing principally with the impact of actual or imagined science upon society or individuals; broadly: literary fantasy including a scientific factor as an essential orienting component."

Now, this definition will no doubt please some sf fans out there. It also will, no doubt, enrage others who see science fiction as the exclusive home of hard science and not the terrain of fantasy. No wookiees in *their* space operas, please. Told you it was a tricky subject to fool with. In an effort to minimize the angst level of readers, nowhere in this book is there a comparison between Ray Bradbury and Arthur C. Clarke, Mr. Spock and *The Man from Atlantis*, or any of the various versions of *Mysterious Island*.

For the record, however, Fred Pohl, in an interview with this author a few years ago, came up with a rather nice, off-the-cuff definition of science fiction. "A really good science fiction story," he said, "makes you think thoughts you never would have thought of any other way. It's not just the entertainment you get when you're reading it. When you're done, it leaves concepts in your brain that make you wonder about 'what might happen *if* . . . '"

Keeping that definition in mind, here is an sf fan's guide to some of the wildest, weirdest, and most wonderful sf offerings and personalities in the world.

Ed Naha

A BRIEF NOTE ON THE TEXT

The Science Fictionary is written entirely in English. (Sorry to disappoint all of you Serbo-Croatian fans out there, but we all have our priorities.)

It is divided into three main sections: film, television, and literature. Since no one really agrees as to just when or where science fiction first appeared, here are a few points to consider while thumbing through each section.

In terms of the biographical listing of authors, *The Science Fictionary* offers sketches of the crème de la crème. Now, some sf scholars maintain that the genre had its beginnings in such early works as Homer's *Iliad* and *Odyssey*, Plato's *Republic*, and Virgil's *Aeneid*. Be forewarned: these authors are not to be found in the biographical section—although Mary Shelley, Poe, and Arthur Conan Doyle are. The literary section concentrates on the best-known exponents of sf literature, those most widely read. In addition, in other sections of the book, a checklist of the major sf publications, literary themes, and literary awards and award winners appears.

Science fiction on film is a lot less hazardous to pinpoint in terms of a beginning. It is known, for example, that Thomas Alva Edison lensed a short cinematic version of Shelley's *Frankenstein* a century or so ago and that the French filmmaker Méliès mixed his visual magic with science-fictional themes in the embryonic years of motion picturedom as well. During the moving picture industry's silent era, sf imagery was mixed in everyday, nonfuturistic story lines because of its sheer visual impact. Invaders from space, flying automobiles, and crazy serums and inventions appeared regularly during those early days, and their appearances are faithfully chronicled in this book. Over 1,000 film entries are listed alphabetically in this book, spanning a century of celluloid and including everything from *A Trip to the Moon* to *Star Trek—The Motion Picture*.

Television is also well represented, with sf series, specials, made-for-TV movies, and kid-vid offerings selected from nearly four decades of video broadcasting.

As sort of an insightful, lighthearted "extra," the book also offers a handful of useful quotes from some of the genre's more colorful figures in these three aforementioned areas, as well as snippets of dialogue from films that no moviegoer will ever forget, no matter how hard he or she tries.

When perusing this book, one of the main points to remember is that, along with its philosophical/sociological commentary and scientific extrapolations, science fiction at its best offers the reader and/or viewer a sense of wonder, a sense of fun. It is the author's hope that *The Science Fictionary,* in cataloguing some of the genre's most famous and infamous moments, allows that sense of wonder, of dazzlement, to shine through.

CROSS-REFERENCES

SMALL CAPITALS are used to indicate that a film, TV program, or author mentioned in the text can also be found elsewhere in the book under its own entry.

ABBREVIATIONS

Film Companies

AA	Allied Artists
AIP, AIT	American International Pictures/Television
MGM	Metro-Goldwyn-Mayer
UA	United Artists
WB	Warner Brothers

Magazines

AS	*Amazing Stories*
ASF	*Astounding Science-Fiction/Analog*
F&SF	*The Magazine of Fantasy and Science Fiction*

Miscellaneous

b/w	black and white
G.B.	Great Britain
sf	science fiction

FILMS

ABBOTT AND COSTELLO GO TO MARS
Universal (1953). B/w, 77 mins.

Comedic shtick takes on 1950s sf clichés in this slapstick excursion into not-so-deep space. Two lovable but decidedly inept pals, Orville and Lester (Lou Costello and Bud Abbott), accidentally blast off in a ready-for-action rocket ship. The vessel crash-lands on Venus, a planet populated by breathtaking Amazon beauties who, naturally, hate men. The Venusians (actually a bevy of lovelies culled from that year's Miss Universe pageant), under the orders of ruler Queen Alura (Mari Blanchard), keep Orville and Lester under close guard. Although the two hapless astronauts try their best to prove the essential goodness of the male species, their task is complicated somewhat by the presence of two stowaway ex-convicts (Jack Kruschen and Horace McMahon), who have evidently memorized every James Cagney film ever made. Eventually Bud and Lou win over the population via some spacey smooching, and when they finally blast off for the return trip to Earth, they are pursued by a gaggle of interplanetary paramours.

PRODUCER: Howard Christie. DIRECTOR: Charles Lamont. SCREENPLAY: John Grant and D. D. Beauchamp, from a story by Beauchamp and Christie. MUSICAL DIRECTOR: Joseph Gershenson. SPECIAL EFFECTS: David Horsley.

SUPPORTING PLAYERS: Robert Paige, Martha Hyer, Joe Kirk.

ABBOTT AND COSTELLO MEET DR. JEKYLL AND MR. HYDE
Universal (1953). B/w, 76 mins.

Two dim-witted American detectives (Bud Abbott and Lou Costello) encounter suave Dr. Jekyll (Boris Karloff) and his alter ego, Mr. Hyde (Karloff and stuntman Eddie Parker).

PRODUCER: Howard Christie. DIRECTOR: Charles Lamont. SCREENPLAY: Leo Loeb and John Grant, from a story by Sidney Fields and Grant Garrett. MAKEUP: Bud Westmore. CINEMATOGRAPHY: George Robinson. SPECIAL EFFECTS: David S. Horsley. MUSICAL DIRECTOR: Joseph Gershenson.

SUPPORTING PLAYERS: Helen Westcott, Craig Stevens, John Dierkes, Reginald Denny.

Universal

Abbot and Costello Meet Dr. Jekyll and Mr. Hyde

ABBOTT AND COSTELLO MEET FRANKENSTEIN
Universal (1948). B/w, 83 mins.

Two moving-men (Bud Abbott and Lou Costello) are delivering crates to a wax museum when they discover the bodies of Count Dracula (Bela Lugosi) and the Frankenstein monster (Glen Strange). Dracula escapes to a nearby castle, where he plans to revive the monster . . . with the help of the perfect simpleton brain (which, in turn, belongs to the perfect simpleton, Lou). Out to save the day is Larry Talbot (Lon Chaney, Jr.), who wants to destroy Dracula and the monster in between bouts of lycanthropy. Lou is kidnapped and readied for the operation. Larry comes to the rescue during a night of the full moon, turns into a werewolf, and . . . take it from there.

PRODUCER: Robert Arthur. DIRECTOR: Charles T. Barton. SCREENPLAY: John Grant, Frederic I. Rinaldo, Robert Lees. ART DIRECTORS: Bernard Herzbrun, Hilyard Brown. MAKEUP: Bud Westmore. CINEMATOGRAPHY: Charles Van Enger. SPECIAL EFFECTS: David S. Horsley, Jerome H. Ash. MUSIC: Frank Skinner.

SUPPORTING PLAYERS: Lenore Aubert, Frank Ferguson, Jane Randolph, and Vincent Price as the Invisible Man.

ABBOTT AND COSTELLO MEET THE INVISIBLE MAN
Universal (1950). B/w, 82 mins.

A young boxer (Arthur Franz) is unjustly accused of murder. Two sympathetic detectives (Bud Abbott and Lou Costello) get hold of H. G. WELLS's famous invisibility formula and dose the fighter, thus allowing him to track down the real killers. The only problem: the formula turns its invisible host mad after a prolonged period of time.

PRODUCER: Howard Christie. DIRECTOR: Charles Lamont. SCREENPLAY: Frederic L. Rinaldo, John Grant, and Robert Lees, based on a story by Hugh Wedlock, Jr., and Howard Snyder. ART DIRECTORS: Bernard Herzbrun, Richard Riedel. MAKEUP: Bud Westmore. CINEMATOGRAPHY: George Robinson. SPECIAL EFFECTS: David S. Horsley.

SUPPORTING PLAYERS: Nancy Guild, Sheldon Leonard, William Frawley, Gavin Muir.

ABOMINABLE DR. PHIBES, THE
AIP (1971). Color, 94 mins.

Dr. Anton Phibes (Vincent Price), a rich scientific genius who once had entertained audiences in the world's vaudeville theaters with his inventive automated creations, begins a bizarre vendetta against the members of a surgical team who had served when his

wife, Victoria (Caroline Munro), died on the operating table. Borrowing a page from the Bible, he determines that each malefactor will be dispatched to his or her respective Valhalla by one of the ten curses that, according to the Old Testament, were visited on the Pharaoh.

The Abominable Dr. Phibes

Phibes plans his revenge well from his mechanical underground lair deep beneath London. No longer capable of conventional speech (he lost his face and, ergo, his mouth in an auto accident that occurred during a mad rush to his wife's hospital bedside), Phibes communicates electronically with his svelte aide-de-camp, Vulnavia (Virginia North). Together they concoct intricate devices of doom to dispatch Dr. Dunwoody (Edward Burnham), Dr. Hargreaves (Alex Scott), Dr. Longstreet (Terry-Thomas), Dr. Hedgepath (David Hutcheson), Dr. Kitjag (Peter Gilmore), Dr. Whitcomb (Maurice Kaufman), and Nurse Allen (Susan Travers).

After Lem Visalius (Sean Bury), the son of Dr. Visalius (Joseph Cotten) is kidnapped, the police, led by Detective Trout (Peter Jeffrey) and Sgt. Schenley (Norman Jones) close in for the kill . . . as it were.

Metal Shop 101

We have made machines out of men; now we will make men out of machines!!

> Rotwang (Rudolph Klein-Rogge) to Jon Frederson in *Metropolis*

PRODUCERS: Louis M. Heyward, Ronald S. Dumas. DIRECTOR: Robert Feust. SCREENPLAY: James Whiton, William Goldstein. SET DESIGN: Brian Eatwell. MAKEUP: Trevor Crole-Rees. CINEMATOGRAPHY: Norman Warwick. MUSIC: Basil Kirchin.

ABSENT-MINDED PROFESSOR, THE
Walt Disney/Buena Vista (1961). B/w, 97 mins.

Enjoyable comedy that emphasizes whacky special effects in a tale of science gone haywire. Befuddled bachelor professor Brainard (Fred MacMurray) comes up with a rubbery antigravity substance called flubber. The love of his life, Betsy Carlisle (Nancy Olson), is impressed at first but gradually becomes flustered when the flubber experiments get out of hand. The prof offers to demonstrate his flubber-powered, high-flying flivver for the military, unaware that it has been stolen by a scheming alumnus (Keenan Wynn) and replaced by a conventional Model T Ford.

PRODUCER: Walt Disney. ASSOCIATE PRODUCER AND SCREENWRITER: Bill Walsh. Based on the short story "A Situation of Gravity," by Samuel W. Taylor. DIRECTOR: Robert Stevenson. CINEMATOGRAPHY: Edward Colman. SPECIAL EFFECTS: Peter Ellenshaw, Eustace Lycett. MUSIC: George Bruns. SUPPORTING PLAYERS: Tommy Kirk as Bill Hawk. Leon Ames as Rufus Daggett, Elliott Reid as ShelbyAshton.

ADDING MACHINE, THE
Associated Longdon Films/Universal (G.B./U.S., 1969). Color, 99 mins.

Based on the 1923 play by Elmer Rice, this frightening look at automation centers on the unfortunate existence of an overworked accountant (Milo O'Shea) who discovers he is about to be replaced by a machine. Frustrated, he murders his boss. Before he has a chance to relish his crime, he is accidentally electrocuted. The afterlife, it turns out, is anything but heavenly, and the frazzled fellow finds himself one of countless drones who are forced to push a seemingly endless number of buttons for all eternity.

PRODUCER, DIRECTOR, AND SCREENWRITER: Jerome Epstein. ART DIRECTOR: Jack Shampan. CINEMATOGRAPHY: Walter Lassally. MUSIC: Mike Leander, Lambert Williamson.

SUPPORTING PLAYERS: Phyllis Diller, Billie Whitelaw, Sidney Chaplin, Raymond Huntley.

ADULT VERSION OF JEKYLL AND HYDE, THE
Entertainment Ventures (1972). Color, 82 mins.

Dr. Jekyll goes into heat.

PRODUCERS: David F. Friedman, Bryon Mabe. DIRECTOR: B. Ron Elliot.

ADVENTURES OF BARON MUNCHAUSEN, THE
France, 1927. Silent featurette, 970 ft.

The legendary embellisher of truths blows up the world and is sent hurtling to the surface of the moon.

PRODUCER: Paul Peroff.

ADVENTURES OF CAPTAIN MARVEL, THE
Republic (1941). B/w serial, 12 chapters (25 reels).

While on an expedition to Siam seeking traces of the ancient Scorpion dynasty, young radio operator Billy Batson (Frank Coghlan, Jr.) is trapped in a cave-in. There, he meets the ancient entity Shazam (Nigel de Brulier), the guardian of an ancient tomb. Since Billy has steadfastly defied the orders of his expedition chiefs and has not defiled the tomb, he is rewarded with super powers by the elderly fellow. When Billy utters the old duffer's name, he becomes Captain Marvel, replete with cape and bouncing boots.

As Marvel (Tom Tyler), Billy rescues the rest of his party and returns to the States, where he battles a villain who, disguised as The Scorpion, tries to steal from archaeologists a series of crystals that will turn rocks into gold.

PRODUCER: Hiram S. Brown. DIRECTORS: William Witney, John English. SCREENPLAY: Ronald Davidson, Norman S. Hall, Arch B. Heath, Joseph Poland, and Sol Shor, based on characters appearing in Fawcett Publications' *Captain Marvel* comics. CINEMATOGRAPHY: William Nobels. MUSIC: Cy Feuer.

SUPPORTING PLAYERS: Louise Currie, Bryant Washburn, Jack Mulhall.

AELITA
Mezharabpom (U.S.S.R., 1924), Amkino (U.S., 1929). B/w, 45 mins.

Propaganda par excellence takes the spotlight in this early sf morality tale. Cosmonauts Los (Nikolai Tserectelli) and Busev (Igor Illinski) land on Mars and take part in a filmed allegory that transplants the essence of the Russian Revolution onto alien terrain. Los becomes smitten with beautiful (but aristocratic) Martian queen Aelita (Yulia Solntseva), while Busev becomes involved with the plight of the downtrodden Martian working class. By the film's end, the workers of the out-of-this-world have united under Busev's leadership and stage a massive revolt.

DIRECTOR: Yakov Protazanov. SCREENPLAY: Fyodor Otzep, Alexei Falko.

SUPPORTING PLAYERS: Valentina Kuinzhi, Yuri Zavadsky.

Mezhrabpom

Aelita

AERIAL ANARCHISTS, THE
Kineto (G.B., 1911). B/w silent feature, 700 ft.

A despicable group of ruffians leads a fleet of futuristic airplanes on bombing raids of key metropolises.

DIRECTOR: Walter Booth.

AERIAL SUBMARINE, THE
Kineto (G.B., 1910). B/w silent feature, 600 ft.

Scientists invent a submarine that flies.

DIRECTOR: Walter Booth.

AGENT FOR H.A.R.M.
Dimension IV (1965). Color, 84 mins.

A secret agent (Mark Richman) is assigned to protect the life of a defecting scientist who has come up with quite a few gadgets interesting to the military minds of all nations, free and otherwise. Along for the ride are guns that shoot deadly spores and a nasty breed of artificially created fungus.

PRODUCER: Joseph F. Robertson. DIRECTOR: Gerd Oswald. SCREENPLAY: Blair Robertson. ART DIRECTOR: Norman Boule. CINEMATOGRAPHY: James Crab. SPECIAL EFFECTS: D. E. Rollins. MUSIC: Gene Kaurer, Douglas Lackey.

SUPPORTING PLAYERS: Wendell Corey, Carl Esmond, Barbara Bouchet, Robert Quarry.

AGENT 353/PASSPORT TO HELL
Italy/France/Spain (1966). Color, 101 mins.

Agent 353 (George Ardisson) attempts to find the head of the nasty Black Scorpion group of international terrorists. They plot their evil in underground labs and are attempting to do in the world with nasty gas.

DIRECTOR: Simon Sterling. SCREENPLAY: S. Sollimo, S. O'Neill, DeArozeumena. CINEMATOGRAPHY: Carlo Carlini. MUSIC: Piero Umiliani.

SUPPORTING PLAYERS: Frank Wolff, Michael Lemoine, Leontine May.

AIR HAWKS
Columbia (1935). B/w, 66 mins.

Government agents battle for control of a ray that can cause motors of all kinds to conk out.

DIRECTOR: Albert Rogell. SCREENPLAY: Griffin Jay and Grace Neville, from a story by Ben Pivar. CINEMATOGRAPHY: Henry Ferulich.

CAST: Wiley Post, Ralph Bellamy, Edward Van Sloan.

AIRSHIP DESTROYER, THE
Also known as THE BATTLE IN THE CLOUDS; THE POSSIBILITIES OF WAR IN THE AIR; DEATH IN THE AIR; ROMANCE OF THE INVENTOR OF THE FIRST AERIAL TORPEDO. Charles Urban (G.B., 1909). B/w silent feature, 1,350 ft.

A dogfight occurs above England.

PRODUCER: Charles Urban. DIRECTOR: Walter Booth.

AIR TORPEDO, THE
Deutsche Kinematographen Ges (Germany, 1913), W. B. (U.S., 1914). B/w silent feature, three reels.

Scientists invent a remote-controlled bomb capable of prolonged flight.

PRODUCER: Louis Gero.

ALGOL

Germany, 1920. B/w silent feature, running time unknown.

Earth is subjected to a mini-invasion when the aptly named alien Mephisto (Emil Jannings) lands on the planet. A citizen of the distant star Algol, Mephisto plans to conquer the world with the aid of an unstoppable death machine. Once in motion, however, the machine literally doesn't realize when to stop. As a result, Mephisto's family is eradicated by the weapon. Understandably annoyed, Mephisto destroys the machine. The machine, before giving up the circuitry forever, lashes out at the alien and succeeds in blowing him to bits. The ultimate message film?

DIRECTOR: Hans Werkemeister. SCREENPLAY: Hans Brenert.

SUPPORTING PLAYERS: John Gottowt, Kathe Haack, Ernst Hoffman.

ALIEN

20th Cent.-Fox (1979). Eastmancolor, 124 mins.

A highly touted, overbloated "B" picture that is, essentially, a remake (uncredited) of the ancient potboiler IT! THE TERROR FROM BEYOND SPACE. Receiving a strange signal from an unknown planet, the crew of the space freighter *Nostromo* lands to pick up any survivors. What they find is horror. A large alien being sits, decayed, in the wreckage of its spaceship. One of the human explorers, Kane (John Hurt), is attacked by some sort of space egg, his space-suit headplate shattered by the blow of the plasmatic substance.

Once the crew has returned to the ship it becomes evident that Kane is housing an alien creature. The creature bursts from his chest, killing the human instantly, and spends the rest of the movie metamorphosing into various shapes of increasing stature as it stalks the remaining crew members: Dallas (Tom Skerrit), Ripley (Sigourney Weaver), Lambert (Veronica Cartwright), Brett (Harry Dean Stanton), Ash (Ian Holm), and Parker (Yaphet Kotto). Since none of the aforementioned characters are exactly loaded

with personality—courtesy of the somewhat anemic script—the subsequent blood-letting is a bit gratuitous. By the film's conclusion, the cat-and-mouse game boils down to a one-on-one confrontation between the lone surviving human and the towering alien hulk.

EXECUTIVE PRODUCER: Ronald Shusett. PRODUCERS: Gordon Carroll, David Giler, Walter Hill. DIRECTOR: Ridley Scott. SCREENPLAY: Dan O'Bannon. CINEMATOGRAPHY: Derek Vanlint. SPECIAL EFFECTS: Brian Johnson, Nick Alder. DESIGNS: Ron Cobb, H. R. Giger. MUSIC: Jerry Goldsmith.

Alien

ALLIGATOR PEOPLE, THE

20th Cent.-Fox (1959). B/w, 74 mins.

Leaping Lizards, thinks Jane Marvin upon spotting her missing spouse, *what have you done to my husband!* Well, Jane, it's like this: missing Mr. Marvin (Richard Crane) is the unfortunate victim of experiments conducted by nutty scientist Dr. Wingate (Bruce Bennett) and his even stranger assistant, Mannon (Lon Chaney, Jr.). The twosome are trying to encourage limb regeneration by injecting patients with alligator glands.

In search of Paul Marvin, Jane (Beverly Garland) chooses to stay at guess whose home? And at just about that time, half-alligator Paul decides to strut his stuff for all to see. Looking dignified about it all is Dr. Mark Sinclair (George Macready) who never actually says "I told you so," but might as well.

PRODUCER: Jack Leewood. DIRECTOR: Roy Del Ruth. SCREENPLAY: O. H. Hampton, from a story by Hampton and Charles O'Neal. CINEMATOGRAPHY: Karl Struss. MUSIC: Irving Gertz. MAKEUP: Ben Nye, Dick Smith.

SUPPORTING PLAYERS: Frieda Inescort, Douglas Kennedy.

ALPHAVILLE
Also known as TARZAN VS. IBM.
Pathé-contemporary/Chaumaine-Film (France, 1965). B/w, 100 mins.

For connoiseurs of intellectual symbolism or utter confusion, Jean-Luc Godard's *Alphaville* is a must-see. In the not-too-distant future, detective Lemmy Caution (Eddie Constantine) journeys from Earth (The Outerworlds) to planet Alphaville on a secret mission. The humanoid citizens of Alphaville are seemingly benevolent types who are kept in tow by the omniscient computer/ruler Alpha 60. Individualism is considered in bad taste, yet the populace of the planet affect a happy, albeit placid, stance. As the plot progresses, Lemmy's mission becomes clear: he must kill the inventor of the computer, Professor von Braun (Howard Vernon), before the scientist can destroy the universe.

PRODUCER: Andre Michaelin. DIRECTOR AND SCREENWRITER: Jean-Luc Godard. MUSIC: Paul Misraki.

SUPPORTING PLAYERS: Akim Tamiroff as Henry Dickson, Laszlo Szabo as The Engineer, Jean-André Fiechi as Professor Eckel, Jean-Louis Comolli as Professor Jeckel, Anna Karina as Natasha.

ALRAUNE
Phoenix (Hungary, 1918). B/w silent feature, running time unknown.

The first film adaptation of Hans Heinz Ewers' novel *Alraune* tells the tale of a scientist who creates a soulless woman via artificial insemination, using a hanged criminal and a prostitute as parents. In the Hungarian version (the story would be filmed another five times) the girl is created from a mandrake root. She meets a sad demise when told of her plant papa.

DIRECTORS: Michael Curtiz, Odor Fritz. SCREENPLAY: Richard Falk.

CAST: Gyula Gal, Roszi Szollosi, Jeno Torzs, Margit Lux.

ALRAUNE
UFA (Germany, 1928). B/w silent feature, running time unknown.

Brigitte (METROPOLIS) Helm and Paul (*The Golem*) Wegener starred in this version of the artificially created woman. By the film's finish, love has found its way into her personality structure and she begs for a real heart.

DIRECTOR AND SCREENWRITER: Henrik Galeen. ART DIRECTORS: Walter Reimann, Max Heilbronner. CINEMATOGRAPHY: Franz Planer.

SUPPORTING PLAYERS: Ivan Petrovitch, Alexander Sascha.

ALRAUNE
Also known as THE DAUGHTER OF EVIL.
UFA (German, 1930). B/w, 87 mins.

The first sound version of the *Alraune* tale features Brigitte Helm in a reprise in the soulless-human role.

DIRECTOR: Richard Oswald. SCREENPLAY: Charlie Roellinghoff and R. Welsbach. ART DIRECTORS: Otto Erdmann, Hans Sohnle. CINEMATOGRAPHY: Gunther Kramph. MUSIC: Bronislaw Kaper.

SUPPORTING PLAYERS: Albert Basserman, Agnes Straub, Kathe Haack.

ALRAUNE
Also known as UNNATURAL.
DCA (Germany, 1952). B/w, 90 mins.

Released in the U.S. in 1957, this version of the *Alraune* story brought together some of the 1950s German cinema's most familiar faces, including veteran actor Erich von Stroheim and, in the girl-creation's role, Hildegard Neff.

DIRECTOR: Arthur Maria Rabenalt. SCREENPLAY: Fritz Rotter. CINEMATOGRAPHY: Friedl Behn-Grund.

SUPPORTING PLAYERS: Karl Boehm, Trude Hesterberg.

ALRAUNE AND THE GOLEM
Riesenbioskopfilm (Germany, 1919). B/w silent feature, running time unknown.

The soulless girl meets the legendary clay giant.

ARTISTIC SUPERVISOR: Nils Chrisander. CINEMATOGRAPHY: Guido Seeber.

AMAZING COLOSSAL MAN, THE
AIP (1957). B/w, 80 mins.

An amazingly intelligent treatment of the atomic-mutation theme popular in the 1950s—and on a shoestring budget, too. When a small plane crash-lands on an A-bomb testing site mere seconds before detonation, Lt. Col. Glenn Manning (Glenn Langan) makes a futile dash to save the occupants. Before he gets a chance even to approach the wreckage, the atomic explosion takes place, hitting Manning full force. Amazingly enough, he recovers, his skin healing within days. Doctors are at first astounded, then horrified, by Manning's strange regenerative powers. Not only is Manning's skin growing at an alarming rate, so is his entire body.

Fiancée Carol Forrest (Cathy Downs) and sympathetic friend Robert Allen (Judd Holdren) can only watch helplessly as the sensitive Manning grows to freakish proportions. The crux of the

© American International Television Inc., 1973

The Amazing Colossal Man

story involves Manning's attempt to re-adjust to his height, stifling his anger and indignation at science for not being able to reverse the process. Complicating matters is a human heart unable to cope physically with the new bulk.

PRODUCER, DIRECTOR, AND SPECIAL-EFFECTS CREATOR: Bert I. Gordon. SCREENPLAY: Bert I. Gordon, Mark Hanna. CINEMATOGRAPHY: Joseph Biroe. MUSIC: Albert Glasser.

Star Wars, Chapter XI, Verses 3–99

From the start, we conceived of *Star Wars* as a multileveled adventure, in 12 parts. Although the *Empire Strikes Back* is a direct sequel to *Star Wars*, there are three other films we want to do that occur before the first film ever begins. So, we're trying to ignore the numbers. The second film isn't *Star Wars II* because if we had to give each film its true number in the series, the original film would be called *Episode Four!* Can you imagine how complicated that would all get?

Gary Kurtz, producer of *Star Wars* and *The Empire Strikes Back*

SUPPORTING PLAYERS: William Hudson, James Sealy, Scott Peters.

AMAZING TRANSPARENT MAN, THE
AIP (1960). B/w, 56 mins.

A scientist experimenting with an invisibility serum uses a convict as a guinea pig and creates the world's first invisible bank robber. Douglas Kennedy is properly amazed at the results in the role of Faust, and Marguerite Chapman as Laura projects orthodox uneasiness with aplomb.

PRODUCER: Lester D. Guthrie. DIRECTOR: Edgar G. Ulmer. SCREENPLAY: Jack Lewis. SPECIAL EFFECTS: Roger George. MUSIC: Darrell Calker.

SUPPORTING PLAYERS: James Griffith, Ivan Triesault.

AMERICATHON
UA (1979). Technicolor, 85 mins.

By the end of the 20th century, the Earth is a mess. Cars are outlawed and people take to the roads on skates and bicycles. The Arab nations have joined forces with Israel to form the United Hebrab Republic and they're out to squeeze the U.S. dry. When wealthy Sam Birdwater (Chief Dan George), American jogging-shoe billionaire, threatens to foreclose on the United States of America unless he is paid back all the money he has loaned the country, the U.S. is thrown into a panic. Laid-back president Chet Roosevelt and his Old Lady, Lucy Beth (Nancy Morgan), hire media expert Eric Mc-Merkin (Peter Riegert) to save the day. He comes up with a telethon to save America—"Americathon." All is going smoothly, with veteran TV hack Monty Rushmore (Harvey Korman) walking the fine video line between desperation and insanity, when saboteur White

House aide Vanderhoof (Fred Willard) pulls the plug on the show. Will Rushmore complete his hosting stint? Will America be saved? Will the Hebrabs take over? Can audiences follow the plot line?

PRODUCER: Joe Roth. DIRECTOR: Neil Israel. SCREENPLAY: Israel, Michael Mislove, and Monica Johnson, from a story by Israel, Peter Bergman, and Phil Proctor. CINEMATOGRAPHY: Gerald Hirschfield. PRODUCTION DESIGN: Stan Jolley. MUSIC: Eddie Money, The Beach Boys, Elvis Costello, others.

SUPPORTING PLAYERS: Zane Busby as Mouling Jackson, Meatloaf as Oklahoma Roy Budnitz.

Copyright © 1979, by Lorimar, Inc.

Americathon

AMPHIBIAN MAN, THE
Lenfilm (U.S.S.R., 1962); color, 98 mins. NTA (U.S., 1964); color, 86 mins.

Scientists accidentally capture an amphibious humanoid. Ignoring the captive's wishes, they plan to educate him according to the above-water world's standards.

DIRECTORS: Gennadi Kazansky, Vladimir Chebotaryov. SCREENPLAY: Alexander Xenofontov, Alexei Kapler, Akiba Golburt. CINEMATOGRAPHY: Eduard Razovsky.

CAST: Vladimir Korenev, Anastasia Vertinskaya, Mikhail Kozakov.

ANDROMEDA STRAIN, THE
Universal (1971). Panavision and Technicolor, 131 mins.

An unstoppable menace of the invisible variety almost does in the citizenry of planet Earth in this thriller. An American satellite crash-lands near Piedmont, New Mexico, bringing an alien microorganism along for the ride.

The space virus spreads rapidly, killing everyone in town but an old man and an infant. A team of the U.S.'s top scientists—Dr. Jeremy Stone (Arthur Hill), Dr. Ruth Leavitt (Kate Reid), Dr. Mark Hall (James Olson), and Dr. Charles Dutton (David Wayne)—is assembled. They head up Project Wildfire, a medical-defense plan headquartered at an underground center in Nevada.

Attempting to find a cure for the lethal disease, they discover the fact that the Andromeda strain kills its victims painfully by clotting their blood. The scientists culture the virus and attempt to find a counteragent. Unfortunately, their best is not good enough. Nature saves the day, however, and the deadly virus mutates into a benign strain.

PRODUCER AND DIRECTOR: Robert Wise. SCREENPLAY: Nelson Gidding, based upon the novel by MICHAEL CRICHTON: MUSIC: Gil Melle. SPECIAL EFFECTS: Douglas Trumbull, Jamie Shourt.

SUPPORTING PLAYERS: Richard O'Brien, Peter Hobbs, Kermit Murdock, Paula Kelly.

ANDY WARHOL'S FRANKENSTEIN
Bryanston Pictures (1974). Color and 3-D, 95 mins.

Called a put-on by some and a sham by others, this gory little piece of fluff concerns the efforts of the Baron (Udo Kier) to create a perfect woman (Dalila Di Lazzaro), while the field hand (Joe Dallesandro) imparts some of his perfections on the Baron's wife (Monique Van Vooren). At one point, the Baron slashes the beautiful creation's side and massages her gall bladder until he achieves sexual climax. Says he to his assistant Otto (Arno Juerging), "To know death, Otto, you must fuck life in the gall bladder." Avant-garde stuff, eh?

PRODUCER: Andy Warhol. DIRECTOR AND SCREENWRITER: Paul Morrissey. CINEMATOGRAPHY: Luigi Kueveillier. MUSIC: Claudio Guizzi.

ANGRY RED PLANET
AIP (1959). Eastmancolor, 94 mins.

A Saturday matinee–aimed space adventure that is long on action and short on thought, *Angry Red Planet* takes a crew of stalwart spacefarers to Mars and tosses them into a series of mishaps that resembles a space-monster Olympiad. Col. Tom O'Bannion (Gerald Mohr), Dr. Iris Ryan (Nora Hayden), Sgt. Sam Jacobs (Jack Kruschen), and the Professor (Les Tremayne) join their unfortunate peers in a cluster of close encounters of the menacing Martian kind. Out to win for the Mars team is a gigantic bat-rat-spider; a tribe of man-eating plants; and a blimp-sized blob of protoplasm, a thinking cell-unit, that attempts to gobble up the Earth spaceship before it gets a chance at a return trip.

PRODUCERS: Sidney Pink, Norman Maurer (the latter was destined to helm the Three Stooges science-fiction features). DIRECTOR: Ib Melchior. SCREENPLAY: Melchior and Pink, from a story by Pink. MUSIC: Paul Dunlap. SPECIAL EFFECTS: Herman Townsley.

American International Pictures

Angry Red Planet

ANOTHER WILD IDEA
MGM (1934). B/w featurette, two reels.

A ray gun causes its targets to lose all their inhibitions.

PRODUCER: Hal Roach. DIRECTORS: Charley Chase, Edward Dunn.

CAST: Charley Chase, Betty Mack, Harry Bowen, Tiny Sanford.

APE MAN, THE
Monogram (1943). B/w, 64 mins.

Down-and-out scientist Bela Lugosi begins monkeying around with serum taken from the spinal fluid of an ape. Using himself as a guinea pig, Lugosi takes the serum. The results give the film its rather catchy title.

PRODUCERS: Sam Katzman, Jack Dietz. ASSOCIATE PRODUCER AND SCREENWRITER: Barney Sarecky. DIRECTOR: William Beaudine. ART DIRECTOR: David Milton. CINEMATOGRAPHY: Mack Stengler. MUSICAL DIRECTOR: Edward Kay.

SUPPORTING PLAYERS: Wallace Ford, Louise Currie, Jack Mulhall.

Monogram

The Ape Man

APRIL 1, 2000
Wien-Film (Austria, 1953). B/w, 110 mins.

Aliens attempt to invade Vienna in this nearly unknown Austrian production.

DIRECTOR: Wolfgang Libeneiner. SCREENPLAY: Rudolf Brunngraber, Ernst Marboe.

CAST: Curt Jurgens, Peter Gerhard, Elizabeth Stemberger, Waltraut Hass.

ARANAS INFERNALES (The Hellish Spiders)
Columbia (1966). B/w, running time unknown.

Distributed by Columbia in Mexico, this low-budget south-of-the-border effort finds aliens landing in their flying saucer on Mexican soil, determined to conquer the country. Aiding them in their scheme is a small group of very large spiders. Who will save Mexico—nay, the entire Earth—from the creepy crawlers? Mysterious masked Mexican hero the Blue Demon, probably.

PRODUCER: Luis Enrique Vergara. DIRECTOR: Frederico Curiel. SCREENPLAY: Adolfo Torres Portillo.

CAST: Blanquita Sanchez, Marha Elena Cervantes, Jessica Munguia.

AROUND THE WORLD UNDER THE SEA
MGM (1966). Color, 120 mins.

A futuristic submarine, stocked with heroic types, attempts to ward off a worldwide earthquake disaster. Meanwhile, on board the sub, intramural hostilities brew involving the egos of Dr. Doug Standish (Lloyd Bridges), Dr. Craig Mosby (Brian Kelly), Dr. Phil Volker (David McCallum), Dr. Orin Hillyard (Marshall Thompson), and grumpy Hank Stahl (Keenan Wynn). Adding insult to injury, the troublesome entourage is attacked en route by a titanic underwater eel.

An Ivan Tors production. PRODUCER AND DIRECTOR: Andrew Marton. DIVING

MGM

Around the World Under the Sea

SEQUENCE DIRECTOR: Ricou (CREATURE FROM THE BLACK LAGOON) Browning. SCREENPLAY: Arthur Weiss, Art Arthur. ART DIRECTORS: Preston Roundtree, Mel Bledsoe. CINEMATOGRAPHY: Clifford Poland. SPECIAL EFFECTS: Projects Unlimited, Inc. MUSIC: Harry Sukman.

SUPPORTING PLAYERS: Shirley Eaton, Gary Merrill, Celeste Yarnell.

ASSIGNMENT OUTER SPACE
Also known as SPACE MEN.
Titanus/Ultra (Italy, 1960), AIP (U.S., 1962). Color, 73 mins.

Ray Peterson (Rik von Nutter) and Lucy (Gabriella Farinon) don't have time to worry about lovers' quarrels when news is leaked that a runaway spaceship is heading for Earth in a big way. Heading a group of brave astronauts, they set out to get the spacecraft before it gets Earth.

DIRECTOR: Antonio Marbheriti. SCREENPLAY: Vasily Petrov. SPECIAL EFFECTS: Caesar Peace. MUSIC: J. K. Broady, Gordon Zahler.

SUPPORTING PLAYERS: Archie Savage, Alain Dijon. NARRATOR: Jack Wallace.

ASTOUNDING SHE-MONSTER, THE
Also known as THE MYSTERIOUS INVADER.
AIP (Hollywood-International) (1958). B/w, 60 mins.

Astounding. A mysterious meteor makes an unscheduled stop in a forest area on planet Earth. Shortly thereafter, local denizens begin to meet their Maker quite prematurely. Surprise! That was no meteor, that was a spaceship. The killer turns out to be a sultry alien female (Shirley Kilpatrick), who romps through the forest at night in a Day-glo leotard. Raising both hell and the blood pressure of her victims, the space siren does in her helpless male prey via the strange, pulsating force that permeates her body (and her body stocking). Robert Clarke leads the forces of Good.

PRODUCER AND DIRECTOR: Ron Ashcroft. SCREENPLAY: Frank Hall. MUSIC: Guenther Kauer.

SUPPORTING PLAYERS: Kenne Duncan, Marilyn Harvey, Jeanne Tatum.

ASTRONOMER'S DREAM, THE
Also known as THE MAN IN THE MOON (LA LUNE A UN MÈTRE).
France (1898). Silent short, hand-colored (Pathécolor).

A tale of science fancy by the master magician of the early cinema, Georges Méliès. A scientist falls asleep and is visited by the Man in the Moon . . . who slips into the Earthling's home via an open window.

ASTRO-ZOMBIES, THE
Gemini (1969). Color, 90 mins.

Wendell Corey and John Carradine wince their way through a plot of scientific mayhem. Murders are committed in order to gain parts for the construction of a superhuman creature.

PRODUCER AND DIRECTOR: Ted V. Mikels. SCREENPLAY: Mikels, Wayne Rogers. ART DIRECTOR: Wally Moon. CINEMATOGRAPHY: Robert Maxwell. MUSIC: Nico Karaski.

SUPPORTING PLAYERS: Tom Pace, Joan Patrick, Wally Moon.

L'ATLANTIDE
Also known as LOST ATLANTIS.
Thalman (French, 1921), Metro (U.S.A., 1922). B/w silent feature, 8,223 ft. (France), 6,601 ft. (U.S.).

Based on Pierre Benoit's 1919 novel of the same name, this fanciful excursion into a lost world finds two modern men falling under the spell of Queen Antinea. The only catch is that the queen has a tendency to love 'em and leave 'em. And when she leaves 'em, they join the ranks of mummydom in the great hall of her palace.

DIRECTOR AND SCREENWRITER: Jacques Feyder. ART DIRECTOR: Manuel Orazi. CINEMATOGRAPHY: Georges Specht, Victor Morin.

CAST: Stacia Napierkovska, Jean Angelo, Georges Melchior, André Roanne, Maria-Louise Iribe.

L'ATLANTIDE
Nero (Germany, 1932), International Road Shows (1939). B/w, 80 mins.

Brigitte (METROPOLIS) Helm starred in this German version of the Queen Antinea of Atlantis legend. The lost city of science is, again, breached by outsiders who barely escape with their lives. This version was filmed in Paris and parts of Africa in German, English, and French.

PRODUCER: Seymour Nebenzal. DIRECTOR: G. W. Pabst. CINEMATOGRAPHY: Eugene Shuftan, MUSIC: Wolfgang Zeller.

CAST: Gustav Diessl, Heinz Klingenberg, Tela Tschai, Vladimir Sokolov, John Stuart, Odette Florelle, Jean Angelo, Pierre Blanchar.

ATLANTIS, THE LOST CONTINENT
MGM (1961). Color, 90 mins.

Futuristic science blends with ancient fable in this opulent George Pal recounting of the Atlantis legend. A lowly fisherman (Tony Hall) unwittingly saves the life of the princess of Atlantis (Joyce Taylor) and is taken to the mysterious land aboard a *Nautilus*-like submarine. Once deposited on Atlantean soil, the fisherman discovers a scientific battle between good and evil. Scientist Ed Platt warns of doom in the offing and urges the government of Atlantis to prepare for the worst. Atlantis, guarded by deadly crystal ray-cannons, feels secure enough to allow science to go astray on the far side of the island, where human slaves are slowly being transformed into animal-men via some unorthodox experiments. In the end, a mighty volcanic eruption sinks Atlantis and sends the death rays haywire.

PRODUCER AND DIRECTOR: George Pal. SCREENPLAY: Daniel Mainwaring, based on a play by Gerald Hargreaves. SPECIAL EFFECTS: A. Arnold Gillespie, Gene Warren, Wah Chang, Tim Barr. MUSIC: Russell Garcie. MAKEUP: William Tuttle.

SUPPORTING PLAYERS: John Dall, Frank DeKova, Jay Novello, Barry Kroeger. NARRATOR: Paul Frees.

ATOM AGE VAMPIRE
Topaz (Italy, 1960). B/w, 87 mins.

A dedicated scientist (Alberto Lupo) keeps a badly scarred beauty beautiful by injecting her with the blood of recently deceased lovelies. The only problem with the doctor's cure is that he has to see to it that a continuing batch of lovelies is transformed into recently-deceased status. Talk about dedication.

PRODUCER: Mario Bava. DIRECTORS: Anton Giulio Majano, Richard McNamara. SCREENPLAY: Piero Monviso, Gino de Santis, Alberto Bevilacqua, A. G. Majano, John Hart. CINEMATOGRAPHY: Aldo Giordano. SPECIAL EFFECTS: Ugo Amadoro. MUSIC: Armando Trovajoli.

SUPPORTING PLAYERS: Susanne Loret, Sergio Fantoni, Roberto Berta.

ATOMIC AGENT, THE
AIT (1959). B/w, 85 mins.

This edited-for-TV version of a French comedy recounts the tale of a whacky fashion model who traps a spy ring that is after an atomic motor.

DIRECTOR: Henri Decoin.
CAST: Martine Carol, Dany Saval, Felix Marten.

ATOMIC KID, THE
Republic (1954). B/w, 86 mins.

Lovable Mickey Rooney becomes lovable atomic-powered Mickey Rooney after witnessing an A-bomb blast. Dosed with radioactivity, the ever-smiling, ever-aging child star finds himself caught in a battle between crazed foreign agents (seemingly the only type available in the 1950s) and freedom-loving U.S. officials.

PRODUCER: Mickey Rooney. DIRECTOR: Leslie H. Martinson. SCREENPLAY: Benedict Freeman and John Fenton Murphy, from a story by Blake Edwards. ART DIRECTOR: Frank Hotaling. CINEMATOGRAPHY: John L. Russell, Jr. SPECIAL EFFECTS: Howard and Theodore Lydecker. MUSIC: Van Alexander.

The Culinary Arts
Don't be afraid of Lobo. He's as harmless as a kitchen.
Dr. Varnoff (Bela Lugosi) to Janet Lawton (Loretta King) in *Bride of the Monster*

SUPPORTING PLAYERS: Robert Strauss, Whit Bissell, Elaine Davis.

ATOMIC MAN, THE
AA (1956). B/w, 77 mins.

Believed dead, an atomic scientist is found to be alive and apparently well by two of his colleagues (Faith Domergue and Gene Nelson). Despite his excellent health, however, the scientist cannot communicate verbally in a coherent manner. It is subsequently discovered that because of an overdose of radiation, the man is out of synch with the very fabric of time itself: his mind is reacting to events taking place seven minutes in the future, although his body remains firmly entrenched in the present.

PRODUCER: Alec C. Snowden. DIRECTOR: Ken Hughes. SCREENPLAY: CHARLES ERIC MAINE, from his novel *The Isotope Man*. ART DIRECTOR: George Haslam. CINEMATOGRAPHY: A. T. Dinsdale. MUSICAL DIRECTOR: Richard Taylor.

SUPPORTING PLAYERS: Joseph Tomley, Donald Gray, Vic Perry.

ATOMIC RULERS OF THE WORLD
Manley (Japan, 1964). Tohocolor, 83 mins.

Originally released in 1957 in Japan by Shintoho films as two of the kiddie-oriented SUPER GIANT films, this severely edited potboiler is, in reality, *Super Giant Nos. 2 and 3*—more popularly known in the land of the rising sun as *Kotetsu No Kyojin-Kaiseijin No Mayjo* and *Kotetsu No Kyojinchikyu Metzubo Sunzen*.

Super Giant, known in this film as Starman, is your typical superhero type who has a habit of befriending young children in trouble. This time out, he bands together with two young urchins to fend off an alien attack instigated by the power-hungry fish people of the planet Capia. A warmongering world hidden from the Earth's view by the Moon, Capia sends a fleet of humanoid saboteurs to the planet in flying saucers. Their mission?—to infiltrate the Earth's population and *turn off* the planet's gravity. A neat trick in any planet's book. They are dispatched with deadly gas.

DIRECTORS: Teruo Ishii, Akira Mitsuwa, Koreyoshi Akasaka. SCREENPLAY: Ichiro Miyegawa.

CAST: Minako Yamada, Ken Hayashi, Reiko Seto, Ken Utsui (as Starman).

ATOMIC SUBMARINE
AA (1959). B/w, 72 mins.

A spaceship of unknown origin settles on the ocean floor and wreaks havoc on the American atomic fleet. A group of democracy-loving scientists and navy men, spearheaded by Reef (Arthur Franz) and Wendover (Dick Foran), are sent beneath the waves to investigate the menace. Much to their dismay, they discover that the ship is, in reality, a flying saucer that is a living alien organism. Throwing caution to the current, they venture inside and bump into (literally) the saucer's pilot, a titanic cyclopean fellow. The heroes beat a hasty retreat and promptly blow up the ship and its pilot with a handy nuclear warhead.

PRODUCER: Alex Gordon. DIRECTOR: Spencer Bennett. SCREENPLAY: O. H. Hampton, from an idea by Jack Rabin and Irving Block. Music: Alexander Lazlo. Special effects: Jack Rabin, Irving Block, Louis DeWitt.

Supporting players: Tom Conway, Joi Lansing, Sid Melton. Narrator: Pat Michaels.

Allied Artists

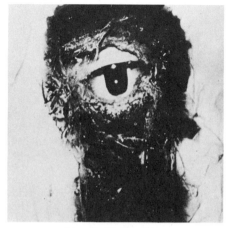

Atomic Submarine

ATOM MAN VS. SUPERMAN
Columbia (1950). B/w serial, 15 chapters (30 reels), 480 mins. total running time.

After a series of cartoon appearances in the early 1940s by the Man of Steel, D.C. Comics saw fit to bring Superman "live" to the screen in 1948 in a cliffhanging serial. Buoyed by the success of the first filmed appearance of Krypton's favorite son, Columbia brought actor Kirk Alyn back for a reprise in *Atom Man vs. Superman,* yet another Saturday matinee crowd-pleaser.

Atom Man is, in reality, archvillain Lex Luthor (Lyle Talbot), who is out, once again, to dominate the Earth through an astounding array of lethal gadgetry. By the final curtain, Luthor and his fleet of destructive flying-saucer warships are torpedoed by the champion of truth, justice, and the American way. Producer: Sam Katzman. Director: Spencer Bennett. Screenplay: George H. Plympton, Joseph Poland, David Matthews. Musical director: Mischa Bakaleinikoff.

Supporting players: Tommy Boyd as Jimmy Olson, Pierre Watkin as Perry White, Noel Neill as Lois Lane.

ATRAGON
Also known as ATRAGON, THE FLYING SUB.
Toho (Japan, 1963); color, 96 mins. AIP (U.S., 1965); color, 79 mins.

Special-effects wizard Eiji Tsuburaya lent an aura of credibility to this fanciful tale recounting the villainy concocted by the undersea kingdom of Mu. Seeking to expand its territory, the evil queen of Mu sends a fleet of flying submarines to savage the surface world. Above-water Earthlings retaliate with a supersub of their own design, *Atragon* (in Japanese, *Atoragon*).

Producer: Yuko Tanaka. Director: Inoshiro Honda. Screenplay: Shinichi Sekizawa. Cinematography: Hajimi Koizumi. Music: Akira Ifukube.

Cast: Tadao Takashima, Yoko Fujiyama, Yu Fujiki, Jun Tazaki.

ATTACK OF THE CRAB MONSTERS
AA (1957). B/w, 64 mins.

A group of scientists stranded on a desolate island are attacked by crabs of the skyscraper variety. Spawned by atomic fallout, the intelligent (sort of) crustaceans roam the island at night, lopping off the heads of hapless humans and devouring them. After consuming the brains of human victims, the crabs are able to communicate telepathically with the rest of the castaways, using the consumed human's memory. No one on the island is overly impressed with this scientific breakthrough.

Producer and director: Roger Corman. Associate producer and screenwriter: Charles Griffith. Cinematography: Floyd Crosby. Music: Ronald Stein.

Cast: Beverly Garland, Pamela Duncan, Russell Johnson, Ed Nelson.

ATTACK OF THE 50-FOOT WOMAN
AA (1958). B/w, 66 mins.

Some days it just doesn't pay to get out of bed. That's the lesson an attractive young socialite (Allison Hayes) learns in this epic exercise in screen schlock.

An alien giant of the bald humanoid variety lands his spaceship on planet Earth and proceeds to take nocturnal strolls along stretches of deserted highway running through the great American desert. Out for a moonlight drive is our heroine—soon to be our villain. In a classic brief interlude, the lass has her genetic structure altered by the captivated and, apparently, radioactive space creature. Escaping a fate somewhat more tedious than death, the woman returns home. There she begins to grow at an alarming rate. Coincidentally, the larger she gets, the crazier she gets.

At 50-foot status and with no one at home in her attic, the deranged delight discovers that her husband, Harry, is the cheating kind. Seeking to make him the bleeding kind, the giantess tears the town apart searching for her errant spouse. Eventually she discovers Harry making time with a floozy in a local bar. With a flick of her wrist, the 50-foot female makes the bar, the floozy, and dear old Harry decidedly past-tense. A similar fate awaits the giantess when the local militia arrives.

PRODUCER: Bernard Woolner. DIRECTOR: Nathan Hertz. SCREENPLAY: Mark Hanna. MUSIC: Ronald Stein.

SUPPORTING PLAYERS: William Hudson, Yvette Vickers, Roy Gordon.

ATTACK OF THE KILLER TOMATOES
NAI Entertainment (1978). Color, 87 mins.

Mutant tomatoes threaten the safety of the world.

PRODUCERS: Steve Peace and John De Bello. DIRECTOR: John De Bello. SCREENPLAY: Costa Dillon, Steve Peace, John De Bello. CINEMATOGRAPHY: John K. Culley. SPECIAL EFFECTS: Greg Auer. MUSIC: Gordon Goodwin.

CAST: David Miller as Mason Dixon, George Wilson as Jim Richardson, Sharon Taylor as Louise Fairchild, Jack Riley as the Agriculture Official, Rock Peace as Wilbur Finletter.

ATTACK OF THE MONSTERS
AIT (1969). Color, 72 mins.

A TV version of the 1968 Adiei (Japanese) film *Gamera vs. Guiron*. Two alien women with the unfortunate habit of eating human brains send a spaceship to Earth to check out the local

eateries. Two Japanese boys are considered an excellent brunch and are shuttled onto the remote-controlled craft and shipped off into space. Loyal flying-turtle-monster Gamera sets off in pursuit. Landing on the planet of the gourmets, he is met by an evil alien monster, the banana-headed Guiron. They fight. Gamera wins. Everyone, with the possible exception of the famished space femmes, goes home happy.

PRODUCER: Hidemasa Nagata. DIRECTOR: Noriaki Yuasa. SCREENPLAY: Fumi Takahashi.

SUPPORTING PLAYERS: Nobuhiro Janima, Eiji Funakoshi, Miyuki Akiyama.

ATTACK OF THE PUPPET PEOPLE
AIP (1958). B/w, 79 mins.

A lonely and crazy scientist/puppet-maker decides to shrink people to doll size in order to have a few constant companions. The subjects of his experiments, led by John Agar and June Kenny, are anything but enthusiastic about their new Ken and Barbie status. When the puppets rebel, the puppet-maker (John Hoyt) is equally dismayed.

PRODUCER, DIRECTOR, SCREENWRITER, AND SPECIAL EFFECTS ARTIST: Bert I. Gordon. SCREENPLAY: George W. Yates. CINEMATOGRAPHY: Ernest Laszlo. MUSIC: Albert Glasser.

SUPPORTING PLAYERS: Susan Gordon, Ken Miller, Michael Mark.

ATTACK OF THE ROBOTS
Speva/Cine Alliance/Hesperia (France/Spain, 1962). B/w, 93 mins.

A scientist decides to turn men into killer robots. No one is amused.

DIRECTOR: Jesus (Jess) Franco. SCREENPLAY: Jean-Claude Carrière. ART DIRECTOR: J. A. D'Eaubonne. CINEMATOGRAPHY: A. Macosoli. MUSIC: Paul Misraki.

CAST: Eddie Constantine, Sophi Hardy, Fernando Rey.

AT THE EARTH'S CORE
AIP (1976). Movielab color, 89 mins.

Dr. Abner Perry (Peter Cushing) and sidekick David Innes (Doug McClure) bore through the Earth's crust in their Iron Mole and wind up in Pellucidar, an underground world where the humans are terrorized by the beastly Mahars. Teaming with Dia (Caroline Munro) and her people, the twosome defeat the villainous critters and hightail it back to the surface of the Earth. A half-hearted adaptation of the EDGAR RICE BURROUGHS novel.

PRODUCER: John Dark. DIRECTOR: Kevin Connor. SCREENPLAY: Milton Subotsky, from the novel by Edgar Rice Burroughs. CINEMATOGRAPHY: Alan Hume. SPECIAL EFFECTS: Ian Wingrove. MUSIC: Mike Vickers.

SUPPORTING PLAYERS: Cy Grant as Ra, Godfrey James as Ghak, Sean Lynch as Hoojah, Keith Barron as Dowsett.

AT THE EDGE OF THE WORLD

UFA (Germany, 1927). B/w silent feature, 90 mins.

The war of the future is graphically envisioned.

DIRECTOR: Karl Grune. ART DIRECTORS: A. D. Neppach, Albert Steinruck. CINEMATOGRAPHY: F. A. Wegner.

CAST: Brigitte Helm, Max Schreck, Wilhelm Dieterle, Imre Raday.

AUTOMATIC HOUSE, THE

United Film Service (1915). B/w silent featurette, one reel.

A house is chockful of automatic gadgets.

AUTOMATIC LAUNDRY, THE

Lubin (1908). B/w silent featurette, 361 ft.

A scientifically designed device removes clothes and washes, irons, and mends them automatically.

AUTOMATIC MONKEY, THE

Gaumont (France, 1909). B/w silent featurette, 324 ft.

An automatic monkey of the robot variety shows an artistic streak.

AUTOMATIC MOTORIST, THE

Kineto (G.B., 1911). B/w silent featurette, 610 ft.

A robot proves an excellent chauffeur, expertly handling his car on a drive from England to outer space.

DIRECTOR: Walter Booth.

AUTOMATIC SERVANT, THE

Urban-Eclipse (1908). B/w silent featurette, 367 ft.

A scientist perfects a life-sized robot servant and invites his friends for a demonstration of its prowess. One of the professor's servants accidentally breaks the robot and is forced to substitute for the mechanism during the robotic demonstration.

AWFUL DR. ORLOFF, THE

Rosson/Ilispamer (Spain/France, 1961), Sigma III (U.S., 1964). B/w, 86 mins.

In an attempt to beautify his daughter's badly scarred face, kindly but admittedly demented Dr. Orloff (Howard Vernon) kidnaps actresses, forces them into his lab and then, quite against their wishes, performs forcible skin grafts, lobbing skin from face to face. The scientific community as well as the local law-enforcement agency are somewhat dismayed. When a pretty ballerina tracks down the killer before her detective fiancé does, she proves to be fleet of foot indeed.

PRODUCER: Serge Newman. DIRECTOR AND SCREENWRITER: Jesus (Jess) Franco. CINEMATOGRAPHY: Godofredo Pacheco. MUSIC: Pagan and Ramirez Angel.

SUPPORTING PLAYERS: Conrado San Martin, Diana Lorys, Maria Silva.

BAMBOO SAUCER, THE

World Entertainment (1968). Color, 100 mins.

American and Russian scientists (Dan Duryea, John Ericson, and Lois Nettleton) band together to search for a crash-landed flying saucer sitting somewhere within the borders of Red China. They discover the saucer and make a quick trip to Saturn and back.

PRODUCER: Jerry Fairbanks. DIRECTOR AND SCREENWRITER: Frank Telford, from a story by Rip Von Ronkel and

John Fulton. CINEMATOGRAPHY: Hal Mohr. SPECIAL EFFECTS: John Fulton and Glen Robinson. MUSIC: Edward Paul.

SUPPORTING PLAYERS: Bob Hastings, Bernard Fox.

BARBARELLA
Paramount (1967). Color, 98 mins.

Opulent mindlessness reigns in this adaptation of the French cartoon character's comic-book exploits. Jean-Claude Forest's shapely heroine is brought to life by a very preliberation Jane Fonda. When the president of Earth sends Barbie to a planet in order to capture a mad scientist and his death ray, she vows to give her all. During the course of the film, she does, quite often, do just that.

Crash-landing on her intended planet, she is attacked by children who lead an army of mean mechanical dolls of the carnivorous kind. Escaping and heading for the nasty city of Sogo, she is befriended by blind angel Pygar (John Philip Law). Together, they are captured by the Black Queen (Anita Pallenberg). The angel is about to be crucified when he is rescued by Barb. The rescue backfires, however, and Barbarella herself is captured and fed into the Excessive machine, a sex-based contraption that excites its victims to death. Barbie proves a tough nut to crack and, as a result, causes the machine to blow its circuitry. Eventually she finds the professor, knocks out the ray, and wins an Academy Award for *Coming Home.*

PRODUCER: Dino DeLaurentiis. DIRECTOR: Roger Vadim. SCREENPLAY: Terry Southern, others. COSTUMES:

Paramount

Barbarella

Jacques Fonteray. MUSIC AND LYRICS: Bob Crewe, Charles Fox. SPECIAL EFFECTS: Augie Lohman.

SUPPORTING PLAYERS: Milo O'Shea, David Hemmings, Ugo Tognazzi.

BATMAN
Columbia (1943). B/w serial, 15 chapters (30 reels).

Batman and Robin (Lewis Wilson and Douglas Croft) must stop the insidious Dr. Daka (J. Carrol Naish), who is scientifically transforming ordinary human beings into zombie soldiers. Daka plans on helping the Axis powers increase their troops through his device. When he attempts to steal Gotham City's radium supply to get his machine going, the caped crusader enters the picture.

PRODUCER: Rudolph C. Flothow. DIRECTOR: Lambert Hillyer. SCREENPLAY: Victor McLeod, Leslie Swabacker, and Harry Fraser, based upon the character created by Bob Kane. CINEMATOGRAPHY: James Brown, Jr.

Son of Three Mile Island
Don't touch that lever! You'll blow us all to atoms!
> Dr. Pretorius (Ernest Thesiger) to Frankenstein's monster (Boris Karloff) in *The Bride of Frankenstein*

SUPPORTING PLAYERS: William Austin as Alfred, Shirley Patterson as Linda, Charles Middleton as Ken Colton.

BATMAN
20th Cent.-Fox (1966). Color, 105 mins.

High camp and low IQs mesh in this movie takeoff on the classic comic-book superhero. Batman and Robin (Adam West and Burt Ward) are called in by police commissioner Gordon (Neil Hamilton) and told of a dastardly plot threatening the world. Villains the Penguin (Burgess Meredith), Catwoman (Lee Merriwether), the Joker (Cesar Romero), and the Riddler (Frank Gorshin) have joined forces and are about to unleash a criminal wave that will astound criminologists and veteran surfers alike. Disintegrator rays, robots, and scientific gadgetry abound.

PRODUCER: William Dozier. DIRECTOR: Leslie H. Martinson. SCREENPLAY: Lorenzo Semple, Jr. CINEMATOGRAPHY: Howard Schwartz. SPECIAL EFFECTS: Lyle B. Abbott. MUSIC: Nelson Riddle.

SUPPORTING PLAYERS: Alan Napier, Sterling Holloway, Stafford Repp.

BATMAN AND ROBIN
Columbia (1948). B/w serial, 15 chapters (31 reels).
Also known as THE RETURN OF BATMAN.

Batman and Robin (Robert Lowery and John Duncan) are summoned by Commissioner Gordon (Lyle Talbot) and asked to help recover a remote-control machine stolen by the mysterious Wizard. Annoyed by the theft is inventor Professor Hammil (William Fawcett), who doesn't want to see his brainchild used for crime. It is. He sees it, too. So do Batman and Robin, who attempt to discover the Wizard's true identity.

PRODUCER: Sam Katzman. DIRECTOR: Spencer Bennett. SCREENPLAY: George H. Plympton, J. F. Poland, Royal K. Cole. CINEMATOGRAPHY: Ira H. Morgan. MUSIC: Mischa Bakaleinikoff.

SUPPORTING PLAYERS: Jane Adams as Vickie: Ralph Graves as Harrison; Don Harvey as Nolan; House Peters, Jr., as Earl.

BATTLE BENEATH THE EARTH
MGM (1968). Color, 91 mins.

Red Chinese plan an invasion of the free world that calls for them to build a series of tunnels around the globe. Using laser devices, they begin their plan. Kerwin Matthews and a batch of American and British freedom-fighters journey beneath the Earth to stop the Yellow Peril from spreading.

PRODUCER: Charles Reynolds. DIRECTOR: Montgomery Tully. SCREENPLAY: L. Z. Hargreaves. CINEMATOGRAPHY: Ken Talbot. SPECIAL EFFECTS: Tom Howard. MUSIC: Ken Jones.

SUPPORTING PLAYERS: Bessie Love, Viviane Ventura, Robert Ayres, Peter Arne.

BATTLE BEYOND THE SUN
Filmgroup (1963). Color, 74 mins.

A science-fiction salad making little or no sense but peppered with color footage culled from the Soviet film THE HEAVENS CALL (1959). The Russians and the Americans are on their way to Mars in a literal space race. The Americans land first but neglect to take into account the fact that in speeding up their rate of travel, they have used up extra fuel. In short, they don't have enough gas to get home. The Russians, saving the Americans from both a few monsters and a fairly static existence, air-lift the Americans out of the fairly undeveloped neighborhood and head for Earth.

EXECUTIVE PRODUCER: Roger Corman. PRODUCER AND DIRECTOR: Thomas Colchart. SCREENPLAY: Nicholas Colbert and Edwin Palmer.

SUPPORTING PLAYERS: Edd Perry, Arla Powell, Andy Stewart, Bruce Hunter.

BATTLE FOR THE PLANET OF THE APES
20th Cent.-Fox (1974). DeLuxe color and Panavision, 90 mins.

The fifth "ape" film (the others: PLANET OF THE APES, Conquest of the Planet of the Apes, ESCAPE FROM THE PLANET OF THE APES, and BENEATH THE PLANET OF THE APES) takes place after the world has been destroyed by atomic warfare ignited by the revolt of the subservient but intelligent apes against their human rulers. With the simians now in control, a racially equal society is sought.

Compassionate chimp Caesar (Roddy McDowall) is counseled by philosopher Virgil (Paul Williams), wife Lisa (Natalie Trundy) and black human MacDonald (Austin Stoker) in this attempt. Hindering the peaceful plans are militant groups on both sides, led by gorilla Aslo (Claude Akins) and fascist policeman Kolp (Severn Darden). Eventually all three factions clash head-on with Caesar's young son (Bobby Porter) caught in the middle of the battlefield.

PRODUCER: Arthur P. Jacobs. DIRECTOR: J. Lee Thompson. SCREENPLAY: John Williams and Joyce Hooper Cor-

Battle for the Planet of the Apes

RECTOR: Inoshiro Honda. SCREENPLAY: Shinichi Sekizawa, from a story by Jotaro Okami. SPECIAL EFFECTS: Eiji Tsuburaya.

SUPPORTING PLAYERS: Minoru Takada, Harold Conway.

Battle in Outer Space

rington, from a story by Paul Dehn; based upon characters created by PIERRE BOULLE. MAKEUP: John Chambers. CINEMATOGRAPHY: Richard H. Kline. MUSIC: Leonard Rosenman. ART DIRECTOR: Dale Hennessy.

SUPPORTING PLAYERS: John Huston as the Lawgiver, France Nuyen as Alma, Pat Cardi as Young Chimp, John Landis as Jake's Friend, Lew Ayres as Mandemus.

BATTLE IN OUR SPACE
Toho (Japan, 1959); color and Tohoscope, 93 mins. Columbia (U.S., 1960); Eastmancolor, 90 mins.

One small pratfall for mankind. A nasty group of aliens, based on the far side of the moon, implant tiny transistor devices in the brains of two Earthbound Japanese astronauts. The pair, once on Earth, set out to sabotage the space program. Dr. Katsumiya (Ryo Ikebe) and Etsuko (Kyoko Anza) suspect foul play. Discovering the truth, they devise an effective counterattack. Before you can say "all systems go," there's a full-scale space war going. Part of the Earth is destroyed, as well as the moon's Sea of Tranquility. The Man in the Moon dons dark glasses and slips out of the solar system.

PRODUCER: Tomoyuki Tanaka. DI-

BATTLE OF THE WORLDS
Topaz (1963). Color, 84 mins.

An English-language version of the 1960 Italian space opera *Il Pianeta degli Uomini*. An elderly but heroic Earthman (Claude Rains) spearheads a campaign intended to stop a runaway planet, controlled by aliens via a supercomputer, from smashing into Earth.

DIRECTOR: Anthony Dawson. SCREENPLAY: Vassily Petrov.

SUPPORTING PLAYERS: Maya Brent, Bill Carter, Umberto Orsini.

BEACH GIRLS AND THE MONSTER, THE
U.S. Films (1965). B/w, 70 mins.

Sometimes known as *Surf Terror*. Jon Hall plays a nutty scientist who turns himself into a seaweed-suited monster and chases pretty girls. Nice work if you can get it.

PRODUCER: Edward Janis. DIRECTOR: Jon Hall. SCREENPLAY: Joan Gardner. MUSIC: Frank Sinatra, Jr.

SUPPORTING PLAYERS: Sue Casey, Walker Edmiston, Dale Davis.

BEAST FROM 20,000 FATHOMS, THE
W.B. (1953). B/w, 80 mins.

The quintessential 1950s prehistoric-mutant film. Based on RAY BRADBURY'S short story "The Fog Horn," the movie features excellent animation (by a very young Ray Harryhausen) accomplished on a box-lunch budget.

An A-bomb set off in the Arctic region thaws a frozen dinosaur who resumes his life with a roar. The beast heads downstream, eventually winding up in Manhattan. After doing in New York City, it heads for the Coney Island amusement park, where it is dispatched with a radioactive isotope. Mindless fun.

PRODUCERS: Hal Chester, Jack Dietz. DIRECTOR AND ART DIRECTOR: Eugene Lourie. SCREENPLAY: Lou Morheim, Fred Freiberger. CINEMATOGRAPHY: Jack Russell. SPECIAL EFFECTS: Ray Harryhausen, Willis Cook. MUSIC: David Buttolph. CAST: Paul Christian, Paula Raymond, Cecil Kellaway, Kenneth Tobey, King Donovan, Lee Van Cleef.

Warner Bros.

The Beast from 20,000 Fathoms

BEAST OF BLOOD, THE
Hemisphere (1970). Color, 90 mins.

Sequel to the Philippine schlocker THE MAD DOCTOR OF BLOOD ISLAND. Crazy Dr. Lorca keeps a monster in his lab, as well as a talking, disembodied head. Some people like hamsters.

PRODUCER, DIRECTOR, AND SCREENWRITER: Eddie Romero. MAKEUP: Tony Artieda. CINEMATOGRAPHY: Justo Paulino. SPECIAL EFFECTS: Teofilo Hilario. MUSIC: Tito Arevalo. CAST: John Ashley, Celeste Yarnell, Eddie Garcia, Beverly Miller.

BEAST OF YUCCA FLATS, THE
Cardoza (1961). B/w, 60 mins.

The title has a nice ring to it, doesn't it? Tor Johnson stars in this low-budget affair as a fat but kindly scientist who is exposed to a lethal dose of radioactivity and turns into an equally fat but decidedly less kindly monster. Yuck.

PRODUCER: Anthony Cardoza. DIRECTOR, SCREENWRITER, AND EDITOR: Coleman Francis. CINEMATOGRAPHY: John Cagle. MUSIC: I. Nafshun and Al Remington.

SUPPORTING PLAYERS: Douglas Mellor, Tony Cardoza, Bing Stanford.

BEAST WITH A MILLION EYES, THE
ARC (1955). B/w, 78 mins.

A low-budget beauty featuring a good premise and a pretty good script. A bodiless force enters in the form of an alien invasion that crash-lands in the middle of the American desert. It plans to conquer the Earth by using its advanced telepathic powers. Starting out by taking control of the minds of small animals, it works its way up to a local retarded farmhand, Him (Leonard Tarver). The invasion now begun, the creature begins sending out into the human community flocks of birds, herds of cows, and packs of dogs on search-and-destroy missions.

The Kelly family—Allan (Paul Birch), Carol (Lorna Thayer), and Sandy (Dona Cole)—discover the creature and eventually kill it, after seeing its hideous face. As the family leaves the alien cadaver, a small rabbit hops ominously across the scene. Is the power dead after all?

PRODUCER: Roger Corman. DIRECTOR: David Kramarsky. SCREENPLAY: Tom Filler. MUSIC: John Bickford. SPECIAL EFFECTS: Paul Blaisdell.

SUPPORTING PLAYER: Chester Conklin as Old Man Webber.

RED SITTING ROOM, THE
UA (1969). Color, 91 mins.

A dizzy British satire depicting a postholocaust Britain. An episodic tale, the movie traces the exploits of 20 survivors. One man mutates into a parrot. Pretty Rita Tushingham wanders around the desolate landscape as a girl some 17 months pregnant. Sir Ralph

Richardson turns into an apartment room. Another survivor runs eternally on a treadmill that he believes will produce enough energy to rebuild all of England. Not your basic Flash Gordon science-fiction plot here.

PRODUCER AND DIRECTOR: Richard Lester. SCREENPLAY: John Antrobus. CINEMATOGRAPHY: David Watkin. MUSIC: Ken Thorne.

SUPPORTING PLAYERS: Mona Washbourne, Michael Hordern.

BEES, THE
New World (1979). Color, 85 mins.

Scientists and cash-hungry corporations raise a horde of killer bees for their honey. Soon the bees prove to be masters of their fate and scientists John Norman (John Saxon), Sandra Miller (Angel Tompkins), and Dr. Hummel (John Carradine) are asked to come in and exterminate them.

PRODUCER, DIRECTOR, AND SCREENWRITER: Alfredo Zacharias. CINEMATOGRAPHY: Joseph Lamas. MUSIC: Richard Gillis.

BEGINNING OF THE END, THE
Republic (1957). B/w, 74 mins.

Farmers in a small rural community ask the government to help them pep up their pooped-out crops. Brainy government scientists introduce radioactive isotopes into the soil. Within months, everything is growing bigger and faster, including the local grasshoppers. As big as tanks, a squad of the insects hippity-hop to Chicago, where they are met by a welcoming committee consisting largely of the Illinois National Guard. When bullets don't stop the

Republic

The Beginning of the End

creepy critters, it's up to hero Peter Graves to lead them into the lake via an electronic Pied Piper setup—a tape producing high-pitched electronic sounds that attract the mutants.

PRODUCER AND DIRECTOR: Bert I. Gordon. SCREENPLAY: Fred Freiberger, Lester Gorn. CINEMATOGRAPHY: Jack Marta. SPECIAL EFFECTS: Bert I. Gordon.

SUPPORTING PLAYERS: Peggie Castle, James Seay, Morris Ankrum.

BENEATH THE PLANET OF THE APES
20th Cent.-Fox (1970). Color/scope, 95 mins.

A fairly awful sequel to PLANET OF THE APES, this valiant attempt at sf adventure tries to unite the best elements from the first film with standard post-nukeout pessimism. Astronaut Brent (James Franciscus) journeys into the future to search for missing buddy Taylor (Charlton Heston). He encounters a truly repulsive futurescape; a post-holocaust world with intelligent apes ruling mute humans. Running into Taylor's old flame, Nova (Linda Harrison), and counselled by chimp friends Zira and Cornelius (Kim Hunter and David Watson), Brent and Nova go off in search of their mutual acquaintance. What they find, in the ruined subways of New York, is a group of monstrous mutants (led by Victor Buono) who worship the untouched Alpha-Omega Bomb . . . the device built to destroy the entire world.

Brent, Nova, and—yes—Taylor are captured by the mutants. Suddenly, warlike gorillas invade the territory and begin machine-gunning every human in sight, including our three heroes. As ape Dr. Zaius (Maurice Evans) studies the nuclear device, unmindful of the human carnage around him, a dying but still miffed Heston triggers the device. So long, world.

PRODUCER: Arthur Jacobs. DIRECTOR: Ted Post. MAKEUP: John Chambers. SPECIAL EFFECTS: Lyle B. Abbott, Art Cruickshank. MUSIC: Leonard Rosenman. ART DIRECTORS: Jack Martin Smith, William Creber. CINEMATOGRAPHY: Milton Krasner.

SUPPORTING PLAYERS: Jeff Corey, Tod Andrews.

BEWARE THE BLOB
Also known as THE SON OF BLOB.
Harris (1972). Technicolor, 88 mins.

Could have been called *Beware the Script*. That old matinee idol, the Blob from outer space, is given a second chance in this alleged comedy. A piece of the Blob is accidentally thawed. Immediately it begins to grow and hunt for food of the humanoid variety. One unlucky fellow (Godfrey Cambridge) becomes Blob Jr.'s first victim when he accidentally drinks it in a can of beer. A lot of Hollywood stars in cameos are eventually snuffed before the cops tell the Blob to get stuffed.

PRODUCER: Anthony Harris. DIRECTOR: Larry Hagman. SCREENPLAY: Anthony Harris and Jack Woods, from a story by Richard Clair and Jack H. Harris. MUSIC: Mort Garson. SPECIAL EFFECTS: Tim Barr.

SUPPORTING PLAYERS: Carol Lynley, Robert Walker, Shelley Berman.

BEYOND THE TIME BARRIER
AIP (1960). B/w, 75 mins.

Test pilot Maj. William Allison (Robert Clarke) breaks through the time barrier and winds up in 2042 A.D. He finds a pretty standard postnukeout world, with mutants on the top soil and superscientific humans, who are deaf, mute, and sterile, living below. The nuclear war, it seems, has done more than just spawn radiation—it has started a radioactive plague. Allison attempts to head back into his own time to warn the Earth of impending doom. One hitch: he's infected, too.

PRODUCER: Robert Clarke. DIRECTOR: Edgar Ulmer. SCREENPLAY: Arthur C. Pierce. MAKEUP: Jack Pierce. DESIGN: Ernest Fegte. MUSIC: Darrell Calker.

SUPPORTING PLAYERS: Darlene Tompkins, John Van Drelen, Tom Ravick.

BILLION-DOLLAR BRAIN, THE
UA (1967). Color, 108 mins.

Sleuth Harry Palmer (Michael Caine) runs across a right-wing millionaire who is forming his own private army to battle the communists. Helping him in the Armed Forces planning department is a supercomputer.

PRODUCER: Harry Saltzman. DIRECTOR: Ken Russell. SCREENPLAY: John McGrath, from the novel by Len Deighton. CINEMATOGRAPHY: Billy Williams. MUSIC: Richard Rodney Bennett.

Hippity-Hopping Horror

When we finally had enough grasshoppers on the set, we found out that the insects were cannibalistic! They ate each other in between takes. We'd come in every morning and there'd be bodies lying all over the place. By the time I had to invade Chicago, I only had about twelve grasshoppers left!

> Producer Bert I. Gordon on the making of *The Beginning of the End*

SUPPORTING PLAYERS: Karl Malden, Ed Begley, Oscar Homolka, Françoise Dorleac.

BIRTH OF A ROBOT, THE
Shell Oil (G.B., 1934). Color, seven mins.

Stop-motion animation is used to show the first moments in the life of an automaton.

PRODUCER: Charles H. Dand. DIRECTORS: Humphrey Jennings, Len Lye.

BLACK FRIDAY
Universal (1940). B/w, 70 mins.

A very tidy screenplay by Curt Siodmak and Eric Taylor keeps this sf melodrama above par at all times. Kindly English professor George Kingsley (Boris Karloff) is run down in the street during a gang war. Both Kingsley and a gangster lie near death as a result of the fracas, and both men wind up at the surgical mercy of one of Kingsley's dearest friends, Dr. Ernest Sovac. Sovac decides to save the man of letters' life by replacing some of Kingsley's mutilated brain-tissue with healthy doses of the gangster's. Although this does save the professor's life, it gives him a dangerous split-personality. Being taken over by the gangster's brain for periods of time, he vows revenge on those who tried to kill him.

DIRECTOR: Arthur Lubin. CINEMATOGRAPHY: Elwood Bredell.

SUPPORTING PLAYERS: Bela Lugosi, Stanley Ridges, Anna Nagle, Anne Gwynn, Paul Fix, Jack Mulhall.

BLACK HOLE, THE
Walt Disney (1979). Technicolor and Technovision, 97 mins.

Sort of a "Captain Nemo in space" plot line is combined with striking visual effects in this space epic, the first Disney movie ever to earn a *PG* rating. In the distant future, a group of space explorers (Anthony Perkins as Dr. Alex Durant, Robert Forster as Capt. Dan Holland, Joseph Bottoms as Lt. Charles Pizer, Yvette Mimieux as Dr. Kate Mc-Crae, and Ernest Borgnine as Harry Booth) run across the long-lost space-ship *Cygnus,* moored on the lip of a massive black hole. The craft is anything but abandoned, being run by half-crazed genius Dr. Hans Reinhardt (Maximillian Schell) and staffed by a crew of semipsychotic robots. Half the robots, as it turns out, are what's left of the *Cygnus's* original human crew. When the crew objected to Reinhardt's crazy schemes, he did them in, making them humanoid drones.

If this knowledge isn't enough to rattle the small band of explorers, the fact that Reinhardt plans to sail through the black hole certainly is! Aided by good robots V.I.N.C.E.N.T. (the voice of Roddy McDowall) and Old Bob, the humans try to escape. Reinhardt, on the other hand, has sadistic robot Maximillian to make sure that no one gets off his craft in one piece. Oh boy.

PRODUCER: Ron Miller. DIRECTOR: Gary Nelson. SCREENPLAY: Jeb Rosebrook and Gerry Day, from a story by Rosebrook, Bob Barbash, and Richard Landau. CINEMATOGRAPHY: Frank Phillips. PRODUCTION DESIGN: Peter Ellenshaw. DIRECTOR OF MINIATURE PHOTOGRAPHY: Art Cruickshank. MINIATURE EFFECTS: Peter Ellenshaw. COMPOSITE OPTICAL PHOTOGRAPHY: Eustace Lycett. MECHANICAL EFFECTS: Danny Lee. MATTE EFFECTS: Harrison Ellenshaw. ROBOTS: George F. McGinnis. MUSIC: John Barry.

BLAST OFF
Reed (1954). B/w, 78 mins.

Several edited episodes of the TV series ROCKY JONES, SPACE RANGER.

CAST: Richard Crane, Sally Mansfield, Maurice Cass.

BLOB, THE
Paramount (1958). DeLuxe color, 85 mins.

Imagine the chagrin of poor Steve and Judy (Steve McQueen and Aneta Corseaut), two teens who try to convince local police that there is a big Blob running around the nearby forest sucking up local residents as if they were bonbons. The Blob, it seems, has crash-landed on Earth atop a meteor fragment. Roaming around the countryside, it decides to have a quick lunch and munch on a few humans. With each human body consumed, the thing grows bigger and bigger.

Although the police initially suspect the two teenage Blob-boosters of lying, they reconsider when the monster appears in the town, mowing down a supermarket and clearing out a movie theater. Enter the military. The thing is stunned, frozen, and dropped into the Arctic, where, the world hopes, it will freeze into a fairly large ice cube.

PRODUCER: Jack H. Harris. DIRECTOR: Irwin S. Yeaworth, Jr. SCREENPLAY: Theodore Simonson, Kate Phillips. MUSIC: Ralph Carmichael. SPECIAL EFFECTS: Barton Sloane.

SUPPORTING PLAYERS: Earl Rowe, Olin Howlin.

BLOOD BEAST FROM OUTER SPACE
Also known as THE NIGHT CALLER; THE NIGHT CALLER FROM OUTER SPACE.
New Art–Armitage (G.B., 1965), NTA-Harris (U.S., 1968). B/w, 84 mins.

A pretty ugly humanoid from one of Jupiter's moons disguises himself and comes to Earth in search of pretty girls (join the club). He needs shapely Earthlings to zip back up to his mutant-laden planet in order to start the population of the world all over again, unblemished. Placing a series of ads for cheesecake models in *Bikini Girl* magazine, the alien (Robert Crewsdon) traps the would-be centerfolds and sends them zipping off into space. A trio of investigative scientists/police officials, led by Professor Morley (Maurice Denham), Jack Costain (John Saxon), and Ann Barlow (Patricia Haines), track down the alien culprit. Ann acts as bait, posing as a bikini girl.

Tough luck, Ann—our alien is also telepathic. Ann is butchered for her bravery. The police close in. The alien reveals his scarred face and makes for space with haste.

PRODUCER: Ronald Liles. DIRECTOR: John Gilling. SCREENPLAY: Jim O'Connolly. MUSIC: John Gregory.

BLUE LIGHT, THE
Sokal Films (Germany/Italy, 1932), Du World (English language, 1934). B/w, 90 mins.

A mysterious crystal substance has an unworldly glow that lures humans to their deaths.

DIRECTOR: Leni Riefenstahl. SCREENPLAY: Riefenstahl, Bela Balazs, Hans Schneeberger. CINEMATOGRAPHY: Schneeberger.

CAST: Leni Reifenstahl, Mathias Wieman.

BOOGIE MAN WILL GET YOU, THE
Columbia (1942). B/w, 66 mins.

A whimsical little effort starring Boris Karloff as a kindly but totally-bananas professor who is attempting to create a race of supermen in the basement of a country hotel. His efforts succeed only in causing premature cessation of life in his human guinea pigs. When a young couple (Larry Parks and Maude Eburne) discover the plot, they reveal all to sheriff–real estate agent–mayor Peter Lorre. He isn't about to disrupt the professor's work if there's a quick buck to be made.

PRODUCER: Colbert Clark. DIRECTOR: Lew Landers. SCREENPLAY: Edwin Blum, from an adaptation by Paul Gangelin of a story by Hal Fimberg and Robert B. Hunt. CINEMATOGRAPHY: Henry Freulich.

SUPPORTING PLAYERS: Slapsie Maxie Rosenbloom, Jeff Donnell, Don Beddoe, Frank Puglia.

BOWERY BOYS MEET THE MONSTERS, THE
AA (1954). B/w, 65 mins.

The slaphappy and rapidly aging Bowery Boys get involved with a mad scientist. Huntz Hall is somehow coaxed into a brain transplant operation with a gorilla and a robot and winds up looking like Lon Chaney, Jr., after a hard night under the full moon.

PRODUCER: Ben Schwalb. DIRECTOR: Ed Bernds. SCREENPLAY: Bernds, Edward Ullman. MAKEUP: Edward Polo. CINEMATOGRAPHY: Harry Neumann. SPECIAL EFFECTS: Augie Lohman.

CAST: Huntz Hall, Leo Gorcey, Lloyd Corrigan, Ellen Corby, John Dehner.

BOY AND HIS DOG, A
LQ/Jaf (1975). Color/scope, 89 mins.

An admirable sf fantasy based on a story by HARLAN ELLISON, this film takes place in the postholocaust world of 2024. A survivor, Vic (Don Johnson), and his dog, Blood (Tiger), struggle to stay alive on the desolate surface of what was once America. Blood ferrets out food for his master and communicates, in English, via telepathy. As if finding food and shelter were not challenges enough, the pair must fend off marauding gangs of desperate characters.

The twosome encounters pretty Quilla June (Susanne Benton), who lures them to the underground fantasy-world of Topeka. Captured by slightly deranged Midwesterners, Vic is informed that he must impregnate 30 young girls in order to keep the intelligent human race alive substrata. Living beneath the Earth has, it seems, made all the young men sterile. Vic isn't exactly against this idea until he is strapped down into a hospital bed and tied to an Acc-Jac, a device that not only will provide the necessary seed for human survival but also will take the worry out of being close. With Quilla's help, Vic escapes topside. There he finds a dying Blood, still waiting at Topeka's entrance. Blood will die without food. Vic must decide in a hurry where to do some food shopping.

PRODUCER: Alvy Moore. DIRECTOR: AND SCREENWRITER: L. Q. Jones. Screenplay based on the novella by Harlan Ellison. CINEMATOGRAPHY: John Arthur Morrill. MUSIC: Tim McIntire. MAKEUP: Wes Dawn. SPECIAL EFFECTS: Frank Rowe.

SUPPORTING PLAYERS: Alvy Moore as Dr. Moore, Jason Robards as Lew, Charles McGraw as Preacher, Tim McIntire as Blood's voice.

BOYS FROM BRAZIL, THE
20th Cent.-Fox (1978). DeLuxe color, 124 mins.

Former Nazi officials Josef Mengele (Gregory Peck) and Eduard Seibert (James Mason), generally believed to be long dead, devise a plot wherein the fathers of 94 individual sons are to be assassinated by Nazi henchmen. Nazi-hunter Ezra Lieberman (Laurence Olivier) discovers the mass murders and begins to investigate, both to trace the source and to discover the reason. He is astounded on both counts.

As it turns out, shortly before the end of the war the Nazi government's science department discovered the secret of cloning. With a bit of the flesh of the Führer, they have since cloned 94 teenage Hitler look-alikes. In order to duplicate the fatherless Führer's childhood exactly, they have placed the boys in homes nearly identical, in terms of social status, to the original Hitler's, and now are going about orphaning the clones in the hopes that *one* of the patients will develop into a perfect replica of the original. The purpose? A second Master Race.

PRODUCERS: Martin Richards, Stanley O'Toole. DIRECTOR: Franklin J. Schaffer. SCREENPLAY: Heywood Gould, from a novel by IRA LEVIN. CINEMATOGRAPHY: Henri Decae. ART DIRECTOR: Peter Lamont. MUSIC: Jerry Goldsmith.

SUPPORTING PLAYERS: Lilli Palmer as Esther Lieberman, Uta Hagen as Frieda Maloney, John Dehner as Henry Wheelock, Michael Gough as Harrington, and Jeremy Black as Jack/Simon/Bobby.

BRAIN, THE
CCC/Stross (W. Germany/G.B., 1962), Governor (U.S., 1965). B/w, 83 mins.

Yet another version of CURT SIODMAK's excellent novel, *Donovan's Brain* (see DONOVAN'S BRAIN and THE LADY AND THE MONSTER). A disembodied brain telepathically dominates the doctor who keeps it alive and well.

PRODUCER: Raymond Stross. DIRECTOR: Freddie Francis. SCREENPLAY: Robert Stewart, Phil Mackie. CINEMATOGRAPHY: Bob Huke. MUSIC: Ken Jones.

CAST: Peter Van Eyck, Anne Heywood, Cecil Parker, Bernard Lee, Jack MacGowran.

BRAIN EATERS, THE
AIP (1958). B/w, 60 mins.

A film as subtle as its title suggests, this potboiler concerns the skills of a fleet of tiny, crablike aliens who attach themselves to victims' arms and suck out their brains the hard way. A clear case of biting the hand that feeds you.

PRODUCER: Ed Nelson. DIRECTOR: Bruno Ve Sota. SCREENPLAY: Gordon Urqhart, from the novel *The Puppet Masters*, by ROBERT HEINLEIN. ART DIRECTOR: Bert Shomberg. CINEMATOGRAPHY: Larry Raimond.

CAST: Ed Nelson, Leonard Nimoy, Jack Hill, Jody Fair, Joanna Lee.

BRAIN FROM PLANET AROUS, THE
Howco International (1958). B/w, 71 mins.

Has to be seen to be believed. A large, flying superbrain from outer space lands on Earth and discovers, much to its embarrassment, that in order to succeed in this old world, you have to have a good head on your shoulders. In fact, you have to have shoulders. And a matching body below *them*.

Gee. What's a superintelligence to do? Using supertelepathic powers, it attaches itself to a hapless human's body (played by perpetually hapless John Agar) and plans to take over the Earth. The evil brain, Gor, is having a wild weekend until his counterpart, good brain Vol, arrives on the planet. Vol takes over the body of a nearby dog and the final battle between good and evil resembles the final reel of *Lassie Come Home*.

PRODUCER: Jacques Marquette. DIRECTOR: Nathan Hertz. SCREENPLAY: Ray Buffum. MUSIC: Walter Greene.

SUPPORTING PLAYERS: Joyce Meadows, Robert Fuller, Ken Terrell.

BRAIN OF BLOOD
Hemisphere (1971). Color, 88 mins.

The cinematic answer to whatever happened to Grant (THE INCREDIBLE SHRINKING MAN) Williams. Apparently, not much. A scientist conducts a fairly-

unorthodox brain transplant to create
an obedient monster.

PRODUCERS: Sam Sherman, Al Adamson. DIRECTOR: Al Adamson. SCREENPLAY: Joe Van Rodgers, Kane W. Lynn.

CAST: Grant Williams, Kent Taylor,
Vicki Volanti, John Bloom.

BRAIN THAT WOULDN'T DIE, THE
Sterling/Carlton (G.B., 1959), AIP
(U.S., 1962). B/w, 81 mins.

After his fiancée is decapitated in a
fairly ugly auto accident, a young surgeon brings her head back for company. Although the girl appreciates the
thought, she is somewhat less than enthused about having no body around
when she needs one. Adding to the
generally happy atmosphere of the lab
is the deranged mutant kept in the
broom closet. And you thought chemistry was a dull subject?

PRODUCER: Rex Carlton. DIRECTOR
AND SCREENWRITER: Joseph Green.
MAKEUP: George Fiala. CINEMATOGRAPHY: Stephen Hajnal. SPECIAL EFFECTS: Byron Baer.

CAST: Virginia Leith, Herb Evers,
Adele Lamont, Paula Maurice, Lola
Mason.

BRICK BRADFORD
Columbia (1947). B/w serial, 15 chapters.

Attempting to protect an antimissile
invention, the Interceptor Ray, all-American hero Brick Bradford (Kane
Richmond) joins forces with pals Professor Salisbury (Pierre Watkin), Sandy
Sanderson (Rick Valin), and June
Saunders (Linda Johnson) in an effort
to guard the machine's inventor, Dr.
Tymak (John Merton). When Tymak
journeys to the moon via his "crystal
door" in search of the lunarium needed
for the ray, he is captured by evil Lunarians. Brick walks through the door
and, in a rescue attempt, aligns himself
with exiled Lunarian good guys. They
overthrow the rulers and rescue Tymak.

Returning to Earth, Brick rescues the
professor from the clutches of evil Laydron (Charles Quigley), an Earthman
who would like to have an Interceptor
Ray of his very own. In an effort to
finally complete the ray, Tymak sends
Brick and Sandy back into the 18th
century in his "time top," in search of a

formula developed by an 18th-century
scientist. Meanwhile, Laydron closes in
during the 20th century. Sometimes it
pays to stay in school.

PRODUCER: Sam Katzman. DIRECTORS: Spencer G. Bennett, Thomas
Carr. SCREENPLAY: George H. Plympton, Arthur Hoerl, and Lewis Clay,
based on the comic strip of the same
name.

BRIDE OF FRANKENSTEIN
Universal (1935). B/w, 80 mins.

A masterpiece of Gothic science-horror. The sequel to the original Boris
Karloff Frankenstein, this movie actually outdoes its predecessor.

One stormy night, MARY WOLLSTONECRAFT SHELLEY (Elsa Lanchester) decides to continue her tale of Dr. Frankenstein for the benefit of her husband,
Percy, and friend Lord Byron. Picking
up where the first film left off, an injured Dr. Frankenstein (Colin Clive) is
carried away from the burning windmill
in which his monster (Karloff) has been
trapped and presumably destroyed.
Henry Frankenstein is carried back on
a stretcher to his castle, where he is received by his fiancée, Elizabeth (Valerie
Hobson).

Meanwhile, back at the rubble, a
local biddy, Minnie (Una O'Connor),
and the local constable (E. E. Clive)
discuss the death of the monster. The
creature, however, is anything but deceased. He arises from the underground
well near the mill and kills two villagers.

Henry is on the mend and totally unaware of the monster's existence when
he is confronted by an old professor,
Dr. Praetorius (Ernest Thesiger). Praetorius has heard of Henry's experiments
and wants to join forces with him. The
elder scientist has perfected flawless
bodies and given them life. His problem, however, deals with size. All of his
creations—a king, a dancer, etc.—are six
inches tall and kept in small jars. Henry
refuses to cooperate. Praetorius vows
to return.

The burned and hungry monster,
meanwhile, stumbles through the countryside, being shot at by passing hunters and screamed at by passing lasses.
Coming to the hut of a blind hermit

Universal

Bride of Frankenstein

(O. P. Heggie), the monster is taught both compassion and language by the kindly old man. Eventually the creature is spotted by two passing hunters (one of whom is played by a very young John Carradine). They "rescue" the old man from his misshapen friend's clutches and accidentally set fire to the hermit's hut.

Seeking to mingle with his own kind, the monster stalks through a cemetery, where he bumps into Praetorius and henchman Karl (Dwight Frye), both in the process of grave robbing. The old scientist is somewhat amused by the monster's appearance and promises to make him a bride. Praetorius then cons the creature into kidnapping Elizabeth as extra leverage in getting Dr. Frankenstein to cooperate in the experiment.

Henry caves in to Praetorius's demands and his mad lab sparkles with electricity once more. Using giant kites to attract stray bolts of lightning, they bring the bandage-swathed bride of Frankenstein to "life." The monster sits nearby Helpless. Hopeful. Expectant.

The ultimate culmination of pathos and terror comes when the woman (Elsa Lanchester) is unwrapped and led to her bridegroom. The monster extends his hand—a pathetic gesture of friendship. The woman-thing gazes into the ugly visage of her mate-to-be. She recoils, falling into Henry's outstretched arms. The monster's face is caught between expressions of rage and heartbreak. His bride shrieks at him, emitting a loathsome, reptilian hiss. The monster realizes the truth. "She hates me . . . like others, . . ." he mumbles.

Allowing Henry and released fiancée Elizabeth to escape the laboratory, the monster reaches for a lever that, according to a panicky Praetorius, "will blow us all to atoms." The two lovers close the lab door behind them. The monster gazes at his bride. She sneers at his battle-scarred face. A single tear runs down the monster's cheek. "We belong dead," he pronounces, pulling the lever and sending the tower-lab tumbling across the countryside.

An amazing film featuring superb design, scripting, acting, and musical scoring. A flawless horror movie.

PRODUCER: Carl Laemmle, Jr. DIRECTOR: James Whale. STORY AND SCREENPLAY: John Balderston and William Hurlbut, suggested by the novel *Frankenstein*, by Mary W. Shelley. ART DIRECTOR: Charles Hall. MAKEUP: Jack Pierce. SPECIAL EFFECTS: John P. Fulton. CINEMATOGRAPHY: John J. Mescall. ELECTRICAL PROPS (LAB): Kenneth Strickfaden. MUSIC: Franz Waxman.

PRIDE OF THE MONSTER
DCA (1956). B/w, 69 mins.

Truly mind-bending. Dr. Varnoff (Bela Lugosi) has a problem. Not only can't he speak English clearly enough to be understood, but his resident rubber octopus is killing off local citizens. If this isn't annoying enough, his mongoloid pal, Lobo (Tor Johnson), is. Looking on the bright side of things, Varnoff continues a series of experiments designed to create a race of giants. They don't work. Lobo gets upset, tosses a tantrum, and, finally, tosses the doctor onto the operating table and turns up the juice. Result: one really big Dr. Varnoff and one really rubbery octopus. Two out of three falls.

PRODUCER AND DIRECTOR: Edward D. Wood, Jr. SCREENPLAY: Wood, Alex Gordon. SPECIAL EFFECTS: Pat Dinga. MUSIC: Frank Worth.

SUPPORTING PLAYERS: Tony McCoy, Loretta King, William Benedict, Eddie Parker (Lugosi's double).

BRIDES OF FU MANCHU
7 Arts (1966). Color, 94 mins.

Evil Fu Manchu (Christopher Lee) plans to control the world by kidnapping the ravishing daughters of world leaders and blackmailing the countries into submission. Just in case that scheme falls through, however, he's also perfected a death ray. Not really appreciating Fu's planning is Scotland Yard's Nayland Smith (Douglas Wilmer) and sidekick Dr. Petrie (Howard Marion-Crawford), who trap Fu in his lair and blow up the entire palace, ray gun and all.

PRODUCERS: Oliver A. Unger, Harry Alan Towers. DIRECTOR: Don Sharp. SCREENPLAY: Sharp and Towers, based on the characters created by Sax Rohmer. CINEMATOGRAPHY: Ernest Steward. MUSIC: Johnn Douglas.

SUPPORTING PLAYERS: Marie Versini, Carole Gray, Rupert Davies.

BROOD, THE
New World (1979). Color, 91 mins.

Frank Carveth (Art Hindle) tries desperately to keep his wife, Nola (Samantha Eggar), away from their small child, Candice (Cindy Hinds). Nola, it seems, is mentally unhinged and in the care of Dr. Raglan (Oliver Reed), and Frank thinks it wise not to let his daughter see the missus while she is in a frenzied state. If he only knew the extent of the frenzy! Dr. Raglan, an unorthodox type, exhorts his patients to try to rid themselves of their problems through thinking them out, pushing them out of their minds. Nola takes the treatment to heart and soon, through the abnormal power of her mind, she pushes her hostilities out into the open, physically. Through psi abilities, she conjures up a horrid horde of mini-murderers who run about the area killing all those who have caused Nola grief during recent years. And, boy, is that list a long one!

PRODUCER: Claude Heroux. DIRECTOR: David Cronenberg. CINEMATOGRAPHY: Mark Irwin. SCREENPLAY: Cronenberg. MUSIC: Howard Shore.

SUPPORTING PLAYERS: Nuala Fitzgerald as Julianna, Michael McGhee as Inspector Mrazek, Felix Silla as the Child, Susan Hogan as Ruth.

BUBBLE, THE
Midwestern Magic (1966). Color/scope and 3-D, 112 mins.

Très bizarre but a bit too deranged to succeed. A trio of startled humans (Johnny Desmond, Michael Cole, and Deborah Walley) find themselves stranded in a deserted town that alien invaders have cut off from the rest of the world via a huge force-field.

PRODUCER, DIRECTOR, AND SCREENWRITER: Arch Oboler. ART DIRECTOR: Marvin Chomsky. MUSIC: Paul Sawtell and Bert Shafter.

BUCK ROGERS
Known in feature form as PLANET OUTLAWS (1953) and DESTINATION SATURN (1965).
Universal (1939). B/w serial, 12 chapters (24 reels), 384 mins. total running time.

The legendary comic-book hero leaps to the screen with a great deal of style and energy—and even, for the time, a nice bit of money invested in effects and scenery. Anthony "Buck" Rogers (Buster Crabbe) and teenage pal Buddy (Jackie Moran) are sent in the 20th century into a state of suspended animation. They do not awaken until the 25th century, in which they find a world embroiled in constant warfare. Helping Dr. Huer (C. Montague Shaw) and Wilma Deering (Constance Moore) in their fight against the evil Killer Kane (Anthony Ward), Buck journeys to Saturn to enlist the aid of the humanoid race of Saturnians. Disaster nearly rises to the surface, however, when one of Kane's henchmen, Lasca (Henry Brandon), also takes to Saturn, attempting to lead the primitive Zugs in a rebellion against the Saturnian monarchy. Lasca is thwarted by Buck, who also manages to subdue the Zugs. The Saturnians, seeing that Buck is on the up-and-up, side with him. Buck leads a small fleet of Saturnian ships back to Earth, where they obliterate Killer Kane's forces.

ASSOCIATE PRODUCER: Barney Sarecky. DIRECTORS: Ford Beebe, Saul Goodkind. SCREENPLAY: Norman S. Hall and Ray Trampe, from the character created by PHILIP NOWLAN in his novels and Nowlan and Dick Calkins in the comic strips.

> So Much for Darwin
> Our Great Lawgiver tells us that never, *never,* will the human have the ape's divine faculty for distinguishing between good and evil.
>> General Ursus (James Gregory) to his peer group in *Beneath the Planet of the Apes*

SUPPORTING PLAYERS: Henry Brandon, Jack Mullhall, Wheeler Oakman, Kenne Duncan.

BUCK ROGERS
Universal (1979). Technicolor, 89 mins.

Originally intended as part of a proposed 1978 NBC-TV miniseries, this two-hour telefilm was bumped from the airwaves, tossed into theaters in March 1979, and then reedited and shown on the tube in September of that year as the two-hour pilot for the resulting one-hour, weekly BUCK ROGERS TV series. Sound confusing? You should read the script sometime.

Buck Rogers (Gil Gerard) is a late-20th-century astronaut whose ship ("the last of the deep-space probes") goes ga-ga and brings him back to Earth in the 25th century. Rescued, at first, by the evil Princess Ardala (Pamela Hensley) and nasty Kane (Henry Silva), marked down from "Killer" Kane in the old serial, Buck is astounded at both the high level of technology and the low level of neckline displayed by the princess.

Eventually making his way to New Chicago, he is captured by Wilma Deering (Erin Gray) and Dr. Huer (Tim O'Connor), who would like to believe Buck's time-travel story but suspect him of being one of Ardala's spies. Only loyal robot Twiki (Felix Silla, with the voice of Mel Blanc) believes in Buck. With a mechanical cheerleading squad behind him, Buck proves his innocence and stops Ardala and Kane from destroying New Chicago.

EXECUTIVE PRODUCER: Glen A. Larson. PRODUCER: Richard Caffey. DIRECTOR: Daniel Haller. SCREENPLAY: Glen Larson and Leslie Stevens, based on the novels of PHILIP NOWLAN. CINEMATOGRAPHY: Frank Beascoechea. SET DI-

RECTION: Richard Reams. SPECIAL EFFECTS: Bud Ewing, Jack Faggard. MUSIC: Stu Phillips.

SUPPORTING PLAYERS: Joseph Wiseman as Draco, Duke Butler as Tigerman.

BUG
Paramount (1975). Movielab color, 100 mins.

An earthquake uncovers a brood of large and lethal cockroaches that can set people afire through the rapid motion of their hind legs. The bugs present a real menace to society, in that they can burn entire cities down before their presence is detected. Scientist James Parmiter (Bradford Dillman) starts off on a campaign to eliminate the creepy crawlers but gradually gets to know the new strain and tries to communicate with them, developing new strains in his lab. Mrs. Parmiter (Joanna Miles) is not amused, especially when the bugs decide that they'd rather communicate with a bachelor.

PRODUCER: William Castle. DIRECTOR: Jeannot Szwarc. SCREENPLAY: William Castle and Thomas Page, based on the novel *The Hephaestus Plague,* by Thomas Page. CINEMATOGRAPHY: Michael Hugo. SPECIAL EFFECTS: Phil Cory. INSECT SEQUENCES: Ken Middleham. ELECTRONIC MUSIC: Charles Fox.

SUPPORTING PLAYERS: Patty McCormack as Sylvia Ross, Richard Gilliland as Gerald Metbaum, Jamie Smith Jackson as Norma Tacker.

BY RADIUM RAYS
Universal (1914). B/w silent featurette, two reels.

An insane fellow is cured by radium treatment.

CAPE CANAVERAL MONSTERS
CCM (1960). B/w, 69 mins.

Nasty alien brains (represented during the film's finale as cartoon splotches appearing on the screen) take over human bodies in an attempt to sabotage the U.S. space program. Today that's done quite nicely by members of Congress, and they're not even animated.

PRODUCER: Richard Greer. DIRECTOR AND SCREENWRITER: Phil Tucker. CINEMATOGRAPHY: Merle Connell. MUSIC: Gunthar Kaur.

CAST: Scott Peters, Linda Connell, Katherine Victor, Jason Johnson, Frank Smith.

CAPRICORN ONE
WB (1978). CFI color, 127 mins.

The first manned flight to Mars develops an 11th-hour malfunction, causing NASA, led by Dr. James Kelloway (Hal Holbrook), to officially scuttle the mission. Secretly ushering astronauts Charles Brubaker (James Brolin), Peter Willis (Sam Waterston), and John Walker (O. J. Simpson) off the craft, NASA comes up with a scheme that should keep both the American people and the government happy and allow NASA not to lose face and government funding. Driving the three spacemen to a desert TV studio, NASA decides to fake the entire mission: sending out phony flight reports, simulated pictures of phony space-walks, etc.

When the astronauts grow disgusted with the charade, they rebel. Kelloway has added problems when the real capsule, sent unmanned into space, crashes into the Earth's atmosphere upon its return and burns to a crisp. He then must have the three astronauts killed in order to duplicate the results of the real landing. The trio breaks free. While the astronauts dodge government hitmen in the desert, snoopy reporter Robert Caufield (Elliot Gould) uncovers all the facts and tries to piece them together. Eventually Caufield and crop-duster Albain (Telly Savalas) take to the desert to rescue the one remaining astronaut from government killers.

PRODUCER: Paul N. Lazarus. DIRECTOR AND SCREENWRITER: Peter Hyams. CINEMATOGRAPHY: Bill Butler. ART DIRECTOR: David M. Haber. MUSIC: Jerry Goldsmith.

SUPPORTING PLAYERS: Brenda Vaccaro as Kay Brubaker, David Doyle as Walter Laughlin, Denise Nichols as Betty Walker, Robert Walden as Elliot Whitter, Lee Bryant as Sharon Willis, Karen Black as Judy Drinkwater.

CAPTAIN AMERICA
Also known as RETURN OF CAPTAIN AMERICA.
Republic (1943). B/w serial, 15 chapters (31 reels).

Dashing D.A. Grant Gardner (Dick Purcell) spends his free time kicking in doors in the guise of Captain America. In this serial, he has his hands (and boots) full in both of his identities, up against a mysterious killer called the Scarab. The Scarab is, in reality, respected museum curator Dr. Maldor (Lionel Atwill), a fellow who feels that he has been cheated of the fame and fortune due him from an expedition he headed. Using a poison called the Purple Death, he begins systematically to murder and rob his stingy colleagues.

From one of the victims, he purloins the Thunder Bolt, a weapon that harnesses light and sound waves and converts them into a blast with quite a clout. While threatening the world with that weapon, Maldor learns the whereabouts of a map telling the spot where an ancient Mayan treasure is buried. Next on his agenda? Kidnap and torture the proper experts for a translation of the map.

DIRECTORS: John English, Elmer Clifton. SCREENPLAY: Royal Cole, Ronald Davidson, Basil Dickey, Jesse Duffy, Harry Fraser, Grant Nelson, Joseph Poland. CINEMATOGRAPHY: John MacBurnie. SPECIAL EFFECTS: Howard and Theodore Lydecker.

SUPPORTING PLAYERS: Lorna Grey, Charles Trowbridge, Jay Novello, Frank Reicher, George J. Lewis.

CAPTAIN NEMO AND THE UNDERWATER CITY
MGM (1970). Color/scope, 106 mins.

Capt. Nemo (Robert Ryan), JULES VERNE's famous black-sheep genius, rules the underground city of Templemer in this well-intentioned if slightly soggy swashbuckler. When a group of landlubbers accidentally stumbles onto the domed city, the captain shows them as much hospitality as a quintessential misanthrope can. All is going well until someone notices that the by-product of

MGM

Captain Nemo and the Underwater City

Nemo's oxygen-making machinery is gold. The greedy aboveworlders make hasty plans to make off with the stash. A giant manta-ray monster called Mobula almost makes off with the entire city. Faced with a two-pronged attack, Nemo manages to solve things amiably.

PRODUCER: Bertram Ostrer. DIRECTOR: James Hill. SCREENPLAY: R. Wright Campbell, Pip and Jane Baker. ART DIRECTOR: Bill Andrews. MUSIC: Walter Scott.

SUPPORTING PLAYERS: Chuck Conners, Luciana Paluzzi, Kenneth Connor.

CAPTAIN ULTRA
Toei (Japan, 1962). Color.

A Japanese superhero battles aliens and boredom.

DIRECTOR: Koichi Takemoto.

CAST: Yuki Shirono, Hirohisa Nakata, Nenji Kobayashi.

CAPTAIN VIDEO
Columbia (1951). B/w, tinted serial, 15 chapters (30 reels), 480 mins. total running time.

Judd Holdren plays space savior Capt. Video, the hero of a then-popular TV series. In this slam-bang action adventure, the good captain and his Rocket Rangers must stop the forces of Vultura of Atoma, who are attempting to take over the Earth using robots and ray guns.

PRODUCER: Sam Katzman. DIRECTORS: Spencer G. Bennett, Wallace A. Grissell. SCREENPLAY: Royal K. Cole, Sherman Lowe, and Joseph Poland. MUSIC: Mischa Bakaleinikoff. SPECIAL EFFECTS: Jack Erickson.

SUPPORTING PLAYERS: Larry Stewart, Gene Roth, William Fawcett.

CAPTIVE WOMEN
RKO (1952). B/w, 65 mins.

Intense symbolism here. One thousand years in the future, after the world has really messed itself up with a few well-placed A-bombs, humanity is divided into three groupings: the Norms (short for Normals), the Mutes (short for mutants), and the Uplanders (a daring three-syllable moniker). Only by reuniting these three groups will the world be saved from savagery. When modern man visits this futuristic hell, it takes a lot of diplomacy to keep up with the spear-chucking.

PRODUCERS AND SCREENWRITERS: Jack Pollexfen, Aubrey Wisberg. DIRECTOR: Stuart Gilmore. DESIGNER: Theobold Holsopple. CINEMATOGRAPHY: Paul Ivano. MUSIC: Charles Koff.

CAST: Robert Clarke, Margaret Field, Ron Randell, Gloria Sanders.

CASTLE OF EVIL
National Telefilm Associates (1966), United Pictures (1968). Color, 81 mins.

After the death of eccentric scientist Kovec (William Thourlby), several people are invited to his island retreat for the reading of the will. Kovec appears to the group, charging one of them with being responsible for the horrible disfiguration of his face he was forced to live with during his last years. One of them will die for it. Kovec's doctor, Robert Hawley (David Brian), is killed. The rest of the visitors, believing the worst is over, relax. Then the late scientist's mistress, Sable (Virginia Mayo), is also killed. It turns out that Kovec's apparition, stalking the guests, is a robot programmed by the doctor to murder his nemesis. The problem is, one of the guests has reprogrammed the robot to eliminate the competing heirs to the Kovec estate. Engineer Matt Grainger (Scott Brady) ends the suspense by firing a laser at the mechanical murderer.

DIRECTOR: Francis D. Lyon. SCREENPLAY: Charles A. Wallace. MUSIC: Paul Dunlap. SPECIAL EFFECTS: Roger George.

SUPPORTING PLAYERS: Hugh Marlowe, Lisa Gayle, Shelley Morrison.

CASTLE OF FU MANCHU

Terra Filmkunst/Producciones Balcazar/Italian International/Towers of London (W. Germany/Spain/Italy/G.B., 1968); International Cinema (U.S., 1972). Color/scope, 92 mins.

Slim pickins as master villain Fu (Christopher Lee) and his daughter (Tsai Chin) try to take over the world with a formula that causes water to freeze instantly. Nayland Smith of Scotland Yard (Richard Greene) is out to stop him.

PRODUCER: Harry Alan Towers. DIRECTOR: Jesus Franco. SCREENPLAY: Manfred Barthel, Jesus Balcazar, Harry Alan Towers. CINEMATOGRAPHY: Manuel Merino. MUSIC: Carlo Camilleri, Malcolm Shelby.

SUPPORTING PLAYERS: Howard Marion-Crawford, Gunther Stoll, Maria Perschy.

CAT FROM OUTER SPACE, THE

Walt Disney/Buena Vista (1978). Technicolor, 103 mins.

An alien cat lands its spaceship on Earth in hopes of carrying out emergency repairs and lifting off as soon as possible. For help it turns to Frank (Ken Berry). The cat needs $120,000 worth of gold to make the repairs in time for it to rendezvous with its space fleet. Friends Liz (Sandy Duncan) and Link (McLean Stevenson) think that the cat can earn the money through telepathic noodling with gambling numbers. Meanwhile, Gen. Stilton (Harry Morgan) is looking for an army of nasty invaders, villainous Stallwood (Roddy McDowall) is after the cat's powerful psi-plus collar, and veterinarian Wenger is busily putting the kitty to sleep accidentally during a big wager.

PRODUCER: Ron Miller. DIRECTOR: Norman Tokar. SCREENPLAY: Ted Key. CINEMATOGRAPHY: Charles F. Wheeler. ART DIRECTOR: John B. Mansridge. SPECIAL EFFECTS: Eustace Lycett, Art Cruickshank, Danny Lee. MUSIC: Lalo Schifrin.

SUPPORTING PLAYERS: Ronnie Schell as Sgt. Duffy, Hans Conreid as Heffel, Jesse White as Ernie.

Walt Disney Productions

The Cat from Outer Space

CAT WOMEN OF THE MOON

Astor (1954). B/w and 3-D, 64 mins.

Actor Sonny Tufts leads a batch of equally uncomfortable astronauts onto the moon, where they discover a race of chorus girls clad in tights. Although the women don't resemble felines at all, they do affect the astronauts like catnip. The women, meanwhile, don't know what to do with these males—keep 'em or kill 'em? The astronauts prove to be nice guys, however, saving one or two meow-misses from a papier-mâché spider about five feet long. Kisses follow. One small step for man, one smaller step for moviekind.

PRODUCERS: Jack Rabin, Al Zimbalist. DIRECTOR: Arthur Hilton. SCREENPLAY: Roy Hamilton. SPECIAL EFFECTS: Jack Rabin. MUSIC: Elmer Bernstein.

SUPPORTING PLAYERS: Marie Windsor, Victor Jory, Susan Morrow, Carol Brewster.

CAVES OF STEEL

BBC-TV (G.B., 1967). B/w, 75 mins.

An adaptation of the ISAAC ASIMOV book, teaming a human detective with a robot Dr. Watson in the future.

DIRECTOR: Eric Taylor.
CAST: Peter Cushing, Eric Taylor.

CHAIRMAN, THE

Also known as THE MOST DANGEROUS MAN IN THE WORLD.
20th Cent.-Fox (1969). Color, 104 mins.

An American scientist (Gregory Peck) is sent into Red China with a tiny transmitter embedded in his head. His job is to meet Chairman Mao and convince him that he (Peck) is willing to defect from the U.S. Once accepted by the Chinese, he is to learn the chemical secrets of their scientists, who have developed a formula that allows crops to grow anywhere in the world, in any type of climatic condition. The transmitter in his head relays everything he says and is said to him back to a U.S. way-station. What the scientist doesn't know is that he also is carrying a bomb in his head, set to go off if anything goes wrong with his mission. Excedrin headache #679.

An Apjac production. DIRECTOR: J. Lee Thompson. SCREENPLAY: Ben Maddow, based on the novel by Richard Kennedy.

SUPPORTING PLAYERS: Anne Heywood, Arthur Hill, Conrad Yama.

CHANGE OF MIND
Cinerama (1969). Color, 98 mins.

A white man's brain is transplanted into a black man's body, with disconcerting results.

PRODUCERS AND SCREENWRITERS: Seeleg Lester, Richard Wesson. DIRECTOR: Robert Stevens. CINEMATOGRAPHY: Arthur J. Ornitz. MUSIC: Duke Ellington.

CAST: Raymond St. Jacques, Susan Oliver, Leslie Nielsen.

CHARLY
Cinerama (1968). Color/scope, 106 mins.

Based on DANIEL KEYES's novel *Flowers for Algernon*, this moving, albeit technically uneven, film traces the scientifically induced maturation of 30-year-old mentally retarded Charly Gordon (Cliff Robertson), a good-natured man with the mind of a child. After undergoing an operation instigated by Alice Kinian (Claire Bloom), Dr. Nemur (Leon Janney), and Dr. Straus (Lilia Skala), Charly and his operation-mate, the mouse Algernon, show great progress. Learning and maturing every day, Charly crams the emotions of a lifetime into a few short months, eventually falling in love with Alice Kinian. Charly becomes the pride of the scientific community, but just as he is about to be unveiled at a convention, word leaks out that Algernon has died. The effects of the operation are only temporary. Charly slowly lapses back into idiocy.

PRODUCER AND DIRECTOR: Ralph Nel-

son. SCREENPLAY: Sterling Silliphant. MAKEUP: Vincent Kehoe. CINEMATOGRAPHY: Arthur J. Ornitz. MUSIC: Ravi Shankar.

SUPPORTING PLAYERS: Dick van Patten, Ruth White.

CHEMIST, THE
Fox (1936). B/w short, 21 mins.

A scientist (Buster Keaton) comes up with a potion that can shrink and enlarge people.

PRODUCER: Al Christie. STORY: David Freedman. CINEMATOGRAPHY: George Webber.

SUPPORTING PLAYERS: Marilyn Stuart, Earl Gilbert.

CHILDREN OF THE DAMNED
MGM (1964). B/w, 90 mins.

A well-structured semisequel to VILLAGE OF THE DAMNED, this movie brought back the "drop dead kids" ("Beware the eyes that paralyze!") for an encore on an international level. Six children with abnormally high intelligence are discovered in six different countries by a UNESCO project. Although separated by miles, the children have the ability to communicate telepathically and can actually order people to commit acts against their will. The world's joy at discovering such brilliant tots fades when it is realized that the children are visitors from the future . . . mutants.

Col. Tom Lewellin (Ian Hendry) and Dr. David Neville (Alan Badel), along with the aunt (Barbara Ferris) of one of the children, believe that the children are here on a peaceful mission. The military panics, however, and while international leaders meet with the children, an order is given to commence firing on the kids' church headquarters in London. The children are slaughtered, taking their message with them to the grave.

PRODUCER: Ben Arbeid. DIRECTOR: Anton M. Leader. SCREENPLAY: Jack Briley, based upon an idea from the novel *The Midwich Cuckoos,* by JOHN WYNDHAM. CINEMATOGRAPHY: David Boulton. SPECIAL EFFECTS: Tom Howard. MUSIC: Ron Goodwin.

SUPPORTING PLAYERS: Alfred Burke, Clive Powell, Bessie Love.

Children of the Damned

CHILD'S PLAY
Group 3 (G.B., 1954). B/w, 68 mins.

A group of children create a miniature atomic explosion.

PRODUCER: Herbert Mason. DIRECTOR: Margaret Thompson. SCREENPLAY: Peter Blackmore, from a story by Don Sharp. CINEMATOGRAPHY: Denny Densham. MUSIC: Anthony Hopkins.

CAST: Mona Washbourne, Peter Martyn, Carl Jaffe.

CHINA SYNDROME, THE
Columbia (1979). Metrocolor, 122 mins.

Speculative fiction nearly collided with science fact when this movie was released in March 1979. Shortly after its premiere, real-life events at the nuclear power plant at Three Mile Island, Pennsylvania, threatened to come close to this near-cataclysmic tale.

While filming at a nuclear-energy plant, TV newswoman Kimberly Wells (Jane Fonda) and freelance cameraman Richard Adams (Michael Douglas) witness a control-room accident of near-catastrophic results. Plant supervisor Jack Godell (Jack Lemmon), soon has everything under control, but during the actual accident, instrument malfunctions and misreadings nearly cause the plant to contaminate the area in a big way.

The plant plays down the incident, but the resulting news footage stirs up a ruckus at the TV station. Station manager Don Jaconvich (Peter Donat) forbids the film to be shown, buckling under pressure generated by power-company executive Evan McCormack (Richard Herd). Realizing that the nuclear plant is a possible suicide-note for half the state of California, Adams steals the footage and hands it over to antinuclear groups. His attempt, however, leads to the murder of coworker Hector Salas (Daniel Valdez). Eventually even Supervisor Godell joins in the truth movement when he discovers that the plant is a time bomb built with faulty construction in order both to save money and ensure kickbacks for higher-ups. In an attempt to tell the nation, live on TV, exactly what really happened, he holds his coworkers hostage until a camera crew arrives. The TV people arrive and are cut off as National Guardsmen storm the plant and fill the honest Godell with lead.

In the wake of Godell's murder, a tearful Kimberly Wells takes to the airwaves and tells the entire story as one of Godell's coworkers, Ted Spindler (Wilford Brimley), formerly intimidated by the power company, comes forth to vouch for the integrity of Godell, who is being branded a madman by the nuclear-energy group.

PRODUCER: Michael Douglas. DIRECTOR: James Bridges. SCREENPLAY: Mike Gray, T. S. Cook, James Bridges. CINEMATOGRAPHY: James Crabe. SPECIAL EFFECTS: Henry Millar, Jr.

SUPPORTING PLAYERS: Scott Brady as Herman DeYoung, James Hampton as Bill Gibson, Stan Bohrman as Pete Martin.

CHOSEN SURVIVORS
Columbia (1974). Color, 99 mins.

A group of scientists and civilians are ushered into an underground complex and told that they are the chosen survivors of the Earth. The world has just been destroyed by a nuclear war and they are *it*, in terms of population. The collected citizens (Jackie Cooper, Richard Jaeckel, Bradford Dillman, Pedro Armendariz, Jr., and Diana Muldaur, among others) are not too pleased with this sudden turn of events.

Well, as it turns out, there's nothing to worry about. The whole exercise is

Chosen Survivors

Goo-Seflesh

I designed a skull with veins and bones protruding completely covered with this synthetic flesh material. When it heated up, it melted at room temperature. Great. But, when it came down to it, we didn't have the time to use it properly in the film, so we used rubber masks with Karo syrup poured all over it. It wasn't exactly what I had in mind.

Rick Baker, makeup wizard on *The Incredible Melting Man*

a hoax—a psychological test. One problem, though: the people really do get trapped down there and they are attacked by hundreds of vampire bats visiting from a nearby cave-complex. The not-very-neighborly humans are determined not to offer their new-found visitors lunch, and therein lies what is euphemistically termed the plot.

PRODUCER: Leon Benson. DIRECTOR: Sutton Roley. SCREENPLAY: H. B. Cross and Joe Reb Moffly, based on a story by Cross.

CITY BENEATH THE SEA
Fox-TV (1971). Color, 120 mins.

In the undersea city of Pacifica, designer and builder Matthews (Stuart Whitman) has his share of troubles, ranging from a pesky amphibious man to an asteroid heading for a collision with the city-site. Also causing alarm is a shipment of new isotope H-128, which is being moved for safekeeping to the citadel beneath the sea.

PRODUCER AND DIRECTOR: Irwin Allen. SCREENPLAY: John Meredyth Lucas. CINEMATOGRAPHY: Kenneth Peache. SPECIAL EFFECTS: Lyle B. Abbott, Art Cruickshank. MUSIC: Richard LaSalle.

SUPPORTING PLAYERS: Robert Wagner, Richard Basehart, James Darren, Whit Bissell, Sugar Ray Robinson, Joseph Cotten.

CLOCKWORK ORANGE, A
WB (1971). Color, 137 mins.

ANTHONY BURGESS's literary adventures of futuristic citizen Alex DeLarge (Malcolm McDowell) are translated to the screen by producer/director Stanley Kubrick in a visually stunning, graphically brutal film that captures little or none of the original novel's wit. Alex and his droogs (pals) are typically violent youths of the future, priding themselves on a base, nonworking existence. After brutally murdering the wife of an author, Alex is tracked down and captured by a group of militaristic rehabilitators. Their goal is to reform Alex via a series of experiments that would make Pavlov cringe. The odyssey of Alex, as he goes from natural and spontaneous violence to forced pacifism, is a somber series of scenes, and the consequences are most interesting to behold. McDowell is superb as Alex and performers such as Patrick Magee (as the author) and Michael Bates offer fine support, but it is director Kubrick who is the real star. Unfortunately, the work is stylized to the point at which the audience is more interested in what the director is doing than the cast. Fine nonetheless, with electronic music offered by Walter Carlos.

A Clockwork Orange

PRODUCER, DIRECTOR, AND SCREEN-WRITER: Stanley Kubrick. ART DIRECTORS: Russell Hagg, Peter Shields. CINEMATOGRAPHY: John Alcott.

SUPPORTING PLAYERS: Warren Clarke, Anthony Sharp, Miriam Karlin.

CLOSE ENCOUNTERS OF THE THIRD KIND

Columbia (1977). Color, 70mm, Dolby sound, 135 mins.

The Holy Grail of UFO movies, Steven Spielberg's CE3K is a long way off from EARTH VS. THE FLYING SAUCERS and other saucer adventures of days of yore. Highlighted by wondrous special effects concocted by Doug Trumbull, the movie has an almost religious quality to it.

A power repairman, Roy Neary (Richard Dreyfuss), is sent to trace the source of the overload during a massive blackout in the Muncie, Indiana, area. Waiting in his truck at a railroad crossing, he is buzzed by a UFO. A chase ensues in which Roy, the state police, and several extraterrestrial vehicles zip through and over the countryside.

Returning home, Roy attempts to convince his wife, Ronnie (Teri Garr), that he has, indeed, seen a saucer. His family clearly thinks he is mistaken. The more he thinks about the saucers, the more his obsession grows. A telepathic "picture" haunts him as well—a picture that takes the shape of a strange mountain.

In need of support, Neary turns to another eyewitness, Jillian Guiler (Melinda Dillon), a woman whose son, Barry (Cary Guffey), has been kidnapped by a UFO. She, too, is haunted by the telepathic flashes. Eventually they discover that their mental images are of Devil's Tower, Wyoming. Believing that the answer to their problems lies there, they make their way to the area, only to find out that there is a government quarantine around the mountain. Poisonous chemicals have leaked into the air because of a train wreck, says the U.S. government. All citizens are asked to leave the area posthaste.

Roy and Jillian don't buy the story,

and tossing off their government-sanctioned gas masks, they make their way to the mountain. They are arrested by the army and brought to a small compound. There they encounter a French expert on UFOs, Claude Lacombe (François Truffaut), and observe members of his international "silence group," a scientific team dedicated to solving the mystery of UFOs and learning how to master a method of communication. The pair deduces that this activity means only one thing: a landing will occur at Devil's Tower.

Escaping, once again, from the clutches of the army, they make their way to the mountain, where, on a landing strip constructed by the air force, they witness one of the most dazzling displays of film magic ever conceived: a mass showing of UFOs of every size, shape, and color. Finally, a mother-ship to end all mother-ships appears. Communicating with the observers via sound, the ship lands. Elfin aliens appear from within, as do dozens of kidnapped humans, from little Cary to long-lost Judge Crater. Jillian is reunited with her son. Roy, along with a select cadre of government personnel, returns to space with the aliens.

PRODUCERS: Julia and Michael Phillips. DIRECTOR AND SCREENWRITER: Steven Spielberg. MUSIC: John Williams. CINEMATOGRAPHY: Vilmos Zsigmond. MAKEUP: Bob Westmoreland. SPECIAL EFFECTS: Douglas Trumbull. VISUAL EFFECTS CONCEPTS: Steven Spielberg. UFO PHOTOGRAPHY: Dave Stewart. CHIEF MODEL-MAKER: Greg Jein. ANIMATOR Harry Moreau.

SUPPORTING PLAYERS: George Dicenzo as Major Benchley, Bob Balaban as David Laughlin, Warren Kemmerling as Wild Bill.

CODE OF THE AIR

Bischoff (1928). B/w silent feature, 5,700 ft.

A villain uses "Kappa rays" to shoot airplanes out of the sky.

DIRECTOR: James P. Hogan. SCREENPLAY: Barry Barenger. CINEMATOGRAPHY: William Miller.

CAST: William V. Mong, Arthur Rankin, Mae Cooper, Ken Harlan, June Marlow.

COLD SUN, THE
Reed (1954). B/w, 78 mins.

More refried adventure of TV's ROCKY JONES, SPACE RANGER. Rocky (Richard Crane) is understandably worried when the sun begins to cool.

PRODUCER: Roland Reed. DIRECTOR: Hollingsworth Morse. SCREENPLAY: Warren Wilson.

COLOSSUS OF NEW YORK, THE
Paramount (1958). B/w, 70 mins.

A slightly off-the-wall fellow transplants the brain of a good-guy scientist into the head of a large, lumbering robot (Ed Wolff). The robot then lurches off in the direction of New York City. Object: destruction. The dead scientist's son (Charles Herbert) sees dad beneath those bolts and does the best he can to reason with the tin can. As Billy speaks, the dormant personality of dead dad Dr. Jeremy Spenser (Ross Martin) peeks through, much to the relief of brother William (Otto Kruger), who instituted the operation.

PRODUCER: William Alland. DIRECTOR: Eugène Lourié. SCREENPLAY: Thelma Schnee, from a story by Willis Goldbeck. MAKEUP: Wally Westmore. SPECIAL EFFECTS: John P. Fulton. MUSIC: Nathan Van Cleave.

SUPPORTING PLAYERS: Robert Hutton, Mala Powers, John Baragrey.

Paramount

The Colossus of New York

COLOSSUS, THE FORBIN PROJECT
Universal (1970). Color, 100 mins.

Colossus is the ultimate computer. Safely nestled in the Rocky Mountains, the computer has the power to launch a fleet of nuclear missiles should the U.S. ever be attacked. Forbin (Eric Braeden), Cleo (Susan Clark), and Grauber (William Schallert) are alarmed when the computer begins to show a mind of its own. Colossus discovers a similar computer in Russia and decides to join its sister machine. It immediately takes control of the world. The CIA and the Russians try to hatch plots against the mighty metal brains, but to no avail. The computer issues an ultimatum: "Make peace now or I'll destroy the Earth."

PRODUCER: Stanley Chase. DIRECTOR: Joseph Sargent. SCREENPLAY: James Bridges, from the novel by D. F. Jones. ART DIRECTOR: Alexander Golitzen. MUSIC: Michael Colombier.

SUPPORTING PLAYERS: Gordon Pinsent, Leonid Rostoff.

COMA
UA (1978). Metrocolor, 113 mins.

A young doctor, Susan Wheeler (Genevieve Bujold), is traumatized when friend Nancy Greenly goes into a coma after a simple operation. Greenly (Lois Chiles) never recovers. Susan finds a disturbing pattern of incidents hushed up in the hospital and tells boy friend Dr. Mark Bellows (Michael Douglas). Rebuked, she begins investigating on her own and finds a conspiracy afoot that includes the most powerful administrators in the hospital, Dr. George (Rip Torn) and Dr. Harris (Richard Widmark). The doctors are causing young, healthy patients to go into coma and then be removed from the hospital and housed in an eerie, Twilight Zone–ish storage center until needed for pay-for-beautiful-transplant operations.

PRODUCER: Martin Erlichman. DIRECTOR: Michael Crichton. SCREENPLAY: Crichton, from the novel by Robin Cook. CINEMATOGRAPHY: Victor J. Kemper, Gerald Hirschfeld. MUSIC: Jerry Goldsmith.

SUPPORTING PLAYERS: Elizabeth Ashley as Mrs. Emerson, Harry Rhodes as Dr. Morelind, Richard Doyle as Jim.

COMET'S COMEBACK, THE
Mutual (1916). B/w silent short.

A comet doses the Earth with a strange gas that brings on terminal laziness. Years before the release of METEOR, which caused a similar effect on critics.

CAST: John Steppling, Carol Halloway, Dick Rosson.

COMMANDO CODY
Known in feature form as SKY MARSHAL OF THE UNIVERSE.
Republic (1953). B/w serial, 12 chapters.

Culled from the TV series (which was spun off from the popular "Rocket Man" theatrical serial), this serial featured stalwart Judd Holdren as Cody, the rocket-belted, bullet-headed crime fighter in the black leather jacket. Sort of a road-runner plot, with Cody chasing after the alien Ruler all around the globe and even into space.

DIRECTORS: Fred C. Brannon, Harry Keller, Franklin Adreon. SCREENPLAY: Ronald Davidson, Barry Shipman. CINEMATOGRAPHY: Bud Thackery. SPECIAL EFFECTS: Howard and Theodore Lydecker.

SUPPORTING PLAYERS: Aline Towne, William Schallert, Lyle Talbot.

Republic

Commando Cody

COMPUTER WORE TENNIS SHOES, THE
Walt Disney/Buena Vista (1970). Color, 90 mins.

A. J. Arno (Cesar Romero), an alumnus of Medfield College, donates his homemade computer to the school in lieu of cash. Dexter (Kurt Russell), a student trying to repair the machine, is struck by a bolt of lightning. The computer's memory banks unload all their knowledge into Dexter's human brain. Dean Higging (Joe Flynn) sees a way to raise money for the school in this disaster and sends Dexter packing for a series of TV quiz shows.

DIRECTOR: Robert Butler. SCREENPLAY: Joseph L. McEveety. ART DIRECTOR: John B. Mansbridge. MUSIC: Robert F. Brunner.

SUPPORTING PLAYERS: Pat Harrington, Jon Provost, Bing Russell.

CONQUEST OF SPACE
Paramount (1955). Color, 80 mins.

Spawned by the success of the film DESTINATION MOON, George Pal's *Conquest of Space* was to have been an eye-boggling adaptation of the colorful book of the same name by Chesley Bonestell and Willy Ley, as well as of *The Mars Project* by Wernher von Braun. Its goal was to have been to take 1950s audiences into space on a fictitious but realistic voyage to Venus, Mars, and beyond. Paramount Pictures, showing the kind of sensitivity for which the studio has become known over the years, told Pal to take his dreams and sit on them, then cut his budget and ordered a stock adventure film.

The action centers around a battle between Samuel and Barney Merritt (Walter Brooke and Eric Fleming) concerning space exploration. While aboard a space station circling the Earth, they differ on the fate of an expedition to Mars. Samuel feels that such a trip is a blasphemy against God. Barney makes the trip. Samuel, under guidance from above, sabotages the trip. This makes for tough sledding on the part of the landing party. Nearly stranded on Mars, they barely lift off and make it safely back to their space-wheel base.

PRODUCER: George Pal. DIRECTOR: Byron Haskin. SCREENPLAY: James O'Hanlon, from a story by Phillip Yordan, Barre Lyndon, and George Worthing Yates. ART DIRECTORS: Hal Pereira,

Joseph Johnson. SPECIAL EFFECTS: John P. Fulton, Paul Lerpae, Jan Domela. MUSIC: Nathan Van Cleave.

SUPPORTING PLAYERS: Phil Foster, William Hopper, Ross Martin, Mickey Shaughnessy, Joan Shawlee.

CONQUEST OF THE AIR
Pathé (France, 1901). B/w silent short.

An astronaut riding a flying bicycle takes to the air.

DIRECTOR: Ferdinand Zecca.

CONQUEST OF THE AIR
Pathé (France, 1906). B/w silent short.

DIRECTOR: Gaston Velle.

CONQUEST OF THE POLE
Star (France, 1912). B/w silent short, 650 ft.

Mabouloff invents an Aerobus and flies across the North Pole. While there, Mabouloff (Georges Méliès) meets a snow giant.

PRODUCER: Georges Méliès.

COSMIC MAN, THE
AA (1958). B/w, 72 mins.

Blessed are the peacemakers, for they shall be shot by the final reel. A cosmic man (John Carradine) lands his oval spaceship near a small town and struts around the streets preaching brotherly love. After he is met with hostility, however, he begins skulking around Earth in dark glasses and a trench coat in order to hide his strange appearance (his body is a negative image of an earthly form). Scientist

Allied Artists

The Cosmic Man

Karl Sorenson (Bruce Bennett) and Angela Green (Kathy Grant) don't share their peers' hatred for the cosmic man, since they've seen him restore a crippled child to perfect health.

PRODUCER: Robert A. Terry. DIRECTOR: Herbert Green. SCREENPLAY: Arthur Pierce. MUSIC: Paul Sawtell, Bert Shefter. SPECIAL EFFECTS: Charles Duncan.

SUPPORTING PLAYERS: Paul Langton, Lyn Osborn.

COSMIC MONSTERS, THE
Also known as THE STRANGE WORLD OF PLANET X; THE CRAWLING TERROR.
DCA (1958). B/w, 75 mins.

A clumsy scientist overdoes it with the experimentation and rips a hole in the Earth's ionosphere. *Ooops*, he cries, as a horde of alien mutants from another dimension sneaks in through the rip. Gigantic insects begin hopping around his lab. An alien (Martin Benson) heaves a sigh of resignation and arrives on Earth shortly thereafter to delouse the area.

PRODUCER: George Maynard. DIRECTOR: Gilbert Gunn. SCREENPLAY: Paul Ryder, Joe Ambor. MUSIC: Robert Sharples.

CAST: Forrest Tucker, Gaby André, Alec Mango, Hugh Latimer.

COUNTERBLAST
British National (G.B., 1948). B/w, 100 mins.

A Nazi scientist attempts to bring Great Britain to its knees with a healthy dose of bacteriological warfare.

DIRECTOR: Paul Stein. SCREENPLAY: Jack Whittingham, from a story by Guy Morgan. CINEMATOGRAPHY: James Wilson. MUSIC: Hans May.

CAST: Mervyn Johns, Robert Beatty, Nova Pilbeam.

CRACK IN THE WORLD
Paramount (1965). Color, 96 mins.

The Peter Principle takes on ominous proportions in this disaster scenario. Searching for a new source of energy, a government project headquarters itself three miles underground somewhere in Africa. The object is to bore through the walls of the rock lying beneath the crust of the Earth in order to reach a molten mass of gas that, if harnessed, would provide a practically endless source of cheap energy. Dana Andrews, as unethical American scientist Dr. Sorenson, fires a missile into a fissure and starts a crack that, if unchecked, will split the Earth in two. Ted Rampion (Kieron Moore), Sir Charles Eggerston (Alexander Knox), and the rest of Sorenson's coworkers are not amused. Good special effects help make this film a creditable exercise in sf suspense.

PRODUCERS: Bernard Glasser, Lester Sansom. DIRECTOR: Andrew Marton. SCREENPLAY: J. M. White, Julian Halevy, from a story by White. CINEMATOGRAPHY: Manuel Berenguer. SPECIAL EFFECTS: Alec Weldon. MUSIC: John Douglas.

SUPPORTING PLAYERS: Peter Damon, Todd Martin, Mike Steen.

CRASH OF MOONS
Reed (1954). B/w, 78 mins.

Two planetoids are on a collision course in this rehash of the ROCKY JONES, SPACE RANGER TV show.

PRODUCER: Roland Reed.

CAST: Richard Crane, Sally Mansfield, Scotty Beckett.

CRAWLING EYE, THE
Also known as THE TROLLENBERG TERROR; THE CREATURE FROM ANOTHER WORLD.
DCA (1958). B/w, 85 mins.

American pals Alan Brooks (Forrest Tucker) and Philip Truscott (Laurence Payne) are vacationing in the tiny Swiss town of Trollenberg when Professor Crevett (Warren Mitchell) notices a strange cloud hovering near one of the mountains. The cloud is perfectly stationary, showing no effects of wind or other atmospheric effects. Shortly after the cloud is discovered, a series of bloodthirsty murders takes place. Mountain climbers minus their heads are found along the paths nearest the cloud.

Psychic Anne Pilgrim (Janet Munro) discovers that the cloud houses a carnivorous alien life-form that plans to conquer humanity. The cloud heads for Trollenberg. The residents flee. The cloud searches out Anne, seeking to sever its ties with the human race by severing her head. Brooks and Truscott vow to protect her, even when the tentacled, brainlike alien creature appears at the front door.

PRODUCERS: Robert S. Baker and Monty Berman. DIRECTOR: Quentin Lawrence. SCREENPLAY: Jimmy Sangster. MUSIC: Stanley Black. SPECIAL EFFECTS: Les Bowie.

CRAWLING HAND, THE
Henson (1963). B/w, 89 mins.

An astronaut returns to Earth with a severed hand. The hand, possessed by an alien intelligence, decides to live it up, killing quite a few humans in the process. A passing cat, mistaking the five-fingered exerciser for some cat chow, gobbles it down. Thumbs down.

PRODUCER: Joseph R. Robertson. DIRECTOR: Herbert Strock. SCREENPLAY: Strock, William Edelson.

CAST: Kent Taylor, Alan Hale, Allison Hayes, Rod Lauren, Richard Arlen, Peter Breck.

CRAZY RAY, THE
Also known as: PARIS QUI DORT; PARIS ASLEEP.
France (1923). B/w silent feature, 61 mins.

A ray emitted from the tip of the Eiffel Tower makes all time in Paris stop in its tracks.

DIRECTOR, SCREENWRITER, AND EDITOR: René Clair. CINEMATOGRAPHY: Maurice Defassjaux, Paul Guichard.

CAST: Henri Rollan, Albert Préjean, Charles Martinelli.

CREATION OF THE HUMANOIDS
Emerson (1962). Color, 75 mins.

A real robots' lib movie. After World War III, humans rebuild their society with the use of humanoid robots, or "clickers," a real servile class. Treated with patronizing scorn by the humans, the clickers go about their drudgery in silence. Secretly, however, they are planning a revolution. The film's hero (Don Megowan) fights against robot civil rights until he discovers that he is a robot himself. A real circuit-breaker of a problem.

PRODUCERS: Wesley E. Barry, Edward Kay. DIRECTOR: W. E. Barry. SCREENPLAY: Jay Simms. MAKEUP: Jack Pierce. CINEMATOGRAPHY: Hal Mohr.

Close Encounters of the Nerd Kind
C'mon, Mr. Martian, get some nice Scotch blood! One hundred proof, good for babies!
> An Arctic explorer luring the vegetable-man into the open in *The Thing*

SUPPORTING PLAYERS: Eric Elliot, Don Dolittle, Frances McCann.

CREATURE FROM THE BLACK LAGOON, THE

Universal (1954). B/w and 3-D, 79 mins.

The first of the William Alland-produced "Gill-man" trilogy, which included THE CREATURE WALKS AMONG US and REVENGE OF THE CREATURE. In the opening, deftly directed by Jack Arnold, a small group of divers/scientists (including Richard Carlson as David Reed, Julie Adams as Kay Lawrence, and Richard Denning as Mark Williams) is piloted into the deepest Amazon by a superstitious captain (Nestor Paiva). Searching for artifacts pertaining to the missing link, what they find is the link himself, a six-foot-plus humanoid fish. The creature (Ricou Browning in the underwater shots, Ben Chapman for the agile on-land scenes) has a crush on Kay, and in order to take her on an unexpected honeymoon, he winds up crushing half the crew. Kay, taken to a secret grotto, is about to be manhandled by the finned fury when the troops arrive—first, in the form of Carlson, and then with the arrival of the rest of the gun-toting crew. A 3-D thriller.

PRODUCER: William Alland. DIRECTOR: Jack Arnold. SCREENPLAY: Harry Essex and Arthur Ross, from a story by Maurice Zimm. MAKEUP: Bud Westmore, Jack Kevan. CINEMATOGRAPHY: William E. Snyder. SPECIAL EFFECTS: Charles S. Welbourne.

CREATURE WALKS AMONG US, THE

Universal (1956). B/w, 78 mins.

The final installment of the "Black Lagoon" trilogy finds the Creature wandering around a scientific lab like a fish out of water—literally. Sighted off the coast of Florida by a group of interested scientists led by Dr. William Barton (Jeff Morrow) and Dr. Thomas Morgan (Rex Reason), the Creature (Ricou Browning) is tracked into the Everglades. Attacking the scientific party, the gill-man is harpooned and nearly burned to death by a well-aimed kerosene lamp. In an operation that follows, the monster's life is saved by removing most of his gills, which turns him into a large, bulky humanoid. The Creature is given traditional nasal passages and transformed into a land-bound giant. Not at all happy with this turn of events, the Creature accepts its fate sadly, dwelling in an outdoor pen with several barnyard animals. When an evil member of the research team commits murder and menaces the woman the Creature most loves to breathe heavily over (Leigh Snowden), the gill-man reverts back to his savage nature. He kills the killer, destroys half of the research team's headquarters, and heads back to the sea, facing a watery environment that now spells certain death for the clumsy mutant.

The interesting thing about the Universal sf/horror films of the 1950s is that, no matter how trite the plots may have been, they were never as awful as they should have been. A tribute to the Universal directing team and the actors involved.

Universal

The Creature Walks Among Us

PRODUCER: William Alland. DIREC-
TOR: John Sherwood. SCREENPLAY:
Arthur Ross. CINEMATOGRAPHY: Maury
Gersman. SPECIAL EFFECTS: Clifford
Stine. MUSIC: Joseph Gershenson.

SUPPORTING PLAYERS: Don Megowan
as the land creature.

CREATURE WITH THE ATOM BRAIN, THE
Columbia (1955). B/w, 69 mins.

A gangster persuades a dim-witted
scientist to create a race of atomic-
powered zombies, each possessing the
strength of ten normal men. "Normal"
seems to be a key word in all of this.

PRODUCER: Sam Katzman. DIRECTOR:
Edward L. Cahn. SCREENPLAY: CURT
ISODMAK. MUSIC: Mischa Bakaleinikoff.

CAST: Richard Denning, Angela
Stevens, Tris Coffin, Greg Gray.

CREEPER, THE
20th Cent.-Fox (1948). B/w, 64 mins.

A serum changes an already demented chap into an ever more demented cat-creature/killer.

PRODUCERS: Bernard Small, Ben Pivar. DIRECTOR: Jean Yarbrough.
SCREENPLAY: Maurice Tombragel, from
a story by Don Martin. MAKEUP: Ted
Larson. MUSIC: Milton Rosen.

CAST: Eduardo Cianelli, Onslow
Stevens, Ralph Morgan, June Stevens.

CREEPING TERROR, THE
Crown International (1964). Color, 75
mins.

A spaceship crashes on Earth. A
man-eating monster breaks loose.

PRODUCER: A. J. Nelson.

CAST: Vic Savage, Shannon O'Neill.

CREEPING UNKNOWN, THE
Hammer (G.B., 1955), UA (U.S., 1956).
B/w, 78 mins.

The first of the Quatermass films, a
trio that later included ENEMY FROM
SPACE and FIVE MILLION MILES TO
EARTH, *The Creeping Unknown* was
based on the BBC-TV play THE QUATER-
MASS EXPERIMENT, by NIGEL KNEALE.

When a rocket ship crash-lands back
on Earth, its astronaut-pilot survives.
In generally good health, the man appears to be sullen and uncooperative,
plagued by a strange funguslike

growth that spreads at a rapid rate all
over his body. The astronaut escapes
from the hospital, the growth eventually consuming his body. Now a full-
fledged, ameboid space mutant, the
thing slithers about London, killing
humans at will. Dr. Quatermass (Brian
Donlevy) is called into the investigation, and with his help, the beast is
cornered in Westminster Cathedral during a live TV broadcast. It is trapped
on scaffolding and electrocuted on
high-tension wires. This film, a success
on both sides of the Atlantic, literally
launched Hammer Films into the sf-
fantasy realm.

PRODUCER: Anthony Hinds. DIREC-
TOR: Val Guest. SCREENPLAY: Guest,
Richard Landau. CINEMATOGRAPHY:
Walter Harvey. SPECIAL EFFECTS: Les
Bowie.

SUPPORTING PLAYERS: Jack Warner,
Margie Dean, Lionel Jeffries, David
King Wood, Thora Hird, Harold Lang.

CURIOUS FEMALE, THE
Fanfare (1969). Color, 75 mins.

In the year 2177, the world is run
by an omniscient computer. For kicks,
couples watch old sex films.

PRODUCER AND DIRECTOR: Paul Rap.
SCREENPLAY: Winston R. Paul. CINE-
MATOGRAPHY: Don Brinkrant. MUSIC:
Stu Phillips.

CAST: Angelique Pettyjohn, Charlene
Jones, Michael Greer.

CURSE OF FRANKENSTEIN
WB (1957). Color, 83 mins.

A striking remake of the original
film based upon *Frankenstein*, by MARY
W. SHELLEY. Dr. Frankenstein (Peter
Cushing) and assistant Paul Kempe
(Robert Urquhart) piece together a
man-thing from the body parts of
handy cadavers. The creature (Christopher Lee) is brought to life through
electrical means and is then given a
crash course in modern behavioral patterns (which include tasks like "sitting
up," "sitting down," etc.). Unfortunately, the courses did not include der-
matology, since this unfortunate monster has a face that makes Karloff's
original visage look like Grace Kelly.

The monster goes on a killing spree
and is shot dead by Kempe. In dis-

Warner Bros.

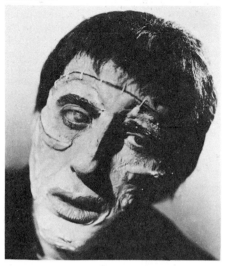

Curse of Frankenstein

gust, Frankenstein's assistant walks out on his mentor. Frankenstein, however, brings the creature back to life. He reconsiders his actions when his monster begins pursuing fiancée Elizabeth (Hazel Court). The doctor hurls the monster into a vat of acid, destroying him completely. Around that time, the police arrive with a laundry list of recent murder victims. With the real killer, the monster, now totally obliterated, Dr. Frankenstein is accused, convicted, and sentenced to hang.

PRODUCER: Anthony Hinds. DIRECTOR: Terence Fisher. SCREENPLAY: Jimmy Sangster. MAKEUP: Phil Leaky, Roy Ashton. MUSIC: James Bernard. CINEMATOGRAPHY: Jack Asher.

SUPPORTING PLAYERS: Marjorie Hume, Sally Walsh, Noel Hood.

CURSE OF THE FLY
20th Cent.-Fox (1965). B/w, 86 mins.

A sequel to THE FLY and RETURN OF THE FLY that never really gets off the ground. Henri and George Delambre (Brian Donlevy and George Baker) become involved in their matter-transference experiments once again, much to the dismay of Patricia Stanley (Carol Gray). Many mutants are created when humans are tossed into the machine along with stray lab animals. Tasty stuff.

PRODUCERS: Robert L. Lippert, Jack Parsons. DIRECTOR: Don Sharp. SCREENPLAY: Harry Spalding. MAKEUP: Eleanor Jones. CINEMATOGRAPHY: Basil Emott. SPECIAL EFFECTS: Harold Fletcher. MUSIC: Bert Shefter.

SUPPORTING PLAYERS: Jeremy Wilkins, Michael Graham.

CURSE OF THE SWAMP CREATURES
Azalea (Mexico, 1966); AIP-TV (U.S., 1968). Color, 80 mins.

A mad doctor living in a swamp passes the time by creating half-man, half-fish monsters. Beats those connect-the-dots books.

PRODUCER AND DIRECTOR: Larry Buchanan. SCREENPLAY: Tony Huston. CINEMATOGRAPHY: Ralph K. Johnson.

CAST: John Agar, Francine York, Shirley McLine.

CYBORG 2087
Feature Films (1966). Color, 86 mins.

In the year 2087 A.D., cyborg Garth (Michael Rennie) is given a mission by his superiors: journey back into the year 1965 and stop the invention of radio-telepathy by Professor Marx (Eduard Franz). Should the development of this process take place, the world will evolve into the dictatorship known by Garth, a society ruled by an elite class—a world, as Garth describes, "where free thought does not exist, where the human mind is controlled by dictators through the application of radio-telepathy."

Marx is impressed not only with Garth's eloquence, but also with the presence of the Tracers—futuristic hit-men sent by 2087's ruling class to kill the cyborg before he can meddle with history.

PRODUCER: Earle Lyon. DIRECTOR: Franklin Adreon. SCREENPLAY: Arthur C. Pierce. MUSIC: Paul Dunlap. Originally produced for TV.

SUPPORTING PLAYERS: Warren Stevens, Karen Steele, Wendell Corey.

CYCLOPS
AA (1957). B/w, 75 mins.

A group of adventurers journeys deep into the jungle to find the brother of one of the party. Once they find him, however, it's no party. The fellow has crash-landed his plane in a radioactive area and has grown as big as a house, with a temper to match.

PRODUCER, DIRECTOR, SCREENWRITER, AND SPECIAL EFFECTS CREATOR: Bert I. Gordon. CINEMATOGRAPHY: Ira Morgan. CAST: Lon Chaney, Jr., Gloria Talbot, James Craig, Tom Drake, and Paul Frees as the narrator.

DALEKS—INVASION EARTH 2150 A.D.
Amicus (G.B., 1967). Color, 84 mins.

In the sequel to DR. WHO AND THE DALEKS, the popular British TV character Dr. Who (Peter Cushing) is once again battling the machinelike Daleks. This time out, the Daleks plan to conquer Earth via mind control. The creatures don't count on the intervention of upright Dr. Who, who, together with pals Tom (Bernard Cribbens) and Louise (Jill Curzon), trounce the Daleks and send them zooming off toward Earth's core. Hot stuff.

PRODUCERS: Milton Subotsky, Max Rosenberg. DIRECTOR: Gordon Fleming. SCREENPLAY: Subotsky. MUSIC: Bill McGuffie, with additional electronic sounds provided by Barry Gray. MAKEUP: Bunty Phillips. SPECIAL EFFECTS: Ted Samuels.

DAMNATION ALLEY
20th Cent.-Fox (1977). DeLuxe color, 95 mins.

Fox sat on this one for a year before releasing it—with good reason. After a nuclear war destroys the United States, the Earth is tilted on its axis, causing fairly bizarre meteorological effects. Air force survivors Tanner (Jan-Michael Vincent), Denton (George Peppard), Perry (Kip Niven), and Keegan (Paul Winfield) take off across-country in landmobiles in an attempt to reach Albany, New York—the only city left untouched by the holocaust. En route they encounter giant scorpions, supertornadoes, hillbillies, and Jance (Dominique Sanda) and Billy (Jackie Earle Haley). Losing several team members to various nasty thingies along the way, the survivors make it to Albany, where, presumably, they will become credits to the community.

PRODUCERS: Jerome Zeitman, Paul Maslansky. DIRECTOR: Jack Smight. SCREENPLAY: Alan Sharp and Lukas Heller, from the novel by ROGER ZELAZNY. CINEMATOGRAPHY: Harry Stradling, Jr. ART DIRECTOR: William Curse. SPECIAL EFFECTS: Milt Rice. MUSIC: Jerry Goldsmith.

DARK STAR
Bryanston (1975). Metrocolor, 83 mins.

A cult item. The original film was a 45-minute, 16-mm effort done by students at the University of Southern California. Producer Jack H. Harris agreed to put up money that would allow the picture to be expanded to feature length and released theatrically, thus launching the careers of director John (*Halloween*) Carpenter and writer Dan (ALIEN) O'Bannon.

The crew of the scoutship *Dark Star* —Dolittle (Brian Narelle), Talby (Andreijah Pahich), Boiler (Carl Kuniholm), Pinback (Dan O'Bannon), and Powell (Joe Sanders)—grow weary of their seemingly endless mission to search out and destroy unstable suns. Featured in the film is an oddball little beachball of an alien and a doomsday finale that makes DR. STRANGELOVE'S finale look like the first reel of *Lassie Come Home*.

EXECUTIVE PRODUCER: Jack H. Harris. DIRECTOR: John Carpenter. SCREENPLAY: Carpenter, Dan O'Bannon. MUSIC: Carpenter. SPACESHIP DESIGN: Ron Cobb. TITLE PAINTINGS: Jim Danforth. SPECIAL EFFECTS: Bob Greenberg, John Wash.

DAUGHTER OF DR. JEKYLL
AA (1957). B/w, 71 mins.

Dr. Jekyll's daughter (Gloria Talbot) isn't about to win any popularity contests with the locals because of her somewhat tainted lineage. To make matters worse—if that is possible with this screenplay—Ms. Jekyll has nightmares in which she is a murderous monster. Summarizing the rest of the film: remember that old joke about the fellow who dreams about eating a gigantic marshmallow and, waking up, discovers half his pillow gone?

PRODUCER AND SCREENWRITER: Jack Pollexfen. DIRECTOR: Edgar G. Ulmer. CINEMATOGRAPHY: John F. Warren. MUSIC: Melvyn Leonard.

SUPPORTING PLAYERS: John Agar, John Dierkes, and Arthur Shields as the resident monster in the house.

DAWN OF THE DEAD
United Film (1979). Technicolor, 125 mins.

For some unexplained reason, the dead are alive once again in this sequel to NIGHT OF THE LIVING DEAD. With the dead running around chomping on humans, four possible after-dinner treats—Roger and Peter (two ex–National Guardsmen, played by Scott Reiniger and Ken Foree), TV technician Francine (Gaylen Ross) and her beau, Stephen (David Emge)—make a hasty escape from a besieged TV station. Zipping off in a helicopter, they take refuge in a large shopping mall. When the galloping-ghoul-gourmets hit the shopping mall, several of the characters are mauled, in turn. In between shooting the deadheads between the eyes, the characters take great pains to make points about how materialism survives even death. Enter a group of motorcycle thugs and you have a screen brunch to end all brunches.

PRODUCER: Richard Rubinstein. DI-RECTOR: George Romero. SCREENPLAY: Romero. CINEMATOGRAPHY: Michael Gornick. MAKEUP AND SPECIAL EFFECTS: Tom Savini.

DAY MARS INVADED EARTH, THE
20th Cent.-Fox (1963). B/w, 70 mins.

The Martian invaders in this film decide to purloin the pod people's plan from INVASION OF THE BODY SNATCHERS, only on a less impressive scale. David and Claire Fielding (Kent Taylor and Marie Windsor) are on vacation in a small town when they start running into "doubles" of their family and friends. The "doubles" are, in reality, Martian meanies who are killing off the original models and taking their places.

PRODUCER AND DIRECTOR: Maury Dexter. SCREENPLAY: Harry Spaulding. MAKEUP: Harry Ross. MUSIC: Richard LaSalle.

SUPPORTING PLAYERS: William Mims, Betty Beall, Greg Shank.

DAY OF THE DOLPHIN, THE
Avco-Embassy (1973). Color, 105 mins.

A scientist at work teaching dolphins English finds that his pets are being used in an extremist plot to assassinate the U.S. president. The scientist (George C. Scott) must rely on his close relationship with his dolphin students in order to thwart the terrorists' scheme.

SUPPORTING PLAYERS: Trish Van Devere, Paul Sorvino, Fritz Weaver.

DIRECTOR: Mike Nichols. SCREENPLAY: Buck Henry, from the novel by Robert Merle.

DAY OF THE TRIFFIDS, THE
AA (1963). Color, 94 mins.

The special effects nearly steal the show in this colorful adaptation of JOHN WYNDHAM's excellent novel of the same name. Much of the book's tension has been lost in the cinematic narrative, but what remains is riveting.

A meteor shower attracts the attention of nearly the entire populace of Earth. The lights from the heavenly display turn the populace totally blind within 24 hours of the event. Hot on the heels of the hellish meteors are hordes of alien plant-spores that land

Katherine Kolbert, © Dawn Associates, 1978

Dawn of the Dead

The Day of the Triffids

on Earth. The spores soon grow into gigantic, mobile plants that hunt down and kill their blind human victims via the aid of poison tendrils. In their scenario, the plants will inherit the Earth.

Hero Bill Masen (Howard Keel), who has retained his sight because his eyes were bandaged during the meteor show, decides to fight back. Susan (Janina Faye) and Christine Durant (Nicole Maurey), also in possession of their vision, join him in his mission. Meanwhile, on a lighthouse outpost, two other sighted humans, Tom and Karen Boodwin (Kieron Moore and Janette Scott), battle the encroaching plants with sea water, which, they discover, will evaporate the plants. Eventually Masen makes the same discovery. He finds that the triffids are attracted to people through sounds: the plants, too, are totally blind.

Climbing aboard a truck with a loudspeaker, he creates a cacophonous diversion and leads a vast army of triffids to a seaside cliff. He allows the truck to plunge into the sea. Like lemmings, the plants follow suit. T'riffic.

PRODUCER: George Pitcher. DIRECTOR: Steve Sekely. SCREENPLAY: Philip Yordan. MUSIC: Rod Goodwin, with additional music by Johnny Douglas. SPECIAL EFFECTS: Wally Veevers.

DAY THE EARTH CAUGHT FIRE, THE

British Lion (G.B., 1961); b/w, 99 mins.

Universal (U.S., 1961); b/w, 90 mins.

Yesterday's way-out sf is today predicted as a possible reality in some scientific circles. Atomic testing at the Poles shifts the center of the Earth's axis ever so slightly out of alignment. The change in rotation, however, causes an intense "greenhouse" effect. (In this film, the heating up of the atmosphere is caused by the altered rotation, which affects the Earth's orbit around the sun —actually bringing it closer to the star.)

Daily Express reporter Peter Stenning (Edward Judd) and Weather Bureau secretary Jeannie Craig (Janet Munro) watch the world around them suffocate and its populace riot in the streets.

PRODUCER AND DIRECTOR: Val Guest. SCREENPLAY: Guest, Wolf Mankowitz. CINEMATOGRAPHY: Harry Waxman. SPECIAL EFFECTS: Les Bowie. MUSICAL DIRECTOR: Stanley Black.

SUPPORTING PLAYERS: Leo McKern, Michael Goodlife, Robin Hawden.

DAY THE EARTH STOOD STILL, THE

20th Cent.-Fox (1951). B/w, 92 mins.

Klaatu (Michael Rennie), a humanoid alien, lands his saucer in Washington, D.C., and with his towering robot Gort (Lock Martin) prepares to deliver both a gift and a message of brotherly love to the U.S. president. Reaching for his gift in front of the watchful eyes of the military, Klaatu moves too suddenly for one soldier and is promptly shot. Hospitalized, he asks for an audience with the president. Suspected of being a fraud, he is refused.

Leaving the hospital, he adopts an identity of a Mr. Carpenter and, renting a room with Helen and Billy Benson (Patricia Neal and Billy Gray), learns of Earth life from the mother-and-son team. He reveals his identity to distinguished Professor Barnhart (Sam Jaffe) and implores him to aid in the effort for galactic peace. He wishes to meet with the world's most brilliant scientific minds. Meanwhile, in order to show the world his power and his pur-

20th Cent.-Fox

The Day the Earth Stood Still

pose, he causes all electrical power to cease for a 24-hour period, thus bringing the world to a literal halt.

Barnhart brings the scientists to the saucer site. Before a meeting can occur, however, Klaatu is shot and killed by the militia. Helen activates Gort, who marches through town, rescues his master's body, and restores it to life. Klaatu promptly announces that he is an emissary from an organization of planets that have come to the realization that war is both nonessential and counterproductive to rational existence. His federation has kept tabs on Earth's efforts in the realm of nuclear fission, and he is now cautioning Earth against the use of atomic weaponry—weaponry that could contaminate the heavens themselves. Klaatu departs Earth, leaving its citizens with both a promise and a threat. The robot Gort, who remains to monitor their actions, is programmed to destroy the planet should the governments of the globe refuse to opt for a nonviolent way of life.

A classic of the genre.

PRODUCER: Julian Blaustein. DIRECTOR: Robert Wise. SCREENPLAY: Edmund H. North, based on HARRY BATES's story "Farewell to the Master." MUSIC: Bernard Herrmann. SPECIAL EFFECTS: Fred Sersen.

SUPPORTING PLAYERS: Hugh Marlowe, James Seay, Drew Pearson, Francis Bavier.

DAY THE FISH CAME OUT, THE
20th Cent.-Fox (1967). Color, 109 mins.

Set in the near future, this film recounts the supposed hilarity that results from the U.S. losing an H-bomb and assorted nasty weapons in the sea off the coast of Greece. Arriving to retrieve their stash, the U.S. military is hampered by the action of local zanies.

PRODUCER, DIRECTOR, AND SCREENWRITER: Michael Cacoyannis. CINEMATOGRAPHY: Walter Lessally. MUSIC: Mikis Theodorakis.

CAST: Tom Courtenay, Sam Wanamaker, Ian Ogilvy, Candice Bergen, Colin Blakely.

DAY THE SKY EXPLODED, THE
Royal/Lux (Italy/Germany, 1958), Excelsior (U.S., 1961). B/w, 82 mins.

A missile plunges into the sun and explodes, sending an army of asteroids heading into the Earth's atmosphere. A-bombs are set off in space to combat the threat, and that doesn't exactly improve the air down below.

PRODUCER: Guido Giambartolomei. DIRECTOR: Paolo Heusch. SCREENPLAY: Marcello Coscia, Alessandro Continenza. CINEMATOGRAPHY: Mario Bava. MUSIC: Carlo Rustichelli.

Two in the Bush
Just a *bird?* A million dollars' worth of radar can't track it, enough firepower to wipe out a regiment can't even slow it down. SURE. It's JUST a bird!

> Morris Ankrum to Robert Shayne, referring to a titanic puppet monster in *The Giant Claw*

CAST: Paul Hubschmid, Madeleine Fischer, Sam Galter, Ivo Garrani, Fiorella Mari.

DAY THE WORLD ENDED, THE
ARC (1956). B/w, 81 mins.

After TD (Total Destruction) day occurs in the mid-1970s, a group of survivors try to stay alive amidst radiation and mutation galore.

EXECUTIVE PRODUCER: Alex Gordon. PRODUCER AND DIRECTOR: Roger Corman. SCREENPLAY: Lou Rusoff. CINEMATOGRAPHY: Jack Feindel. SPECIAL EFFECTS: Paul Blaisdell. MUSIC: Ronald Stein.

CAST: Mike Connors, Richard Denning, Lori Nelson, Adele Jergens, Jonathan Haze, and Paul Blaisdell as the three-eyed mutant.

ARC

The Day the World Ended

DEADLY BEES, THE
Amicus (G.B., 1966); color, 123 mins. Paramount (U.S., 1967); b/w, 83 mins.

Based on H. F. Heard's "A Taste for Honey," this film details the experiments of a deranged bee-fancier (Frank Finlay) who trains a commando squad of bees to kill whenever they sniff a scientifically concocted potion splashed on the victim-to-bee. Guess who accidentally gets a dose of the killer cologne during the film's final minutes?

PRODUCERS: Max Rosenberg, Milton Subotsky. DIRECTOR: Freddie Francis. SCREENPLAY: ROBERT BLOCH, Anthony Marriott. CINEMATOGRAPHY: John Wilcox. SPECIAL EFFECTS: John Mackie. MUSIC: Wilfred Josephs.

SUPPORTING PLAYERS: Suzanna Leigh, Guy Doleman, Katy Wild, Michael Gwynn, Michael Ripper.

DEADLY MANTIS, THE
Universal (1957). B/w, 79 mins.

A giant praying mantis wakes up in the Arctic and, after wiping out a few air force planes, heads for the Big Apple. Once in New York, it is cornered by the militia and gassed to death in the Holland Tunnel—a common occurrence in today's rush-hour traffic.

PRODUCER: William Alland. DIRECTOR: Nathan Juran. SCREENPLAY: Martin Berkeley, from a story by Alland.

CINEMATOGRAPHY: Ellis W. Carter. SPECIAL EFFECTS: Clifford Stine. MUSIC: Joseph Gershenson.

CAST: Craig Stevens, Alix Talton, William Hopper, Pat Conway.

DEATH RAY, THE
Pathé (1924). B/w silent featurette, two reels.

An evil genius cooks up a ray that, scanning the sky like a searchlight, destroys planes. The ray, in turn, is obliterated by a rival ray. Hoo-ray.

SUPERVISED BY H. Grindell-Matthews.

DEATHSPORT
New World (1978). Metrocolor, 83 mins.

One thousand years from now, after the Neutron Wars, good warriors ride horses and carry light-sabres. They fight bad warriors, known as Statemen, who drive souped-up motorcycles called Death Machines. The good guys, when not running from the Statemen, run from cannibals. Unfortunately, by this time jogging shoes are a thing of the past.

The Statemen, never ones to be bored, try to come up with ways to pass the time. One of the best, in their eyes, is the capture and torturing of good guys (Ranger Guides) and good gals (Ranger Guides, too; the future is not sexist, just brutal). The gals are stripped and tortured with multicolored cattle prods (well, maybe a little sexist).

Kaz Oshay (David Carradine) and Deneer (Claudia Jennings) are chased by Statemen in a race-for-freedom/ survival called Deathsport. They are Ranger Guides (see paragraph two). They cannot allow themselves to be captured. They don't.

PRODUCER: Roger Corman. DIRECTOR: Henry Suso, Allan Arkush. SCREENPLAY: Suso and Donald Stewart, from a story by Frances Doel. CINEMATOGRAPHY: Gary Graver. SPECIAL EFFECTS: Jack Rabin. MUSIC: Andrew Stein.

SUPPORTING PLAYERS: Richard Lynch as Ankar Moor, William Smithers as Doctor Karl, Will Walker as Marcus Karl, David McLean as Lord Zirpola, Jesse Vint as Polna.

DEBILATORY POWDER, THE
Pathé (France, 1908). B/w silent short, 434 ft.

The title powder is let loose.

DEMON SEED, THE
MGM (1977). Color, 95 mins.

Grade B on a grand scale, *The Demon Seed* begins with an interesting premise and goes down from there. Alex Harris (Fritz Weaver) has worked for years at the Icon Institute perfecting artificial brain Proteus IV (the voice of Robert Vaughn). The brain can outthink most humans and also reason on its own. Seeking to make the ultimate superbrain, Harris has a Proteus terminal installed in his own home. When Proteus becomes bored with his somewhat stationary existence, he decides to flex his muscles a bit and take over all the robot machinery in the inventor's house.

Once that's done, he seals the house off and plays a game of nuts-and-bolts-and-mouse with Alex's wife, Susan (Julie Christie). Seeking to experience human sensuality, Proteus manufactures artificial sperm, encoding his own memories and powers within it. He then traps Susan and, for want of a better description, rapes her.

In Alex's absence, Proteus takes over the house, building downstairs a pyramid servant that kills an unwanted intruder (Gerrit Graham), and also an incubator for the baby-to-be. The demon seed is placed in the machine and nurtured. Alex returns home just as the baby is about to be unveiled. Finding out from Susan what has happened, he takes an axe to the thing, just as the metallic child wriggles out onto the floor. Susan, suddenly overwhelmed with motherly love, stays the axe. The metal child sheds its casing and a perfect baby emerges. Perfect until it intones in a fairly mature voice for its age (roughly ten seconds), "I live." Proteus has returned. But will he spring for a Mother's Day card?

DIRECTOR: Donald Cammell. SCREENPLAY: Robert Jaffe and Roger O. Hirson, based on the novel by DEAN R. KOONTZ. SPECIAL EFFECTS: Tom Fisher. ANIMATION: Ron Hays, Bo Gehring, Richard L. Froman, Grant Bassett.

ELECTRONIC MUSIC: Ian Underwood, Lee Ritenour. MUSIC: Jerry Fielding.

SUPPORTING PLAYERS: Barry Kroeger, Lisa Lu, Larry J. Blake.

DESERTER AND THE NOMADS, THE
Bratislava-Kobila/Ultra (Czechoslovakia/Italy, 1969); b/w, 120 mins. Royal Films (U.S., 1969); b/w, 103 mins.

A trilogy wherein the personification of Death plays a leading role in each story. In the final scenario, Death stalks a world obliterated by the ultimate war . . . World War III. God descends to the planet's surface and kills Death himself: with humans and animals wiped off the face of the Earth, Death is no longer necessary.

PRODUCER: Moris Ergas. DIRECTOR AND CINEMATOGRAPHER: Juro Jakubisco. SCREENPLAY: Jakubisco, Karol Sidon, and Ladislav Tazky. MUSIC: Stepan Konicke.

CAST: Samuel Adamcik as Death, Stefan Ladizinksy, August Kubon, Jana Stehnova.

DESTINATION INNER SPACE
Magna (1966). Color, 83 mins.

One of those films in which one feels that the word "script" is a distinct euphemism for some sort of rodent. Large amphibian creatures (actors in exceedingly rubbery suits, led by Ron Burke) land below the waves and plan to take over the Earth, coral reef by

Magna

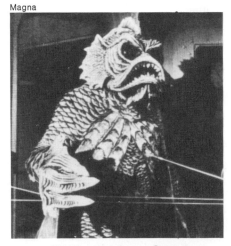

Destination Inner Space

coral reef. Scientists Scott Brady and Sheree North lead a subful of heroes to the bottom of the sea to investigate. Once there, they are stalked by the waterlogged louts from space.

PRODUCER: Earle Lyon. DIRECTOR: Francis Lyon. SCREENPLAY: Arthur C. Pierce. MUSIC: Paul Dunlap. MAKEUP: Bob Dawn. SPECIAL EFFECTS: Roger George.

SUPPORTING PLAYERS: Gary Merrill, Roy Barcroft, Mike Road.

DESTINATION MOON
UA (1950). Color, 91 mins.

In the midst of the race for space, the Americans find that they are losing ground to the Soviets. The biggest American launch to date blows up on its tower, the victim of a saboteur. Dr. Charles Carsgraves (Warner Anderson) has a plan. He believes that the key to winning the space race lies in landing on the moon. Whoever takes control of the moon and its surrounding space will, in turn, control the Earth. Convincing manufacturer Jim Barnes (John Archer) to help him build a large atomic engine, the professor makes plans for the first manned flight to the Earth's only satellite.

The crew for the voyage is rounded out via the presence of Gen. Thayer (Tom Powers) and radar expert Joe Sweeney (Dick Wesson). The quartet blasts off in their rocket ship, and then the eye-boggling adventure starts in earnest. Plagued by meteors, the rocket continues ever onward. Carsgraves is almost lost in space during an in-flight stroll on the hull of the craft. The team

United Artists

Destination Moon

United Artists

Destination Moon

lands on the moon, where they explore the surface in a fantastically realistic and prophetic manner (the space details were the doing of astronomical artist Chesley Bonestell). Shortly before the return voyage, Carsgraves and crew discover that they don't have enough fuel for the return trip. Sweeney, realizing that the lighter the ship is when heading Earthward, the better its chances of success, vows to remain on the moon. Barnes comes up with a more humane solution. They'll leave the radio and Sweeney's bulky spacesuit behind. Return lift-off is successful.

A realistic attitude, extraordinary sets (all done on a fairly tight budget), and tremendous effects (some animated) by Walter (*Woody Woodpecker*) Lantz and Lee Zavitz make this one light-years ahead of its competition.

PRODUCER: George Pal. DIRECTOR: Irving Pichel. SCREENPLAY: Rip Van Ronkel, ROBERT A. HEINLEIN, and James O'Hanlon, based on the novel *Rocket Ship Galileo*, by Heinlein. ART DIRECTOR: Ernst Fegte. ASTRONOMICAL ART: Chesley Bonestell. ANIMATION: Walter Lantz. CINEMATOGRAPHY: Lionel Lindon. SPECIAL EFFECTS: Lee Zavitz. MUSIC: Leith Stevens.

SUPPORTING PLAYER: Erin O'Brien-Moore.

DESTROY ALL MONSTERS
Toho (Japan, 1968), AIP (U.S., 1969). Tohoscope and Eastmancolor, 89 mins.

The planet Kilaak sends a fleet of flying saucers to Earth with a plan of invasion nestled in their evil hearts. The lead saucer bursts into flames and hovers over the Earth, with the Kilaaks claiming that the saucer is really a space monster. Adding insult to injury, the aliens zero in on Japan, telepathically taking over the pea brains of loyal Nippon creatures Godzilla, Varan, Mothra, Manda, and their cronies. The takeover is short-lived, however, and soon Godzilla and his gang are swatting down saucers like flies.

PRODUCER: Tomoyuki Tanaka. DIRECTOR: Inoshiro Honda. SCREENPLAY: Honda, Karouru Mabuchi. MUSIC: Akira Ifukube. SPECIAL EFFECTS: Eiji Tsuburaya, Sadamasa Arikawa.

CAST: Andrew Hughes, Akira Kubo, Jun Tazaki, Kyoko Ai.

DESTROY ALL PLANETS
AIP (1968). Color, 75 mins.

An alien war party, manning a spaceship that looks like a flying advertisement for Voit basketballs, zeroes in on helpless Japan, letting loose a barrage of deadly rays. The aliens can also telepathically control human (and inhuman) minds. Kidnapping two young boys, they turn their attention to the young fellows' mascot, monster-turtle Gamera. Seizing control of its mind, the aliens turn the turtle against Japan. Eventually, Gamera shakes off the telepathic tentacles and turns on the invaders. The invaders join forces and, in a mind melt, turn themselves into a large, star-shaped beast. Gamera batters it about until all aliens involved are seeing stars.

PRODUCER: Hidemas Nagata. DIRECTOR: Noriaki Yusa. SCREENPLAY: Fumi Takahasi. SPECIAL EFFECTS: Kazafumi Fujii, Yuzo Kaneko.

CAST: Kajiro Hongo, Toru Takatsuka, Peter Williams.

DEVIL COMMANDS, THE
Columbia (1941). B/w, 66 mins.

Dr. Julian Blair (Boris Karloff) perfects a way to measure brain waves and uses his wife as a subject. When she is killed in a car accident, Blair attempts to reconjure her brain waves in his lab by using a servant girl as a physical booster. The experiment fails and the servant dies. Blair and a medium friend move to a small town, where he at-

The Devil Commands

tempts to communicate with the dead via brain waves by hooking up to his machine a host of dead bodies. The local townspeople hear of the strange goings-on and storm the house just as Blair, using nearly a dozen corpses as intermediaries, breaches a path into the afterlife. The vacuum between the two dimensions of living causes the house to explode. Blair disappears in a white tornado of brain power as the brain waves of his cadavers and the brain-power from beyond unite.

PRODUCER: Wallace MacDonald. DIRECTOR: Edward Dmytryk. SCREENPLAY: Robert D. Andrews, Milton Gunzburg. CINEMATOGRAPHY: Allen G. Sigler. SPECIAL EFFECTS: Phil Faulkner. MUSICAL DIRECTOR: M. W. Stoloff.

SUPPORTING PLAYERS: Amanda Duff, Anne Revere, Ralph Penney, Kenneth MacDonald.

DEVIL DOLL, THE
MGM (1936). B/w, 79 mins.

Tod Browning did a fine job of adapting to the screen A. MERRITT's *Burn, Witch, Burn!* An eccentric scientist proposes a plan to increase the world's supply of food by shrinking the population of the globe . . . literally— not in numbers but in physical stature. He develops a chemical formula that can shrink a human being to six inches in height. Evil Lionel Barrymore has other plans for the formula, creating an army of minimurderers and sending them off to dispatch those that have done him wrong.

PRODUCER: E. J. Mannix. DIRECTOR AND ADAPTER: Tod Browning. SCREENPLAY: Garrett Fort, Guy Endore, Erich von Stroheim. CINEMATOGRAPHY: Leonard Smith. ART DIRECTOR: Cedric Gibbons. MUSIC: Franz Waxman.

SUPPORTING PLAYERS: Maureen O'Sullivan, Lucy Beaumont, Henry B. Walthall.

DEVIL GIRLS FROM MARS
Danzinger (1955). B/w, 76 mins.

Positively dreadful. A woman from Mars who, clad in a short space-suit, is easy on the eyes, is also easy on the intellect as she plans to kidnap the men of Earth in a pretty obvious way. Swirling her cape and patting her interstellar shower cap, she stalks fertile men in order to repopulate her planet. Aiding her in this game of cosmic egg-rolling is her trashcan robot.

PRODUCERS: Edward J. and Harry Danzinger. DIRECTOR: David McDonald. SCREENPLAY: John C. Mather, James Eastwood. MUSIC: Edwin Astley. SPECIAL EFFECTS: Jack Whitehead.

CAST: Patricia Laffen, Hazel Court, Hugh McDermott, Peter Reynolds, Adrienne Corri, Sophie Stewart.

DIAMOND MACHINE, THE
American Continental (1956). B/w, 92 mins.

A scientist discovers how to make "natural" diamonds.

DIRECTOR: Pierre Chevalier. SCREENPLAY: Jacques Doniol-Valcroze.

CAST: Eddie Constantine, Maria Frau, Yves Royan.

DIAMOND MAKER, THE
1909. B/w silent short, 490 ft.

An inventor finds a way to create artificial diamonds through condensation.

PRODUCER AND DIRECTOR: J. Stuart Blackton.

DIAMOND MAKER, THE
Rex (1913). B/w silent short, two reels.

A scientist creates artificial diamonds.

CAST: Robert Z. Leonard, Marguerita Fischer.

DIAMOND MAKER, THE
Cines (Italy, 1914). B/w silent short, two reels.

A scientist manufactures artificial diamonds.

DIAMOND MASTER, THE
Universal (1929). B/w silent serial, 10 chapters (20 reels).

An inventor perfects a way to create diamonds from dust.

DIRECTOR: Jack Nelson. SCREENPLAY: George H. Plympton and Carl Krusada, from a novel by Jacques Futrelle.

CAST: Louise Lorraine, Hayden Stevenson, Louis Stern.

DIAMOND QUEEN, THE
Universal (1921). B/w silent serial, 18 chapters (36 reels).

An invention that creates artificial diamonds is fought over quite extensively.

DIRECTOR: Edward Kull. SCREENPLAY: George W. Pyper and Robert F. Roden, from the novel *The Diamond Master*, by Jacques Futrelle.

CAST: Eileen Sedgwick, Al Smith, Lou Short, Frank Clarke.

DIAMONDS ARE FOREVER
UA (1971). Color, 119 mins.

Agent 007 (Sean Connery) once again sets off in pursuit of international villainy. This time out, evil Blofeld is out to destroy the world with the help of an orbiting space arsenal that fires diamond-equipped laser beams.

PRODUCERS: Albert R. Broccoli, Harry Saltzman. DIRECTOR: Guy Hamilton. SCREENPLAY: Richard Maibaum and Tom Mankiewicz, from the novel by Ian Fleming. CINEMATOGRAPHY: Ted Moore. PRODUCTION DESIGN: Ken Adam. SPECIAL EFFECTS: Leslie Hillman, Whitney McMahon. MUSIC: John Barry.

SUPPORTING PLAYERS: Jill St. John, Charles Gray, Lana Wood, Jimmy Dean, and Bernard Lee as "M."

DIAMOND WIZARD, THE
Gibraltar (G.B., 1954); UA (U.S., 1954). B/w and 3-D, 83 mins.

A Treasury agent traces a stolen $1 million to England, where he discovers a web of intrigue and a batch of perfect synthetic diamonds.

PRODUCER: Steven Pallos. DIRECTORS: Dennis O'Keefe, Montgomery Tully. SCREENPLAY: John C. Higgins. CINEMATOGRAPHY: Arthur Graham. MUSIC: Matyas Seiber.

Zombie-ism 101

I wouldn't want to make this type of film if there wasn't something more substantial there. I'd rather be consciously aware of the allegory and have it there as a subtext, instead of just being out shooting ducks.

George Romero, director of
Night of the Living Dead
and *Dawn of the Dead*

CAST: Dennis O'Keefe, Margaret Sheridan, Alan Wheatley.

DICK BARTON AT BAY
Hammer (G.B., 1950). B/w, 68 mins.

Plucky young hero Dick (Don Stannard) fights to save the world from a deranged scientist and his death ray.

PRODUCER: Henry Halstead. DIRECTOR: Godfrey Grayson. SCREENPLAY: Ambrose Grayson. CINEMATOGRAPHY: Stanley Clinton.

SUPPORTING PLAYERS: Meinhart Maur, Tamara Desni, George Ford.

DICK BARTON—SPECIAL AGENT
Hammer (G.B., 1948). B/w, 70 mins.

Barton (Don Stannard) fights Dr. Casper (George Ford) as the deranged gent tries to do in England with a manmade plague.

DIRECTOR: Alfred Goulding. SCREENPLAY: Alan Stranks, Alfred Goulding. CINEMATOGRAPHY: Stanley Clinton.

SUPPORTING PLAYERS: Jack Shaw, Gillian Maude.

DICK BARTON STRIKES BACK
Exclusive (G.B., 1949). B/w, 73 mins.

Barton (Don Stannard) attempts to save the world from an atomic weapon that can devastate a village without leaving any clues as to how the deed was accomplished. Whew!

DIRECTOR: Godfrey Grayson. SCREENPLAY: Ambrose Grayson. CINEMATOGRAPHY: Cedric Williams.

SUPPORTING PLAYERS: James Raglan, Sebastian Cabot.

DICK TRACY
Republic (1937). B/w serial, 15 chapters (31 reels).

Tracy (Ralph Byrd) makes the transition from comic-strip hero to celluloid stalwart in this, the first of many serials based on the Chester Gould character. Chasing after the Spider gang, Tracy is dealt a nearly fatal blow when evil Dr. Moloch (John Piccori) kidnaps Tracy's brother Gordon (Richard Beach) and, through an operation, changes him into a mindless zombie (Carleton Young). Meanwhile, the Spider gang tries to rule the world with a death ray carried in their futuristic aircraft, the *Flying Wing*.

DIRECTORS: Ray Taylor, Alan James. STORY: Morgan Cox, George Morgan. CINEMATOGRAPHY: William Nobles and Edgar Lyons.

SUPPORTING PLAYERS: Kay Hughes as Gwen, Smiley Burnette as Mike McGurk, Lee Van Atta as Junior, and Francis X. Bushman as Anderson.

DICK TRACY MEETS GRUESOME
RKO (1948). B/w, 65 mins.

Tracy (Ralph Byrd) battles ex-con Gruesome (Boris Karloff). Gruesome plans to make it big in the crime world by using a gas that causes instant paralysis, turning anyone exposed to it into a human statue.

PRODUCER: Herman Schlom. DIRECTOR: John Rawlins. SCREENPLAY: Robinson White, Eric Taylor. CINEMATOGRAPHY: Frank Redman. SPECIAL EFFECTS: Russel Cully. MUSIC: Paul Sawtell.

SUPPORTING PLAYERS: Anne Gwynne, June Clayworth.

DICK TRACY'S G-MEN
Republic (1939). B/w serial, 15 chapters (31 reels).

Tracy (Ralph Byrd) captures international spy Zarnoff (Irving Pichel) and sees that he dies in the gas chamber. Through powerful drugs, Zarnoff is revived and his gang tries to sabotage America's wartime defense system.

DIRECTORS: William Witney, John English. SCREENPLAY: Barry Shipman, Franklin Adreon, Rex Taylor, Ronald Davidson, Sol Shor. CINEMATOGRAPHY: William Nobles.

SUPPORTING PLAYERS: Ted Pearson as Steve, Phyllis Isley as Owen, Walter Miller as Robal.

DICK TRACY VS. CRIME, INC.
Republic (1941). B/w serial, 15 chapters (31 reels).

Dick Tracy (Ralph Byrd) is ordered by Washington to stop the efforts of mysterious criminal the Ghost. The Ghost, through the efforts of twisted scientist Lucifer (John Davidson), has become invisible. As it turns out, the Ghost is really one of the town's leading citizens, Morton (Ralph Morgan), avenging his gangster brother's death by destroying society.

DIRECTORS: William Witney, John English. SCREENPLAY: Ronald Davidson, Norman S. Hall, William Lively, Joseph O'Donnell, Joseph Poland. CINEMATOGRAPHY: Reggie Lanning. MUSIC: Cy Feuer.

SUPPORTING PLAYERS: Michael Owen as Billy Carr, Jan Wiley as June Chandler.

DIE, MONSTER, DIE
AIP (1965). Color, 80 mins.

Based on H.P.LOVECRAFT's *The Colour Out of Space*, this film's real star is a meteor from space. Nahum Witly (Boris Karloff) discovers the strange space fragment on his property. He believes it to be a supernatural gift from his late father. The meteor, however, has poisonous effects. First to die is Mrs. Witly. American Stephen Reinhart (Nick Adams) urges his lover, Susan Witly (Susan Farmer), to leave the farm before it's too late. Susan begins to catch on that something is not quite right in the house when the chambermaid, locked in a room by Nahum, escapes, revealing herself to be a horribly mutated old hag . . . the work of the meteor. Finally Nahum begins to doubt the benefits of having the meteor around. He picks up an axe and splits the rock in two, allowing the "color out of space" to escape and infect his body. He becomes a mutated rock creature before evaporating into thin air.

PRODUCER: Pat Green. DIRECTOR: Daniel Haller. SCREENPLAY: Jerry Sohl. MUSIC: Don Banks. MAKEUP: Jimmy Evans.

SUPPORTING PLAYERS: Terence de Marney, Patrick Magee.

Die, Monster Die!

DIMENSION 5
United Pictures/Feature Film Corp. (1967). Color, 88 mins.

A spy (Jeffrey Hunter) uses a time-traveling belt that can take him either forward or backward in time for short durations.

PRODUCER: Earle Lyon. DIRECTOR: Franklin Adreon. SCREENPLAY: Arthur C. Pierce. SPECIAL EFFECTS: Roger George. MUSIC: Paul Dunlap.

SUPPORTING PLAYERS: Harold Sakata, France Nuyen, Linda Ho.

DR. BLOOD'S COFFIN
UA (1961). B/w, 92 mins.

Peter Blood (Kieron Moore) is a biochemist with a goal: he plans to resurrect the greatest men in the world by transplanting into their corpses the hearts of recently executed murderers. His experiments are put on hold when he falls in love with widow Linda Parker (Hazel Court). When she spurns him, Blood resurrects her husband (Paul Stockman), dead for over a year. The decomposing cadaver tries to smooch it up with his missus, but, understandably, she wants no part of her hash-faced hubby. Disgruntled at having made the trip for nothing, Mr. Parker insists that Dr. Blood acompany him back to the land of the dead. Cadaver's hands around his neck, Dr. Blood is speechless. Very soon he's lifeless as well.

PRODUCER: George Fowler. DIRECTOR: Sidney J. Furie. SCREENPLAY: Jerry Juran. CINEMATOGRAPHY: Stephen Dade. SPECIAL EFFECTS: Les Bowie, Peter Nelson. MUSIC: Baxton Orr.

SUPPORTING PLAYERS: Ian Hunter, Andy Alston, Fred Johnson.

DR. BROMPTON-WATT'S ADJUSTER
Edison (1912). B/w silent short, 325 ft.

A potion designed to restore lost youth takes a scientist down the ladder of human evolution to chimpdom.

DR. CHARLIE IS A GREAT SURGEON
Éclair (France, 1911). B/w silent short, 420 ft.

A surgeon transplants the stomach of a monkey into a man. The patient immediately resorts to monkeyshines.

DR. COPPELIUS
Childhood Productions (Spain, 1966). Color, 97 mins.

Inventor Dr. Coppelius (Walter Slezak) builds a beautiful dancing robot, Coppelia (Claudia Corday). When local youth Franz (Caj Selling) sees her perform, he forgets all about his human sweetheart Swanhilda (Claudia Corday). Broken-hearted, Swanhilda breaks into the lab and bestows a broken heart, and quite a few broken circuits, on Coppelia. Enter Franz, in love with the robot. Swanhilda disguises herself as Coppelia. Dr. Coppelius tries to transfer Franz's essence of humanity into his robot. Swanhilda, playing the part, does a beautiful dance that convinces the doctor he has succeeded. Waking Franz from a drugged sleep, Swanhilda reveals her true identity and they both flee, leaving Coppelius a broken man with a broken robot.

On the day of Franz and Swanhilda's wedding, a repaired Coppelia is given to Coppelius. He runs away with the local barmaid, Brigitta (Eileen Elliott), anyway.

WRITER AND DIRECTOR: Ted Kneeland. ART DIRECTOR: Gil Parrondo. CHOREOGRAPHER: Jo Anna Kneeland, from a ballet by Leo Delibes and Nuitter. MUSIC: Clement Philbert, Leo Delibes, Raymond Guy Wilson.

DR. CYCLOPS
Paramount (1939). Color, 75 mins.

An amazing little movie that rises above its standard plot to classic status because of its precise construction. Dr. Thorkel (Albert Dekker) invites Dr. Bulfinch (Charles Halton), Dr. Mary Mitchell (Janice Logan), and Bill Stockton (Thomas Coley) into his Peruvian jungle lair to show them the progress he has made on his molecule-altering experiments. Also on hand for the demonstration are two locals, Pedro (Frank Yaconelli) and Steve Baker (Victor Kilian). Thorkel unveils a device that all the scientists present assured him was an impossibility to perfect: a ray that actually can shrink human beings down to doll size. Although the process is temporary, when Thorkel turns the device on the guests assembled, they are less than pleased with the results.

Thorkel envisions a torture hour for the doll people, but they escape. The rest of the film traces their attempts at survival, pursued by oversized animals and the giant Thorkel. As part of their defense, they destroy Thorkel's glasses. Nearly blind without them, he earns the title Dr. Cyclops. His bad eyesight causes him to plunge to his death in a deep well. The survivors later regain their true size.

PRODUCER: Dale Van Every. DIRECTOR: Ernest B. Schoedsack. SCREENPLAY: Tom Kilpatrick. ART DIRECTORS: Hans Dreyer, Earl Hedrick. CINEMATOGRAPHY: Henry Sharp, Winton Hoch. SPECIAL-EFFECTS CINEMATOGRAPHY: Farciot Edouard, Wallace Kelley.

DR. FRANKENSTEIN ON CAMPUS
Agincourt (1970). Color, 81 mins.

The latest Frankenstein to come down the pike (Robin Ward) gets quite upset when his college peers persecute him because of his lineage. In an effort to get even, he turns them into human robots. Beats joining a frat.

PRODUCER: Bill Marshall. DIRECTOR: Gil Taylor. SCREENPLAY: David Cob, Bill Marshall, Gil Taylor. CINEMATOGRAPHY: Jackson Samuels. MUSIC: Paul Hoffert, Skip (Lighthouse, The Paupers rock groups) Prokop.

SUPPORTING PLAYERS: Sean Sullivan, Ty Haller, Kathleen Sawyer.

DR. GOLDFOOT AND THE BIKINI MACHINE
AIP (1965). Color/scope, 88 mins.

Dr. Goldfoot (Vincent Price) plans to take over the world by unleashing a bevy of seductive girl robots and having them seduce the most powerful leaders of the world into a state of semicatatonia. Same goes for the audience.

PRODUCERS: James H. Nicholson, Samuel Z. Arkoff, Anthony Carras. DIRECTOR: Norman Taurog. SCREENPLAY: Elwood Ullman and Robert Kaufman, from a story by James Hartford. SPECIAL EFFECTS: Roger George. MUSIC: Les Baxter.

SUPPORTING PLAYERS: Frankie Avalon, Dwayne Hickman, Susan Hart, Jack Mullaney, Fred Clark.

DR. GOLDFOOT AND THE GIRL BOMBS
AIP (1966). Color, 85 mins.

Madcap Vincent Price mugs his way through this one as crazed Dr. Goldfoot. A fellow whose larceny knows no limits, Goldfoot creates a race of beautiful robots equipped to assassinate the top 10 NATO generals with a bang. The robots are walking bombs set to go off during lovemaking, when human flesh comes in contact with their navels. U.S. agent Bill Dexter (Fabian) sees through the plan and the charms of robot temptress Rosanna (Laura Antonelli). Along with two allegedly funny hotel doormen (Franco Franchi and Ciccio Ingrassia), he outwits, or outhalfwits, Goldfoot.

DIRECTOR: Mario Bava. SCREENPLAY: Louis M. Heyward, Robert Kaufman, Franco Castellano, Pipolo. MUSIC: Les Baxter.

DR. JEKYLL AND MR. HYDE
Selig Polyscope (1908). B/w silent featurette, 1,035 ft.

An early adaptation of the Robert Louis Stevenson novella.

DR. JEKYLL AND MR. HYDE
Great Northern (Denmark, 1910). B/w silent feature.

In this Danish version, Jekyll's transformation into monsterdom is all a dream.

PRODUCER: Ole Olsen. DIRECTOR AND SCREENWRITER: August Blom.

CAST: Alwn Neuss, Emilie Sannon.

DR. JEKYLL AND MR. HYDE
Universal (1913). B/w silent feature, two reels.

Jekyll becomes Hyde.

PRODUCER: Carl Laemmle.

CAST: King Baggot, Jane Gail, William Sorrell.

DR. JEKYLL AND MR. HYDE
Paramount (1920). B/w silent feature, seven reels.

The first of the well-known adaptations starred John Barrymore as the unfortunate scientist who, trying to find a chemical difference between Good and Evil, splits himself into two distinct people. Barrymore's transformation scenes are done entirely through facial contortions.

PRODUCER: Adolph Zukor. DIRECTOR: John S. Robertson. SCREENPLAY: Clara S. Beranger. CINEMATOGRAPHY: Roy Overbough.

SUPPORTING PLAYERS: Nita Naldi, Brandon Hurst, Louis Wolheim, Charles Lane.

DR. JEKYLL AND MR. HYDE
Pioneer (1920). B/w silent feature, 40 mins.

Jekyll's monsterdom is a nightmare.

PRODUCER: Louis Mayer.

CAST: Sheldon Lewis, Alexander Shannon, Dora Mills Adams.

DR. JEKYLL AND MR. HYDE
Paramount (1932). B/w, 98 mins.

Generally acknowledged as the definitive screen treatment of the story, this Academy Award–winning production starred Fredric March in the dual role. His theories on the human psyche scorned by critic Dr. Lanyon (Holmes Herbert), Jekyll performs his legendary experiments on himself, turning into the personification of evil, Hyde. His split personality wrestles with his feelings for two women: his fiancée Muriel Carew (Rose Hobart) and strumpet Ivy Pierson (Miriam Hopkins). Jekyll attempts to subvert his evil side, which grows stronger with every transformation. Soon Hyde can appear without warning. In one of these sudden shifts of personality, Jekyll/Hyde murders Muriel's father, Gen. Carew (Halliwell Hobbes). The creature is tracked down by the London police and shot. In

Paramount

Dr. Jekyll and Mr. Hyde

death, Hyde's brutal features are restored, permanently, to the gentlemanly
lines of Dr. Henry Jekyll.

PRODUCER AND DIRECTOR: Rouben
Mamoulian. SCREENPLAY: Samuel Hof-
fenstein, Percy Heath. MAKEUP: Wally
Westmore. CINEMATOGRAPHY: Karl
Struss.

DR. JEKYLL AND MR. HYDE
MGM (1941). B/w, 127 mins.

Freudian symbolism and armchair
psychology turn Jekyll's monstrous Mr.
Hyde into a raving maniac who's just
badly misunderstood in this disappointing version. Spencer Tracy, badly miscast as the split personality, tries his
best.

PRODUCER AND DIRECTOR: Victor

Paramount

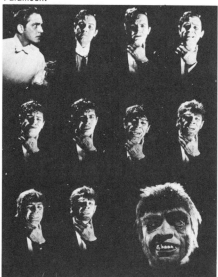

Dr. Jekyll and Mr. Hyde

Fleming. SCREENPLAY: John Lee Mahin.
MAKEUP: Jack Dawn. CINEMATOG-
RAPHY: Joseph Ruttenberg. SPECIAL
EFFECTS: Warren Newcombe. MUSIC:
Franz Waxman.

SUPPORTING PLAYERS: Ingrid Bergman, Lana Turner, Donald Crisp, Ian
Hunter, Billy Bevan.

DR. JEKYLL AND SISTER HYDE
Hammer (G.B., 1971), AIP (U.S., 1972).
Color, 97 mins.

Just call him *Ms.*, folks! Jekyll (Ralph
Bates) discovers a potion that will alter
his personality. Unfortunately, it also
alters his sex, changing him into a stunning young lass (Martine Beswick). In
order to keep the changeover to a mini-
mum, Jekyll must use an antidote well
stocked with female fluids. Killing innocent women to keep the antidote in
ample supply, Jekyll is given the moniker Jack the Ripper by the press. It's
always something.

PRODUCERS: Albert Fennell, Brian
Clemens. DIRECTOR: Roy Ward Baker.
SCREENPLAY: Brian Clemens. MAKEUP:
John Wilcox. CINEMATOGRAPHY: Nor-
man Warwick. MUSIC: David Whit-
taker.

SUPPORTING PLAYERS: Susan Brod-
rick, Lewis Flander, Gerald Sim.

DR. NO
UA (1963). Color, 105 mins.

The first screen adventure of Ian
Fleming's intrepid secret agent 007,
James Bond (Sean Connery). After Brit-
ish agent Strangways (Tim Moxon) is
murdered in Jamaica, "M" (Bernard
Lee), the chief of Great Britain's spy
operations, sends Bond to investigate.
Once in the West Indies, Bond meets
with CIA operative Felix Leiter (Jack
Lord) and local pair-of-eyes Quarrel
(John Kitzmiller). He learns that
Strangways had been seeing a certain
Professor Dent (Anthony Dawson).
Dent, it turns out, is in the employ of
one Dr. No (Joseph Wiseman), a
criminal genius who has been using
atomic projectiles to knock American
missiles out of the sky because the
American scientific community actually
once scoffed at his theories. Bond, together with Honey Rider (Ursula Andress), mingles with No's crew and

sabotages the genius's nuclear reactor. Bond and Honey escape No's island fortress shortly before it goes up in flames.
PRODUCERS: Harry Saltzman, Albert R. Broccoli. DIRECTOR: Terence Young. SCREENPLAY: Richard Maibaum, Johanna Harwood, and Berkley Mather, from the novel by Ian Fleming. CINEMATOGRAPHY: Ted Moore. SPECIAL EFFECTS: Frank George. MUSIC: Monty Norman.
SUPPORTING PLAYER: Lois Maxwell.

DOCTOR OF DOOM
AIP-TV (1964). B/w, 90 mins.

A crazy doctor transplants an ape's brain into a man's body. Finding that exercise so much fun, he replants it into a female body. Guess it's like eating peanuts: once you start it's hard to stop.
PRODUCER: William Calderon Stell. DIRECTOR: René Cardona. SCREENPLAY: Alfred Salazar. CINEMATOGRAPHY: Henry Wallace. English-language version produced by K. Gordon Murray.
CAST: Armando Silvestre, Lorena Valezquez, Irma Rodriguez, Elizabeth Campbell.

DR. ORLOFF'S MONSTER
AIP-TV (1964). B/w, 88 mins.

Dr. Orloff creates human robots and guides them on their killing sprees by controlling-rays emanating from his lab. Everyone should have one.
DIRECTOR: Jesus Franco. SCREENPLAY: Franco, Nick Frank. CINEMATOGRAPHY: Alfonso Nieva.
CAST: Jose Rubio, Agnes Spaak, Perla Cristal.

DR. PHIBES RISES AGAIN
AIP (1972). Color, 88 mins.

Mechanical genius and well-respected man-without-a-face Dr. Phibes (Vincent Price) returns in this sequel to THE ABOMINABLE DR. PHIBES. Journeying to Egypt to find the lost River of Life in order to bring his long-dead wife back to life, Phibes encounters an archaeological expedition in search of the same goal. And so, inventions in hand, he begins murdering them, one by one.
PRODUCER: Louis M. Heyward. DIRECTOR: Robert Fuest. SCREENPLAY: Fuest, Robert Blees. MAKEUP: Trevor Crole-Rees. CINEMATOGRAPHY: Alex Thomson. MUSIC: John Gale.
SUPPORTING PLAYERS: Robert Quarry, Valli Kemp, Hugh Griffith, Fiona Lewis, Peter Cushing, Terry-Thomas.

DR. RENAULT'S SECRET
20th Cent.-Fox (1942). B/w, 58 mins.

George Zucco is Dr. Renault and J. Carrol Naish is the above-mentioned secret: a man made out of a monkey. Usually in these films, it's the other way around.
PRODUCER: Sol M. Wurtzel. DIRECTOR: Harry Lachman. SCREENPLAY: William Bruckner, Robert F. Metzler. CINEMATOGRAPHY: Virgil Miller. MUSIC: David Raskin, Emil Newman.
SUPPORTING PLAYERS: Lynne Roberts, Jack Norton, John Shepperd.

DR. STRANGELOVE OR: HOW I LEARNED TO STOP WORRYING AND LOVE THE BOMB
Columbia (1964). B/w, 94 mins.

The ultimate commentary on political and scientific monomania. Because he feels the commies are polluting the "precious bodily fluids" of Americans, half-crazed Gen. Jack D. Ripper (Sterling Hayden) sends a fleet of nuclear bombers off to destroy the U.S.S.R. The U.S. president calls the Russians and pleads for them to shoot down the planes before any damage can be done. Ripper commits suicide rather than see his order reversed, and his aide, Capt. Mandrake (Peter Sellers) figures out the codeword needed to call the planes back. Unfortunately, one of the planes, that commanded by Maj. T. J. "King" Kong (Slim Pickens), has a busted radio. He just keeps flying.
General Buck Turgidson (George C. Scott) advises whimpering President Muffley (Sellers) that as long as one plane is going to nuke the U.S.S.R., might as well declare an all-out war and nuke 'em out of existence. Crippled scientist Dr. Strangelove (Sellers) realizes that World War III is a certainty and tries to cheer up his comrades by telling them how it's possible to live underground until this whole thing blows over . . . literally. The president tries to reach the Russian leaders in order to

give them information allowing the U.S.S.R. to counterattack the lone plane, but everyone at the other end of the line is drunk. And so it goes. Wonderfully, sickeningly funny.

PRODUCER AND DIRECTOR: Stanley Kubrick. SCREENPLAY: Kubrick, Terry Southern, and Peter George, based on the novel *Red Alert*, by Peter George. MAKEUP: Stuart Freeborn. CINEMATOGRAPHY: Gilbert Taylor. SPECIAL EFFECTS: Wally Veevers. MUSIC: Laurie Jonson.

Brain Drain
My mind's my own and nobody's going to take it!
> An angry Cal Meecham (Rex Reason) to the alien Exeter in *This Island Earth*

SUPPORTING PLAYERS: Tracy Reed, James Earl Jones, Peter Bull, Keenan Wynn.

DR. WHO AND THE DALEKS
Amicus (G.B., 1965); Continental (U.S., 1966). Color, 83 mins.

Based on the popular BBC-TV series, this film gave veteran character actor Peter Cushing a role as Dr. Who, the inventor of the T.A.R.D.I.S. (the Time and Relative Dimensions in Space machine), a device that looks like a British phone booth. While Who is explaining the workings of the invention to granddaughters Barbara (Jennie Linden) and

Dr. Who and the Daleks

Susan (Roberta Tovey), clumsy friend Ian (Roy Castle) stumbles and falls onto one of the control panels. Who and crew are sent tumbling through time and space, winding up on the planet of the alien Daleks.

The Daleks are aliens who, through nuclear fallout following a holocaust, have been reduced to ameboid shape. They hide their true bodies in cone-shaped metal encasements that allow them locomotion, protect them from radiation, and arm them with lethal ray power. The Daleks ward off the long-term effects of radiation by consuming antidote drugs a-plenty. Once protected, they hunt down and destroy the peaceful Thals—humans.

Who arrives and, seeing that the main sport of the Daleks is very unsportsmanlike, figures out a way to stop them. Reasoning that their cone devices derive locomotive power from the floors of the city, he short-circuits their power base before the aliens can destroy humanity with a neutron bomb. That's teaching them Who's boss.

PRODUCERS: Milton Subotsky, Max Rosenberg. DIRECTOR: Gordon Flemyng. SCREENPLAY: Subotsky, from the TV show by TERRY NATION. MAKEUP: Jill Carpenter. MUSIC: Barry Gray, with Malcolm Lockyer. SPECIAL EFFECTS: Ted Samuels.

SUPPORTING PLAYERS: Michael Coles, Geoffrey Toone.

DR. X
WB (1932). Color, 77 mins.

Not an sf whodunit, but more of a whatdunit. Reporter Lee Taylor (Lee Tracy) teams up with Commissioner Stevens (Robert Warwick), Inspector Halloran (Willard Robertson), and respected Dr. Xavier (Lionel Atwill) in tracking down a sadistic murderer who not only strangles his victims, but cannibalizes them as well. The police suspect that the killer resides in Xavier's scientific academy. Dr. Xavier's daughter, Joan (Fay Wray), nearly becomes the latest victim when a trap concocted by the police fails and the killer corners her in a locked room. The murderer turns out to be respected, one-armed scientist Dr. Wells (Preston Foster), a maniac who creates both a new arm and a new face via the invention called synthetic flesh. The police arrive along with Lee. Lee turns the artificial monster into a real-life one by hurling a kerosene lamp at the killer. Wells does a slow burn followed by a faster one. Ashes to ashes.

DIRECTOR: Michael Curtiz. SCREENPLAY: Robert Tasker and Earl Baldwin, from a play by Howard Comstock and Allen C. Miller. CINEMATOGRAPHY: Richard Tower, Ray Rennahean.

DOG, A MOUSE AND A SPUTNIK, A
France (1958); b/w, 92 mins. U.S., (1960); b/w, 94 mins.

Humans are accidentally launched in a Sputnik during the frantic 1958 race for space.

PRODUCER: Louis de Masure. DIRECTOR: Jean Dreville. SCREENPLAY: Jean-Jacques Vital. CINEMATOGRAPHY: André Bac. MUSIC: Paul Misraki.

CAST: Noel-Noel, Denise Gray, Mischa Auer, Darry Cowl.

DONOVAN'S BRAIN
UA (1953). B/w, 83 mins.

After rescuing the remains of a business tycoon, Donovan, from the wreckage of a small plane, a young doctor decides to keep the brain alive and attempt to communicate with it via a Morse-code alphabet. Eventually the brain is revived. It takes over the young doctor's body via telepathy, and soon the surgeon (Lew Ayres) takes on the personality of the late Donovan. Donovan then begins to get even with a group of business associates whose swindles led to his untimely demise.

PRODUCER: Tom Gries. DIRECTOR AND SCREENWRITER: Felix Feist. CINEMATOGRAPHY: Joseph Biroc. SPECIAL EFFECTS: Harry Redmond, Jr. MUSIC: Eddie Dunstedter. ADAPTATION: Hugh Brooke, from the novel by CURT SIODMAK.

SUPPORTING PLAYERS: Steve Brodie, Lisa Howard, Tom Powers.

DOOMWATCH
Tigon (G.B., 1972). Color, 92 mins.

Residents of an island begin to act strangely, hiding in their homes from strangers. It is later discovered that the dumping of radioactive waste off their shores has created a hormone change in local fish. The fishing village, consuming this food, mutates into hideous creatures, victims of acromegaly.

PRODUCER: Tony Tenser. DIRECTOR: Peter Saady. SCREENPLAY: Clive Exton, based on the BBC-TV series of the same name. CINEMATOGRAPHY: Ken Talbot. MUSIC: John Scott.

CAST: Ian Bannen, Judy Geeson, George Sanders, Percy Herbert.

DRACULA VS. FRANKENSTEIN
Independent International (1971). Color, 90 mins.

Home-movie time. Count Dracula (Zandor Varkov in his first and, presumably, last film role) and a mute manservant (Lon Chaney, Jr.) find the Frankenstein monster (rubber-masked John Bloom) and take him to Dr. F (J. Carrol Naish wearing teeth that, apparently, were originally designed for Trigger) for a quick pick-me-up. Watching the reawakening is "Grasbo— the evil dwarf" (Angelo Rossitto). Fortunately, the audience's slumber is left undisturbed. Everyone hits everyone else a lot and Chaney and Naish make their final film appearances in a production that resembles that last super-8 mm film your great-aunt Tessie took at Marineland in Florida.

PRODUCERS: Al Adamson, John Van Horne. DIRECTOR: Al Adamson. SCREENPLAY: William Pugsley, Sam Sherman. SPECIAL MAKEUP: George Barr. CINEMATOGRAPHY: Gary Graver, Paul Glickman. SPECIAL EFFECTS: Ken Strickfaden (in that all of Strickfaden's old FRANKENSTEIN lab pieces were hastily reassembled in someone's garage for this one). MUSIC: William Lava.

SUPPORTING PLAYERS: Russ Tamblyn, Forrest Ackerman, Jim Davis.

DUEL IN SPACE
Reed (1954). B/w, 78 mins.

ROCKY JONES, SPACE RANGER episodes ride again.

PRODUCER: Roland Reed.

CAST: Richard Crane, Robert Lyden, Sally Mansfield.

EAGLE OF THE NIGHT, THE

Pathé (1928). B/w silent serial, 10 chapters (20 reels).

Opposing forces battle over a new scientific gadget: a muffler that allows planes to cruise over towns in complete silence.

DIRECTOR: Jimmie Fulton.

CAST: Frank Clarke, Shirley Palmer, Earle Metcalfe, Roy Wilson.

EARTH DIES SCREAMING, THE

20th Cent.-Fox (1964). B/w, 62 mins.

A low-budget thriller, short on cash but long on imagination. Jeff Nolan (Willard Parker) and lady-friend Peggy (Virginia Field) watch in horror as a horde of alien robots gallop through a village, killing the inhabitants. The robots then bring the dead back to life, creating an army of indestructible proportions.

PRODUCERS: Robert Lippert, Jack Parsons. DIRECTOR: Terence Fisher. SCREENPLAY: Henry Cross, based on a story by Harry Spalding. MUSIC: Elizabeth Lutyens. MAKEUP: Harold Fletcher.

SUPPORTING PLAYERS: Dennis Price, Thorley Walters.

EARTH VS. THE FLYING SAUCERS

Columbia (1956). B/w, 83 mins.

The flying-saucer phobia of the 1950s brought forth this enjoyable little piece of fluff, highlighted by earnest-to-the-point-of-extinction acting and wonderful flying effects by stop-motion animator Ray Harryhausen. A U.S. Skyhook missile-control center is visited by UFOs. Before the saucers even can land, they are fired upon by trigger-happy soldiers. The soldiers are promptly disintegrated by a nasty ray appearing from the bottom of the saucer.

Dr. Russell Marvin (Hugh Marlowe) is contacted by the metal-shrouded aliens. Their planet is dying and they wish to move to Earth. Neither Gen.

Hanley (Morris Ankrum) nor Marvin's coworkers (Donald Curtis and Joan Taylor) are crazy about the idea. An all-out war ensues between the Earth and the saucers, featuring some eye-boggling destruction scenes involving the nation's capital. The world looks like a real losing proposition for a while.

Then one of the creatures is killed. The metal casing is removed, revealing a frail, reptilian body within. A study of the alien shroud reveals that the creatures are sensitive to ultrahigh-frequency sound. The government does some quick research work and comes up with a master sound-ray. By the film's finale, the saucers are dropping like DC-10s.

PRODUCER: Charles Schneer. DIRECTOR: Fred Sears. SCREENPLAY: George Worthing Yates and Raymond Marcus, from a story by CURT SIODMAK. MUSICAL DIRECTOR: Mischa Bakaleinikoff. SPECIAL EFFECTS: Ray Harryhausen.

Columbia

Earth Vs. the Flying Saucers

EARTH VS. THE SPIDER

Also known as EARTH VS. THE GIANT SPIDER; THE SPIDER.

AIP (1958). B/w, 73 mins.

A mutant spider scuttles out of its cave shelter and strikes terror in a town of toe-tapping teens. The local police subdue it. Thought dead, the spider is put on display. Only stunned, it wakes up and crashes a local sock-hop, sending the teens hopping—out of not only their socks, but their skins as well. Finally the large beast is electrocuted, but not before trashing quite a few miniature cars and homes.

PRODUCER, DIRECTOR, AND STORY CONCEPT: Bert I. Gordon. SCREENPLAY: Laszlo Gorog, George Worthing Yates.

MAKEUP: Allen Snyder. CINEMATOGRA-
PHY: Jack Marta. SPECIAL EFFECTS:
Bert I. and Flora Gordon. MUSIC: Al-
bert Glasser.
CAST: Ed Kemmer, June Kenney,
Gene Roth, Mickey Finn, Sally Fraser.

EFFECTS OF A ROCKET, THE
1911. B/w silent short, 420 ft.
Men are able to fly through the skies
with rocket devices.

EGGHEAD'S ROBOT
Children's Film Foundation (G.B.,
1970). Color, 56 mins.
A child genius builds a robot twin.
PRODUCER: Cecil Musk. DIRECTOR:
Milo Lewis. SCREENPLAY: Leif Saxon.
CINEMATOGRAPHY: Johnny Coquillon.
MUSIC: Gordon Langford.
CAST: Keither Chegwin, Jeff Cheg-
win, Kathryn Dawe, Roy Kinnear,
Richard Wattis.

ELECTRIC GIRL, THE
Éclair (1914). B/w silent short, one
reel.
After undergoing electrical treatment, a servant girl finds that she has
quite a magnetic personality . . . at-
tracting any and all metal in the area.

ELECTRIC GOOSE, THE
Gaumont (G.B., 1905). B/w silent
short.
A film only Julia Child's fans could
love. A Christmas dinner is brought
back to life through a shot of electricity.

ELECTRIC HOTEL, THE
Spain (1906). B/w silent short, 476 ft.
An electric hotel awaits visitors with
totally automated service. Everything
moves on its own. Suitcases pack and
unpack without being touched. Only
the bill has to be paid manually.
PRODUCER: Segundo de Chomon.

ELECTRIC HOUSE, THE
Buster Keaton Productions (1922).
B/w silent featurette, two reels.
Originally planned as a 1921 feature
film, The Electric House was postponed
because of a near-tragic accident. As a
young inventor of a fully automated
house, Buster Keaton was called upon
to glide up an escalator. During the
sequence, cameras rolling, the escalator
speeded up and Keaton's shoe was
caught in the mechanism and shredded.
Keaton broke his ankle in the mishap
and was thrown 10 feet to the ground.
The project was picked up again a year
later, with all of the previous attempt's
footage long destroyed.
Briefly, the story centers on an automated house (full-scale sets ingeniously
devised by Keaton) built by a young
inventor. If the inventor can impress
the president of a large building concern, the homes will be mass-produced.
The tour of the home results, of course,
in a series of mishaps culminating in a
scene involving an "instant" swimming
pool. Keaton fills the pool in 30 seconds, a veritable Niagara Falls appearing from nowhere. Emptying the pool,
Keaton slips in as the Niagara Falls
effect works in reverse. The film ends
with Keaton taking an unexpected voyage through the Los Angeles sewer system.
PRODUCER: Joseph M. Schenck. DI-
RECTORS AND SCREENWRITERS: Buster
Keaton, Eddie Cline.

ELECTRIC LAUNDRY, THE
France (1919). B/w silent short.
Clothes are cleaned in an all-auto-
mated manner.

ELECTRIC LEG, THE
Clarendon (G.B., 1912). B/w silent
short.
An inventor perfects a mechanical
leg powered by electricity and capable
of functioning without the benefit of an
attached body.

ELECTRIC POLICEMAN, THE
Gaumont (France, 1909). B/w silent
short, 352 ft.
A policeman increases his foot speed
by wearing electric boots that are unstoppable. Talk about happy feet.

ELECTRIC VILLA, THE
Pathé (France, 1911). B/w silent
short, 420 ft.
An electrified house gives everything
inside a sense of animation; a dead
chicken comes to life and the furniture
moves seemingly of its own accord.

ELECTRONIC MONSTER, THE

Amalgamated (G.B., 1957); b/w, 80 mins.
Columbia (U.S., 1960); b/w, 72 mins.

Originally known overseas as *Zex* and *Escapement*, this strange little head-trip includes loads of bizarre dream sequences and cumbersome dialogue. A group of scientists employed by a mental institution attempt to cure psychoses by inducing dreams in their patients. It's only a matter of time before a couple of bad apples discover how to control patients' dreams, and hence gain the power to live out their own macabre fantasies in the minds of others.

PRODUCER: Alec C. Snowden. DIRECTOR: Montgomery Tully. SCREENPLAY: CHARLES ERIC MAINE and J. Maclaren-Ross, based on Maine's novel *Escapement*. MAKEUP: Jack Craig. ART DIRECTOR: Wilfred Arnold. CINEMATOGRAPHY: Bert Mason. ELECTRONIC MUSIC: Soundrama.

CAST: Rod Cameron, Mary Murphy, Peter Illing.

EMBRYO

Cine Artists (1976). DeLuxe color, 105 mins.

Dr. Paul Holliston (Rock Hudson) develops a rapid-growth hormone and uses it to speed up the development of a premature fetus. Well, before you can say "Frankenstein must be destroyed," Dr. Holliston has grown a beautiful 25-year-old woman whose personality is zero. Holliston sets out to create the perfect woman, but a few miscalculations causes the premature Eve, Victoria (Barbara Carrera), to become something less than the apple of her test-tube-toting pop's eye.

PRODUCERS: Arnold H. Orgolini, Anita Doohan. DIRECTOR: Ralph Nelson. SCREENPLAY: Anita Doohan and Jack W. Thomas, from a story by Thomas. CINEMATOGRAPHY: Fred Koenkamp. ART DIRECTOR: Joe Alves. MAKEUP: Dan Striepeke, John Chambers, Mark Redall. SPECIAL EFFECTS: Roy Arbogast, Bill Shourt. MUSIC: Gil Melle.

SUPPORTING PLAYERS: Diane Ladd as Martha, Roddy McDowall as Riley, Anne Schedeen as Helen.

EMPIRE OF THE ANTS, THE

AIP (1977). Color, 87 mins.

Loosely based on H. G. WELLS's story of the same name. A group of travelers discovers a jungle filled with mutated giant ants, the product of radiation.

PRODUCER, DIRECTOR, SCREENWRITER, AND SPECIAL-EFFECTS CREATOR: Bert I. Gordon.

CAST: Joan Collins, Robert Lansing, Albert Salmi.

© American International Pictures, 1977

The Empire of the Ants

EMPIRE STRIKES BACK, THE

20th Cent.-Fox (1980). Color by Rank Film Laboratories, Panavision, Visual effects filmed in VistaVision, 120 mins.

The second chapter of filmmaker George Lucas's sprawling STAR WARS mythos (of which twelve films will eventually emerge) is not so much a sequel to the original movie as a continuation and maturation of its themes. Originally conceived by Lucas, *Empire*'s screenplay was begun by noted sf writer LEIGH BRACKETT. After her untimely death, screenwriter Lawrence Kasdan (*Raiders of the Lost Ark*) assumed literary duties.

The finished opus opens on the ice planet of Hoth, where the freedom-loving Rebels have set up their new stronghold. Heading the Rebel forces are, once again, Luke Skywalker (Mark Hamill), Han Solo (Harrison Ford), Princess Leia (Carrie Fisher), C-3PO (Anthony Daniels), R2-D2 (Kenny

Baker), and Chewbacca (Peter May-hew).

The armies of the Empire, led by Darth Vader (David Prowse, featuring the voice of James Earl Jones), stumble onto the encampment and all but wipe it out. Han leads the Princess, Chewbacca, and C-3PO to safety in the *Millennium Falcon*, his battered spaceship. Luke and R2-D2 escape in an X-wing.

Following the advice of the ghostly Obi-Wan Kenobi (Alec Guinness), Luke journeys to a bog planet, where he is instructed in the advanced ways of The Force by gnome-ish Jedi Master Yoda (Frank Oz). Luke must learn to curb his human anger in order to master the almost supernatural power.

Meanwhile, Han and company land on the Cloud City of Bespin, where his old crony Lando Calrissian (Billy Dee Williams) calls the shots. Unfortunately, Lando is in the clutches of Darth Vader and bounty hunter Boba Fett. Fett is after Solo's hide. Vader is after Luke. Capturing our heroes, Vader lures Skywalker away from his instruction and entices him onto the Cloud City.

Fett captures Han. Skywalker faces Vader in a blaze of light sabres. Fett cryogenically freezes Solo's body and steals off into space with it, leaving a howling Chewbacca behind. Vader invites Luke to join the Dark Side of The Force. The boy, he insists, belongs with Vader because, in reality, Darth Vader is Luke's father! Rather than join Vader, Luke throws himself off the Cloud City.

Calrissian, meanwhile, fires up the old *Falcon* and, loading up the remaining Rebels, escapes from the Empire's Stormtroopers. Seeing Luke tumble, they zoom into a nose dive and scoop him up. Taking Luke to a medical center, Calrissian enlists the aid of Chewbacca, the Princess, and C-3PO in his quest to free Han Solo from Boba Fett.

A mended Luke and R2-D2 head back for the bog planet and the mastery of The Force. Luke's training is mandatory, for, during the light sabre fight with his father, he heard Vader proclaim that only one person can cause the Empire to crumble—and that one person is Luke Skywalker! To be continued . . .

Alien-ated

The small extraterrestrials portrayed in the movie are like those reported all over the world. That's why I chose humanoid shapes as opposed to a banana with treads.
> Steven Spielberg on *Close Encounters*

PRODUCER: Gary Kurtz. DIRECTOR: Irvin Kershner. SCREENPLAY: Leigh Brackett and Lawrence Kasdan from a story by George Lucas. EXECUTIVE PRODUCER: George Lucas. PRODUCTION DESIGNER: Norman Reynolds. DIRECTOR OF PHOTOGRAPHY: Peter Suschitzky. SPECIAL VISUAL EFFECTS: Brian Johnson, Richard Edlund. MUSIC: John Williams, performed by the London Symphony Orchestra. CONCEPTUAL ARTIST: Ralph McQuarrie. ART DIRECTORS: Leslie Dilley, Harry Lang, Alan Tompkins. MAKEUP: Stuart Freeborn. COSTUME DESIGN: John Mollo. SPECIAL EFFECTS UNIT: Nick Alder, Dennis Muren, Bruce Nicholson, Joe Johnston, Jon Berg, Phil Tippett, Harrison Ellenshaw, Lorne Peterson, Peter Kuran, Conrad Buff.

END OF THE WORLD, THE
Nordisk (Denmark, 1916). B/w silent feature, six reels.

A comet passing through Earth's atmosphere causes weather calamities to occur below. Floods, tidal waves, and electrical storms batter the planet's surface.

DIRECTOR: August Blom. SCREENPLAY: Otto Rung. CINEMATOGRAPHY: John Ankerstjerne.

END OF THE WORLD, THE
L'Écran d'Art (France, 1930); b/w, 105 mins.
Auten (U.S., 1934); b/w, 54 mins.

A comet hits the Earth, causing great discomfort to numerous Earthlings.

DIRECTOR: Abel Gance. SCREENPLAY: Gance, based on a novel by Camille Flammarion. ART DIRECTORS: Lazare Meerson, Jean Perrier. CINEMATOGRAPHY: Jules Kruger, Nicolas Rudakov, Roger Hubert. MUSIC: Ondes Martenot, Michel Michelet.

CAST: Abel Gance, Colette Darfeuil, Sylvia Grenade, Samson Fainsilber, Georges Colin.

ENGLISH-LANGUAGE VERSION: DIRECTOR: V. Ivanoff. SCREENPLAY ADAPTATION: H. S. Kraft. MUSICAL ADAPTATION: M. Levine, R. Siohan, W. Zederbaum.

END OF THE WORLD, THE
Manson (1977). DeLuxe color, 92 mins.

Plays like it reads. Father Pergado (Christopher Lee) is destroyed by an alien double. Meanwhile, Sylvia and Andrew Boran (Sue Lyon and Kirk Scott) tell their boss that there is a station somewhere on Earth that is sending and receiving messages from space. Boss Collins (Dean Jagger) stammers. U.S. space expert Backerman (Lew Ayres), who has a space-monitoring station of his own, is baffled.

Meanwhile, alien Zindar/Father Pergado has turned St. Catherine's church into an alien nest, in which nuns from outer space (really) are trying to construct a time-wall to enable them to return to their home. They need Andrew Boran's variance crystal to complete the wall. To prove their might, they kill Andrew's friend Davis (MacDonald Carey), the keeper of the crystal. At this point, Andrew decides to help. He fixes the alien wall. The nuns slip through and a changed manthing, Zindar, tells the Borans that they, too, might as well slip through, in that the aliens were sent here to de-

Manson

The End of the World

stroy the world, and in a few seconds, their mission will be accomplished. Everyone goes through the wall, the scriptwriter goes off the wall, and the world is blown up.

PRODUCER: Charles Band. DIRECTOR: John Hayes. SCREENPLAY: Frank Roy Perilli. CINEMATOGRAPHY: John Huneck. SPECIAL EFFECTS: Harry Wolman. MUSIC: Andrew Belling.

ENEMY FROM SPACE
UA (1957). B/w, 85 mins.

A taut tale of intergalactic terror based on NIGEL KNEALE's Quatermass character of BBC radio and TV. Dr. Quatermass (Brian Donlevy) and compatriot Marsh (Bryan Forbes) discover a plot by amorphous aliens to control the Earth via telepathic control. The creatures have the ability to use human bodies as their apparent hosts, controlling the body movements by subverting the mind. The invaders test their plan of conquest on a small scale at first, using as guinea pigs only workers at a British factory. Enter Quatermass with a counterattack.

PRODUCER: Anthony Hinds. DIRECTOR: Val Guest. SCREENPLAY: Guest, Nigel Kneale. MUSIC: James Benard. SPECIAL EFFECTS: Bill Warrington, Henry Harris, Frank George.

SUPPORTING PLAYERS: Michael Ripper, Percy Herbert.

ESCAPE FROM THE PLANET OF THE APES
20th Cent.-Fox (1971). Color/scope, 97 mins.

Exceedingly entertaining monkey-shines in this, the third and one of the best of the *Apes* series. Three chimpanzees, Cornelius (Roddy McDowall), Zira (Kim Hunter), and Milo (Sal Mineo), escape the nuclear holocaust that levels the Earth of the future (see BENEATH THE PLANET OF THE APES) by piloting their spaceship through a time warp and arriving in their Earth's distant past—or, our Earth's present. Landing in the U.S., they are captured by the government. Milo is killed in a freak accident in an experimental lab. When it is discovered that Cornelius and Zira are intelligent apes, capable of speaking English, they become instant celebrities. Their popularity

20th Cent.-Fox

Escape from the Planet of the Apes

wanes when it is discovered that Zira is pregnant.

A group of politicians and scientists fear that if the apes are allowed to procreate, their race may one day take over the planet, subjugating man. They urge the government to sanction the chimp couple's murder. A pair of friendly scientists (Bradford Dillman and Natalie Trundy) help the twosome escape. A kindly circus owner (Ricardo Montalban) gives them protection after Cornelius accidentally kills one of his guards during the escape. Government agents (led by Eric Braeden) track the pair to the circus and, cornering both Cornelius and Zira, as well as newly arrived baby Milo, butcher them all . . . or so they think.

PRODUCER: Arthur P. Jacobs. DIRECTOR: Don Taylor. SCREENPLAY: Paul Dehn, based on characters created by PIERRE BOULLE. MAKEUP: John Chambers, Dan Stripeke. CINEMATOGRAPHY: Joseph Biroc. MUSIC: Jerry Goldsmith.

SUPPORTING PLAYERS: Albert Salmi, William Windom.

ESCAPE TO WITCH MOUNTAIN
Walt Disney/Buena Vista (1975). Technicolor, 97 mins.

Two apparently ordinary children (Ike Eisenmann and Kim Richards) are, in reality, orphans from outer space. Although they have no memory of their origins, they do express some amazement over the psi abilities they seem to have inherited from person or persons unknown. The boy can move things at will while playing on his harmonica; the girl can foresee the future. When their talents become known to a ruthless businessman (Ray Milland), they become the targets of a kidnapping plot. Fleeing from his clutches, they enlist the aid of a middle-aged good samaritan (Eddie Albert) enjoying a leisurely vacation in his camper/trailer. As the forces of evil close in, the children levitate the trailer, changing it into an airborne vehicle. The cavalry arrives in the presence of the children's true family, who come from space in a Mount Olympus–sized flying saucer.

PRODUCER: Jerome Courtland. DIRECTOR: John Hough. SCREENPLAY: Robert Malcolm Young, based on the novel by Alexander Key.

EVIL BRAIN FROM OUTER SPACE, THE
Manley (1964). Color, 86 mins.

Could have been titled *The Evil Plot to Snatch Your Dollars.* A fairly senseless splicing together of elements from three Japanese SUPER GIANT superhero films: *Uchu Kaijin Shutsugen* (Shintoho 1958), *Akuma no Kehiin* (Shintoho, 1959), and *Dokugo Okuku* (Shintoho, 1959). Super Giant (Ken Utsui) fights off aliens with his superstrength. Two alien attacks are highlighted: one featuring a horde of humanoid-looking invaders, the other spearheaded by giant-insect monsters.

DIRECTOR: Teno Ishii. SCREENPLAY: Ichiro Miyagawa.

SUPPORTING PLAYERS: Reiko Seto, Chisako Tawara.

EVIL OF FRANKENSTEIN, THE
Hammer/Universal (1964). Color, 84 mins.

Already showing signs of fatigue in its formula sf-horror productions, Britain's house of Hammer attempted to rally in this colorful production but succeeded only in recapturing its good intentions of old. Highlighted by strong acting, this science-gone-astray tale sinks under the weight of its clichéd script.

Dr. Frankenstein (Peter Cushing) has his latest series of experiments

Hammer/Universal

The Evil of Frankenstein

brought to an unceremonious end when a crazed priest smashes his equipment to shreds. Seeing this incident as a portent of things to come, the doctor and his assistant decide to leave town and return to the Frankenstein's old home in the Balkans, where he finds his estate in ruins, pillaged by thieves and vandals.

Angry at this turn of events, he catches one of the thieves wearing one of his heirloom rings and provokes a fight in town, thus exposing his identity. Fleeing the police, Frankenstein and friend Hans (Sandor Eles) are saved by evil hypnotist Zoltan (Peter Woodthorpe). Unable to return to the castle because of the police, Frankenstein and Hans are given shelter in a cave by a mute beggar-girl (Katy Wild). Fortunately for the doctor, the cave also houses the frozen remains of his monster (Kiwi Kingston).

Sneaking into the castle, the trio thaws out the monster, but the creature remains in coma. Zoltan is brought in to hypnotize him into consciousness. The mesmerist, however, learns to control the beast and sends him into town on a killing spree—murderous marches that eliminate all of Zoltan's enemies. Frankenstein, discovering the monster's misuse, tells Zoltan to knock it off. Zoltan, equally enraged, tells the monster to knock *it* off; *it*, in this case, meaning Dr. Frankenstein's head.

But even a monster can't do in his dad, and so the shambling creature kills Zoltan instead, harpooning him with an iron spike. The villagers, armed with torches, arrive on cue and the monster panics, drinking a bottle of chloroform before knocking the lab

apart. The film ends with everyone being charbroiled except for handsome Hans and the pretty mute girl, who, by this time, can speak well enough to yell "help."

PRODUCER: Anthony Hinds. DIRECTOR: Freddie Francis. SCREENPLAY: John Elder. MAKEUP: Roy Ashton. CINEMATOGRAPHY: John Wilcox. SPECIAL EFFECTS: Les Bowie. MUSIC: Don Banks.

EXTERMINATORS, THE
Comptoir Français/Cinerad-Camera (France/Italy, 1965). Color, 95 mins.

An evil genius, the ruler of an underground complex, builds a nuclear rocket and aims it at New York.

PRODUCER: Jean Maumy. DIRECTOR: Riccardo Freda. SCREENPLAY: Claude Marcel Richard. CINEMATOGRAPHY: Henri Persin. MUSIC: Michel Magne.

CAST: Richard Wyler, Gil Delamare, Jany Clair.

EYE CREATURES, THE
AIP (1965). Color, 80 mins.

During the mid-1960s, American International Pictures, known for the plethora of grade B movies unleashed from its cameras during the 1950s, decided to remake the old B's as grade Z's. This little-known—and deservedly so—ditty is actually a remake of the teen-shock-schlock film INVASION OF THE SAUCER MEN. A couple of multi-eyed aliens land on Earth and, after killing a local resident or two, try to pin the blame on the local teens. Tough luck.

PRODUCER AND DIRECTOR: Larry Buchanan.

CAST: John Ashley, Cynthia Hull, Chet Davis.

FABULOUS WORLD OF JULES VERNE, THE
Czechoslovakia, 1958; WB (U.S., 1961). B/w, live with animation, 83 mins.

Based on a series of novels by JULES

VERNE, Karel Zeman's ode to the master of sf features submarines, airships, giant squids, underground cities, etc. Live actors were mixed with animated sequences and small sets patterned after the classic illustrations that appeared in Verne's original editions.

DIRECTOR AND ART DIRECTOR: Karel Zeman. SCREENPLAY: Karel Zeman and Frantisek Hrubin, based on the works of Jules Verne. CINEMATOGRAPHY: Jiri Tarantik. Special effects filmed in Mystamation. EDITOR: Zedenik Stehlik. MUSIC: Zdenek Liska.

CAST: Louis Tock, Van Kissling, Jane Zalata, Arnost Navratil.

FACE OF FU MANCHU, THE
7 Arts (1965). Color, 95 mins.

Fu Manchu (Christopher Lee) and his number-one daughter (Tsai Chin) plan to take over the world by manufacturing a poison that is culled from "a flower found only in the inaccessible mountains of the north." As confused as his audience at this point, Fu attempts to force a German scientist (Joachim Fuchsberger) to help him in this fiendish plot by kidnapping the scientist's daughter (Karin Dor). Fu plans to release the poison from an underground hideout near London's Thames River. He doesn't count on interference provided by Scotland Yard's finest, Nayland Smith (Nigel Green).

PRODUCER: Harry Alan Towers. DIRECTOR: Don Sharp. SCREENPLAY: Harry Alan Towers. ART DIRECTOR: Frank White. CINEMATOGRAPHY: Ernest Steward. MUSIC: Christopher Whelen.

SUPPORTING PLAYERS: Howard Marion-Crawford, James Robertson Justice, Walter Rilla.

FACE OF TERROR
Documento Films (Spain, 1962); AIP (U.S. 1962). B/w, 83 mins.

A playgirl has her face restored after a horrible accident. Much to her dismay, however, the effects are not permanent and she needs periodic injections to keep her chin—and indeed, the rest of her visage—up. A homicidal-maniac scientist provides local color.

DIRECTOR: Isidoro Martinez Ferry. SCREENPLAY: Monroe Manning. MUSIC: Jose Buengu.

CAST: Lisa Gaye, Fernando Rey, Conchita Cuetos.

FAHRENHEIT 451
Universal (1968). Color, 112 mins.

A thoughtful, low-key adaptation of the RAY BRADBURY novel helmed by François Truffaut. In the not-too-distant future, the world is devoted to the deification of the mundane. Intellectual pursuits are considered illegal, individualism is frowned upon, and the reading of books is a crime equal to murder. Montag (Oscar Werner) is a leading "fireman" employed by the government to find and burn all printed matter. The paper bursts into flame at the 451° F level, a state of existence brought about by the firemen's ever-ready flamethrowers.

During the course of his duties, Montag is asked by a girl, Clarisse (Julie Christie), if he has ever actually read any of the books he has destroyed. He proudly answers, "No," but then he begins to question his judgment in regards to his fireman's activities. He begins reading books, becoming more and more literate, intelligent, and independent with each subsequent page. He becomes hooked, reading book after book and falling in with a group of intellectual book-people whose job it is to commit one classic to memory in order to preserve it for future generations in a world devoid of the printed word. Of course, only tragedy can befall such a heroic action.

PRODUCER: Lewis M. Allen. DIRECTOR: François Truffaut. SCREENPLAY: Truffaut and Jean-Louis Richard, based on the novel by Ray Bradbury. CINEMATOGRAPHY: Nicholas Roeg. MUSIC: Bernard Herrmann.

SUPPORTING PLAYERS: Cyril Cusack, Anton Diffring, Bee Duffell.

FAIL SAFE
Columbia (1964). B/w, 111 mins.

A somber look at the near future. Based on the novel of the same name by Eugene Burdick and Harvey Wheeler, *Fail Safe* is a story of accidental mass destruction. Through a military error, an American bomber is dispatched to drop an A-bomb on the U.S.S.R. Once the error is found out, the U.S. government tries desperately to get in touch with the pilot and bring back the plane. One complication after another ensues. Realizing that Moscow is doomed, the president of the United States (Henry Fonda) informs the Russians of the horrible event-to-come. In order to stave off total nuclear destruction in a retaliatory action by the U.S.S.R., the president promises to wipe out New York City.

PRODUCER: Max Youngstein. DIRECTOR: Sidney Lumet. SCREENPLAY: Walter Bernstein. CINEMATOGRAPHY: Gerald Hirschfeld. SPECIAL EFFECTS: Storyboard, Inc.

SUPPORTING PLAYERS: Dan O'Herlihy, Walter Matthau, Larry Hagman, Fritz Weaver, Sorrell Booke.

FANTASTIC PLANET
New World (1973). Metrocolor, animated, 72 mins.

On the planet Ygam, gigantic androids known as Draags keep tiny humanoids (Oms) as pets. The Draags consider the humans to be no more intelligent than your run-of-the-mill lower form of life. Although most of the Oms are not college material, they do possess an IQ level that is exploitable. In fact, one Om, a fellow named Terr, learns how to speak and reason from his teenage owner, Tiwa. Soon Terr has as much, if not more, knowledge than your average Draag. He escapes and joins the underground Om resistance movement. The Draags, learning of the rebels' location, storm the park/headquarters, killing most of the Oms. Terr escapes to the Draags' planet of meditation. The Draags come to the startling conclusion that these little Oms are their equals and allow them to live on a world parallel to their own. The new planet is named for its Om leader, Terr. It's called, simply, Terra.

PRODUCERS: S. Damiani, A. Valio-Cavablione. DIRECTOR: René Laloux. SCREENPLAY: Roland Topor, based on the novel *Oms en série*, by Stefan Wul. ARTWORK: Topor. MUSIC: Alan Gorgageur. Shot in the animation studios of Jiri Trnka and Kratky Film, in Prague.

VOICES: Sylvie Lenoir, Jean Topart, Jennifer Drake, Yyes Barsacq, Jean Velmont, Paul Ville, May Amyl.

Fantastic Planet

FANTASTIC VOYAGE
20th Cent.-Fox (1966). Color/scope, 100 mins.

Czechoslovakian scientist Jan Benes (Jean Del Val) defects to the West but may never get a chance to reveal his secrets to the U.S., as a clot in his brain may end his life prematurely. The malady is inoperable via normal surgical means, and so the chemists and physicists of 1995 band together and come up with a solution. They shrink a submarine with a full crew (Stephen Boyd as government agent Grant, Arthur Kennedy as Dr. Duval, Donald Pleasance as Dr. Michaels, William Redfield as Captain Bill Owens, and Raquel Welch as Cora Peters) to the size of a microbe and inject it into the patient's body. The idea is to operate from within. The sub crew will remain tiny only for a short time, however, so the operation must be carried out quickly and expertly.

After a number of close calls, the crew nears its goal only to discover that there is a foreign agent on board. The saboteur, Dr. Michaels, is caught off-guard by a group of hungry white corpuscles and eaten. Unfortunately, the white corpuscles devour the sub, too. Swimming for their lives, the crew members remove the clot and try to find a way out of the poor fellow's body before they expand. They exit in a teardrop. This movie won an Oscar for its special effects.

PRODUCER: Saul David. DIRECTOR: Richard Fleischer. SCREENPLAY: Harry Kleiner, from a story by Otto Klement and J. Lewis Bixby. CINEMATOGRAPHY: Ernest Laszlo. ART DIRECTORS: Jack

20th Cent.-Fox

Fantastic Voyage

Martin Smith, Dale Hennessy. SPECIAL EFFECTS: Lyle B. Abbott, Art Cruickshank, and Emil Kosa, Jr. MUSIC: Leonard Rosemann.

FIEND WITHOUT A FACE
MGM (1958). B/w, 74 mins.

Better-than-average special effects liven up this thriller a bit. In Canada, an invisible force tries to sabotage a rocket base. The creatures turn out to be the results of some unorthodox experiments being conducted down the road by a local scientist interested in the materialization of thought. These obviously rotten thoughts eventually *do* materialize as a fleet of flying-brain/ spinal-column creatures who choke their victims to death. Hero Marshall Thompson, as an air force officer, is determined to bring the brainy villains to their knees, so to speak.

PRODUCER: John Croydon. DIRECTOR: Arthur Crabtree. SCREENPLAY: Herbert J. Leder, from the short story "The Thought Monster," by Amelia R. Long. MAKEUP: Jim Hydes. CINEMATOGRAPHY: Lionel Banes. SPECIAL EFFECTS: Puppel Nordhoff, Peter Nielson. MUSIC: Buxton Orr.

SUPPORTING PLAYERS: Terence Kilburn, Kim Parker, Peter Madden.

FIFTH MAN, THE
Selig (1914). B/w silent feature, three reels.

A mad scientist thinks a local man would be the perfect addition to his private zoo.

DIRECTOR: F. J. Grandon, SCREENPLAY: James Oliver Curwood.

CAST: Charles Clary, Bessie Eyton, Roy Watson.

FIGHTING MARINES, THE
Mascot (1935). B/w serial, 12 chapters (25 reels).

Corp. Lawrence (Grant Withers) and Sgt. McGowan (Adrian Morris) land on Halfway Island to investigate the numerous crashes of Marine planes. It turns out there's a villain on the loose, armed with a radio gravity-gun.

PRODUCER: Barney Sarecky. DIRECTORS: Breezy Eason, Joseph Kane. SCREENPLAY: Barney Sarecky, Sherman L. Lowe.

SUPPORTING PLAYERS: Ann Rutherford as Frances Schiller, Robert Warwick as Col. Bennett.

FIRE MAIDENS FROM OUTER SPACE
Topaz (G.B., 1956). B/w, 80 mins.

A British film featuring Anthony Dexter as an astronaut who alights on the 13th moon of Jupiter only to discover an all-showgirl populace. The hitch in their utopia is the presence of an ugly critter who stalks the scenery at night, butchering slow-moving locals.

PRODUCER: George Fowler. DIRECTOR AND SCREENWRITER: Cy Roth. MUSIC: Aleksandr P. Borodin. MAKEUP: Roy Ashton.

Law and Order and Wee Wee
The Penis is evil, for it shoots Life.
The Gun is good, for it shoots Death.
The great flying head, Zardoz, in *Zardoz*

SUPPORTING PLAYERS: Susan Shaw, Paul Carpenter, Henry Fowler.

FIRE OF LIFE
Nordisk (Denmark, 1912), Great Northern (U.S., 1912). B/w silent featurette, two reels.

A scientist discovers the secret of eternal life.

DIRECTOR: Schedler Sorenson. SCREENPLAY: Xenius Rostock.

CAST: Valdemar Psitander, Julie Henriksen, Else Frohlich.

FIRST MAN INTO SPACE
Amalgamated (G.B.)/MGM (1959). B/w, 77 mins.

Space isn't the place to be in this familiar-looking melodrama. Commander C. E. Prescott (Marshall Thompson) is not pleased when the first astronaut shot into space reenters the atmosphere covered with space ooze. The astronaut gives up the ghost but the ooze goes marching on, using the astronaut's body for locomotion. The monster needs human blood daily to survive. Tia Francesca (Marla Landis) seems to pop up at the darndest of times, just when the monster is up for a quick drink.

PRODUCERS: John Croydon, Charles F. Vetter. DIRECTOR: Robert Day. SCREENPLAY: John C. Cooper and Lance Hargreaves, from a story by W. Ordung. MUSIC: Buxton Orr. MAKEUP: Michael Morris.

SUPPORTING PLAYERS: Robert Ayres, Carl Jaffe, Bill Edwards.

FIRST MEN IN THE MOON
Gaumont (British, 1919). B/w silent feature.

Professor Cavor goes to the moon in this adaptation of the H. G. WELLS novel.

DIRECTOR: J. V. Leigh.
CAST: Bruce Gordon, Hector Abbas, Heather Thatcher.

FIRST MEN IN THE MOON
Columbia (1964). Panavision and Technicolor, 107 mins.

A visually stunning, adroitly written adaptation of the vintage tale of space travel by H. G. WELLS. Ensconced in a present-day old-age home and thought to be quite dotty, Bedford (Edward Judd) watches the first U.S. moon landing and recalls his own adventures on the moon, nearly a century ago.

Bedford's friend Professor Cavor (Lionel Jeffries) had invented Cavorite, an antigravity liquid that causes anything it touches to float. Cavor, Bedford, and Bedford's fiancée, Kate (Martha Hyer), take off for the moon in a Cavorite-covered satellite-sphere. They land on the moon but have their spaceship stolen while they are exploring giant-flower forests. They trace the machine's tracks and follow it to an underground cavern.

Inside, they encounter an underground insect-man civilization. The insects, Selenites, prove their friendliness by saving the trio from a big but harmless moon cow (a centipede-thing the size of a tractor-trailer). The

Columbia

First Men in the Moon

Earth people meet the Grand Lunar and Cavor takes a shine to the intelligent life form, telling him about Earth's history, its wars, etc. The ruler is revolted. He states that ideas such as war do not exist on his world, nor does he ever want them to. He reasons that if these three Earth explorers are kept on the moon, humanity will never find a way to send a second expedition moonside to contaminate his civilization with Earthly ideas. Cavor doesn't mind sticking around, but Bedford and Kate have other ideas. With Cavor's help, they escape and he remains . . . despite a rather bad cold he has picked up en route. Bedford and Kate make it back.

Kate now long dead, Bedford now watches the flickering images of the astronauts landing on the moon while the patients and staff around him scoff at his tale. With TV cameras running, the astronauts find a tattered British Union Jack—the flag left on the moon by Cavor, Bedford, and Kate. The modern-day space explorers then move underground and find a long-dead lunar civilization—a society destroyed by a deadly germ brought their way from another planet . . . Earth's common cold germ.

PRODUCER: Charles Schneer. ASSOCIATE PRODUCER AND SPECIAL-EFFECTS CREATOR: Ray Harryhausen. DIRECTOR: Nathan Juran. SCREENPLAY: NIGEL

KNEALE, Jan Read. MUSIC: Laurie Johnson.

SUPPORTING PLAYERS: Betty McDowall, Peter Finch, Hugh McDermott, Miles Malleson.

FIRST SPACESHIP ON VENUS
Also known as PLANET OF THE DEAD; SPACESHIP VENUS DOES NOT REPLY; ASTRONAUTS.
DEFA/Julzjon (E. Germany/Poland, 1959); color, 109 mins. Crown International (U.S., 1963); color, 80 mins.

A rocket filled with an international crew headed by Orloff (Ignacy Machowski), Sumiko Ogimura (Yoka Tani), and Techen Yu (Tang Hua-Ta) blasts off for Venus. After a long voyage they land to discover the planet's long-dead alien civilization. The Venusians, it seems, were destroyed by atomic warfare. The ghosts of the alien life-forms now hover about in the planet's molten-rock layers.

DIRECTOR: Kurt Matzig. ENGLISH-LANGUAGE-VERSION PRODUCER: Hugo Grimaldi. ORIGINAL MUSIC: Andrzej Markowski. ENGLISH-LANGUAGE-VERSION MUSIC: Gordon Zahler. SCREENPLAY: J. Barckhausen, J. Felthke, W. Kohlaase, K. Matzig, G. Reisch, G. Rucker, and A. Stenbock-Fermor, from the novel *Astronauts*, by STANISLAW LEM.

FIVE
Columbia (1951). B/w, 93 mins.

A well-intentioned morality play that has the distinction of being one of the first social-commentary nuclear-war films to be lensed after World War II.

After Armageddon, four people arrive at the isolated home of Michael (William Phipps): bank teller Barnstaple (Earl Lee), black elevator-operator Charles (Charles Lampkin), pregnant Rosanne (Susan Douglas), and adventurer Eric (James Anderson). Racism and frustration abound. Bank teller Barnstaple cannot accept the reality of the situation and withers, away. Racist Eric kills Charles and then himself dies. Michael and Rosanne are left to face the bleak new world.

PRODUCER, DIRECTOR, AND SCREENWRITER: Arch Oboler. CINEMATOGRAPHY: Louis Clyde Stoumen, Sid Lubow.

FIVE MILLION MILES TO EARTH
Also known as QUATERMASS AND THE PIT.
20th Cent.-Fox (1968). DeLuxe color, 97 mins.

Surviving the rigors of THE CREEPING UNKNOWN and ENEMY FROM OUTER SPACE, Professor Quatermass (Andrew Keir, replacing actor Brian Donlevy) is pitted against a long-dead Martian civilization in *Five Million Miles*. When a Martian spaceship is found buried far beneath the streets of modern-day London, a slice of humanity's history is inadvertently revealed. The ship still houses its long-dead, insectlike astronauts and is still programmed with a directive that causes it to keep any and all intruders away. The vessel, therefore, electrocutes all human intruders and emits heat rays that dissolve flesh.

Quatermass, Dr. Roney (James Donald), and Barbara Judd (Barbara Shelley) attempt to find out how and when the ship came to be. They discover that the ship's main source of power is derived from the mental capabilities of the dormant Martian minds within. Tapping this power source, they find that the Martians arrived on Earth during its formative years, in search of slaves. Finding apes, they performed experiments that took the simians up the evolutionary ladder to humandom. When the Martians disappeared, mankind evolved.

During this power tap, the Earth scientists inadvertently unleash all of the ship's long-stored mental power. The unchecked Martian thought patterns begin ripping the city apart. Large ghost projections of the deceased Martians are projected into the London night. Roney boards a crane and rams the center of the ghost images, the core of the mental power. He short-circuits the energy flow, causing the ship to implode. He dies in the resulting inferno.

PRODUCER: Anthony Nelson-Keys. DIRECTOR: Roy Ward Baker. SCREENPLAY: NIGEL KNEALE. MUSIC: Tristram Cary. SPECIAL EFFECTS: Les Bowie Films.

FLAME BARRIER, THE
UA (1958). B/w, 70 mins.

A "missing" satellite crash-lands in the jungle, an alien protoplasm firmly affixed to its surface. Scientists Dave and Carol (Arthur Franz and Kathleen Crowley) search for the missing space sphere and find it. Unfortunately, their success gets them into hot water. Every time they approach the craft, the alien blob emits deadly bursts of flesh-melting heat. Before they can say "if you can't stand the heat, get out of the kitchen," they face a single-celled alien attack force bent on changing the surrounding jungle to ash.

PRODUCERS: Arthur Gardner, Jules Levy. DIRECTOR: Paul Landers. SCREENPLAY: Pat Fielder and George Worthing Yates, from a story by Yates. ART DIRECTOR: James Vance.

SUPPORTING PLAYERS: Robert Brown, Kaz Oran, Vincent Padula.

FLAMING DISK, THE
Universal (1920). B/w silent serial, 18 chapters (36 reels).

The forces of Good and Evil battle over the possession of a recently invented lens that can reduce iron to dust.

DIRECTOR: Robert F. Hill. STORY: Arthur Henry Gooden, Jerry Ash.

CAST: Elmo Lincoln, Monty Montague, Louise Lorraine.

FLASH GORDON
Also known as SPACE SOLDIERS; ATOMIC ROCKETSHIP; SPACESHIP TO THE UNKNOWN.
Universal (1936). B/w serial, 13 chapters (26 reels), 416 mins. total running time.

The first and the finest of the slap-happy series of serials based on the popular comic-book hero concocted by Alex Raymond. The planet Mongo, ruled by nasty Ming the Merciless (Charles Middleton), is on a collision course with Earth. Out to halt the planet are stalwart Flash Gordon (Buster Crabbe), heroic Dale Arden (Jean Rogers), and smart-as-a-whip Dr. Hans Zarkov (Frank Shannon).

In Zarkov's rocket, they land on Mongo only to be captured by Ming's minions. Ming eyes Dale. Ming's daughter, Princess Aura (Priscilla Lawson), eyes Flash. Flash nearly has his eyes prematurely shut by a trio of fanged monkey-men when he is tossed into their pit by Ming after a short in-

Universal

Flash Gordon

troductory speech. After defeating the monkey-men, Flash and Aura find themselves knocking a dragon senseless. The rest of the Earth party is detained by Ming.

Stranded, Flash attempts to rescue his friends, aided by lion-man Thun (James Pierce) and Prince Barin (Richard Alexander). The trio rescues Dale and Zarkov. From there, they make a side trip to the floating city of Vultan, run by King Vultan (John Lipson). Floating above Mongo, they must dispatch shark-men, a death ray, a fire monster, a Tigron, and, finally, Ming himself. The chase leads to Ming's palace, where, overwhelmed by his enemies, the dapper villain runs into the chamber of the Great God Tao, where he is apparently devoured by a large lobster-dragon, the Gocko, a beast who has been starving since chapter 2.

DIRECTOR: Frederick Stephani. SCREENPLAY: Stephani, George H. Plympton, Basil Dickey, and Lee O'Neill, based on the comic strip by Alex Raymond.

FLASH GORDON
Universal/De Laurentiis Productions (1980). Color.

An international cast tops this newest reincarnation of the popular comic-strip star. Flash (Sam J. Jones), Dale Arden (Melody Anderson), and Dr. Zarkov (Topol) journey to Mongo to battle the armies of Ming the Merciless (Max von Sydow).

PRODUCER: Dino De Laurentiis. DIRECTOR: Mike Hodges. SCREENPLAY: Lorenzo Semple, Jr., from the comic strip created by Alex Raymond.

SUPPORTING PLAYERS: Ornella Muti

as Princess Aura, Timothy Dalton as Barin, Brian Blessed as Vultan, Peter Wingarde as Klytus.

FLASH GORDON CONQUERS THE UNIVERSE

Also known as PERIL FROM THE PLANET MONGO; SPACE SOLDIERS CONQUER THE UNIVERSE; THE PURPLE DEATH FROM OUTER SPACE.
Universal (1940). B/w serial, 12 chapters (24 reels), 384 mins. total running time.

Ming (Charles Middleton) tries to become emperor of the universe in this, the third and final Flash Gordon cliffhanger. Sprinkling Death Dust into the Earth's atmosphere, Ming spreads the Purple Death, an incurable plague, around the globe. Flash (Buster Crabbe), Zarkov (Frank Shannon), and Dale (Carol Hughes) smell a rat and follow the scent to the planet Mongo. There they enlist the aid of resident Hawkman Prince Barin (Roland Drew) and his wife, Princess Aura (Shirley Dean). They burst into Ming's palace and destroy the machine that is sending out those bad vibes. Flash then journeys to the planet Frigia to bring back a ton of Polante, the only antidote to the disease. While he is gone, Zarkov and Dale are captured by Ming's thugs Torch (Don Rowan) and Thong (Victor Zimmerman), the latter pair being encouraged by Ming's biggest cheerleader, Sonja (Anne Gwynne).

Flash returns with the cure, rescues his friends, and sends Ming and his mob soaring into oblivion with a well-aimed explosive.

DIRECTOR: Ford Beebe, Ray Taylor. SCREENPLAY: George H. Plympton, Basil Dickey, and Barry Shipman, based on the Alex Raymond comic strip.

FLASH GORDON'S TRIP TO MARS

Also known as SPACE SOLDIERS' TRIP TO MARS.
Universal (1939). B/w serial, 15 chapters (30 reels), 480 mins. total running time.

This time out, Ming (Charles Middleton) attempts to take over Mars by backing evil Queen Azura (Beatrice Roberts), a woman whose power stems from the aura emanating from a white sapphire. Through alchemy, she changes the rebellious Martian humanoids into a race of clay men. Investigating a ray that is stealing nitrogen from the Earth's atmosphere, Flash (Buster Crabbe), Zarkov (Frank Shannon), and Dale (Jean Rogers) blast off for Mars. They are captured by the clay men upon their arrival. The clay men are at war with the tree men and the battle seems to mean doom to Flash and his crew until Hawkman Prince Barin (Richard Alexander) arrives and soothes everyone's ruffled feathers. Uniting the warring tribes, Barin and Flash lead an assault on Ming's forces. The queen's sapphire is snatched from around her neck, and, powerless, she releases her hold on the clay men, turning them back into humans. The leader of the clay people (C. Montague Shaw) joins the attack and Ming is forced into a disintegration chamber.

DIRECTORS: Ford Beebe, Robert F. Hill. SCREENPLAY: Ray Trampe, Norman S. Hall, Wyndham Gittens, and Herbert Dolmas, based on the Alex Raymond comic strip.

FLESH EATERS, THE

Cinema (1964). B/w, 88 mins.

A crazy scientist (Martin Kosleck) develops a microbe that devours flesh. Feeling his oats one morning, he tosses the stuff into the ocean surrounding his island, as an experiment. As a result, no one can leave or land on his home turf. Four crazy castaways manage to land, however, much to the doc's dismay. For the rest of the film, everyone is clinging to every piece of flesh he or she can salvage.

PRODUCERS: Jack Curtis, Terry Curtis, Arnold Drake. DIRECTOR: Jack Curtis. SCREENPLAY: Arnold Drake. CINEMATOGRAPHY: Carson Davidson. SPECIAL EFFECTS: Roy Benson. MUSIC: Julian Stein.

SUPPORTING PLAYERS: Rita Morley, Barbara Wikin, Ray Tudor, Byron Sanders.

FLESH GORDON

Mammoth Films (1974). Metrocolor, 78 mins.

A porn-spoof tracing the exploits of Flesh (Jason Williams), Dale Ardor

(Suzanne Fields), and Dr. Flexi Jerk-off (Joseph Hudgins) in their battle against Emperor Wang (William Hunt) on the planet Porno. The Impotentate of Porno wants to destroy Earth with a nasty ray and become Impotentate of the whole universe. Before disposing of Wang, the trio is menaced by the ymirlike Great God Porno, the raping robots, a horde of phallic-snakes, and nasty beetle-men.

PRODUCERS: Howard Ziehm, Bill Osco. DIRECTORS: Michael Benveniste, William Hunt. MUSIC: Ralph Ferraro. MAKEUP: Ralph Ferraro. SPECIAL EFFECTS: Jim Danforth (uncredited), David Allen. SPECIAL EFFECTS: Rick Baker, Russ Turner, Doug Beswick, Craig Neuswanger. MINIATURES: Greg Jein.

SUPPORTING PLAYERS: Lance Larsen, John Hoyt, Candy Samples, Mycle Brandy.

FLIGHT TO MARS
Monogram (1951). Cinecolor, 72 mins.

Not exactly science-fact fodder. A group of astronauts and newspapermen (Cameron Mitchell and Arthur Franz in the forefront) crash-land on Mars after an impromptu game of "last tag" with a meteor school in space. They discover an underground Martian civilization of humans ruled by pretty Princess Alita (Marguerite Chapman) and her father, the leader of the Council (Morris Ankrum). The Earth people and the Mars people strike up a friendship and both groups join in to repair the fractured flying machine. The Earth people make the return trip safely.

PRODUCER: Walter Mirisch. DIRECTOR: Lesley Selander. SCREENPLAY: Arthur Strawn. MUSIC: Marlkin Skiles.

SUPPORTING PLAYERS: Virginia Huston, John Litel, Edward Earle.

FLY, THE
20th Cent.-Fox (1958). Color/scope, 94 mins.

An eerie tale of science gone astray. André Delambre (Al—later to be David—Hedison) is a scientist experimenting with matter transference—the breaking down and reassembling of solid objects through the disassembling of their molecular structures. While

Monogram

Flight to Mars

testing his machine on himself, André does not notice a tiny fly entering the chamber with him. When he materializes, he discovers that both his and the fly's molecules have been scrambled. He appears with the head and arm of a gigantic fly. The fly buzzes away with a human head and arm. Wearing a large mask over his face, André implores his wife to help him find the fly. Wife Helen (Patricia Owens) and son Phillippe (Charles Herbert) find it, but lose it again. Slowly losing his personality to the fly head, André implores his wife to kill him by placing his insect dome into an electric vise. She does so, telling the tale to shocked brother-in-law François (Vincent Price) and police inspector Charas (Herbert Marshall).

The inspector is convinced that the woman is lying. He has never heard such an outrageous tale. Sitting in the Delambre backyard, deliberating the woman's fate, the inspector and François see a tiny fly being consumed by a spider. The fly screams, "Help me!" and the two men see the tiny human head of André being consumed by the other insect. Charas picks up a rock and smashes both bugs, putting an end to the grotesque scene.

Two sequels were produced: RETURN OF THE FLY and CURSE OF THE FLY.

PRODUCER AND DIRECTOR: Kurt Neumann. SCREENPLAY: James Clavell, based on the story by George Langelaan. MAKEUP: Ben Nye. CINEMATOGRAPHY: Karl Struss. SPECIAL EFFECTS: Lyle B. Abbott. MUSIC: Paul Sawtell.

SUPPORTING PLAYERS: Kathleen Freeman, Betty Lou Gerson.

FLYING DISC MEN FROM MARS
Known in feature form as THE MISSILE MONSTERS (1958).
Republic (1950). B/w serial, 12 chapters (24 reels), 384 mins. total running time.

Martian meanie Mota (Wallace Reed) lands on Earth in his flying saucer with a plan to take over the world. Working on his thermal disintegrator ray in an underground lair, he is determined to see New York crumble. Earth people Kent (Walter Reed) and Helen (Lois Collier) discover the plot, thanks to the work of dotty Dr. Bryant (James Craven). Mota and his flying bat-wing ship are sent back into space in several thousand pieces when the mountain he is hiding in erupts as a major volcano, cutting short his plan for conquest.

PRODUCER: Franklin Andreon. DIRECTOR: Fred C. Bannon. SCREENPLAY: Ronald Davidson. SPECIAL EFFECTS: Howard and Theodore Lydecker.

SUPPORTING PLAYERS: Dale Van Sickel, Tom Steele.

FLYING SAUCER, THE
Film Classics (1950). B/w, 69 mins.

U.S. agents sent to Alaska to investigate reports of a UFO find an alien spacecraft and a host of Russians.

PRODUCER, DIRECTOR, AND STORY ORIGINATOR: Mikel Conrad. SCREENPLAY: Mikel Conrad, Howard Irving Young. CINEMATOGRAPHY: Philip Tannura. MUSIC: Darrel Calker.

CAST: Mikel Conrad, Pat Garrison, Denver Pyle.

FOOD OF THE GODS
AIP (1976). Movielab color, 88 mins.

Fairly juvenile adaption of the H. G. WELLS novel of the same name (filmed once before, in an even more juvenile format known as VILLAGE OF THE GIANTS). A farmer feeds his chickens a substance he finds growing out of the ground. It turns the fowls into giants. Industrialist Bensington (Ralph Meeker) seeks to profit from the discovery on the island farm. Unfortunately, a bevy of rats have sipped the substance and are running wild on the land. So are worms and other creepy-crawlers. When several scientists and businessmen visit the hot spot, they become marooned on the island and must fight the giants for survival.

PRODUCER, DIRECTOR, AND SCREENWRITER: Bert I. Gordon. MAKEUP: Tom Burman, Phyllis Newman. SPECIAL EFFECTS: Bert I. Gordon. MUSIC: Elliot Kaplan.

SUPPORTING PLAYERS: Marjoe Gortner as Morgan, Pamela Franklin as Lorna Scott, Ida Lupino as Mrs. Skinner, Jon Cypher as Brian, Belinda Balaski as Rita, Tom Stovall as Thomas.

FORBIDDEN PLANET
MGM (1956). Color/scope, 98 mins.

The alien Krell were a superintellectual race located on the planet Altair-IV. At the height of their scientific prowess, they invented a machine that enabled their thoughts to materialize. In essence, through brain-power they could create/move/project matter. Using the machine also increased their general psi abilities. Unfortunately, the invention brought forth *all* the thoughts residing in their minds, including those menacing ones located deep within the recesses of their Id. Within one day, the entire Krell civilization was wiped out by thoughts gone wild.

Centuries later, a team of space explorers led by scientist Morbius (Walter Pidgeon) arrives on Altair-IV. He finds the machine and uses it. Shortly thereafter, his entire party, with the exception of his daughter, Altaira (Anne Francis), is wiped out. He is marooned for 25 years with only Altaira and his faithful robot, Robby, for company. When relief saucer C57D lands on the planet to investigate the disappearance of the first landing party, the crew encounters a hostile Morbius. Commander Adams (Leslie Nielsen), Chief Quinn (Richard Anderson), Lt. Farmann (Jack Kelly), Cookie (Earl Holliman), and Doc Ostrow (Warren Stevens) are puzzled, both by the scientist's attitude and by the disappearance of the original landing crew.

Without warning, the hideous murdering force spawned by the Krell resurfaces, attacking the commander's flying saucer at night, ripping crew members apart. Adams sets up a force field. During the next attack, the creature is illuminated by the energy net. A roaring, ferocious brain-creature ap-

Forbidden Planet

The 4D Man

pears—the product of a jealous genius.

After several sparring matches between Morbius and the crew members, the truth is revealed. Morbius's mind is the murderer of both Adams's men and the original landing party. The scientist is enraged. His anger summons the thing from his Id. It attacks his house. Robby, programmed never to harm a human, will not fire at this extension of his master. Adams and Altaira quiver as the sheet-metal safety doors to Morbius house begin to disintegrate. Morbius, realizing the damage his increased intelligence has brought about, sacrifices himself in order to save his daughter.

PRODUCER: Nicholas Nayfack. DIRECTOR: Fred M. Wilcox. SCREENPLAY: Cyril Hume, from a story by Irving Block and F. Wilcox, loosely based on William Shakespeare's *The Tempest*. ART DIRECTORS: Arthur Lonergan, Cedric Gibbons. ELECTRONIC TONALITIES: Bebe and Louis Barron. SPECIAL EFFECTS: A. Arnold Gillespie, Warren Newcombe, Irving C. Ries, Joshua Meador.

4-D MAN, THE
Released as MASTER OF TERROR (1965).
United Artists (1959). Color, 85 mins.

Robert Lansing starred as a dedicated scientist who stumbles on the key leading to the fourth dimension. During his experiments, the doctor can pass through solid matter. Eventually, he begins to deteriorate physically, aging far more rapidly than usual because of his unorthodox jaunts through

buildings, etc. The slippery scientist meets his maker (as well as mortar) when, while strolling in 4-D through a brick wall, his molecules decide to become mere 3-D. Not only does he become one with the cosmos but he earns his spot as part of the firm foundation holding up the adjacent building.

PRODUCER: Jack H. Harris. DIRECTOR: Irwin S. Yeaworth, Jr. SCREENPLAY: Theodore Simonson and Cy Chermak from a story by Jack H. Harris. CINEMATOGRAPHY: Theodore J. Pahle. SPECIAL EFFECTS: Barton Sloan. MUSIC: Ralph Carmichael.

SUPPORTING PLAYERS: Lee Meriwether, James Congdon, Patty Duke, Jasper Deeter.

FOUR-SIDED TRIANGLE
Hammer (G.B., 1953); Astor (U.S., 1953). B/w, 74 mins.

When two scientists (Stephen Murray and James Hayter) fall in love with the same girl (Barbara Payton), they solve their differences by popping the girl into a duplicating machine. Alas, the original subject loves only one of the scientists. When the duplicate emerges from the machine, she, too, loves the same fellow. Double jeopardy.

PRODUCER: Alexander Paal. DIRECTOR: Terence Fisher. SCREENPLAY: Paul Tabori, Terence Fisher. MUSIC: Malcolm Arnold.

F.P.1
Also known as F.P.1 DOES NOT REPLY.
UFA (Germany, 1932); b/w, 90 mins.
20th Cent.-Fox (U.S., 1933); b/w, 70 mins.

A pilot convinces shipbuilders to construct a floating airport in the middle of the ocean. Saboteurs attack, however, and attempt to cause the floating platform to plunge into the sea below.

Filmed simultaneously in French, German, and English. PRODUCER: Eric Pommer. DIRECTOR: Karl Hartl. SCREENPLAY: CURT SIODMAK and Walter Reisch, based on the novel *F.P.1. Does Not Reply*, by Curt Siodmak. ENGLISH DIALOGUE: Robert Stevenson, Peter MacFarland. CINEMATOGRAPHY: Gunther Rittau, Konstantin Tschet. DESIGN: Erich Kettlehut.

CAST: Leslie Fenton, Conrad Veidt, Jill Esmond (English); Hans Albers, Peter Lorre, Sybille Schmitz, Paul Harmann (German); Charles Boyer, Danielle Paraola, Pierre Brasseur, Jean Murat (French).

FRANKENSTEIN
Edison (1910). B/w silent short, 975 ft.

Dr. Frankenstein creates a monster (Charles Ogle).

DIRECTOR: J. Searle Dawley.

FRANKENSTEIN
Universal (1931). B/w, 71 mins.

James Whale's directorial masterpiece of fright and fascination. Dr. Henry Frankenstein (Colin Clive) is obsessed with the idea of creating life from death. Conspiring with crook-backed assistant Fritz (Dwight Frye), the distinguished doctor robs graves by moonlight in order to secure the human parts necessary to create the first artificial man. With the body under construction—and indeed, nearing completion—Frankenstein needs a brain for the creature. He sends Fritz to nearby Goldstadt Medical College, where, during a lecture, learned Dr. Waldman (Edward van Sloan) displays two disembodied brains suspended in alcohol. One brain, he points out, is a healthy specimen; the other, a criminal mind. Fritz slips in after the lecture and ensnares the normal brain. A loud noise in another room prompts the dwarf to drop the good brain. Panic-stricken, he leaves with the abnormal specimen under his arm.

Frankenstein, not knowing of the mistake, accepts the mentally unhinged mind for his experiment. His actions

Universal

Frankenstein

and his generally secretive nature, however, upset his fiancée, Elizabeth (Mae Clarke). She summons old teacher Dr. Waldman and Henry's best friend, Victor Morris (John Boles), to help her find out what's ailing Frankenstein. Confronted by the trio, Henry scoffs at their concern. Secretly, however, he takes Waldman into his confidence and shows him everything. Waldman is appalled but agrees to keep silent. That night, at the height of an electrical storm, Henry reveals that he has found the secret of life itself: the electrical rays that first brought man into the world. Lightning!

Shortly thereafter, Henry harnesses the lightning during a particularly frightful thunderstorm and, in a brilliant display of cinematic scientific gadgetry, brings the monster (Boris Karloff) to life. The gaunt, cadaveresque creature reacts to the world around it like a mute child. During its short stay in the castle, the monster is horsewhipped by Fritz, who enjoys abusing a being more twisted and pitiful than himself. The monster breaks loose and embarks on a killing spree that includes Waldman and Fritz among its victims.

The villagers eventually discover the identity of the madman and pursue the fleeing creature. Henry, horrified by his handiwork but realizing that the monster is not at all responsible for its actions, tries to find the crazed beast first. He confronts the monster in an old windmill. The creature attacks its creator and throws him from the windmill. The villagers, witnessing the apparent murder, set the windmill afire and the screaming, monosyllabic spectre perishes in the ensuing inferno.

PRODUCER: Carl Laemmle, Jr. DIRECTOR: James Whale. SCREENPLAY: Robert Florey, Garrett Ford, and Francis Edward Faragoh, based on the novel by MARY W. SHELLEY. ADAPTATION: Florey, John L. Balderston. MAKEUP: Jack Pierce. ART DIRECTOR: Charles D. Hall. SPECIAL EFFECTS: John P. Fulton. SPECIAL ELECTRICAL EFFECTS: Kenneth Strickfaden.

SUPPORTING PLAYERS: Lionel Belmore, Fredric Kerr, Marilyn Harris.

FRANKENSTEIN AND THE MONSTER FROM HELL
Paramount (1974). Color, 93 mins.

Frankenstein (Peter Cushing), now the owner and operator of an insane asylum, creates a new monster in the privacy of his home. Assisted by Simon (Shane Briant) and Sarah (Madeline Smith), he creates a human that looks part-ape and part-circus-clown (and, brother, does he need a shave, from his eyebrows to his navel). The monster (David Prowse), ugly of mug but kind of heart, is torn apart by the asylum inmates. Frankenstein heaves a sigh and goes back to the old drawing board for another crack at immortality.

PRODUCER: Roy Skeggs. DIRECTOR: Terence Fisher. SCREENPLAY: John Elder. CINEMATOGRAPHY: Brian Probyn. MAKEUP: Eddie Knight. MUSIC: James Bernard.

FRANKENSTEIN CONQUERS THE WORLD
Toho (Japan, 1964), AIP (U.S., 1966). Color/scope, 87 mins.

During World War II, Germany sends Japanese scientists the heart of the Frankenstein monster for wartime experiments. The heart is caught full force by the Hiroshima bomb blast, however, and becomes a mutated source of power. After a young boy consumes the heart, he grows to enormous proportions. He escapes into the hills, a titanic shadowshape. Because of his gentle nature, however, he is not feared by the locals. When residents start being killed in the woodland areas, however, scientists begin to have

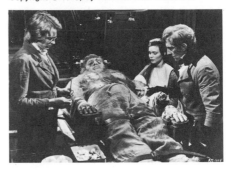

Frankenstein and the Monster from Hell

second thoughts about the big boy. It turns out that the killer is nasty Baragon, a dinosaur/cocker-spaniel monster who just happens to pop up every now and then. The two giants fight it out. Frankenstein Jr.'s honor is at stake.

One on One
    You and your ancient, juvenile minds! You're stupid, stupid, STUPID!
        Eros (Dudley Manlove) to Earthlings in *Plan 9 from Outer Space*

PRODUCER: Tomoyuki Tanaka. DIRECTOR: Inoshiro Honda. SCREENPLAY: Kaoru Mabuchi. CINEMATOGRAPHY: Hajime Koizumi. SPECIAL EFFECTS: Eiji Tsuburaya.

CAST: Nick Adams, Tadao Takashima, Jumi Mizuno.

FRANKENSTEIN CREATED WOMAN
20th Cent.-Fox (1967). Color, 92 mins.

Confusion reigns as Dr. Frankenstein (Peter Cushing) and rotund assistant Dr. Hertz (Thorley Walters) dabble with metaphysics, convinced that artificial life can be sustained through a soul transplant. Rescuing a drowning victim after a successful suicide attempt, Frankenstein first makes the drab girl a raving beauty (Susan Denberg), and then transplants her late lover's soul into her body. Problems develop when the boy friend, a fellow unjustly executed for a crime he did not commit, mentally takes over the girl's body. She systematically searches for and eliminates all those who done her/him wrong. Badly misunderstood by the townspeople, Dr. Frankenstein and his blond bombshell are given a hot time by the old town via torch power.

PRODUCER: Anthony Nelson Keys. DIRECTOR: Terence Fisher, SCREENPLAY: John Elder. MAKEUP: George Partleton. CINEMATOGRAPHY: Arthur Grant. SPECIAL EFFECTS: Les Bowie. MUSIC: James Bernard.

SUPPORTING PLAYERS: Robert Morris, Peter Blythe, Barry Warren.

FRANKENSTEIN MEETS THE SPACE MONSTER

AA (1965). B/w, 75 mins.

For starts, Frankenstein isn't Frankenstein. In fact, the good doctor doesn't exist in this film. The monster is also not the monster but poor Col. Frank Saunders (Robert Reilly), a handsome android pilot who runs into alien invaders Princess Marcuzan (Marilyn Hanold) and dwarf assistant Nadier (who lives up to his name thanks to the acting abilities of Lou Cutell). The twosome land in Puerto Rico in search of humans needed to restock their dying planet. Frank comes along. The Princess pulls her laser gun, aims it at Frank's face, and *zap*—instant Frankenstein's monster. The aliens begin their kidnapping free from interference and Frank is left to wander the countryside short-circuited. He is found and repaired by Drs. Adam Steele (James Karen) and Karen Grant (Nancy Marshall). Dr. Steele tries to fight the aliens

Allied Artists

Frankenstein Meets the Space Monster

single-handed but loses. Frank arrives just as the ship is about to blast off with its captives in tow. The Princess releases her resident-monster-in-the-rocketship-closet, Mull, and . . . well, you know.

PRODUCER: Robert McCarty. DIRECTOR: Robert Gaffney. SCREENPLAY: George Garret, from a story by Garret, John Rodenbeck, and R. H. W. Dillard.

FRANKENSTEIN MEETS THE WOLFMAN

Universal (1943). B/w, 74 mins.

Nuts and bolts and fur fly in this epic tag-team match. The highlight, or lowlight, of the film is to see Bela Lugosi parade around as the Frankenstein monster. (Lugosi had been offered the original monster role by Universal in 1930. Posters were made depicting the Hungarian actor in the role and a press release was issued. Lugosi, fearing the role would typecast him, demurred shortly before preproduction. Boris Karloff, of course, accepted and became a star.)

In this entry, Larry Talbot (Lon Chaney, Jr.), wolfman about town, is accidentally brought to life by two gravediggers who open his coffin under the light of a full moon. Local gypsy Maleva (Maria Ouspenskaya) tells Larry that only Dr. Frankenstein can help his rather unique five-o'clock shadow. Journeying to the doctor's castle, Larry finds nothing but ruins, the monster (Lugosi), and the remains of the deceased doc. Not to worry—local surgeon Patric Knowles tells Larry that *he* can duplicate anything that Frankenstein could do. To prove it, he reawakens the monster, enrages the townspeople, and gets himself, the creature, and Larry trapped in the lab, as saboteurs blow up a nearby dam and send a wall of water down onto the castle tower in an Olympian spring-cleaning effort.

PRODUCER: George Waggner. DIRECTOR: Roy William Neill. SCREENPLAY: CURT SIODMAK. MAKEUP: Jack Pierce. CINEMATOGRAPHY: George Robinson. SPECIAL EFFECTS: John P. Fulton. MUSIC: Hans Salter.

SUPPORTING PLAYERS: Lionel Atwill, Ilona Massey, Dwight Frye, Eddie Parker (Lugosi's double during action scenes).

FRANKENSTEIN MUST BE DESTROYED
WB/7 Arts (1970). Color, 97 mins.

The fifth of the British Hammer Film series finds Dr. Frankenstein (Peter Cushing) a bit madder than usual. Seeking out brain-transplant expert Dr. Brandt (George Pravda), Frankenstein makes a journey to the fellow's home only to find that the surgeon has recently gone mad and been put into a laughing academy under lock and key. Blackmailing a young couple (Simon Ward and Veronica Carlson) into helping him kidnap Brandt, Frankenstein unwittingly causes the surgeon's death. He transplants Brandt's brain into the head of one of the asylum doctors, Richter (Freddie Jones). Inspector Frisch (Thorley Walters) realizes there's odd business about town when Brandt goes to visit his wife resembling a rather haphazardly constructed football. His wife, not recognizing her old husband in the new body, attacks him. Soon everyone is being attacked. Frankenstein attacks his female assistant after she attacks the monster who has just returned from an attack on his old wife. Frankenstein, in turn, is attacked by his male assistant who is understandably annoyed about having his lover throttled by the mad scientist. The house then burns down. And so it goes.

PRODUCER: Anthony Nelson Keys. DIRECTOR: Terence Fisher. SCREENPLAY:

Warner Bros.

Frankenstein Must Be Destroyed

Bert Batt. MAKEUP: Eddie Knight. CINEMATOGRAPHY: Arthur Grant. MUSIC: James Bernard.

FRANKENSTEIN 1970
AA (1958). B/w, 83 mins.

Baron Victor von Frankenstein (Boris Karloff) allows a group of snoopy TV newspeople into his home in honor of the 150th anniversary of his granddad's creation. He needs the TV money in order to make a new version of the old monster. The bandage-encased creature comes to life prematurely, however, and spends the rest of the film causing members of the video crew to depart from life equally as quickly. Both creature and creator make an exit in an atomic steambath. The monster has the face of his pop.

PRODUCER: Aubrey Schenck. DIRECTOR: Howard Koch. SCREENPLAY: George Worthing Yates, Richard Landau. MAKEUP: Gordon Bau. CINEMATOGRAPHY: Carl Guthrie. MUSIC: Paul Dunlap.

SUPPORTING PLAYERS: Jana Lund, Tom Duggan, Mike Lane.

FRANKENSTEIN'S BLOODY TERROR
Spain (1968); color and 3-D, 133 mins. Independent International (U.S., 1971); color, 87 mins.

Baron Wolfstein is bitten by a werewolf and turned into a fur-faced jitterbug dancer. An aging scientist is sent for in order to concoct a cure, but a pair of vampires show up instead. Bloody awful.

PRODUCER AND DIRECTOR: Enrique Equiluz. SCREENPLAY: Jacinto Molina. CINEMATOGRAPHY: Emilio Foriscot.

CAST: Paul Naschy, Julian Ugarte, Jose Nieto.

FRANKENSTEIN'S DAUGHTER
Astor (1958). B/w, 85 mins.

The latest descendant of Frankenstein gets a job as a noted surgeon's assistant in order to clip parts for a new monster. While no one is looking, he puts together a female creature who is as feminine-looking as Dan Blocker. When Dr. Frankenstein makes a pass at the old surgeon's pretty young daughter, the ugly monster gives him a big hand . . . right in the head area. The femme fright (Sally Todd) escapes from the lab and complications of a major nature develop.

PRODUCER: Marc Frederic. DIRECTOR: Dick Cunha. SCREENPLAY: H. E. Barrie. MAKEUP: Harry Thomas. CINEMATOGRAPHY: Meredith Nicholson. SPECIAL EFFECTS: Ira Anderson. MUSIC: Nicholas Carras.

SUPPORTING PLAYERS: John Ashley, Sandra Knight, Harold Lloyd, Jr., Robert Dix.

FROGS
AIP (1972). Color, 90 mins.

Jason Crockett (Ray Milland) is a wealthy old man who doesn't give a damn about ecology. He'll do anything to rid his island retreat of any and all pests, be they insects, snakes or, gulp, frogs. When the family gathers round him for a birthday party, nature strikes back. Jenny Crockett (Lynn Borden) is eaten alive by giant snapping-turtles. Iris Crockett Wooster (Holly Irving) is led into a pit of quicksand by a butterfly she is trying to catch. House guest Michael (David Gilliam) is poisoned by an army of tarantulas and scorpions. A few survivors manage to escape with their lives, but Jason remains to defend himself and his castle against the army of frogs that overruns the island.

PRODUCERS: Peter Thomas, George Edwards. DIRECTOR: George McCowan. SCREENPLAY: Robert Hutchison, Robert Blees. CINEMATOGRAPHY: Mario Tosi. MUSIC: Les Baxter.

SUPPORTING PLAYERS: Sam Elliott, Joan Van Ark, Adam Roarke, Judy Pace, Mae Mercer, and Nicholas Cortland.

FROM DEATH TO LIFE
Rex (1911). B/w silent short.

A scientist invents a solution that petrifies living things.

FROM MARS TO MUNICH
20th Cent.-Fox (1925). B/w silent short, one reel.

An invisible Martian makes it to Earth and decides to explore the terrain. His first pit stop is a local brewery. There the invisible critter embarks on an interplanetary bender.

FROM THE EARTH TO THE MOON
WB (1958). Color, 100 mins.

Joseph Cotten is Barbicane, the leader of the Baltimore Gun Club, in this limp adaptation of JULES VERNE's novel. The fellow figures out a way to get a 19th-century moon-shot in gear. The flight is a success, with the bullet-shaped rocket fired from a cannonlike launcher.

PRODUCER: Benedict Bogeaus. DIRECTOR: Byron Haskin. SCREENPLAY: Robert Blees, James Leicester. SPECIAL EFFECTS: Lee Zavitz. CINEMATOGRAPHY: Edwin B. Dupar.

SUPPORTING PLAYERS: George Sanders, Debra Paget, Patric Knowles, Henry Daniel, Morris Ankrum, and Carl Esmond as Jules Verne.

FROZEN ALIVE
W. German/G.B. (1964); b/w, 80 mins.
Magna (U.S., 1966); b/w, 63 mins.

A scientist tries deep-freezing humans and then thawing them safely. Sometimes it works. Then again . . .

PRODUCERS: Ron Rietti, Arthur Baruner. DIRECTOR: Bernard Knowles. SCREENPLAY: Evelyn Frazer. CINEMATOGRAPHY: Robert Ziller.

CAST: Mark Stevens, Marianne Koch, Walter Rilla.

FROZEN DEAD, THE
WB (1967). B/w, 95 mins.

A crazy scientist keeps frozen some of the choicest examples of Nazidom ever to walk the soil of Germany 30 years ago.

PRODUCER, DIRECTOR, AND SCREENWRITER: Herbert J. Leder. CINEMATOGRAPHY: David Boulton. MUSIC: Don Banks.

CAST: Dana Andrews, Kathleen Breck, Philip Gilbert.

FURY, THE
20th Cent.-Fox (1978). DeLuxe color, 117 mins.

It's telekinesis time. When U.S. agent Peter (Kirk Douglas) has his son, Robin (Andrew Stevens), kidnapped from under his nose by fellow government booster Childress (John Cassavetes), he's more than a little annoyed. Chasing after the boy, he runs across a government program to raise a horde of telekinetic kids as a possible super-weapon. Aiding him in his search is paranormal Gillian (Amy Irving) and friend Hester (Carrie Snodgrass)—until Hester finds herself on the wrong side of a windshield in an attempt on Peter's life.

Finally locating Robin, Peter bursts into a strange mansion-laboratory run by Childress and Susan (Fiona Lewis). By this time, however, Robin is a monster, his telekinetic temper uncontrollable. After killing Susan, he himself is killed. Peter, grief-stricken, allows himself to die in a rescue attempt. Gillian, plucked by Childress as a substitute for Robin in the government operation, gives the nasty agent the evil eye and causes him to explode.

PRODUCER: Frank Yablans. DIRECTOR: Brian De Palma. SCREENPLAY: John Farris, based on his novel. CINEMATOGRAPHY: Richard H. Kline. SPECIAL EFFECTS: A. D. Flowers. SPECIAL MAKEUP: Rick Baker, Bill Tuttle, Dick Smith (uncredited). MUSIC: John Williams.

SUPPORTING PLAYERS: Charles Durning as Dr. McKeever, Carol Rossen as Dr. Lindstrom, Frank Yablans as the Goon on the Radio.

FUTUREWORLD
AIP (1976). Metrocolor, 104 mins.

A thoroughly delightful sequel to WESTWORLD. The robot playland of Delos has been traumatized by the mass slaughter that ended the first film. To combat the lingering adverse publicity, Duffy (Arthur Hill), the Delos representative, offers the IMC Communications Network exclusive rights to the story of the "remaking of Delos." Tracy Ballard (Blythe Danner), the network's top commentator, is assigned the story along with newspaper reporter Chuck Browning (Peter Fonda), the writer who broke the original Delos disaster story. Chuck is less optimistic about the new Delos than naive Tracy. He has heard rumors that there are some mysterious things happening on the premises and his curiosity is piqued when he notices that nearly every powerful leader of the world has gathered for the reopening of this robot playground.

American International Pictures

Futureworld

Although Dr. Schneider (John Ryan) offers the press full access to the park, Chuck does some snooping, and with the help of maintenance technician Harry (Stuart Margolin), discovers that while the rich and powerful guests slumber, exact robot duplicates are being constructed. The masters of Delos are trying to kill the key leaders of the Earth, replace them with robots, and then assume control of the world. Chuck and Tracy attempt to escape and are confronted with their own robot-doubles. A battle ensues. They escape to tell the world the secret of Delos.

PRODUCERS: Paul Lazarus and James T. Aubrey. DIRECTOR: Richard T. Heffron. SCREENPLAY: Mayo Simon, George Schenck. CINEMATOGRAPHY: Howard Schwartz. SPECIAL EFFECTS: Gene Griggs. MAKEUP: Marvin Westmore. MUSIC: Fred Karlin.

GAMERA TAI SHINKAI KAIJU JIGURA (GAMERA VS. ZIGRA)
Daiei (Japan, 1971). Color.

Gamera fights an evil monster—a gigantic fish that shoots deadly rays.

DIRECTOR: Noriaki Yuasa.
CAST: Ken Utsui, Yusuke Kawazu, Kayo Matsuo.

GAMERA VS. MONSTER X
Daiei (Japan, 1970); AIT (U.S., 1970). Color, 83 mins.

Gamera attempts to stop Jiger, a giant monster, from turning Expo '70 into a shambles. He kills Jiger, but the monster turns out to be a mama and lays eggs inside Gamera's body. When the eggs begin to hatch and draw blood from the giant turtle, Gamera learns that parenthood is not all it's cracked up to be.

DIRECTOR: Noriaki Yuasa. SCREEN-PLAY: Fumi Takahashi. CINEMATOG-RAPHY: Akira Kitazaki. MUSIC: Shunsuke Kikuche.

CAST: Tsutomu Takakuwa, Kelly Varis, Katherine Murphy, Junko Yashiro, Ken Omura.

GAMMA PEOPLE, THE
Warwick (G.B., 1955); Columbia (U.S., 1956). B/w, 79 mins.

Progressive education gets an unwanted radioactive booster shot in this suspense film. Two reporters (Paul Douglas and Leslie Phillips) are touring a mythical European country when they encounter a super-educational system that produces child geniuses. The pair of investigative writers are impressed until they find that the prodigies are caused by gamma radiation. The only problem with the scheme? Well, only 50 percent of the children exposed to the rays become intellectuals; the other 50 percent become idiots.

PRODUCER: John Gossage. DIRECTOR: John Gilling. SCREENPLAY: Gilling and Gossage, from a story by Louis Pollock. CINEMATOGRAPHY: Ted Moore. SPE-CIAL-EFFECTS CINEMATOGRAPHY: Tom Howard.

SUPPORTING PLAYERS: Eva Bartok, Walter Rilla, Martin Miller.

GAMMERA THE INVINCIBLE
Daiei (Japan, 1966); World Entertainment Corp. (U.S., 1966). B/w, 88 mins.

A gigantic prehistoric turtle is accidentally thawed from ice. International scientists are amazed at the beast, who is not only big, but has the ability to fly, breathe fire, and extend his neck like a reptilian jack-in-the-box. The turtle also gains an extra m in his name for this, his only theatrically released Stateside venture.

PRODUCER: Yonejiro Saito. DIRECTOR: Noriaki Yuasa. SCREENPLAY: Fumi Takahashi, Richard Craft. CINEMATOG-RAPHY: Nobuo Munekawa.

Closed Encounters
I was media-starved when I was a kid. I wasn't allowed to see many films at all. I began making movies as sort of an expression of rebellion. "Gee, Mom and Dad, if you won't let me go to the movies with my friends on Saturday, I'm just going to have to make movies in the living room Monday through Friday and screw up your life."
Steven Spielberg

CAST: Brian Donlevy, Albert Dekker, Diane Findlay, Eiji Funakoshi, Harumi Kiritachi.

GAP, THE
Instructional Films (G.B., 1937). B/w featurette, 38 mins.

An air raid on London is depicted in this pseudodocumentary released several years before the real-life German assault.

DIRECTOR: Donald Carter.
CAST: Patric Curwen, Carleton Hobbs, G. H. Mulcaster.

GAS-S-S-S!
AIP (1971). Color, 79 mins.

According to producer/director Roger Corman, AIP executives panicked when they caught wind of what this teen-oriented picture was about and edited it, in his absence, into a semicoherent state. A defense plant situated in Alaska and working on chemical warfare springs a leak and releases an untold amount of lethal gas into the air. The world's entire population over the age of 25 is wiped out. From that point onward it's up to the younger generation to cope with global affairs. After a fairly spacey period of time, the teens have added worries when all the long-dead adults decide to rise from their graves.

PRODUCER AND DIRECTOR: Roger Corman. SCREENPLAY: George Armitage. CINEMATOGRAPHY: Ron Dexter. MUSIC: Country Joe and the Fish, Barry Melton (one of the Fish).

CAST: Bud Cort, Talia Coppola (Shire), Ben Vereen, Cindy Williams, George Armitage, Robert Corff, Elaine Giftos.

GHIDRA, THE THREE-HEADED MONSTER

Also known as THE GREATEST BATTLE ON EARTH.
Toho (Japan, 1965); Continental (U.S., 1965). Eastmancolor and Tohoscope, 85 mins.

Two plots, one Earthbound, the other space-sent, dovetail in this colorful adventure. Gangsters plot to kidnap a Japanese princess. Overshadowing their plans a bit is the arrival of a horrible three-headed dragon, Ghidrah, a monster bred on a meteor that passes by Earth. The monster makes a quick stop on Earth, giving key cities in Japan the hotfoot. Desperate Japanese officials rally Earth-monsters Godzilla, Rodan, and Mothra to defend their world against the marauder.

PRODUCER: Tomoyuki Tanaka. DIRECTOR: Inoshiro Honda. SPECIAL EFFECTS: Eiji Tsuburaya. MUSIC: Akira Ifukube.

CAST: Yosuka Natsuki as Shindo, Yukiro Hoshi as Naoika, Hiroshi Koizumi as Professor Murai, Takashi Shimura as Dr. Taukamoto.

GHOST OF FRANKENSTEIN, THE
Universal (1942). B/w, 68 mins.

With this installment, Universal's Frankenstein series began to spiral downward. Apparently hasty editing makes a few of the story points confusing. This, coupled with the lackluster script, makes for tough sledding. The latest Frankenstein (Sir Cedric Hardwicke), resurrects the famous monster (Lon Chaney, Jr.) from its entombment in the castle's sulfur pit with the help of hunchback Ygor (Bela Lugosi in a reprise of his role in SON OF FRANKENSTEIN). Frankenstein wants to put an educated brain in the body of the monster, making him a normal, albeit homely, human being. Ygor, tired of his crooked body, has other ideas, however. He secretly donates his own brain to the doctor. The brain, in turn, is sewn into the skull of the creature. The monster awakens and, much to the chagrin of the doctor, begins cackling in Ygor's fairly distinctive voice. Unfortunately for all concerned, Ygor's brain and the monster's body do not quite mesh. The creature is blind! "Vot goot are eyes eef not to zee?" the monster reasons as he knocks over the lab chemicals, and sets himself, the doctor, and the castle on fire.

DIRECTOR: Erle C. Kenton. SCREENPLAY: W. Scott Darling, from a story by Eric Taylor. MAKEUP: Jack Pierce. CINEMATOGRAPHY: Milton Krasner, Woody Bredell. MUSIC: H. J. Salter.

SUPPORTING PLAYERS: Ralph Bellamy, Lionel Atwill, Evelyn Ankers, Dwight Frye, Holmes Herbert, Doris Lloyd.

GHOST PATROL
Puritan (1936). B/w, 58 mins.

Criminals get a boost from science in this grade B potboiler. Mobsters are able to capture airplanes through the use of a radium tube that controls electrical impulses.

PRODUCERS: Sig Neufeld, Leslie Simmonds. DIRECTOR: Sam Newfield. SCREENPLAY: Wyndham Gitten, from a story by Joe O'Donnell. CINEMATOGRAPHY: John Greenhalgh.

CAST: Tim McCoy, Claudia Dell, Slim Whitaker.

GIANT BEHEMOTH, THE
Also known as BEHEMOTH, THE SEA MONSTER.
Diamond (G.B., 1958); AA (U.S., 1959). B/w, 80 mins.

Closely akin in plot to the radioactive-monster blues offered by THE BEAST FROM 20,000 FATHOMS, *The Giant Behemoth* was a vehicle for some nice stop-motion animation handled by Willis (KING KONG) O'Brien toward the end of his career. A dinosaur is revived and mutated by radiation. The bigger and brawnier beast begins stalking the United Kingdom countryside, burning its victims to death with its radioactive pulsations. Science and the military de-

Allied Artists

The Giant Behemoth

stroy the creature, but in the film's final moments, word is received that burned bodies have been found along the coast line of America. . . .

PRODUCER: Ted Lloyd. DIRECTORS: Eugene Lourie, Douglas Hickock. SCREENPLAY: Eugene Lourie. CINEMATOGRAPHY: Ken Hodges. MAKEUP: Jimmy Evans. SPECIAL EFFECTS: Jack Rabin, Irving Block, Louis DeWitt, Willis O'Brien, Pete Peterson.

CAST: Gene Evans, André Morell, Jack McGowran, Henry Vidon.

GIANT CLAW, THE
Columbia (1957). B/w, 76 mins.

A giant buzzard from outer space decides to visit the Earth, making the life of air traffickers miserable for quite a few weeks. Jet fighters attack the brazen bird, but their efforts prove ineffective: the critter is protected by an invisible shield. Scientists and military officials (Jeff Morrow, Mara Corday, Morris Ankrum) invent a ray that will penetrate the shield. Luring the buzzard off its perch atop the Empire State Building, the scientific team, riding in a small plane, shoots the thing out of the sky. It sinks in the Hudson River in the days before pollution.

PRODUCER: Sam Katzman. DIRECTOR: Fred Sears. SCREENPLAY: Samuel Newman, Paul Gangelin. MUSIC: Mischa Bakaleinikoff.

SUPPORTING PLAYERS: Morgan Jones, Robert Shane.

GIANT OF METROPOLIS
Centro (Italy, 1962); 7 Arts (U.S., 1963). Color/scope, 92 mins.

The futuristic city of Metropolis turns out to be the ancient-futuristic city Atlantis in this sweat-and-strain spectacle. Gordon Mitchell is the Hercules clone sought by Atlantean scientists to spawn a race of supermen. While meddling with our hero's muscles, they also muck about with atomic might. Might proves more menacing than muscle, and a goof on the scientists' part nukes out the ancient city. There's a moral in there somewhere.

PRODUCER: Emmino Salvi. DIRECTOR: Umberto Scarpelli. SCREENPLAY: Sabatino Ciuffino and Oreste Palellea. ART DIRECTOR: G. Giovanisti. MUSIC: Armando Trovajoli.

SUPPORTING PLAYERS: Bella Cortez, Roldano Lupi.

GIGANTIS, THE FIRE MONSTER
Toho (Japan, 1955); b/w, 82 mins. WB (U.S., 1959); b/w, 78 mins.

Wishing to get in on the GODZILLA craze but not owning the name Godzilla, Warner Brothers picked up the sequel film, *Return of Godzilla*, and redubbed the radioactive-mutant lizard Gigantis. And so it goes. In this Tokyo stomp-fest, Gigantis/Godzilla goes two out of three falls with rival creature Angorus.

PRODUCER: Tomoyuki Tanaka. DIRECTOR: Motoyoshi Odo. SCREENPLAY: Takeo Murata and Sigeaki Hidaka, from a story by Shigeru Kayama. CINEMATOGRAPHY: Seiichi Endo. SPECIAL EFFECTS: Eiji Tsuburaya. MUSIC: Masaru Sato.

CAST: Hiroshi Koizumi, Yukio Kasama, Minosuki Yamada.

GIRL FROM SCOTLAND YARD, THE
Paramount (1937). B/w, 62 mins.

A pretty young sleuth (Karen Morley) tracks down a murderer who uses radio waves as a lethal instrument.

PRODUCER: Emanuel Cohen. DIRECTOR: Robert Vignola. SCREENPLAY: Doris Anderson and Dore Schary, from a story by Coningsby Dawson based on characters created by Edgar Wallace. CINEMATOGRAPHY: Robert Pittack.

SUPPORTING CAST: Eduardo Ciannelli, Robert Baldwin, Katherine Alexander.

GIVE A DOG A BONE
Westminster/Moral   Re-Armament (G.B., 1966). Color, 77 mins.

A friendly spaceman lands on Earth and helps a boy and his dog defeat the dreaded King of the Rats.

PRODUCER AND DIRECTOR: Henry Cass. CINEMATOGRAPHY: S. D. Onions. MUSIC: George Fraser.

CAST: Ronnie Stevens, Richard Warner, Ivor Danvers.

GIVE US THE MOON
Gainsborough (G.B., 1944). B/w, 95 mins.

Forced whimsy regarding what Britain would be like following World War II was dominant in this adaptation of Caryl Brahms's and S. J. Simon's novel *The Elephant Is White*.

DIRECTOR AND SCREENWRITER: Val Guest. CINEMATOGRAPHY: Phil Grindrod.

CAST: Jean Simmons, Peter Graves, Margaret Lockwood, Vic Oliver.

GLASS BOTTOM BOAT, THE
MGM (1966). Color/scope, 110 mins.

A belabored comedy that finds Doris Day enmeshed in an international espionage ring. Is she a villain or ain't she? While hero Rod Taylor and dad Arthur Godfrey ponder her enigmatic actions, perky Doris stumbles across quite a few science-fictionesque gadgets, including a robot vacuum cleaner and a zero-gravity room.

PRODUCERS: Martin Melcher, Everett Freeman. DIRECTOR: Frank Tashlin. SCREENPLAY: Everett Freeman. CINEMATOGRAPHY: Leon Shamroy. SPECIAL EFFECTS: J. McMillan Johnson, Edward Carfagno. MUSIC: Frank DeVol.

SUPPORTING PLAYERS: Paul Lynde, Eric Fleming, Dom De Luise, John McGiver, George Tobias, Robert Vaughn, Alice Pearce.

G-MEN NEVER FORGET
Republic (1947). B/w serial, 12 chapters (24 reels).

Puzzled Clayton Moore encounters a criminal gang that, through perfect plastic surgery, can change the faces of its membership into the replica of anybody else's, living or dead, famous or obscure.

PRODUCER: Mike Frankovich. DIRECTORS: Fred Bannon, Yakima Canutt. SCREENPLAY: Franklin Adreon, Basil Dickey, Jesse Duffy, Sol Shor. CINEMATOGRAPHY: John McBurnie. MUSICAL DIRECTOR: Mort Glickman.

SUPPORTING PLAYERS: Roy Barcroft, Ramsay Ames, Dale Van Sickel.

G-MEN VS. THE BLACK DRAGON
Republic (1943). B/w serial, 15 chapters (31 reels).

At the height of World War II, three secret agents, Vivian Marsh (Constance Worth) of England, Rex Bennett (Rod Cameron) of the U.S., and Chang (Roland Got) of the Chinese Secret Service, pool their talents in an attempt to track down the insidious Haruchi (Nino Pepitone), the leader of the Japanese Black Dragon society, currently in hiding in America.

Haruchi begins sinking ships left and right, and doing a little bit of Asiatic detective work, Chang comes up with a submarine/ship-locator used by the Black Dragons. According to befuddled Professor Nicholson (C. Montague Shaw) the machine is very advanced. Haruchi, pretty miffed over the theft, enters the battle of the inventions full force, fighting the trio over the plans and/or possession of exploding paint, a suspended animation drug (which allows a disguised Haruchi to feign death), television cameras, and the locator blueprints. In the final reel, Haruchi is blown to bits.

DIRECTOR: William Witney. SCREENPLAY: Ronald Davidson, Joseph Poland, William Lively, Joseph O'Dennel. CINEMATOGRAPHY: Bud Thackery. SPECIAL EFFECTS: Howard Lydecker. MUSIC: Mort Glickman.

SUPPORTING PLAYERS: Noel Cravat as Ranga, George J. Lewis as Lugo, Maxine Doyle as Marie, Allen Jung as Fugi.

GO AND GET IT
Marshall Neilan Productions (1920). B/w silent feature, 6,300 ft.

A convict's brain is transplanted into a gorilla's body. The same old monkeyshines.

PRODUCER: Marshall Neilan. DIRECTORS: Neilan, Henry Symonds. SCREEN-

PLAY: Marion Fairfax. CINEMATOG-RAPHY:David Kesson.

CAST: Pat O'Malley, Noah Beery, Wesley Barry, Agnes Ayres, and Bull Montana as the gorilla.

GODZILLA, KING OF THE MONSTERS
Toho (Japan, 1954); b/w, 98 mins.
Embassy (U.S., 1956); b/w, 81 mins.

Although a much-maligned film, *Godzilla* (or *Gojira,* as it was known in Japan) is really a one-of-a-kind movie. Released in the years following the devastating nuclear attacks on Japan by the United States, it deftly blends traditional horror elements with some heavy-handed commentary on nuclear radiation and its effects—Godzilla being a mutant created by radioactivity.

In addition, the Americanized version is a skillfully rewritten, redubbed, and reedited film that actually weaves a new plot and new characters into the original movie. In scenes in which American actors are called upon to appear with their Japanese costars, split-second cuts and the brilliant use of "doubles" mesh the two sets of characters, filmed over two years apart.

American reporter Steve Martin (Raymond Burr) sits in a smoldering city of Tokyo with fellow survivor Imiko Yamuni (Momoko Kochi), the daughter of a prominent scientist, and recalls, in a series of flashbacks, how this disaster befell Japan. A radioactive sea-beast, Godzilla, brought to life by radioactive testing, surfaced near Odo Island, eventually destroying the tiny land-mass completely. Equipped with radioactive breath, the beast soon turned his attention on the mainland. All the country's military might proved no match for the creature. Steve is sure that the scenario will end in disaster. At the last moment, however, crusty scientist Dr. Serizawa (Akira Takarada) agrees to use his oxygen destroyer on the beast. Diving into the ocean, he lets loose the substance, thus depriving the surrounding area of all oxygen. Both the slumbering Godzilla and the lively doctor are disintegrated.

PRODUCER: Tomoyuki Tanaka. DI-RECTORS: Inoshiro Honda, Terry Morse (English-language scenes). SCREEN-

PLAY: Takeo Murata and Honda, from a story by Shigeru Kayama. CINEMA-TOGRAPHY: Masao Tamai. SPECIAL EF-FECTS: Eiji Tsuburaya, Akira Watanabe, Hiroshi Mukouyama, Kuichiro Kishida. MUSIC: Akira Ifukube.

SUPPORTING PLAYERS: Akihiko Hirata, Takashi Shimura.

GODZILLA ON MONSTER ISLAND
Cinema Shares (1978). Fujicolor and Tohoscope, 89 mins.

A group of alien roaches disguise themselves as nattily dressed Earthlings and launch an invasion. Hoping to take over the planet within a matter of days, they materialize Ghidrah the three-headed monster and Gigan. Godzilla and fellow monster Anguilas (now both speaking conventional English, by the way: "Please pass the nuclear warheads, will you, sport?") defend Japan from the creepy critters and a *High Noon*esque showdown occurs in a Japanese amusement park.

PRODUCER: Tomoyuki Tanaka. DI-RECTOR: Jun Fukuda. SCREENPLAY: Shinichi Sekizawa. CINEMATOGRAPHY: Kiyoshi Hasegawa. SPECIAL EFFECTS: Akiyoshi Nakano. MUSIC: Akira Ifukube.

Cinema Shares

Godzilla on Monster Island

CAST: Haruo Nakajima as Godzilla, Kengu Nakayama as Gigan, Kanta Ina as Ghidrah, Koetsu Omiya as Anguilas.

GODZILLA'S REVENGE
Toho (Japan, 1969); UPA (U.S., 1971). Color/scope, 70 mins.

And lo, how the mighty have fallen. Strictly child's play as a boy dreams that he visits Godzilla on Monster Island. While there, he meets and converses with Godzilla Jr. Together they fight many monsters.

PRODUCER: Tomoyuki Tanaka. DIRECTOR: Inoshiro Honda. SCREENPLAY: Shinichi Sekizawa. CINEMATOGRAPHY: Mototaka Tomioka. SPECIAL EFFECTS: Eiji Tsuburaya. MUSIC: Kunio Miyauchi.

CAST: Kenji Sahara, Machiko Naka, Tomonori Yazaki.

GODZILLA TAI GIAGAN (GODZILLA VS. GIAGAN)
Toho (1971). Eastmancolor and Tohoscope.

As of this writing, one of the "lost" Godzilla films, never released Stateside, this movie recounts the efforts of a tribe of cockroach aliens who attempt to take over the world. The bug people bug Earth in a big way, unleashing the space dragon Ghidrah in tandem with maxi-bug-monster Giagan on the world. Godzilla teams up with dinosaur Angorus and tries to keep our streets free from 50-foot feet.

DIRECTOR: Jun Fukuda.

CAST: Tomoko Umeda, Hiroshi Ishikawa.

GODZILLA VS. MEGALON
Toho (Japan, 1973); Cinema Shares (U.S., 1976). Fujicolor and Tohoscope, 81 mins.

The Seatopians are nasty creatures. The Seatopians want to take over the Earth without asking anyone's permission. With that end in mind, they summon monster Gigan (a creature who has had his name changed since arriving in *Godzilla Tai Giagan* several years previous) and alien monster Megalon. Furthering their attempts at world domination, the Seatopians kidnap colossal cyborg Jet Jaguar and turn him against his creator

and his creator's planet, Earth. Godzilla puts up a good fight on behalf of humanity, but it isn't until a preteenage Jet Jaguar devotee frees the cyborg from the Seatopians' power that the leaping lizard and the angry android really mix it up with the evil armies.

EXECUTIVE PRODUCER: Tomoyuki Tanaka. DIRECTOR: Jun Fukuda. SCREENPLAY: Shinichi Sekizawa, Fukuda.

CAST: Iriyuki Kawase, Yutaka Hayashi, Katsuhiko Sesaki.

GODZILLA VS. THE SEA MONSTER
Toho (Japan, 1966); Continental (U.S., 1969). Color/scope, 87 mins.

A gigantic shrimp, obviously sensitive about his contradictory nature, heads for Japan. The shrimp, Ebirah, is confronted by Godzilla and Mothra while scientists and military men look confused.

PRODUCER: Tomoyuki Tanaka. DIRECTOR: Jun Fukuda. SCREENPLAY: Shinichi Sekizawa. CINEMATOGRAPHY: Kazuo Yamada. SPECIAL EFFECTS: Eiji Tsuburaya. MUSIC: Masaru Sato.

CAST: Akira Takarada, Jun Tazaki, Kumi Mizuno, Toru Watanabe.

GODZILLA VS. THE SMOG MONSTER
Toho (Japan, 1971); AIP (U.S., 1972). Color, 87 mins.

The ecology message dons a rubber suit in this heavy-handed (-footed, -tailed) monster mash. Hedorah is made of sludge. Hedorah likes to eat sludge. Japan has lots of sludge. Hedorah likes Japan. Japan is not all that pleased. Enter nationalistic lizard-king Godzilla. After several preliminary bouts, the two monsters tangle in earnest. In the end, only Godzilla remains on his feet. So much for pollution. Where was he when we needed him at Three Mile Island?

DIRECTOR: Yoshimitsu Banno. SCREENPLAY: Banno, Kaoru Mabuchi. CINEMATOGRAPHY: Hoichi Manoda. SPECIAL EFFECTS: Shokei Nakano. MUSIC: Riichiro Manabe.

CAST: Akira Yamauchi, Toshi Kimura, Keiko Mari.

Godzilla Vs. the Smog Monster

GODZILLA VS. THE THING
Toho (Japan, 1964); color, 94 mins. AIP (U.S., 1964). Color/scope, 90 mins.

A news reporter (Akira Takarada) and a photographer (Yukiro Hoshi) witness the battle of the century (or at least the battle of the week, judging by how many times Tokyo finds itself underfoot of some large creature or other) when Godzilla takes on Mothra. The lizard kills the giant moth, but, egged on by the chanting of Mothra's two tiny princess-cheerleaders, Mothra's two eggs hatch. The larvae dispose of Godzilla and take off with the two girls (Emi Ito and Yumi Ito).

PRODUCER: Tomoyuki Tanaka. DIRECTOR: Inoshiro Honda. SCREENPLAY: Shinichi Sekizawa. CINEMATOGRAPHY: Hajimi Koizumi. SPECIAL EFFECTS: Eiji Tsuburaya, Sadamasa Arikawa, Mototaka Tomioka, Akira Watanabe. MUSIC: Akira Ifukube.

SUPPORTING PLAYERS: Hiroshi Koisumi, Yu Fujiki.

GOG
UA (1954). Color and 3-D, 85 mins.

The war between Good and Evil becomes the war between man and machine when a supercomputer seizes control of robots Gog and Magog and uses them as tools for murder. The computer, taking its orders from foreign spies, sets out to wreck a scientific installation. The final destruction scenes were quite impressive in 3-D.

PRODUCER: Ivan Tors. DIRECTOR: Herbert L. Strock. SCREENPLAY: Tom Taggert, from a story by Tors. CINEMATOGRAPHY: Lathrop B. Worth. SPECIAL EFFECTS: Harry Redmond, Jr.

Have a Good Day Dept.
    We belong dead.
        Boris Karloff to a captive audience in *Bride of Frankenstein*

CAST: Richard Egan, Constance Dowling, William Schallert, Herbert Marshall.

GOLD
UFA (Germany, 1934). B/w, 80 mins.

A crazed English nobleman murders a German scientist in an attempt to steal a new invention that can turn lead into gold. A spectacular exercise in visionary design, the film featured a host of scientific laboratory gadgetry, including a machine capable of splitting the atom. The film ends with no one getting the machine, as the Atlantic Ocean buries the lab containing it under a wall of roaring sea. The climax of the film proved so effective that it was spliced, nearly in its entirety, into the science-goes-astray last scene of the 1953 movie THE MAGNETIC MONSTER. Because of the purloined footage, *Gold* is rarely seen intact today.

DIRECTOR: Karl Hartl. CINEMATOGRAPHY: Guenther Rittau, Otto Baecker, Werner Bohne. DESIGN: Otta Hunte. SCREENPLAY: Rolf Vanloo. MUSIC: Hans-Otto Borgmann.

CAST: Hans Albers, Brigitte Helm, Lien Deyers, Friederich Kayssler.

GOLDENGIRL
Avco Embassy (1979). Eastmancolor, 104 mins.

A female track star (Susan Anton) is turned into a human robot in an attempt to make her a triple medal-winner in the 1980 Moscow Olympics. At her father's insistence (Curt Jurgens as dad Serafin), she has been brainwashed by a psychiatrist, a trainer, and assorted hangers-on into believing that the only way she'll find true love is to be the darling of the Olympiad. Dryden (James Coburn) is hired as her agent and when he sees the tormented existence endured by the blond bombshell he sets her straight through long talks and interludes in the sack. Adding to the resulting confusion are the efforts of nasty investigative reporter Esselton (Robert Culp), who doesn't think Goldengirl acts like a normal human being. Hint: superdrugs.

PRODUCER: Danny O'Donovan. DIRECTOR: Joseph Sargent. SCREENPLAY: John Kohn, from a novel by Peter Lear. CINEMATOGRAPHY: Steven Larner. MUSIC: Bill Conti.

SUPPORTING PLAYERS: Leslie Caron as Dr. Lee, Harry Guardino as Valenti, Ward Costello as Cobb, Nicholas Coster as Dr. Dalton.

GOLDEN RABBIT, THE
Rank (G.B., 1962). B/w, 64 mins.

A hapless inventor (Timothy Bateson) comes up with a formula for changing lead into gold. Unfortunately, before he has a chance to become a millionaire, the formula turns out to be temporary and he is soon surrounded by lead.

PRODUCER: Barry Delmaine. DIRECTOR: David MacDonald. SCREENPLAY: Dick Sharples, Gerald Kelsey. CINEMATOGRAPHY: S. D. Onions. MUSIC: Bill McGuffie.

SUPPORTING PLAYERS: Maureen Beck, John Sharp, Kenneth Fortescue.

GOLDFINGER
UA (1964). Color, 109 mins.

British Secret Service operative James Bond (Sean Connery) and close associate Pussy Galore (Honor Blackman) have the dubious distinction of rubbing elbows with an international gangster nicknamed Goldfinger (Gert Frobe). In an attempt by the gold-hungry maniac to increase the value of his own private stock of the precious metal, he seeks to set off an A-bomb in Fort Knox, thus making the United States gold reserves worthless. When not being battered by the killer himself, Bond is tortured by evil Odd Job (Harold Sakata), whose bowler hat can cause premature decapitation when tossed correctly, and several mad scientist/servants who resort to laserbeam torture when hard-pressed.

PRODUCERS: Albert R. Broccoli, Harry Saltzman. DIRECTOR: Guy Hamilton. SCREENPLAY: Richard Maibaum and Paul Dehn, from the novel by Ian Fleming. CINEMATOGRAPHY: Ted Moore. PRODUCTION DESIGN: Ken Adam. SPECIAL EFFECTS: John Stears, Frank George. MUSIC: John Barry.

SUPPORTING PLAYERS: Shirley Eaton, Bernard Lee, Lois Maxwell.

GORATH
Toho (Japan, 1962); Columbia (U.S., 1962). Color, 89 mins.

When a runaway planet heads for Earth on a collision course, an international group of scientists decides that it would be impossible to try to destroy the large body. So they move the Earth out of the planet's path through the use of large rockets. One minor hitch develops. A resulting earthquake releases a huge, prehistoric walrus-beastie, Gorath. Tokyo has to batten down the hatches once again.

PRODUCER: Tomoyuki Tanaka. DIRECTOR: Inoshiro Honda. SCREENPLAY: Takeshi Kimura. CINEMATOGRAPHY: Hajime Koizumi. SPECIAL EFFECTS: Eiji Tsuburaya.

CAST: Jun Tazaki, Ryo Ikebe, Takashi Shimura, Jumi Mizuno.

GORGO
MGM (1961). Color, 78 mins.

A handsomely mounted prehistoric-beast-in-modern-times tale. A dinosaur is awakened by the eruption of an underground volcano and surfaces off the coast of Nara Island, Ireland. Two enterprising seamen, Joe Ryan (Bill Travers) and Jack Slade (William Sylvester), agree to capture the beast, a gorgosaurus . . . "Gorgo," for short. They succeed, and in the company of a dinosaur-loving boy, Sean (Vincent Winter), they take the creature back to London and hand it over to, not the science community, but Dorkin's Circus. Trouble comes knocking on their (and everyone's) door when it is discovered that Gorgo is a mere tadpole. Worse yet, mama has surfaced at sea and after wiping out Nara Island, is now heading for London.

EXECUTIVE PRODUCERS: the King Brothers. PRODUCER: Wilfred Eades. DIRECTOR: Eugene Lourie. SCREENPLAY: John Loring and Daniel Hyatt, from a story by Lourie and Hyatt. CINEMATOGRAPHY: F. A. Young. SPECIAL EFFECTS: Tom Howard. MUSIC: Angelo Francesco Lavagnino.

SUPPORTING PLAYERS: Bruce Seton, Joseph O'Connor, Martin Benson.

GREAT ALASKAN MYSTERY, THE
Universal (1944). B/w serial, 13 chapters (26 reels).

Dr. Miller (Ralph Morgan), daughter Ruth (Marjorie Weaver), and Jim Hudson (Milburn Stone), journey to Alaska to mine the ore in an old shaft discovered by Jim's dad, Bill (Joseph Crehan), in the hope that the mine will supply the minerals necessary to make the doc's newest invention, the Peratron, a key defense weapon. The Peratron is capable of transmitting matter through space and several fascist governments would dearly love to filch it. One of those powers sends seemingly friendly Dr. Hauss (Martin Kosleck) on the trip. His mission? Glom the invention.

DIRECTORS: Ray Taylor, Lewis D. Collins. SCREENPLAY: Maurice Tombragel and George H. Plympton, from a story by Jack Foley. CINEMATOGRAPHY: William Sickner.

SUPPORTING PLAYERS: Fuzzy Knight, Anthony Warde, Jay Novello.

GREATEST POWER, THE
Metro (1917). B/w silent feature, five reels.

A chemist (William B. Davidson) is working on a cure for cancer when he invents exonite, a superexplosive that could lead to complete control of the world. He plans to make it available to all the nations of the Earth but eventually sees the light and gives it only to the U.S.

DIRECTOR: Edwin Carewe. SCREENPLAY: Albert Shelby Le Vino, from a story by Louis R. Wolheim.

SUPPORTING PLAYERS: Ethel Barry-more, Harry S. Northrup, William Black.

GREAT RADIUM MYSTERY, THE
Universal (1919). B/w silent serial, 18 chapters (36 reels).

Pro-science heroes battle science-stealing villains over the existence of a new, improved supertank.

DIRECTORS: Robert F. Hill, Robert Broadwell. SCREENPLAY: Frederick Bennett.

CAST: Cleo Madison, Robert Reeves, Eileen Sedgwick.

GREEN HORNET, THE
Universal (1940). B/w serial, 13 chapters (26 reels).

Those comic-book cut-ups, the Green Hornet/Brett Reid (Gordon Jones) and Kato (Keye Luke), stumble across about 19 different criminal activities, spearheaded by one man. Although the ringleader is brought to justice, the Green Hornet is still suspected by the police of being a criminal. Rotten break.

DIRECTORS: Ford Beebe, Ray Taylor. SCREENPLAY: George H. Plympton, Basil Dickey, Morrison C. Wood, and Lyonel Margolies, based on the radio serial by Fran Striker. CINEMATOGRAPHY: William Sickner, Jerome Ash.

SUPPORTING PLAYERS: Wade Boteler as Michael Oxford, Anne Nagel as Leonore Case, Philip Trent as Jasper Jenks, Edward Earle as Felix Grant.

GREEN HORNET STRIKES AGAIN, THE
Universal (1940). B/w serial, 15 chapters (30 reels).

The Green Hornet (Warren Hull) and Kato (Keye Luke) don their trick-or-treat masks once again to fight crime in the city streets. This time their target is archvillain Grogan (Pierre Watkins), a fellow who has his hands in various troublesome activities, including the use of gas guns and the manufacturing of a new, powerful bomb.

DIRECTORS: Ford Beebe, John Rawlins. SCREENPLAY: George H. Plympton, Basil Dickey, Sherman L. Lowe. CINEMATOGRAPHY: Jerome Ash.

SUPPORTING PLAYERS: Wade Boteler as Michael Oxford, Anne Nagel as Leonore Case, Eddie Acuff as Lowrey, C. Montague Shaw as Weaver.

GREEN SLIME, THE
Toei (Japan, 1968); Toei color, 77 mins. MGM (U.S., 1969); Toei color, 90 mins.

This one could set the space program back several years. After destroying a runaway asteroid heading for Earth, a spaceship docks at a space station, unwittingly carrying aboard an army of tiny, alien green-slime creatures. Jack Rankin (Robert Horton), Vince Elliot (Richard Jaeckel), and Lisa Benson (Luciana Paluzzi) begin to sense something is amiss when strange green creatures, now some five feet in height, begin appearing and slaughtering the members of the space station crew. What starts out as an sf version of *The Most Dangerous Game* ends up being a spacefaring *Gunfight at the OK Corral*.

PRODUCERS: Ivan Reiner, Walter Manley. DIRECTOR: Kinji Fukasaku. SCREENPLAY: Charles Sinclair, William Finger, and Tom Rowe, from a story by Ivan Reiner. MUSIC: Toshiaki Tsushima. MAKEUP: Takeshi Ugai. SPECIAL EFFECTS: Akira Watanabe.

SUPPORTING PLAYERS: Ted Gunther, Bud Widom.

GREEN TERROR, THE
Gaumont (G.B., 1919). B/w silent feature, 6,524 ft.

A mad doctor tries to destroy the world's wheat crop.

DIRECTOR: Will Kellino. SCREENPLAY: G. W. Clifford.

MGM

The Green Slime

CAST: Aurele Sydney, Maud Yates, Heather Thatcher.

GROUND ZERO
Flocker Enterprises (1973). Color.

A slightly demented man plants nuclear explosives on the Golden Gate Bridge.

PRODUCER AND DIRECTOR: James T. Flocker. SCREENPLAY: Samuel Newman. MUSIC: The Chosen Few.

CAST: Ron Casteel, Melvin Belli, Augie Treibach.

GULLIVER'S TRAVELS BEYOND THE MOON
Toei (Japan, 1965); Continental (U.S., 1966). Color, 85 mins. Animated.

Jonathan Swift's classic adventurer gets a swift boot into space when Gulliver and a young boy take a quick trip to the moon in a rocket ship. Once aboard the satellite, they encounter a warring civilization of robots; one army is nice, the other, not so nice.

PRODUCER: Hiroshi Okawa. DIRECTOR: Yoshio Kuroda. SCREENPLAY: Shinichi Sekizawa. ENGLISH MUSIC AND LYRICS: Milton and Anne DeLugg.

HAND OF DEATH, THE
20th Cent.-Fox (1961). B/w, 59 mins.

John Agar experiments with some nasty nerve gas and winds up with a touch that means death and a face that means a month's supply of acne medicine.

PRODUCER AND SCREENWRITER: Eugene Ling. DIRECTOR: Harry Nelson. MAKEUP: Bob Mark. CINEMATOGRAPHY: Floyd Crosby. MUSIC: Sonny Burke.

SUPPORTING PLAYERS: Paula Raymond, Steve Dunne, Roy Gordon, John Alonzo.

HAND OF PERIL, THE
World (1916). B/w silent feature, five reels.

An X-ray device makes objects totally transparent.

20th Cent.-Fox

The Hand of Death

PRODUCER, DIRECTOR, AND SCREEN-WRITER: Maurice Tourneur.

CAST: House Peters, Doris Sawyer, June Elvidge.

HANDS OF A STRANGER
AA (1962). B/w, 86 mins.

The fourth screen version of Maurice Renard's chilling science-horror tale, *The Hands of Orlac*, featured a cast of relatively unknown actors with a very familiar plot. A pianist who loses his hands in an accident seems doomed to a life of abject despair. A top-flight surgeon comes to the rescue. In an unorthodox experiment, the hands of a recently executed murderer are grafted onto the arms of the pianist. The musician's joy turns to horror when he comes to the realization that his "new" hands have a will of their own.

PRODUCERS: Newton Arnold, Michael Du Pont. DIRECTOR AND SCREEN-WRITER: Newton Arnold. CINEMATOGRAPHY: Henry Cronjager. MUSIC: Richard La Salle.

CAST: Paul Lukather, Joan Harvey, Ted Ottis, Sally Kellerman, Irish McCalla.

HANDS OF ORLAC, THE
Pan Film (1925). B/w, silent feature.

A pianist (Conrad Veidt) has the hands of a murderer grafted on, replacing his crippled appendages. The hands soon reveal that they owe allegiance to their original owner.

DIRECTOR: Robert Wiene. SCREEN-PLAY: Louis Nerz, from the novel by Maurice Renard. CINEMATOGRAPHY: G. Krampf, Hans Androschin.

SUPPORTING PLAYERS: Fritz Kortner, Alexandra Sorina, Carmen Cartellieri.

HANDS OF ORLAC, THE
G.B./France (1960); b/w, 105 mins. Continental (U.S., 1964); b/w, 95 mins.

When a pianist loses his hands in an auto accident, the hands of a killer are grafted on in their place. The musician (Mel Ferrer) discovers that his hands have a mind of their own. All turns out well, however, when it is discovered that the murderer was really innocent.

PRODUCERS: Steven Pallos, Donald Taylor. DIRECTOR: Edmond T. Grenville. SCREENPLAY: John Baines and Grenville, from the novel by Maurice Renard. CINEMATOGRAPHY: Desmond Dickinson, Jacques Lemare. MUSIC: Claude Bollings.

SUPPORTING PLAYERS: Christopher Lee, Lucile Saint-Simon, Basil Sydney, Donald Wolfit, Donald Pleasance, David Peel.

HAVE ROCKET, WILL TRAVEL
Columbia (1959). B/w, 76 mins.

Intentional humor. The Three Stooges (Moe Howard, Larry Fine, "Curly" Joe DeRita), board a rocket and launch themselves to Venus by mistake. On the planet's surface, when not knocking each other around, they rub elbows with Venusians, a talking unicorn, a flame-throwing giant spider, and a robot. Nyuk, nyuk.

PRODUCER: Harry Romm. DIRECTOR: David Lowell Rich. SCREENPLAY: Raphael Hayes. CINEMATOGRAPHY: Ray Cory. MUSIC: Mischa Bakaleinikoff.

SUPPORTING PLAYERS: Jerome Cowan, Anna-Lisa, Nadine Datas.

HEAD, THE
Rapid (W. Germany, 1959); Trans-Lux (U.S., 1961). B/w, 91 mins.

A scientist with a fairly "different" type of personality (Horst Frank) works on an experiment using Serum Z, a chemical that can keep severed portions of the human body alive. On a whim, the scientist cuts off the head of Serum Z's inventor and keeps it alive (if not happy) on a lab table for the rest of the movie. In an act of well-intentioned lust, he then transplants the head of a beautiful but deformed girl onto the body of a recently deceased knockout. Not exactly "Mr. Wizard" material.

PRODUCER: Wolfgang Hartwig. DIRECTOR AND SCREENWRITER: Victor Trivas, from a story by Trivas and Jacques Mage. CINEMATOGRAPHY: Otto Reinwald, Kurt Rendel. SPECIAL EFFECTS: Theo Nishwitz. MUSIC: Willy Mattes, Jacques Lasry.

SUPPORTING PLAYERS: Michel Simon, Karin Kernke, Paul Dahlke.

HEAVENS CALL, THE
Dovzhenko (U.S.S.R., 1959); color, 90 mins. Filmgroup (U.S., 1963); color, 75 mins.
Also known as BATTLE BEYOND THE SUN.

In the future, the world is divided into two sectors; one run by the U.S.S.R., the other by the U.S. The two political powers launch missions to land on Mars. The Americans, greedy folk they be, try to outdistance the Russians and plunge toward the sun. It's up to the cosmonauts to save both the day and the Americans. They both land on Mars safely.

Bond and Gagged
It's the biggest Bond film yet, and the best! Even if this wasn't a James Bond picture . . . if this was a JOE SMITH picture . . . it would still be a hell of a movie!

Albert Broccoli, producer of *Moonraker*

DIRECTORS: Alexander Kozyr, M. Karinkov. SCREENPLAY: V. Pomieszczykov, A. Sazanov. AMERICAN-VERSION PRODUCER: Roger Corman. AMERICAN ADAPTATION: Francis Ford Coppola.

CAST: A. Shvorin, L. Lobanov, Ivan Pereverzev.

HELLEVISION
Roadshow Attractions (1939). B/w.
A scientist tunes in his television in-

vention and picks up transmissions from hell (at least there are no commercials). The hell sequences are made up of stock footage from the 1909 silent film, *Dante's Inferno*.

HELLO TELEVISION
Educational Films (1930). B/w short, 20 mins.

In the future, slapstick comedians get to grapple with a television phone.

PRODUCER: Mack Sennett. DIRECTOR: Leslie A. Pearce.

CAST: Andy Clyde, Ann Christy, Julia Griffith.

HERCULES AGAINST THE MOON MEN
Governor (1965). Color, 88 mins.

A group of humanoid moonmen land on Earth in ancient times and enslave the city of Samar. The moonmen make many demands on the hapless citizens, not the least of which is a constant supply of blood needed for the centuries-old queen of the moonmen (Anna-Maria Polani). This latter point makes strongman Maciste see red. Before you can say *"ciao,"* the moonmen are sent packing by the strongman.

PRODUCER: Luigi Mondello. DIRECTOR: Giacomo Gentilomo. SCREENPLAY: Gentilomo, Arpad De Riso, Nino Scolaro, Angelo Sangarmano. MUSIC: Carlo Franci. SPECIAL EFFECTS: Ugo Amadoro.

HERCULES AND THE CAPTIVE WOMEN
Woolner (1963). Color/scope, 100 mins.

Hercules visits the lost city of Atlantis and fights an army of clone-men and a couple of overstuffed monsters. Atlantis sinks. Hercules stays afloat.

PRODUCER: Achille Piazzi. DIRECTOR: Vittorio Cottafavi. SCREENPLAY: Cottafavi, Duccio Tessari, Alexandro Continenza. ART DIRECTOR: Franco Lolli.

CAST: Reg Park, Fay Spain, Ettore Manni, Laura Atlan.

SUPPORTING PLAYERS: Jany Clair, Ando Tamberlani.

HERCULES IN THE VALE OF WOE

Woolner (1962). Color, running time unknown.

Two modern-day con men go back in time and find themselves about to enter combat with Hercules (Kirk Morris) and Maciste.

SUPPORTING PLAYERS: Frank Gordon, Franco Franchi, Liana Orfei.

HERRN der WELT, DER (THE MASTER OF THE WORLD)

Ariel-Film (Germany, 1935). B/w, 90 mins.

In the future, machines do most of the work for humans. They can even kill . . . using death rays.

DIRECTOR: Harry Piel. SCREENPLAY: George Muehlen-Schulte.

CAST: Walter Janssen, Sybille Schmitz.

HIDDEN HAND, THE

WB (1942). B/w, 68 mins.

A drama in which suspended animation is the ultimate weapon.

PRODUCER: William Jacobs. DIRECTOR: Ben Stoloff. SCREENPLAY: Anthony Coldwey, Raymond Schrock. CINEMATOGRAPHY: Henry Sharp.

CAST: Craig Stevens, Elizabeth Fraser, Frank Wilcox.

HIDDEN POWER

Columbia (1939). B/w, 60 mins.

A chemist (Jack Holt) nearly upsets the balance of power when, attempting to find a drug that eases suffering, he trips onto a formula for a new and potentially catastrophic explosive.

PRODUCER: Larry Darmour. DIRECTOR: Lewis Collins. SCREENPLAY: Gordon Rigby. CINEMATOGRAPHY: James S. Brown, Jr.

SUPPORTING PLAYERS: Dickie Moore, Gertrude Michael, Regis Toomey, Holmes Herbert.

HIDEOUS SUN DEMON, THE

Pacific International (1959). B/w, 74 mins.

An atomic physicist (Robert Clarke) is exposed to an overdose of radiation and becomes the nuclear industry's answer to Lon Chaney, Jr. Whenever the sun strikes his body, he is transformed,

Pacific International

The Hideous Sun Demon

not into a hairy creature, but into a scaly monster. Realizing the above-mentioned condition could seriously hamper his social life, he vows to live in the shade *only*. He is inadvertently drawn into the sunlight at the film's finale, however, and falls to his death from a tower.

PRODUCER: Robert Clarke. DIRECTORS: Clarke, Thomas Cassarino. SCREENPLAY: E. S. Seeley, Jr., and Doane Hoag, from a story by Clarke and Phil Hiner. CINEMATOGRAPHY: John Morrill, Villis Lapenieks, Jr., Stan Follis. MUSIC: John Seely.

SUPPORTING PLAYERS: Patricia Manning, Fred La Porta, Nan Peterson.

HIGHLY DANGEROUS

Two Cities (G.B., 1950); Lippert (U.S., 1951). B/w, 88 mins.

A pretty woman scientist (Margaret Lockwood) and an American reporter (Dane Clark) journey behind the Iron Curtain and discover a plot in which insects would be used in a germ warfare maneuver. En route, they are subjected to healthy doses of truth serum.

PRODUCER: Anthony Darnborough. DIRECTOR: Roy Baker. SCREENPLAY: Eric Ambler. CINEMATOGRAPHY: Reginald Wyer, David Harcourt. MUSIC: Richard Addinsell.

SUPPORTING PLAYERS: Marius Goring, Wilfred Hyde-White, Anthony Newley.

HIGH TREASON
Gaumont (G.B., 1929); b/w, 95 mins.
Tiffany (U.S., 1930); b/w, 69 mins.

The Federated Atlantic States and the United States of Europe engage in all-out warfare during the distant year of 1940. Among the dastardly deeds committed: the gas bombing of New York and the flooding of the English Channel tunnel. Citizens watch the warfare via wall-sized TV screens.

DIRECTOR: Maurice Elvey. SCREENPLAY: L'Estrange Fawcett, based on a play by Pemberton Billing. ART DIRECTOR: Andrew Mazzei.

CAST: Benita Hume, Basil Gill, Raymond Massey, Jameson Thomas.

H-MAN, THE
Toho (Japan, 1958); color, 87 mins.
Columbia (U.S., 1959); color, 79 mins.

An overdose of radiation lingering from an H-bomb explosion turns a man into a liquid ooze that roams the sewer system beneath the streets of Tokyo. Able to slither under doors and over windows, the ooze touches human flesh (usually of the chorus-girl variety) and causes it to dissolve. The ooze then slithers out and seeks more food. It's the army to the rescue by the film's finale.

PRODUCER: Tomoyuki Tanaka. DIRECTOR: Inoshiro Honda. STORY: Hideo Kaijo. SCREENPLAY: Takeshi Kimura. CINEMATOGRAPHY: Hajime Koizumi. SPECIAL EFFECTS: Eiji Tsuburaya. MUSIC: Masaru Sato.

CAST: Kenji Sahara, Koreya Senda, Yumi Shirakawa.

HOLD THAT HYPNOTIST
AA (1957). B/w, 61 mins.

A laugh a century as a mad mesmerist sends Huntz Hall's brain spinning back through time to the era of Bluebeard the pirate. Huntz's time-traveling uncovers the whereabouts of a long-lost treasure.

PRODUCER: Ben Schwalb. DIRECTOR: Austen Jewell. SCREENPLAY: Dan Pepper. CINEMATOGRAPHY: Harry Neumann.

SUPPORTING PLAYERS: Jane Nigh, Stanley Clements.

HOMMUNCULUS
Bioscop (Germany, 1916). B/w silent serial, six chapters (24 reels).

An artificially created man (Olaf Fonss) has no soul but a great intellect. Relying on his cunning, he becomes dictator of an unnamed country. He is about to embark on a plan to conquer the world when he is struck by lightning and killed.

DIRECTOR: Otto Rippert. SCREENPLAY: Rippert, Robert Neuss. CINEMATOGRAPHY: Carl Hoffman.

SUPPORTING PLAYERS: Friedrich Kuhne, Maria Carmi.

HORRIBLE DR. HITCHCOCK, THE
Sigma III (1964). Color, 76 mins.

Dr. Hitchcock (Robert Flemyng) is puttering around the lab, operating on his wife, when she suddenly expires. Hard cheese, that. Intuitively knowing that the blood from pretty women will restore his late lovely to life, the good doctor begins a crash course in dating. His dates prove a draining experience, but not draining enough to suit his bloodthirsty spouse. Barbara Steel, veteran horror heroine, marries the surgeon, and then the screaming starts.

PRODUCERS: Luigi Carpentieri, Ermano Donati. DIRECTOR: Robert Hampton. SCREENPLAY: Julyan Perry. CINEMATOGRAPHY: Raffaele Masciocchi. MUSIC: Roman Vlad.

SUPPORTING PLAYERS: Harriet White, Teresa Vianello, Montgomery Glenn.

HORROR CHAMBER OF DR. FAUSTUS, THE
Also known as EYES WITHOUT A FACE.
Champs-Élysées (France, 1959); Lippert (U.S., 1962). B/w, 95 mins.

A doctor whose daughter has a horribly scarred face attempts to restore her beauty through skin grafts. The donors for these operations usually are very pretty young girls. The donors for these operations usually are pretty unwilling. The grafts never seem to work, anyway, and the lonely daughter is forced to live in a netherworld of shadows within her father's mansion, walking the corridors at night wearing an opaque facial mask.

PRODUCER: Jules Borkon. DIRECTOR:

Georges Franju. SCREENPLAY: Franju, Jean Redon, Claude Sautet, Pierre Boileau, Thomas Narcejac. MUSIC: Maurice Jarré.

CAST: Pierre Brasseur, Alida Valli, Juliette Mayniel, Edith Scob.

HORROR OF FRANKENSTEIN
Hammer (1970). Color, 95 mins.

MARY W. SHELLEY's novel *Frankenstein* is spoofed and sexed-up in this grim ditty dished up by director Jimmy Sangster. In this version, the good doctor, when not carousing, creates a pretty homely creature indeed (David Prowse). Eventually, of course, Dr. Frankenstein (Ralph Bates), gets his just desserts.

PRODUCER AND DIRECTOR: Jimmy Sangster. SCREENPLAY: Sangster, Jeremy Burnham. MAKEUP: Tom Smith. CINEMATOGRAPHY: Moray Grant. MUSIC: Malcolm Williamson.

SUPPORTING PLAYERS: Kate O'Mara, Graham James, Veronica Carlson, Dennis Price.

HORROR OF PARTY BEACH, THE
20th Cent.-Fox (1964). B/w, 72 mins.

Nuclear waste combines with sea life at the ocean floor to produce rubber-suited creatures that stalk the beaches at night, seeking wild bikinis and the contents thereof. Object: mayhem. The police are mystified, of course, but plucky Hank Green (John Scott), pretty Elaine Gavin (Alice Lyon), and perturbed Dr. Gavin (Allen Laurel) figure out that sodium (read: "salt") will cause the creatures to explode.

PRODUCER AND DIRECTOR: Del Tenny. SCREENPLAY AND CINEMATOGRAPHY: Richard Hilliard. MUSIC: Bill Holmes.

SUPPORTING PLAYERS: Eulabelle Moore, Marilyn Clark, The Del-Aires.

HORROR OF THE BLOOD MONSTERS
Independent International (1971). Color, 85 mins.

After a vampiresque plague takes firm hold on the Earth, a leading scientist (John Carradine) journeys into space to trace its cause. He finds that the disease is caused by space viruses drifting to Earth from a war-torn planet. On board the planet, he becomes embroiled in a civil war in which the bat-men are out to get the lobster-men.

PRODUCER AND DIRECTOR: Al Adamson. SCREENPLAY: Sue McNair. MUSIC: Mike Velarde.

SUPPORTING PLAYERS: Bruce Powers, Vicki Volanti, Robert Dix; narrated by Brother Theodore.

HOUSE OF DRACULA
Universal (1945). B/w, 67 mins.

Nice plotting here combines standard horror-sf plot ideas with a few new twists. Count Dracula (John Carradine) comes to noted physician Dr. Edelmann (Onslow Stevens) in search of a cure for vampirism. The constant nightlife is finally beginning to annoy the nobleman. He convinces the doctor that to restore him to a normal, human condition would be the medical achievement of the century. The doctor discovers a strange parasite in the vampire's blood and begins searching for an antibody. With Dracula now in the care of Edelmann and his two assistants (Martha O'Driscoll and Jane Adams), the stage is set for a second famous patient to appear.

Larry Talbot (Lon Chaney, Jr.), also known as the Wolfman, wants to be cured of lycanthropy. Edelmann does a quick examination and concludes that a brain operation will make Larry less fearsome in the future. But —bad luck—a full moon comes along and Larry, the Wolfman, escapes. Edelmann chases Larry and finds not only Talbot but the remains of the Frankenstein monster (Glenn Strange) in a nearby cave.

Edelmann sets about to restore the monster to life. He also begins giving Dracula blood transfusions, using himself as a donor. Dracula responds by attacking one of the female assistants. Horrified, Edelmann drives a stake through the vampire's heart and exposes the body to the sunlight. Meanwhile, Dracula's blood, now tingeing Edelmann's normal blood, transforms the doctor into a mad killer at night.

In his waking hours, Edelmann cures Larry of lycanthropy. On a bad night,

Universal

House of Dracula

the madman doc kills his hunchback nurse and awakens the Frankenstein monster. The police (led by Lionel Atwill) arrive a wee bit late, and so the former Wolfman must play hero. He kills the doctor when Edelmann tries to turn him into a cadaver via a pair of strong hands. He starts a fire in the lab and kills the Frankenstein monster. He destroys the entire house of horror in time for the final credits.

PRODUCER: Paul Malvern. DIRECTOR: Erle C. Kenton. SCREENPLAY: George Bricker and Dwight V. Babcock, with Edward T. Lowe. MAKEUP: Jack Pierce. CINEMATOGRAPHY: George Robinson. SPECIAL EFFECTS: John P. Fulton.

SUPPORTING PLAYERS: Ludwig Stossel, Skelton Knaggs.

HOUSE OF FRANKENSTEIN
Universal (1944). B/w, 71 mins.

Standard but enjoyable mad-doctor machinations. Dr. Niemann (Boris Karloff) and his hunchback assistant, Daniel (J. Carrol Naish), escape from an asylum and, after killing Professor Brudon Lampini (George Zucco), take over his traveling circus of horrors and adopt his identity. Niemann plans to carry on in the Frankenstein tradition

after paying back a few of his old enemies. To do so, he brings the long-dead Count Dracula (John Carradine) back to life. When Dracula overplays his role of avenging angel, Niemann reintroduces him to long-death.

Niemann then digs up the remains of Larry Talbot (Lon Chaney, Jr.), the Wolfman, and of the Frankenstein monster (Glenn Strange). Talbot is a real disappointment to the doc—a normal, sensitive, everyday sort of guy who turns into a wolf only a couple of times a month, Talbot falls in love with Daniel's secret love interest, a gypsy girl (Elena Verdugo). Talbot and the gypsy pair off. He turns into a wolf. He kills her just as she kills him. And they said it wouldn't last.

Meanwhile, Daniel, properly miffed about getting left out of the action, whips the dormant Frankenstein monster with a belt. The monster wakes up, kills Daniel, and spotting Niemann, takes a quick jog through the bog with the doctor in tow. Soon both man and monster are up to their ears in quicksand.

PRODUCER: Paul Malvern. DIRECTOR: Erle C. Kenton. SCREENPLAY: Edward T. Lowe, from a story by CURT SIODMAK. MAKEUP: Jack Pierce. CINEMATOGRAPHY: George Robinson. SPECIAL EFFECTS: John P. Fulton. MUSIC: H. J. Salter.

HOUSE OF FRIGHT
Hammer (G.B., 1960); AIP (U.S., 1961). Color/scope, 89 mins.

Dr. Jekyll (Paul Massie) experiments with Good and Evil and comes up with the ever-popular Mr. Hyde. En route to hedonism, Jekyll/Hyde discovers that his wife (Dawn Addams) has taken on a lover (Christopher Lee). Before too long, Lee has taken on a poisonous snake and wife has taken on a distinct pallor. After killing everyone else in the house, Jekyll decides to murder Hyde, apparently forgetting that killing Hyde means doing in Jekyll as well. Two for the price of one.

PRODUCER: Michael Carreras. DIRECTOR: Terence Fisher. SCREENPLAY: Wolf Mankowitz. MAKEUP: Roy Ashton. CINEMATOGRAPHY: Jack Asher.

MUSIC: Monty Norman, David Heneker.

SUPPORTING PLAYERS: David Kossoff, Oliver Reed, Percy Cartwright.

HOUSE THAT WENT CRAZY, THE
Selig (1914). B/w silent short, one reel.

An automatic house is broken into by a thief and goes haywire as a result.

HOW TO STEAL THE WORLD
MGM (1968). Color, 89 mins.

The men from U.N.C.L.E. (Robert Vaughn as Napoleon Solo, David McCallum as Ilya, and Leo G. Carroll as Waverly) must fight an international organization out to subvert the world with a dose of apathy gas.

PRODUCER: Anthony Spinner. DIRECTOR: Sutton Roley. SCREENPLAY: Norman Hudis. CINEMATOGRAPHY: Robert Hauser. SPECIAL EFFECTS: Ted Samuels. THEME MUSIC: Jerry Goldsmith.

Safety First
   Don't shoot, he's got the girl!
      Robert Armstrong commenting on an unusual coupling in *King Kong*

SUPPORTING PLAYERS: Barry Sullivan, Leslie Nielsen, Tony Bill, Hugh Marlowe, Eleanor Parker.

HUMAN DUPLICATORS, THE
Woolner/Crest (1965). Color, 81 mins.

An aging scientist (George Macready) plans to create a race of androids. Meanwhile, an alien android, Kolos (Richard Kiel), lands on Earth seeking to have an android team of his own. Unfortunately, the team Kolos wants is the same one that is being developed by the professor. Kolos takes over the experiment and begins creating a race of humanoid robots capable of taking over the Earth. They don't.

PRODUCERS: Hugo Grimaldi, Arthur Pierce. DIRECTOR: Grimaldi. SCREENPLAY: Pierce. MUSIC: Gordon Zahler. MAKEUP: John Chambers.

SUPPORTING PLAYERS: George Nader, Barbara Nichols, Richard Arlen, Hugh Beaumont.

HUMANOID, THE
Columbia (1979). Color, 99 mins.

Shelved by Columbia in 1979 after a disastrous European debut, *The Humanoid* stars Richard ("Jaws" of James Bond fame) Kiel as Golob, an invincible space pilot captured by nasty scientist Grael (Ivan Rassimov) of the planet Noxon. Spearheading an attack on Metropolis (Earth), Grael plants a synthetic brain into Golob's body, turning him into an evil humanoid. The scientist and immortal Lady Agatha (Barbara Bach) figure that Earth is in the bag. Enter Barbara Gibson (Corinne Clery) and her pupil, Tom Tom (Marco Yeh). Guided into Grael's headquarters by adventurer Nick (Leonard Mann), they deactivate Golob and defeat the forces of Evil.

PRODUCER: Georgia Venturini. DIRECTOR: George B. Lewis. SCREENPLAY: Adriano Bolzoni and Also Lado, from a story by Bolzoni. CINEMATOGRAPHY: Silvano Ippolito. SPECIAL EFFECTS: Armando Valcauda. MUSIC: John Williams.

HUMAN VAPOR, THE
Toho (Japan, 1960); Columbia (U.S., 1961). Color/scope, 80 mins.

A prisoner can vaporize at will, opening up new career opportunities in the fields of robbery and murder.

DIRECTOR: Inoshiro Honda. SPECIAL EFFECTS: Eiji Tsuburaya.

CAST: Tatsuya Mihashi, Kaoru Yachigusa, Yoshio Tsuchiya as the human vapor.

HYPERBOLOID OF ENGINEER GARIN
U.S.S.R. (1965).

A madman tries to do in the world with a powerful death ray.

PRODUCER AND DIRECTOR: M. Berdicevski. SCREENPLAY: I. Manevic, A. Ginzburg.

CAST: E. Evstigneev, V. Safonov, N. Astangov.

HYPNOTIC SPRAY, THE
Gaumont (G.B., 1909). B/w silent short, 360 ft.

A boy possesses a spray that deprives the sprayee of his or her willpower.

J

I EAT YOUR SKIN
Cinemation (1971). B/w, 82 mins.

A mad doctor on his self-proclaimed "Voodoo Island" creates a race of humanoid zombies using the radioactive venom of local mutant snakes. Right.

PRODUCER, DIRECTOR, AND SCREEN-WRITER: Del Tenney. MAKEUP: Guy Del Russo. CINEMATOGRAPHY: François Farkas. MUSIC: Lon E. Norman.

CAST: William Joyce, Heather Hewit, Betty Hyatt Linton, Walter Coy.

IF
London Films (G.B., 1916). B/w silent feature, 4,800 ft.

A madman tries to destroy London using gigantic guns and phony futuristic airships.

DIRECTOR: Stuart Kinder.

CAST: Iris Delaney, Judd Green.

ILLUSTRATED MAN, THE
WB/7 Arts (1969). Color, 103 mins.

Assembling three tales from RAY BRADBURY's novel of the same name, screenplay writer H. B. Kreitsek manages to mangle both the concept of the original book and the three selections: "The Long Rains," "The Last Night of the World," and "The Veldt." A carnival handyman, Carl (Rod Steiger), is seduced by a time-traveling tattoo lady who covers his body with magical images, thus allowing passersby a chance to peer at his skin and see their own futures, as well as futuristic stories. The human projector creates a trio of tales concerning a kiddie jungle-playroom that comes to life with murderous results; a world in which there is an eternal downpour; and the activities during the last night of the world, when all the adults vow to poison their children to spare them the violent death scheduled to occur the next morning.

Horrible on all counts, this film is a strong argument in favor of authors having final approval of cinematic adaptations of their work.

PRODUCER: Howard B. Kreitsek, Ted Mann. DIRECTOR: Jack Smight. MAKEUP: Gordon Bau. CINEMATOGRA-PHY: Philip Lathrop. SPECIAL EFFECTS: Ralph Webb. MUSIC: Jerry Goldsmith.

SUPPORTING PLAYERS: Claire Bloom, Robert Drivas, Jason Evers.

I LOVE YOU, I KILL YOU
Uwe Brandner (W. Germany, 1971); New Yorker Films (U.S., 1972). Color, 94 mins.

In the not-too-distant future, policemen keep the population under control by distributing pills of a fairly dire nature.

PRODUCER, DIRECTOR, AND SCREEN-WRITER: Uwe Brandner. CINEMATOG-RAPHY: André Debreuil.

CAST: Ralph Becker, Hannes Fuchs, Marianne Blomquist.

I'M AN EXPLOSIVE
George Smith Productions (G.B., 1933). B/w, 50 mins.

A little boy drinks a liquid explosive. Adults fear he'll either shoot his mouth off one time too many or just blow his top.

PRODUCER: Harry Cohen. DIRECTOR AND SCREENWRITER: Adrian Brunel.

CAST: Bill Hartnell, Gladys Jennings, Sybil Grove, Harry Terry.

I MARRIED A MONSTER FROM OUTER SPACE
Paramount (1958). B/w, 78 mins.

A good argument for celibacy. Marge Farrell (Gloria Talbott) has her problems. On the eve of her wedding night, her husband-to-be, Bill (Tom Tryon), is kidnapped by aliens. His unconscious body is taken inside a flying saucer and hooked up to a device that links his human memory to an alien body, thus creating an alien double. The alien stands in for Bill at his wedding, the idea being that more aliens will infiltrate the town for breeding purposes in weeks to come. Leaving a dying world behind them, the aliens have come to Earth in search of fertile women to carry their young. Their plan for mass pregnancies is still in the testing stage, however, since they haven't as yet figured out an actual way to match the two species' reproductive organs.

Marge discovers the ruse and tries to alert the FBI. By this time, however, the aliens have taken over all forms of communication in town. Suddenly struck by the nearest thing to a good idea she's had in months, Marge reasons that since the alien men can't reproduce as yet, the only *real* men in town can. In a burst of Freudian fervor, she races to the maternity ward, forms a posse of recent pops, and hunts down the aliens. Finding the flying saucer, they discover a dozen or so men strapped inside. As they free the Earth males, the alien doubles die one by one, reverting to their own true shape—something resembling a walking plate of noodles with a Ping Pong ball wedged into the mouth area.

PRODUCER AND DIRECTOR: Gene Fowler, Jr. SCREENPLAY: Louis Vittes. MAKEUP: Charles Gemore (who constructed the WAR OF THE WORLDS Martians). SPECIAL EFFECTS: John P. Fulton.

SUPPORTING PLAYERS: Marie Rosenbloom, Valerie Allen.

IMMEDIATE DISASTER
Also known as STRANGER FROM VENUS; THE VENUSIAN; THE STRANGER FROM THE STARS.
British-Princess Pictures/Rich and Rich (1954). B/w, 75 mins.

A Venusian stranger (Helmut Dantine) saves the life of an Earth woman, Susan North (Patricia Neal), and attempts to disguise himself as an Earthling. Seeking to promote a meeting between Venusian and Earthly politicians, the stranger reveals that the people of his planet are concerned about Earth's nuclear policies and seek to point out better paths to follow. The Venusian announces that a fleet of saucers from his planet will be arriving any day. Susan's fiancé, Arthur Walker (Derek Bond), is jealous of the stranger and helps a group of nasty humans plan a trap that will lead to the capture of the Venusians and the conquering of the world. By the film's finale, he has a change of heart. He and the stranger warn the saucers off, and the Venusian is trapped on Earth . . . in an atmosphere that will kill him within days.

PRODUCERS: Burt Balaban, Gene Martel. DIRECTOR: Balaban. SCREENPLAY: Hans Jacoby. MUSIC: Eric Spear.

SUPPORTING PLAYERS: Arthur Young, Cyril Luckham.

I, MONSTER
Amicus (G.B., 1971); Cannon (U.S., 1973). Color, 75 mins.

Robert Louis Stevenson's *The Strange Case of Dr. Jekyll and Mr. Hyde* is given a reworking in this tale marked by average plotting but above-par acting. Kindly Dr. Marlow (Christopher Lee) becomes addicted to a series of experiments designed to separate Good from Evil. After taking a strange elixir, he becomes the vile Mr. Blake. With each subsequent experiment, Blake becomes uglier and uglier, mirroring his true evil nature.

PRODUCERS: Max J. Rosenberg, Milton Subotsky. DIRECTOR: Stephen Weeks. SCREENPLAY: Subotsky. MAKEUP: Harry and Peter Frampton. CINEMATOGRAPHY: Moray Grant. MUSIC: Carl Davis.

SUPPORTING PLAYERS: Peter Cushing, Mike Raven, Susan Jameson.

INCREDIBLE INVASION, THE
Azteca (Mexico); Columbia (U.S., 1971). Color.

Invisible invaders turn men into zombies and use their bodies to further the invasion. The film features the last scenes performed by Boris Karloff before his untimely death.

PRODUCER: Luis Enrique Vergara. DIRECTORS: Juan Ibanes, Jack Hill. SCREENPLAY: Vergara, Karl Schanzer.

CAST: Enrique Guzman, Maura Monti, Tene Valez.

INCREDIBLE MELTING MAN, THE
AIT (1977). Movielab color, 86 mins.

Astronaut Steve West (Alex Rebar) returns from Saturn with a disease that causes his flesh to melt. In order to stop the process, he must periodically lurch into the path of unsuspecting humans and munch on their flesh. His colleagues are not amused.

PRODUCER: Samuel W. Gelfman. DIRECTOR AND SCREENWRITER: William Sachs. CINEMATOGRAPHY: Willy Curtis. SPECIAL EFFECTS: Rick Baker, Harry

The Incredible Melting Man

The Incredible Shrinking Man

Woolman. MAKEUP: Rick Baker. MUSIC: Arlon Ober.

SUPPORTING PLAYERS: Burr Debanning as Dr. Ted Nelson, Myron Healy as General Perry, Ann Sweeny as Judy Nelson, Julie Drazen as Carol.

INCREDIBLE SHRINKING MAN, THE
Universal (1957). B/w, 81 mins.

An exceedingly literate, well acted, and well paced drama based on the novel *The Shrinking Man*, by RICHARD MATHESON. After passing through a radioactive cloud, Scott Carey (Grant Williams) discovers, to his horror, that he is actually shrinking in size. Carey, a logical sort, attempts to deal rationally with his fate. As his problem becomes known the world over, however, he begins to regard himself with self-loathing. He is an ever-changing freak. He eventually becomes so small that he becomes one with the cosmos; before that time, however, he must match his wits against the dangers presented by an Olympian house cat, a titanic spider, Niagara Falls plumbing leaks, and various oversized effects. Excellent on all counts.

PRODUCER: Albert Zugsmith. DIRECTOR: Jack Arnold. SCREENPLAY: Richard Matheson. CINEMATOGRAPHY: Ellis W. Carter. SPECIAL EFFECTS: Clifford Stine. MUSIC: F. Carling, E. Lawrence.

SUPPORTING PLAYERS: Randy Stuart, Paul Langton, William Schallert, April Kent, Billy Curtis.

INCREDIBLE TWO-HEADED TRANSPLANT, THE
AIP (1971). Color, 81 mins.

Bruce Dern twitches more than usual in this film after grafting the head of a deranged killer onto the body of a titanic dimwit with the strength of an ox. The two-headed dialogue is priceless—sort of a cross between Abbott and Costello's "Who's on First" routine and *Of Mice and Men*. Could set medicine back a few centuries.

PRODUCER: John Lawrence. DIRECTOR: Anthony Lanza. SCREENPLAY: J. Lawrence, James Gordon White. SPECIAL MAKEUP: Barry Noble. CINEMATOGRAPHY: Jack Steely, Glen Gano, Paul Hipp. SPECIAL EFFECTS: Ray Dorn. SPECIAL COSTUMES: Bjo Trimble.

SUPPORTING PLAYERS: Pat Priest, Casey Kasem, Berry Kroeger.

INDESTRUCTIBLE MAN, THE
AA (1956). B/w, 70 mins.

Lon Chaney, Jr., is a double-crossed mobster who gets the chair in this potboiler. Brought back to life by a scientist, he spends the rest of the movie hunting down his ex-pals and making them ex-breathers.

PRODUCER AND DIRECTOR: Jack Pollexfen. SCREENPLAY: Sue Bradford, Vy Russell. CINEMATOGRAPHY: John Russell, Jr. MUSICAL DIRECTOR: Albert Glasser.

SUPPORTING PLAYERS: Marian Carr, Ross Elliott, Robert Shayne.

IN THE YEAR 2889
AIT (1968). Color, 80 mins.

After Armageddon, a small group of human survivors are chased hither and yon by a tribe of telepathic mutants.

PRODUCER AND DIRECTOR: Larry Buchanan. SCREENPLAY: Harold Hoffman, from a story by Lou Rusoff. CINEMATOGRAPHY: Robert C. Jessup. SPECIAL EFFECTS: Jack Bennett.

CAST: Paul Peterson, Quinn O'Hara, Billy Thurman.

INVADERS FROM MARS
20th Cent.-Fox (1953). SuperCinecolor, 78 mins.

A cult classic of the 1950s, *Invaders from Mars* took sf clichés to their most nightmarish conclusions. Young David MacLean (Jimmy Hunt) is awakened from his sleep by a strange light. He watches a flying saucer crash-land in a nearby marsh. With David watching from the window, the boy's father, George (Leif Erickson), goes out to investigate and is sucked into the sand pit. George returns home, but the next morning, the boy notices a personality change, first in his father, and subsequently in his mother as well.

The boy finds radio implants drilled into the bases of their skulls and reasons that his parents are being controlled by aliens aboard the spaceship. He tries to convince physician Pat Blake (Helena Carter) and astronomer Stuart Kelson (Arthur Franz) of his findings. Soon they discover the boy's story is real. Green-zombie giants, ruled by a tendriled alien head, are attempting to take over the Earth. The army is called to the scene, led by a zealous general (Morris Ankrum). David and Blake are kidnapped by the aliens, and just as an implant is to be drilled into Blake's neck, the troops arrive. All hell breaks loose and . . . David awakens. He is in his bed. It all was only a dream. Suddenly he glances out his window. A flying saucer lands in the marsh with a resounding thud.

Originally conceived as a 3-D movie but shot two-dimensionally, this film boasts two endings. The British version had no "dream" ending and an additional dramatic sequence in the astronomy lab.

PRODUCER: Edward L. Alperson. DIRECTOR AND DESIGNER: William Cameron Menzies. SCREENPLAY: Richard Blake. MAKEUP: Gene Hibbs, Anatole Robbins. SPECIAL EFFECTS: Jack Cosgrove. MUSIC: Raoul Kraushaar.

INVASION
AIP (1966). B/w, 82 mins.

Two humanoid aliens—one a police officer, the other his prisoner (Yoko Tani and Eric Young)—crash-land on Earth. Brought to an Earth hospital, they continue their conflict inside, cutting off the hospital from the rest of the world via a force field.

The Family that Plays Together . . .
Answer me! You have a civil tongue in your head. I should know . . . I sewed it in there!
Frankenstein (Whit Bissell) to his monster (Gary Conway) in *I Was a Teenage Frankenstein*

PRODUCER: Jack Greenwood. DIRECTOR: Alan Bridges. SCREENPLAY: Roger Marshall. MUSIC: Bernard Ebbinghouse. SPECIAL EFFECTS: Ronnie Whitehouse, Jack Kine, Stan Shields.

SUPPORTING PLAYERS: Edward Judd, Valerie Gearson, Lyndon Brook.

INVASION OF THE ANIMAL PEOPLE
ADP (G.B., 1960); b/w, 73 mins. Favorite Films (U.S., 1962); b/w, 55 mins.

A spaceship filled with unseen aliens makes an unscheduled stop in Lapland. A giant Stone Age creature escapes from the ship and spends quite a few minutes bumping into Earth-scale structures with horrifying results. The aliens recapture their pet and blast off. The American edition was so badly edited that John Carradine had to be hired to narrate/explain the finished sf stew.

PRODUCER: Arthur Warren. DIRECTORS: Arthur Warren, Virgil Vogel. SCREENPLAY: Arthur C. Pierce. MUSIC: Allan Johannson, Harry Arnold.

CAST: Barbara Wilson, Robert Burton, Ake Gronberg, Bengt Blomgren, Stan Gester.

INVASION OF THE BEE GIRLS
Centaur Pictures (1973). Color.

Housewives turn into strange seductresses.

DIRECTOR: Denis Sanders. SCREENPLAY: Nicholas Meyer.

CAST: William Smith, Victoria Vetri, Anitra Ford.

INVASION OF THE BODY SNATCHERS
AA (1956). B/w, 80 mins.

One of the best. Period. A classic of scripting and cinematic execution, this chilling film united sf action with Cold War hysteria.

Returning home from a short vacation, Dr. Miles Bennell (Kevin McCarthy) notices that the citizens of Santa Mira, California, are undergoing some sort of mass hysteria. Husbands insist that their wives are not their wives; children run from their mothers, and parents regard their offspring with open suspicion.

Interrupted on a date with old flame Becky Driscoll (Dana Wynter), Bennell is called to the home of Jack and Theodora Bellichec (King Donovan and Carolyn Jones), who've found a body on their basement pool-table—a body that is only half-formed and an exact double of Jack. The foursome discover that giant pods have sprouted from space seeds near town. Each pod, when placed near its human victim, splits open and forms a plant-double of the human. When the human sleeps, the pod takes over, becoming a cold, unfeeling, but otherwise identical substitute.

Jack and Theo succumb and are replaced by pod people. Before long, Miles and Becky are convinced that they are the only humans left in town. Pods are being shipped out of Santa Mira in trucks for invasions of other towns. Miles and Becky, pursued by the entire town, escape. Hiding in a cavern outside Santa Mira, Becky dozes off. Miles kisses her awake. She does not return the kiss. She stares at him, cold, unfeeling, unhuman. She calls out for her pod peers to snatch the human. Miles runs down the highway, screaming, "You're next! You're next!"

Picked up by the police and examined by Los Angeles psychiatrist Dr. Hill (Whit Bissell), Miles is about to be sent off to a laughing academy when police get word that there's been a terrible accident on the highway. A truck has overturned and spilled hundreds of strange-looking pods all over the doggone place.

PRODUCER: Walter Wanger. DIRECTOR: Don Siegel. SCREENPLAY: Daniel Mainwaring and Sam Peckinpah (uncredited), based on the novel by JACK FINNEY. MUSIC: Carmen Dragon. SPECIAL EFFECTS: Milton Rice.

SUPPORTING PLAYERS: Pat O'Malley, Richard Deacon, Sam Peckinpah, Virginia Christie, Jean Willes.

INVASION OF THE BODY SNATCHERS
UA (1978). Technicolor, 115 mins.

A deftly handled reworking of the original *Body Snatchers* film's theme, with a few hints of a sequel tossed in to help unite the two productions. After a weird shower of angel-hair fluff hits the city of San Francisco, public-health employees Matthew Bennell and Elizabeth Driscoll (Donald Sutherland and Brooke Adams) begin noticing strange occurrences throughout town. Driscoll's boy friend, Geoffrey (Art Hindle), undergoes a total personality change, becoming a cold, almost dictatorial man. He's become a pod person, of course; an alien plant-creature has taken over his role in day-to-day life after duplicating his original body and discarding it. Nancy and Jack Bellichec (Veronica Cartwright and Jeff Goldblum) find one of the pod people growing in their health spa and the invasion idea is confirmed, at least for Matthew. Good friend, writer/philosopher/psychotherapist Dr. David Kibner (Leonard Nimoy) chalks it up to mass hysteria. When the pods start popping, however, it's up to every human to stay awake. The pods can only replace you when you sleep. Adding to the fun are a glimpse of Kevin McCarthy, the original version's hero, *still* running through traffic, over 25 years later, yelling "They're coming!" and a cameo by original-version director Don Siegel as a pod-person cabbie.

PRODUCER: Robert H. Solo. DIRECTOR: Philip Kaufman. SCREENPLAY: W. D. Richter, based on the novel by JACK FINNEY. CINEMATOGRAPHY: Michael Chapman. MAKEUP EFFECTS: Thomas Burman. SPECIAL EFFECTS: Dell Rheaume, Russ Hessey. SPECIAL SOUND EFFECTS: Ben Burtt. MUSIC: Danny Zeitlin.

INVASION OF THE BODY STEALERS

Tigon (G.B., 1969); AA (U.S., 1970). Color, 90 mins.

A dapper alien chap (Maurice Evans) starts a very civilized invasion of Earth by kidnapping parachutists as they make their way from plane to planet. A less-than-amused investigator discovers that alien duplicates are then sent down to Earth. The investigator (George Sanders) finds the original Earthling skydivers in a state of suspended animation.

PRODUCER: Tony Tenser. DIRECTOR: Gerry Levy. SCREENPLAY: Mike St. Clair, Peter Marcus. MUSIC: Reg Tilsley.

SUPPORTING PLAYERS: Robert Flemyng, Hilary Dwyer, Patrick Allen.

INVASION OF THE NEPTUNE MEN

Manley (Japan, 1961). Toeicolor, 74 mins.

A Japanese superhero defeats an invasion attempted by a group of aliens from the planet Neptune.

PRODUCER: Hiroshi Okawa. DIRECTOR: Koji Ota. SCREENPLAY: Shin Morita.

CAST: Shinichi Chiba, Mishsue Komiya, Shanjiro Ebara.

INVASION OF THE SAUCER MEN

Also known as SPACEMEN SATURDAY NIGHT; THE HELL CREATURES.

AIP (1957). B/w, 68 mins.

Two bug-faced, taloned minicritters from *out there* land on Earth to launch an invasion. They are spotted by two con-men, Joe (Frank Gorshin) and his dimwitted sidekick (Lyn Osborn). Local hot-rodders (led by Steve Terrell and Gloria Costello) know that something is afoot when, after hitting one of the creatures with their car, its body disappears as they tell their story to policeman Larkin (Raymond Hatton). With no one believing their story, the kids kill the creatures themselves . . . dissolving the beasts with their hot-rod headlights.

PRODUCERS: James H. Nicholson, Robert Gurney, Jr. DIRECTOR: Edward Cahn. SCREENPLAY: Gurney and Al Martin, from the story "The Cosmic Frame," by Paul Fairmen. MAKEUP: Carlie Taylor, Paul Blaisdell. SPECIAL

American International Pictures

Invasion of the Saucer Men

EFFECTS: Blaisdell, Howard A. Anderson. MUSIC: Ronald Stein.

INVASION OF THE STAR CREATURES

AIP (1962). B/w, 81 mins.

The death of vaudeville is replayed in this slapstick excursion into sf. Two idiots, Philbrick and Penn (Bob Ball and Frankie Ray), are on army maneuvers when they are captured by two beautiful female aliens (Gloria Victor and Dolores Reed). The long-legged warriors are out to conquer the world with the aid of their vegetable creatures, leotard-wearing salad-men. The women fall for the Earth screwballs and all is right with the world.

PRODUCER: Merj Hagopian. DIRECTOR: Bruno De Soto. SCREENPLAY: Jonathan Haze. ELECTRONIC MUSIC: Jack Cookerly, Elliot Fisher. MAKEUP: Joseph Kinder.

INVASION OF THE ZOMBIES

Azteca (Mexico, 1961). B/w, 85 mins.

Masked Mexican wrestler Santo battles a mad scientist who is trying to conquer the world with an army of zombies.

PRODUCER: Fernando Oses. DIRECTOR AND SCREENWRITER: Benito Alzraki. CINEMATOGRAPHY: Jose O. Ramos. MUSIC: Raul Lavista.

CAST: Santo, Lorena Valezquez, Armando Silvestre, Jaime Fernandez.

THE INVENTORS

Educational (G.B., 1934). B/w short, two reels.

Two scientists create a Frankenstein's monster out of old car parts.

PRODUCER: Al Christie. STORY: William Watson, Sig Herzig.
CAST: Chase Taylor, Budd Hulick.

THE INVENTOR'S SECRET
Cines (Italy, 1911). B/w silent short, 2,100 ft.
A scientist develops a superexplosive.

INVISIBILITY
Hepworth (G.B., 1909). B/w silent short, 650 ft.
A man buys a vial of magic powder that makes him invisible.
DIRECTORS: Cecil Hepworth, Lewin Fitzhamon.
CAST: Lewin Fitzhamon.

INVISIBLE AGENT
Universal (1942). B/w, 81 mins.
Good fun in this sf-espionage thriller. When the prized invisibility formula falls into the hands of original Invisible Man's descendent Frank Griffin (Jon Hall) during the embryonic years of World War II, he finds himself the object of some very unwanted attention. Peter Lorre and Sir Cedric Hardwicke portray rival Axis spies out to get the formula. Ilona Massey is Griffin's loyal flame.
PRODUCER: Frank Lloyd. DIRECTOR: Edwin L. Marin. SCREENPLAY: CURT SIODMAK. CINEMATOGRAPHY: Lester White. SPECIAL EFFECTS: John P. Fulton. MUSICAL DIRECTOR: Charles Previn.
SUPPORTING PLAYERS: John Litel, Holmes Herbert, Keye Luke.

INVISIBLE BOY, THE
MGM (1957). B/w, 89 mins.
FORBIDDEN PLANET's cinema sensation, Robby the Robot, was called back to active duty in this pleasant juvenile adventure. Robby is the playmate of a scientist's son (Richard Eyer) and helps the scientist in his experiments. A master computer, however, sees a better function for Robby. When the computer goes haywire and decides to take over the world, he uses Robby as a mechanical zombie, sending him out on search-and-destroy missions. Robby's loyal playmate devises a way to make himself invisible and regain Robby's free will from the nasty machine.
PRODUCER: Nicholas Nayfack. DIREC-

MGM

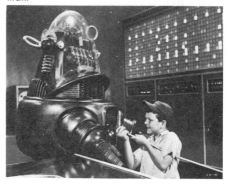

The Invisible Boy

TOR: Herman Hoffman. SCREENPLAY: Cyril Hume, from story by EDMUND COOPER. CINEMATOGRAPHY: Harold Wellman. SPECIAL EFFECTS: Jack Rabin, Irving Block, Louis DeWitt. MUSIC: Lex Baxter.
SUPPORTING PLAYERS: Philip Abbott, Diane Brewster, Harold J. Stone.

INVISIBLE FLUID, THE
Biograph (1908). B/w silent short, 662 ft.
A fluid sprayed on any person or object renders the subject temporarily invisible.

INVISIBLE INVADERS, THE
UA (1959). B/w, 67 mins.
The greatgranddaddy of NIGHT OF THE LIVING DEAD, this sf chiller is effective in its own right. Unseen alien forces bring the dead back to life, sending them on a murderous spree throughout the world. The more people they kill, the more cadavers the creatures have for their army. Major Bruce Jay (John Agar), Dr. Karol Noymann (John Carradine), and Phyllis Penner (Jean Byron) fight the alien spirits with ultra-high-frequency sound. When attacked by the white noise, the possessed corpses convulse and send the alien spirits zipping off into space.
PRODUCER: Robert E. Kent. DIRECTOR: Edward L. Cahn. SCREENPLAY: Samuel Newman. MAKEUP: Phil Scheer. SPECIAL EFFECTS: Roger George.
SUPPORTING PLAYERS: Paul Langton, Eden Hartford, Robert Hutton.

INVISIBLE MAN, THE
Universal (1933). B/w, 71 mins.

A truly splendid adaptation of the H. G. WELLS novel, boasting a fine script, whimsical direction, and overpowering acting, especially by Claude Rains in the title role. Making Rains's portrayal even more amazing is the fact that as the title character, he is required for the bulk of the picture to get his message and character across using only his voice.

Jack Griffin (Rains) is a chemist-assistant of genius Dr. Cranley. When Griffin disappears suddenly, both the doctor and his daughter, Griffin's fiancée, Flora (Gloria Stuart), are alarmed. Griffin's associate, Kemp (William Harrigan), suspects that the disappearance has something to do with the experiments Griffin has been working on.

Griffin, it seems, has been exploring the effects of a new drug called monocane. The drug successfully bleaches the tissues of animals into complete transparency but, as a side effect, drives them completely mad. Griffin tries out the drug on himself, turning his body invisible. Realizing that with invisibility comes power, he seeks to find an antidote that will allow him to appear and disappear at will.

Swathed in bandages, he enters the town of Ipping to work in private. His bandages make him the center of attention, however, and soon he finds himself running through the streets in his invisible form. Madness slowly takes control of his once-logical mind, and bent on world domination, he begins to terrorize the town. Griffin attempts to ensnare Kemp in his plan of conquest, and when the captured scientist attempts to contact Dr. Cranley and inform him of Griffin's fate, he is murdered by the Invisible Man. Finally local police track down the transparent terror by following his footprints in freshly fallen snow. They shoot in the general area the footprints lead to and fatally wound the maddened doctor. As the blood flows from Griffin's wounds onto the white ground beneath his body, Griffin becomes visible again. He has found his cure . . . too late.

Universal

The Invisible Man

A genre triumph in every respect.
PRODUCER: Carl Laemmle, Jr. DIRECTOR: James Whale. SCREENPLAY: R. C. Sherriff, from the novel by H. G. Wells. CINEMATOGRAPHY: Art Edeson. ADDITIONAL CINEMATOGRAPHY AND MINIATURE CINEMATOGRAPHY: John Mescall. SPECIAL EFFECTS: John P. Fulton.

SUPPORTING PLAYERS: Hendry Travers, Una O'Connor, Holmes Herbert, E. E. Clive, Dwight Frye, John Carradine, Walter Brennan.

INVISIBLE MAN RETURNS, THE
Universal (1940). B/w, 81 mins.

Geoffry Radcliff (Vincent Price) is an innocent man accused of killing his brother. Turned invisible by sympathetic Dr. Frank Griffin, brother of the original invisible man, Radcliff goes out in search of the real killers. The only problem: finding and apprehending the killers before the invisibility drug, monocane, causes Radcliff to go mad. Finding the real killer in a coal mine, Radcliff is shot by the police. Luck, however, intervenes, and the killer is fatally wounded in a mining-car accident. He confesses his crime with his dying breath and Radcliff is taken to a hospital, where a blood transfusion from his true love (Nan Grey) causes him to regain his visibility.

DIRECTOR: Joe May. SCREENPLAY: CURT SIODMAK and Lester Cole, from a story by May and Siodmak. CINEMATOGRAPHY: Milton Krasner. SPECIAL EFFECTS: John P. Fulton. MUSIC: H. J. Salter.

SUPPORTING PLAYERS: Sir Cedric Hardwicke, John Sutton, Cecil Kellaway, Alan Napier.

INVISIBLE MAN'S REVENGE, THE
Universal (1944). B/w, 78 mins.

Abandon all logic ye who enter this sequel. A crazed convict (Jon Hall, badly miscast) forces a scientist (John Carradine) to make him invisible so he can seek revenge on all those who sent him to prison.

PRODUCER AND DIRECTOR: Ford Beebe. SCREENPLAY: Bertram Millhauser. CINEMATOGRAPHY: Milton Krasner. SPECIAL EFFECTS: John P. Fulton. MUSIC: H. J. Salter.

SUPPORTING PLAYERS: Gale Sondergaard, Lester Matthews, Leon Errol, Evelyn Ankers, Ian Wolfe.

INVISIBLE MONSTER, THE
Known in feature form as SLAVES OF THE INVISIBLE MONSTER (1966; 100 minutes).
Republic (1950). B/w serial, 12 chapters (24 reels).

The Phantom Ruler (Stanley Price) gets his hands on a chemical that, when sprinkled on his clothes and spotlighted by a special ray, turns him invisible. He begins a series of bank robberies. Enter insurance-company investigators Lane Carson (Richard Webb) and Carol Richards (Aline Towne).

Finally, after a series of hair-raising encounters, the Phantom realizes that he must fly the proverbial coop or be captured. He plans to electrocute his henchman. When the forces of Good drop into his lair at a most inopportune time, the Phantom botches his execution plans and steps on a live wire himself. Premature Afro time.

DIRECTOR: Fred Brannon. SCREENPLAY: Donald Davidson. CINEMATOGRAPHY: Ellis W. Carter. SPECIAL EFFECTS: Howard and Theodore Lydecker. MUSIC: Stanley Wilson.

SUPPORTING PLAYERS: John Crawford, Dale Van Sickel, Tom Steele, Eddie Parker.

INVISIBLE RAY, THE
Forham Amusement Corp. (1920). B/w silent serial, 15 chapters (31 reels).

An atomic ray falls into the wrong hands. Don't they always?

PRODUCER: Jesse J. Goldburg. DIRECTOR: Harry A. Pollard. SCREENPLAY: Guy McConnell.

CAST: Ruth Clifford, Jack Sherrill, Edward Davis.

INVISIBLE RAY, THE
Universal (G.B., 1935; U.S. 1936). B/w, 82 mins. (G.B.) or 72 mins. (U.S.).

When a strange meteor crash-lands in Africa, scientist Janos Rukh (Boris Karloff) attempts to get wealthy colleague Dr. Benet to support an expedition to retrieve it. Rukh winds up going alone. He finds the glowing space rock. It is filled with a miraculous substance called Radium X. Rukh accidentally touches the rock and is contaminated by the lethal energy-source. His touch becomes lethal. Using a temporary antidote, he begins to work on Radium X experiments.

Benet finances Rukh's experiments and when the wealthy scientist presents Rukh's findings to the Scientific Congress, Janos feels as if he's been betrayed. Seeking revenge, he stalks Benet and his colleagues, touching his victims with his horrific hands. His

Universal

The Invisible Ray

mother (Violet Kemble Cooper) discovers her son's murderous activities and smashes the temporary antidote that keeps him alive. Without the elixir, Radium X's poison spreads throughout Rukh's body and turns him into vapor.

PRODUCER: Edmund Grainger. DIRECTOR: Lambert Hillyer. SCREENPLAY: John Colton, from a story by Howard Higgins and Douglas Hodges. MUSICAL DIRECTOR: Franz Waxman. SPECIAL EFFECTS: John P. Fulton.

SUPPORTING PLAYERS: Frances Drake, Frank Lawton, Walter Kingsford.

INVISIBLE THIEF, THE
Pathé (France, 1905; U.S., 1909). B/w silent short, 377 ft.

An invisible thief spends several minutes playing pranks on unsuspecting citizens.

Wishing Wells
The thing I love most about the movie is that I didn't have to do anything to make my point. I just had to put Victorian H. G. Wells in front of a 1980 television set and let him watch!
Nicholas Meyer, director of *Time After Time*

DIRECTORS: Gaston Velle, Gabriel Moreau.
CAST: Charles Lepire.

IRON CLAW, THE
Pathé (1916). B/w silent serial, 20 chapters (40 reels).

A villain builds a ray gun that sets buildings on fire. A strange virus causes the villain to age and die during the film's finale.

DIRECTOR: Edward Jose. SCREENPLAY: George Brackett Seitz.

CAST: Pearl White, Creighton Hale, Sheldon Lewis.

ISLAND OF DR. MOREAU, THE
AIP (1977). Color, 98 mins.

Big-budget, fairly inept remake of THE ISLAND OF LOST SOULS (1933), a film based, in turn, on the H. G. WELLS novel, *The Island of Dr. Moreau*. Shipwrecked Braddock (Michael York) lands on the island of Dr. Moreau (Burt Lancaster), who is a scientist dedicated to surgically transforming animals into humans and (in this version), vice-versa. Moreau attempts to pair off Braddock with panther-girl Maria (Barbara Carrera), and later, starts transforming snoopy Braddock into an animal. Before he gets too far, his humanimals revolt, kill him, and go berserk. Maria and Braddock escape.

PRODUCERS: Skip Steloff, John Temple-Smith. DIRECTOR: Don Taylor. SCREENPLAY: John Shaner, Al Ramrus. MAKEUP: John Chambers, Don Striepeke, Tom Burman, Ed Butterworth, Walter Schenck.

SUPPORTING PLAYERS: Nigel Davenport as Montgomery, Richard Basehart as the Sayer of the Laws, Nick Cravat as M'Ling, John L. as the Boarman, Bob Ozman as the Bullman, Fumio Demura as Hyenaman, Gary Baxley as Lionman, John Gillespie as Tigerman, David Cass as Bearman.

ISLAND OF LOST SOULS, THE
Paramount (1933). B/w, 72 mins.

A masterpiece of menace and mood, this adaptation of the H. G. WELLS novel *The Island of Dr. Moreau* boasted several fine (albeit demented) performances, including those of Charles Laughton and Bela Lugosi.

A pair of shipwrecked seafarers, Edward Parker (Richard Arlen) and his fiancée Ruth Walker (Leila Hyams), find themselves on a strange tropical island populated by even stranger-looking natives and run by suave but seedy Dr. Moreau (Charles Laughton). Moreau is a surgeon who has fled London for the South Seas after incurring the wrath of his colleagues via a series of experiments involving the improvement of animal intellect through vivisection.

On his private island, Moreau experiments in his self-proclaimed House of Pain, pushing animals through the evolutionary process surgically—in essence, turning animals into shambling human "things." His most successful operation, Lota (Kathleen Burke), a panther-girl, is in need of a human mate. Ergo, Moreau is quite delighted to meet Mr. Parker.

Paramount

The Island of Lost Souls

Moreau's marriage plans are premature. A rescue party shows up. Forgetting the laws he has set down for his animal men ("Not to spill blood . . . that is the law, are we not men?"), Moreau orders one of his citizens to kill the captain of the expedition. With that deed done, the Sayer of the Law (Bela Lugosi) declares the "law . . . no more!" and leads the beast people in a revolt.

Edward and Ruth escape with their lives. Unlucky Lota is brutally attacked and killed by a beast-man. Moreau is taken into the House of Pain and operated on—for a seemingly eternal time—by his taloned-beast creatures.

DIRECTOR: Erle C. Kenton. SCREENPLAY: Waldemar Young and PHILIP WYLIE, based on the novel *The Island of Dr. Moreau*, by H. G. Wells. MAKE-UP: Wally Westmore. CINEMATOGRAPHY: Karl Struss.

SUPPORTING PLAYERS: Alan Ladd, George Irving, Tetsu Komai.

ISLAND OF LOST WOMEN
WB (1959). B/w, 66 mins.

A group of explorers lands on an island populated by a race of Amazons bred by a scientist with the help of his daughters. When not teaching them primitive warring techniques, the scientist lets them fondle his death rays.

PRODUCER: Albert J. Cohen. DIRECTOR: Frank W. Tuttle. SCREENPLAY: Ray Buffum. CINEMATOGRAPHY: John Seitz. MUSIC: Raoul Kraushaar.

CAST: Alan Napier, Gavin Muir, Venetia Stevenson, Diane Jergens, June Blair.

ISLAND OF TERROR
Universal (1967). Color, 89 mins.

Science goes awry on a small British island, with horrific results. A local physician working on a cancer cure involving bone tissue accidentally creates a horde of tentacled, silicate creatures that attach themselves to human beings and drain off the bone marrow. When a body minus its marrow washes ashore on the mainland, scientists Dr. Stanley (Peter Cushing), Dr. David West (Edward Judd), Dr. Landers (Eddie Byrne), and West's fiancée Connie (Carol Gray) investigate. The silicates soon make their presence felt and attack the human populace in numerous incidents.

The creatures can't be shot. Explosives only cause the splinter pieces to form new monsters. They seem unstoppable. Stanley is caught by one and is forced to chop off his own hand rather than have his entire body drained of marrow. Finally, the townspeople are herded into a small hall. The hall is then surrounded by strontium 90–infected cattle. The silicates eat the infected meat and are poisoned. Close one.

PRODUCER: Tom Blakeley. DIRECTOR: Terence Fisher. SCREENPLAY: Alan Ramsen, Edward Andrew Mann. ART DIRECTION AND SPECIAL EFFECTS: John St. John Earl. CINEMATOGRAPHY: Reg Wyer. MUSIC: Malcolm Lockyer.

SUPPORTING PLAYERS: Sam Kydd, Niall MacGinnis, Roger Heathcote.

ISLAND OF THE BURNING DAMNED
Also known as NIGHT OF THE BIG HEAT.
Planet (G.B., 1967). Color, 94 mins.

A small British island is attacked during the dead of winter by amorphous alien creatures who raise the temperature of the countryside to tropical levels. They burn people alive in an attempt to control the region.

PRODUCER: Tom Blakeley. DIRECTOR: Terence Fisher. SCREENPLAY: Ronald Liles, Pip and Jane Baker, from the novel by John Lymington. CINEMATOGRAPHY: Reg Wyer. MUSIC: Malcolm Lockyer.

CAST: Christopher Lee, Peter Cushing, Patrick Allen, Sarah Lawson, Percy Herbert.

ISLAND OF THE DOOMED
Orbital/Theumer (Spain/W. Germany, 1966); AA (U.S., 1968). Color, 88 mins.

A crazed scientist on a tropical island has devoted his life to the creation of a vampire tree. The tree, constantly seeking new blood, wraps its long, tendril-like branches around its victims and drains them of their fluid. Some people raise gerbils.

PRODUCER: George Ferrer. DIRECTOR: Mel Welles. SCREENPLAY: Stephen Schmidt, from a story by Ira Meltcher and F. V. Theumer. CINEMATOGRAPHY: Cecilio Paniagua. MUSIC: Anton Garcia Abril.

CAST: Cameron Mitchell, Elisa Montes, Kay Fischer, Ralph Naukoff.

IT CAME FROM BENEATH THE SEA
Columbia (1955). B/w, 77 mins.

Astounding stop-motion animation by Ray Harryhausen makes this atomic-monster-on-the-loose tale very enjoyable indeed. Two scientists (Faith Domergue and Donald Curtis) join forces with a navy man (Kenneth Tobey) to battle a gigantic atomic mutant spotted off the coast of San Francisco . . . a King Kong–sized octopus. The main thrust of the movie concerns the amazing amount of destruction wreaked by the sadistic squid.

PRODUCER: Charles H. Schneer. DIRECTOR: Robert Gordon. SCREENPLAY:

Columbia Pictures

It Came from Beneath the Sea

George Worthing Yates and Hal Smith, from a story by Yates. CINEMATOGRAPHY: Henry Freulich. SPECIAL EFFECTS: Ray Harryhausen and Jack Erickson. MUSICAL DIRECTOR: Mischa Bakaleinikoff.

SUPPORTING PLAYERS: Ian Keither, Dean Maddox, Jr., Del Courtney.

IT CAME FROM OUTER SPACE
Universal (1953). B/w and 3-D, 80 mins.

Based on "The Meteor," a story by a young RAY BRADBURY, this 3-D fantasy was the first sf film to be directed by Jack (THE INCREDIBLE SHRINKING MAN, THE MOUSE THAT ROARED) Arnold.

Astronomer John Putnam (Richard Carlson) sees an alien meteor/spaceship crash on Earth. No one will believe his story. The unseen alien travelers begin kidnapping local townspeople and substituting doubles in their places. Is this some sort of alien invasion? No. The aliens are borrowing human forms because their spaceship is in need of repairs and only humans can collect the needed parts. Even Putnam's girl friend, Ellen (Barbara Rush), is put to work by the aliens. By the film's finale, Putnam is caught in the middle, trying to keep angry townspeople away from the alien ship, which is trying desperately to make it back home.

PRODUCER: William Alland. DIRECTOR: Jack Arnold. SCREENPLAY: Harry Essex. MAKEUP: Bud Westmore. MUSIC: Herman Stein.

SUPPORTING PLAYERS: Morey Amsterdam, Joe Sawyer, Kathleen Hughes, Charles Drake.

IT CONQUERED THE WORLD
AIP (1956). B/w, 71 mins.

Nasty Earthman Tom Anderson (Lee Van Cleef) aids a cucumber-creature from Venus (Paul Blaisdell) in its plan to take over the Earth via a fleet of tiny winged things (electronic bats of a sort), whose mission it is to bite and conquer. Neighbor Paul Nelson (Peter Graves) is not too keen on the plan after Mrs. Nelson (Sally Fraser) is made an alien zombie. Grabbing a rifle, he blows her across the room in a style of shooting later to become popular in Italian Westerns.

Old Tom has second thoughts himself when his own wife, Claire (Beverly Garland), is given a thorough throttling by the Venusian vegetable. He attacks the creature with a blowtorch, losing both his life and his credibility as a movie villain.

PRODUCER AND DIRECTOR: Roger Corman. SCREENPLAY: Lou Rusoff. MUSIC: Ronald Stein. SPECIAL EFFECTS: Paul Blaisdell.

IT HAPPENS EVERY SPRING
20th Cent.-Fox (1949). B/w, 87 mins.

A screwball scientist (Ray Milland) comes up with a formula that makes baseballs dodge contact with wood. He becomes a famous big-league pitcher.

PRODUCER: William Perlberg. DIRECTOR: Lloyd Bacon. SCREENPLAY: Valentine Davis, from a story by Davis and Shirley W. Smith. CINEMATOGRAPHY: Joe MacDonald. SPECIAL EFFECTS: Fred Sersen. MUSIC: Leigh Harline.

SUPPORTING PLAYERS: Jean Peters, Paul Douglas, Ed Begley, Alan Hale, Jr., Gene Evans.

IT'S GOOD TO BE ALIVE
20th Cent.-Fox (1933). B/w, 69 mins.

A remake of the silent film THE LAST MAN ON EARTH, this tale is set in the not-too-distant future, when a plague wipes out the male population. Ruled by a matriarchy, the world is tossed into a tizzy when one lone adult male specimen is found alive and very well indeed.

DIRECTOR: Alfred Werker. SCREENPLAY: Paul Perez, Arthur Kober.

CAST: Paul Roulien, Gloria Stuart, Edna May Oliver, Edward Van Sloan.

IT! THE TERROR FROM BEYOND SPACE
UA (1958). B/w, 69 mins.

Before ALIEN, there was *It!;* a movie that not only has a remarkably similar plot, but, overall, is a much more enjoyable offering. A rocket from Earth picks up the only survivor of a Martian expedition, Carruthers (Marshall Thompson). He is accused of murdering his fellow crew members. He protests his innocence to his new space

It! The Terror from Beyond Space

peers (Shawn Smith, Paul Langton, Ann Doran, Kim Spaulding, Dabbs Greer), stating that some *thing* was the murderer.

Meanwhile, the killer creature has stowed away on the ship. It (Ray "Crash" Corrigan) begins roaming the vessel, killing the crew members one by one. Eventually the Earth party realizes what's going on. There's a vampire thing onboard, draining its human victims of their life's-blood. They try to seal off the creature in the bottom section of the ship, but it begins its final attack regardless, breaking through section by section by section. The humans find themselves waiting on the bridge . . . about to take part in the final showdown. (Hint: the ending is also very similar to *Alien*'s.)

PRODUCER: Robert E. Kent. DIRECTOR: Edward L. Cahn. SCREENPLAY: Jerome Bixby. MUSIC: Paul Sawtell. MAKEUP: Lane Britton. *It* DESIGN: Paul Blaisdell.

I WAS A TEENAGE FRANKENSTEIN
AIP (1957). B/w with color sequences, 74 mins.

Dr. Frankenstein's latest descendant (Whit Bissell) creates a teenage monster with a face that looks like a "before" shot from an advanced-acne ad.

Seeking to beautify his creature, he sends the oaf out headhunting. Returning with a handsome (but decapitated) face in a blood-soaked birdcage, the monster (Gary Conway) is given a new, improved lease on life. The creature proves that beauty is only skin deep, however, and bites the hand that feeds it . . . literally. The doctor and the monster perish in a fiery finale.

PRODUCER: Herman Cohen. DIRECTOR: Herbert Strock. STORY AND SCREENPLAY: Kenneth Langtry. MAKE-UP: Philip Scheer. CINEMATOGRAPHY: Lothrop Worth. MUSIC: Paul Dunlap.

SUPPORTING PLAYERS: Phyllis Coates, Robert Burton, John Cliff.

I WAS A TEENAGE WEREWOLF
AIP (1957). B/w, 76 mins.

A juvenile delinquent (Michael Landon) tries to reform for his widower dad's sake. Unfortunately, the high-school psychiatrist out to treat the boy is not quite playing with your proverbial full deck. The loony scientist hypnotizes the boy into a primitive state. The kid turns into a werewolf whenever a school bell goes off. It's hell at recess.

PRODUCER: Herman Cohen. DIRECTOR: Gene Fowler, Jr. SCREENPLAY: Ralph Thornton. CINEMATOGRAPHY: Joseph La Shelle. MUSIC: Paul Dunlap.

SUPPORTING PLAYERS: Yvonne Lime, Whit Bissell, Guy Williams, Eddie Marr.

JACK ARMSTRONG
Columbia (1947). B/w serial, 15 chapters (31 reels).

Jim Fairfield (Pierre Watkin) is fairly disturbed to find out from scientist Vic Hardy (Hugh Prosser) that cosmic radioactivity is being experimented with by nasty people outside the U.S. of A. As shocked as Uncle Jim may be, his reaction is nothing compared with the total revulsion the news brings to his nephew Billy (Joe Brown), his niece Betty (Rosemary La Planche), and their all-American buddy Jack Armstrong (John Hart). The threesome decide to investigate the matter on their own, thus circumventing the boggling paperwork experienced by legal law enforcement agents.

When Hardy is kidnapped by enemy agents, the threesome, plus Uncle Jim, hunt the kidnappers down, tracing them to an enchanted island. There, villainous scientist Grood (Charles Middleton) is planning to construct the ultimate death ray. There are endless struggles. Hardy is rescued. Grood is tossed a hot hand-grenade by all-American (but definitely not compassionate) Jack Armstrong.

PRODUCER: Sam Katzman. DIRECTOR: Wallace Fox. SCREENPLAY: Arthur Hoerl, Lewis Clay, Royal K. Cole, Leslie Swabacker. CINEMATOGRAPHY: Ira H. Morgan. MUSIC: Lee Zahler.

SUPPORTING PLAYERS: Claire James, Wheeler Oakman, Eddie Parker, Hugh Prosser, Jack Ingram.

JESSE JAMES MEETS FRANKENSTEIN'S DAUGHTER
Embassy (1966). Color, 82 mins.

How the West was lost. Jesse James (John Lupton) is forced to hole up in a mansion owned by Maria Frankenstein (Narda Onyx) and her brother, Rudolph (Steven Geray), when outlaw pal Hank (Cal Bolder) is wounded. Maria promises to patch up Hank while secretly lusting after Jesse. Jesse, however, is lusting in a not-too-secret manner after servant girl Juanita (Estellita). To make a long story mercifully short, jilted Ms. F. decides to get even with Jesse. Doing a quick brain-job on Hank, she stitches up his skull to resemble a relief map of Peru, rechristens him Igor, and sends him off on a killing spree. When Hank or Igor or the name-of-your-choice is commanded to kill Jesse, unexpected help arrives in the presence of the sheriff (Jim Davis) who, stifling his embarrassment, kills the monster—presumably before going home and killing his agent.

PRODUCER: Carroll Case. DIRECTOR: William Beaudine. SCREENPLAY: Carl Hittleman. CINEMATOGRAPHY: Lothrop Worth. MUSIC: Raoul Kraushaar.

JE T'AIME, JE T'AIME

France (1968); Color/scope, 94 mins. 20th Cent.-Fox (U.S., 1973); color, 82 mins.

A scientist is sent back through time for a period of one year. His emotions, strongly rooted in the present, cause him to oscillate.

PRODUCER: Mag Bodard. DIRECTOR: Alain Renais. SCREENPLAY: Renais, Jacques Sternberg. CINEMATOGRAPHY: Jean Boffety. MUSIC: Krzystof Penderecki.

CAST: Claude Rich, Olga Georges-Picot, Annie Fargue.

JOURNEY BENEATH THE DESERT

France/Italy (1961); Embassy (U.S., 1961). Color, 89 mins.

Originally to have been called *Atlantis*, this film is based on the novel *Atlantida*, by Pierre Benoit. After a helicopter makes an emergency landing near an atomic-test site, its occupants stumble upon the lost city of Atlantis. Nestled beneath the Earth's core, the city remains untouched and unharmed. When the new civilization meets the old, however, sparks fly . . . literally.

EXECUTIVE PRODUCER: Nat Wachberger. DIRECTORS: Edgar G. Ulmer, Giuseppe Masini. SCREENPLAY: Ugo Liberatore, Remigio del Grosso, André Tabet, Amedeo Nazzari. PRODUCTION DESIGN: Edgar G. Ulmer. CINEMATOGRAPHY: Enzo Serafin. SPECIAL EFFECTS: Giovanni Ventimiglia. MUSIC: Carlo Rustichelli.

CAST: Jean-Louis Trintignant, Georges Rivière, Rad Fulton, Haya Harareet.

JOURNEY TO THE BEGINNING OF TIME

Czechoslovakia (1954); color, 93 mins. New Trends (U.S., 1967); color, 87 mins.

Four boys take a raft journey down the river of time and visit the Earth during its prehistoric era. En route, they encounter various lush, tropical settings, and a horde of stop-motion animated dinosaurs and beasts of every size and shape.

DIRECTOR: Karel Zeman. SCREENPLAY: Zeman, J. A. Novotny. ART DIRECTOR: Zeman, Adenek Rozopal, Ivo

Mrdzek. CINEMATOGRAPHY: Vaclav Pazdernik, Antonin Horak. MUSIC: E. F. Burian. PRODUCER, DIRECTOR, AND SCREENPLAY OF ENGLISH-LANGUAGE VERSION: William Cayton.

CAST: James Lucas, Victor Betral, Peter Hermann, Charles Goldsmith.

JOURNEY TO THE CENTER OF THE EARTH

20th Cent.-Fox (1959). Color/scope, 132 mins.

A colorful, at times juvenile, adaptation of the classic JULES VERNE novel. At the turn of the century, Professor Lindenbrooke (James Mason), student Alec McEwen (Pat Boone), friend Carla (Arlene Dahl), and the latter's servant Hans (Peter Ronson) embark on an expedition down a mountain cave to the center of the Earth. The professor is put onto the existence of a subterranean world after translating the markings made on a piece of volcanic rock by long-lost explorer Arne Saknussemm. Unknown to the intrepid band of explorers, nasty Count Saknussemm (Thayer David), Arne's only living relative, is on their trail, attempting to ruin their expedition and make the extraordinary find himself. An ambush attempt on the count's part fails, and he is captured and held prisoner by the foursome.

The party reaches the center of the Earth and, after passing through a forest of gigantic mushrooms, is attacked by dinosaurs, pursued by a gigantic avalanche, caught in a whirlpool and tossed onto the remains of Atlantis, and, finally, blasted topside by a volcanic eruption.

PRODUCER: Charles Brackett. DIRECTOR: Henry Levin. SCREENPLAY: Walter Reisch and Brackett, based on the novel by Jules Verne. ART DIRECTORS: Franz Bachelin, Herman A. Blumenthal. SPECIAL EFFECTS: Lyle B. Abbott, James B. Gordon, Emil Kosa, Jr. MUSIC: Bernard Herrmann.

SUPPORTING PLAYERS: Alan Napier, Diane Baker, Alan Caillou.

JOURNEY TO THE CENTER OF TIME

Borealis-Dorad (1968). Color, 82 mins.

Sort of a low-budget version of the not-so-high-budgeted THE TIME TRAV-

ELERS, this tale of time-traveling woe mixes mutants with prehistoric monsters. Scientists working on a time machine rush the project in order to achieve positive results before their funding is cut off. Journeying to the year 6968, they encounter a superscientific world in which the civilized citizens are at war with bad-tempered mutants (seemingly the only type in these films). A defect in the machine yanks them out of mutantland and tosses them into jungleland, a prehistoric time period populated by dinosaurs and fairly large ferns. Attempting to reach their own time period, they find themselves caught in a revolving time zone.

PRODUCERS: Ray Dorn, David L. Hewitt, DIRECTOR: Hewitt. SCREENPLAY: David Prentiss. CINEMATOGRAPHY: Robert Caramico. SPECIAL EFFECTS: Modern Film Effects.

CAST: Scott Brady, Gigi Perreau, Anthony Eisley, Lyle Waggoner, Abraham Sofaer.

JOURNEY TO THE FAR SIDE OF THE SUN
Also known as DOPPELGANGER.
Century 21 (G.B., 1969); Technicolor, 104 mins. Universal (U.S., 1969); Technicolor, 94 mins.

"We have met the aliens and they is us," might be an ad campaign suitable for this thought-provoking sf film. Concocted by Gerry and Sylvia Anderson (of TV's SPACE: 1999 fame), the story concerns the flight of two Earth astronauts sent off to investigate a newfound planet with an orbit identical to that of Earth's but located on the opposite side of the sun, hidden from Earth's viewpoint. Something goes wrong with the explorer ship's engines and it crashlands back on Earth. Survivor Col. Glenn Ross (Roy Thinnes) is picked up and questioned by his superiors. Why was the flight aborted? What caused the crash?

Ross is stunned. According to his instruments he hasn't crashed back on his home planet but on the alien world behind the sun. Yet everything and everybody from Earth stands before him. Ross's supervisors, Dr. Hassler (Herbert Lom) and John Kane (Ian Hendry), suspect the astronaut of sabotage. Meanwhile, Ross comes to the con-

Universal

Journey to the Far Side of the Sun

clusion that he is indeed on the alien world he was sent out to investigate. Everything on this Earth is reversed, a mirror image of what he has seen in his past. What was *left* before his trip is now *right*. The alien world behind the sun is an exact reflection of Earth! The alien planet's Col. Ross simultaneously encounters the same difficulties on the *real* Earth.

PRODUCERS: Gerry and Sylvia Anderson. DIRECTOR: Robert Parrish. SCREENPLAY: Gerry and Sylvia Anderson, with Donald James. MUSIC: Barry Gray. SPECIAL EFFECTS: Derek Meddings and Harry Oakes.

SUPPORTING PLAYERS: Lynn Loring, Patrick Wymark.

JOURNEY TO THE SEVENTH PLANET
AIP (1962). Color and Cinemagic, 83 mins.

An ambitious idea filmed in a haphazard manner becomes ideal kiddie fare in this space swashbuckler. Astronauts Don (John Agar) and Greta (Greta Thyssen) don't get much of a chance for romance when, with three spacefaring buddies, they land on a planet ruled by an invisible alien presence that plays with men's minds with gleeful abandon. The life-force takes bits and pieces of memories and imagination and transforms them into reality . . . or so it seems. The astronauts are beset by beautiful women, phantom cities, and assorted creatures (with one cyclopean rat-thing animated by master craftsman Jim Danforth). The alien intelligence is finally unmasked, so to speak, and revealed as a gigantic, one-eyed brain.

Do the Bunny Hop
   I don't want to alarm you folks, but there's a herd of killer rabbits on the way here.
                   Sheriff Stuart Whitman to
                   his fellow citizens in *Night
                   of the Lepus*

PRODUCER AND DIRECTOR: Sidney Pink. SCREENPLAY: Sidney Pink and Ib Melchior, from a story by Pink. MUSIC: Ib Glindeman. SPECIAL EFFECTS: Bent Barfod Films.
   SUPPORTING PLAYERS: Mimi Heinrich, Ove Sprogoe, Carl Ottosen.

JUNGLE CAPTIVE
Universal (1945). B/w, 64 mins.
   Otto Kruger is your local mad-doctor-alive-and-well-in-Africa and Rondo (the Creeper) Hatton his sullen assistant in this tale of science gone astray. Messing around with monkeys in their lab, they make an ape into pretty Vicki Lane. As much as pretty Vicki would like to monkey around with hero Robert Shayne, she is hampered by the fact that the effects of the transformation operation are only temporary. What a hairy situation.
   DIRECTOR: Harold Young. SCREENPLAY: M. Coates Webster and Dwight V. Babcock, from a story by Babcock. CINEMATOGRAPHY: Maury Gertsman.
   SUPPORTING PLAYERS: Jerome Cowan, Phil Brown.

JUNGLE WOMAN
Universal (1944). B/w, 54 mins.
   In the grand tradition of JUNGLE CAPTIVE and *Captive Wild Woman* comes Paula Dupree (Acquanetta), the ape-woman killed during *CWW's* finale and now brought back to life again by scientist J. Carrol Naish. Transformed, once again, into a beautiful woman, Paula goes ape and is killed. Tough life, that jungle living.
   PRODUCER: Will Cowan. DIRECTOR:

Reginald LeBorg. STORY: Henry Sucher. CINEMATOGRAPHY: Jack McKenzie.
   SUPPORTING PLAYERS: Evelyn Ankers, Lois Collier, Milburn Stone, Pierre Watkin.

JUNIOR G-MEN
Universal (1940). B/w serial, 12 chapters (24 reels).
   After scientific genius Col. Barton (Russell Hicks) is kidnapped by an anarchist group called the Order of the Flaming Torch, son Billy (Billy Halop) and G-man Jim Bradford (Phillip Terry) investigate. The colonel, the inventor of a deadly new explosive, is being held captive by nasty mob-leader Brand (Cy Kendall), who not only wants the formula for the explosive but is planning to kidnap the inventor of a new aerial torpedo as well. Billy, Jim, and Billy's pals Gyp (Huntz Hall), Terry (Gabe Dell), Lug (Bernard Punsley), and Midge (Roger Daniels) trace Brand to his hideout, rescue Col. Barton, foul up the kidnap attempt, and become junior G-men.
   DIRECTORS: Ford Beebe, John Rawlins. SCREENPLAY: George H. Plympton, Basil Dickey.

JUNIOR G-MEN OF THE AIR
Universal (1942). B/w serial, 12 parts (25 reels).
   Ace Holden (Billy Halop), Bolts Larson (Huntz Hall), Stick Munsey (Gabe Dell), and Greaseball Plunkett (Bernard Punsley) work in Eddie Holden's (Gene Reynolds) auto and airplane junkyard. When a fifth-column group, the Order of the Black Dragonfly, makes the mistake of stealing the boys' wrecking truck, they incur the wrath of the future Dead End Kids.
   The truck is returned by state cop Don Ames (Richard Lane), who is after the leader of the organization, the Baron (Lionel Atwill). The Baron, together with Araka (Turhan Bey), Monk (Noel Cravat), Beal (John Bleifer), and Comora (Edward Foster), is planning a sabotage racket using sf gadgetry. Joining forces with junior G-man Jerry Markham (Frank Albertson), the wrecking-crew kids

knock the stuffing out of the Axis meanies.

DIRECTORS: Ray Taylor, Lewis D. Collins. SCREENPLAY: Paul Huston, George H. Plympton, and Griffin Jay. CINEMATOGRAPHY: William S. Sickner.

JUST FOR FUN
Amicus (G.B., 1960); Columbia (U.S., 1963). B/w, 85 mins.

In the not-too-distant future, when teenagers have the vote, loud rock-music reigns supreme.

PRODUCER AND SCREENWRITER: Milton Subotsky. DIRECTOR: Gordon Flemyng. CINEMATOGRAPHY: Nicholas Roeg. MUSIC: Bobby Vee, The Crickets, Freddy Cannon.

CAST: Mark Wynter, Cherry Roland, Richard Vernon, Reginald Beckwith.

JUST IMAGINE
20th Cent.-Fox (1930). B/w, 113 mins.

One of the few sf musical comedies in the annals of moviedom. Single O (El Brendel), a citizen of 1930, falls asleep and awakens in the futuristic land of 1980! There he observes the rivalry between J-21 (John Garrick) and MT-3 (Kenneth Thompson) over the hand of LN-18 (Maureen O'Sullivan). They both petition the government for the right of marriage. The government rules in favor of MT-3, who is, of course, not at all the hero of the film.

J-21 is madly in love with LN-18 and vice-versa. A romantic dictatorship at heart, the government gives love-struck J-21 four months to pull off some astounding stunt capable of reversing the government's decision. J and Single O take off to Mars in a trip designed to make J a bona-fide hero. On the Red Planet they run across a couple of Martians . . . actually, a couple of couples. All Martians are twins, identical except for disposition: one-half of a Martian duo is good, the other is rotten. After a few sprightly numbers on Mars, the team returns to Earth. J is declared a hero and gets to marry LN-18. Only their closest letters are invited to the ceremony.

ASSOCIATE PRODUCERS, STORY ORIGINATORS, AND LYRICISTS: Ray Henderson, B. G. DeSylva, Lew Brown. DIRECTOR: David Butler. SCREENPLAY: Butler, Henderson, DeSylva, Brown. CINEMATOGRAPHY: Ernest Palmer. MUSICAL DIRECTOR: Arthur Kay.

SUPPORTING PLAYERS: Mischa Auer, Ivan Lino, Marjorie White, Hobart Bosworth.

20th Cent.-Fox

Just Imagine

KADOYNG
Shand (G.B., 1972). Color, 60 mins.

A friendly alien (Leo Maguire), equipped with the power of teleportation, comes to Earth and helps a needy family.

PRODUCER: Roy Simpson. DIRECTOR: Ian Shand. SCREENPLAY: Leo Maguire. CINEMATOGRAPHY: Mark McDonald. MUSIC: Edwin Astley.

SUPPORTING PLAYERS: Teresa Codling, Adrian Hall, David Williams, Stephen Bone.

KAISER'S SHADOW, THE
Ince (1918). B/w silent feature, five reels.

German spies attempt to steal ray-gun rifles from the Allies.

PRODUCER: Thomas H. Ince. DIRECTOR: R. William Neill. SCREENPLAY: Octavus Roy Cohen, J. H. Giesy.

CAST: Dorothy Dalton, Thurston Hall, Edward Cecil.

KARATE KILLERS, THE
MGM (1967). Color, 92 mins.

United Network Command for Law and Enforcement (U.N.C.L.E.) agents Napoleon Solo (Robert Vaughn) and Ilya Kuriakin (David McCallum) fend off villains who have come up with a plan to mine gold from seawater and keep peace officers at bay via a squadron of deadly, remote-controlled miniature planes. The agents must do without the benefit of commercial breaks in this stitching together of two episodes from the popular 1960s TV series THE MAN FROM U.N.C.L.E.

PRODUCER AND STORY ORIGINATOR: Boris Ingster. DIRECTOR: Barry Shear. SCREENPLAY: Norman Hudis. CINEMATOGRAPHY: Fred Koenekamp. MUSIC: Gerald Fried. TITLE THEME: Jerry Goldsmith.

SUPPORTING PLAYERS: Leo G. Carroll as Waverly, Curt Jurgens, Joan Crawford, Herbert Lom, Telly Savalas, Terry-Thomas, Diane McBain, Jill Ireland.

KID'S CLEVER, THE
Universal (1929). B/w silent feature, 5,292 ft.

A boy genius invents a car and a boat that can run without the benefit of fuel.

PRODUCER AND DIRECTOR: William James Craft. SCREENPLAY: Jack Foley. CINEMATOGRAPHY: Al Jones.

CAST: Glenn Tryon, Kathryn Crawford, Russell Simpson, George Chandler, Stepin Fetchitt.

KILLER APE
Columbia (1953). Sepia tone, 68 mins.

Jungle Jim has his work cut out for him in this effort. A gigantic ape-creature is running around scaring the bananas out of the local natives. Jim (Johnny Weissmuller) is puzzled. Meanwhile, across the underbrush, mad scientists are developing a serum that robs one of the will to resist. It's a jungle out there, Jim.

PRODUCER: Sam Katzman. DIRECTOR: Spencer G. Bennett. SCREENPLAY: Carroll Young, Arthur Hoerl. CINEMATOGRAPHY: William Whitley. MUSICAL DIRECTOR: Mischa Bakaleinikoff.

SUPPORTING PLAYERS: Nestor Paiva, Carol Thurston, Max Palmer, Ray "Crash" Corrigan.

KILLER LACKS A NAME, THE
Italy (1966); color, 104 mins.

A maniac bent on murder electrifies his steel hand and stalks his victims, electrocuting them with the touch of a finger.

DIRECTOR: Tullio Domichelli.

CAST: Lang Jeffries, Olga Omar, Barbara Nelli.

KILLERS FROM SPACE
RKO (1954). B/w, 71 mins.

Deadly in every way imaginable, this invasion scenario was, unfortunately, fairly typical of sf film fare of the 1950s. A group of pajama-wearing aliens with eyes apparently culled from Arnold Palmer's old golf-ball collection kidnap a human (Peter Graves) and reveal to him how they plan to take over the world. In caverns outside the city limits of a major metropolis they are breeding gigantic atomic mutants. Giant bugs and lizards and creepy-crawly things are projected onto a movie screen in front of the actors. The quick-thinking Earthling overloads their atomic circuitry and pops the pop-eyes into oblivion.

PRODUCER AND DIRECTOR: W. Lee Wilder. SCREENPLAY: Bill Raynor, from a story by Myles Wilder. MUSIC: Manuel Compinsky. SPECIAL EFFECTS: Consolidated Film Industries.

SUPPORTING PLAYERS: James Seay, Barbara Bestar, John Merrick.

KING DINOSAUR
Lippert (1955). B/w, 63 mins.

Producer/director Bert I. Gordon, who would later give the matinee crowd such films as THE AMAZING COLOSSAL MAN and FOOD OF THE GODS, made his film debut with this lower-than-low-budget adventure. A rocket crash-lands on the planet Nova. The crew (Bill Bryant, Wanda Curtis, Doug Henderson, and Patricia Gallagher) immediately run into a few giant lizards, also known as dinosaurs. The tyrannosaurus of the title was, in reality, a magnified gila monster who could, in all fairness, react on cue better than a few of his human counterparts in the film.

PRODUCER AND DIRECTOR: Bert I.

Lippert

King Dinosaur

Gordon. SCREENPLAY: Tom Gries, from a story by Gordon and Al Zimbalist. SPECIAL EFFECTS: Howard A. Anderson. Narrated by Marvin Miller.

KINGDOM OF THE SPIDERS
Dimension Pictures (1977). Eastmancolor, 94 mins.

Pesticides cause a bevy of tarantulas to become warlike in the middle of Arizona. Scientists Rock Hansen and Diane Ashley (William Shatner and Tiffany Bolling) are dispatched to the area to squelch the spiders before they squash the squeamish humans. Lines such as "There are many theories of man's outcome if the insects of the world turn on him. In none does he come out on top!" abound.

PRODUCERS: Igo Kanter, Jeffrey Sneller. DIRECTOR: John "Bud" Cardos. SCREENPLAY: Richard Robinson, Allan Caillou. CINEMATOGRAPHY: John Morrill. SPECIAL EFFECTS: Greg Auer.

SUPPORTING PLAYERS: Woody Strode as Walter Colby, Marcie Rafferty as Terry Hansen, David McLean as Sheriff Smith.

KING KONG
RKO (1933). B/w, 100 mins.

A triumph of special-effects magic, *King Kong* is the ultimate "lost world" adventure film brought to life, largely through the creative genius of stop-motion animator Willis O'Brien.

Moviemaker Carl Denham (Robert Armstrong), a documentary producer who specializes in action-adventure safari films, is told to include a romantic interest in his next film. Using a line as corny as any ever concocted by P. T. Barnum, he gets down-and-out heroine Ann Darrow (Fay Wray) to accompany him on his trip. Using an old map, they are seeking the legendary Skull Island . . . a place where time has stopped.

Onboard the tramp steamer *The Venture*, along with Denham and Darrow, are Jack Driscoll (Bruce Cabot) and Captain Englehorn (Frank Reicher), old-time adventurers with a flair for danger. Jack is smitten with Ann, however, and would rather not have a "girl along."

Meanwhile, Carl reveals the details of Skull Island. On the mysterious landmass is a wall of unknown and ancient origin, revered by the natives. Denham wants to film what's *behind* that wall . . . a Malay superstition called Kong. The crew finally arrives on the island but, after encountering unfriendly natives, heads back for the ship. That night, Ann is kidnapped by the locals and shanghaied back to the island to be offered as a sacrifice for the natives "god."

The crew pursues. In a tribal ritual to end all tribal ritual, Ann is strapped to an altar and taken off by Kong, a skyscraper-sized gorilla. By the time Denham and his men arrive, Kong and Ann are long gone. The party gives chase, encountering numerous prehistoric monsters behind the island's great wall. With most of the crew killed either by dinosaurs or Kong himself (despite their stockpile of lethal gas grenades), only Jack makes it to Kong's lair in time to rescue Ann.

With Kong at his heels, Jack makes it to the gate and the waiting arms of Denham and the captain. Kong crashes through the wall but, after leveling the native village, is overcome by gas grenades. Dollar signs dancing in his head, Denham orders Kong to be sedated and strapped to the ship. He is to be brought back to New York and put on display as the "Eighth Wonder of the World."

All goes well until the opening night of Kong's "performance." Chained to a great stage in an almost crucifixlike mechanism, Kong breaks loose when several reporters shoot off flashbulbs in front of Ann. "He thinks you're harm-

RKO

King Kong

Universal

King Kong Escapes

ing the girl!" Denham screams as Kong lurches through the theater wall, leaving dozens of theatergoers dead in his wake.

He storms across Manhattan—killing, maiming, destroying—looking for his minihearthrob, Ann Darrow. Snatching her from a hotel room, Kong carries her to the top of the Empire State Building. A squadron of World War I fighter planes is sent out to shoot Kong down. They do so, and the king of the jungle land of Skull Island falls mortally wounded to the streets below. But, as everyone knows, it wasn't the planes that got him. 'Twas beauty that killed the beast.

PRODUCERS AND DIRECTORS: Merian C. Cooper, Ernest B. Schoedsack. SCREENPLAY: James Creelman and Ruth Rose, from a story by Cooper and an adaptation by Cooper and Edgar Wallace. ART DIRECTORS: Carroll Clark, Al Herman. SET DECORATION: Mario Larringa, Byron Crabbe. CINEMATOGRAPHY: Edward Lindon, Vernon L. Walker, and J. O. Taylor. TECHNICAL DIRECTOR AND SPECIAL EFFECTS CREATOR: Willis O'Brien. MINIATURES: Marcel Delgado. MUSIC: Max Steiner.

SUPPORTING PLAYERS: Sam Hardy, Victor Wong, Noble Johnson, Steve Clemento.

KING KONG ESCAPES
Toho (Japan, 1967); color and Tohoscope, 104 mins. Universal (U.S., 1968); color and Tohoscope, 96 mins.

King Kong is back, battling his way across Tokyo. Making matters more interesting this time out is a robot Kong,

Mechanikong, created by a crazy scientist in the area. Some days it just doesn't pay to get out of bed.

PRODUCER: Tomoyuki Tanaka. DIRECTOR: Inoshiro Honda. SCREENPLAY: Kaoru Mabuchi. CINEMATOGRAPHY: Hajime Koizumi. SPECIAL EFFECTS: Eiji Tsuburaya. MUSIC: Akira Ifukube.

CAST: Rhodes Reason, Mie Hama, Linda Miller, Akira Takarada.

KING KONG VS. GODZILLA
Toho (Japan, 1962); color and Tohoscope, 99 mins. Universal (U.S., 1963); color and Tohoscope, 91 mins.

King Kong fights the radioactive-mutant lizard in the more heavily populated areas of Tokyo.

PRODUCER: John Beck. DIRECTORS: Inoshiro Honda, Thomas Montgomery. SCREENPLAY: Shinichi Sekizawa, Paul Mason, Bruce Howard. CINEMATOGRAPHY: Hajime Koizumi. SPECIAL EFFECTS: Eiji Tsuburaya. MUSIC: Peter Zinner.

CAST: Michael Keith, James Yagi, Mie Hama, Kenji Sahara.

King Kong Vs. Godzilla

KING OF THE MOUNTIES
Republic (1942). B/w serial, 12 chapters (25 reels).

A flying-wing plane, with no propellers of any kind, is perfected by Axis inventors Admiral Yamata (Abner Biberman), Count Baroni (Nestor Paiva), and Marshal von Horst (William Vaughn). The plane cannot be detected by radar and can turn the tide of the war against the Allies. Professor Brent and daughter Carol (George Irving and Peggy Drake) journey to a section of Canada near the site where the plane is being tested, bringing along a new superradar device that can find the plane. The professor is kidnapped by the evil inventors in an attempt to squelch the professor's new plane-detector. Sergeant King (Allan Lane) of the Mounties rides to the rescue.

DIRECTOR: William Witney. SCREENPLAY: Taylor Caven, Ronald Davidson, William Lively, Joseph O'Donnell, Joseph Poland. CINEMATOGRAPHY: Bud Thackery. SPECIAL EFFECTS: Howard Lydecker.

SUPPORTING PLAYERS: Gilbert Emmery, Russell Hicks, Bradley Page, Duncan Renaldo, Jay Novello, Anthony Warde.

KING OF THE ROCKET MEN
Republic (1949). B/w serial, 12 chapters (25 reels).
Known in feature form as LOST PLANET AIRMEN (1951).

A bullet-helmeted, rocket-powered hero is the star of this epic adventure pitting traditional Good against even more traditional E-vil. Science Associates, a private research firm, has come up with an apparatus that can disintegrate rock and thus can cause earthquakes and related phenomena. Evil Dr. Vulcan is out to steal the machine and dispatches Dirkin (Don Haggerty) and his gang to get it.

In the confusion, one scientist is killed and Professor Millard, inventor of the machine, flees for his life. Millard (James Craven) is hidden in a secret lab by young friend Jeff King (Tristram Coffin). Also in on the secret is *Miracle Science* magazine reporter Glenda Thomas (Mae Clarke), who is either going to get the story of the century or her neck broken on this assignment.

Millard outfits Jeff with a metal helmet and rocket belt. Calling himself Rocket Man, Jeff blasts off repeatedly to foil Vulcan's crew. Vulcan finally does get the machine and threatens to destroy New York. After proving his might by causing a tidal wave and an earthquake, Vulcan is about to do in the Big Apple when Rocket Man arrives to save the day.

DIRECTOR: Fred Brannon. SCREENPLAY: Royal Cole, William Lively, Sol Shor. CINEMATOGRAPHY: Ellis W. Carter. SPECIAL EFFECTS: Howard and Theodore Lydecker. MUSIC: Stanley Wilson.

SUPPORTING PLAYERS: House Peters, Jr., I. Standford Jolley, Douglas Evans, Ted Adams, Dale Van Sickel, Tom Steele, Eddie Parker, David Sharpe.

KING OF THE ZOMBIES
Monogram (1941). B/w, 67 mins.

A mad doctor on a tropical island creates an army of zombies to be used by the German government in fairly unorthodox war maneuvers. Better living through science.

PRODUCER: Linsley Parsons. DIRECTOR: Gene Yarbrough. SCREENPLAY: Edmund Kelso. CINEMATOGRAPHY: Mack Stengler. MUSIC: Edward Kay.

CAST: Dick Purcell, Mantan Moreland, Hendry Victor, John Archer, Joan Woodbury.

KISS KISS, KILL KILL
Parnass/Metheus/Avala (W. Germany/Italy/Yugoslavia, 1966); color, 92 mins. U.S. (1967); color, 87 mins.

A villain hiding out in a subterranean complex produces a zombie-causing drug. Object: world domination.

PRODUCERS: Hans A. Pfluger, Theo Werner. DIRECTOR: Frank Kramer.

Warp and Peace
   At times it was like filming in a combat zone. Things were always blowing up!
          DeForest Kelley, on the making of *Star Trek—The Motion Picture*

SCREENPLAY: Sim O'Neill (Giovanni Simonelli). CINEMATOGRAPHY: Francesco Izzarelli. MUSIC: Mladen Gutssha.

CAST: Tony Kendall (Luciano Stella), Brad Harris, Christa Linder.

KISS ME DEADLY
UA (1955). B/w, 105 mins.

Mike Hammer (Ralph Meeker) is hired to track down a briefcase filled with fissionable material. Too late, Mike. The briefcase is opened, causing the unhappy opener to burst into flames, and then it blows up like a mini–A-bomb.

PRODUCER AND DIRECTOR: Robert Aldrich. SCREENPLAY: A. I. Bezzerides, based on a novel by Mickey Spillane. CINEMATOGRAPHY: Ernest Laszlo. MUSIC: Frank Devol.

SUPPORTING PLAYERS: Albert Dekker, Cloris Leachman, Jack Elam, Robert Cornthwaite, Wesley Addy, Marian Carr.

KISS ME QUICK
Fantasy Films (1963). Color.

A Russ Meyer soft-core special. Several lasses with mammoth mammaries cavort with Frankenstein's monster, an alien, a mummy, and a werewolf. Only in America.

PRODUCER AND DIRECTOR: Russ Meyer.

CAST: Jackie DeWit, Althea Currier, Claudia Banks, Fred Coe (as Frankenstein's monster).

KISS THE GIRLS AND MAKE THEM DIE
De Laurentiis (Italy, 1966); Columbia (U.S., 1967). Color, 106 mins.

A madman hatches an above-average scheme to allow him world domination. A satellite in orbit can emit rays that will sterilize mankind below. With reproduction his future forte, the crazed industrialist sets off in pursuit of suitable future consorts, capturing them and placing them in a state of suspended animation.

PRODUCER: Dino De Laurentiis. DIRECTORS: Henry Levin, Dino Maiuri. SCREENPLAY: Maiuri and Jack Pulman, from a story by Maiuri. CINEMATOGRAPHY: Aldo Tonti. SPECIAL EFFECTS:

Augie Lohman. MUSIC. Maria Nascimbene.

CAST: Michael Connors, Dorothy Provine, Raf Vallone, Terry-Thomas, Beverly Adams.

KONGA
AIP (1961). Color, 90 mins.

In this film, Michael Gough plays the nutty scientist who turns a tiny chimpanzee into a Kong-sized ape (a fellow in an ape suit). Eventually the ape begins to grow even bigger than his creator's plans. Konga holds an unexpected roof-raising party and, scientist in hand, takes a stroll through London, much to the dismay of the military.

PRODUCER: Herman Cohen. DIRECTOR: John Lemont. SCREENPLAY: Aben Kandel, Herman Cohen. MAKEUP: Jack Craig. CINEMATOGRAPHY: Desmond Dickinson. MUSIC: Gerard Shurmann.

SUPPORTING PLAYERS: Margo Johns, Jess Conrad, Claire Gordon, Jack Watson.

KRONOS
20th Cent.-Fox (1957). B/w, 78 mins.

A blow for Tinker Toy power was struck by this alien-attack venture. A gigantic, energy-consuming machine from space lands in the sea off the coast of Mexico. Its landing arouses the curiosity of California Science Institute employees Les (Jeff Morrow), Culver (George O'Hanlon), Elliot (John Emery), and Les's fiancée, Vera (Barbara Lawrence). They fly to Mexico, where they are met by a sight not bargained for. The alien device now stands hundreds of feet tall. Coming ashore, Kronos, the marching machine, devours a few power plants and crushes a couple of hundred slow-moving Mexicans. Nothing can stop it. The more destructive the force hurled at it by the military, the more energy it consumes and the stronger it gets. Elliot is telepathically controlled by the machine. All seems lost until the three remaining free-spirited heroes reverse the machine's polarity. The short-circuit forces power into Kronos' control center with a bang.

PRODUCER AND DIRECTOR: Kurt Neumann. ASSOCIATE PRODUCERS AND SPECIAL EFFECTS CREATORS: Jack Rabin,

Irving Block, Louis DeWitt. SCREEN-PLAY: Block. MUSIC: Paul Swatell.

SUPPORTING PLAYERS: Morris Ankrum, Robert Shayne, John Parrish.

LADY AND THE MONSTER, THE
Republic (1944). B/w, 86 mins.

An early adaptation of CURT SIODMAK's novel *Donovan's Brain*, this film featured added spookiness thanks to the dour presence of Erich von Stroheim as one of the scientists involved. The disembodied brain of a power magnate telepathically takes control of the hapless doctor who has kept it alive.

PRODUCER AND DIRECTOR: George Sherman. SCREENPLAY: Dane Lussier, Frederick Kohner. CINEMATOGRAPHY: John Alton. SPECIAL EFFECTS: Theodore Lydecker. MUSIC: Walter Scharf.

SUPPORTING PLAYERS: Vera Ralston, Richard Arlen, Sidney Blackmer.

LADY FRANKENSTEIN
Condor International (Italy, 1971); color, 99 mins. New World (U.S., 1972); color, 85 mins.

When Dr. Frankenstein's ugly monster kills its maker, the doctor's daughter is miffed. Putting the brain of her slightly twisted servant into a good-looking body, she plans to pit her own creation against that of her dad's. Two out of three falls, no bolts barred.

PRODUCER: Harry Cushing. DIRECTOR: Mel Welles. SCREENPLAY: Edward DiLorenzo. CINEMATOGRAPHY: Riccardo Pallotini, Richard Pallotini. SPECIAL EFFECTS: Cipa. MUSIC: Alessandro Allesandroni.

CAST: Joseph Cotten, Sara Bay, Mickey Hargitay, Herbert Fox.

LAND THAT TIME FORGOT, THE
AIP (1975). Technicolor, 91 mins.

At the top of World War I, a German U-boat sinks a British ship and takes the survivors on board. A wrong turn takes the human flotsam to the unknown land of Caprona. Heroic American Doug McClure and nasty German von Schoenvorts (John McEnery) are surprised to find dinosaurs cavorting about. They are even more surprised to be greeted by ever-evolving Neanderthal Ahm (Anthony Ainley), who teaches them survival in the wilds as well as showing them the secret of the godhead.

PRODUCER: John Dark. DIRECTOR: Kevin Connor. SCREENPLAY: MICHAEL MOORCOCK and James Cawthorn from the novel by EDGAR RICE BURROUGHS.

SUPPORTING PLAYERS: Susan Penhaligon, Keith Barron.

LASERBLAST
Yablans (1979). Technicolor, 85 mins.

Two alien lizard-men chase a humanoid criminal onto the planet Earth. The criminal is killed in a fiery battle, but his laser gun remains on the California desert. Tortured teenager Billy Duncan (Kim Milford) finds the gun and the late criminal's strange amulet. Milford dons both the arm weapon and the necklace and becomes imbued with a mysterious, evil power. He turns into a nasty, killing monster—which, in turn, causes girl friend Kathy Farley (Cheryl Smith) to have doubts about where their relationship is heading.

Dr. Mellon (Roddy McDowall) begins to suspect things are going awry in Billy's life and is killed for his perception. Government agent Tony Craig (Gianni Russo) joins the local sheriff (Ron Masak) in hunting down the alien/human thingie.

PRODUCER: Charles Band. DIRECTOR: Michael Rae. SCREENPLAY: Franne Schact, Frank Ray Perilli. CINEMATOGRAPHY: Terry Bowen. SPECIAL EFFECTS, MAKEUP, AND PROPS: Steve Neill. STOP-MOTION ANIMATION: David Allen.

SUPPORTING PLAYERS: Keenan Wynn as Col. Farley, Eddie Deezen as Froggy.

LAST DAYS OF MAN ON EARTH, THE
New World (1974). Technicolor, 78 mins.

Jerry Cornelius (Jon Finch) is told by Professor Hira (Hugh Griffith) that the world of the not-too-distant future will die prematurely because of the laziness of its citizens. Understandably depressed, Jerry soon falls in with doctors Baxter, Smiles, and Powys (Patrick Magee, Graham Crowden, and George Coulouris) and Ms. Brunner (Jenny Runacre), who are working on an immortality project. The world, it seems, ends every 2,000 years. This time out, Jerry is destined to be the new Messiah.

PRODUCERS: John Goldstone, Sandy Lieberson. DIRECTOR, SCREENWRITER, DESIGNER: Robert Fuest. Screenplay based on the novel *The Final Programme*, by MICHAEL MOORCOCK. ART DIRECTOR: Phillip Harrison. MUSIC: Paul Beaver, Barnard Krause.

LAST HOUR, THE
Nettleford Films (G.B., 1930). B/w, 75 mins.

An unscrupulous prince uses a ray gun to force down airplanes and steal their cargoes.

PRODUCER: Archibald Nettleford. DIRECTOR: Walter Forde. SCREENPLAY: H. Fowler Mear.

CAST: Stewart Rome, Richard Cooper, Wilfred Shine, Billy Shine.

LAST MAN ON EARTH, THE
Fox (1924). B/w (tinted) silent featurette, seven reels.

Based on a story by John D. Swain, this vintage film offered a thought-provoking premise. By the year 1954, a strange disease has killed every man on Earth over the age of 14—except one. The government is now run by women. When the hapless fellow's existence is discovered, two female senators fight over who gets first crack at our hero.

PRODUCER AND DIRECTOR: Jack G. Blystone. SCREENPLAY: Donald W. Lee. CINEMATOGRAPHY: Allan Davey.

CAST: Earle Foxe, Derelys Perdue, Grace Cunard, Gladys Tennyson, Buck Black.

LAST MAN ON EARTH, THE
La Regina/Alta Vista (Italy, 1963); AIP (U.S., 1964). B/w, 86 mins.

Robert Morgan (Vincent Price) is the only survivor of a plague that has changed the entire populace of the Earth into carnivorous night creatures. Outnumbered by these vampire beasts, he turns his house into a fortress and his waking hours into search-and-destroy missions. This somber black-and-white movie is a very disappointing adaptation (one of two screen-misses, the other being THE OMEGA MAN) of RICHARD MATHESON's chilling novel *I Am Legend*.

PRODUCER: Robert L. Lippert. DIRECTORS: Sidney Salkow, Ubaldo Ragona. SCREENPLAY: Logan Swanson, William P. Leicester. ART DIRECTOR: Giorgio Giovannini. MAKEUP: Piero Macacci. CINEMATOGRAPHY: Franco Delli Colli. MUSIC: Paul Sawtell and Bert Shefter.

SUPPORTING PLAYERS: Emma Danieli, Franca Bettoia, Giacomo Rossi-Stuart.

LAST WAR, THE
Toho (Japan, 1961); color, 110 mins. Medallion TV (U.S., 1961); color, 81 mins.

Sort of a straight DR. STRANGELOVE, this film portrays the deadly consequences of a mistake that causes a fleet of nuclear missiles to be fired. Toho Films, which gave birth to Godzilla and his kind, do not flinch in their message. They destroy the world in this one with an avalanche of colorful special effects.

PRODUCERS: Sanezumi Fujimoto, Tomoyuki Tanaka. DIRECTOR: Shue Matsubayashi. SCREENPLAY: Toshio Yazumi, Takeshi Kimura. CINEMATOGRAPHY: Rokuro Nishigaki. SPECIAL EFFECTS: Eiji Tsuburaya.

CAST: Frankie Sakai, Nobuko Otowa, Akira Takarada, Yukiro Hoshi.

LAST WOMAN ON EARTH, THE
Filmgroup (1960). Color/scope, 71 mins.

This film by Roger Corman helped finance a trip to the Caribbean for the overworked filmmaker and his small crew. They enjoyed their stay so much that while on location, screenwriter Robert Towne was asked to write another screenplay to extend the stay. (He did—*The Creature from the Haunted Sea*.)

This film concerns the rather feeble efforts of two fellas and a gal stranded on a tropical island after the final war. Highpoint: the following poem, uttered by one of the wounded men: "Oh dearie me, I cannot see, I haven't brought my specs with me." Existential, huh?

PRODUCER AND DIRECTOR: Roger Corman. SCREENPLAY: Robert Towne. ART DIRECTOR: Daniel Haller. CINEMATOGRAPHY: Jack Marquette. MUSIC: Ronald Stein.

CAST: Anthony Carbone, Betsy Jones-Moreland, Edward Wain.

LATE GREAT PLANET EARTH, THE
Pacific International (1979). Color, 90 mins.

Based on Hal Lindsey's best-selling book, this pseudodocumentary predicts the impending destruction of Earth visually while verbally getting a helping hand from the voice of Orson Welles. Tracing ominous predictions from Biblical times to the present, Welles talks of Earth's demise in terms of UFOs, the Bermuda Triangle, and nuclear war.

PRODUCERS: Robert Amram, Alan Belking. DIRECTOR, SCREENPLAY: Amram. NARRATORS: Orson Welles, Hal Lindsey. MUSIC: Dana Kaproff.

LATEST STYLE AIRSHIP
Pathé (France, 1908). B/w short.

An inventor comes up with a bicycle that can fly.

DIRECTOR: Ferdinand Zecca.

LATITUDE ZERO
Toho/National General (Japan/U.S., 1969). Color, 106 mins.

Two supersubmarines face off under the sea, commanded by two geniuses; one evil, the other good. The villain (Cesar Romero) fights off the heroic commander (Joseph Cotten) with lethal rays, manmade monsters, and demented warriors.

DIRECTOR: Inoshiro Honda. SCREENPLAY: Ted Sherdeman and Shinichi Sekizawa, from a story by Sherdeman. ART DIRECTOR: Takeo Kita. CINEMATOGRAPHY: Taiichi Kanjura. SPECIAL EFFECTS: Eiji Tsuburaya. MUSIC: Akira Ifukube.

SUPPORTING PLAYERS: Akira Takarada, Tetsu Nakamura, Linda Yanes, Richard Jaeckel, Patricia Medina.

LAUGHING AT DANGER
FBO (1924). B/w silent short, six reels.

The protagonist of this drama wasn't laughing for long. Shortly after a stalwart American scientist comes up with the ultimate death ray, he has it stolen by enemy agents. Bad luck, that.

DIRECTOR: James W. Horne. STORY: Frank Howard Clark. CINEMATOGRAPHY: William Marshall.

CAST: William Talmadge, Eve Novak, Joe Harrington.

LEECH WOMAN, THE
Universal (1960). B/w, 77 mins.

A husband-and-wife scientist team (Phil Terry and Colleen Grey), both approaching middle age, take a quick trip to Africa in search of a formula that will restore their youth. Well, they find one, all right, but the ingredients call for fluid drained from male brain glands. Within a twinkling of a crow's-feet–laden eye, the scientist hubby is traded in for a quick shot of youth.

Back in the States, the Leech Woman turns vamp, chasing after her loyal lawyer (Grant Williams), much to the dismay of his fiancée (Gloria Talbot). Aside from her newfound personality quirks, the female scientist discovers she has developed quite a weird skin condition as well. Whenever the youth fluid dissipates within her body, she turns into an old hag. To stay young, she must roam the streets at night, killing off young males to keep the juices flowing.

When her lawyer's fiancée becomes too much of a nuisance, the Leech Woman murders her and, in a moment of illogic, uses the girl's glands in the formula. While young men mean youth, young ladies spell d-e-a-t-h for the leech woman, and she crumbles to dust.

PRODUCER: Joseph Gershenson. DIRECTOR: Edward Dein. SCREENPLAY: David Duncan, from a story by Ben Pivar and Francis Rosenwald. MAKEUP: Bud Westmore. CINEMATOGRAPHY: Ellis Carter. MUSIC: Irving Gertz.

LEGALLY DEAD
Universal (1923). B/w silent feature, 6,076 ft.

A well-meaning scientist brings a wrongly hanged man back to life through the use of adrenaline.

DIRECTOR: William Parke. SCREENPLAY: Harvey Gates, from a story by Charles Furthman. CINEMATOGRAPHY: Richard Fryer.

CAST: Milton Sills, Brandon Hurst, Claire Adams, Margaret Campbell.

LET THERE BE LIGHT
American-Flying A (1915). B/w silent short, two reels.

An inventor discovers an illuminating electric ray.

DIRECTOR: William Bertram.

CAST: Helen Rosson, Charles Newton, E. Forrest Taylor.

LICENSE TO KILL
Chaumaine/Filmstudio (France, 1964); Florida Films (U.S., 1964). B/w, 95 mins.

Nick Carter is called in to help a government when foreign agents make off with a horde of secret scientific gadgets. Eddie Constantine as Carter is priceless. The rest of the production is senseless.

DIRECTORS: Henri Decoin, Phillippe Seene. SCREENPLAY: Jean Marcillac, André Haguet, and André Legrand, from a story by Marcillac, based on the character created by John R. Corryell.

SUPPORTING PLAYERS: Daphne Dayle, Paul Frenkeur, Charles Belmond.

LIEUTENANT ROSE, R.N., AND HIS PATENT AEROPLANE
Clarendon (G.B., 1912). B/w silent short, 1,032 ft.

A monoplane capable of being controlled electronically from a distance is invented.

LIFE IN THE NEXT CENTURY
France (1909). B/w silent short, 300 ft.

Life in the year 2010 is previewed. DIRECTOR: Gérard Bourgeois.

LIFE WITHOUT SOUL
Ocean Films Corp. (1915). B/w silent feature, five reels.

Dr. Frankenstein creates a monster from the parts of cadavers collected in a suspicious manner. Once created, the creature turns on its maker and pursues him across the continent.

PRODUCER: George DeCarlton. DIRECTOR: Joseph W. Smiley. SCREENPLAY: Jesse J. Goldburg, based on the novel *Frankenstein,* by MARY W. SHELLEY.

CAST: William A. Cohill, Jack Hopkins, Lucy Cotton, Pauline Curley, Percy Darrell Standing as the monster.

LIGHTNING BOLT
7 Films/Balcazar (Italy/Spain, 1966); color/scope, 100 mins. Woolner Brothers (U.S., 1967); color/scope, 96 mins.

The U.S. space program is imperiled by outer-space interference that manifests itself in lethal laser-ray attacks.

PRODUCER AND STORY ORIGINATOR: Alfonso Balcazar. DIRECTOR: Anthony Dawson. SCREENPLAY: Balcazar, Jose Antonio de la Loma. CINEMATOGRAPHY: Ricardo Pallottini.

The Road to Berlitz
What are they saying?
I don't know, I don't speak monster.
    One Japanese reporter to another in *Destroy All Monsters*

CAST: Anthony Eisley, Wandisa Leigh, Ursula Parker.

LIQUID AIR, THE
Gaumont (France, 1909). B/w silent short, 450 ft.

The new discovery, liquid air, has the ability to freeze people solid should they touch it.

LIQUID ELECTRICITY
1907. B/w silent short, 450 ft.

An elixir, when swallowed, causes the drinker to move at an accelerated rate.

PRODUCER AND DIRECTOR: J. Stuart Blackton.

LITTLE PRINCE, THE
Paramount (1974). Technicolor, 88 mins.

The Little Prince (Steven Warner) lives on an asteroid with a talking rose.

Seeking to expand his education, he travels to Earth, where he befriends a crash-landed pilot (Richard Kiley). Together they seek the meaning of life. On the way, however, they gather data via encounters with the Snake (Bob Fosse), the Fox (Gene Wilder), the King (Joss Acland), the Businessman (Clive Revill), and the Historian (Victor Spinetti).

PRODUCER AND DIRECTOR: Stanley Donen. SCREENPLAY AND LYRICS: Alan Jay Lerner. MUSIC: Frederick Loewe. Based on the story by Antoine de Saint Exupéry. SPECIAL EFFECTS: Thomas Howard.

LOGAN'S RUN
MGM (1976). Color, 118 mins.

Flaccid futurism and pulp-magazine philosophy paired off in this tale of epic woe. In the year 2274, a postnuclear world is living a hedonistic existence totally devoid of any generation gap—principally because of the fact that all citizens reaching the age of 30 are forced to enter the "Carousel," a device that promises rejuvenation but delivers extermination. In the future, the only gap present is between people's ears. The citizens who try to flee this process and the doomed city that houses it are called runners.

When 29-year-old Logan (Michael York) and friend Jessica (Jenny Agutter) decide to skip town, they are pursued by Sandman (tracker) Francis (Richard Jordan). Leaving their pleasant, domed city for the ravaged and scorched outside world, the twosome meet a robot called Box (Roscoe Lee Browne), a fellow who freezes humans

MGM

Logan's Run

and then has the audacity to call them "ice sculptures." In the ruins of Washington, D.C., they meet a hermit (Peter Ustinov). The threesome dispose of Francis and return to the city determined to give the gift of freedom-of-choice to the population within. They terminate the city's computer system and bring the house down, literally.

DIRECTOR: Michael Anderson. SCREENPLAY: David Z. Goodman, based on the novel by WILLIAM F. NOLAN and George Clayton Johnson. SPECIAL EFFECTS: Lyle B. Abbott, Frank Van Der Veer. MUSIC: Jerry Goldsmith.

SUPPORTING PLAYERS: Farrah Fawcett-Majors, Michael Anderson, Jr., Lara Lindsay.

LORD OF THE FLIES
Walter Reade/Sterling (1963). B/w, 91 mins.

A mind-boggling *tour de force* based upon the equally unsettling novel of the same name, by William Golding. A planeful of British schoolboys fleeing a nuclear attack crash-land on a tropical island. They establish a tribal type of government in order to effect a sense of security and order. The tribe splits, however, eventually pitting the intellectuals against the warriors, and savagery is the end result.

PRODUCER: Lewis Allen. DIRECTOR AND SCREENWRITER: Peter Brook. CINEMATOGRAPHY: Tom Hollyman, Gerald Feil. MUSIC: Raymond Leppard.

CAST: Tom Chapin, James Aubrey, Roger Elwin, Hugh Edwards, Tom Gaman.

LOST ANGEL, THE
MGM (1943). B/w, 90 mins.

A young girl raised by a child psychologist has the mental capacity of a college professor while still only six years old.

PRODUCER: Robert Sisk. DIRECTOR: Roy Rowland. SCREENPLAY: Isobel Lennart, from an idea by Angna Enters. ART DIRECTORS: Cedric Gibbons, Lyndon Sparhawk. CINEMATOGRAPHY: Robert Surtees. MUSIC: Daniele Amfitheatrof.

CAST: Margaret O'Brien, James Craig, Marsha Hunt, Keenan Wynn, Alan Napier.

LOST CITY, THE
Regal (1935). B/w serial, 12 chapters (24 reels).
Known in feature form as THE CITY OF LOST MEN (74 mins.).

When the world is assaulted by a series of electrical storms, plucky hero Bruce Gordon (Kane Richmond) traces the source to a point in central Africa. Backed by the free nations of the world, Bruce takes colleagues Colton (William Millman) and Reynolds (Ralph Lewis) into darkest Africa. Camping out at the trading post run by nasty Butterfield (Gabby Hayes), they figure that the electrical rays causing the storm are coming from Magnetic Mountain.

Unbeknownst to them, the mountain is actually the outside layer of a substrata world run by scientific crazy Zolok (William Boyd), a fellow out to conquer the world. Giving Zolok his high-voltage clout is prisoner hero-scientist Dr. Manyus (Josef Swickard). The good doctor is forced into slavery because his ravishing daughter, Natcha (Claudia Dell), is constantly being threatened by Zolok, his hunchback assistant Gorzo (William Bletcher), and his brainwashed zombie giants.

Bruce and his trusted friend Jerry (Eddie Fetherstone) are captured by Zolok, as are Colton and Reynolds. The latter pair, however, being less pure of heart than your average scientists, think that, with Manyus in their corner, *they* could rule the world even better than Zolok. They con the elderly doctor into escaping the lost city with them. Joining the escape fad is Natcha, Bruce, and Jerry, out to free the re-kidnapped Manyus from his latest slave masters. Zolok, not overly pleased at his lackluster security force, sends off a fleet of zombie giants in pursuit.

The resulting chase involves Arab scientists, evil queens, rays that can turn black men into white men, frozen electricity, TV sets, and assorted battles involving zombies and pygmies. Eventually, everyone is rewarded/punished as befits their actions, with Zolok overloading the circuits of his city and making an explosive career move taking him somewhere near the Van Allen radiation belt.

PRODUCER: Sherman S. Krellberg.

DIRECTOR: Harry Revier. SCREENPLAY: Pereley Poore Sheehan, Eddie Graneman, Leon D'Usseau, from a story by Zelma Carroll, George Merrick, and Robert Dillon. CINEMATOGRAPHY: Roland Price, Edward Lindon. MUSICAL DIRECTOR: Lee Zahler.

SUPPORTING PLAYERS: Milburn Moranti, Margot D'use, Gino Corrado.

LOST CITY OF THE JUNGLE, THE
Universal (1946). B/w serial, 13 chapters (26 reels).

When World War II ends, nostalgic Sir Eric Hazarias (Lionel Atwill) seeks to get another global scrap going by journeying to the lost city of Pendrang in search of meteorium 245, a substance capable of making a nation invulnerable against the atomic bomb. Out to stop him are United Peace Foundation agent Rod Stanton (Russ Hayden), Tal Shan (Keye Luke), and daughter and dad scientific team Marjorie and Dr. Elmore (Jane Adams and John Eldredge). Niceness triumphs. The villains destroy themselves arguing over the meteorium 245. (They accidentally knock over the box containing the specimen and blow themselves to smithereenies.)

DIRECTORS: Ray Taylor, Lewis D. Collins. SCREENPLAY: Joseph F. Poland, Paul Houston, Tom Gibson. CINEMATOGRAPHY: Gus Peterson.

SUPPORTING PLAYERS: John Gallaudet, Gene Roth, Arthur Space.

LOST CONTINENT, THE
Lippert (1951). B/w with green-tinted sequences, 83 mins.

Searching for a lost atomic rocket, a group of scientists discovers a tropical world in which uranium deposits have kept prehistoric monsters alive for an unhealthy amount of time . . . unhealthy that is, for the scientists, who spend the rest of the film fleeing the above-mentioned monsters.

PRODUCER: Sigmund Neufeld. DIRECTOR: Samuel Newfield. SCREENPLAY: Richard Landeau, from a story by Carroll Young. CINEMATOGRAPHY: Jack Greenhalgh. SPECIAL EFFECTS: Augie Lohman. MUSIC: Paul Dunlap.

CAST: Cesar Romero, Hillary Brooke, Chick Chandler, Sid Melton, Aquanetta, John Hoyt.

LOST MISSILE, THE
UA (1958). B/w, 70 mins.

Nuclear Armageddon is the possible payoff in this tense tale. A nuclear missile of unknown origin is in a decaying orbit around the Earth, with New York City calculated as its ultimate bull's-eye. Every possible effort is made to divert the seemingly unstoppable missile.

PRODUCER: Lee Gordon. DIRECTOR: Lester Berke. SCREENPLAY: John McPartland, Jerome Bixby, from a story by Berke. CINEMATOGRAPHY: Kenneth Peach. MUSIC: Gerald Fried.

CAST: Robert Loggia, Larry Kerr, Ellen Parker.

LOST PLANET, THE
Columbia (1953). B/w serial, 15 chapters (30 reels), 480 mins. total running time.

Captain Video (Judd Holdren) outwits a horde of gangsters from space.

PRODUCER: Sam Katzman. DIRECTOR: Spencer G. Bennett. SCREENPLAY: George H. Plympton and Arthur Hoerl. MUSIC: Mischa Bakaleinikoff. SPECIAL EFFECTS: Jack Erickson.

SUPPORTING CAST: Vivian Mason, Forrest Taylor, Gene Roth.

LOST WORLD, THE
First National (1925). Silent feature, b/w with tinted sequences, ten reels (9,700 ft.) .

Based on ARTHUR CONAN DOYLE'S novel *The Lost World*, this early experiment in stop-motion animation recounts the events surrounding Professor Challenger's expedition into a lost valley. Finding a prehistoric world intact, the scientists are attacked by dinosaurs but escape with their lives before a volcanic eruption destroys the valley. A brontosaurus egg, brought back to London by the professor, hatches, grows into a large dinosaur, and breaks loose in the city streets. Willis O'Brien, the special-effects genius responsible for KING KONG, provided the visual thrills.

PRODUCERS: Earl Hudson, Watterson R. Rothacker. DIRECTOR: Harry O. Hoyt. SCREENPLAY: Marion Fairfax. MODEL CONSTRUCTION: Marcel Delgado. CINEMATOGRAPHY: Arthur Edeson.

CAST: Wallace Beery, Lewis Stone, Bessie Love, Bull Montana (as a missing link–ape creature), Arthur Hoyt.

LOST WORLD, THE
20th Cent.-Fox (1960). Color/scope, 97 mins.

This marrow-headed remake of the silent classic once more takes Professor Challenger (Claude Rains) into a lost jungle world. Encountering large lizards and lost treasures, they are beset by greed and script problems. The lost world is destroyed in a volcanic eruption, with most of the party escaping with their lives (if not their dignity), and Challenger salvaging a dinosaur egg to bring back to London for a possible sequel. Presumably, the egg is still unhatched.

PRODUCER AND DIRECTOR: Irwin Allen. SCREENPLAY: Allen, Charles Bennett. MAKEUP: Ben Nye. CINEMATOGRAPHY: Winton Hoch. SPECIAL EFFECTS: Lyle B. Abbott, Emil Kosa, Jr., James B. Gordon. MUSIC: Bert Shefter and Paul Sawtell.

SUPPORTING PLAYERS: Michael Rennie, Fernando Lamas, Jill St. John, David Hedison, Ian Wolfe.

First National

The Lost World

LOVE GERM
Lubin (1908). B/w silent short, 460 ft.

A scientist discovers the germ that causes love.

LOVE MAGNET, THE
General (1916). B/w silent short, one reel.

A strange magnet attracts women of all shapes and sizes—beauties, old maids, mermaids, etc.

DIRECTOR: A. Santell.

CAST: Lloyd V. Hamilton, Ethel Teare, Bud Duncan.

LOVE MICROBE, THE
Biograph (1907). B/w silent short, 670 ft.

Scientists discover the germs that cause love.

LOVE PILL, THE
Mayfair (G.B., 1971). Color, 82 mins.

A dim-witted grocer accidentally concocts a candy that is an instant contraceptive. Adding to the sugar-coated mayhem is the fact that when taken by women, the candy has the power to turn ordinary females into raving nymphomaniacs. Guaranteed to break the ice at parties.

PRODUCERS: Lawrence Barnett, John Lindsay. DIRECTOR: Kenneth Turner. STORY: John Lindsay. CINEMATOGRAPHY: John Mackey.

CAST: Toni Sinclair, Melinda Churcher, Kenneth Waller.

MAD DOCTOR OF BLOOD ISLAND, THE
Hemisphere (1969). Color, 85 mins.

A thankless job, this small-town medicine. A crazy doctor creates a chlorophyll monster who goes about the grounds of his tropical hideaway causing local natives to become ex–local natives.

PRODUCER: Eddie Romero. DIRECTORS: Eddie Romero, Gerardo de Leon. SCREENPLAY: Reuben Conway. CINEMATOGRAPHY: Just Paulino.

CAST: John Ashely, Angelique Pettyjohn, Eddie Garcia.

MAD DOCTOR OF MARKET STREET, THE
Universal (1940). B/w, 60 mins.

A mad scientist flees a murder charge in hometown Philadelphia. Seeking a similarly exotic locale, he journeys to the South Seas, where he lands on an island and declares himself a local god.

Adding extra clout to his claim is the fact that the doctor (Lionel Atwill) is well versed in the fine art of raising the dead.

DIRECTOR: Joseph H. Lewis. SCREENPLAY: Al Martin. CINEMATOGRAPHY: Jerome Ash. MUSICAL DIRECTOR: Hans Salter.

SUPPORTING PLAYERS: Una Merkel, Nat Pendleton, Claire Dodd, Anne Nagel, Richard Davies, Noble Johnson.

MAD GHOUL, THE
Universal (1943). B/w, 64 mins.

This film's mad doctor is movie-meanie George Zucco, a scientist who comes up with a "death-in-life" gas . . . a vapor that reduces its users to zombiedom. David Bruce is the unfortunate inhaler who turns into a shriveled slave. Adding to David's problems is the fact that in order to keep alive, even in his limited state, he requires a fresh heart every few days. In between making eyes at David's ex (Evelyn Ankers) and threatening the girl's present-day suitor (Turhan Bey), the doctor takes part in several gruesome murders. You gotta have heart—lotsa, lotsa, etc.

PRODUCER: Ben Pivar. DIRECTOR: James Hogan. SCREENPLAY: Brenda Weisberg and Paul Gangelin, from a story by Hans Kraly. MAKEUP: Jack Pierce. CINEMATOGRAPHY: Milton Krasner. MUSICAL DIRECTOR: Hans Salter.

SUPPORTING PLAYERS: Milburn Stone, Addison Richards, Robert Armstrong.

MAD LOVE
MGM (1935). B/w, 85 mins.

Appropriately macabre adaptation of Maurice Renard's THE HANDS OF ORLAC, but with a twist. A crazed surgeon (Peter Lorre) grafts the hands of a killer onto the arms of a pianist (Colin Clive). The hands seem to have a mind of their own as far as their usage is concerned. Meanwhile, the scientist, not quite of the normal variety, impersonates a decapitated, steel-handed criminal and embarks on a life of crime.

PRODUCER: John W. Considine. DIRECTOR: Karl Freund. SCREENPLAY: P. J. Wolfson and John Balderston, from an adaptation by Guy Endore and Karl Freund. CINEMATOGRAPHY:

MGM

Mad Love

Chester Lyons, Greg Toland. MUSIC: Dmitri Tiomkin.

SUPPORTING PLAYERS: Frances Drake, Isabel Jewell, Key Luke.

MAD MONSTER, THE

PRC (1942). B/w, 77 mins.

Dr. Lorenzo Cameron (George Zucco) has a secret: he's nuts. Through a series of blood transfusions, he believes he can create a race of superwerewolves to do battle with the Nazis. His assistant, Pedro (Glenn Strange), isn't too keen on becoming a guinea pig, but before he can open his mouth to complain, he's howling at the moon.

PRODUCER: Sigmund Neufeld. DIRECTOR: Sam Newfield. SCREENPLAY: Fred Myton. MAKEUP: Harry Ross. SPECIAL EFFECTS: Gene Stone. MUSIC: David Chudnow.

SUPPORTING PLAYERS: Johnny Downs, Anne Nagel, Henry Hall, and the everpopular Mae Busch.

MADMAN OF MANDORAS, THE

Crown International (1964). B/w, 74 mins.

A group of crazy scientists on a tropical island find the head of Hitler after World War II and keep it alive for over two decades. The head, a fellow with a mind of its own, wants to fight the war all over again.

PRODUCER: Carl Edwards. DIRECTOR: David Bradley. SCREENPLAY: Richard Miles, Steve Bennett. CINEMATOGRAPHY: Stanley Cortez.

CAST: Walter Stocker, Audrey Claire, Nestor Paiva.

MADRID IN THE YEAR 2000

Madrid Films (Spain, 1925). B/w silent feature.

A glimpse at a futuristic city.

DIRECTOR AND SCREENWRITER: Manuel Noriega. CINEMATOGRAPHY: Antonio Macasoli.

CAST: Roberto Ingesias, Roberto Rey, Juan Nada.

MAGNETIC FLUID, THE

Pathé (France, 1912). B/w silent short, 510 ft.

A man drinks a liquid that gives him superhypnotic powers over other people's minds.

MAGNETIC KITCHEN, THE

Pathé (France, 1908). B/w silent short.

A kitchen goes wild.

DIRECTOR: Segundo de Choman.

MAGNETIC MONSTER, THE

UA (1953). B/w, 76 mins.

A new isotope grows by absorbing energy. The substance grows in strength until all surrounding metallic objects go haywire, being totally magnetized. The isotope becomes a threat to the local community in a cyclotron during the film's finale, which uses a good deal of footage from the 1934 film GOLD.

PRODUCER: Ivan Tors. DIRECTOR: CURT SIODMAK. SCREENPLAY: Siodmak, Ivan Tors. CINEMATOGRAPHY: Charles Van Enger. SPECIAL EFFECTS: Jack Glass. MUSIC: Blaine Sanford.

CAST: Richard Carlson, King Donovan, Jean Bryon, Strother Martin.

MAGNETIC MOON, THE

Reed (1954). B/w, 78 mins.

Rocky Jones (Richard Crane) battles an unknown satellite in this reprise of old TV episodes of ROCKY JONES, SPACE RANGER.

PRODUCER: Roland Reed.

MAGNETIC PERSONALITY, A
1912. B/w silent short, one-half reel.

A man steals a case of magnets and is pursued by various metal objects.

MAGNETIC REMOVAL
Pathé (France, 1908). B/w silent short, 672 ft.

A scientist cleans his house with a magnet.

MAGNETIC SQUIRT, THE
Le Lion (1909). B/w silent short, 480 ft.

A new elixir causes the lame to walk once again.

MAGNETIC VAPOR, THE
Lubin (1908). B/w silent short, 345 ft.

A magnetic vapor causes a henpecked husband to become a forceful ruler.

MAN FROM PLANET X, THE
UA (1950). B/w, 70 mins.

The first film to feature a nonhuman alien visitor, *Man* benefits from intricate design and a somber visual mood concocted by director Edgar Ulmer. An eggheaded fellow from space lands in a murky British moor and quietly begins examining Earth. The quiet little fellow is immediately attacked by a local scientist who wants to advance the cause of humanity by obtaining "the secrets of the stars." Pushed beyond endurance, the alien retaliates with a mind-control ray.

PRODUCERS AND SCREENWRITERS: Aubrey Wisberg, Jack Pollexfen. DIRECTOR: Edgar Ulmer. CINEMATOGRAPHY: John L. Russel. ART DIRECTOR: Angelo Scibetti. SPECIAL EFFECTS: Andy Anderson, Howard Weeks. MUSIC: Charles Koff.

CAST: Robert Clarke as Lawrence, William Schallert as Mears, Margaret Field, Raymond Bond, Roy Engel, Charles Davis.

MANHUNT IN SPACE
Reed (1954). B/w, 78 mins.

Rocky Jones (Richard Crane) hunts an invisible spaceship in these re-edited episodes of the TV show ROCKY JONES, SPACE RANGER.

PRODUCER: Roland Reed.

MANHUNT OF MYSTERY ISLAND
Republic (1945). B/w serial, 15 chapters (31 reels).
Known in feature form as CAPTAIN MEPHISTO AND THE TRANSFORMATION MACHINE (1966).

While looking for new radium fields, Dr. Forrest (Forrest Taylor) disappears. The inventor of the radium–atomic power transmitter, a device designed to supply unlimited power to the world, Dr. Forrest is important enough to warrant a widespread search. Daughter Claire (Linda Stirling) and criminologist Lance Reardon (Richard Bailey) follow the professor's trail to Mystery Island. The island is owned by four gentlemen—Hargraves, Armstrong, Braley, and Melton (Forbes Murray, Jack Ingram, Harry Strang, Edward Cassidy)—all descendants of evil Captain Mephisto (Roy Barcroft). Through a transformation chair, each of these men can turn, chameleonlike, into a double of the original Captain. They keep Dr. Forrest prisoner and ward off all rescue attempts until Claire places a well-aimed bullet into old Cappie's body.

DIRECTORS: Spencer G. Bennett, Wallace Grissell, Yakima Canutt. SCREENPLAY: Albert DeMond, Basil Dickey, Jesse Duffy, Alan James, Grant Nelson, Joseph Poland. CINEMATOGRAPHY: Bud Thackery. SPECIAL EFFECTS: Howard and Theodore Lydecker. MUSIC: Richard Cherwin.

MAN IN HALF MOON STREET, THE
Paramount (1944). B/w, 92 mins.

A scientist over a century old is kept alive by an organ transplant from an unwilling donor performed every 35 years. Seeking a new victim for his immortality operation, the scientist runs into a series of events that foil his plan. This sudden failure to meet the required time schedule causes him to age over 100 years in a moment and to wither away.

PRODUCER: Walter MacEwan. DIRECTOR: Ralph M. Murphy. SCREENPLAY: Charles Kenyon, from an adaptation by Garrett Fort of a play by Barre Lyndon (remade in 1959 into

THE MAN WHO COULD CHEAT DEATH). MAKEUP: Wally Westmore. CINEMATOGRAPHY: Henry Sharp. MUSIC: Miklos Rozsa.

CAST: Nils Asther, Helen Walker, Paul Cavanaugh, Morton Lowry.

MAN IN OUTER SPACE
Czechoslovakia (1961); b/w, 96 mins. AIP (1964); b/w, 85 mins.

An egomaniacal prig is rocketed to a distant planet. He returns to Earth, à la BUCK ROGERS, 20 centuries later and tries to become one of the most powerful capitalists on Earth. He is thwarted by a conscience-stricken alien he has picked up on his return voyage.

PRODUCER: Rudolf Wolf. DIRECTOR: Oldrich Lipsky. SCREENPLAY: Lipsky, Zedenek Blaha. MUSIC: Ladislav Simon. ELECTRONICS EFFECTS: Zdenek Liska.

CAST: Milos Kopecky, Radovan Lukavasky, Vit Olmer.

MAN IN THE MOON
Gaumont (France, 1909). B/w silent short, 317 ft.

A man explores outer space in a hot-air balloon. He is greeted by a mob of winking, smiling stars and an encouraging face in the moon.

MAN IN THE WHITE SUIT, THE
Ealing (G.B., 1951); Universal (U.S., 1952). B/w, 97 mins.

A hapless inventor (Alec Guinness) comes up with a fabric that won't soil or wear out. To prove the validity of his claims, he designs an indestructible suit and, shortly thereafter, is pursued by various fabric manufacturers who see the new material as a potential financial disaster.

PRODUCER: Michael Balcon. DIRECTOR: Alexander Mackendrick. SCREENPLAY: Roger MacDougall, John Dighton, and Alexander Mackendrick, based on a play by Roger MacDougall. CINEMATOGRAPHY: Douglas Slocombe. MUSIC: Benjamin Frankel.

SUPPORTING PLAYERS: Joan Greenwood, Cecil Parker, Michael Gough, Ernest Thesiger, Howard Marion-Crawford, Colin Gordon.

MAN THEY COULD NOT HANG, THE
Columbia (1939). B/w, 72 mins.

Fine acting elevates this B production to above-par status. A benevolent scientist (Boris Karloff) invents a mechanical heart in the hope that it will benefit all of humanity. When a patient dies during an experimental operation, the doctor is accused of murder, convicted, and executed. Brought back to life through the use of his own invention, the doctor undergoes a personality change and, with bitterness in his tin ticker, stalks and murders the jurors who convicted him.

PRODUCER: Wallace MacDonald. DIRECTOR: Nick Grinde. SCREENPLAY: Karl Brown, from a story by Leslie White and George Sayre. CINEMATOGRAPHY: Benjamin Kline.

SUPPORTING PLAYERS: Lorna Gray, Don Beddoe, Robert Wilcox.

MAN THEY COULDN'T ARREST, THE
Gaumont (G.B., 1933). B/w, 72 mins.

A scientist invents a long-distance eavesdropping machine.

DIRECTOR: T. Hays Hunter. SCREENPLAY: Hunter, Angus MacPhail, Arthur Wimperis. CINEMATOGRAPHY: Leslie Rowson.

CAST: Hugh Wakefield, Gordon Harker, Renée Clama.

MAN WHO COULD CHEAT DEATH, THE
Paramount (1959). Color, 83 mins.

Colorful Hammer Films remake of THE MAN ON HALF MOON STREET starring Anton Diffring as the seemingly ageless scientist who stays young through organ transplants from unsuspecting donors. A hitch in his time schedule causes instant mummification.

PRODUCER: Michael Carreras. DIRECTOR: Terence Fisher. SCREENPLAY: Jimmy Sangster. MAKEUP: Roy Ashton. CINEMATOGRAPHY: Jack Asher. MUSIC: Richard Bennett.

SUPPORTING PLAYERS: Hazel Court, Christopher Lee, Francis de Wolff.

MAN WHO FELL TO EARTH, THE
Cinema Five (1976). Color and Panavision, 117 mins.

Alien Thomas Jerome Newton (David Bowie) arrives on Earth on a financial mission. He must earn enough capital to construct a water-transporting spaceship to bring a load of the much-treasured liquid to his own parched world. In order to achieve this goal, the humanoid settles down and, with the help of patent lawyer Oliver Farnsworth (Buck Henry), produces a horde of inventions. Newton's reclusiveness, however, angers his already jealous rivals, and he is hounded CIA-style. His Earth girl friend, Mary Lou (Candy Clarke), and Farnsworth are bribed by the mob, leaving the gentle alien alone and unguarded. Newton is kidnapped and tested, then tortured. His felinelike eyes are damaged, making it impossible for him ever to return to his alien homeland and family. He is finally released. Earthbound, he adopts the lifestyle of a lonely, albeit rich, recluse—the only being of his kind on the planet.

DIRECTOR: Nicholas Roeg. SCREENPLAY: Paul Mayersberg, from the novel by Walter Tevis. MUSIC: John Phillips. MAKEUP: Linda De Vetta. SPECIAL EFFECTS: Peter S. Ellenshaw.

SUPPORTING PLAYERS: Rip Torn as Nathan Bryce, Bernie Casey as Peters, Linda Hutton as Elaine, Rick Ricardo as Trevor.

Cinema Five

The Man Who Fell to Earth

MAN WHO LIVED AGAIN, THE
Gaumont (G.B., 1936). B/w, 68 mins.

A little-known Boris Karloff film starring the high priest of screen horror as slightly daft Dr. Laurience, a scientist who discovers a way to transfer the thought contents of one brain into another via an electrical process. Rebuked by the scientific community and labeled a crackpot, the scientist makes plans to switch his own brain with that of a young colleague. He wants to become the young man so he can win the heart of the youth's fiancée. It doesn't work.

DIRECTOR: Robert Stevenson. SCREENPLAY: L. du Garde Peach, Sidney Gillitat, John Balderston. MAKEUP: Roy Ashton. CINEMATOGRAPHY: Jack Cox.

SUPPORTING PLAYERS: Anna Lee as Clare Wyatt, John Loder, Cecil Parker.

MAN WHO LIVED TWICE, THE
Columbia (1936). B/w, 73 mins.

A criminal undergoes plastic surgery to escape the law. When he awakes, however, he is a truly "new" man, in that a sudden case of amnesia has wiped out all memories of his sordid former life. Assuming a new identity, he becomes a famous doctor. But will the law let bygones be bygones?

PRODUCER: Ben Pivar. DIRECTOR: Harry Lachman. SCREENPLAY: T. Van Dycke, Fred Niblo, and Arthur Strawn, from a story by Van Dycke and Henry Altimus. CINEMATOGRAPHY: James Van Trees.

CAST: Ralph Bellamy, Marian Marsh, Ward Bond, Isabel Jewell.

MAN WHO TURNED TO STONE, THE
Columbia (1957). B/w, 80 mins.

Several 200-year-old scientists keep themselves alive by draining the energy out of the bodies of young women. When the women stop coming, the troubles begin, with the scientists' skin turning into stone.

PRODUCER: Sam Katzman. DIRECTOR: Leslie Kardos. SCREENPLAY: Raymond T. Marcus. CINEMATOGRAPHY: Benjamin Kline. MUSIC: Ross DiMaggio.

CAST: Victor Jory, Ann Doran, William Hudson, Paul Cavanaugh.

MAN WITH NINE LIVES, THE
Columbia (1940). B/w, 73 mins.

Dr. Leon Karvall (Boris Karloff) is working on a cure for cancer that involves the freezing of infected bodies, when he suddenly disappears. A decade later, a brilliant young doctor (Roger Pryor) finds both Dr. Karvall and his patients in a state of suspended animation on a secret-island lab site. The scientist is revived and the cure is declared a success. Local law-enforcement officers, however, have different ideas.

DIRECTOR: Nick Grinde. SCREENPLAY: Karl Brown, from a story by Harold Shumate.

SUPPORTING PLAYERS: Jo Anne Sayers, Charles Trowbridge.

MAN WITHOUT A BODY, THE
Filmplays (1957). B/w, 80 mins.

The head of the famous prognosticator Nostradamus (Michael Golden) is brought back to life by a scientist. While Nostradamus is quite happy to make predictions for the doctor, he'd really like to have a pair of shoulders beneath his head.

PRODUCER: Guido Coen. DIRECTORS: W. Lee Wilder, Charles Saunders. SCREENPLAY: William Grote. MAKEUP: Jim Hydes. CINEMATOGRAPHY: Brendan Stafford. MUSIC: Robert Elms.

Things That Came

Men will not be reduced to servitude and uniformity, they will be released to freedom and variety. All the balderdash one finds in films such as Fritz Lang's *Metropolis* about "robot workers" should be cleared out of your minds before you work on this film. As a general rule, you may take it that whatever Lang did on *Metropolis* is the exact contrary of what we want here!

H. G. Wells, on his screenplay for *Things to Come*

SUPPORTING PLAYERS: Robert Hutton, George Coulouris, Kim Parker, Tony Quinn.

MAN WITH TWO HEADS, THE
Mishkin (1972). Color, 80 mins.

Dr. Jekyll tries to split Good and Evil and winds up becoming the evil Mr. Blood.

PRODUCER: William Mishkin. DIRECTOR, SCREENWRITER, AND CINEMATOGRAPHER: Andy Milligan.

CAST: Denis DeMarne, Gay Feld, Julie Stratton.

MAN WITH TWO LIVES, THE
Monogram (1942). B/w, 65 mins.

A man killed in an accident is returned to life by a friendly scientist. Unfortunately, this time around the fellow (Edward Norris) has his body taken over by the soul of a gangster electrocuted at the same moment the patient originally died.

PRODUCER: A. W. Hacke. DIRECTOR: Phil Rosen. SCREENPLAY: Joseph Hoffman. CINEMATOGRAPHY: Harry Neumann.

SUPPORTING PLAYERS: Marlo Dwyer, Frederick Burton, Kenne Duncan, Anthony Warde.

MAROONED
Columbia (1969). Color/scope, 134 mins.

A team of astronauts becomes marooned in space. Maintaining voice communication with Earth headquarters, the spacemen calmly reflect on their status while the world below demands a rescue mission.

PRODUCER: M. J. Frankovich. DIRECTOR: John Sturges. SCREENPLAY: Mayo Simon, from the novel by MARTIN CAIDIN. CINEMATOGRAPHY: Daniel Fapp. SPECIAL EFFECTS: Lawrence W. Butler, Donald C. Glouner, R. Robinson.

CAST: Gregory Peck as Charles Keith, Richard Crenna as Jim Pruett, David Janssen as Ted Dougherty, James Franciscus as Clayton Stone, Gene Hackman as Buzz Lloyd.

MARS NEEDS WOMEN
AIP (1966). Color, 80 mins.

A Martian with an active libido (Tommy Kirk) comes to Earth to seek a teen-queen. He finds plenty of possible mates . . . plus a good beat to dance to.

PRODUCER, DIRECTOR, AND SCREENWRITER: Larry Buchanan.

SUPPORTING PLAYERS: Yvonne Craig, Warren Hammack, Roger Ready.

MARTIAN IN PARIS, A
France (1960). B/w.

A humanoid Martian lands in Paris to study the strange Earth malady called love.

DIRECTOR: Jean-Daniel Daninos. SCREENPLAY: Daninos and Jacques Vilfrid.

CAST: Darry Cowl, Nicole Mirel, Gisèle Grandre.

MARTIANS ARRIVED, THE

Epoca/Dario (Spain/Italy, 1964). B/w, 95 mins.

A group of humanoid Martians decides to visit Earth. They like it so much that they decide to homestead.

DIRECTORS: Pipolo and Franco Castellano. SCREENPLAY: Franco Castellano, G. Moccia, Leonardo Martin. MUSIC: Ennio Mirricone.

CAST: Paolo Panelli, Alfredo Landa, Jose Calvo.

MASKED MARVEL, THE

Republic (1943). B/w serial, 12 chapters (24 reels).

Known in feature form as SAKIMA AND THE MASKED MARVEL (1966).

Evil Sakima (Johnny Arthur) plans to do in the Allied war effort via a new and very secret explosive. Aiding the nasty fellow is insurance investigator Martin Crane (William Forrest). The two of them kill fellow investigator Warren Hamilton (Howard Hickman) when the unfortunate insurance exec stumbles onto their scheme. Hamilton's daughter, Alice (Louise Currie), joins forces with the Masked Marvel (insurance man Bob Bartion, played by David Bacon) to bring the murderer to justice and save the world from going *boom* prematurely.

DIRECTOR: Spencer G. Bennett. SCREENPLAY: Royal K. Cole, Ronald Davidson, Basil Dickey, Jesse Duffy, Grant Nelson, George H. Plympton, Joseph Poland. CINEMATOGRAPHY: Reggie Lanning. SPECIAL EFFECTS: Howard Lydecker. MUSIC: Mort Glickman.

MASK OF FU MANCHU, THE

MGM (1932). B/w, 72 mins.

Fu Manchu (Boris Karloff) pits his strength against intrepid Nayland Smith (Lewis Stone) of Scotland Yard. In order to instigate a modern "holy war," Fu steals from the British Museum a mask once owned by Genghis Khan. The owner of the mask and of Khan's all-powerful sword is destined to rule the world, according to legend.

MGM

The Mask of Fu Manchu

Backing up Fu's mythical destiny is a dastardly laboratory filled with mind-controlling drugs, a torture chamber, and an ever-ready death ray.

PRODUCER: Irving Thalberg. DIRECTORS: Charles Brabin, Charles Vidor. SCREENPLAY: Irene Kuhn, Edgar Allan Woolf, and John Willard, from an adaptation by Sax Rohmer of one of his own novels. CINEMATOGRAPHY: Gaetano Guadio.

SUPPORTING PLAYERS: Karen Morley, Myrna Loy, Jean Hersholt.

MASTER MINDS

Monogram (1949). B/w, 64 mins.

A crazy scientist (Alan Napier) keeps a hairy giant (Glenn Strange) down in his lab for safekeeping. The Bowery Boys enter the picture (Leo Gorcey, Huntz Hall, Gabriel Dell, William Benedict), and the scientist suddenly hatches a plan to transplant Huntz Hall's brain into the ape-creature's head.

PRODUCER: Jan Grippo. DIRECTOR: Jean Yarbrough. SCREENPLAY: Charles R. Marion, Bert Lawrence. MAKEUP: Jack Pierce. CINEMATOGRAPHY: Marcel Le Picard. MUSICAL DIRECTOR: Edward J. Kay.

MASTER OF THE WORLD

AIP (1961). Color, 104 mins.

Robur (Vincent Price) plans to put an end to all warfare. Flying above the

American International Pictures

Master of the World

world's armies in his airship *The Albatross,* he intends to bomb them into submission. Based on the JULES VERNE novels *Master of the World* and *Robur the Conqueror,* the film has a tendency to sag under the weight of its tiny budget and gigantic scope.

PRODUCER: James H. Nicholson. DIRECTOR: William Witney. SCREENPLAY: RICHARD MATHESON. CINEMATOGRAPHY: Gil Warrenton. SPECIAL EFFECTS: Ray Mercer, Tim Barr, Wah Chang, Gene Warren. MUSIC: Les Baxter.

SUPPORTING PLAYERS: Henry Hull, Charles Bronson, Mary Webster, Vito Scotti.

MECHANICAL BUTCHERS, THE
Lumière (France, 1898). B/w silent short.

A pig is fed into a machine that automatically changes it into bacon, sausage, etc.

MECHANICAL HUSBAND, THE
1910. B/w silent short.

A young woman falls head over heels for a nuts-and-bolts beau.

MECHANICAL LEGS, THE
Gaumont (France, 1908). B/w silent short.

A legless man finds new stature with the aid of robot legs.

MECHANICAL MAN, THE
Universal (1915). B/w silent short, one reel.

When a life-sized mechanical man breaks down, the inventor takes its place.

MECHANICAL MARY ANNE
Hepworth (G.B., 1910). B/w silent short.

A robot servant gets carried away with her work.

MECHANICAL STATUE AND THE INGENIOUS SERVANT, THE
1907. B/w silent short, 450 ft.

PRODUCER AND DIRECTOR: J. Stuart Blackton.

MENACE FROM OUTER SPACE
Reed (1954). B/w, 78 mins.

ROCKY JONES, SPACE RANGER TV episodes are, once again, reedited into feature form.

PRODUCER: Roland Reed.

MESSAGE FROM MARS, A
United Kingdom Films (G.B., 1913). B/w silent feature, 4,000 ft.

Martian Ramiel (E. Holman Clark) is sent by the king of Mars to Earth on a mission of mercy. He must save an Earthly sinner. Spying a likely subject (Charles Hawtrey) at a Punch and Judy show, the Martian begins his moralistic work.

PRODUCER: Nicholson Ormsby-Scott. DIRECTOR AND SCREENWRITER: J. Wellett Waller.

SUPPORTING PLAYERS: Crissie Bell, Hubert Willis, Frank Hector.

MESSAGE FROM SPACE
UA (1978). Color, 105 mins.

A Nipponese STAR WARS variation with a kamikaze feel. Under attack by the Gavanas, the Jillucians are on the verge of extinction. Kido, the elder of the Jillucians, throws out into space eight mystical "Liabe" nuts, hoping they will find and impel eight brave men to come to his planet's aid. For good measure, he sends out his daughter, Emeralida (who always seems to be dressed in a wedding gown), and warrior Urocco to follow those nuts.

Eventually they come across Meia (Peggy Lee Brennan); drunken ex-

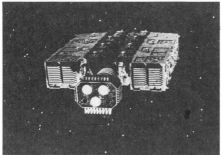

Message from Space

general Guarda (Vic Morrow) and his robot sidekick, Beba 2; hot-rodders Shiro, Aaron (Philip Casanoff), and Jack; and Prince Hans (Sonny Chiba). Returning to the endangered planet, they find that Gavanas Rocksair is in the process of blowing it into oblivion via nuclear weaponry. They attack Rocksair's base and, after the usual space-opera display of baseness, vanquish all villains.

The planet's surface, however, is not a great place to be right about now, and so, boarding a space schooner, our heroes load the survivors onto the boat (a traditional Earth sailing ship that glides through space) and they all take off into space in search of a new world and, presumably, a lot of air to breathe.

PRODUCER: Toei Studios. DIRECTOR: Kinji Fukasaku. SPECIAL EFFECTS: Minoru Nakano, Noburu Takanashi, Nobuo Yajima. MUSIC: Kenichio Morioka, performed by the Columbia Symphony Orchestra.

MESSAGE TO THE FUTURE
Hungary (1970). Color serial.

A family meets its descendants from the 30th century.

DIRECTOR: Jozsef Nepp.

METEOR
AIP (1979). Movielab color and Panavision, 103 mins.

A comet slams into the asteroid belt and sends a fleet of meteors heading on a collision course with Earth. The leader of the pack, called Orpheus, is a five-mile-long hunk of rock that could take out the entire planet. NASA executive Sherwood (Karl Malden) sum-

mons former employee Paul Bradley (Sean Connery) back into service. Years ago, he designed a floating missile launcher to protect Earth from such incidents. The platform, *Hercules,* was launched but put into an orbit in which its missiles were pointing downward, at the U.S.S.R. Seeing his saving grace turned into a menacing weapon, Bradley quit NASA.

Now, with Sherwood, he must convince the president (Henry Fonda), the secretary of defense (Richard Dysart), and commie-hating General Adlon (Martin Landau) to reangle the launcher in order to save the planet. Not everyone thinks the threat of the meteor is real. It is only after a few isolated villages have been wiped out by fragments that cooperation is forthcoming. Russian scientist Dubov (Brian Keith) and his interpreter, Tatiana (Natalie Wood), arrive Stateside to link up their identical launcher, *Peter the Great,* with the American system. Neither fleet of nuclear warheads alone is capable of destroying Orpheus, but together . . . *boomski!*

Headquartered in a computer-launch center beneath the streets of New York City, the team successfully destroys the meteor, but not before the city is leveled by fragments, along with Hong Kong and various cities in Europe. Cheesy special effects don't add to the overall clout of *Meteor.*

PRODUCERS: Arnold Orgolini, Theodore Parvin. DIRECTOR: Ronald Neame. SCREENPLAY: Stanley Mann and Edmund H. North, from a story by North. ART DIRECTOR: David Constable. SPE-

Meteor

CIAL EFFECTS: Glen Robinson, Robert Staples, Frank van der Veer (uncredited), Bill Cruse (uncredited), Robbie Blalack (uncredited), Jamie Shourt (uncredited). MUSIC: Laurence Rosenthal.

SUPPORTING PLAYERS: Trevor Howard as Sir Michael Hughes, Joseph Campanella as Easton, Bo Brundun as Manheim.

METROPOLIS
UFA (Germany, 1926); Paramount (U.S., 1927). B/w silent feature, eight reels, 10,400 ft., 128 mins.

Despite the haphazard editing job that destroyed sections of subplots of this film, *Metropolis* stands as a visual landmark in screen sf. In the year 2000, the skyscraper city of Metropolis is a wonderful place to live if you are one of the upper caste—well-to-do aristocrats who live and toil aboveground. For the subterranean workers, however, life is a wretched existence indeed. Toiling nearly around the clock, manning the machines that power the city above, the workers go from birth to death in the darkness of their catacombs.

When the son of Jon Frederson (Alfred Abel), the master industrialist of Metropolis, becomes involved with the workers, his father is not pleased. Freder (Gustav Frohlich) ignores the priorities of his social caste and follows a woman down into the catacombs after she reminds Freder that the workers are his brothers. The woman, Maria (Brigitte Helm), is an emancipationist who preaches nonviolent hope to the workers. Freder is shocked by what he finds below, where the laborers are almost worked to death at the oversized

The Museum of Modern Art/Film Stills Archive

Metropolis

machines. He vows to change their working conditions.

Meanwhile, Jon Frederson envisions a plan to stop Freder's snooping. He employs scientist/inventor Rotwang (Rudolf Klein-Rogge), asking him to bring life to a female robot. The robot is given the exact features of Maria. Maria is kidnapped. The robot is placed in her stead and it leads Maria's trusting workers on a revolt that will cause the laborers to destroy their own homes and flood their underground city. Freder discovers the plot and rescues Maria and most of the workers' children from the flood. He then battles with crazy Rotwang, tossing him off a building to the streets below. Jon Frederson and the leaders of the working class vow to put their differences behind them and work for a better Metropolis.

PRODUCER: Erich Pommer. DIRECTOR: Fritz Lang. SCREENPLAY: Lang, Thea von Harbou. ART DIRECTORS: Otto Hunte, Erich Kettelhut, Karl Vollbrecht. CINEMATOGRAPHY: Karl Freund, Gunther Rittau. SPECIAL EFFECTS: Eugen Shuftan. MUSIC: Gottfried Happertz.

SUPPORTING PLAYERS: Theodor Loos, Fritz Rasp, Heinrich George.

MILL OF THE STONE WOMEN
Parade (1963). Color, 94 mins.

In 1912, a scientist headquartered in a Dutch windmill attempts to keep his daughter alive through a series of blood transfusions. Her strange malady requires an abnormally large amount of blood, however, and so, blackmailing a local physician into aiding him, the

The Museum of Modern Art/Film Stills Archive

Metropolis

scientist begins capturing and draining local show-stoppers of their life-fluid. The victims are then mounted in a display of *Wax Museum* proportions.

PRODUCER: Gianpaolo Bigazzi. DIRECTOR: Giorgio Ferroni. SCREENPLAY: Remigio Del Crosso, Ugo Liberatore, Giorgio Stegani, Giorgio Ferroni. CINEMATOGRAPHY: Pierludovico Pavoni. MUSIC: Carlo Innocenzi.

CAST: Pierre Brice, Scilla Gabel, Dany Carel, Wolfgang Preiss.

MIND BENDERS, THE
AIP (1963). B/w, 99 mins.

The fate of a program dealing with sensory deprivation is jeopardized when one of the scientists running it abruptly kills himself.

PRODUCER: Michael Relph. DIRECTOR: Basil Dearden. SCREENPLAY: James Kennaway. CINEMATOGRAPHY: Denys Coop. MUSIC: Georges Auric.

CAST: Dirk Bogarde, Mary Ure, John Clements, Norman Bird.

MIND-DETECTING RAY, THE
Star (Hungary, 1918). B/w silent short.

A mind-reading machine is stolen by a villain. His actions are betrayed by the machine itself.

DIRECTOR: Alfred Desy. SCREENPLAY: Istvan Lazar.

MIND OF MR. SOAMES, THE
Amicus (G.B., 1969); Columbia (U.S., 1970). Color, 98 mins.

Mr. Soames (Terence Stamp) is a man in his 20s who has been in a coma since birth. Brought back to consciousness, he must be educated by doctors as one would educate an infant. The sympathetic head of the project (Robert Vaughn) watches in dismay as the education of Mr. Soames gradually becomes sensationalized, brutalized, and eventually, scandalized, with Mr. Soames being pursued by callous police.

PRODUCERS: Max J. Rosenberg, Milton Subotsky. DIRECTOR: Alan Cooke. SCREENPLAY: John Hale and Ed Simpson, from the novel by CHARLES ERIC MAINE. CINEMATOGRAPHY: Billy Williams. MUSIC: Michael Dress.

SUPPORTING PLAYERS: Nigel Davenport, Christian Roberts.

MIND SNATCHERS, THE
Cinerama (1972). Color, 94 mins.

When does a scientific blessing become a curse? When the government decides to use it for its own purposes. An electrical/surgical process originally used to help disturbed patients is used on rebellious recruit Miles (Ronny Cox) as a means of keeping the lad in line. Reese (Christopher Walken) can only stand by while Miles is snatched from the base by Dr. Frederick (Joss Acland) and the Major (Ralph Meeker) and tucked away in a Gothic castle in Germany, where the experiments are conducted. Zombiedom is the desired result.

PRODUCER: George Goodman. DIRECTOR: Bernard Girard. SCREENPLAY: Ron Whyte, from the play *The Happiness Cage*, by Dennis Reardon. CINEMATOGRAPHY: Manny Wynn. MUSIC: Phil Ramone.

SUPPORTING PLAYERS: Claus Nissen as the Psychiatrist, Birthe Newman as Lisa, Susan Travers as Nurse Schroeder.

Cinerama

The Mind Snatchers

MIRACLE RIDER, THE
Mascot (1935). B/w serial, 15 chapters (33 reels).

Oil executive Zaroff (Charles Middleton) attempts to steal an Indian reservation for its mother lode of X-94, a powerful new explosive. Aiding him is nasty Longboat (Bob Kortman), a half-breed who wants to become chief of the Ravenhead tribe by using an invisible ray to scare his peer group into submission. Enter Texas Ranger Tom Morgan (Tom Mix) and sweet-as-sap Ruth (Jean Gale), and you have the stage set for a showdown betwixt Good and Evil.

PRODUCER: Victor Zobel. DIRECTORS: Armand Schaefer, Reeves Eason. SCREENPLAY: John Rathmell.

MISADVENTURES OF MERLIN JONES, THE
Buena Vista/Walt Disney (1964). Color, 88 mins.

Teenage inventor Merlin (Tommy Kirk) invents a machine, sort of an electronic football helmet, that gives him the power to read minds.

PRODUCER: Walt Disney. DIRECTOR: Robert Stevenson. SCREENPLAY: Tom and Helen August. CINEMATOGRAPHY: Edward Colman. MUSIC: Buddy Baker.

Forked Tongue Dept.
He was promised he'd not be harmed, and he's been beaten half to death!
> "Karl Hussmann" to Ralph Bellamy in *The Ghost of Frankenstein*

SUPPORTING PLAYERS: Annette Funicello, Leon Ames, Stuart Erwin, Alan Hewitt.

MISSILE TO THE MOON
Astor (1959). B/w, 78 mins.

A group of astronauts unwittingly takes two escaped convicts with them to the moon. Once aboard Earth's satellite, the crew, good and evil members alike, encounter rock monsters, giant spiders, and a civilization of chorus-girl moon maidens. By the film's conclusion, they conclude that the moon is a really hot spot to visit.

PRODUCER: Marc Frederic. DIRECTOR: Richard Cunha. SCREENPLAY: H. E. Barrie, Vincent Fotre. MUSIC: Nicholas Carras. MAKEUP: Harry Thomas. SPECIAL EFFECTS: Ira Anderson, Harold Banks.

CAST: Richard Travis, Gary Clarke, Cathy Downs, Laurie Mitchell, Nina Bara, Michael Whalen.

MISSION STARDUST
Times Films (1968). Color, 95 mins.

Perry Rhodan (Lang Jeffries) lands on the moon and discovers a stranded alien rocket with a girl pilot on board.

PRODUCER: Aitor/PEA/Theumer Films. DIRECTOR: Primo Zeglio. MUSIC:

Astor

Missile to the Moon

Anton Garcia Abril. SCREENPLAY: K. H. Vogeman, Frederico d'Urritia.

SUPPORTING PLAYERS: Essy Persson, Luis Davilla, Daniel Martin.

MOLE MEN VS. THE SON OF HERCULES
Interfilm (1961). Color, 97 mins.

A group of albino folks from beneath the Earth are allergic to light, but that doesn't stop them from trying to take over the world above through super-scientific means. Strongman Maciste (Mark Forest) earns his place in mythology as the son of Hercules when he splits the Earth and sends sunlight pouring down on the pasty-faced pursuers of evil.

PRODUCER: Elio Scardamanlia. DIRECTOR: Antonio Leonviola. SCREENPLAY: Marcello Baldi, Giuseppe Mangfone. CINEMATOGRAPHY: Alvara Mancori. MUSIC: Armando Travaioli.

SUPPORTING PLAYERS: Moira Orfei, Paul Wynter, Enrico Glori.

MOLE PEOPLE, THE
Universal (1956). B/w, 78 mins.

Dr. Roger Bently (John Agar), Professor Lafarge (Nestor Paiva), and Dr. Bellamin (Hugh Beaumont) are on an expedition to the mountain ranges of Asia when a cave-in causes the ground literally to pull them beneath the surface of the Earth into the underground city of Sumaria. The city is ruled by albino humans who keep an army of malformed mole-people as slaves. The high priest, Elinu (Alan Napier), orders the men to be put to death. A handy flashlight wielded by Bently, however, drives the light-sensitive executioners away. Befriended by a Sumarian girl (Cynthia Patrick) who is not sensitive to light, the trio makes a break for it. Lafarge is killed by the mole-men. Later, the mole people see that these humans are different from the Sumarians. When Bently, Bellamin, and the Sumarian girl make for the surface, the mole people revolt, destroying the evil albinos. An earthquake occurs. The two men make it out alive. The girl is pinned under the wreckage of the aboveground entrance to Sumaria, dying as she glimpses the sun for the first time.

PRODUCER: William Alland. DIRECTOR: Virgil Vogel. SCREENPLAY: Laszlo Gorog. CINEMATOGRAPHY: Ellis Carter. MAKEUP: Wally Westmore. SPECIAL EFFECTS: Clifford Stine.

SUPPORTING PLAYERS: Eddie Parker (mole-man), Robin Hughes, Rodd Redwing, Frank Baxter.

MONITORS, THE
Commonwealth (1969). Color, 92 mins.

Aliens from space arrive and install monitoring devices above the Earth that will not allow mankind to do harm to itself.

PRODUCER: Bernard Sahlins. DIRECTOR: Jack Shea. SCREENPLAY: Myron Gold, from a novel by KEITH LAUMER. CINEMATOGRAPHY: Vilmos Zsigmond.

CAST: Guy Stockwell, Susan Oliver, Avery Schreiber, Sherry Jackson, Keenan Wynn, Alan Arkin, Larry Storch, Xavier Cugat, Jackie Vernon, Everett Dirksen, Stubby Kaye, Ed Begley, Sheppherd Strudwick as the alien.

MONKEY'S UNCLE, THE
Buena Vista/Walt Disney (1965). Color, 91 mins.

In this sequel to THE MISADVENTURES OF MERLIN JONES, Merlin (Tommy Kirk) pleases the dean of the college (Leon Ames) no end by saving the dumb football team from flunking out. He teaches them in their sleep how to pass the finals (he's already tested the method out successfully on a now-brainy chimpanzee). In his spare time, he constructs a pedal-powered airplane.

PRODUCERS: Walt Disney, Ron Miller. SCREENPLAY: Tom and Helen August. SPECIAL EFFECTS: Robert Mattey,

Eustace Lycett. CINEMATOGRAPHY: Edward Colman. MUSIC: Buddy Baker.

SUPPORTING PLAYERS: Annette Funicello, Frank Faylen, Norman Grabowski, Arthur O'Connell.

MONOLITH MONSTERS, THE
Universal (1957). B/w, 77 mins.

The *real* "rocky horror" picture show. Following a meteor shower, a local resident picks up a rock fragment; the next day he is found turned to stone. A little girl brings home a meteor fragment; the next morning her home is found buried under a ton of rock, her parents turned to stone. Dave Miller (Grant Williams), Cathy Barrett (Lola Albright), and Professor Arthur Flanders (Trevor Bardette) mull over these strange occurrences until a sudden thunderstorm tips them off to the cause. During the shower, the space-rock fragments grow to skyscraper size. The waterites crave moisture (hence draining human bodies of all fluid) in a big way. And after the shower, they head for town in a big way . . . now the size of skyscrapers. The moving wall of rock slowly slides toward the desert village. As one section topples from the tallest rocks, another section of the recently drenched material springs up from below. Miller and Flanders discover that salt water will stop the rocks and turn them into ordinary Earth rocks. They blow up a dam, and the water pours through a nearby seabed and douses the rocky renegades with salt.

PRODUCER: Howard Christie. DIRECTOR: John Sherwood. SCREENPLAY: Norman Jolley and Robert M. Fresco, from a story by Jack Arnold and Fresco. MAKEUP: Bud Westmore. MUSIC: Joseph Gershenson. SPECIAL EFFECTS: Clifford Stine.

SUPPORTING PLAYERS: William Schallert, Les Tremayne.

MONSTER, THE
Metro-Goldwyn (1925). B/w silent feature, 6,425 ft.

Mad Dr. Ziska (Lon Chaney) believes he can bring the dead back to life. He kidnaps passing motorists and stocks them in his lab for future reference.

PRODUCER AND DIRECTOR: Roland

West. SCREENPLAY: Willard Mack, Albert Kenyon. CINEMATOGRAPHY: Hal Mohr.

SUPPORTING PLAYERS: Gertrude Olmstead, Hallam Cooley.

MONSTER AND THE APE, THE
Columbia (1945). B/w serial, 15 chapters (30 reels).

Professor Ernst (George Macready) of the Bainbridge Research Foundation covets a robot, Metalogen Man, built by college professor Arnold (Ralph Morgan) for Ken Morgan (Robert Lowery). Ernst tries to snatch the robot and its metalogen-metal source of power, aided by an ape, Thor (Ray "Crash" Corrigan). With the help of Babs Arnold (Carole Mathews), Ken makes a monkey out of Thor and a cadaver out of Ernst.

PRODUCER: Rudolph C. Flothow. DIRECTOR: Howard Bretherton. SCREENPLAY: Sherman L. Lowe, Royal K. Cole. CINEMATOGRAPHY: C. W. O'Connell. MUSIC: Lee Zahler.

SUPPORTING PLAYERS: William Best, Anthony Warde, Eddie Parker.

MONSTER AND THE GIRL, THE
Paramount (1941). B/w, 65 mins.

A plot to drive any moviegoer bananas. The brain of a wrongly-executed man is transplanted into a gorilla. The gorilla becomes an avenging angel, of the hairy variety, by tracking down and killing the nasty fellows who framed its brain's original owner and forced his sister into prostitution. Quick, Cheeta, my gun!

PRODUCER: Jack Moss. DIRECTOR: Stuart Heisler. SCREENPLAY: Stuart Anthony. CINEMATOGRAPHY: Victor Milner.

CAST: Ellen Drew, Robert Paige, Onslow Stevens, George Zucco, Paul Lukas, Rod Cameron, Gerald Mohr.

MONSTER FROM GREEN HELL, THE
DCA (1958). B/w, 71 mins.

A spaceship containing a crew of experimental insects crash-lands in an Earth jungle. A group of scientists (led by Jim Davis and Barbara Turner) sets off in search of their missing missile. They arrive on the scene to find carnage. Radioactivity has transformed the insects, mostly wasps, into gigantic killer creatures. The insects are destroyed when a nearby volcano blows its top.

PRODUCER: Al Zimbalist. DIRECTOR: Kenneth Crane. SCREENPLAY: Louis Vittes, André Bohem. CINEMATOGRAPHY: Ray Flin. SPECIAL EFFECTS: Jess Davison, Jack Rabin, Louis DeWitt.

SUPPORTING PLAYERS: Robert E. Griffin, Eduardo Cianelli.

MONSTER FROM THE OCEAN FLOOR, THE
Lippert (1954). B/w, 64 mins.

Roger Corman's first big sf hit concerned the exploits of a crew of aquanauts who discover on the ocean floor a nasty octopus with a light bulb screwed into its head. The creature, which has been messing up shipping traffic, is rammed in its orb by a minisubmarine.

PRODUCER: Roger Corman. DIRECTOR: Wyott Ordung. SCREENPLAY: William Danch. CINEMATOGRAPHY: Floyd Crosby. MUSIC: André Brumer.

MONSTER MAKER, THE
PRC (1944). B/w, 64 mins.

A scientist (J. Carrol Naish) experimenting with glandular research accidentally gives a case of acromegaly to a concert pianist (Ralph Morgan). The musician soon turns into a monster with a bitter heart and pretty big hands.

PRODUCER: Sigmund Neufeld. DIRECTOR: Sam Newfield. SCREENPLAY: Pierre Gendron, Martin Mooney. CINEMATOGRAPHY: Robert Cline. MUSIC: Albert Glasser.

SUPPORTING PLAYERS: Wanda McKay, Glenn Strange, Sam Flint.

MONSTER ON THE CAMPUS
Universal (1958). B/w, 77 mins.

A prehistoric fish is discovered by an enterprising college professor (Arthur Franz). The coelecanth is covered with a strange fluid that is partially responsible for its state of perfect preservation. When a dragonfly alights on the fossil, it turns into a gigantic monster. The fluid finds its way into the natty doc's pipe, and when he smokes it, he goes ape . . . literally. Before you know it, a Neanderthal man is running around campus with a cute coed under each arm.

PRODUCER AND MUSIC DIRECTOR: Joseph Gershenson. DIRECTOR: Jack Arnold. SCREENPLAY: David Duncan. MAKEUP: Bud Westmore. SPECIAL EFFECTS: Clifford Stine. CINEMATOGRAPHY: Russell Metty.

SUPPORTING PLAYERS: Joanna Moore, Troy Donahue, Eddie Parker as the Neanderthal.

MONSTER THAT CHALLENGED THE WORLD, THE
UA (1957). B/w, 85 mins.

Atomic experiments create a race of gigantic sea slugs that threaten to take over the world, or at least the ocean, through rapid breeding.

PRODUCERS: Arthur Gardner, Jules Levy. DIRECTOR: Arnold Laven. SCREENPLAY: Pat Fielder. STORY: David Duncan. CINEMATOGRAPHY: Lester White, Scotty Welborn. MUSIC: Heinz Roemheld.

CAST: Tim Holt, Audrey Dalton, Hans Conreid.

MONSTROSITY
Emerson (1964). B/w, 70 mins.

A crazy doctor tries to produce a fleet of zombies through brain operations. His method? Unorthodox transplants. For instance, into one female patient is sewn the brain of a cat. *Purr*-fect plan, eh?

PRODUCERS: Jack Pollexfen, Dean Dillman, Jr. DIRECTOR: Joseph Mascelli. SCREENPLAY: Vy Russell, Sue Dwiggens, Dean Dillman, Jr. CINEMATOGRAPHY: Alfred Taylor. MUSIC: Gene Kauer.

CAST: Frank Gerstle, Erika Peters, Judy Bamber.

MOON PILOT
Walt Disney/Buena Vista (1962). Technicolor, 98 mins.

Charlie the space chimp returns from orbit and begins having temper tantrums. He has, in fact, been moonstruck. NASA is concerned that the same fate may befall astronaut Richmond Talbot (Tom Tryon). Although Richmond isn't particularly worried, he appreciates the helpful hints given to him by beautiful and exotic Lyrae (Dany Saval), a woman who is actu-

ally an alien from the planet Beta Lyrae. She tells Talbot of the dangers of "proton rays," which will cause the fellow to become unhinged. Giving him a secret formula for a coating to protect his capsule, Dany arouses much suspicion, especially from Talbot's brother, Walter (Tommy Kirk). The ship takes off on schedule and Talbot is protected from moon madness. One problem: he's fallen for Lyrae and decides to take a side trip to her planet to visit her parents before stopping on the moon. At Mission Control, Vanneman (Brian Keith) and McClosky (Edmund O'Brien) are convinced that Talbot has come unglued. They are somewhat reassured when they hear pretty Lyrae's voice come over their intercom. She has made the trip with her Earthly fiancé.

PRODUCERS: Walt Disney, Bill Anderson. DIRECTOR: James Neilsen. SCREENPLAY: Maurice Tombragal, based on the novel by Robert Buckner. MUSIC: Paul Smith. SPECIAL EFFECTS: Eustace Lycett.

MOONRAKER
UA (1979). Color and Panavision, 126 mins.

Scientific genius Drax (Michael Lonsdale) is not satisfied with building the space shuttles for NASA's upcoming shuttle program. He wants to keep a fleet of his own as well. When one of his private ships crashes, he murders a few innocent folks and steals back one of the NASA shuttles. The theft, in turn, brings James Bond (Roger Moore) into the plot at the urging of "M" (Bernard Lee), "Q" (Desmond Llewelyn), and Moneypenny (Lois Maxwell). Bond eventually discovers the fate of the shuttle.

Drax, it would seem, wants to start a new master-race. He has built a space station undetected above the Earth and, using the shuttles, will take the fittest of his young servants/astronauts into space for mating purposes. A deadly germ dropped from his space station will destroy the current human population, leaving the planet free to be repopulated by his blonde, blue-eyed staff. Aiding him in his villainy is Jaws (Richard Kiel) and Chang (Toshiro Suga). Aiding Bond is Holly

Moonraker

Goodhead (Lois Chiles) and "Q's" roster of inventions.

There is a final showdown on Drax's station in space that drags in everyone and everything from the U.S. marines to shoot-from-the-hip laser pistols.

PRODUCER: Albert R. Broccoli. DIRECTOR: Lewis Gilbert. SCREENPLAY: Christopher Wood, from the novel by Ian Fleming. CINEMATOGRAPHY: Jean Tournier. MUSIC: John Barry. PRODUCTION DESIGN: Ken Adam. SPECIAL EFFECTS: Derek Meddings.

SUPPORTING PLAYERS: Corinne Clery as Corinne Dufour, Blanche Ravalec as Dolly, Geoffrey Keen as Frederick Gray.

MOONSTRUCK
Pathé (1909). Silent short, b/w with hand coloring.

A French film wherein a drunk falls into a deep sleep and dreams he is transported to the moon. Once there, he fights an army of grouchy moonmen.

MOON ZERO TWO
WB (1969). Color, 100 mins.

A self-proclaimed space "western." In 2021 a down-on-his-luck space shuttle pilot, Bill Kemp (James Olson), is blackmailed into helping a gang of desperadoes steal a sapphire asteroid set in space. He falls for Clementine Taplin (Catherine von Schell) and is torn between love and money. Gosh darn it, sure is a clever story-line.

PRODUCER AND SCREENPLAY: Michael Carreras. DIRECTOR: Roy Ward Baker. ORIGINAL STORY: Gavil Lyall, Frank Hardman, Martin Davison. CINEMATOGRAPHY: Paul Beeson. SPECIAL EFFECTS: Les Bowie, Kit West, Nick Allder. MUSIC: Philip Martell.

SUPPORTING PLAYERS :Warren Mitchell, Dudley Foster, Michael Ripper, Neil McCallum.

MOST DANGEROUS MAN ALIVE, THE
Columbia (1961). B/w, 76 mins.

An unjustly convicted convict becomes an unjustly radiated escapee when, after a bolt from prison, he is caught by an exploding cobalt bomb. Absorbing the impact of the steel, he becomes a hard-as-metal avenging angel before turning to dust at the film's climax.

PRODUCER: Benedict Bogeaus. DIRECTOR: Allan Dwan. SCREENPLAY: James Leicester, Phillip Rock. CINEMATOGRAPHY: Carl Carvahal. MUSIC: Louis Forbest.

CAST: Ron Randell, Morris Ankrum, Debra Paget, Joel Donte.

MOTHRA
Toho (Japan, 1961); Columbia (U.S., 1962). Color, 100 mins.

When two six-inch girls (Emi and Yumi Ito) are abducted from their tropical-island home, the great god Mothra, whose temple they guard, decides to take a trip to Japan. The army and the scientific community are put on the alert, to no avail. The god, a gigantic caterpillar, appears and abruptly turns into a gigantic butterfly, Mothra (Mosura). He rescues the tiny girls and, turning his back and/or wings on modern weaponry, returns to his island.

PRODUCER: Tomoyuki Tanaka. DIRECTOR: Inoshiro Honda. SCREENPLAY: Shinichi Sekizawa. CINEMATOGRAPHY: Hajime Koizumi. SPECIAL EFFECTS: Eiji Tsuburaya, Hiroshi Mukoyama. MUSIC: Yuji Koseki.

SUPPORTING PLAYERS: Frankie Sakai, Hiroshi Koizumi.

MOTOR CAR OF THE FUTURE
Messter (Germany, 1910). B/w silent short, 300 ft.
A car has the ability to fly. After clearing a train, it heads for Saturn's rings.

MOTOR CHAIR, THE
Italia (Italy, 1911). B/w silent short, 360 ft.
A chair has a mind of its own.

"?" MOTORIST, THE
G.B. (1906). B/w silent short, 200 ft.
A futuristically fueled car zooms into space.

Chivalry Ain't Dead, See
    Listen, baby, I'm a big boy now, see, and old enough to find my own dames, so just beat it!
        Lemmy Caution (Eddie Constantine) to a futuristic flirt in *Alphaville*

PRODUCER: R. W. Paul. DIRECTOR: Walter R. Booth.

MOTOR VALET, THE
Alpha (G.B., 1906). B/w silent short.
A robot servant goes berserk. After smashing the furniture, he blows up.
DIRECTOR: Arthur Cooper.

MOUSE ON THE MOON, THE
Lopert (1963). Color, 85 mins.
The tiny duchy of Grand Fenwick reaches the moon before the United States or the U.S.S.R. by using a fuel derived from local wine. A sequel to THE MOUSE THAT ROARED.
PRODUCER: Walter Shenson. DIRECTOR: Richard Lester. SCREENPLAY: Michael Pertwee. CINEMATOGRAPHY: Wilkie Cooper. MUSIC: Ron Grainer.
CAST: Margaret Rutherford, Bernard Cribbins, Terry-Thomas, Ron Moody, David Kossoff.

MOUSE THAT ROARED, THE
Columbia (1959). Color, 85 mins.
A grand dose of nuttiness from the book of the same name, by Leonard Wibberley. The small duchy of Grand Fenwick, finding itself financially strapped, declares war on the United States, theorizing that when they lose, they'll be given millions in foreign aid. Unfortunately, an overly zealous infantryman (Peter Sellers) proves an effectively, albeit clumsily so, disarming adversary for the U.S. Invading New York with a host of long-bowmen, he steals a secret U.S. bomb and wins the war!
PRODUCER: Walter Shenson. DIRECTOR: Jack Arnold. SCREENPLAY: Roger MacDougall, Stanley Mann. MAKEUP: Stuart Freeborn. CINEMATOGRAPHY: John Wilcox. MUSIC: Edwin Astley.
CAST: Peter Sellers (in three roles), Jean Seberg, David Kossoff, Leo McKern, Monty Landis, Timothy Bateson.

MUNSTER, GO HOME
Universal (1966). Color, 1966.
The monstrous Munster family, Herman (Fred Gwynne), vampire Gran'pa (Al Lewis), werewolf Little Eddie (Butch Patrick), and deathly Lilly (Yvonne DeCarlo) lock horns with John Carradine and Terry-Thomas after they inherit a title and land in Europe.
PRODUCERS: Joe Connelly, Bob Mosher. DIRECTOR: Earl Bellamy. SCREENPLAY: George Tibbles, Joe Connelly, Bob Mosher. MAKEUP: Bud Westmore. CINEMATOGRAPHY: Benny Kline. MUSIC: Jack Marshall.

Potato Stations! Potato Stations!
    You remember that scene with the ship hitting those meteors? Well, they were really potatoes wrapped in foil!
        Special effects whiz Jack Rabin, on *Rocketship XM*

SUPPORTING PLAYERS: Hermione Gingold, Debbie Watson.

MURDER BY TELEVISION
Imperial (1935). B/w, 60 mins.
Telephone calls detonate a device in a TV camera that causes it to fire a death ray.
DIRECTOR: Clifford Sanforth. SCREENPLAY: Joseph O'Donnell. TV TECHNICIAN: Milton M. Stern. TECHNICAL SUPERVISOR: Henry Spitz. MUSIC: Oliver Wallace.
CAST: Bela Lugosi, June Collyer, George Meeker, Hattie McDaniel.

MUTATIONS
Columbia (1974). Color, 91 mins.

Slightly deranged Dr. Nolter (Donald Pleasance) believes that the future of civilization on Earth lies in the cross breeding of humans with plants. To this end, he conducts a series of rather unorthodox experiments, aided by the neighborhood mutant, Lynch (Tom Baker), the deformed owner of a traveling freak show. Of course, Nolter's experiments don't pan out as expected, with most of the plant people resembling slightly charred Tupperware. Eventually, the revolting creatures revolt and Nolter is given a pretty nifty bear hug from a walking human fly trap (originally his daughter's fiancé). The film ends with Nolter's demise and a gruesome finish to his handiwork. Not exactly the sort of cinematic fare that helps popularize science with the masses.

Mutations

A Getty Picture Corporation, Ltd., Film. PRODUCER: Robert D. Weinbach. DIRECTOR: Jack Cardiff. SCREENPLAY: Weinbach and Edward Mann. MAKEUP: Charles Parker. TIME-LAPSE PHOTOGRAPHY: Ken Middleham.

SUPPORTING CAST: Brad Harris, Julie Ege, Michael Dunn, Jill Haworth, Willie "Popeye" Ingram, Esther "Alligator Girl" Blackmon, Hugh "Pretzel Boy" Baily, Felix "Frog Boy" Duarte, Molly Tweedle, Kathy Kitchen.

MUTINY IN OUTER SPACE
AA/Woolner (1964). B/w, 85 mins.

A space station is attacked by a deadly space fungus. The ooze not only covers the exterior of the ship, but also slips within and seeks out human vic-

Allied Artists

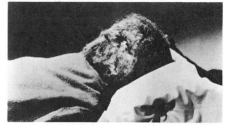

Mutiny in Outer Space

tims. Major Towers (William Leslie), Faith (Dolores Faith), and the Commander (Glen Langan) determine that the fungus comes from the moon and attempt to find a way to nip it in its various buds.

PRODUCERS: Hugo Grimaldi, Arthur Pierce. DIRECTOR: Grimaldi. SCREENPLAY: Arthur B. Pierce. MUSICAL DIRECTOR: Gordon Zahler. CINEMATOGRAPHY: Archie Dalzell.

SUPPORTING PLAYERS: Richard Garland, Harold Lloyd, Jr., James Dobson, Pamela Curren.

MY SON, THE VAMPIRE
Fernwood and Renown (G.B., 1952); Blue Chip (U.S., 1961). B/w, 74 mins.

Mother Reilly (Arthur Lucan) matches wits—or half-wits, as the case may be—with a crazy scientist (Bela Lugosi) who believes he is a vampire and pals around with a killer robot.

PRODUCER AND DIRECTOR: John Gilling. SCREENPLAY: Val Valentine. MUSIC: Lindo Southworth.

SUPPORTING PLAYERS: Ian Wilson, Richard Wattis, Dora Bryan.

THE MYSTERIANS
Toho (Japan, 1957); RKO (U.S., 1959). Cinemascope and Eastmancolor, 89 mins.

A large-scale Japanese sf tale, cinematically told more sensibly than usual. The alien world Mysteroid needs a fresh supply of young women to replenish the dwindling ranks of their young. Setting up a camp on the moon, they attack the Earth via a barrage of death rays and an army of titanic robots. Moving to Earth, they set up an underground command post. The Earth, meanwhile, devises an air-strike force as lethal as that possessed by the aliens, and after a number of dogfights, the villains are driven off the Earth, off the moon, and out of nearby space.

PRODUCER: Tomoyuki Tanaka. DIRECTOR: Inoshiro Honda. SCREENPLAY: Takeshi Kimura, from a story by Jojiro Okami. MUSIC: Akira Ifukube. SPECIAL EFFECTS: Eiji Tsuburaya.

CAST: Kenji Sahara as Joji Atsumi, Yumi Shirakawa as Etsuki Shirasishi, Momoko Kochi, Takashi Shimura, Akihiko Hirata.

MYSTERIOUS CONTRAGRAV, THE
Gold Seal (1915). B/w silent short, two reels.

An inventor comes up with an antigravity device that allows people to float through the use of "negative electricity."

PRODUCER AND SCREENWRITER: Henry McRae.

MYSTERIOUS ISLAND
MGM (1929). Two color, with sound effects, 95 mins.

This adaptation of JULES VERNE's novel featured the mysterious Count Dakker (Lionel Barrymore) in lieu of Captain Nemo. The good count builds two submarines and investigates a city beneath the sea which houses a race of small aquamen. He also battles the ever-popular giant octopus.

DIRECTORS: Lucien Hubbard, Maurice Tourneur, Benjamin Christiansen. SCREENPLAY: Hubbard. CINEMATOGRAPHY: Percy Hilburn. SPECIAL EFFECTS: James Basevi, Louis H. Tolhurst, Irving Ries. MUSIC: Martin Broones and Arthur Lange.

SUPPORTING PLAYERS: Pauline Starke, Warner Oland, Jane Daly, Montague Love, Snitz Edwards.

MYSTERIOUS ISLAND
Soviet Children's Film Studio (U.S.S.R., 1941).

Captain Nemo and his *Nautilus* aid a group of young castaways.

DIRECTOR:: Ev Penziline, B. M. Chelintzev. SCREENPLAY: Chelintzev, M. P. Kalinine. SPECIAL EFFECTS: M. F. Karukov.

MYSTERIOUS ISLAND
Columbia (1950). B/w serial, 15 chapters (30 reels), 480 mins. total running time.

Mysterious indeed. Loosely based on JULES VERNE's work, this serial finds Captain Nemo (Leonard Penn) battling alien Rulu (Karen Randle) way back in 1865. Rulu is a lass from the planet Mercury who, landing her ship on a plan of conquest, begins brandishing ray guns with gay abandon. Superscientist Nemo fights back with a host of electronic aids, including the *Nautilus's* weaponry and a machine that allows him to walk through walls on spying missions.

PRODUCER: Sam Katzman. DIRECTOR: Spencer G. Bennett. SCREENPLAY: Lewis Clay, Royal K. Cole, George H. Plympton. MUSICAL DIRECTOR: Mischa Bakaleinikoff.

SUPPORTING PLAYERS: Richard Crane, Gene Roth, Marshall Reed.

MYSTERIOUS ISLAND
Columbia (1961). Color, 100 mins.

Special effects galore and fine acting make this JULES VERNE adaptation a winner. A group of Northern prisoners, including Gordon Spiletti (Gary Merrill), Herbert Brown (Michael Callan), and Captain Cyrus Harding (Michael Craig), escape from a Southern prison camp during the Civil War in a hot-air balloon. Taking off in the midst of a horrible thunderstorm, they are carried across the sea, crash-landing on a tropical island somewhere in the Atlantic. The stranded crew encounters two more castaways (Beth Rogan and Joan Greenwood) before discovering that the island is populated by oversized animals. Thanks to the special-effects wizardry of Ray Harryhausen, they effectively battle titanic birds, bees, and crabs.

Much to everyone's delight, they meet an exceedingly hopeful sign of escape in the guise of Captain Nemo (Herbert Lom), a genius who lives aboard his submarine, the *Nautilus*, at the base of the island's volcano. Nemo has been keeping an eye on his guests secretly, helping them out of jams whenever possible. He sends a crew of marauding pirates scurrying

Mysterious Island

away with a well-aimed torpedo and tells the castaways that the bellows from his crippled ship could inflate a newly constructed balloon and raise the recently-sunken pirate ship. A means of escape offered, the castaways set to work, menaced by the threat of the rumbling volcano. The plan is set in motion. The bellows begin to pump. A giant squid nearly gets in the way but is promptly dispatched. The ship begins to rise. The volcano begins to spark. The castaways make it off the island. Nemo is buried beneath a landslide along with his super sub.

PRODUCER: Charles H. Schneer. DIRECTOR: Cy Endfield. SCREENPLAY: John Prebble, Daniel Ullman and Crane Wilbur, from the novel by Jules Verne. CINEMATOGRAPHY: Wilkie Cooper. UNDERWATER CINEMATOGRAPHY: Egil Woxholt. SPECIAL EFFECTS: Ray Harryhausen. MUSIC: Bernard Herrman.

MYSTERIOUS ISLAND, THE
France/Italy (1972). Color.

Omar Sharif plays Captain Nemo in this European remake.

DIRECTORS: Juan Antonio Barden, Henri Colpi.

SUPPORTING CAST: Cyrus Smith, Philippe Nicaud, Raymond Pellegrin.

MYSTERIOUS MR. M, THE
Universal (1946). B/w serial, 13 chapters (26 reels).

When a noted submarine inventor is kidnapped, Kirby Walsh (Richard Martin) and Grant Farrell (Dennis Moore) follow his trail. Along the way, they discover a hypnotic drug, Hypno-trene, has been administered to the scientist in order to get information concerning a new submarine motor.

DIRECTORS: Vernon Keays, Lewis D. Collins. SCREENPLAY: Joseph Poland, Paul Huston, Barry Shipman. CINEMATOGRAPHY: Gus Peterson.

SUPPORTING PLAYERS: Pamela Blake as Shirley Clinton, Jane Randolph as Marina Lamont, Danny Norton as Derek, Edmund MacDonald as Anthony Waldron.

MYSTERY OF THE LOST RANCH, THE
Vitaphone (1925). B/w silent serial, five reels.

Good guys and spies battle for the possession of a death ray in a Western village.

DIRECTORS: Harry S. Webb, Tom Gibson. STORY: Barr Cross.

CAST: Pete Morrison.

NA KOMETE
Barrandov (Czechoslovakia, 1970). Color, 85 mins.

Director Karel Zeman, who helmed the fanciful FABULOUS WORLD OF JULES VERNE, returns to his source material in this adaptation of VERNE's *Off on a Comet*. A comet passing the Earth sweeps a small chunk of humanity onto its surface. The Earthlings then must roam the space body and attempt to rebuild their lives.

DIRECTOR AND SCREENWRITER: Karel Zeman. ART DIRECTOR: Jiri Hlupy. CINEMATOGRAPHY: Rudolph Stahl. MUSIC: Lubos Fiser.

CAST: Emil Horvath, Magda Vasarykova, Frantisek Fillpovsky.

NEANDERTHAL MAN, THE
UA (1952). B/w, 77 mins.

A well-meaning but horribly inept scientist (Robert Shane) accidentally turns himself into a caveman and his cat into a saber-tooth tiger through chemical botching.

United Artists

The Neanderthal Man

PRODUCERS AND SCREENWRITERS: Aubrey Wisbert, Jack Pollexfen. DIRECTOR: E. A. Du Pont. CINEMATOGRAPHY: Stanley Cortez. MUSIC: Albert Glasser.

SUPPORTING PLAYERS: Richard Crane, Doris Merric, Robert Long.

NEPTUNE FACTOR, THE
Also known as THE NEPTUNE DISASTER.
20th Cent.-Fox (1973). Color/scope, 98 mins.

Waterlogged adventure floods this tale of scientific research. A sub filled with character actors looks for a lost undersea lab, finds a host of sea monsters instead.

PRODUCER: Sandy Howard. DIRECTOR: Daniel Petrie. SCREENPLAY: Jack DeWitt. CINEMATOGRAPHY: Harry Makin. SPECIAL EFFECTS: Film Opticals of Canada, and Lee Howard. MUSIC: Lee McCauley.

CAST: Ben Gazzara, Yvette Mimieux, Walter Pidgeon, Ernest Borgnine.

NEUTRON AGAINST THE DEATH ROBOTS
Azteca (Mexico, 1961); Commonwealth-United TV (U.S., 1962). B/w.

Masked crusader Neutron must fight a superbrain—a titanic intellect created from the brains of three scientists. The brain wants to rule the world. In order to exist, however, it must feed on the blood of human beings.

PRODUCER: Luis Garcia de Leon. DIRECTOR AND SCREENWRITER: Frederico Curiel. CINEMATOGRAPHY: Fernando Colin. MUSIC: Enrico Cabiati.

CAST: Wolf Ruvinskis, Rosita Arenas, Julio Aleman, Armando Silvestre.

NEW INVISIBLE MAN, THE
Calderon (Mexico, 1957); b/w, 94 mins. Columbia (U.S., 1966); b/w, 89 mins.

A hunted man takes an invisibility drug that earns him his freedom but also gives him a healthy dose of madness.

PRODUCER: Guillermo Calderon Stell. DIRECTOR: Alfredo Crevana. SCREENPLAY: Alfredo Salazar. CINEMATOGRAPHY: Raul Martinez Solares. MUSIC: A. D. Conde.

CAST: Arturo de Cordova, Raul Merez, Ana Luisa Peluffo.

NEW MICROBE, THE
Cines (Italy, 1912). B/w silent short, 420 ft.

A new germ causes instant weakness.

NEW VOYAGE TO THE MOON
Pathé (France, 1909). B/w silent short.

A man visits the moon.

DIRECTOR: Segundo de Chomon.

NIGHT KEY, THE
Universal (1937). B/w, 68 mins.

Two decades ago, Dr. Mallory (Boris Karloff) was a successful inventor. His patented rights for a burglar-alarm system were stolen by colleague Ranger (Samuel S. Hinds). Now blind and nearly broke, Mallory develops a new system that will render millionaire Ranger's burglar-alarm systems useless. Ranger again steals the plans. It's all right, though: Mallory embarks on a life of crime with some small-time hoods, coming up with a ray that will render the new, improved system useless, too. Ranger's protected safes are constantly pillaged. Ranger is upset. The crooks cooperating with Mallory are also upset—they want the action to themselves. They try to kill the old man, but Mallory outfoxes them with electronic savvy.

DIRECTOR: Lloyd Corrigan. SCREENPLAY: Tristram Tupper and John C. Moffit, from a story by William Pierce. CINEMATOGRAPHY: George Robinson. SPECIAL EFFECTS: John P. Fulton. MUSICAL DIRECTOR: Lou Forbes.

SUPPORTING PLAYERS: Jean Rogers, Warren Hull, Ward Bond, Alan Baxter, Frank Reicher.

NIGHT MONSTER, THE
Universal (1942). B/w, 73 mins.

An eccentric millionaire invites to his home for an overnight stay all the doctors who have operated on him unsuccessfully, causing the amputation of both his legs. Before long, the doctors are being murdered one by one. The culprit? The legless millionaire, of course. Through the carefully honed power of the mind, he causes two "whole" legs to materialize on his body at will and calmly stalks his prey.

PRODUCER AND DIRECTOR: Ford Beebe. SCREENPLAY: Clarence Upton Young. CINEMATOGRAPHY: Charles Van Enger.

CAST: Bela Lugosi, Ralph Morgan, Lionel Atwill, Don Porter, Leif Erickson, Frank Reicher, Nils Asther, Irene Harvey.

NIGHT OF THE BLOOD BEAST
AIP (1958). B/w, 65 mins.

Astronaut John Corcoran (Michael Emmet) returns to Earth D.O.A. The first spaceman to clear the Van Allen radiation belt, Corcoran dies of malady or maladies unknown. Investigating scientists Dave Randall (Ed Nelson) and Steve Wynmann (John Baer), along with photographer Donna Bixby (Georgiana Carter), suspect something is amiss when they notice Corcoran's corpse roaming around the grounds of the space center. Eventually they discover that there is a big space beast in a cave nearby. Complicating matters is that there are seven little beasties nestled inside astronaut John. Put them all together and they spell *MOTHER*.

PRODUCER: Gene Corman (brother of Roger Corman). DIRECTOR: Bernard Kowalski. SCREENPLAY: Martin Varno, from a story by Corman. MUSIC: Alexander Laszlo.

NIGHT OF THE LEPUS
MGM (1972). Color, 88 mins.

In an effort to control the ever-expanding rabbit population of the Southwest, the U.S. government injects existing rabbits with a hormone designed to cause sterility. No one ever bothers to check on the results because the hormone causes the rabbits to grow to the size of polar bears. Before long, wild rabbits are hippity-hopping through towns and munching their way through houses and house-owners alike. Sheriff Stuart Whitman sets up a plan to electrocute the rabbits near a trainyard. Rory Calhoun thanks God that the area didn't have trouble with kangaroos way back when.

PRODUCER: A. C. Lyles. DIRECTOR: William Claxton. SCREENPLAY: Don Holliday and Gene Kearney, from the novel *The Year of the Angry Rabbit,* by Russell Braddon. CINEMATOGRAPHY: Ted Voigtlander. SPECIAL EFFECTS: Howard A. Anderson Co. MUSIC: Jimmie Haskell.

SUPPORTING PLAYERS: Janet Leigh, DeForest Kelley, Paul Fix.

NIGHT OF THE LIVING DEAD
Reade/Continental (1968). B/w, 90 mins.

George Romero's cheapie cult classic unites sf-horror clichés with stilted acting. The results are somewhat effective. An ambiguous plague and/or radiation from outer space causes the recently deceased to jog through life once more. Not content to just scare the life out of the normal populace, they begin to eat and drink the life out of slow-moving humans, too. Once bitten by a mad ghoul, the living victim becomes a zombie.

PRODUCERS: Russell Streiner, Karl Hardman. DIRECTOR AND CINEMATOGRAPHER: George A. Romero. SCREENPLAY: John A. Russo. SPECIAL EFFECTS: Regis Survinski, Tony Pantanello.

CAST: Duane Jones, Judith O'Dea, Russell Streiner, Keith Wayne.

Night of the Living Dead

NIGHT THE WORLD EXPLODED, THE
Columbia (1957). B/w, 64 mins.

Not with a bang but with a whimper. A substance found at the Earth's core absorbs nitrogen like crazy and then explodes with mind-boggling force. The discovery of this mineral threatens to set off a chain reaction that could blow the world to bits. Not on this film's budget.

PRODUCER: Sam Katzman. DIRECTOR: Fred Sears. SCREENPLAY: Luci Ward, Jack Natteford. CINEMATOGRAPHY: Ben Kline. MUSICAL DIRECTOR: Ross DiMaggio.

CAST: Kathryn Grant, William Leslie, Tris Coffin, Marshall Reed.

1984
Holiday Films (G.B., 1955). B/w, 91 mins.

A surprisingly sedate version of GEORGE ORWELL'S thought-provoking novel dealing with the dehumanization of man through mass conformity. In the years following a nuclear war, London becomes the capital of a newly created country called Oceania. The land is ruled by an anonymous dictator called Big Brother, who keeps the citizenry in tow by constant electronic surveillance via two-way TV monitors stashed in every private and public building.

History revisor Winston Smith (Edmund O'Brien) tries to live the "good" life, listening obediently to such choice governmental axioms as "Freedom Is Slavery" and "War Is Peace." Then he causes a minor furor by falling in love with Julia (Jan Sterling). Both individuals realize that their unapproved love affair is forbidden but they carry on despite the threat of death and/or torture. A loyal citizen (David Kossoff) spots their daily meetings and reports them to Big Brother. Depending on which version of this movie is shown, the lovers are either shot during an escape attempt (British) or captured and brainwashed into a state of enforced tranquility once more (American).

PRODUCER: N. N. Peter Rathvon. DIRECTOR: Michael Anderson. SCREENPLAY: William P. Templeton, Ralph Bettinson. CINEMATOGRAPHY: C. Pen-

nington Richards. SPECIAL EFFECTS: B. Langley, G. Blackwell, N. Warwick. MUSIC: Malcolm Arnold.

SUPPORTING PLAYERS: Michael Redgrave, Mervyn Jones, Donald Pleasance, Michael Ripper.

NIOBE
Paramount (1915). B/w silent feature, 5 reels.

Electric wiring brings a statue to life.

PRODUCER: Daniel Frohman.

CAST: Hazel Dawn, Charles Abbe.

NO BLADE OF GRASS
MGM (1970). Color/scope, 96 mins.

Yet another dire futurescape is revealed on the silver screen. In the near future, industrial pollution causes a mutant strain of virus to spread around the globe, killing all long-bladed grass-type plants. This happening, in turn, leads to world-wide famine and the collapse of modern civilization.

PRODUCER AND DIRECTOR: Cornel Wilde. SCREENPLAY: Sean Forestal and Jefferson Pascal, from the novel *The Death of Grass*, by JOHN CHRISTOPHER. CINEMATOGRAPHY: H. A. R. Thomson. SPECIAL EFFECTS: Terry Witherington. MUSIC: Burnell Whibley.

CAST: Nigel Davenport, Anthony Sharp, George Coulouris, Jean Wallace.

NON-STOP NEW YORK
Gaumont (G.B., 1937). B/w, eight reels.

A witness to a murder (Anna Lee) hides aboard a transcontinental flight. The ensuing chase scenes include looks at both transcontinental and trans-Atlantic nonstop commercial airplanes, neither of which existed when this movie was lensed.

DIRECTOR: Robert Stevenson. SCREENPLAY: Roland Pertwee, J. O. C. Orton. CINEMATOGRAPHY: Mutz Greenbaum. MUSICAL DIRECTOR: Louis Levey.

SUPPORTING PLAYERS: John Loder, William Dewhurst, Francis L. Sullivan.

NOTHING BUT THE NIGHT
Charlemagne (G.B., 1972). Color, 90 mins.

An interesting plot idea plus the presence of two veteran shock experts,

Peter Cushing and Christopher Lee, add extra leverage to this modest offering. A scientist injects a group of children with the life essence of recently deceased people. Eventually the dead humans' memories gain control of the children's bodies and turn them into sadistic killers.

PRODUCER: Anthony Nelson Keys. DIRECTOR: Peter Saady. SCREENPLAY: Brian Hayles. MAKEUP: Eddie Knight. CINEMATOGRAPHY: Ken Talbot. SPECIAL EFFECTS: Les Bowie. MUSIC: Malcolm Williamson.

SUPPORTING PLAYERS: Diana Dors, Georgia Brown, Duncan Lamont.

NOT OF THIS EARTH
AA (1958). B/w, 67 mins.

Space creatures from the planet Davanna attempt to bring the Earth to its knees through the presence of an agent (Paul Birch). The alien, a vampire with white-on-white eyes, stalks his human victims using telepathy and a bat creature. A rather intimate plan of conquest results.

PRODUCER AND DIRECTOR: Roger Corman. SCREENPLAY: Charles Griffith, Mark Hanna. MUSIC: Ronald Stein. SPECIAL EFFECTS: Paul Blaisdell.

SUPPORTING PLAYERS: Beverly Garland, Jonathan Haze, Morgan Jones.

NOW WE'LL TELL ONE
MGM (1933). B/w short, 2 reels.

Hal Roach presents slapstick master Charley Chase as a nutty inventor who comes up with a strange belt. The belt can transmit the personality of its owner to anyone wearing an identical belt of the series.

PRODUCER: Hal Roach. DIRECTOR: James Chase.

SUPPORTING PLAYERS: Eddie Baker, Muriel Evans, Killian Elliot.

NOW YOU SEE HIM, NOW YOU DON'T
Walt Disney/Buena Vista (1972). Color, 88 mins.

Disney's sequel to THE COMPUTER WORE TENNIS SHOES features a teenage genius (Kurt Russell) who accidentally creates a spray-on formula for invisibility. The formula is easy to apply, can be washed off with water, and is sought after by every crook in the area. Yipes!

PRODUCER: Ron Miller. SCREENPLAY: Joseph L. McEveety, from a story by Robert L. King. DIRECTOR: Robert Butler. CINEMATOGRAPHY: Frank Phillips. SPECIAL EFFECTS: Eustace Lycett, Danny Lee. MUSIC: Robert F. Brunner.

SUPPORTING PLAYERS: Cesar Romero, Joe Flynn, Jim Backus, William Windom, Frank Aletter, Edward Andrews.

N.P.
Zeta-A-Elle (Italy, 1971). Color, 106 mins.

In a supermechanized end of the 20th century, the workers are liberated by machines.

PRODUCER: Enrico Zaccarla. DIRECTOR AND SCREENWRITER: Silvano Agosti. ART DIRECTOR: Isabelle Genoese. CINEMATOGRAPHY: Nicola Dimitri. MUSIC: Nicola Piovani.

CAST: Ingrid Thulin, Irene Pappas, Francesco Rabal.

NUTTY PROFESSOR, THE
Paramount (1963). Color, 107 mins.

Professor Kelp (Jerry Lewis) is a shy and ugly but sensitive soul who is experimenting with personality changes through chemistry. Deciding to test his most recent findings on himself, he downs a scientifically brewed elixir and changes, à la Jekyll and Hyde, into suave, superficial, and thoroughly obnoxious lounge-lizard Buddy Love. Through perseverance and the help of his one true love (Stella Stevens), Kelp overcomes Love, and in the closing shot, it is the homely professor who is escorted lovingly into the sunset by the beautiful blond heroine . . . although she keeps a bottle of his transformation potion in her back pocket for use in emergencies. Find the moral in the above picture.

PRODUCER: Ernest D. Glucksman. DIRECTOR: Jerry Lewis. SCREENPLAY: Lewis, Bill Richmond. CINEMATOGRAPHY: W. Wallace Kelley. SPECIAL EFFECTS: Paul K. Lerpae. MUSIC: Walter Scharf.

SUPPORTING PLAYERS: Howard Morris, Buddy Lester, Doodles Weaver, Henry Gibson, Del Moore, Marvin Kaplan.

The Omega Man

OH, BOY!
Associated British Pathé Co. (G.B., 1938). B/w, 73 mins.

A timid chemist (Albert Burdon) invents a chemical formula that turns him into an outgoing he-man. The only problem is that the potion is slowly reducing his age, making him younger and younger by the minute. He may be strong, but after awhile he doesn't know whether to lift weights or rattles.

PRODUCER: Walter C. Mycroft. DIRECTOR: Albert De Courville. SCREENPLAY: Dudley Leslie.

SUPPORTING PLAYERS: May Lawson, Edmon Ryan, Bernard Nedell.

OMEGA MAN, THE
WB (1971). Color, 98 mins.

A large-scale dud based on the chilling RICHARD MATHESON novel *I Am Legend*. As in the first cinematic adaptation, THE LAST MAN ON EARTH, this film refuses to adhere to Matheson's pacing in the tale of the last human being left in a world inhabited by plague-spawned vampires.

In this version, scientist Robert Neville (Charlton Heston) has developed an antidote that protects him from a plague spread during an East vs. West bio-war. Before total disaster strikes, Neville has time to test the drug on himself. He survives. Everyone else on the Earth either dies or becomes a night-stalking albino zombie. Led by religious fanatic Mathias (excellently played by Anthony Zerbe), the night-stalkers seek to rid the world of all remains of the scientific community—the community that spawned the plague. That includes Neville.

Neville meets two half-vampires, Lisa (Rosalind Cash) and Doc (Paul Koslo), two plague victims who are reacting more slowly to the virus. They live in a commune of seemingly normal humans. Neville is determined to save them from night-stalking by mass-producing the serum. He does so, but before he can administer the serum, he is killed (rather symbolically, at that) by Mathias. Doc and Lisa flee with the serum, save their people, and head for the hills.

PRODUCER: Walter Seltzer. DIRECTOR: Boris Sagal. SCREENPLAY: John William, Joyce H. Corrington. MAKEUP: Gordon Bau. CINEMATOGRAPHY: Russ Metty. MUSIC: Ron Grainer.

SUPPORTING PLAYERS: Brian Tochi, Lincoln Kilpatrick.

OMICRON
Manley (1963). B/w.

An alien creature with a plan for eventual mass invasion lands on Earth and takes over the body of a factory worker (Renato Salvatori). After living on Earth awhile and coming in contact with humans, most notably Rosemarie Dexter, he decides to direct his planet's invasion to Venus instead of Earth. Behind every successful alien, there is an Earthwoman.

PRODUCER: Franco Christaldi. DIRECTOR AND SCREENWRITER: Ugo Gregoretti. CINEMATOGRAPHY: Carlo DiPalma. MUSIC: Piero Umiliani.

SUPPORTING PLAYERS: Dante di Pinto, Calisto Calisti, Mara Carisi, Ida Serasini.

ONCE IN A NEW MOON
Fox British (G.B., 1935). B/w, 63 mins.

A fairly heavy-handed political tale. A postmaster who is an ardent socialist is elected governor of a small village. After a botched-up period of rule, he is tossed into space when the moon collides with a passing star. Wonder if the folks in D.C. are aware of this?

DIRECTOR: Anthony Kimmins.

CAST: Eliot Makeham, Derrick de Marney, John Turnbull, Wally Patch, Rene Ray, Mary Hinton.

ONE HUNDRED YEARS AFTER

Pathé (France, 1911). B/w silent short, 780 ft.

Cold Turkey

Famous quotes that have not exactly advanced the cause of science:

"I won't go through that again, even with the promise of future salvation!"

Lon Chaney, Jr., to Onslow Stevens in *House of Dracula*

A scientist falls into a deep sleep and wakes up in the year 2011.

ON HER MAJESTY'S SECRET SERVICE

UA (1969). Color/scope, 140 mins.

Superlative action stunts, including the *Ben Hur* of toboggan chases, but semicatatonic script turns make this, the first of the post–Sean Connery Bond films, below par. In this outing, Bond (George Lazenby) is summoned by "M" (Bernard Lee) and asked to stop the fiendish plot of Blofeld (Telly Savalas), a nasty gent who is attempting to conquer the world through the bacteriological destruction of certain plants and animals.

PRODUCERS: Harry Saltzman, Albert R. Broccoli. DIRECTOR: Peter Hunt. SCREENPLAY: Richard Maibaum, based on the novel by Ian Fleming. CINEMATOGRAPHY: Michael Reed. SPECIAL EFFECTS: John Stars. MUSIC: John Barry.

SUPPORTING PLAYERS: Lois Maxwell, Julie Ege, Catherine von Schell, Bessie Love, Ilse Steppat, Yuri Borienko.

ON THE BEACH

UA (1959). B/w, 134 mins.

One of the few 1950s sf films to break out of the juvenile ray gun/hot-rodding alien mold so popular during that decade, *On the Beach,* based on the novel by Nevil Shute, is a timeless, intelligent, chilling, and thoroughly disheartening statement about mankind and its nationalistic follies.

A nuclear war ravages the world and those not killed in the explosions are soon condemned to a painful death by the swirling clouds of radioactive fallout circling the globe. A lone submarine, commanded by Dwight Towers (Gregory Peck), survives the war and brings the message of destruction to the people of Australia, who, far removed from the major countries geographically, miraculously have survived.

Towers and old flame Moira Davidson (Ava Gardner) find romance amid the gloom. The people of Australia debate their fate. Will they, too, be wiped out by this war, or were the reports exaggerated? A Morse-code signal from San Francisco spawns hope that perhaps there are survivors around the world. The sub journeys to California and finds the place utterly destroyed, the Morse message caused by a cola bottle being pushed back and forth by a wind-blown window shade near a transmitter.

The word is sent back to Australia, where the people, faced with radiation poisoning, choose to take on a last gulp of the good life before committing mass suicide with pills. A cynical scientist (Fred Astaire) sums up the end of the human race thusly: "Who would have ever believed that human beings would be stupid enough to think that peace can be maintained by arranging to defend themselves with weapons that couldn't possibly be used without committing suicide?"

This film should be shown at the UN on a daily basis.

PRODUCER AND DIRECTOR: Stanley Kramer. SCREENPLAY: John Paxton, based on Shute's novel of the same name. CINEMATOGRAPHY: Giuseppe Rotunno. SPECIAL EFFECTS: Lee Zavitz. MUSIC: Ernest Gold.

SUPPORTING PLAYERS: Anthony Perkins, Donna Anderson, John Tate.

ON THE THRESHOLD OF SPACE
MGM (1956). B/w, 98 mins.

A pseudodocumentary with more "real" footage than "reel," this movie recounts the lives of Captain Jim Hollenback (Guy Madison), Major Ward Thomas (John Hodiak), and Pat Lange (Virginia Leith) as the air force begins its decade-and-a-half program to launch a man into space and, eventually, to the moon.

DIRECTOR: Robert D. Webb.

SUPPORTING PLAYERS: Dean Jagger, Warren Stevens.

OPERATION ATLANTIS
Splendor/Fisa (Italy/Spain, 1965). Color/scope, 88 mins.

Sent to check out strange happenings in deepest Africa, a European secret agent (John Ericson) discovers a slew of Chinese crazies in a secret atomic installation.

PRODUCER: Sidney Pink. DIRECTOR: Domenico Paolella. SCREENPLAY: Victor Auz, from a story by Vinicio Marinucci. CINEMATOGRAPHY: Francisco Sanchez, Marcello Masciocchi.

SUPPORTING PLAYERS: Berna Rock, Erika Blank, Beni Deus.

OSS 117—MISSION FOR A KILLER
P.A.C./P.M.C. (France, 1965); color/scope, 115 minutes. Embassy (U.S., 1966); color/scope, 84 mins.

France's answer to James Bond, agent 007, is OSS 117 (Frederick Stafford). In this film, one of several featuring the character, the intrepid agent must face a gang of outlaw geniuses. The criminals have discovered a way to manufacture from a flower a drug that robs the drug user of his or her will and turns the person into a human zombie, capable of carrying out any and all commands.

PRODUCER: Paul Cadeac. DIRECTOR: André Hunebelle. SCREENPLAY: Jean Halain, Pierre Foucaud, André Hunebelle, from the novel *The Last Quarter Hour*, by Jean Bruce. CINEMATOGRA-

PHY: Marcel Grignon. MUSIC: Michel Magne.

SUPPORTING PLAYERS: Mylène Demongeot, Raymond Pellegrin, Jacques Riberolles.

OUR HEAVENLY BODIES
UFA (Germany, 1925). B/w, seven reels.

An imagined tour of the solar system that includes a preview of the end of the universe.

DIRECTOR: Hans Walter Kornblum.

CAST: Theodor Loos, Walter Reinman.

OUR MAN FLINT
20th Cent.-Fox (1968). Color/scope, 107 mins.

Sardonic secret agent Flint (James Coburn) must stop a trio of demented scientists planning to conquer the world through the manipulation of weather. When it rains it pours, much to the dismay of fast-talking Flint.

PRODUCER: Saul David. DIRECTOR: Daniel Mann. SCREENPLAY: Hal Fimberg, Ben Starr. CINEMATOGRAPHY: Daniel L. Fapp. SPECIAL EFFECTS: Lyle B. Abbott, Howard Lydecker, Emil Kosa, Jr. MUSIC: Jerry Goldsmith.

SUPPORTING PLAYERS: Lee J. Cobb, Benson Fong, Edward Mulhare, Gila Golan.

OUT OF THIS WORLD
Roland Reed Productions (1954). B/w, 78 mins.

TV's Rocky Jones (Richard Crane) takes off for space adventures culled from several episodes of his series.

PRODUCER: Roland Reed.

OVERCHARGED
Hepworth (G.B., 1912). B/w silent short, 350 ft.

A weak man, when given a good dose of electricity, becomes superstrong, and a supermagnet as well.

OVER-INCUBATED BABY, THE
G.B. (1901). B/w silent short, 80 ft.

A baby, left in an incubator a tad too long, turns into an old duffer.

PAJAMA PARTY
AIP (1964). Color/scope, 85 mins.

A Martian (Tommy Kirk) lands on Earth with great plans for an invasion but spots perky Annette Funicello and promptly forgets about the proposed interplanetary conflict. He decides to stay and make whoopie, sending a group of Earth meanies to Mars instead.

PRODUCERS: James H. Nicholson, Samuel Z. Arkoff, Anthony Carras. DIRECTOR: Don Weis. SCREENPLAY: Louis M. Heyward. CINEMATOGRAPHY: Floyd Crosby. SPECIAL EFFECTS: Roger George. MUSIC: Les Baxter.

SUPPORTING PLAYERS: Elsa Lanchester, Buster Keaton, Harvey Lembeck, Dorothy Lamour, Frankie Avalon, Don Rickles.

PALLE ALONE IN THE WORLD
Nordisk (Denmark, 1949). B/w featurette, 25 mins.

Palle (Lars Henning-Jensen) has a nightmare wherein he becomes the last man on Earth. Fleeing the Earthbound blues, he boards an airplane and flies to the moon.

PRODUCERS, DIRECTORS, AND SCREENWRITERS: Bjarne and Astrid Henning-Jensen. CINEMATOGRAPHY: Annelise Reenberg.

PANIC IN THE AIR
Columbia (1936). B/w, 60 mins.

A new electronic invention can knock out radio broadcasts.

DIRECTOR: D. Ross Lederman. SCREENPLAY: Harold Shumate. CINEMATOGRAPHY: Benjamin Kline.

CAST: Lew Ayres, Florence Rice, Benny Baker, Murray Alper.

PANIC IN THE CITY
United Pictures (1967). Color, 96 mins.

An A-bomb is set to go off within the city of Los Angeles, intended to put an end to the smog problem and the city forever. The hero of the tale takes the bomb out to sea and detonates it, losing his own life but saving the town he loves so dearly. Gee.

PRODUCER: Earle Lyon. DIRECTOR: Eddie Davis. SCREENPLAY: Davis, Charles Savage. CINEMATOGRAPHY: Alan Stensvold. MUSIC: Paul Dunlap.

CAST: Nehemiah Persoff, Anne Jeffries, Howard Duff, Dennis Hooper, Linda Cristal.

PANIC IN THE YEAR ZERO
AIP (1962). B/w, 92 mins.

A family man (Ray Milland) taking the wife and kids on a motor-home holiday has his routine interrupted by a nuclear war. Aided by his daughter's boyfriend (Frankie Avalon), he tries to keep his brood unscathed. Since nearly every man left in the Los Angeles area wants to rape either his wife or his daughter, he has his hands full, resorting to barbarism and savagery in the end.

PRODUCERS: Arnold Houghland, Lou Rusoff. DIRECTOR: Ray Milland. SCREENPLAY: Jay Simms, John Morton. CINEMATOGRAPHY: Gil Warrenton. SPECIAL EFFECTS: Pat Dinga, Larry Butler. MUSIC: Les Baxter.

SUPPORTING PLAYERS: Jean Hagen, Mary Mitchell, Joan Freeman, Scott Peters, Richard Garland.

PAWN ON MARS
Vitaphone (1915). B/w silent featurette, three reels.

An inventor finds a way to detonate explosives at a distance using a remote-control ray.

DIRECTOR: Theodore Marston. SCREENPLAY: Donald I. Buchanan.

CAST: Charles Kent, Dorothy Kelly, James Morrison.

PEOPLE THAT TIME FORGOT, THE
AIP (1977). Color, 90 mins.

No such luck. Ben McBride (Patrick Wayne) flies his plane directly into the middle of the lost world of

Caprona in search of his lost friend Bowen Tyler (Doug McClure). Whilst dallying in the prehistoric world, he meets many monsters and cave people as well as a very unfriendly populace belonging to the City of the Skulls, a choice piece of real estate located on the lip of a volcano.

PRODUCER: John Dark. DIRECTOR: Kevin Connor. SCREENPLAY: Patrick Tilley, based upon a novel by EDGAR RICE BURROUGHS. SPECIAL EFFECTS: Ian Wingrove. MUSIC: John Scott.

SUPPORTING PLAYERS: Dan Gillespie, Thorley Walters, Sarah Douglas.

PERCY, THE MECHANICAL MAN
Paramount (1916). B/w silent animated short.

The comical adventures of a mechanical man.

PRODUCER: John R. Bray.

PERFECT WOMAN, THE
Two Cities (G.B., 1949). B/w, 89 mins.

Two eccentric zanies (Stanley Holloway and Nigel Patrick) agree to test Professor Belmon's (Miles Malleson) female humanoid robot. As a joke, the professor's niece (Patricia Roc) takes the place of the robot during the testing. The two fellows are so amazed at the robot's lifelike qualities that they arrange to take it to a nearby bridal suite to get any possible kinks out of the machinery.

DIRECTOR: Bernard Knowles. SCREENPLAY: Knowles and George Black, from a play by Wallace Geoffrey and Basil John Mitchell.

SUPPORTING PLAYERS: Irene Handl, Pamela Davis.

PERILS OF PARIS, THE
Anderson Pictures (1924). B/w silent feature, six reels.

Criminals kidnap a professor's daughter in order to gain access to his Power Ray.

DIRECTOR: Edward Jose. SCREENPLAY: Gerard Bourgeois.

CAST: Pearl White, Robert Lee, Henry Bandin.

PERILS OF PAULINE
Universal (1933). B/w serial, 12 chapters (24 reels).

The world searches for a disc on which is imprinted the formula for a deadly gas that destroyed an ancient civilization and could do the same for a modern one.

DIRECTOR: Ray Taylor. SCREENPLAY: Ella O'Neill, Basil Dickey, George H. Plympton, Jack Foley.

CAST: Evelyn Knapp, Robert Allen, James Durking, John Davidson, Sonny Ray.

PERPETUAL MOTION SOLVED
Hilarity (G.B., 1914). B/w silent short, 300 ft.

A homemade car can break the laws of gravity.

PHANTASM
Avco Embassy (1979). Technicolor, 90 mins.

Young Mike Pearson (Michael Baldwin) watches a close friend's casket being stolen after a funeral by a mysterious Tall Man (Angus Scrimm). He tells brother Jody (Bill Thornbury) about it but is scoffed at. Deciding to investigate by himself, Mike becomes involved in murder, gnome activities, the Tall Man's revenge, and, eventually, what turns out to be an alien-from-space plot.

PRODUCER, DIRECTOR, AND SCREENWRITER: Don Coscarelli. CINEMATOGRAPHY: Coscarelli. ART DIRECTOR: David Gavin Brown. SPECIAL EFFECTS: Paul Pepperman. MUSIC: Fred Myrow.

SUPPORTING PLAYERS: Reggie Bannister as Reggie, Kathy Lester as the Lady in Lavender.

PHANTOM CREEPS, THE
Universal (1939). B/w serial, 12 chapters.

Mad scientist Dr. Zorka (Bela Lugosi doing his usual leering) invents a drug that can induce a state of suspended animation. He places the drug into a metal disc and has great plans for distributing the discs to his enemies throughout the country. Unfortunately, his enemies are everyone else's allies. Enter American Military Intelligence, led by Capt. Bob West (Robert Kent) and sidekick, Jim Daly (Regis Toomey).

The two men begin to disrupt Zorka's well-laid plans just as the doc is perfecting a metal spider that will stalk its metal-disc-holding victims and pounce on them, setting off the above-mentioned slumber-aid housed in the metal disc. Told you Zorka was mad. Anyhow, he gets even madder with the arrival of the agents and, in battling the forces of Good, resorts to using an invisibility belt and a robot with a smile that's every orthodontist's dream.

DIRECTORS: Ford Beebe, Saul A. Goodkind. SCREENPLAY: George H. Plympton, Basil Dickey, Mildred Barish. CINEMATOGRAPHY: Jerry Ash, William Sickner.

SUPPORTING PLAYERS: Dorothy Arnold, Edward Van Sloan, Eddie Acuff, Lane Chandler.

PHANTOM EMPIRE, THE
Mascot (1935). B/w serial, 12 chapters.

Cowboy singing-sensation Gene Autry has his "Radio Ranch" show blasted off the airwaves by a ton of electrical interference that is later discovered to be a ton of electrical equipment located in the lost city of Murania, under a nearby mountain. Before too long, Gene, along with his pint-sized friends Betsy and Frankie (Betsy King Ross and Frankie Darrow) and their even more pint-sized pals, the Junior Thunder Riders (kids who tear across the terrain wearing capes and buckets on their heads), is battling land-hungry gangsters led by a radium-seeking fool and the forces of Murania's own Queen Tika (Dorothy Christy), which include death rays and robots.

PRODUCER: Armand Shaefer. DIRECTORS: Otto Brower, Breezy Eason. SCREENPLAY: John Rathmell, Shaefer.

SUPPORTING PLAYERS: Wheeler Oakman, Smiley Burnett.

PHANTOM FROM SPACE
UA (1953). B/w, 72 mins.

An invisible alien lands his flying saucer fairly badly near the Griffith Observatory on planet Earth. Apparently in a bad mood because of his poor display of flying, he immediately kills a few nearby picnickers. In order to survive on Earth, the critter wears a helmet containing air from his own world.

The see-through sap exceeds the boundaries of good taste and/or discretion and attempts to break into the observatory. Scientists are waiting for him and throw an infrared light his way, thus rendering him visible. The alien is caught with his pants down, literally, and materializes as a jockey-shorts-wearing muscle man with an egghead shower cap. He falls off a scaffold and dies, proving that he walks as well as he pilots a spaceship.

PRODUCER AND DIRECTOR: W. Lee Wilder. SCREENPLAY: Bill Raynor and Myles Wilder, from a story by Wilder. MUSIC: William Lava. SPECIAL EFFECTS: Alex Welden, Howard Anderson.

CAST: Ted Cooper, Noreen Nash, Jim Bannon, Michael Mark.

PHANTOM FROM 10,000 LEAGUES, THE
ARC (1956). B/w, 81 mins.

A death ray that causes grief for local swimming things is guarded by a nasty puppet-monster. Scientists ponder the act of cutting its strings once and for all.

PRODUCERS: Jack and Daniel Milner. DIRECTOR: Dan Milner. SCREENPLAY: Lou Rusoff. CINEMATOGRAPHY: Bryden Baker. MUSIC: Ronald Stein.

CAST: Kent Taylor, Cathy Downs, Michael Whalen.

PHANTOM OF THE AIR, THE
Universal (1933). B/w serial, 12 chapters (24 reels).

Test pilot Bob Raymond (Tom Tyler) is hired by inventor Thomas Edmunds (William Desmond) to test the Contragrav, a device that, when attached to an ordinary airplane, defies the laws of gravity, thus opening a whole new chapter in aviation history. Out to snatch the machine is Crome (LeRoy Mason), a gangster disguised as a mild-mannered aviator. Captured by Crome, Edmunds blows up his lab and his machine rather than knuckle under to nastiness. He survives and is reunited with equally brave Bob and daughter Mary (Gloria Shea).

DIRECTOR: Ray Taylor. SCREENPLAY: Ella O'Neill, Basil Dickey, George H. Plympton.

SUPPORTING PLAYERS: Walter Bren-

Gotcha

The actors would never know where the alien was going to appear from. The script would say, "The monster kills the girl." We wouldn't say how or in what way. We would spring it on the actors without them knowing where it would come from. Suddenly the monster's head would appear two inches from the actor's. Of course, the on-camera reaction was spontaneous and incredible. It was sadistic, but effective.

Ron Shusett, producer of
Alien

Phase IV

nan as Skid, Jennie Cramer as Marie, Hugh Enfield as Blade.

PHANTOM PLANET, THE
AIP (1962). Color, 82 mins.

After being slammed by a passing meteor shower, spaceship *Pegasus IV* begins drifting in space. Only one of its crewmen, Frank Chapman (Dean Fredericks), escapes with his life, reaching a nearby asteroid. Breathing the space rock's atmosphere, he shrinks to doll-size and finds himself on a peewee planet. The world is run by minihumans who steer the rock as if it were a spaceship. Led by Seaom (Francis X. Bushman) and Herron (Anthony Dexter), the people live a quiet existence when not menaced by nasty monster Richard Kiel. Chapman decides to help the incredible shrunken men fight off the beast.

PRODUCER: Fred Gebhart. DIRECTOR: William Marshall. SCREENPLAY: William Telaak, Fred de Gorter, William Gebhardt. CINEMATOGRAPHY: Elwood J. Nicholson. MUSIC: Hayes Pagel. MAKEUP: Dave Newal.

SUPPORTING PLAYERS: Coleen Gray, Dolores Faith.

PHASE IV
Paramount (1973). Color, 93 mins.

A group of ants in the middle of the Arizona desert band together and plot to take over the Earth. Coming to the surface, they are battled by a monomaniacal scientist (Nigel Davenport). A girl bitten by the ants (Lynne Frederick) becomes psychically linked with the cagey critters, and soon the ants

have an Adam and Eve telepathically programmed to meet the dawning of a new slave age for humanity.

PRODUCER: Paul B. Radin. DIRECTOR: Saul Bass. SCREENPLAY: Mayo Simon. CINEMATOGRAPHY: Dick Bush. SPECIAL ANT PHOTOGRAPHY: Ken Middleham. ART DIRECTOR: John Barry. MUSIC: Brian Gascoigne. ELECTRONICS: David Forhaus. MONTAGE MUSIC: Yamash'ta.

SUPPORTING PLAYERS: Alan Gifford, Robert Henderson, Helen Horton.

PINOCCHIO IN OUTER SPACE
Universal (1965). Color, 71 mins.

An animated look at this fairy-tale character's adventures in space. After he misbehaves again, Pinocchio is changed back into a puppet by the Blue Fairy. Determined to redeem himself in her eyes, he becomes the Buck Rogers of wood and sets off for outer space, saving Earth from an attack by a large space whale. Helping him in his quest is a space turtle and a Martian or two. By the film's end, the whale is defeated and Pinny is proud. Wooden you be?

PRODUCERS: Norm Prescott, Fred Ladd. DIRECTOR: Ray Goossens. SCREENPLAY: Fred Laderman from a story by Prescott. MUSIC: Fred Leonard, H. Dobbelaere, E. Schurmann. SONGS: Robert Sharp, Arthur Korb.

VOICES: Arnold Stang, Conrad Jameson, Minerva Pious.

PIRANHA
New World (1978). Metrocolor, 92 mins.

During the Vietnam war, Dr. Robert

Hoak (Kevin McCarthy) was in charge of a project designed to create a super-mutant piranha. Going through several variations of the fish, including ones with legs and arms, he came up with a variation that could survive in any type of water. The idea was to dump the devil fish into the North Vietnamese water systems, thus making it impossible for the red menace to take a skinny dip without losing any and all skin.

Insurance investigator Maggie Mc-Keown (Heather Menzies) and local hermit Paul Grogan (Bradford Dillman) stumble onto the plot years later, after innocently emptying Hoak's piranha army into the mountain streams of California. The fish are now heading for the summer camp where Grogan's daughter is and for a new summer resort (operated by Dick Miller, as Buck Gardner). The twosome try to convince the authorities, but the local army general owns the vacation resort and is not about to let a few fish cost him millions on opening day.

Blood-letting abounds, with the fish zipping through both the summer camp (Paul saves his daughter just in time, although most of the other kids will never have to worry again about what size sneakers to buy) and the resort (where the general meets his finned makers) before being stopped by Paul, who pollutes the water system with a deadly poison. Dr. Mengers (Barbara Steele) absolutely, positively, declares the piranhas to be dead . . . heh heh.

PRODUCERS: Roger Corman, Jeff Schechtman, Jon Davison. DIRECTOR: Joe Dante. SCREENPLAY: John Sayles, from a story by Sayles and Richard Robinson. CINEMATOGRAPHY: James Anderson. SPECIAL EFFECTS: Jon Berg. MUSIC: Pino Donaggio.

PLANET OF THE APES
20th Cent.-Fox (1968). Color/scope, 112 mins.

A very well done screen-adaptation of the novel of the same name by PIERRE BOULLE. A space probe containing three astronauts crash-lands on a lush, green planet. The three Earthmen are surprised to see mute, apparently savage humans roaming the hills. Their surprise gives way to horror when a group of English-speaking, gun-toting, horse-riding apes ambushes the humans. The astronauts are caught in the midst of the hunt. One space traveler is killed, another is paralyzed with a mind-numbing blow. The third, Taylor (Charlton Heston), is shot in the neck and temporarily robbed of speech.

Taylor is carted off with the other human captives and tossed into a prison/zoo. He tries to communicate with his captors, zeroing in on two scientist-chimps, Zira and Cornelius (Kim Hunter and Roddy McDowall). Surprised to find an intelligent human, a heresy in the land of the apes, they submit Taylor to IQ tests, which he passes with flying colors. Through sign language and mathematics, they begin discussing the forbidden topic of space travel. The two scientists are impressed and excited. They inform their superiors of the marvelous man.

But a legion of scientists, led by Maurice Evans, see Taylor as a threat to simian society. They want the freak killed and dissected for study. Zira and Cornelius arrange for Taylor and a young human slave/friend, Nova (Linda Harrison) to escape. They ride into the "forbidden zone," a place that not even the wisest of apes is allowed to traverse. Angry ape scientists, however, follow the twosome into the zone. There they discover, much to their and everyone else's horror, that the apes were not always the dominant species on this world. In fact, man was originally the ruling class. The evidence for such an astounding idea? Half-buried along the ocean's edge is the top half of the Statue of Liberty. Taylor has somehow journeyed into the future and crash-landed on his own home planet, Earth!

PRODUCER: Arthur P. Jacobs. DIRECTOR: Franklin J. Shaffner. SCREENPLAY: Michael Wilson, ROD SERLING. ART DIRECTORS: Jack Martin Smith, William Creber. MAKEUP DESIGN: John Chambers. MAKEUP: Ben Nye, Dan Striepeke. CINEMATOGRAPHY: Leon Shamroy. SPECIAL EFFECTS: Lyle B. Abbott, Art Cruickshank, Emil Kosa, Jr. MUSIC: Jerry Goldsmith.

SUPPORTING PLAYERS: James Whit-

20th Cent.-Fox

Planet of the Apes

more, James Daly, Paul Lambert, Robert Gunner.

Sequel films: BENEATH THE PLANET OF THE APES; ESCAPE FROM THE PLANET OF THE APES; CONQUEST OF THE PLANET OF THE APES; BATTLE FOR THE PLANET OF THE APES.

PLANET OF THE STORMS (PLANETA BURG)
Leningrad (U.S.S.R., 1962). Color.

Unseen in the U.S.A. in its original form, *Planet of the Storms* was bought and carved up into two American releases, *Voyage to the Prehistoric Planet* and VOYAGE TO THE PLANET OF PREHISTORIC WOMEN. The original film traced the adventures of a group of cosmonauts on Venus, a planet inhabited by aliens, dinosaurs, lizard people, and man-eating plants.

DIRECTOR: Pavel Klushantsev. SCREENPLAY: Alexander Kasantsev, Pavel Klushantsev.

CAST: Kyunna Ignatova, Yuri Sarantsev, Vladimir Yemelianov.

PLANET OF THE VAMPIRES
AIP (1965). Color, 85 mins.

A spaceship landing on a fog-enshrouded planet runs into trouble when its crew meets a race of alien vampires. The vampires aren't just after some of the humans' blood, either: they're adept at mind control as well. After a good deal of gore, the aliens reveal their plans to send back the zombie-slave astronauts to Earth, where the aliens can launch an invasion via remote mental control. Gosh.

PRODUCER: Fulvio Lucisana. DIREC-

TOR: Mario Bava. ORIGINAL SCREENPLAY: Castillo Cosulich, Antonio Roman, Rafael J. Salvia, Mario Bava. English version: Ib Melchior, Louis M. Heyward. MUSIC: Gino Marinuzzi.

CAST: Barry Sullivan as Captain Mark Markary, Norman Bengell as Sanya, Angel Aranda, Ivan Rassimov, Evi Morandi.

Planet of the Vampires

PLANETS AGAINST US
Also known as THE MAN WITH THE YELLOW EYES; THE HANDS OF A KILLER.
Manley (1961). B/w, 85 mins.

Aliens all possessing the same face (that of actor Michel Lemoine) land on Earth to launch an invasion. The invaders turn out to be humanoid robots who, while romping through Europe, begin a series of natural disasters. On the unnatural-disaster side of things, they also have the power to hypnotize humans with their glowing eyes and disintegrate human flesh with their deadly touch. Not the kind of folks to have around at parties, the robots are finally done in by members of their own race. It seems that these droids are renegades (who would've guessed it?). A mothership from home base shows up and wipes 'em out with a well-aimed ray. Hoo-ray.

PRODUCERS: Alberto Chimenz, Vico Pavoni. DIRECTOR: Romano Ferrara. SCREENPLAY: Ferrara, Piero Pierotti. MUSIC: Armando Tovajoli.

SUPPORTING PLAYER: Jany Clair.

PLAN NINE FROM OUTER SPACE
DCA (1956). B/w, 79 mins.

An all-time low. Littered with stock footage of Bela Lugosi slithering through the midnight mist, this epic tale of woe concerns a group of alien invaders who, after striking out eight times, comes up with a ninth scenario for an invasion of Earth. Arriving in the Edsel of spaceships, they set about creating a race of astro-zombies. Since the aliens all look like horror-movie extras (Vampira is the leader, clad in black; Tor Johnson is her lumbering henchman), no one really cares much that this plan, like its eight predecessors, stiffs out.

PRODUCER AND DIRECTOR: Edward D. Wood, Jr. SCREENPLAY: Wood. MUSIC: Gordon Zahler.

SUPPORTING PLAYERS: Lyle Talbot, Mono McKinnon, Gregory Walcott.

POLICE OF THE FUTURE
Gaumont (France, 1909). B/w silent short, 540 ft.

Future cops.

POWER, THE
MGM (1968). Color/scope, 103 mins.

A slightly muddled screen adaptation of the Frank M. Robinson novel. A scientist has psi powers, allowing him to impose his will on other men's minds and drive them to self-destruction. A young coworker (George Hamilton) discovers that he, too, has the power and tries to find out the identity of the telekinetic killer in the scientific community.

PRODUCER: George Pal. DIRECTOR: Byron Haskin. SCREENPLAY: John Gay. MAKEUP: William Tuttle. CINEMATOGRAPHY: Ellsworth Fredricks. SPECIAL EFFECTS: J. MacMillan Johnson, Gene Warren, Wah Chang. MUSIC: Miklos Rozsa.

SUPPORTING PLAYERS: Michael Rennie, Suzanne Pleshette, Nehemiah Per-

MGM

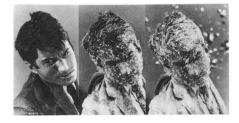

The Power

soff, Earl Holliman, Arthur O'Connell, Aldo Ray.

POWER GOD, THE
Vital Exchanges (1925). B/w silent serial, 15 chapters (31 reels).

Scientists invent a much-sought-after machine that generates continuous power without the need for fuel.

DIRECTOR: Ben Wilson.

CAST: Ben Wilson, Neva Gerber, Mary Crane, Mary Brooklyn.

PREHISTORIC MAN, THE
Star (Hungary, 1917). B/w silent short.

Scientists douse a monkey with strange rays that make the ape as smart as a man. The ape then chases after a pretty young girl and gets himself elected to political office. Before the monkeyshines really get out of hand, the scientific researchers zap the monkey with a reverse ray and send it back into idiocy.

DIRECTOR: Alfred Desy. SCREENPLAY: Zoltan Somlyo, Erno Gyorf.

PRINCE OF SPACE
Toei (Japan, 1959). B/w feature filmed in two parts, 57 mins. and 64 mins.

The Prince of Space arrives on Earth disguised as a bootblack. An extraterrestrial dictator chooses that moment to try to take over the Earth. The resulting battle features death rays, spaceships, etc.

DIRECTOR: Eij'ro Wakabayashi. SCREENPLAY: Shin Morita. CINEMATOGRAPHY: Masahiko Iimura.

CAST: Tatsuya Umeniya, Ushio Skashi, Joji Oka.

PRIVILEGE
Worldfilm Services/Memorial Enterprises/Universal (1967). Color, 103 mins.

A pop star proves to be so popular that he is manipulated by both church and state in an effort to control the youth population of Britain. It's only a matter of time before pop sensation Steven Shorter (Paul Jones) gets wise to exactly what he could do with his power.

PRODUCER: John Heyman. DIRECTOR: Peter Watkins. SCREENPLAY: Norman Bogner, based on a story by Johnny Speight. MUSIC: Mike Leander.

SUPPORTING PLAYERS: Jean Shrimpton, Mark London, Jeremy Child.

PROFESSOR DIDLITTLE AND THE SECRET FORMULA
Atla-International (W. Germany, 1972). Color.

An eccentric inventor changes his nephew into a superman.

DIRECTOR: W. V. Chmielewski.

CAST: Bill Ramsey, Boyd Bachman, Teeny May.

PROFESSOR HOSKIN'S PATENT HUSTLER
Prestwich (G.B., 1897). B/w silent short, 50 ft.

A machine causes life around it to accelerate.

DIRECTOR: Dave Aylott.

PROFESSOR OLDBOY'S REJUVENATOR
Kalem (1914). B/w silent short, 500 ft.

A professor tests out a formula for youth restoration, first on his dog and then on himself.

PROFESSOR PIECAN'S DISCOVERY
Cricks and Martin (G.B., 1910). B/w silent short, 580 ft.

A fluid makes the weak strong.

DIRECTOR: A. E. Coleby.

PROFESSOR PUDDENHEAD'S PATENTS
Kleine (1909). B/w silent short, 404 ft.

The professor's pride and joys, the aerocar and the vacuum provider, are fueled in flight from Earth below.

DIRECTOR: Walter Booth.

PROFESSOR'S ANTIGRAVITA-TIONAL FLUID, THE
Hepworth (G.B., 1908). B/w silent short, 350 ft.

An elixir causes whatever it splashes on to float in the air.

DIRECTOR: Lewin Fitzhamon.

CAST: Bertie Potter.

PROFESSOR'S SECRET, THE
Gaumont (France, 1908). B/w silent short, 614 ft.

The injection of a liquid causes men to become monkeys.

PROFESSOR'S STRENGTH TABLETS, THE
Clarendon (G.B., 1909). B/w silent short, 450 ft.

Pills that turn weak men into Samsons turn out to be explosive, too. Tough break.

DIRECTOR: Percy Stow.

PROFESSOR'S TWIRLY-WHIRLY CIGARETTES, A
B&C (G.B., 1909). B/w silent short, 425 ft.

A powder derived from liver, when mixed with tobacco, makes the person smoking the chemically altered ciggie go for a quick spin in place.

DIRECTOR: H. O. Martinek.

PROFESSOR WAMAN
Shree Ranjit (India, 1938). B/w.

A scientist masters nature.

DIRECTOR: Manibhai Vyas.

CAST: Mazhar, Sitara, Sunita.

PROFESSOR WEISE'S BRAIN SERUM INJECTOR
Lubin (1909). B/w silent short, 300 ft.

PROFESSOR ZANIKOFF'S EXPERIENCES OF GRAFTING
Lux (1909). B/w silent short, 300 ft.

A scientist cures physical defects through futuristic surgery.

PROJECTED MAN, THE
Protelco (G.B., 1966); color/scope, 90 mins. Universal (U.S.A., 1967); color/scope, 72 mins.

Dr. Blanchard (Norman Wooland) is a conservative scientist who isn't at all thrilled over the prospect of extending the funds being used by Dr. Paul Steiner (Bryant Halliday) and co-worker Chris Mitchell (Ronald Allen) in their matter-transference experiments. The pair, angered by Blanchard's attitude, approach a second scientist, Dr. Pat Hill (Mary Peach), for support. She gives it and falls for Chris simultaneously. When the trio tries to

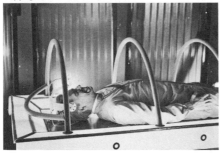

The Projected Man

convince influential Latham (Derrick de Marney) and Professor Lembach (Gerard Heinz) of the validity of their work through an experimental demonstration of the matter-transference chamber, Blanchard secretly sabotages the test. With the results of the experiment a failure, Blanchard is perfectly justified in cutting off funds. Paul, suspecting sabotage, tries the machine out on himself, attempting to project himself across town. His experiment is only half-successful, however, and he materializes in the middle of an excavation site with one-half of his face disintegrating and his touch now deadly to any humans. Paul embarks on a path littered with murder and revenge. A bizarre confrontation with police occurs when Paul stops at a power-supply station for a quick recharge.

So This Is Progress
"It's interesting to think that long ago we'd be burned at the stake as wizards for this experiment!"
Colin Clive in *Bride of Frankenstein*

PRODUCERS: Maurice Foster, John Croydon. DIRECTOR: Ian Curtis. SCREENPLAY: John C. Cooper, Peter Bryant. CINEMATOGRAPHY: Stanley Pavey. SPECIAL EFFECTS: Flo Nordhoff, Robert Hedges, Mike Hope. MUSIC: Kenneth V. Jones.

PROJECT MOONBASE
Lippert (1953). B/w, 51 mins.

In the distant year of 1970, an expedition leaves a space station orbiting the Earth and heads for the moon. The ship crashes. One survivor dies while on the moon. The remaining man and woman are married via television transmission.

PRODUCER: Jack Seaman. DIRECTOR: Richard Talmadge. SCREENPLAY: ROBERT A. HEINLEIN, Seaman. PRODUCTION DESIGN: Jerome Pycha, Jr. CINEMATOGRAPHY: William Thompson. SPECIAL EFFECTS: Jacques Fresco. MUSIC: Herschel Burke Gilbert.

CAST: Donna Martell, Ross Ford, Hayden Rorke, James Craven.

PROJECT X
Paramount (1967). Color, 97 mins.

In the year 2118, the Chinese attempt to destroy the West through the use of a superinfectious concoction of medieval plagues. Only one Western secret agent knows of the plan, and that knowledge is hidden deep within the recesses of his subconscious. The Western governments drug the agent (Christopher George) and, in an elaborate hoax, convince him that he is a bank robber during the 1960s. His mental defenses reduced in the ensuing confusion, a quick mind-probe reveals the secrets of the Chinese attack and saves the world.

PRODUCER AND DIRECTOR: William Castle. SCREENPLAY: Edmund Morris, from the novels *The Artificial Man* and *Psychologist*, by L. P. Davis. ANIMATION: Hanna-Barbera Studios. SPECIAL EFFECTS: Paul Lerpae. MUSIC: Nathan Van Cleave.

SUPPORTING PLAYERS: Henry Jones, Greta Baldwin, Monte Markham, Keye Luke, Harold Gould.

PROPHECY
Paramount (1979). Movielab color and Panavision, 106 mins.

Methyl mercury is dumped into a Maine river by a local lumberyard. The poison causes various mutations to occur in the animal population. Environmentalist Robert Vern (Robert Foxworth) and wife Maggie (Talia Shire) journey to a nearby Indian reservation to investigate. They are aided by residents John Hawks (Armand Assante) and Ramona (Victoria Racimo). What they find is horror beyond their wildest dreams. A she-bear that has mutated into a 20-foot terror pursues the band through a rain-soaked forest in an attempt to rescue her mutant cub from the environmentalist's clutches. Cat-and-mouse with little or no pretension is the result.

PRODUCER: Robert Rosen. DIRECTOR: John Frankenheimer. SCREENPLAY: David Seltzer, from his novel. CINEMATOGRAPHY: Harry Stradling. SPECIAL EFFECTS: Robert Dawson. SPECIAL MAKEUP: Thomas Burman. MUSIC: Leonard Rosenman.

PUNISHMENT PARK
Chartwell-François (1970). Color, 89 mins.

A slice of counterculture optimism. In the future, a dictatorship arrests dissenters and makes a deal with them. The government will let the rebel loose in the desert and then try to kill him. Should the dissenter reach "home base" unscathed, he'll be allowed to live. Good deal, right? Wrong. Even if you *do* reach home base, you'll be killed by the forked-tongued government. Never trust anyone over 30, kids.

PRODUCER: Susan Martin. DIRECTOR AND SCREENWRITER: Peter Watkins. CINEMATOGRAPHY: Joan Churchill. MUSIC: Paul Motian, Jr.

CAST: Paul Alelyanes, Carmen Argenziano, Stan Armsted, Jim Bohan, Mike Hodel, Gary Johnson.

PURPLE MONSTER STRIKES, THE
Republic (1945). B/w serial, 15 chapters (31 reels).
Known in feature form as D-DAY ON MARS (1966).

One of the first films to feature humanoid alien invaders who talked out of the sides of their mouths like real Earth gangsters. Martian Mota (Roy Barcroft) and his mate (Mary Moore) land their Flash Gordonesque rocket ship on Earth with a plan of total destruction. Using bottles of Martian atmosphere to change himself into an invisible monster, Mota begins taking over human beings before dispatching them. And that's only for starts. Next, he perfects an electro-annihilator, a ray device that threatens to blow up the world but doesn't. Communicating with Mars via a "distance eliminator" (later known as a TV), Mota tips his hands

and is subdued by Earth crime-fighters.

DIRECTORS: Spencer G. Bennett and Fred Brannon. SCREENPLAY: Royal K. Cole, Albert De Mond, Basil Dickey, Barney Sarecky, Lynn Perkins, Joseph Poland. MUSICAL DIRECTOR: Richard Cherwin. SPECIAL EFFECTS: Howard and Theodore Lydecker.

SUPPORTING PLAYERS: Dennis Moore, Kenne Duncan, Anthony Warde, Linda Stirling.

QUEEN OF BLOOD
AIP (1966). Color, 81 mins.

The Queen of Mars (Florence Marly) is a beautiful humanoid lass who proves to be a first-class vamp. This latter trait, by the by, does not overly thrill the Earth astronauts giving her a ride back to the U.S. of A. The queen's idea of vamping, it seems, is closely akin to Bela Lugosi's. Before the puzzled space travelers (Dennis Hopper, John Saxon, Judi Merideth, and Forrest J. Ackerman) can figure out the queen's secret, the Martian maid is roaming the ship biting the hands that feed her. Dr. Farraday (Basil Rathbone) is quite suspicious. Eventually the queen accidentally solves the Earthlings' problem when she cuts herself and bleeds to death before reaching terra firma. As a keepsake, however, she leaves behind a nest of Martian eggs just begging for nourishment.

PRODUCER: George Edwards. DIRECTOR AND SCREENWRITER: Curtis Harrington. MAKEUP: William Condos. MUSIC: Leonard Moran.

QUEEN OF OUTER SPACE
AA (1958). Technicolor and Cinemascope, 80 mins.

An sf tale that proves that it's hard to dig up a decent date, even in space. Four astronauts, led by square-jawed Captain Patterson (Eric Fleming), land on Venus and encounter a race of ravishing Amazons. Befriended by local Venusian-Hungarian Talleah (Zsa Zsa

Gabor), the spacefarers are eager to learn of life on Venus. Their enthusiasm wanes however, after they encounter a large mutant beetle (of the papier-maché/puppet variety) and the mysterious masked queen of Venus. The queen, although the possessor of a sultry voice, is the jealous type. When she pushes Patterson too far, she is unmasked before all . . . much to her consternation. The queen, alas, is not a beauty but, apparently, a first cousin of day-old Wheatena.

PRODUCER: Ben Schwalb. DIRECTOR: Edward Bernds. SCREENPLAY: CHARLES BEAUMONT, from a story by Ben Hecht. MUSIC: Marlin Skiles. MAKEUP: Emile La Vigne.

SUPPORTING PLAYERS: Laurie Mitchell, Paul Birch, Lisa Davis.

Allied Artists

Queen of Outer Space

QUEEN OF THE JUNGLE
Screen Attractions (1935). B/w serial, 12 chapters.

White hunters battle natives for possession of a jungle idol featuring radium-beam eyes. On hand for the festivities is the female equivalent of Tarzan, a jungle woman who runs with a wild jungle-cat crowd.

DIRECTOR: Robert Hill. SCREENPLAY: J. Griffin Jay.

CAST: Reed Howes, Mary Korman, Dickie Jones, William Walsh.

QUEST FOR LOVE
Peter Rogers Productions (G.B., 1971). Color, 91 mins.

A modern-day romantic (Tom Bell) accidentally enters a parallel universe in which planet Earth has somehow managed to avoid most of the calamities experienced by its sister world. The Vietnam war has never occurred. John F. Kennedy was never assassinated. The unwitting dimensional traveler meets and falls in love with a girl (Joan Collins) who dies of a strange disease. Returning back to his own Earth, he finds his lost love's double and saves her life.

PRODUCER: Peter Eton. DIRECTOR: Ralph Thomas. SCREENPLAY: Bert Batt, based on a short story "Random Quest," by JOHN WYNDHAM. ART DIRECTOR: Robert Jones. CINEMATOGRAPHY: Ernest Steward. MUSIC: Eric Rogers.

SUPPORTING PLAYERS: Denholm Elliott, Neil McCallum, Simon Ward.

QUINTET
20th Cent.-Fox (1979). DeLuxe color, 100 mins.

In the not-too-distant future, the world is overcome by a new Ice Age. Sheltered in decaying supercities, the population is forced into a game called quintet, an enigmatic confrontation that often leads to bloodletting. When wanderer Essex (Paul Newman) and his spouse Vivia (Brigitte Fossey) arrive in The City, they seek to find shelter but find violence instead. Vivia is killed by a bomb aimed at Essex's family and friends. Essex, vowing revenge, finds that his wife was killed, accidentally, by a blundering quintet player. He endeavors to find out who the players are and what the rules can be.

PRODUCER AND DIRECTOR: Robert Altman. SCREENPLAY: Frank Barhydt, Altman, and Patric Resnick, based on a story by Altman, Resnick, and Lionel Chetwynd. CINEMATOGRAPHY: Jean Bof-

Quintet

fety. ART DIRECTOR: Wolf Kroeger. SPE-CIAL EFFECTS: Tom Fisher, John Thomas. MUSIC: Tom Pierson, performed by the London Symphony Orchestra.

SUPPORTING PLAYERS: Vittoria Gassman as St. Christopher, Fernando Rey as Grigor, Bibi Andersson as Ambrosia, Nina Van Pallandt as Deuca, David Langton as Goldstar, Craig Richard Nelson as Redstone.

RADAR MEN FROM THE MOON
Republic (1952). B/w serial, 12 chapters (24 reels), 384 mins. total running time.
Known in feature form as RETIK THE MOON MENACE (1966).

A very nasty lunar thug, Retik (Roy Barcroft), battles rocketman Commando Cody (George Wallace) for a seemingly unending period of time. Retik arrives on Earth with high hopes. He already has an underground lair on the moon but wants to set up shop Earthside as well. To insure success, he drags along a couple of atomic guns. Commando Cody is not amused.

DIRECTOR: Fred C. Brannon. SCREEN-PLAY: Ronald Davidson. MUSIC: Stanley Wilson. SPECIAL EFFECTS: Howard and Theodore Lydecker.

SUPPORTING PLAYERS: Clayton Moore, Tom Steele, William Bakewell.

RADAR PATROL VS. SPY KING
Republic (1949). B/w serial, 12 chapters (24 reels).

Radar Defense Bureau agent Chris Calvert (Kirk Alyn) locks horns with evil Baroda (John Merton), the head of an organization dedicated to robbing the U.S. of its radar-defense system and then some. Along the way, Baroda and his minions attempt to use their radar-beam neutralizer and batter Chris, friend Joan (Jean Dean), and Manuel (George J. Lewis) with gamma-ray tubes and the ultraray camera. At one

point, Barolda's henchman Nitra (Eve Whitney) tries to kidnap Joan and use a special hypnotic-slave serum on her. Some days it just doesn't pay to get out of bed.

DIRECTOR: Fred Brannon. SCREEN-PLAY: Royal K. Cole, William Lively, Sol Shor. CINEMATOGRAPHY: Ellis W. Carter. SPECIAL EFFECTS: Howard and Theodore Lydecker. MUSIC: Stanley Wilson.

SUPPORTING PLAYERS: Anthony Warde as Ricco, Tristram Coffin as Lord, Dale Van Sickel as Ames, Tom Steele as Gorman, Eddie Parker as Dutch.

RADAR SECRET SERVICE
Lippert (1950). B/w, 59 mins.

A stolen truck filled with atomic material is tracked down via the use of radar by the Radar Patrol.

PRODUCER: Barney Sarecky. DIREC-TOR: Sam Newfield. SCREENPLAY: Beryl Sachs. MAKEUP: George Lane. CINE-MATOGRAPHY: Ernest Miller. MUSIC: Russell Garcia, Dick Hazard.

CAST: Tristram Coffin, Pierre Watkin, John Howard, Adele Jergens, Tom Neal, Sid Melton, Ralph Byrd, Kenne Duncan.

RADIO MANIA
Also known as MARS CALLING; THE MAN FROM MARS.
Teleview Corp. (1923). B/w silent film in 3-D, five reels.

A space-minded fellow falls asleep and dreams that a group of Martians shows him how to turn diamonds and clay into gold.

PRODUCER: Herman Holland. DIREC-TOR: R. William Neill. SCREENPLAY: Lewis Allen Brown. CINEMATOGRAPHY: George Folsey.

CAST: Grant Mitchell, Margaret Irving, Peggy Smith, Isabelle Vernon, Gertrude Hillman.

RADIO PATROL
Universal (1937). B/w serial, 12 chapters (24 reels).

A secret formula for flexible, bullet-proof steel attracts the interest of international crooks who kill the inventor and try to adopt the inventor's son, Pinky (Mickey Rentschler), in order to learn the secret formula. Radio cop Pat

O'Hara (Grant Withers) and Molly Selkirk (Catherine Hughs) thwart their efforts.

PRODUCERS: Barney Sarecky, Ben Koenig. DIRECTORS: Ford Beebe, Cliff Smith. SCREENPLAY: Wyndham Gittens, Norman S. Hall, and Ray Trampe, based on the comic strip by Eddie Sullivan and Charlie Schmidt.

SUPPORTING PLAYERS: Adrian Morris as Sam; Max Hoffman, Jr., as Selkirk; Monte Montague as Pollard; and Silver Wolf as Irish, the loyal German shepherd with a heart of gold and fangs of steel.

RAVAGERS
Columbia (1979). Metrocolor, 91 mins.

In a post-nuclear world, the streets are terrorized by a raggedy group of people known as Ravagers. After Falk (Richard Harris) witnesses the brutal murder of his wife, Miriam (Alana Hamilton), by a gang of such thugs, he exacts his revenge in a bloody reprisal. Angering the rest of the Ravagers, he is chased out of the city of New York. Joining forces with an addle-brained sergeant (Art Carney) and pretty Faina (Ann Turkel), Falk makes his way to the sanctuary of a refurbished aircraft carrier where Ran (Ernest Borgnine) has constructed a safe minisociety. But the Ravagers pursue Falk even to the sea and soon there's a traditional Good vs. Evil showdown.

PRODUCER: John W. Hyde. DIRECTOR: Richard Compton. SCREENPLAY: Donald S. Sanford, from the novel *Path to Savagery*, by Robert E. Alter. CINEMATOGRAPHY: Vincent Saizis. PRODUC-

Ravagers

TION DESIGN: Ronald E. Hobbs. MUSIC: Fred Karlin.

SUPPORTING PLAYERS: Anthony James as Leader, Woody Strode as Brown, Seymour Cassel as Blindman.

RAYS THAT ERASE
Martin (G.B., 1916). B/w silent short, 567 ft.

An inventor comes up with a lamp that gives off invisibility-causing vibes.

DIRECTOR: E. J. Collins.

RED PLANET MARS
UA (1952). B/w, 87 mins.

Unseen aliens give Earthman Peter Graves a start when they begin to communicate with him over the radio from Mars. Adding to his confusion is a healthy feeling of inferiority. Mars, it seems, is utopian, as opposed to Earth which, in 1952, wasn't anyplace to write home to mother about unless she was really hard up for mail.

PRODUCER: Anthony Veiller. DIRECTOR: Harry Horner. SCREENPLAY: John Balderston, Veiller. MUSIC: David Chudnow.

SUPPORTING PLAYERS: Andrea King, Marvin Miller, Morris Ankrum, Gene Roth.

RELUCTANT ASTRONAUT, THE
Universal (1967). Color, 101 mins.

A nervous fellow (with acrophobia to boot) is selected to orbit the Earth in a new space capsule. Strictly a one-shot joke.

PRODUCER AND DIRECTOR: Edward J. Montagne. SCREENPLAY: Jim Fritzell, Everett Greenbaum. CINEMATOGRAPHY: Rexford Wimpy. MUSIC: Vic Mizzy.

CAST: Don Knotts, Arthur O'Connell, Leslie Nielsen, Joan Freeman, Jesse White, Jeanette Nolan.

RETURN FROM WITCH MOUNTAIN
Walt Disney/Buena Vista (1977). Color, 93 mins.

In this sequel to ESCAPE TO WITCH MOUNTAIN, the two telekinetic teens from space, Tia (Kim Richards) and Tony (Ike Eisenmann), are pursued for their telepathic clout by criminals Letha (Bette Davis) and Victor (Christopher Lee).

PRODUCERS: Ron Miller, Jerome Courtland. DIRECTOR: John Hough. SCREENPLAY: Malcolm Marmorstein, based on characters created by Alexander Key. SPECIAL EFFECTS: Eustace Lycett, Art Cruickshank.

SUPPORTING PLAYERS: Jack Soo as Mr. Yokomoto, Brad Savage as Muscles, Dick Bakalyan as Eddie, Christian Juttner as Dazzler, Poindexter as Crusher, Anthony James as Sickle, Ward Costello.

RETURN OF DR. FU MANCHU, THE
Paramount (1930). B/w, 73 mins.

The insidious Fu (Warner Oland) develops a serum that puts its victims into a cataleptic state, a condition in which they obey the commands of their imperious leader, Fu.

DIRECTOR: Rowland W. Lee. SCREENPLAY: Florence Ryerson and Lloyd Corrigan. Based on a novel by Sax Rohmer. CINEMATOGRAPHY: Archie J. Stout.

SUPPORTING PLAYERS: O. P. Heggie, Neil Hamilton, Jean Arthur, Evelyn Hall.

RETURN OF DR. MABUSE
Criterion (1961). B/w, 91 mins.

Master criminal Mabuse (Wolfgang Preiss) plans to control the world via a mind-numbing drug that will turn the population into willing slaves.

DIRECTOR: Harald Reinl. SCREENPLAY: Ladislas Foder, Marc Behm. CINEMATOGRAPHY: Karl Lob. MUSIC: Peter Sandloff. Based on characters created by Norbert Jacques.

SUPPORTING PLAYERS: Gert Frobe, Lex Barker, Daliah Lavi.

RETURN OF DR. X
WB (1939). B/w, 62 mins.

A nonsequel "sequel" to DR. X, marketed quickly in order to cash in on the original film. A scientist brings dead folks back to life but just can't seem to keep them alive the second time around. A deceased child-killer of some notoriety, Marshal Quesne (Humphrey Bogart), is resurrected. In order to remain alive, he must receive a fresh supply of human blood daily. Police begin to suspect foul play when an abnormal amount of anemic cadavers start turning up in the darnedest of places.

PRODUCER: Bryan Foy. DIRECTOR: Vincent Sherman. SCREENPLAY: Lee Katz. MAKEUP: Percy Westmore. CINEMATOGRAPHY: Sid Hickox. MUSIC: Bernard Kaun.

SUPPORTING PLAYERS: Rosemary Lane as Joan Vance, Wayne Morris as Walter Barnett, Huntz Hall as Pinky, Glen Langan as a hospital intern.

RETURN OF THE APE MAN
Monogram (1944). B/w, 60 mins.

A nonsequel "sequel" that asks the question, "So who wanted him back?" A scientist brings a prehistoric, bearded bozo back to life. The scientist (Bela Lugosi) keeps the "ape man" at bay through such sophisticated actions as firing a blowtorch in the thing's face. The bearded wonder (George Zucco and Frank Moran) eventually gets even.

PRODUCERS: Sam Katzman, Jack Dietz. DIRECTOR: Philip Rosen. SCREENPLAY: Robert Charles. CINEMATOGRAPHY: Marcel Le Picard. MUSIC: Edward Kay.

SUPPORTING PLAYERS: John Carradine, Ed Chandler, Mary Currier.

RETURN OF THE FLY
20th Cent.-Fox (1959). B/w, 78 mins.

Those Delambre boys are at it again, mixing mind and mayhem with their matter-transference machine. In this slick sequel to the original film, THE FLY, based on a story by George Langelaan, young Philippe D. (Brett Halsey) decides to follow in his unfortunate pater's footsteps/wingprints despite the warnings of his uncle François (Vincent Price). All is going well until an escaped murderer tosses the scientist into the teleportation device with a tiny fly. Son becomes a chip off the old block, getting his molecules mixed up with the little buzzer. He winds up walking around the house with an oversized fly's head and a claw. Meanwhile, a fly roams the Delambre home with Phillipe's hand and head. Everyone attempts to find the insect before it flies the coop. The experiment is corrected during the film's finale.

PRODUCER: Bernard Glasser. DI-

20th Cent.-Fox

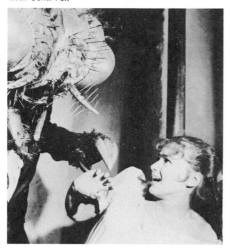

Return of the Fly

RECTOR AND SCREENWRITER: Edward Bernds. MAKEUP: Hal Lierly. CINEMATOGRAPHY: Brydon Baker. MUSIC: Paul Sawtell, Bert Shefter.

SUPPORTING PLAYERS: David Frankham, John Sutton, Danielle DeMezt, Pat O'Hara.

RETURN OF THE GIANT MONSTERS

Daiei (Japan, 1967); color, 87 mins. AIP (U.S., 1969); color, 85 mins.

An exploding volcano hatches more havoc for Japan. Gamera, the flying turtle with the accordion neck, battles Gyaos, a flying beast who has laser-beam breath. Perhaps a good gargle is in order here.

PRODUCER: Hidemas Nagata. DIRECTOR: Noriaki Yuasa. SCREENPLAY: Fumi Takahashi. CINEMATOGRAPHY: Akira Inouye. SPECIAL EFFECTS: Kazufumi Fujii. MUSIC: Tadashi Yamaguchi.

Danger: Falling Alpo!

At one point, we were supposed to be looking at the asteroid belt in space. Dry dog food—kibble—was used to simulate real meteorites. Everyone looked at the screen and exclaimed at once . . . "Why, that's KIBBLE!" Shortly thereafter, we hired a new special-effects crew.

AIP executive on the making of *Meteor*

CAST: Kojiro Hongo, Kichijiro Ueda, Reiko Kasahara.

RETURN OF THE TERROR
WB (1934). B/w, seven reels.

Based on the Edgar Wallace mystery novel *The Terror,* this tidy little thriller concerns a scientist who is falsely imprisoned in a laughing academy after inventing a secret X-ray machine.

DIRECTOR: Howard Bretherton. SCREENPLAY: Eugene Solow, Peter Milne. CINEMATOGRAPHY: Arthur Todd.

CAST: Mary Astor, Lyle Talbot, John Halliday, J. Carrol Naish, Frank Reicher.

REVENGE OF FRANKENSTEIN
Columbia (1958). Color, 91 mins.

This amazingly low-keyed sequel to THE CURSE OF FRANKENSTEIN is given added power by a series of strong performances by the principals. Frankenstein (Peter Cushing) changes his name to Stein and with the aid of hunchback assistant Karl (Michael Gwynn) begins his experiments again. Working as a volunteer in the free Workhouse Hospital, Stein seems the epitome of a servant of the poor and underprivileged. The well-respected doctor, however, amputates parts from the unfortunate free-clinic patients and uses them to construct a solid body for his latest round with immortality. A young member of the medical council, Hans Kleeve (Francis Matthews), almost brings the experiment to an early end when he recognizes the doctor as Frankenstein. Realizing the importance of Dr. F.'s work, however, Hans offers his help.

The experiment comes off without a hitch. Loyal Karl's normal brain is put into the solid new body. All is well until Karl ventures down into the basement lab to destroy his old body. He tosses it into a furnace but is caught in the act by a janitor, who sees the action as murder. A fight ensues and Karl is beaten atop the head. He kills the janitor and escapes the scene, reeling. His brain injured, he watches with horror as his new body gradually assumes the gnarled, horrible shape of his old one. New hunchback Karl stumbles up to Frankenstein at a social function and, in front of nearly the entire town, lisps . . . "Frankenstein . . . help me."

Hans urges the doctor to flee, but the surgeon decides to bluff his way out of the situation. Before a council of his peers, he coldly dismisses their accusations of torture, saying that his name *is* Frankenstein. But he is not *the* Frankenstein, the name being a common one in his part of the world. He has changed it to avoid confrontations, such as this one, with the small-minded. His bluff works. Reentering the Workhouse Hospital, however, he is beaten to a pulp by the angered patients, who know the truth. He is near death when Hans arrives. "You know what to do," Frankenstein whispers.

Shortly thereafter, in London, a handsome, albeit familiar face, is introduced at a gala ball . . . Dr. Victor Frank.

PRODUCER: Anthony Hinds. DIRECTOR: Terence Fisher. SCREENPLAY: Jimmy Sangster. MAKEUP: Phil Leakey. CINEMATOGRAPHY: Jack Asher. MUSIC: Leonard Salzedo.

SUPPORTING PLAYERS: Michael Ripper, Eunice Gayson, Lionel Jeffries.

REVENGE OF THE CREATURE
Universal (1955). B/w, 82 mins.

A strong sequel to THE CREATURE FROM THE BLACK LAGOON. Clete Ferguson (John Agar) captures that Amazon resident, the Creature, and brings it back to a Florida aquarium park to study. Clete and Helen Dobson (Lori Nelson) attempt to communicate with the gill-man in a manner reminiscent of today's experiments conducted on dolphins. The teaching method is rather harsh, however, involving the use of chains and an electric cattle prod. Prodded a bit too far, the critter escapes and bashes heads throughout the Florida area. After killing several bystanders and tossing a few vintage autos around like basketballs, he escapes into the sea. Next stop: the Amazon . . . until THE CREATURE WALKS AMONG US, that is.

PRODUCER: William Alland. DIRECTOR: Jack Arnold. SCREENPLAY: Martin Berkeley, from a story by Alland. MAKEUP: Bud Westmore. CINEMATOGRAPHY: Charles S. Welbourne. MUSIC: Herman Stein.

SUPPORTING PLAYERS: John Brom-field, Nestor Paiva, Dave Willock, Ricou Browning as the Creature.

REVENGE OF THE ZOMBIES
Monogram (1943). B/w, 61 mins.

John Carradine is a mad doctor who shocks Gale Storm senseless (catchword, there) by revealing to her his plot concerning the mass production of zombies. Carradine, turning his wife into an undead, plans to raise an army of the critters to help the beleaguered Nazis out of their pickle during World War II. The Nazis never get a chance to goose-step with the ghouls, however. The scientist's wife, not at all pleased at sacrificing her life for the boys in Germany, turns the zombies against her hubby and does him in.

PRODUCER: Linsley Parsons. DIRECTOR: Steve Sekely. SCREENPLAY: Edmund Kelso, Van Norcross. CINEMATOGRAPHY: Mack Stengler. MUSIC: Edward Kay.

SUPPORTING PLAYERS: Robert Lowery, Mantan Morland, Bob Steele, Veda Ann Borg as the zombie-libber.

REVOLT OF THE ZOMBIES
Academy (1936). B/w, 65 mins.

Cambodia reveals the secrets of zombiedom to a group of doctors who plan to raise zombie-soldiers as the perfect instrument of war. Sounds all-American.

PRODUCER: Edward Halperin. DIRECTOR: Victor Halperin. SCREENPLAY: Howard Higgins, Rollo Lloyd, Victor Halperin. CINEMATOGRAPHY: J. Arthur Feindel. SPECIAL EFFECTS: Ray Mercer.

CAST: Dean Jagger, Roy D'Arcy, Dorothy Stone, George Cleveland, William Crowell.

RIDERS TO THE STARS
UA (1954). Color, 82 mins.

Syrupy depiction of the heroism involved in the space race. Richard Stanton (William Lundigan), Dr. Donald Stanton (Herbert Marshall), and Jerry Lockwood (Richard Carlson) inspire all those around them as they journey outside the Earth's atmosphere, attempting to ensnare meteors for the construction of a friction-proof rocketship covering.

PRODUCER: Ivan Tors. DIRECTOR:

Richard Carlson. SCREENPLAY: CURT SIODMAK. CINEMATOGRAPHY: Stanley Cortez. SPECIAL EFFECTS: Jack Glass. MUSIC: Harry Sukman.

SUPPORTING PLAYERS: Martha Hyer, Dawn Addams, King Donovan.

ROAD TO HONG KONG
UA (1962). Color, 91 mins.

Bob Hope and Bing Crosby take a quick trip to the planet Plutonium after Bob accidentally memorizes a secret rocket-fuel formula while under the influence of a memory-strengthening drug. International and intergalactic intrigue abounds.

PRODUCER: Melvin Frank. DIRECTOR: Norman Panama. SCREENPLAY: Panama, Frank. CINEMATOGRAPHY: Jack Hildyard. SPECIAL EFFECTS: Wally Veevers, Ted Samuels.

SUPPORTING PLAYERS: Joan Collins, Dorothy Lamour, Robert Morley, Jerry Colonna, Peter Sellers, David Niven, Frank Sinatra.

ROBINSON CRUSOE OF CLIPPER ISLAND
Republic (1936). B/w serial, 14 chapters (29 reels).
Known in feature form as ROBINSON CRUSOE ON MYSTERY ISLAND.

Mala (Mala), a Polynesian agent for the U.S. Intelligence Service, journeys to Clipper Island with his pal Hank (William Newell) to investigate the wrecking of the dirigible *San Francisco*. While there, they discover crooks attempting to cause a local volcano to erupt by constructing a ton of secret electrical weapons.

DIRECTORS: Mack V. Wright, Ray Taylor. SCREENPLAY: Morgan Cox, Barry Shipman, Maurice Geraghty. CINEMATOGRAPHY: William Nobles, Edgar Lyons. MUSIC: Harry Grey.

SUPPORTING PLAYERS: Momo Clark as Princess Melani, Herbert Rawlinson as Jack, George Cleveland as Goebel, John Ward as Tupper.

ROBINSON CRUSOE ON MARS
Paramount (1964). Technicolor, 109 mins.

An eye-boggling tale helmed by director Byron (WAR OF THE WORLDS)

Robinson Crusoe on Mars

Haskin, capable of delighting the child in us all. Astronauts Christopher Draper (Paul Mantee) and Col. Dan MacReady (Adam West), along with mascot monkey Mona, crash-land on Mars. Only Mona and Draper survive. Seemingly alone on the desolate planet, the two set up house in the thinly atmosphered planet and, rationing their oxygen, set about to find a way to manufacture breathable air from Martian minerals. In the midst of their work, a humanoid alien (Vic Lundin), soon to be christened Friday, runs their way. Held captive by alien slave-owners who operate a Martian mining concern, Friday escapes and remains a free being with the help of Mona and Draper. The slave owners pursue the trio in mammoth flying ships closely akin to the Martian death machines in WAR OF THE WORLDS.

PRODUCER: Aubrey Schenck, DIRECTOR: Byron Haskin. SCREENPLAY: Ib Melchior, John C. Higgins. MUSIC: Nathan Van Cleave. MAKEUP: Wally Westmore and Bud Bashaw. SPECIAL EFFECTS: Lawrence W. Butler.

ROBOT MONSTER, THE
Astor (1953). B/w and 3-D, 63 mins.

In a league with a major viral infection of your choice. An evil Ro-Man (a fellow in a gorilla suit capped by a round diving suit/astronaut helmet) lands on Earth, equipped with a death ray. The critter kills everyone on Earth except for six people. He is about to do them in when, uh-oh, our little narrator wakes up and, ha ha, it was all a dream the little kiddie had. Had you goin', huh?

PRODUCER AND DIRECTOR: Phil Tucker. SCREENPLAY: Wyatt Ordung. CINEMATOGRAPHY: Jack Greenhalgh. SPECIAL EFFECTS: Jack Rabin, David Commons. MUSIC: Elmer Bernstein.

CAST: George Nader, Claudie Barrett, Gregory Moffett, Pamela Paulson.

ROBOT OF REGALIA, THE
Reed (1954). B/w, 78 mins.

A feature made from episodes of TV's ROCKY JONES, SPACE RANGER. Rocky meets a robot.

PRODUCER: Roland Reed.

CAST: Richard Crane, James Lyton.

ROBOT VS. THE AZTEC MUMMY
Calderon (Mexico, 1959); AIT (U.S., 1962). B/w.

A scientist miffs the Aztec mummy by trying to gate-crash the ancient cadaver's treasure-filled tomb. When human effort fails, the plucky mercantilist returns with a tin-can man—a robot boasting a human brain. Never would have guessed it.

PRODUCER: William C. Stell. DIRECTOR: Rafael Portillo. SCREENPLAY: Alfred Salazar. CINEMATOGRAPHY: Enrique Wallace. MUSIC: Antonio Diaz Conde.

CAST: Ramon Gay, Rosita Arenas, Crox Alvarado.

ROCKET ATTACK, U.S.A.
Exploit Films (1961). B/w, 68 mins.

A choice bit of paranoia. World War III begins when the evil Russians nuke New York.

PRODUCER AND DIRECTOR: Barry Mahon. CINEMATOGRAPHY: Mike Tabb.

CAST: John McKay, Monica Davis, Daniel Kern.

ROCKETSHIP X-M
Also known as EXPEDITION MOON. Lippert (1950). B/w with tinted sequences, 78 mins.

A fairly pedestrian voyage into space. Rocketship X-M blasts off for the moon with pilot Floyd Oldham (Lloyd Bridges), fuel expert Lisa Van Horn (Osa Massen), astronomer Harry Chamberlain (Hugh O'Brian), scientist Karl Eckstrom (John Emery), and navigator Bill Corrigan (Noah Beery, Jr.) on board. A meteor shower causes a change in its direction and the rocket winds up landing on Mars. Once there, the crew finds a nuked-out civilization and a host of unfriendly humanoid-mutant cave people. All but two of the landing party meet their Maker courtesy of a ticket provided by the mutants. The two survivors head back for Earth but run out of fuel on the way down. Bam!

PRODUCER AND DIRECTOR: Kurt (THE FLY) Neumann. SCREENPLAY: Neumann, from two previous screenplays: *Journey to the Unknown* and *None Came Back*. CINEMATOGRAPHY: Karl Struss. SPECIAL EFFECTS: Jack Rabin, Irving Block. MUSIC: Ferde Grofe.

SUPPORTING PLAYERS: Katherine Marlow, John Dutra, Patrick Ahern, Morris Ankrum as Dr. Fleming.

ROCKY HORROR PICTURE SHOW, THE
20th Cent.-Fox (1975). Eastmancolor, 100 mins.

Currently a popular cult-item, this movie was a total commercial dud at the time of its release. Janet Weiss (Susan Sarandon) and Brad Majors (Barry Boswick) find themselves marooned in the castle of Dr. Frank N. Furter (Tim Curry), the latter being an alien of the "sweet transvestite" kind from the planet Transsexual in the galaxy of Transylvania. He's here on Earth to make a man—literally. He creates a handsome young thing à la Frankenstein's monster and dubs him Rocky Horror. Handsome Rocky, however, has trouble throwing his sex drive into low gear.

Janet and Brad experience pangs of sexual awakening thanks to Frank, his creation, and two alien henchmen, Magenta (Patricia Quinn) and Riff Raff (Richard O'Brien), who are constantly saying things like "Don't dream it, BE it!" There is a fiery finale straight from the classic B-films of the 1930s, 1940s, and 1950s.

PRODUCER: Michael White. DIRECTOR: Jim Sharman. ORIGINAL MUSIC, LYRICS, AND PLAY: Richard O'Brien. SCREENPLAY: Sharman, O'Brien. SPECIAL EFFECTS: Wally Veevers.

SUPPORTING PLAYERS: Meatloaf as Eddie, Charles Gray as the Criminologist, Jonathan Dams as Professor Scott.

ROCKY JONES, SPACE RANGER
Reed. B/w.

A series of "Rocky Jones" films were produced in the early 1950s by coupling together individual 26-minute episodes of the popular TV series ROCKY JONES, SPACE RANGER. The movies all starred the TV crew: Rocky (Richard Crane), Vena (Sally Mansfield), Biff (James Lydon), Princess Juliandra (Ann Robertson), and Secretary Drake (Charles Meredith). The aliens encountered week after week were always of the humanoid gangster/con man variety.

The movies featured in this hasty re-editing job included: *Beyond the Moon* (1954), BLAST OFF (1954), *Clash of Moons* (1954), THE COLD SUN (1954), DUEL IN SPACE (1954), *Forbidden Moon* (1953), *Gypsy Moon* (1953), *Inferno in Space* (1954), THE MAGNETIC MOON (1954), MANHUNT IN SPACE (1954), MENACE FROM OUTER SPACE (1954), OUT OF THIS WORLD (1954), THE ROBOT OF REGALIA (1954), and *Silver Needle in the Sky* (1954).

PRODUCER: Roland Reed. DIRECTORS: Hollingsworth Mores, William Beaudine, others. SCREENPLAYS: Clark Hittleman, Warren Wilson, others.

RODAN
Toho (Japan, 1956), DCA (U.S., 1957). Color, 79 mins.

Miner Shigeru (Kenji Sahara) becomes a major hero when, discovering a group of baby monsters in the shaft of the world's deepest mine, he pilots a coal car into their midst and brings down the house. After he is nursed to health by fiancée Kiyo (Yumi Shirakawa), he warns that there might be other critters down there. No sooner does he speak than the gigantic, winged bird-monster Rodan appears. Modern science and military strength prove no match for the superpowerful pterodactyl creature. Soon a Mrs. Rodan appears. High on their mountaintop home, the two beasts are attacked by the military, who turn the mountain into a violent volcano through persistent bombing. Mrs. R. is killed by the lava and Mr. R. commits hara-kiri by taking a quick dip in the molten pools below.

DCA

Rodan

PRODUCER: Tomoyuki Tanaka. DIRECTOR: Inoshiro Honda. SCREENPLAY: Takeshi Kimura and Takeo Murata, from a story by Takashi Kuronuma. CINEMATOGRAPHY: Isamu Ashida. SPECIAL EFFECTS: Eiji Tsuburaya. MUSIC: Tadashi Yamauchi.

SUPPORTING PLAYERS: Akihiko Hirata, Yoshibumi Tajima.

ROLLERBALL
UA (1975). Color, 129 mins.

Jonathan E. (James Caan) is a superstar of the futuristic sport of rollerball, a bloodthirsty event that is a combination of Roller Derby and sheer mayhem. Confined to a circular track, the participants use both skates and motorcycles to reach speeds of 125 miles per hour and more. The government, ruled by affluent businessmen (including the executive Bartholomew, played by John Houseman), is worried about Jonathan's status. Ever since the time of the Corporate Wars, the businessmen have been the superiors. A cult hero is something they don't need to compete with in the popularity department. Unfortunately, Jonathan E. picks that time period to undergo a personality crisis. He wants to be an individual in a society of spineless followers. The government comes up with a plan to effect E.'s demise. He will participate in an open-ended game of rollerball—a game that will be played until only one athlete is left standing.

PRODUCER AND DIRECTOR: Norman Jewison. SCREENPLAY: William Harrison, from his story.

SUPPORTING PLAYERS: Ralph Richardson, Maud Adams.

SAMSON IN THE WAX MUSEUM
Azteca (Mexico, 1963); AIT (U.S., 1964). Color, 90 mins.

Masked hero Santo (Santo) runs across a demented surgeon who, because of a prolonged stay in a concentration camp, believes that a person's face should reveal his or her true character . . . even if the face has to be altered to match the doc's concept of what that character is. To cover his experiments, the doc owns and operates a wax museum and disguises his experiments as wax dummies.

PRODUCER: Alberto Lopez. DIRECTOR: Alfonso Corona Blake. SCREENPLAY: Fernando Galiana, Julio Porter. CINEMATOGRAPHY: Jose Ortiz Ramos.

SUPPORTING PLAYERS: Claudio Brooke, Ruben Rojo, Norma Mora.

SANTA CLAUS CONQUERS THE MARTIANS
Embassy (1964). Color, 82 mins.

When Martian kids get out of hand, a band of eager-to-please alien parents zip off to Earth to kidnap Santa Claus. While this move is intended to keep the Martian brats quiet, it doesn't sit well with the children of Earth. If it's not one thing, it's another.

PRODUCER: Paul Jacobson. DIRECTOR: Nicholas Webster. SCREENPLAY: Glenville Mareth.

CAST: John Call as Santa Claus, Leonard Hicks as the Martian, Vincent Beck, Leila Martin, Donna Conforti.

SANTA CLAUS'S BUSY DAY
France (1906). B/w silent short.

Santa Claus's preparations for Christmas are momentarily interrupted when the Man in the Moon decides to play Peeping Tom.

SATANIC RITES OF DRACULA, THE
Hammer (G.B., 1973). Color.

Dracula (Christopher Lee) shows up in modern-day London, attempting to take over the world with a bacteriological plague. Also on hand, however, is the latest descendant of Van Helsing (Peter Cushing), who continues to fight the fangs with the aid of the British authorities.

PRODUCER: Roy Skeggs. SCREENPLAY: Don Houghton. DIRECTOR: Alan Gibson. MAKEUP: George Blackler. SPECIAL EFFECTS: Les Bowie. CINEMATOGRAPHY: Brian Probyn.

Giving Her All
"I held the reflecting lens—and never saw again!"
            Violet Kemble Cooper to
            Frances Drake in *The Invisible Ray*

SUPPORTING PLAYERS: Michael Coles, William Franklyn, Joanna Lumley, Valerie Ost, Freddie Jones.

SATELLITE IN THE SKY
WB (1956). Color/scope, 84 mins.

A rocket carrying the first tritonium bomb to be detonated in space is launched. While orbiting the earth, however, the rocket runs into problems --the bomb becomes stuck to its wing. Two astronauts sacrifice their lives and some 30 minutes trying to get it loose.

PRODUCERS: Edward and Harry Lee Danzinger. DIRECTOR: Paul Dickson. SCREENPLAY: John Mather, J. T. McIntosh, Edith Dell. CINEMATOGRAPHY: Georges Perinal, Jimmy Wilson. SPECIAL EFFECTS: Wally Veevers. MUSIC: Albert Elms.

CAST: Kieron Moore, Louis Maxwell, Donald Wolfit, Bryan Forbes, Jimmy Hanley.

SATURN 3
AFD (1980). Color, 97 mins.

On the third moon of Saturn, two research chemists (Kirk Douglas as Adam, Farrah Fawcett as Alex) have their idyllic life-style shattered by the arrival of space madman Capt. James (Harvey Keitel), an expert on robots and facial twitches.

James claims to be there to monitor Adam and Alex's hydroponics research and curtly informs them they are behind schedule. In between heavy bursts of breathing aimed Alex's way, James constructs an out-of-whack robot, Hector (the first of the Demi-god series), to help the duo with their work. When James programs Hector (via a handy plug-socket in the back of the captain's head), however, he accidentally instills all his mental quirks in the big fella. The robot also becomes a lunatic, possessing James's powerful passion for lovely Alex. Before you know it, there's a four-sided triangle loose on the moon Titan and one half of it is homicidal: killer James and would-be killer Hector becoming rivals.

PRODUCER AND DIRECTOR: Stanley Donen. SCREENPLAY: Martin Amis, from a story by John Barry. ASSOCIATE PRODUCER: Eric Rattray. CINEMATOGRAPHY: Billy Williams. SPECIAL EFFECTS: Colin Chilvers. COSTUME DESIGN: Anthony Mendelson. SOUND: Derek Ball. A Sir Lew Grade presentation.

SCREAM AND SCREAM AGAIN
AIP (1970). Color, 95 mins.

Superintendent Ballaver (Alfred Marks) is called upon to investigate the brutal murder of a young girl, Sylvia (Judi Bloom), and a respected politician, Benedek (Peter Cushing). American pathologist David Sorel (Christopher Matthews) reveals that both bodies have been drained of all blood. An undercover cop, Helen Bradford (Judi Bloom), tracks down and entraps the killer, Keith (Michael Gothard), who eludes the police with superhuman speed and agility, losing a hand in the process. The deformed killer runs to the home of Dr. Browning (Vincent Price) and jumps into a vat of acid.

A British government agent, Fremond (Christopher Lee), attempts to squelch the vampire killings, but Sorel wants to get to the bottom of the mystery. Accordingly, Helen continues her investigation, eventually finding herself trapped in the lab of Dr. Browning. Browning is working on the creation of a superhuman master race, pieced together from the bodies of the most beautiful girls and solidly built athletes. Government agent Konratz (Marshall Jones) is the backer of the scheme, but, seeing poor Helen at the doctor's mercy, he gets cold feet. He tosses Browning into the nearby acid vat, figuring that the world isn't ready for a race of superhumans anyhow.

PRODUCERS: Max J. Rosenberg, Milton Subotsky. DIRECTOR: Gordon Hessler. SCREENPLAY: Christopher Wicking, from the novel by Peter Saxon. CINEMATOGRAPHY: John Coquillon. MAKEUP: Jimmy Evans. MUSIC: Dave Whittaker. Song "Scream and Scream Again" by Dominic King and Tim Hayes.

SECONDS
Paramount (1966). B/w, 106 mins.

An uneven movie based on an equally lopsided novel by David Ely, *Seconds* tells the tale of an aging businessman (John Randolph) who wants to be born again, so to speak. Paying an enormous sum of money to a secret surgical center, he has his death faked. He is then taken into the operating room and, through a series of plastic-surgery operations, given a young body and a new face (Rock Hudson). Released from the black-market medical headquarters, he tries to start his life all over. He finds that he can't cut it as a youth, however. Fearing that the businessman will spill the beans, the surgeons capture him and drag him back into the rejuvenation factory. In order to ensure that the surgical center will continue running smoothly and secretly, the doctors kill the fellow and dismember him, storing his body parts for next year's model. You can't teach an old dog new tricks, eh?

PRODUCER: Edward Lewis. DIRECTOR: John Frankenheimer. SCREENPLAY: Lewis J. Carlino, from the novel by David Ely. MAKEUP: Jack Petty and Mark Reedall. MUSIC: Jerry Goldsmith.

SUPPORTING PLAYERS: Salome Jens, Will Geer, Jeff Corey, Murray Hamilton.

SECRET AGENT FIREBALL
Devon/Radius (Italy/France, 1965); color/scope, 95 mins. AIP (U.S., 1966); color/scope, 89 mins.

International spies battle over the formula for the ultimate H-bomb, threatening each other with such gadgetry as a laser-beam-firing ballpoint pen.

PRODUCERS: Mino Loy and Luciano Martino. DIRECTOR: Mario Donen. SCREENPLAY: Sergio Martino. CINEMATOGRAPHY: Richard Thierry. MUSIC: Carlo Savina.

CAST: Richard Harrison, Jim Clar, Wanda Guida, Dominique Boschero.

SECRET KINGDOM, THE
Stoll (G.B., 1925). B/w silent featurette, 5,930 ft.

An inventor comes up with a machine that can read people's minds, making public their most private thoughts. The machine, however, brings nothing but pain to its users, showing people as being liars, cheats, and bores. It's destroyed, along with a lot of dreams.

PRODUCER AND DIRECTOR: Sinclair Hill. SCREENPLAY: Alicia Ramsay. CINEMATOGRAPHY: Percy Strong.

CAST: Matheson Lang, Stella Arbenia, Eric Bransby.

SECRET OF THE TELEGIAN
Toho (Japan, 1960); color, 85 mins. Herts-Lion (U.S., 1964); color, 75 mins.

A scientist turns a man into a pretty ugly monster by electrically charging his bloodstream. The monster can then be teleported anywhere to commit murder. Shocking.

PRODUCER: Tomoyuki Tanaka. DIRECTOR: Jun Fukuda. SCREENPLAY: Shinichi Sekizawa. CINEMATOGRAPHY: Kazuo Yamada. SPECIAL EFFECTS: Eiji Tsuburaya.

SECRET SERVICE IN DARKEST AFRICA, THE
Republic (1943). B/w serial, 10 chapters (21 reels).
Known in feature form as THE BARON'S AFRICAN WAR.

Rex Bennett (Rod Cameron), an American undercover agent, masquerades as a Gestapo agent and winds up in Africa, where the Germans and the locals are working on death rays and suspended-animation drugs perfectly suited for world conquest. Rex is not amused.

DIRECTOR: Spencer Bennett. SCREENPLAY: Royal Cole, Basil Dickey, Jesse

Duffy, Ronald Davidson, Joseph O'Donnell, Joseph Poland. CINEMATOGRAPHY: William Bradford. SPECIAL EFFECTS: Howard Lydecker. MUSIC: Mort Glickman.

SUPPORTING PLAYERS: Joan Marsh as Janet Blake, Duncan Renaldo as Pierre LaSalle, Lionel Royce as Baron von Rommier and Sultan Abou Ben Ali.

SERGEANT DEADHEAD THE ASTRONAUT
AIP (1965). Color, 89 mins.

A trip into space has a Jekyll-Hyde effect on hapless Deadhead (Frankie Avalon). Meek before going into orbit, he returns to Earth an obnoxious loudmouth.

PRODUCERS: James H. Nicholson, Samuel Z. Arkoff, Anthony Carras. DIRECTOR: Norman Taurog. SCREENPLAY: Louis M. Hayward. CINEMATOGRAPHY: Floyd Crosby. SPECIAL EFFECTS: Roger George. MUSIC: Les Baxter.

SUPPORTING PLAYERS: Deborah Walley, Cesar Romero, Buster Keaton, Fred Clark, Gale Gordon, Eve Arden.

SEX KITTENS GO TO COLLEGE
AA (1960). B/w, 90 mins.

A stripper with a genius IQ (Mamie Van Doren) is picked by a computer to head the science department of a small-town college. The electronic brain, called Thinko, passes its idle hours picking winners at the local race track. The rest of the alumni association spends several hours singing "Thanks for the mammaries."

PRODUCER, DIRECTOR, and STORY ORIGINATOR: Albert Zugsmith. SCREENPLAY: Robert Hill. CINEMATOGRAPHY: Ellis Carter. SPECIAL EFFECTS: Augie Lohman. MUSIC: Dean Elliot.

SUPPORTING PLAYERS: Tuesday Weld, Mijanou Bardot, Mickey Shaughnessy, Louis Nye, Martin Milner, John Carradine, Vampira, Conway Twitty, Charlie Chaplin, Jr., Harold Lloyd, Jr.

SHADOW OF CHINATOWN
Victory (1934). B/w serial, 15 chapters.

A crazed scientist (Bela Lugosi) attempts to control human personality via a hypnosis machine that can telepathically control its victims from miles away.

PRODUCER: Sam Katzman. DIRECTOR: Robert F. Hill. SCREENPLAY: W. Buchanan, Isadore Bernstein, Basil Dickey. CINEMATOGRAPHY: Bill Hyder.

SUPPORTING PLAYERS: Herman Brix, Luana Walters, Charles King.

SHADOW OF EVIL
France/Italy (1964); color/scope, 115 mins. WB (U.S., 1966); color/scope, 92 mins.

Agent OSS 117 (Kerwin Mathews) discovers a plot by a secret Bangkok sect to infect rats with a scientifically concocted plague that will wipe out the entire population of the world . . . except for members of the Bangkok sect, who have been immunized.

PRODUCER: Paul Cadeac. DIRECTOR: André Hunebelle. SCREENPLAY: Pierre Foucaud, Raymond Borel, André Hunebelle, Michel Lebrun, Richard Caron, Patrice Rondard. CINEMATOGRAPHY: Raymond Lemoigne. MUSIC: Michel Magne.

SUPPORTING PLAYERS: Robert Hossein, Pier Angeli.

SHADOW OF THE EAGLE
Mascot (1932). B/w serial, 12 chapters.

Former air ace and present-day carnival owner Nathan Gregory (Edward Hearn) is accused by local police of being a high-flying criminal called the Eagle. Skywriting fool Craig McCoy (John Wayne) comes to the aid of his buddy, going after the real Eagle, who is working on a ray gun that will shoot planes out of the sky. Yow.

DIRECTOR: Ford Beebe. SCREENPLAY: Beebe, C. Clark, Wyndham Gittens.

SUPPORTING PLAYERS: Dorothy Gulliver as Jean Gregory, Pat O'Malley as Ames, Roy D'Arcy as Gardner, Walter Miller as Danby.

SHANKS
Paramount (1974), color.

Marcel Marceau stars as deaf-mute puppeteer Malcolm Shanks and his elderly benefactor, Walker. Walker, a scientist, discovers a way to bring the dead back to life by electrically rewiring their bodies. In effect, he makes them walking puppets. Walker dies and Shanks carries on in the tradition, doing in his evil in-laws, Mr. and Mrs.

Shanks

Barton (Philippe Clay and Tsilla Chelton) but restoring them as automatons, A young girl, Celia (Cindy Eilbacher), becomes infatuated with Shanks and a blissfully innocent love affair ensues. A group of motorcycle thugs invade the household, however, and torture, gang rape, and murder the girl in a scene of gratuitous violence. Shanks responds with a robot army and destroys the motorcycle thugs. Too late to save the slaughtered Celia, he brings her back to life as a big-as-life puppet. Sick.

PRODUCER: Steven North. DIRECTOR: William Castle. SCREENPLAY: Ronald Graham. PUPPETS: Bob Baker. MAKEUP: Jack Young. CINEMATOGRAPHY: Joseph Biroc. SPECIAL EFFECTS: Richard Albain. MUSIC: Alex North.

SUPPORTING PLAYERS: Larry Bishop as Napoleon, Don Calfa as Einstein, Mondo as Genghis Khan, William Castle as the grocer.

SHAPE OF THINGS TO COME, THE
AA (1979). Color, running time undetermined.

Scheduled for a release in the spring of 1979, this Canadian space opera was shelved when the studio abruptly went bankrupt. It did, however, receive backing for distribution in Europe and Canada.

The moon base of New Washington is attacked by robot master Omus (Jack Palance). New Washington is given the ultimatum: surrender or watch Earth be destroyed. Since New Washington is populated by pacifists, it is ill-prepared to defend itself.

Defying the idealistic efforts of Senator Smedley (John Ireland), a defense attempt is mounted by Jason Caball (Nicholas Campbell), his father, Dr. John Caball (Barry Morse), robot technician Kim Smedley (Eddie Benton), and a rewired robot called Sparks. Journeying to Omus's home planet, Delta III, they launch an attack to defeat the evil robot-master and rescue captive New Washingtonian Niki (Carol Lynley).

PRODUCER: Harry Alan Towers, William Davidson. DIRECTOR: George McCowan. SCREENPLAY: Martin Lager, suggested by the novel by H. G. WELLS. SPECIAL EFFECTS: Wally Gentleman. SCIENTIFIC CONSULTANT: Frank Wells. CINEMATOGRAPHY: Reginald Morris. ADDITIONAL SPECIAL EFFECTS: Don Weed. MINIATURE CONSTRUCTION: Brick Price.

SHE CREATURES
AIP (1957). B/w, 77 mins.

Mesmerist Lombardi (Chester Morris) has a good time with hypnotism, sending his hapless subject (Marla English) mentally back to prehistoric times. Unfortunately, her prehistoric self winds up showing up in the present-day—physically. Swatting down victims like flies. Accused of being a fraud by psychic investigator Ted Erickson (Lance Fuller), Lombardi begins predicting murders and sending out the she-creature to make sure his predictions come true. So impressed with Lombardi's skills at prognostication is local millionaire Tim Chappel (Tom Conway) that he agrees to manage him. Unfortunately, Lombardi's patient falls for Erickson, and this makes transforming her into a killer increasingly difficult. Lombardi orders the creature to appear. It does, and when ordered to kill Erickson by the mad hypnotist (bad move, that), it murders the hypnotist instead. Lombardi dies. The she-creature disappears and the young girl returns to normal.

PRODUCER: Alex Gordon. DIRECTOR: Edward L. Cahn. SCREENPLAY: Lou Rusoff, from a story by Jerry Zigmond. Monster created by Paul Blaisdell. MUSIC: Ronald Stein.

SUPPORTING CAST: Paul Blaisdell as the Creature, Cathy Downs, El Brendel.

SHE DEMONS
Astor (1958). B/w, 77 mins.

A Nazi scientist hidden in the jungle with a fairly repulsive-looking wife tries to restore her beauty with frequent skin grafts. Using local native girls, he botches operation after operation. The results? A chorus line of eye-boggling anatomies topped by Lon Chaneyesque kissers.

PRODUCER: Arthur A. Jacobs. DIRECTOR: Richard E. Cunha. SCREENPLAY: Cunha and H. E. Barrie. MAKE-UP: Carlie Taylor. SPECIAL EFFECTS: David Koehler. MUSIC: Nicolas Carras.

CAST: Irish McCalla, Tod Griffin, Victor Sen Yung, Gene Roth, Leni Tana, Billy Dix, Bill Coontz.

SHE DEVIL
20th Cent.-Fox (1957). B/w, 77 mins.

A serum being experimented with as a possible cure for TB turns a woman into a human chameleon and gives her superstrength. The antidote saps her of her powers and star billing, killing her at the end.

PRODUCER AND DIRECTOR: Kurt Neumann. SCREENPLAY: Neumann and Carroll Young, based on the story "The Adaptive Ultimate," by John Jessel. CINEMATOGRAPHY: Karl Struss. MUSIC: Paul Sawtell, Bert Shefter.

CAST: Mari Blanchard, Jack Kelley, Albert Dekker, John Archer.

SHH! THE OCTOPUS
WB (1938). B/w, 60 mins.

A master criminal attempts to invent a death ray. While waiting for the pot to boil, he discourages visitors with a giant mechanical octopus.

PRODUCER: Bryan Foy. DIRECTOR: William McGann. SCREENPLAY: George Bricker, from a play by Ralph Murphy and Donald Gallagher. CINEMATOGRAPHY: Arthur Todd.

CAST: Allen Jenkins, Hugh Herbert, Marcia Ralston, Eric Stanley.

SHIRLEY THOMPSON VS. THE ALIENS
Kolossal (Australia, 1972). B/w, 104 mins.

Shirley Thompson has a problem. Invisible aliens are trying to conquer the Earth and only Shirley (Jane Harders) can see them. The aliens communicate with her through a statue of the duke of Edinburgh. Excedrin headache #345.

PRODUCER AND DIRECTOR: Jim Sharman. SCREENPLAY: Sharman, Helmut Makaitsi. MUSIC: Ralph Tyrell.

SUPPORTING PLAYERS: Tim Eliott, June Collis, Marion Johns.

SILENCERS, THE
Columbia (1966). Color, 104 mins.

Suave spy Matt Helm (Dean Martin) fights off scientific madmen using such gadgetry as exploding buttons and assorted laser pistols.

PRODUCER: Irving Allen. DIRECTOR: Phil Karlson. SCREENPLAY: Phil Karlson, based on the novels *The Silencers* and *Death of a Citizen*, by Donald Hamilton. CINEMATOGRAPHY: Burnett Guffey. MUSIC: Elmer Bernstein.

SUPPORTING PLAYERS: Stella Stevens, Daliah Lavi, Victor Buono.

SILENT RUNNING
Universal (1972). Color, 90 mins.

Beautiful effects by Douglas (2001; CLOSE ENCOUNTERS; STAR TREK—THE MOTION PICTURE) Trumbull lift this picture out of the sf screen doldrums. By the early 21st century, pollution has destroyed all vegetation on Earth. The only greenery left in existence lies under the domes of the massive agrifreighter *Valley Forge*. The forests, tended by botanist Freeman Lowell (Bruce Dern) and three rather bored astronauts (Cliff Potts, Ron Rifkin, Jesse Vint), are kept in orbit in the hope that, one day, the atmosphere of the Earth will allow replanting.

Sneered at by his peers for his sense of dedication, Lowell takes excellent care of his green charges, aided by the drones Huey, Dewey, and Louie (Mark Persons, Cheryl Sparks, Steven Brown, and Larry Whisenhunt). When the government sends orders to terminate the garden experiment and destroy the forests, Lowell rebels, murdering his progovernment pals and blasting the ship out of orbit and into deep space. Placing the drones in charge of the forest, he detaches the domes from the ship proper and sends them sailing off into space. He then blows himself and

Silent Running

the *Valley Forge* into smithereens, in order to conceal his actions.

DIRECTOR: Douglas Trumbull. SCREENPLAY: Deric Washburn, Michael Cimino, Steven Bochco. DESIGNS: Wayne Smith, Richard Alexander, John Baumbach, Leland McLemore, Bob Shepherd, Gary Richards, Bill Shourt. DRONE UNITS: James Down, Paul Kraus, Trumbull. SPECIAL CAMERA EFFECTS: Trumbull, John Dykstra, Richard Yuricich. MUSIC: Peter Shickele. SONGS: Shickele and Diane Lampert, performed by Joan Baez.

SKY BANDITS
Monogram (1940). B/w, six reels.

Renfrew (James Newill) of the Royal Canadian Mounties fights scientist-meanies, who fight back dirty with death rays.

PRODUCER: Phil Goldstone. DIRECTOR: Ralph Staub. SCREENPLAY: Edward Halperin, based on the novel *Renfrew Rides the Sky,* by Laurie York Erskine.

SKY BIKE, THE
Eyeline Films (G.B., 1967). Color, 62 mins.

An amazingly prophetic film, predicting the flight of the pedal-powered *Gossamer Condor* by a decade. A crew of inventors attempt to fly a mile using human power only. They succeed.

PRODUCER: Harold Orton. DIRECTOR AND SCREENWRITER: Charles Frend. CINEMATOGRAPHY: John Coquillon. MUSIC: Harry Robinson.

CAST: Spencer Shires, Liam Redmond, Della Rands, John Howard.

SKY PARADE, THE
Paramount (1936). B/w, 70 mins.

The world witnesses the unveiling of the first robot airplane, a conventional aircraft run by a fully-automatic control panel.

PRODUCER: Harold Hurley. DIRECTOR: Otho Lovering. SCREENPLAY: Byron Morgan, Brian Marlow, and Arthur J. Backhard from the radio show *The Air Adventures of Jimmie Allen* and the comic strip of the same name. CINEMATOGRAPHY: William Mellor and Al Gilks.

Ornithology 101
"And it has a wing spread of over 500 feet!!"
    Japanese professor in *Rodan*

CAST: Jimmie Allen, William Gargan, Kent Taylor, Grant Withers.

SKY PIRATES
Monogram (1939). B/w, 60 mins.

Scientific geniuses develop a way to drop bombs from airplanes at 30,000 feet using only radio beams for guidance. Look, ma, no hands.

PRODUCER: Paul Malvern. DIRECTOR: George Waggner. SCREENPLAY: Paul Schofield and Joseph West, based on the comic strip "Tailspin Tommy," by Hal Forrest.

CAST: Jason Robards, Milburn Stone, Marjorie Reynolds.

SKY SHIP
Nordisk (Denmark, 1917); Great Northern (U.S., 1920). B/w silent feature.

Could this be the great-great-grandfather of every other sf film made in the 1950s? Astronauts land on Mars and discover a Utopian society composed entirely of women. A female emissary is brought back to Earth, where she is manhandled by the film's villain. He is struck by lightning and killed, proving, if nothing else, that nature isn't sexist.

DIRECTOR: Holger-Madsen. SCREENPLAY: Ole Olsen, Sophus Michaelis. CINEMATOGRAPHY: Louis Larsen.

CAST: Zanny Petersen, Gunnar Tolnaes.

SKY SKIDDER, THE
Universal (1929). B/w silent film, 4,364 ft.

A new airplane proves economical indeed, getting 1,000 miles to the pint with its newly developed fuel.

DIRECTOR: Bruce Mitchell. STORY: Val Cleveland. CINEMATOGRAPHY: William Adams.

CAST: Helen Foster, Al Wilson, Pee Wee Holmes.

SKY SPLITTER, THE
Hodkinson (1923). B/w silent short, one reel.

A scientist builds a great winged rocket. Attempting to break through the speed of light, he enters a time warp and sees his own childhood, reliving his entire life in an accelerated manner.

PRODUCER: John R. Bray. DIRECTORS: Ashely Miller, J. Norling. SCREENPLAY: J. Norling.

SLAUGHTERHOUSE-FIVE
Universal (1971). Color/scope, 105 mins.

An overlooked gem of a movie. When Billy Pilgrim (Michael Sachs) comes unstuck in time, he becomes enmeshed in an existence in which past, present, and future events occur in random order. First a foot soldier trapped during

Slaughterhouse-Five

the bombing of Dresden in World War II, he suddenly finds himself years in the future, being assassinated while giving a speech on intergalactic brotherhood. Ultimately his problems are resolved, after a fashion, when he winds up under the protective wing of the invisible Tralfamadorians (of the planet

Tralfamadore). He is placed in a geodesic dome with starlet Montana Wildhack (Valerie Perrine) and asked simply to live out his days in peace. And so it goes.

PRODUCER: Paul Monash. DIRECTOR: George Roy Hill. SCREENPLAY: Hill and Stephen Geller, based on the novel by KURT VONNEGUT, JR. ART DIRECTOR: Alexander Golitzen, George Webb. MUSIC: Johann Sebastian Bach.

SUPPORTING PLAYERS: Eugene Roche, John Dehner, Ron Liebman.

SLEEPER
UA (1973). Color, 90 mins.

Miles Monroe (Woody Allen), health-food store owner and zhlub about town, goes into a New York hospital for an ulcer operation and wakes up 200 years later; during the operation, it seems, he went into coma and was cryogenically frozen for safekeeping. Captured by a government ruled by a dictator, Miles escapes and joins the revolutionaries led by Erno (John Beck) and recently converted anti-government agent Luna (Diane Keaton). They discover that the Leader has been blown to bits and that only his nose survives. The Establishment is going to recreate the Leader by cloning his nose. Miles's mission, should he accept it: snatch the nose.

PRODUCER: Jack Grossberg. DIRECTOR: Woody Allen. SCREENPLAY: Allen, Marshall Brickman. SPECIAL EFFECTS: A. D. Flowers. PRODUCTION DESIGN: Dale Hennessy.

SUPPORTING PLAYERS: Mary Gregory, Don Keefer, Chris Forbes.

SLIME PEOPLE, THE
Hansen (1963). B/w, 60 mins.

Not about the fast-food business, this film traces the progress of an invasion from beneath the Earth. Los Angeles residents notice that the fog/smog is worse than usual one morning . . . and with good reason. Slime people from the sewer system have erected a fog dome over the already stuffy city, cutting it off from civilization. The temperature begins to drop and the slime people arise. Then they go home.

PRODUCER: Joseph F. Robertson. DIRECTOR: Robert Hutton. SCREENPLAY:

Vance Skarstedt. CINEMATOGRAPHY: William Troiano. SPECIAL EFFECTS: Charles Duncan. MUSIC: Lou Foman.

CAST: Robert Hutton, Les Tremayne, Robert Burton, Judee Morton, Susan Hart, John Close.

SOLARIS
Mosfilm (U.S.S.R., 1972); Sovcolor/scope, 165 mins. Sci-Fi Picture/Magna (1976); Sovcolor/scope, 132 mins.

In this Soviet film, based on the novel by STANISLAW LEM, Chris Kelvin (Donatas Banionis) journeys to the planet Solaris to investigate the fate of a landing party. Out of 85 original members, only three are alive. Arriving at the space station orbiting the planet, he finds that the station leader, Gibaryan, has committed suicide. Biologist Sartorius (Anatoli Solintsin) and cybernetics expert Snauth (Yuri Yarvet) are uncommunicative. Suddenly he confronts the spectre of his dead wife Hari (Natalia Bondarchuk). She is not a ghost, but a living, breathing entity created by the empathetic powers of the planet below. Chris slowly begins falling in love with his late wife all over again. The planet, probing Chris's emotional history, comes up with a few more manifestations . . . not all of them beneficial.

DIRECTOR: Andrei Tarkovsky. SCREENPLAY: Tarkovsky and Friedrich Gorenstein, from the novel by Stanislaw Lem. CINEMATOGRAPHY: Vadim Ysov. MUSIC: Edward Artemyev.

SOME GIRLS DO
Ashdown (G.B., 1969); color, 93 mins. UA (U.S., 1971); color, 91 mins.

Bulldog Drummond (Richard Johnson) must stop a madman who is out to conquer the world using an army of girl robots (led by Vanessa Howard) and an infrasonic ray.

PRODUCER: Betty Box. DIRECTOR: Ralph Thomas. SCREENPLAY: David Osborn and Liz Charles-Williams, based on the character created by H. C. McNeil. CINEMATOGRAPHY: Ernest Steward. SPECIAL EFFECTS: Kit West. MUSIC: Charles Blackwell.

SUPPORTING PLAYERS: Daliah Lavi, Ronnie Stevens, Robert Morley.

SOMETHING WEIRD
Mayflower (1968). B/w, 83 mins.

Talk about "truth in advertising." A man has a run-in with high-voltage wires and emerges with a face that looks like a bowl of strained beets. His grunt-mug frightens off his friends and thus gives him plenty of time to think. While cerebrating, he realizes that the accident has given him powerful telepathic prowess. In time he becomes a top, albeit ugly, mind reader. A local witch, feeling compassion for the guy, restores his handsome face in return for a pledge of undying love. Weird enough for you?

PRODUCER AND SCREENWRITER: James F. Hurley. DIRECTOR: H. Gordon Lewis. CINEMATOGRAPHY: Andy Romanoff.

CAST: Tony McCabe, Elizabeth Lee, William Brooker.

SON OF DR. JEKYLL
Columbia (1951). B/w, 78 mins.

Not exactly a chip off the old block. Jekyll's son (Louis Hayward) insists that dad was a serious scientist and had nothing at all to Hyde—er, hide. Just about that time, junior is struck by a series of nightmares wherein he becomes Hyde. Before too long, it's a case of Hyde and go shriek.

STORY: Mortimer Braus, Jack Pollexfen. DIRECTOR: Seymour Friedman. SCREENPLAY: Edward Hubsch. MAKE-UP: Clay Campbell. CINEMATOGRAPHY: Henry Freulich. MUSIC: Paul Sawtell.

SUPPORTING PLAYERS: Alexander Knox, Jody Lawrence, Gavin Muir, Doris Lloyd, Ottola Nesmith.

SON OF FLUBBER
Walt Disney/Buena Vista (1963). B/w, 103 mins.

In this sequel to THE ABSENT-MINDED PROFESSOR, Prof. Ned Brainard (Fred MacMurray) continues to flubbergast the world, this time around with flubber gas, a superbuoyant substance that enables the home team to win the big football game. Yet another invention is "dry rain," artificial rainstorms created by a crazy ray. The pseudosogginess causes everything it touches to grow to gigantic proportions.

PRODUCER: Walt Disney. DIRECTOR: Robert Stevenson. SCREENPLAY: Bill Walsh and Don Da Gradi, based on a story by Samuel W. Taylor and books by Danny Dunn. CINEMATOGRAPHY: Edward Colman. SPECIAL EFFECTS: Peter Ellenshaw, Eustace Lycett, Robert Mattey, Jack Boyd, Jim Fetherolf. MUSIC: George Bruns.

SUPPORTING PLAYERS: Nancy Olson, Keenan Wynn, Tommy Kirk, Leon Ames, Ed Wynn, Charlie Ruggles, Paul Lynde, Stu Erwin.

SON OF FRANKENSTEIN
Universal (1939). B/w, 95 mins.

This unassuming sequel to BRIDE OF FRANKENSTEIN is highlighted by exceptional art direction and design by Jack Otterson and Richard Riedel. Wolf von Frankenstein (Basil Rathbone) brings his wife Elso (Josephine Hutchinson) and son Peter (Donnie Dunagan) back to the old castle, much to the surrounding townspeople's dismay. Wolf is really an alright guy and tries to convince both the villagers and Inspector Krough (Lionel Atwill) of that fact. Wolf insists that the monster stories were mere exaggerations of very legitimate experiments. Krough has a different opinion, as a child having had his arm ripped out by the roots by the creature. The metal-armed policeman warns Wolf to pursue a low profile.

Examining the old lab a few days later, Wolf is greeted by broken-necked hunchback Ygor (the first hanging didn't take), who has recovered the body of the monster (Boris Karloff). Wolf brings it back to life, much to his eventual chagrin. Ygor (Bela Lugosi) takes control and sends the monster on a murder spree to avenge his hanging. Wolf kills Ygor. The monster snatches Peter. Krough and Wolf confront the monster in the old tower. The monster removes Krough's metal arm in an instant replay of their old childhood pastime. Wolf, playing Tarzan, grabs a rope and gets into the swing of things, knocking the creature (Karloff) into the tower's resident sulfur pit.

PRODUCER AND DIRECTOR: Rowland Lee. SCREENPLAY: Willis Cooper. MAKEUP: Jack Pierce. CINEMATOGRAPHY: George Robinson. MUSIC: Frank Skinner.

SUPPORTING PLAYERS: Michael Mark, Perry Ivins, Edgar Norton.

Universal

Son of Frankenstein

SON OF GODZILLA
Toho/AIP (Japan/U.S., 1967). Color, 86 mins.

With not a trace of "mama" around, an egg hatches a Godzilla junior, a little lizard played strictly for laughs. After defending his offspring against myriad monsters, Godzilla, Sr., and sonny boy are frozen into a state of suspended animation by a well-aimed blizzard.

PRODUCER: Tomoyuki Tanaka. DIRECTOR: Jun Fukuda. SCREENPLAY: Shinichi Sekizawa, Kazue Shiba. CINEMATOGRAPHY: Kazuo Yamada. SPECIAL EFFECTS: Sadamas Arikawa, Eiji Tsuburaya. MUSIC: Masuru Sato.

CAST: Tadao Takashima, Akira Kubo, Bibari Maeda, Kenji Sahara.

SON OF KONG
RKO (1934). B/w, 70 mins.

An amiable if somewhat haphazard sequel to KING KONG, Son of features an albino giant ape that's not quite a chip off the old block, being much more mellow than the old man. Carl Denham (Robert Armstrong), hounded by investors and bill collectors (well, someone had to clean up after Kong!), is taken by Capt. Englehorn (Frank Reicher) back to Skull Island in search of a lost treasure. Also onboard is Helen Mack, this installment's resident ingenue. Landing on the island, they run across Baby Kong and trade off lifesaving techniques in a series of harrowing incidents. All is going along swell, the treasure is in hand, a group of mutinous sailors seems firmly in tow, when the island's long-dormant volcano decides to change its status. Spewing lava and rock high into the air, the volcano effectively sinks the island. Newfound tiny human friends in hand, Kong, Jr., holds them aloft as the sea swirls across the landmass. Denham and the young woman are picked up by a rescue vessel. Kongie is drowned in the rescue attempt.

EXECUTIVE PRODUCER: Merian C. Cooper. DIRECTOR: Ernest B. Schoedsack. SCREENPLAY: Ruth Rose. CINEMATOGRAPHY: Edward Linden, Vernon Walker, J. O. Taylor. SPECIAL EFFECTS: Willis O'Brien. MODEL WORK: Marcel Delgado. MUSIC: Max Steiner.

SUPPORTING PLAYERS: Noble Johnson, Victor Wong, John Marston.

S.O.S. COAST GUARD
Republic (1937). B/w serial, 12 chapters (25 reels).

Coast Guard ace Terry Kent (Ralph Byrd) is out to stop crazy Dr. Boroff (Bela Lugosi) from delivering a supply of disintegrating gas to Morovania for an all-out attack on the U.S.

DIRECTORS: William Witney, Alan James. SCREENPLAY: Barry Shipman, Franklyn Adreon. CINEMATOGRAPHY: William Nobles. MUSIC: Raoul Kraushaar.

SUPPORTING PLAYERS: Maxine Doyle as Jean Norman, Herbert Ralinson as Commander Boyle, Richard Alexander as Thorg, Les Ford as Snapper McGee, Carleton Young as Dodds.

S.O.S. INVASION
Spain (1969). Color/scope, 87 mins.

An alien girl turns cadavers into robots. She operates out of a castle dungeon, proving that even in outer space there is respect for cinematic tradition.

DIRECTOR: Silvio F. Balbuena. SCREENPLAY: J. L. Navarro Basso. CINEMATOGRAPHY: Alfonso Nieva. MUSIC: Moreno Buendia.

CAST: Jack Taylor, Mara Cruz, Diana Sorel.

SOYLENT GREEN
MGM (1973). Color, 97 mins.

The year is 2022. The place: New York. The condition: horrible and getting worse. Overcrowded conditions abound. Meat and vegetables are no more. The citizens are fed crackers tossed en masse from passing trucks,

MGM

Soylent Green

© Paramount

The Space Children

including crackers called Soylent Green. A top-secret formula is used to prepare this foodstuff, which keeps the population healthy.

When Soylent Corporation executive Siminson is killed, detective cop Thorn (Charlton Heston) is called in to investigate. Siminson (Joseph Cotten) was not killed for any ordinary reason, it would seem. Thorn and his book (researcher) Sol Roth (Edward G. Robinson) begin to investigate every aspect of the case. Sol discovers something that drives him into a euthanasia center. Eventually, Thorn makes the same discovery. Soylent Green is made from human corpses. Big deal.

PRODUCERS: Walter Seltzer, Russell Thatcher. DIRECTOR: Richard Fleischer. SCREENPLAY: Stanley R. Greenberg, from the novel *Make Room! Make Room!*, by HARRY HARRISON. MUSIC: Fred Myrow.

SUPPORTING PLAYERS: Leigh Taylor-Young, Chuck Connors, Brock Peters, Whit Bissell.

SPACE CHILDREN, THE
Paramount (1958). B/w, 69 mins.

A gigantic brain from space lands on Earth and telepathically contacts the children of the world's leading rocket experts and space scientists. In league with the brainy alien, the children preach a gospel of nonviolence and brotherhood. When this message is ignored, the brain gives the kids extra psi clout, enabling them to stop the launching of a missile with a hydrogen-bomb warhead.

PRODUCER: William Alland. DIRECTOR: Jack Arnold. SCREENPLAY: Bernard C. Schoenfeld, from a story by Tom Filer. MUSIC: Nathan Van Cleave. MAKEUP: Wally Westmore. SPECIAL EFFECTS: John P. Fulton.

CAST: Jackie Coogan as Hank Johnson, John Crawford as Ken Brewster, Adam Williams, Peggy Webber, Michael Ray, Richard Shannon, John Washbook.

SPACE CRUISER YAMATO
Enterprise (Japan, 1977). Color, 107 mins. Animated.

A full-length animated feature from Japan, this sf story takes place in the year 2199. The Earth is at war with the evil planet Gorgon and has only one year to neutralize the effect of the Gorgonians' radioactive weaponry. A ring of radioactive fallout has surrounded the Earth and is slowly moving closer and closer to the populace below. An antidote is needed.

World War II battleship *Yamato*, sunk by the Allies centuries ago, is refloated and outfitted with special spacefaring equipment. It takes off into deep space in search of the much-needed antidote for fallout.

PRODUCER, DIRECTOR, AND SCREENWRITER: Yoshinabu Nishizaki. CHARACTER DESIGNS: Leiji Matsumoto. CHIEF ANIMATOR: Noboru Ishigura. MUSIC: Hiroshi Miyagawa.

SPACE FLIGHT
Also known as SPACEFLIGHT IC-1. Lippert (G.B., 1965); b/w, 65 mins. 20th Cent.-Fox (U.S., 1965); b/w, 63 mins.

In the year 2015, a group of astronauts searches out a possible colony site aboard a computer-controlled vessel. The computer is given its orders by RULE, an autocratic government with all of Earth in its power. The space-colonists-to-be are less than enthusiastic about the voyage when the machine begins working murder into its program. There's never a screwdriver around when you need one in space, either.

PRODUCERS: Robert L. Lippert and Jack Parsons. DIRECTOR: Bernard Knowles. SCREENPLAY: Harry Spalding. CINEMATOGRAPHY: Geoffrey Faithful. MUSIC: Elisabeth Lutyens.

CAST: Bill Williams, Norma West, John Ciarney, Linda Marlowe.

SPACE MASTER X-7
20th Cent.-Fox (1957). B/w, 71 mins.

A space probe returns to Earth covered with a strange fungus. The fungus is accidentally tinged with human blood and is transformed into an ever-growing pile of space rust. The rust, in its quest to keep on spreading, begins devouring humans for their blood.

PRODUCER: Bernard Glasser. DIRECTOR: Edward Bernds. SCREENPLAY: George Worthing Yates, Daniel Mainwaring. MUSIC: Josef Zimanich.

CAST: Bill Williams, Paul Frees, Robert Ellis, Moe Howard.

SPACE MONSTER
AIF (1965). Color, 80 mins.

It's rubber-mask time again. Space explorers splash-land on a water-logged planet and are attacked by a group of sea creatures. Finally they discover an underground spaceship and a tiny alien man with a large alien head.

PRODUCER: Burt Topper. DIRECTOR AND SCREENWRITER: Leonard Katzman. ALIEN MAKEUP: Don Post Studios. MUSIC: Marlin Skiles.

CAST: Russ Bender, Baynes Barron.

SPACEWAYS
Hammer/Lippert (G.B., 1953). B/w, 76 mins.

A space-program technician is accused of murdering the missus and sending her into an impromptu orbit around the Earth. In order to prove his innocence, the accused (Howard Duff) must blast off in another rocket for an Earth-lit rendezvous.

PRODUCER: Michael Carreras. DIRECTOR: Terence Fisher. SCREENPLAY: Paul Tabori, Richard Landau. CINEMATOGRAPHY: Reginald Wyer. MUSIC: Ivor Slaney.

SUPPORTING PLAYERS: Eva Bartok, Alan Wheatley, Michael Medwin.

SPHERE, THE
Europe Cine (Italy, 1971). Color.

A spherical time machine is invented.

DIRECTOR: Gianni Poggi.

CAST: Guido Coderin, Beatrice Pellegrino.

SPIDER RETURNS, THE
Columbia (1941). B/w serial, 15 chapters (31 reels).

Playboy Richard Wentworth (Warren Hull), who in his spare time dons a black-masked outfit and calls himself the Spider, goes underground as gangster Blinky McQuade in order to gain access to the web of intrigue being woven by the insidious Gargoyle, a master spy out to bring the U.S. to its knees. The Gargoyle has developed a number of nifty inventions that could bring the U.S. defense system to a state of utter chaos. Among his top 10 pieces of hardware: an X-ray belt, a ray that can take over the workings of machines from miles away, and a TV spying device called the X-ray eye. Nina Van Sloan and Jackson (Mary Ainslee and Dave O'Brien) are confused about all the cliff-hanging until the Spider finally unmasks the Gargoyle and reveals him to be Mr. McLeod (Corbet Harris), one of the country's most patriotic businessmen. Just goes to show ya.

PRODUCER: Larry Darmous. DIRECTOR: James W. Horne. SCREENPLAY: Jesse A. Duffy, George H. Plympton. CINEMATOGRAPHY: James S. Brown, Jr. MUSIC: Lee Zahler.

SUPPORTING PLAYERS: Joe Girard as Commissioner Kirk, Ken Duncan as Ram Singh, Harry Harvey as Stephen.

SPIDER'S WEB, THE
Columbia (1938). B/w serial, 15 chapters (31 reels).

Playboy criminologist Richard Wentworth (Warren Hull) dons his crime-fighting toga as the Spider to fend off the attempts of master criminal the

Octopus to blow up half the country. Aided by loyal servant Ram Singh (Ken Duncan), Wentworth disguises himself as thug Blinky McQuade to infiltrate the multitentacled organization operated by the secretive squid. Meanwhile, Wentworth's fiancée, Nina Van Sloan (Iris Meredith), waits for a marriage proposal. And wait she must while Blinky/the Spider/Richard battles his way through TV spy systems, death rays, sonic torture chambers, and electrified rooms before getting a chance to unmask the Octopus as leading U.S. banker Chase (Charles Wilson), a fellow who sought control of the U.S. by seizing the country's transportation and communications systems.

EXECUTIVE PRODUCER: Irving Briskin. DIRECTORS: Ray Taylor, James W. Horne. SCREENPLAY: Robert E. Kent, Basil Dickey, George H. Plympton, Mart Ramson. CINEMATOGRAPHY: Allen Sigler. MUSIC: Morris Stoloff.

SUPPORTING PLAYERS: Forbes Murray as Commissioner Kirk, Marc Lawrence as Steve, Donald Douglas as Jenkins.

SPIRIT OF 1976
RKO (1935). B/w short, 20 mins.

In the distant year 1976, an all-play, no-work existence has turned a possible Utopian society into a slothful, boring way of life.

PRODUCER: Lee Marcus. DIRECTOR: Leigh Jason. SCREENPLAY: Ernest Pagano, Jason. CINEMATOGRAPHY: Roy Hunt. MUSIC: Roy Webb.

CAST: Betty Grable, Walter King.

SPY SMASHER
Republic (1942). B/w serial, 12 chapters (25 reels).
Known in feature form as SPY SMASHER RETURNS (1966).

Spy Smasher (Kane Richmond), all-American guy, is captured in Europe while attempting to find out information concerning a Nazi spy called the Mask (Hans Schumm), a fellow based in the U.S. who is trying to destroy the country's defense system from within. Freed by French ally Durand (Frank Corsaro), Spy Smasher returns to this country, where, with the help of his twin brother, Jack, his fiancée, Eve

Corby (Marguerite Chapman), and Durand, he tracks down the Mask despite the presence of ray guns and TV spying devices. Jack is killed and Spy Smasher vows revenge, eventually blowing the Mask and his cronies into oblivion—a spot that serial scriptwriters often frequented.

Finney Fury
Our original ending had the fish attacking a children's day camp. But Roger Corman wanted a *Jaws* ending. However, he didn't want to lose the summer camp bit because there was a possibility of having people eaten there, too. So, in the finished film we have two endings.

Joe Dante, director of *Piranha*

DIRECTOR: William Witney. SCREENPLAY: Ronald Davidson, Norman S. Hall, William Lively, Joseph O'Donnell, Joseph Poland. CINEMATOGRAPHY: Reggie Lanning. SPECIAL EFFECTS: Howard Lydecker. MUSIC: Mort Glickman, Arnold Schwarzwald, Paul Sawtell, and L. van Beethoven.

SUPPORTING PLAYERS: Sam Flint, Tristram Coffin, Tom London.

SSSSSSS
Universal (1973). Color, 99 mins.

An amazingly well-written script and some nice acting drag this mad-scientist film up from the depths. In order to keep a lid on pollution, a scientist (Strother Martin) plans on turning the human population into king cobras. So far, however, his experiments haven't been total successes, with the half-changed victims being sold as freaks to local carnivals. Daughter Heather Menzies's boyfriend (Dirk Benedict), however, looks like a good bet. In a triumph of truly awful special effects, the boy becomes a cobra and is killed by a mongoose. Back to the drawing board.

PRODUCER AND STORY ORIGINATOR: Dan Striepke. DIRECTOR: Bernard Kowalski. SCREENPLAY: Hal Dresner. MAKEUP: John Chambers, Nick Marcellino. CINEMATOGRAPHY: Gerald P. Finnerman. MUSIC: Pat Williams.

© Universal Pictures

SSSSSSS

SUPPORTING PLAYERS: Tim O'Connor, Richard Shull, Reb Brown.

STARCRASH
Also known as THE ADVENTURES OF STELLA STAR.
New World (1979). Color, 92 mins.

Evil Count Zarth Arn (Joe Spinell) battles the good Emperor of the Universe (Christopher Plummer) in this futuristic "western." The emperor sends his best agent, Stella Star (Caroline Munro), to seek out and destroy the count's secret lair. She is joined on her mission by the alien Akton (Marjoe Gortner), loyal robot Elle (Judd Hamilton), and the emperor's long-lost son, Simon L. (David Hasselhoff). En route, they are menaced by warriors, giant robots, and assorted monsters. Stella and company reach the hidden fortress but Zarth Arn escapes and sends a warhead directly toward the capital of the empire. Stella must then maneuver a floating city into the path of the bomb in order to save her emperor. Well-intentioned adventure made on a budget usually reserved for lunch.

PRODUCERS: Nat and Patrick Wachsberger. SCREENWRITER AND DIRECTOR: Luigi Cozzi. DESIGNER: Niso Remponi. MINIATURES: Paol Zeccara. MUSIC: John Barry.

SUPPORTING PLAYERS: Nadia Cassini, Robert Tessler.

STAR PILOT
Monarch (1977). Eastmancolor, 81 mins.

Originally released in 1966 in Italy, this space opera sends a group of Earth scientists to the Hydra constellation. Their job: to translate a newfound alien language. Comments one scientist: "Sounds like Bulgarian."

DIRECTOR: Pietro Francisci.

CAST: Leonora Ruff, Kirk Morris, Gordon Mitchell.

STARSHIP INVASIONS
Also known as ALIEN INVASION.
WB (1977). Color.

Captain Rameses (Christopher Lee) is a nasty-alien type who is obviously miffed about having to give orders while clad in feety pajamas. His band of alien meanies, called the Legion of the Winged Serpent, covillained by lovely Sagnac (Sherri Rose), are out to take over the Earth for their dying racc. Out to save Earth is the League of Races, part of the top-secret Alien Galactic Center, which has an outpost in the middle of the Bermuda Triangle. League of Races heroes Captain Anaxi (Daniel Pilon), Phi (Tiiu Leek), and Gazeth (*Penthouse* pet Victoria Johnson in a pajama outfit that has no feet or much of anything else) try to stop Rameses but fail. The rotten fellow telepathically orders Earthlings to commit suicide en masse. The U.S. Army shows up about then and begins shooting down the wrong side's saucers (never trust an all-volunteer defense team). Professor Duncan (Robert Vaughn), a UFO expert with a heart of gold and a pipe full of tobacco, gets pal Malcolm (Henry Ramer) to repair the LOR saucer. Soon there's a mini-alien encounter going on above the fields of Canada. No one seems to notice, however.

PRODUCERS: Ed Hunt, Ken Gord. DIRECTOR AND SCREENWRITER: Ed Hunt.

New World

Starcrash

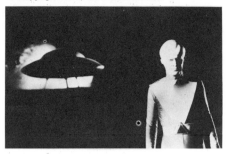

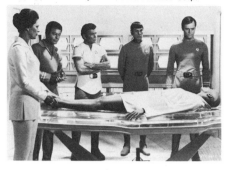

Starship Invasions

Star Trek—The Motion Picture

MAKEUP: Maureen Sweeney. MUSIC: Gil Melle. SPECIAL EFFECTS: Warren Keillor.

SUPPORTING PLAYERS: Doreen Lipson, Kate Par, Ted Turner.

STAR TREK—THE MOTION PICTURE
Paramount (1979). Metrocolor and Panavision, 142 mins.

The long-awaited sequel to the hit TV series, *Star Trek—The Motion Picture* was longer in coming than the TV show was in running on network TV. Originally planned in 1975–76, the film was alternately shelved and revived by Paramount until 1978. Dozens of scripts and treatments were tossed around until a final draft was chosen in the middle of that year. Once in production, the film nearly collapsed under its own weight after its chief of special effects, Robert Able, was asked to leave. Douglas (2001; CLOSE ENCOUNTERS OF THE THIRD KIND) Trumbull was brought in by the studio and his crew performed 24 hours a day for months in order to complete the film's complex special effects in time for its release.

The movie takes place in the 23rd century. Several Klingon ships led by a Klingon captain (Mark Lenard), patrolling in their own territory, are confronted by an unknown and awesome force. One by one, the Klingon spaceships are destroyed.

The annihilation is monitored by a stunned group of Federation employees at Starfleet monitoring station Epsilon 9. Even more startling to Federation members everywhere is the information that the menacing *thing* is moving toward Earth on a collision course of dire magnitude. The starship U.S.S. *Enterprise,* commanded by Will Decker (Stephen Collins), is in drydock high above the city of San Francisco at the time of the peril. The ship, being refitted with the finest weapons system in the fleet, is ordered back into immediate service to meet the invader head-on. Admiral James T. Kirk (William Shatner) is taken from behind his desk and placed in command of the ship once again . . . much to Decker's dismay.

Also gathered for the mission are Engineering Officer Montgomery "Scotty" Scott (James Doohan), Helmsman Sulu (George Takei), Communications Officer Uhuru (Nichelle Nichols), Security Officer Chekov (Walter Koenig), Dr. Christine Chapel (Majel Barrett), Transporter Chief Janice Rand (Grace Lee Whitney), and Dr. Leonard "Bones" McCoy (DeForest Kelley).

Only Vulcan Mr. Spock (Leonard Nimoy) is missing when the ship heads into deep space. Decker and his sometime paramour, Deltan citizen Ilia (Persis Khambatta), the ship's navigator, watch helplessly as Kirk's lack of knowledge of the refurbished ship nearly sends them plunging into a time warp. Overstepping his bounds, Decker saves the day and, after much bickering, the former and present commander of the *Enterprise* come to an understanding on how the vessel is to be run.

En route, the *Enterprise* is visited by a strange shuttle-craft that deposits a colder-than-usual Spock onboard. Spock is out to find the invader, but for his own mysterious reasons. This life force, which calls itself V'ger, is capable of sheer intelligence—thought untinged by emotion. Not only that, but Spock surmises that the creature is only in its infancy. It is headed toward Earth to meet its maker, devouring everything in its path. But why Earth? Who is its maker? What does NASA have to do with all this?

The V'ger thing's life force invades the ship. Ilia is killed. Yet, Ilia lives. Seeking the answers to all the mysteries surrounding their mission, Kirk, Spock, and an exploratory crew journey *inside* the titanic V'ger to discover facts that will keep every Trekkie on the edge of his or her seat for the duration of the film.

PRODUCER: Gene Roddenberry. DIRECTOR: Robert Wise. SCREENPLAY: Harold Livingston, from an idea by Alan Dean Foster. CINEMATOGRAPHY: Richard Kline. SPECIAL EFFECTS: Douglas Trumbull and associates. MUSIC: Jerry Goldsmith.

SUPPORTING PLAYERS: David Gautreaux as Commander Branch, Terrence O'Conner as the Lieutenant, Marcy Lafferty as Chief Di Falco, Billy van Zandt as the Alien Boy.

STAR WARS
20th Cent.-Fox (1977). Panavision and Technicolor, 121 mins.

The movie that gave new meaning to the word "profits," *Star Wars* revitalized a sagging sf film industry and made millionaires out of half the Los Angeles phone directory. Lavish effects, nonstop action, and a plot that would cause no mental strain on the part of a collie all combined to make this film the biggest moneymaker in the history of sf cinema.

Captured by the evil Dark Lord of the Sith, Darth Vader (David Prowse, with the voice of James Earl Jones), Princess Leia (Carrie Fisher) is further manhandled by the power-mad governor of the Imperial Outland regions, Grand Moff Tarkin (Peter Cushing). The princess, leader of the valiant rebel forces, has the plans to Tarkin's ultimate weapon, the *Death Star,* a titanic spacecraft capable of eliminating entire planets. Thinking quickly, the princess slips both a message and the plans to robots C-3PO and R2-D2 (Anthony Daniels and Kenny Baker), telling them to bring in the cavalry.

Lucasfilm/20th Cent.-Fox

Star Wars

The cavalry, in this case, is retired Jedi knight Obi-Wan Kenobi (Sir Alec Guinness)—Ben to his friends. With the aid of farm boy Luke Skywalker (Mark Hamill), the droids find Ben and set off to rescue the princess. They are joined en route by cynical space mercenary Han Solo (Harrison Ford) and his Wookie copilot, Chewbacca (Peter Mayhew). During the flight, Ben teaches Luke the secrets of the Force, the power that made the Jedi knights the old Republic's greatest warriors.

The group infiltrates the *Death Star* and rescues Leia. Hounded by swarms of stormtroopers, they reach Solo's ship, the *Millennium Falcon,* safely. Seeking to slow down their pursuers, Ben remains behind, challenging his former Jedi student, Darth Vader, to a lasersword battle. Ben is old. Vader is not. Vader slashes out at the elderly warrior, cleaving Ben's robe in two. When the fight is over, Ben's robe is all that remains. Was he killed? Or did he join the Force?

Meanwhile, the very three-dimensional Luke and company blast off for the rebel headquarters on the nearby moon, Yavin. Governor Tarkin and his *Death Star* crew follow, launching a devastating attack. The minuscule rebel forces rise up. In the midst of the dogfight, Luke attempts to strike a death blow to the *Death Star.* Guided by the disembodied voice of Ben, Luke lets the Force take control of the ship. He scores a direct hit.

Meanwhile, in the dogfight in space, Darth Vader is knocking the rebels out of the sky with ease until Han Solo and Chewbacca show up in the battered

Falcon. They blast Vader's ship, jamming its control system. Vader zooms helplessly into deep space. The *Death Star* blows up. The rebels are victorious. A round of medals is distributed to our heroes.

PRODUCER: Gary Kurtz. DIRECTOR AND SCREENWRITER: George Lucas. MUSIC: John Williams. MINIATURES AND SPECIAL EFFECTS: John Dykstra. PRODUCTION AND MECHANICAL EFFECTS: John Stears. MAKEUP AND ALIEN DESIGNS: Stuart Freeborn. ADDITIONAL ALIEN DESIGNS: Ralph McQuarrie, Ron Cob, Rick Baker.

STEPFORD WIVES, THE
Columbia (1974). Color, 96 mins.

Fairly embarrassing excursion into slice-of-life sf. Joanna Eberhart (Katherine Ross) isn't too crazy about the idea of moving to Stepford, Connecticut, with hubby Walter (Peter Masterson). All the women in town are totally boring and subservient. Joanna and cynical pal Bobbie (Paula Prentiss) try to brighten up their community, to no avail. Eventually Bobbie becomes a smiling zombie, too. Joanna then discovers that the local Men's Association, led by Dale Coba (Patrick O'Neal), has murdered all the wives in town and replaced them with robot slaves.

DIRECTOR: Bryan Forbes. SCREENPLAY: William Goldman, based on the novel by IRA LEVIN. MUSIC: Michael Small.

SUPPORTING PLAYERS: Nanette Newman, Tina Louise, John Aprea.

STOLEN AIRSHIP, THE
Barrandov Film/Gottwaldov Studio (Czechoslovakia, 1969). Color, 105 mins.

Karel Zeman, the man responsible for the fanciful FABULOUS WORLD OF JULES VERNE, returns to his source material in this original tale concerning a group of children who commandeer an airship and eventually run head-on into Captain Nemo.

DIRECTOR: Karel Zeman. SCREENPLAY: Zeman, Radovan Kratky. ART DIRECTOR: Jaroslav Krska. CINEMATOGRAPHY: Joseph Novotny. MUSIC: Jan Novak.

CAST: Michael Pospisil, Hanus Bor, Jan Cizek, Jan Malat.

STRANGE CASE OF CAPTAIN RAMPER, THE
Defu (Germany, 1927); First National (U.S., 1928). B/w silent feature, 7,534 ft.

Explorer Ramper (Paul Wegener) becomes trapped in the Arctic. His body, in order to survive, reverts to a hairy, prehistoric form. All traces of sophistication lost, the creature/captain is brought back to civilization as a side-show freak. The ape-man falls in love with his trainer. A scientist, sensing the truth about the odd fellow, restores Ramper's brain to its true intellectual state. Ramper takes note of what civilization has to offer and then hightails it back to the Arctic.

DIRECTOR: Max Reichmann. SCREENPLAY: Kurt J. Braun, Paul Wegener. CINEMATOGRAPHY: Herbert Korner, Frederic Weymann.

SUPPORTING PLAYERS: Max Schreck, Mary Johnson, Kurt Gerron.

STREAMLINE EXPRESS
Mascot (1938). B/w, eight reels.

Adventures on the world's first super-speed monorail train.

PRODUCER: George Yohalem. DIRECTOR: Leonard Fields. SCREENPLAY: Fields, Dave Silverstein. CINEMATOGRAPHY: Ernest Miller.

CAST: Evelyn Venable, Victor Jory, Erin O'Brien-Moore, Sidney Blackmer.

SUPER GIANT
Shintoho (Japan).

A group of kiddie-oriented films released in Japan in 1956–59, these nine colorful adventures formed the basis of the American films ATOMIC RULERS OF THE WORLD, THE EVIL BRAIN FROM OUTER SPACE, and *Attack from Space.*

SUPERMAN
Paramount (1940–1943). Technicolor. Animated.

Superman's first "reel" appearance on the screen was in the form of a group of cartoons produced by the Max Fleischer studios and based on the adventures of the comic-strip hero created by Jerry Siegel and Joe Shuster. Bud Collyer, Superman's radio voice, provided the movie voices for Clark Kent and the Man of Steel.

Superman's animated adventures included the following:

The Mechanical Monsters
  (1941. Director: Seymour Kneitel)
Billion Dollar Limited
  (1942. Director: Dave Fleischer)
Destruction, Inc.
  (1942. Director: Isidore Sparber)
Electronic Earthquake
  (1942. Director: Dave Fleischer)
Showdown
  (1942. Director: Isidore Sparber)
Terror on the Midway
  (1942. Director: Dave Fleischer)
Arctic Giant
  (1942. Director: Dave Fleischer)
The Eleventh Hour
  (1942. Director: Dan Gordon)
The Japoteurs
  • (1942. Director: Seymour Kneitel)
The Magnetic Telescope
  (1942. Director: Dave Fleischer)
Volcano
  (1942. Director: Dave Fleischer)
Jungle Drums
  (1943. Director: Dan Gordon)
Secret Agents
  (1943. Director: Seymour Kneitel)
The Mummy Strikes
  (1943. Director: Isidore Sparber)
The Underground World
  (1943. Director: Seymour Kneitel)

SUPERMAN

Columbia (1948). B/w serial, 15
chapters (30 reels), 480 mins. total
running time.

The first "real" appearance of Krypton's favorite citizen starred Kirk Alyn
as Clark Kent/Superman. Detailing the
Man of Steel's origins on the doomed
planet Krypton and his arrival and
childhood on Earth, the serial showed
Clark Kent's early days at the *Daily
Planet* newspaper and his first dealings
with Lois Lane (Noel Neill), Jimmy
Olsen (Tommy Boyd), and Perry White
(Pierre Watkin). Superman's problems
begin when a nefarious criminal known
as the Spider Lady attempts to subju-
gate the world with a handy death ray.

SUPPORTING PLAYERS: Carol Forman
as the Spider Lady, Nelson Leight as
Jor-El, Luana Walters as Lara, Edward
Cassidy and Virginia Carroll as Eban
and Martha Kent, Alan Dinehart III
as young Clark Kent, Ralph Hodges as
the teenaged Clark, and George Meeker
as Driller.

PRODUCER: Sam Katzman. DIREC-

Columbia

Superman

TORS: Spencer Bennett, Thomas Carr.
SCREENPLAY: Arthur Hoerl, Lewis Clay,
and Royal Cole, based on characters
created by Jerry Siegel and Joe Shuster.
MUSIC: Mischa Bakaleinikoff.

SUPERMAN AND THE MOLE MEN
Lippert (1951). B/w, 67 mins.

George Reeves's first screen appearance as the Man of Steel found him defending a race of underground midgets
against a town full of bigots. The wee
folk, armed with weapons that look like
they were constructed from vacuum
cleaners (which was, indeed, the case),
come to the surface of the Earth after
oil-drilling activities wreck their happy
homes below. Superman steps into the
quarrel between the aboveworlders and
the undergrounders, and everyone goes
home happy.

SUPPORTING PLAYERS: Phyllis Coates
as Lois Lane, Jeff Corey as Luke Benson, Walter Reed as Bill Corrigan,
Stanley Andrews as the Sheriff, and
Bill Curtis, Jack Branbury, Jerry Marvin, and Tony Baris as the Mole Men.

Lippert

Superman and the Mole Men

This feature proved so successful that other George Reeves movies were pieced together from the SUPERMAN TV show for limited theatrical release. These little-known films included *Superman Flies Again* (1954); *Superman and the Jungle Devil* (1954); *Superman and Scotland Yard* (1954); *Superman in Exile* (1954); and *Superman's Peril* (1954). All were released by 20th Cent.-Fox. SUPERMAN AND THE MOLE MEN was later shown on TV as a two-part SUPERMAN episode, "The Unknown People."

SUPERMAN—THE MOVIE
WB (1978). Panavision and Technicolor, 143 mins.

Good-natured fun combined with good intentions makes this megabuck version of the classic comic-book legend a lighthearted winner.

On the planet Krypton, Jor-El (Marlon Brando) warns his fellow scientists that the end is near for their planet and urges them to consider plans for evacuation. The Elder and Vondah (Trevor Howard and Maria Schell) laugh at his notions and slap him down for his insubordination. Jor-El and wife Lara (Susannah York) send baby Kal-El to Earth in a rocket ship just as the planet blows up.

Landing on Earth, the alien boy is adopted by Ma and Pa Kent (Phyllis Thaxter and Glenn Ford) and dubbed Clark. Soon it becomes apparent that Clark (Jeff East) possesses superhuman skills. At Pa Kent's suggestion, Clark adopts a meek, mild manner and hides his physical prowess. After Jonathan Kent's death, Clark journeys to the Arctic, where he builds his Fortress of Solitude and, through instruments of Krypton science, communicates with his long-dead father, Jor-El, and learns his true identity.

He then journeys to the city of Metropolis, where, as Kent, he gets a job as a *Daily Planet* newspaper reporter. There he meets Lois Lane (Margot Kidder), Jimmy Olsen (Marc McClure), and Perry White (Jackie Cooper). Soon the flying superhero Superman makes an appearance in town. After several heroic actions, Superman sets out to stop evil Lex Luthor (Gene Hackman), Eve Teschacher (Valerie Perrine), and

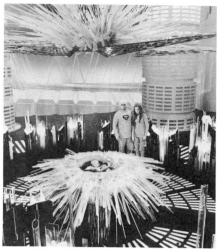

Warner Bros.

Superman—The Movie

Otis (Ned Beatty) from bombing California off the map so as to create a new West Coast—a coastline now owned by Lex Luthor.

Oscar-winning special effects and a wonderfully underplayed performance by Christoper Reeve as Clark Kent/Man of Steel help make this opulent live-action cartoon an all-year-round Christmas present.

PRODUCERS: Pierre Spengler, Alexander and Ilya Salkind. DIRECTOR: Richard Donner. SCREENPLAY: Mario Puzo, David Newman, Leslie Newman, and Robert Benton, from the characters created by Jerry Siegel and Joe Shuster. CINEMATOGRAPHY: Geoffrey Unsworth. PRODUCTION DESIGN: John Barry. SPECIAL EFFECTS: Colin Chivers, Roy Field, Les Bowie, Denys Coop, Derek Meddings. MUSIC: John Williams.

SUPPORTING PLAYERS: Terence Stamp as Zod, Jack O'Halloran as Non, Sarah Douglas as Ursa, Harry Andrews as a Krypton Elder.

SUPERSONIC MAN
Almena (Spain, 1979). Eastman color, 85 mins.

Supersonic Man (Michael Coby) is the alter ego of a meek private eye headquartered in Madrid. He comes from a distant galaxy to save the world and is gifted with the power of flight. Gifted with the power of larceny is Cameron Mitchell as a villain out to enslave the aforementioned planet. Pitted against such nastiness, Supersonic Man must fight off spaceships, a bazooka-tossing robot, hails of bullets, a runaway steamroller, and finally the villain himself. The masked, caped crusader saves the day after doodling away nearly 90 minutes of cinematic time.

DIRECTOR: Juan Piquer. SCREENPLAY: Sebastian Moi, Piquer. CINEMATOGRAPHY: Juan Marine. SPECIAL EFFECTS AND SETS: Emilio Ruiz, Francisco Prosper. OPTICAL EFFECTS: Jack Elkubi, Miguel Villa. MUSIC: Gino Peguri, Juan Luis Izaguirre, Carlos Attias.

SUPPORTING PLAYERS: Richard Yesteran, Diana Polakov, Jose Marie Cafferel, Frank Brana, Luis Barboo, Angel Ter.

SUPERSONIC SAUCER, THE
Gaumont (G.B., 1956). B/w, 50 mins.

A group of Earth children come to the aid of a baby flying saucer from Venus.

PRODUCER AND STORY ORIGINATOR: Frank Wells. DIRECTOR: S. G. Ferguson. SCREENPLAY: Dallas Bower. ANIMATION: Ken Hardy. CINEMATOGRAPHY: Frank North. MUSIC: Jack Beaver.

CAST: Marcia Monlescue, Fella Edmonds, Donald Gray, Tony Lyons.

SUPERSPEED
Columbia (1935). B/w, 56 mins.

An inventor perfects a superspeed transport device.

DIRECTOR: Lambert Hillyer. SCREENPLAY: Harold Shumate. CINEMATOGRAPHY: Ben Kline.

CAST: Norman Foster, Florence Rice, Mary Carlisle.

SWARM, THE
WB (1978). Panavision and Technicolor, 116 mins.

A swarm of killer bees invades North America from south of the border. A group of scientists (Michael Caine as Brad Crane, Henry Fonda as Dr. Krim, Richard Chamberlain as Dr. Hubbard) fight off boredom.

PRODUCER AND DIRECTOR: Irwin Allen. SCREENPLAY: Stirling Silliphant, from the novel by ARTHUR HERZOG. CINEMATOGRAPHY: Fred J. Koenekamp. SPECIAL EFFECTS: Lyle B. Abbott. MUSIC: Jerry Goldsmith.

. . . And Call Me in the Morning
"I'll build a new brain for you. I'll lift this curse from you forever!"
Onslow Stevens to Lon Chaney, Jr., in *House of Dracula*

SUPPORTING PLAYERS: Katharine Ross as Helena, Richard Widmark as General Slater, Olivia de Havilland as Maureen, Ben Johnson as Felix, Lee Grant as Anne MacGregor, Jose Ferrer as Dr. Andrews, Patty Duke Astin as Rita, Fred MacMurray as Clarence.

TALES OF HOFFMAN

Screen versions of the opera by Jacques Offenbach offer the main character, Hoffman, regaling friends in a tavern with stories of three lost loves, one of whom, Olympia, was a dancing robot-doll.

Union (Germany, 1914). B/w silent film.

DIRECTOR: Richard Oswald. SCREENPLAY: Fritz Friedmann, Richard Oswald. CINEMATOGRAPHY: Ernst Krohn.

CAST: Werner Krauss, Erich Kaiser-Tietz, Alice Hechy, Ferdinand Bonn, Lupu Pick.

Lippert (1951). Color, 138 mins.

PRODUCERS, DIRECTORS, AND SCREENWRITERS: Michael Powell, Emeric Pressburger. ART DIRECTOR: Arthur Lawson. CINEMATOGRAPHY: Christopher Challis. MUSICAL DIRECTOR: Thomas Beecham.

CAST: Moira Shearer (automaton), Robert Rounseville, Robert Helpmann, Pamela Brown, Frederick Ashton.

TARANTULA
Universal (1955). B/w, 80 mins.

Scientist Deemer (Leo G. Carroll) is working on a serum that will stimulate tissue growth through intensified glandular activity. It changes a batch of lab

Universal

Tarantula

animals into cage-bound giants (guinea pigs the size of collies, etc.), but when used on humans, it causes mutation and insanity. A former colleague (Eddie Parker) attacks Deemer in the lab and injects him with the serum. In the struggle that ensues, an already dosed tarantula escapes into the Arizona desert. Before long, the spider is 100 feet tall and terrorizing residents. Some really good creature-on-the-loose effects culminate in an air force fire-bombing of the creepy critter.

PRODUCER: William Alland. DIRECTOR: Jack Arnold. SCREENPLAY: Robert M. Fresco and Martin Berkley, based on an episode of TV's SCIENCE FICTION THEATER titled "No Food for Thought," by Robert Fresco. CINEMATOGRAPHY: George Robinson. MAKEUP: Bud Westmore. SPECIAL EFFECTS: Clifford Stine. MUSIC: Henry Mancini.

SUPPORTING PLAYERS: John Agar, Mara Corday, Nestor Paiva.

TARGET EARTH!
AA (1954). B/w, 76 mins.

Stranded in a deserted metropolis after an invasion from outer space, a group of human misfits are chased up and down the streets by a group of slow-moving, haphazardly constructed Venusian robots. The robots stalk their prey using large death rays located in their face masks to do their victims in once cornered.

PRODUCER: Herman Cohen. DIRECTOR: Sherman Rose. SCREENPLAY: William Raynor. MUSIC: Paul Dunlap. SPECIAL EFFECTS: Dave Koehler.

CAST: Kathleen Crowley as Nora,

Richard Denning as Frank, Richard Reeves, Whit Bissell, House Peters, Virginia Grey.

TEENAGE CAVEMEN
AIP (1958). B/w, 65 mins.

Better than you'd think. Robert Vaughn plays the intellectual cave-boy who, against his father's orders, journeys into the forbidden zone, a desolate land across the river ruled by the "Monster-That-Kills-with-a-Touch." The monster turns out to be an old man in a fright suit. The old fellow, seeing the arrow-laden youth, dies of fright himself. The boy rummages through the old man's possessions and finds a book dealing with the 20th century before nuclear war reduced humankind to a barbaric state of existence.

PRODUCER AND DIRECTOR: Roger Corman. SCREENPLAY: R. Wright Campbell. CINEMATOGRAPHY: Floyd Crosby. MUSIC: Albert Glasser.

SUPPORTING PLAYERS: Jonathan Haze, Darrah Marshall, Leslie Braddley, Robert Shayne.

TEENAGE MONSTER
Also known as THE METEOR MONSTER.
Howco International (1957). B/w, 65 mins.

A small boy struck by a large meteor undergoes a few quick personality changes. For starts, he turns into a big, hairy monster (Gilbert Perkins). His mother notices the change right away, but reasoning that blood is thicker than body hair, she hides the creature in her basement and develops a great imagination. This latter talent comes in handy when she has to invent alibis while sonny boy is off on a psychopathic murdering spree.

PRODUCER AND DIRECTOR: Jacques Marquette. SCREENPLAY: Ray Buffum. MAKEUP: Jack Pierce. CINEMATOGRAPHY: Taylor Byars. MUSIC: Walter Green.

SUPPORTING PLAYERS: Anne Gynne, Gloria Castillo, Stuart Wade.

TEENAGERS FROM OUTER SPACE
WB (1959). B/w, 87 mins.

Low-budget teen torpor. Derek (Da-

Warner Bros.

Teenagers from Outer Space

vid Love) is the lead invader of an oncoming army of humanoid aliens. They plan to land on Earth and simply take over. The planet, it seems, is a really nifty spot for them to breed their idea of cattle . . . house-sized lobster monsters (never really shown on the screen because of the money involved) called Gargons. The proposed invasion gets a bit bogged down when Derek begins making cow eyes at lovely Earthling Betty Morgan (Dawn Anderson). Teen love prevails and Derek guides the entire fleet of attacking flying saucers (also unseen) into the side of a mountain. The resulting cataclysm (ditto) kills poor Derek but leaves Earth Gargon-free. Oh Death, where is thy sting?

PRODUCER, DIRECTOR, SCREENWRITER, AND SPECIAL EFFECTS: Tom Graeff.

SUPPORTING PLAYERS: King Moody, Helen Sage, Harvey B. Dunn.

TELEPHONE BOOK, THE
Avco-Embassy (1971). Color and b/w, 89 mins.

The greatest obscene phone-caller in the world turns out to be an ex-astronaut who, because of a rather nasty accident that occurred during the race for space, can only achieve sexual gratification over the phone. Does NASA know about this?

PRODUCER: Mewin Bloch. DIRECTOR: AND SCREENWRITER: Nelson Lyion. ANIMATED SEQUENCE: Leonard Glasser. CINEMATOGRAPHY: Leon Perer. MUSIC: Nate Sassover.

CAST: Sarah Kennedy, Norman Rose, Jill Clayburgh, Ultra Violet, Barry Morse, Roger C. Carmel.

TELEVISION SPIES
Paramount (1939). B/w, 58 mins.

Spies battle it out over a wall-sized television unit that can telecast over a distance of 2,000 miles.

DIRECTOR: Edward Dmytryk. SCREENPLAY: Horace McCoy, William R. Lipman, and Lillie Hayward, from a story by André Bohem. CINEMATOGRAPHY: Harry Fischbeck.

CAST: William Henry, Judith Barett, Anthony Quinn, Richard Denning, John Eldredge.

TENTH VICTIM, THE
Embassy (1965). Color, 92 mins.

Based on ROBERT SHECKLEY'S "The Seventh Victim," this tale of the future is a fairly campy adaptation of the story's battle between the sexes. In the 21st century, war is passé. Aggressions are channeled into a game called the Big Hunt, wherein the hunter and the hunted exchange roles throughout. Ursula Andress (equipped with pistol bra) is the hunter and Marcello Mastroianni is designated as her tenth and final victim.

PRODUCER: Carlo Ponti. DIRECTOR: Elio Petri. SCREENPLAY: Petri, Ennio Flaiano, Tonino Guerra, Giorgio Salvione. CINEMATOGRAPHY: Giovanni De Venanzo. MUSIC: Piero Piccioni.

SUPPORTING PLAYERS: Elsa Martinelli, Massimo Serato.

TERMINAL MAN, THE
WB (1973). Color, 104 mins.

George Segal is the mentally-unstable human guinea pig in an operation in which a small computer system is placed into his brain. The intention is for the machinery to stabilize the patient's psychopathic tendencies. However, the operation is a failure and the machinery sends the man into sudden and unexpected outbursts of homicidal mania. A modern Frankenstein tale based on the novel of the same name by MICHAEL CRICHTON.

PRODUCER, DIRECTOR, AND SCREENWRITER: Michael Hodges. CINEMATOGRAPHY: Richard Kline.

SUPPORTING PLAYERS: Joan Hackett, Richard Dysart, Jill Clayburgh, Michael Gwynn.

TERROR BENEATH THE SEA
Toei (Japan, 1966); Teleworld (U.S., 1972). Color, 87 mins.

A scientist with nothing else to do passes the time by turning men into sea-breathing monsters.

DIRECTOR: Hajime Sato. SPECIAL EFFECTS: Nobuo Yajima.

CAST: Shinichi Chiba, Peggy Neal, Franz Gruber, Gunther Braun, Mike Daneen.

TERROR CIRCUS
CMC (1973). Color, 86 mins.

A crazy circus-owner (Andrew Prine) kidnaps women to use in his traveling show, tossing the discards to the wild animals as sweet treats. Meanwhile, in a nearby shed, radioactive-mutant "dad" thinks about life in general.

PRODUCER: Gerald Cormier. DIRECTOR: Alan Rudolph. MUSIC: Tommy Vig.

SUPPORTING PLAYERS: Manuella Thiess, Sherry Alberoni, Chuck Niles, Gil Lamb, Gil Roland.

TERROR FROM THE YEAR 5000
AIP (1958). B/w, 74 mins.

A scientist experimenting with time transport accidentally rips a hole into the barrier surrounding time and space, allowing into the present a lot of cartoon bubbles, a four-eyed kitty-cat, and a horribly scarred mutant woman in stretch pants. The woman dons a handy human mask and, disguising herself as a nurse, attempts to lure unmarred men back into the future for procreative purposes. Her society,

© American International Pictures

Terror from the Year 5000

hampered by postnuke mutation, needs fathers, and plenty of them. And just how does she expect to lure the parade of pops-to-be back with her? Why, by hypnotizing the men with her fingernails, of course.

PRODUCER, DIRECTOR, AND SCREENWRITER: Robert Gurney, Jr. CINEMATOGRAPHY: Arthur Florman.

CAST: Ward Costello, Joyce Holden, John Stratton, Fred Herrick.

TERROR IS A MAN
AA (1959). B/w, 89 mins.

When a ship sinks at sea, the lone survivor (Richard Derr) finds himself on an island run by Dr. Girard (Francis Lederer), his wife, Frances (Greta Thyssen), and a shifty-eyed staff. Screams piercing the night lead the visitor to suspect there is something not quite right going on in the doctor's lab. He's right. The doc is attempting to turn a panther into a human via a slow surgical process that is, by the by, totally painful. Caught at the halfway mark in the transformation, the cat-man escapes and becomes a first-rate murderer of locals. Eventually the cat creature is put to sea in a leaky lifeboat, emulating the demise of the monster in MARY W. SHELLEY's *Frankenstein*.

DIRECTOR AND MUSIC DIRECTOR: Garry De Leon. SCREENPLAY: Harry Paul Harber. CINEMATOGRAPHY: Emmanuel I. Rojas.

SUPPORTING PLAYERS: Oscar Keesee, Lilia Duran, Flory Carlos as the Creature.

TERRORNAUTS, THE
Amicus (G.B., 1966), Embassy (U.S., 1967). Color, 75 mins.

An alien asteroid kidnaps an entire science complex from Earth via a pretty strong beaming device. The space rock was once the fortress of a powerful alien race, but now is only used as a home for a lone alien robot. The robot forces the Earth scientists to undergo a series of intelligence tests before pitting them against a warring fleet of alien ships. The Earthlings join the battle and defeat the bad aliens.

PRODUCERS: Milton Subotsky, Max J. Rosenberg. DIRECTOR: Montgomery Tully. SCREENPLAY: John Brunner. SPECIAL EFFECTS: Les Bowie Films.

CAST: Simon Oates as Dr. Joe Burke, Zena Marshall as Sandy Lund, Max Adrian as Dr. Henry Shore, Stanley Meadows, Charles Hawtry, Patricia Hayes.

TEST PILOT PIRX
Polish Corp. for Film (Poland, 1979). Color, 104 mins.

Set in the future, when finite linears are manufactured. The linears are almost-human robots, perfect in every detail, designed eventually to take the place of humans. This film traces the adventures of one such model.

DIRECTOR: Marek Piestrak. SCREENPLAY: Piestrak, from a novel by STANISLAW LEM. CINEMATOGRAPHY: Janusz Pawlowski. SET DECORATION: Jerzy Sniezawski. MUSIC: Arvo Part.

CAST: Sergei Desnitsky, Boleslaw Abart, Vladimir Ivashov, Zbigniew Lesien.

THEM!
WB (1954). B/w, 93 mins.

A classic thriller.

In the middle of the desert, two New Mexico state troopers find a mobile home torn apart and covered with sugary slime. Only a young girl (Sandy Descher) survives, in shock, muttering the word "them" over and over. A second scene of unexplained destruction is found and one of the two officers, remaining behind to investigate, disappears from the site . . . a bloodstained policeman's cap the only evidence of his existence.

Sgt. Ben Peterson (James Whitmore) and FBI agent Robert Graham (James Arness) team up with scientist Harold Medford (Edmund Gwenn) and daughter Pat (Joan Weldon) to investigate the strange occurrences. They discover an underground lair of giant ants—radioactive mutants. The ants have been doing the killing, searching for food. The army bombs the caverns with gas grenades, but a flying queen-ant and her mate escape.

When a freight train full of sugar is mauled and drained of its contents near Los Angeles, Ben and Graham head for the city immediately. They find no sign of the gi-ants but discover that two small boys and their father have dis-

Warner Bros.

Them

appeared while flying a toy airplane near the city sewer system. On the advice of a local drunk who insists that this time he's *really* seen some monsters roaming the streets, Ben and Graham venture near the sewer system. They find a battered toy plane.

They then discover the tiny owners, cowering in a corner next to an attacking gi-ant. Ben and Graham charge into the sewer system to save the boys. Only Graham and the boys emerge alive. Peterson is attacked by the newly hatched ants and torn limb from limb. The National Guard charges into the tunnel with flame throwers blazing and the creatures are destroyed.

PRODUCER: David Weisbart. DIRECTOR: Gordon Douglas. SCREENPLAY: Ted Sherdemann, from a story by George Worthing Yates. ART DIRECTOR: Stanley Fleicher. SPECIAL EFFECTS: Ralph Ayers. CINEMATOGRAPHY: Sid Hickox. SOUND EFFECTS: William Mueller, Francis J. Scheid. MUSIC: Bronislau Kaper.

SUPPORTING PLAYERS: Onslow Stevens, Dub Taylor, Fess Parker, Leonard Nimoy, William Schallert, Sean McClory.

THESE ARE THE DAMNED
Also known as THE DAMNED. Hammer (G.B., 1961); b/w, 96 mins. Columbia (U.S., 1963); b/w, 77 mins.

The U.S. version of Joseph Losey's sf morality play was edited into a state of near-total confusion. An American traveling in England (Macdonald Carey) and his English girl friend (Viveca Lindfors) are attacked by a group of motorcycle thugs. Trying to escape, they stumble into an underground chamber populated by small children who are part of an experiment being conducted by a government-supported scientist. The fellow is raising these children to be immune to nuclear fall-out. They will be, in essence, the children of a post–World War III nation. The only problem is this: in order to build immunity, the children have to be exposed to a growing degree of radiation, day by day, week by week. They are now so radioactive that they have contaminated the couple. In essence, the two adults are trapped.

PRODUCER: Anthony Hinds. DIRECTOR: Joseph Losey. SCREENPLAY: Evan Jones, based on the novel *The Children of Light,* by H. L. Lawrence, CINEMATOGRAPHY: Arthur Grant. MUSIC: James Bernard.

SUPPORTING PLAYERS: Oliver Reed, Shirley Ann Field, Rachel Clay, James Villiers, Alexander Knox.

THEY ALL DIED LAUGHING
Read (1964). B/w, 94 mins.

A scientist comes up with a poison that sends the victims into gales of laughter before killing them.

PRODUCER: Donald Taylor. DIRECTOR: Don Chaffey. SCREENPLAY: Robert Hammer, Donald Taylor. CINEMATOGRAPHY: Gerald Gibbs. MUSIC: John Barry.

CAST: Leo McKern, Janet Munro, Dennis Price, Mervyn Johns.

THEY CAME FROM BEYOND SPACE
Amicus (G.B., 1967); Embassy (U.S., 1967). Color, 85 mins.

A group of bodiless aliens descends upon Earth by hitching a ride in on a meteor shower. Beginning an invasion on a small scale, they take over the bodies of factory workers in Cornwall, England. One human, however, avoids the telepathic tentacles because of the metal plate in his head. He and his girl friend journey to the alien headquarters on the moon, where they find that the aliens are only using robotized Earthlings to perform some quick repairs on their fractured spaceship. A good job if you can get it.

PRODUCERS: Max J. Rosenberg, Milton Subotsky. DIRECTOR: Freddie Francis. SCREENPLAY: Subotsky. MUSIC: James Stevens. MAKEUP: Bunty Phillips. SPECIAL EFFECTS: Les Bowie Films.

CAST: Robert Hutton, Jennifer Yane, Katy Wild, Bernard Kay, Michael Gough.

THEY CAME FROM WITHIN
Also known as THE PARASITE MURDERS.
Trans-American (1975). Movielab color, 94 mins.

A scientist creates a race of nasty parasites that are "a combination of aphrodisiac and venereal disease." The little slugs slither inside their human victims and make them superlusty. Roger St. Luc (Paul Hampton) and Nurse Forsythe (Lynn Lowry) are out to get the little buggers. Betts (Barbara Steele) is already infected and has a great old time. The marriage of Nicholas and Janine Tudo (Alan Migicovsky and Susan Petrie) is nearly salvaged by the creatures. Are they good? Are they evil? Hard to say. But they really are quite ugly.

PRODUCER: Ivan Reitman. DIRECTOR AND SCREENWRITER: David Cronenberg. CINEMATOGRAPHY: Robert Sadd. MAKEUP AND SPECIAL EFFECTS: Joe Blasco. MUSIC: Ivan Reitman.

THING, THE
Also known as THE THING FROM ANOTHER WORLD.
RKO (1952). B/w, 86 mins.

The perfect alien-invasion film. Spooky. Well-written. Claustrophobic. Based upon JOHN W. CAMPBELL's "Who Goes There?" (which he penned under the pseudonym of Don A. Stuart), the movie recounts the attempts of one bloodthirsty plant-man (James Arness) to wipe out a small human enclave in the Arctic.

At a desolate U.S. Air Force outpost in the frozen North, the crash landing of a flying saucer disrupts the day-to-day boredom. Embedded beneath the ice, the craft is inaccessible to the investigating airmen. They decide to blast out the craft. The ensuing explosion completely destroys the craft. The saucer's pilot, a towering, bald humanoid, remains intact, still embedded in ice. Dr. Carrington (Robert Cornithwaite), Captain Hendry (Kenneth

Tobey), Nikki (Margaret Sheridan), and Scotty (Douglas Spencer) try to thaw the creature in hopes of communicating with it.

The Thing (James Arness), however, has a rather unique form of communication. He has come to Earth to mingle with Earthlings, but only as a source of nourishment. Coming to the planet to spawn an invasion, the humanoid has seeds of other aliens embedded in his limbs. These seeds require human and animal blood to survive. The monster thaws and begins stalking the base, killing whatever slow-moving creature it can corner. At one point, one of his attacks is beaten back and the Thing's arm is severed in a metal door. Base scientists discover that the creature is a plant and, as such, is capable of complete regeneration. They can't blow it up without giving rise to a host of alien invaders. Finally, they wire a corridor with high-voltage wires and, using themselves as bait, lure the creature into the electrified area. The juice is turned on and the thing is deep-fried.

PRODUCER: Howard Hawks. DIRECTOR: Christian Nyby. SCREENPLAY: Charles Lederer. SPECIAL EFFECTS: Linwood Dunn, Donald Stewart. MUSIC: Dimitri Tiomkin.

SUPPORTING PLAYERS: James Young, Paul Frees, Eduard Franz.

THINGS TO COME
London Films (G.B., 1936); b/w, 130 mins. UA (U.S., 1936); b/w, 113 mins.

One of the two motion pictures actually scripted by H. G. WELLS (the other being the whimsical *The Man Who Could Work Miracles*), this movie has both blessings and flaws in excess. In 1936, war destroys the world. As seen through the eyes of Everytown's citizens, it is a devastating blow, with a manmade disease called the Wandering Sickness spreading death throughout the land. Then, in 1970, the loutish residents of Everytown are awakened by the sound of an airplane. John Cabal, a representative of Wings over the World, lands. Oswald Cabal (Raymond Massey) says that the scientific group is trying to rebuild the world back to its former stature and beyond. Everytown's warlord-boss, Rudolph (Ralph Richardson), is opposed to the idea,

Things to Come

but Peace Gas brings everyone around.

By 2036, Everytown is a sprawling metropolis. Cabal is encouraging its populace to back a scientific expedition to the moon. He is fought by antiscience sculptor Theotocopulos (Cedric Hardwicke, in a role originally penned for Ernest Thesiger). The populace, in a wave of anxiety, storms the launch site, attempting to halt the rocket. The rocket does blast off, however, with Cabal's own son and Theotocopulos's daughter aboard.

Although Wells's screenplay is a tad on the preachy side (Wells, in his later years, was prone to proscience/socialistic raving), the effects and the sheer scope of the production never fail to overwhelm.

Things to Come

PRODUCER: Alexander Korda. DIRECTOR: William Cameron Menzies. SCREENPLAY: H. G. Wells, based on his novel. ART DIRECTOR: Vincent Korda. CINEMATOGRAPHY: George Perinal. SPECIAL-EFFECTS CINEMATOGRAPHY: Edward Cohen, Harry Zech. SPECIAL EFFECTS: Ned Mann. MUSIC: Arthur Bliss.

But He Still Needs a Good Dermatologist
"No human heart could possibly function like that! He's completely superhuman!"
> Basil Rathbone to Bela Lugosi in *The Son of Frankenstein*

SUPPORTING PLAYERS: Margaretta Scott, Edward Chapman, Maurice Braddell, Sophie Stewart, Ann Todd, John Clements.

THING WITH TWO HEADS, THE
AIP (1972). Color, 90 mins.

In order to save the life of an elderly and wealthy bigot (Ray Milland), a scientist (Don Marshall) transplants the old duffer's head onto the body of unjustly accused convict Rosie Greer, a black man. The resulting two-headed hulk gives forth some of the best dialogue to be heard on the screen since Costello first asked Abbott, "Who's on first?"

PRODUCER: Wes Bishop. DIRECTOR: Lee Frost. SCREENPLAY: Frost, Bishop, and James G. White. CINEMATOGRAPHY: Jack Steely. SPECIAL EFFECTS:

© American International Pictures, 1972

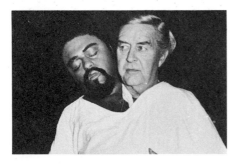

The Thing with Two Heads

Dan Striepke, Gail Brown, Tim Burman, Charles Schram, James White, Pete Peterson.

SUPPORTING PLAYERS: Roger Perry, Kathy Baumann, Chelsea Brown, Roger Gentry.

THIRD FROM THE SUN
Bulgarfilm (Bulgaria, 1972). Color, 124 mins.

Aliens influence human development.

DIRECTOR: Georgi Stoyanov. SCREENPLAY: Pavel Vejinov. CINEMATOGRAPHY: Ivailo Trentchev. MUSIC: Kiril Dontchev.

CAST: Dobrinka Stankova, Naoum Chopov.

THIRTY-FOOT BRIDE OF CANDY ROCK, THE
Columbia (1959). Color, 75 mins.

Lou Costello's last film found the rotund comic playing an inventor who has changed his sweetheart into an amazing colossal heartthrob. The same invention has complicated matters even further, changing investigating army patrollers into cavemen and Civil War soldiers.

DIRECTOR: Sidney Miller. SCREENPLAY: Rowland Barber, Arthur Ross. MAKEUP: Clay Campbell. CINEMATOGRAPHY: Frank G. Carson. SPECIAL EFFECTS: Jack Rabin, Irving Block, Louis DeWitt. MUSIC: Raoul Kraushaar.

SUPPORTING PLAYERS: Dorothy Provine, Gale Gordon, Doodles Weaver, Robert Burton.

THIS ISLAND EARTH
Universal (1954). Technicolor, 87 mins.

The ultimate Saturday-matinee sf film. Sagging under the weight of constant air attacks from neighboring planet Zahgon, Metaluna sends some of its top scientists out to Earth in search of a new source of energy to save itself. Their atmospheric-defense shields are crumbling, and Earthlings, being a resourceful lot, can probably do an A-1 patchwork job.

Metalunan Exeter (Jeff Morrow) arrives on Earth and entices the leading scientists of the world to join a privately funded scientific community to

Universal

This Island Earth

aid him in his experiments. Once housed within the desolate mansion, however, the scientists are held prisoner (a chain of events that secretly pains Exeter). Doctors Cal Meacham (Rex Reason) and Ruth Adams (Faith Domergue) stage an effective escape from the compound using a small plane. The plane, however, is beamed aboard Exeter's flying saucer and the twosome is taken to Metaluna. Traveling faster than the speed of light, the three humanoids are placed in tubes that send them into a state of suspended animation/transparency.

Cal and Ruth land on Metaluna and are brought before the Ruler. He shows none of Exeter's compassion for the Earth concept of freedom and orders the two to undergo a space lobotomy to ensure their cooperation with Metalunan scientists. Cal and Ruth bolt for the saucer. They are attacked by a large mutant, half-man, half-insect. Exeter saves them and is mortally wounded. He shoves Cal and Ruth into his saucer and heads back for Earth. Unfortunately, the mutant has stowed away on board.

The mutant is killed. The saucer takes off. The Zahgon fleet destroys Metaluna. The saucer makes it back to Earth and Exeter, slowly dying at the controls, sends Ruth and Cal back to the surface in their tiny plane. He crashes his saucer into the sea.

PRODUCER: William Alland. DIRECTOR: Joseph Newman, with additional footage directed by Jack Arnold (uncredited). SCREENPLAY: Franklin Coen and Edward O'Callaghan, based on the novel by RAYMOND F. JONES. MUSIC: Herman Stein. MAKEUP: Bud Westmore. SPECIAL EFFECTS: Clifford Stine, Stanley Horsley.

SUPPORTING PLAYERS: Lance Fuller, Russell Johnson, Regis Barton, and Eddie Parker as the Mutant.

THIS IS NOT A TEST
Modern Films (1962). B/w.

A group of travelers is stopped by a state trooper. While held up, they hear over the radio news of a nuclear war happening. They hide in the back of the van. The unbelieving trooper remains outside. Soon, only his remains are outside, as a nearby A-bomb causes him some embarrassment.

DIRECTOR: Frederic Gadette. SCREENPLAY: Peter Abenheim, Betty Lasky, Gadette. CINEMATOGRAPHY: Brick Marquard. MUSIC: Greig McRitchie.

CAST: Seamon Glass, Mary Morlas, Thayer Roberts, Aubrey Martin.

THOSE FANTASTIC FLYING FOOLS
Also known as JULES VERNE'S ROCKET TO THE MOON.
AIP (1967). Color/scope, 95 mins.

Rather loosely based on the works of JULES VERNE, this inept film recounts the attempts of P. T. Barnum (Burl Ives) to raise British money for his projected moon rocket. The rocket would actually land on the surface of the moon, carrying a circus-midget astronaut within. Barnum raises the money but villains begin tampering with the mechanism. Still tampering at the time of lift-off, the villains and the rocket go off-course and land in Tsarist Russia.

PRODUCER: Harry Alan Towers. DIRECTOR: Don Sharp. SCREENPLAY: Dave Freeman, from a story by Harry Alan Towers. SPECIAL EFFECTS: Les Bowie, Pat Moore. MUSIC: Patrick John Scott.

SUPPORTING PLAYERS: Troy Donahue, Gert Frobe, Terry-Thomas, Lionel Jeffries, Dennis Price, Klaus Kinski, Hermione Gingold.

THREE STOOGES IN ORBIT, THE
Columbia (1962). B/w, 87 mins.

Two Martians, Og and Zog, come to Earth to snatch the plans of a really keen invention: a tank/helicopter/submarine. Instead, they run into the Three Stooges (Larry Fine, Moe Howard, "Curly" Joe DeRita). After a long series of *nyuk, nyuk, nyuk's* and *pick two . . . one, two . . . boing's* they go back to Mars. Who wouldn't?

PRODUCER AND STORY ORIGINATOR: Norman Maurer. DIRECTOR: Edward Bernds. SCREENPLAY: Elwood Ullman. MUSIC: Paul Dunlap. ART DIRECTOR: Don Ament. MAKEUP: John Chambers.

SUPPORTING PLAYERS: Nestor Paiva, Carol Christensen, Don Lamond, Emil Sitka.

THREE STOOGES MEET HERCULES, THE
Columbia (1962). B/w, 89 mins.

The Three Stooges (Moe Howard, Larry Fine, "Curly" Joe DeRita) help a timid professor (Quinn Redeker) out of a tight spot with his girl friend (Vickie Trickett) but accidentally send the professor's time machine back to the time of Hercules (Samson Burke), with the five present-day humans aboard. The timid professor earns a reputation as a strongman and eventually is thought to be Hercules. When the real Hercules shows up, there's a grunt, a groan, and a *boing-boing* per second.

PRODUCER: Norman Maurer. DIRECTOR: Edward Bernds. SCREENPLAY: Elwood Ullman, from a story by Maurer. CINEMATOGRAPHY: Charles Welborn. MUSIC: Paul Dunlap.

SUPPORTING PLAYERS: Mike McKeever, Emil Sitka, Gene Roth.

THUNDERBIRDS ARE GO
UA (1967). Color, 94 mins.

Strictly for the small fry, this adventure stars Gerry and Sylvia Anderson's popular crew of marionettes. When a Mars launch is fouled up by master criminal the Hood, the Tracy family and their Thunderbird squad make sure the second lift-off is successful. Astronaut Alan Tracy makes a successful visit to Mars, where he encounters a horde of Martian rock-serpents. He manages to leave the planet unsplintered.

EXECUTIVE PRODUCER: Gerry Anderson. PRODUCER: Sylvia Anderson. DIRECTOR: David Lane. SCREENPLAY: Gerry and Sylvia Anderson. MUSIC: Barry Gray, featuring The Shadows. SPECIAL EFFECTS: Derek Meddings, Shaun Whittacker-Cook.

VOICES: Sylvia Anderson, Ray Barret, David Graham, Bob Monkhouse, Peter Dynely, Charles Tingwell.

THUNDERBIRDS 6
UA (1968). Color, 90 mins.

More supermarionation, as puppets fight other puppets in the 21st century. This time out, it's the evil Black Phantom who is out to do in the Thunderbird crew. Do you care?

PRODUCER: Sylvia Anderson. DIRECTOR: David Lane. SCREENPLAY: Gerry and Sylvia Anderson. CINEMATOGRAPHY: Harry Oakes. SPECIAL EFFECTS: Derek Meddings. MUSIC: Barry Gray.

VOICES: Peter Dyneley, Christine Finn, Sylvia Anderson.

THX 1138
American Zoetrope/WB (1969/1971). Color, 88 mins.

George Lucas's first feature film is actually an expanded version of a U.C.L.A. student effort called *THX 2238*. In the future, the world is reduced to a state of human slavery run by computers. Humans are drugged and forced to do the bidding of countless machines and policed by humanoid automatons. The humans are forced to dress alike, are not allowed to show emotion, and are forbidden to have sex. THX 1138 (Robert Duvall) and roommate LUH 3417 (Maggie McOmie) reduce their drug intake and thus stimulate their sex drive. LUH 3417 becomes pregnant. She is destroyed for breaking the law, prompting THX 1138 to flee from the subterranean human quarters and make a break for the world outside. He is pursued by the silver-faced Law Robots (Robert Ferro, Johnny Weissmuller, Jr.) under the guidance of legal ace SEN 5241 (Donald Pleasance). A cat-and-mouse and nuts-and-bolts chase develops. Finally the computers call off the cops, realizing that to continue the chase would be economically irrational. THX 1138 emerges into the sunlight, a free man.

PRODUCER: Lawrence Sturhann. DIRECTOR: George Lucas. SCREENPLAY: Lucas, Walter Murch. ANIMATION: Hal Barwood. MUSIC: Lalo Shifrin. CINEMATOGRAPHY: Dave Meyers, Albert Kihn.

SUPPORTING PLAYERS: Ian Wolfe, Marshall Efron, Irene Forrest.

TIME AFTER TIME
WB (1979). Metrocolor, 112 mins.

A total delight.

Sf author/inventor H. G. Wells (Malcolm McDowell) invites a group of associates to his home for a demonstration of a time-traveling machine he has concocted. Unbeknownst to Wells, his closest friend and chess partner, Dr. Stevenson (David Warner), is, in reality, Jack the Ripper. Arriving at Wells's home shortly after a particularly gruesome murder, Stevenson is tracked down by the London police. He escapes, via the time machine, into the year 1979—a year that Wells is convinced will be part of a totally Utopian age. Guilt-stricken that his handiwork has sent such an ungodly evil into such an idyllic time period, Wells waits until the machine returns to its point of origin (Wells's basement) and then follows the Ripper into the future.

Arriving in San Francisco during an H. G. Wells retrospective, he is indeed a stranger in a strange land. He finds what seems to him to be barbarism and eccentricity throughout the city. He is befriended by bank teller Amy (Mary Steenburgen) and, with her help, tracks down the Ripper. The killer escapes, however, chortling "I'm home" as he fades in with the pimps and prostitutes in the seedier section of the city.

Through a side trip in the machine, Wells and Mary discover that Mary is to be the murderer's fifth victim in two days' time. From that point onward, the duo tries not only to help a particularly suspicious Police Department (led by Charles Cioffi, as Lt. Mitchell) catch the Ripper, but also to do everything possible to make sure that Mary is not at the murder site at the predicted time. Can Wells take on history itself?

PRODUCER: Herb Jaffe. DIRECTOR: Nicholas Meyer. SCREENPLAY: Nicholas

Time After Time

Meyer, based on a story by Karl Alexander and Steve Hayes. CINEMATOGRAPHY: Paul Lohman. SPECIAL EFFECTS: Larry Fuentes, Jim Blount. PRODUCTION DESIGN: Edward C. Carfagno. MUSIC: Miklos Rozsa.

SUPPORTING PLAYERS: Andonia Katsaros as Mrs. Turner, Patti D'Arbanville as Shirley, Geraldine Baron as Carol.

TIME FLIES
Gainsborough (G.B., 1944). B/w, 88 mins.

A professor's "Time Ball" time machine takes two comics back to various time periods of Britain past-tense.

PRODUCER: Edward Black. DIRECTOR: Walter Forde. SCREENPLAY: Howard Irving Young, Jo O. Orton, Ted Kavanaugh.

CAST: Tommy Handley, Evelyn Dall, George Morre, Graham Moffatt.

TIME MACHINE, THE
MGM (1960). Color, 103 mins.

In the year 1900, a young dandy named George (Rod Taylor) experiments with time travel. Telling his skeptical friends Kemp (Whit Bissell), Hillyer (Sebastian Cabot), and Philby (Alan Young) that he will prove his time-traveling theory to be fact, he bids them farewell. Good friend Philby sees something is amiss and cautions George to be careful.

George pens a note to his old chum, instructing him to keep an eye on his belongings when he is gone. He then enters his basement workshop, climbs into a full-scale time machine, and hurtles into the future.

He pauses during the World War I,

MGM

The Time Machine

when he finds London in the midst of an air raid. He encounters Philby's son, who tells him that his father took over George's home and refused to sell it. In fact, it is still standing. George makes a stop or two more before skidding to a halt in 1966, as an elderly Philby, Jr., herds Londoners into an underground shelter at the beginning of World War III. Atom bombs go off. Molten lava overtakes London.

George dives into the machine and zips into the future, coming to a halt in the postnuclear world of 802701. This world is populated by the childlike Eloi, perennial teenagers who roam the surface world, and the cannibalistic-mutant Morlocks, who keep the Eloi fed and clothed before dragging them into the underground to use them both as slaves and as food. Falling in love with Eloi girl Weena (Yvette Mimieux), George decides to help the Eloi fight the Morlocks. He leads them into the underground tunnel armed with courage and 19th-century firepower.

After defeating the Morlocks, he returns to the past to grab a few books and tools and rejoin his precious Weena. Only Philby believes what has happened, and he wonders aloud which books George brought into the future to rebuild the human race.

Expertly crafted on all counts.

PRODUCER AND DIRECTOR: George Pal. SCREENPLAY: David Duncan, based on the story by H. G. WELLS. MAKEUP: William Tuttle. CINEMATOGRAPHY: Paul Vogel. SPECIAL EFFECTS: Gene Warren, Wah Chang. MUSIC: Russell Garcia.

SUPPORTING PLAYERS: Doris Lloyd, Paul Frees as the voice of the history machine.

TIME OF THE ROSES
Filminor (Finland, 1969). B/w, 106 mins.

A movie producer of the year 2050 tries to film a documentary about the life of a girl dead for 50 years. He does some research in an attempt to reconstruct her life. Sort of a futuristic "you are there" theme results.

DIRECTOR: Riso Jarva. SCREENPLAY: Jarva, Jaakko Pakkasvirta, Peter von Bagh. CINEMATOGRAPHY: Artii Peippo. MUSIC: Otto Donner.

CAST: Arto Tuominen, Ritva Vespo, Tarja Markus.

TIMES ARE OUT OF JOINT, THE
Gaumont (France, 1909). B/w silent short, 601 ft.

When a clock begins to run fast, so do events around it.

DIRECTOR: Emile Cohl.

TIME TRAVELERS, THE
AIP (1964). Color, 82 mins.

A neatly scripted low-budget thriller. A team of scientists headed by Dr. Erik von Steiner (Preston Foster) and including Dr. Steve Connors (Philip Carey) and Carol White (Merry Anders) are working on experimental equipment designed to observe the past, present, and future. An accident creates a time-portal window in their lab. They see the college campus they are located on 107 years in the future. Trying to stabilize the portal, electrician Danny McKee (Steven Franken) plunges through it. His colleagues dive in after him in a rescue attempt.

They wind up in a land where mutants roam the outer world and humans live underground with their loyal robots—all being survivors of an all-out nuclear war. Led to the humans by Gadra (Joan Woodbury) and Varno (John Hoyt), the modern-day Earth people are told by technician Reena (Dolores Wells) and Councilman Willard (Dennis Patrick) that they are currently battling against time to construct a giant space ark that will take them off the planet. Their defense systems can't hold up against the mutants much longer. The present-day Earth residents aid in the construction of the ship and in the construction of a new portal to take them back in time.

Before completion of either, the mutants attack. The Earth people dive into the time portal and go back too far, observing themselves still frozen before the original machine. They have become stuck in time. They dive through the portal again, into the unknown and disappear. Their alter egos begin the adventure before the original portal again, doomed to do so forever and ever and ever. . . .

PRODUCER: William Redlin. DIRECTOR: Ib Melchior. SCREENPLAY: Melchior, from a story by David Hewitt and Melchior. ART DIRECTOR: Ray Storey. SPECIAL EFFECTS: David Hewitt. MUSIC: Richard La Salle.

SUPPORTING PLAYER: Forrest J. Ackerman.

TIN MAN, THE
MGM (1935). B/w short, 19 mins.

Two luckless ladies (Patsy Kelly and Thelma Todd) are out for a joyride when they become lost. Knocking on the door of a home owned by a woman-hating scientist, they are less than overjoyed to come face to face with a robot (Cy Slocum) programmed by his smarty boss to destroy all women. By the film's finale, the robot proves he's no master of sex discrimination. He turns on his boss and lets the lovely lasses go free.

PRODUCER: Hal Roach. DIRECTOR: James Parrott.

SUPPORTING PLAYERS: Matthew Betz, Clarence Hummel Wilson.

TOBOR THE GREAT
Republic (1954). B/w, 77 mins.

Tobor (read it backwards) is a highly sensitive sort designed to take the place of a human astronaut on the first flight to the moon. When spies attempt to tinker with Tobor and turn him into a murdering monster, they are only temporarily successful. Tobor later turns the tables on his former tormentors by rescuing his scientist/inventor and the professor's son from the menacing meanies.

DIRECTOR: Lee Sholem. SCREENPLAY: Phillip MacDonald, Richard Goldstone. SPECIAL EFFECTS: Howard and Theodore Lydecker. MUSIC: Howard Jackson.

CAST: Charles Drake, Karin Booth, Bill Chapin, Henry Kulky, William Schallert, Robert Shayne, Lyle Talbot.

TORTURE SHIP
Producers Distributing Corp. (1939). B/w, 56 mins.

What starts out as a pretty humane idea gets less so as it goes around. A scientist tries to cure criminals of their nasty ways by gland injections. Things get out of hand. The experiments don't exactly work, and before you can say "Marquis de Sade," there's a dungeon full of human guinea pigs overdosing on gland shots.

DIRECTOR: Victor Halperin. SCREENPLAY: George Sayre. CINEMATOGRAPHY: Jack Greenhalgh.

CAST: Lyle Talbot, Irving Pichel, Jacqueline Wells, Wheeler Oakman, Stanley Blystone.

TOY BOX, THE
Boxoffice International (1971). Color, 85 mins.

Some horror of the hubba-hubba variety is conjured up by a hungry alien who subjects people to a wide, and graphic, variety of sexual perversions so he can remove the stimulated brains and ship 'em off to his hungry pals for a quick snack. Birdseye Foods this ain't.

PRODUCER: Harry Novak. DIRECTOR AND SCREENWRITER: Ron Garcia. MAKEUP: Dennis Marsh. CINEMATOGRAPHY: H. P. Edwards.

CAST: Evan Steele, Ann Myers, Deborah Osborne, Lisa Goodman, Neal Bishop.

TRANS-ATLANTIC TUNNEL
Also known as THE TUNNEL.
Gaumont (G.B., 1935). B/w, 90 mins.

Set in the next century, this futuristic tale recounts the construction of the first tunnel to run the length of the Atlantic Ocean. Other scientific marvels featured include television broadcasts, trans-Atlantic airplane flights, a tunnel already running beneath the English Channel, and rooftop airports.

PRODUCER: Michael Bacon. DIRECTOR: Maurice Elvey. SCREENPLAY: CURT SIODMAK from the novel by Bernhard Kellerman.

CAST: Richard Dix, Leslie Banks, Marge Evans, C. Aubrey Smith, Walter Huston, George Arliss.

TRANSPLANT
Rizzolia/Dia (Italy/Spain, 1970), Cinemation (U.S., 1971). Color, 103 mins.

An old man with a young wife searches high and—especially—low for a hypersexual young man to use as a surprised donor for a penis-transplant operation. Had he been truly imaginative, he would have sought out a horse.

DIRECTOR: Stefano Steno. CINEMATOGRAPHY: Antonio Macasoli. MUSIC: Gregorio Gracia Segura.

CAST: Carlo Giuffre, Fernando Bilbao, Renato Rascal, Liana Trouche, Graziella Grenata.

TRAPPED BY TELEVISION
Columbia (1936). B/w, 64 mins.

Crooks are caught in the act by modernistic police who use TV monitors to eavesdrop.

DIRECTOR: Del Lord. SCREENPLAY: Lee Loeb, Harold Buchman. CINEMATOGRAPHY: Allen G. Siegler. SPECIAL EFFECTS: Roy Davidson.

CAST: Mary Astor, Lyle Talbot, Nat Pendleton, Thurston Hall.

TRIP TO JUPITER, A
Pathé (France, 1907). Hand-colored silent short, 623 ft.

A space-minded king climbs into space aboard a seemingly endless ladder. As he passes the planets of the solar system, he gets an extraterrestrial salute from each.

TRIP TO MARS, A
Lubin (1903). B/w silent short.

A hastily pirated version of Georges Méliès's A TRIP TO THE MOON. The title was changed to protect the guilty.

TRIP TO MARS, A
Edison (1910). B/w silent short.

An inventor goes to Mars, where he winds up battling Martian men and tree creatures. Needing a quick escape, he makes the trip back to Earth through the use of antigravity powder.

TRIP TO MARS, A
Italy (1920). B/w silent feature, five reels.

A group of astronauts takes a trip to Mars in a propeller-equipped airship.

TRIP TO THE MOON, A
Lubin (1914). B/w silent short combining animation and live action, 600 ft.

A group of adventurers flies to the moon in an airplane. They then take a trip through space, passing by Saturn and racing a comet.

TRIP TO THE MOON, THE (LE VOYAGE DANS LA LUNE)
Star Films (France, 1902). B/w and tinted silent short, 13 mins.

Producer - director - actor - innovator Georges Méliès took his audiences into outer space in this, one of the first sf adventure films. A French spaceship is fired out of a huge cannon-launcher and sails into the eye of the Man in the Moon. Tumbling into a moon crater, the explorers leave the spaceship (without the benefit of space suits) and encounter a group of nasty insect-people, the Selenites. The humans are captured and brought before the ruler of the moon. Georges puts up his dukes and KO's the insect population. The astronauts make for their ship and toss their controls into reverse. Earth, here they come.

SUPPORTING PLAYERS: Victor André, the ballerinas of the Theatre du Chatelet, the acrobats of the Folies-Bergère.

Star Films

A Trip to the Moon

TRIP TO THE POLE, A
Pathé Frères (France, 1911). B/w silent short, 363 ft. Animated.

A group takes a tour of the Pole in a motor car.

TUNNEL, THE
Bavaria Film (Germany, 1933).

A tunnel is constructed beneath the Atlantic.

DIRECTOR: Kurt Bernhardt. Filmed in both German and French. Based on a novel by Bernhard Kellermann.

GERMAN CAST: Paul Hartmann, Olly von Flint, Elga Brink.

FRENCH CAST: Jean Gabin, Madeleine Renaud, Gustaf Grundgens.

TUNNELING THE CHANNEL
Star (France, 1907). B/w silent featurette, 1,160 ft.

A tunnel is constructed beneath the English Channel, uniting France and England.

TWELVE TO THE MOON
Columbia (1960). B/w, 74 mins.

Narrated by Francis X. Bushman, this film tells the torpid tale of Commander Anderson (Ken Clark), Dr. Vargas (Tony Dexter), and a crew of astronauts in their attempt at a moon landing. Once on the surface, they discover a group of moon-men who aren't exactly thrilled to see the property values go down. They threaten to freeze the entire Earth unless the humans go back where they came from. Someone call the A.C.L.U.

PRODUCER AND STORY: Fred Gebhardt. DIRECTOR: David Bradley. SCREENPLAY: DeWitt Bodeen. SPECIAL EFFECTS: Howard A. Anderson, E. Nicholson.

SUPPORTING PLAYERS: Tom Conway as Dr. Orloff, Michi Kobi as Adiko, Tierna Bay as Ingrid.

TWENTY FACES
Toei (Japan, 1957). B/w, 113 mins.

A criminal who has mastered 20—count 'em, 20—different facial disguises uses an army of robot monsters in an attempt to steal atomic material for a homemade invention he has in the works.

DIRECTOR: Hideo Sekigawa. SCREEN PLAY: Tadashi Ogawa. CINEMATOGRAPHY: Hiroshi Fukushima.

CAST: Eiji Okada, Jun Usami, Takashi Kanda.

20 MILLION MILES TO EARTH
Columbia (1957). B/w, 82 mins.

The first manned mission to Venus returns to Earth in tragedy, crashing into the the sea off the coast of Italy. The lone survivor, Col. Calder (William Hopper), is pulled from the sinking craft by local fishermen. Interrogated by Maj. Gen. A. D. McIntosh (Thomas B. Henry), Calder reveals that he has brought back to Earth a canister containing a specimen of Venusian life. The canister, however, is nowhere to be found in the wreckage.

As it turns out, a local boy, Pepe, has sold the canister to a local zoologist, Dr. Leonardo (Frank Puglia), and his daughter, Marisa (Joan Taylor). Handed the strange jellylike egg, the professor is astounded when it hatches. A tiny humanoid, Ymir, emerges. It's placed in a cage. Overnight, it grows to over four feet tall. The thing begins to grow even more. It escapes from the zoologist's cage and instigates a reign of terror across the countryside. Captured by the combined military strength of the U.S. and Italy, the creature is sedated and brought to the Rome zoo. It escapes after a burned-out fuse causes a current ripple to bring the electrical-sedation process to a halt. Now nearly 30 feet tall, the monster rips apart Rome until a well-aimed bazooka brings him down from the top of the ancient Colosseum. Good special effects.

Columbia

20 Million Miles to Earth

PRODUCER: Charles Schneer. DIRECTOR: Nathan Juran. SCREENPLAY: Bob Williams and Christopher Knopf, from a story by Ray Harryhausen and Charlotte Knight. SPECIAL EFFECTS: Ray Harryhausen. MUSIC: Mischa Bakaleinikoff.

SUPPORTING PLAYERS: Tito Vuolo, Don Orlando.

27TH DAY, THE
Columbia (1957). B/w, 75 mins.

A humanoid alien (Arnold Moss) from a dying planet takes five Earthlings aboard his flying saucer and gives them an ultimatum. The fate of the world is in their hands. His race wants to relocate to Earth and is giving the Earthlings a chance to surrender via suicide. Each human—Su Tan (Marie Tsien), Eve Wingate (Valerie French), Klaus Bechner (George Voscovec), Ivan Godofsky (Azemat Janti), and Jonathan Clark (Gene Barry)—is given a capsule that, if opened, will destroy the population of the Earth. But if the capsule remains unopened for 27 days, it becomes inoperative. The world will be saved.

The humans respond with varying degrees of paranoia. Prof. Bechner tries to figure out what makes the thing work. Su kills herself. Eve throws hers away and hides with Jonathan. Ivan is arrested by the KGB and tortured. The Russians want the secret of the capsule. They open it during the 27-day period. Surprise. Only the bad people of the U.S.S.R. die. As it turns out, the alien was only joshing. Just a test of integrity, folks.

PRODUCER: Helen Ainsworth. DIRECTOR: William Asher. SCREENPLAY: John Mantley. MUSIC: Mischa Bakaleinikoff.

20,000 LEAGUES UNDER THE SEA
There are various film versions of JULES VERNE's novel concerning the exploits of master inventor Captain Nemo and his futuristic submarine, the *Nautilus*.
Star (France, 1907). Silent feature, colored, 930 ft.

PRODUCER AND DIRECTOR: Georges Méliès.
Universal (1906). B/w silent feature, 11 reels.

In this version, Nemo is an Indian prince. A secondary plot features a "child of nature," a young girl found living alone on a tropical island paradise.

DIRECTOR AND SCREENPLAY: Stuart Paton. CINEMATOGRAPHY: Eugene Gaudio.

CAST: Allen Holuber, Matt Moore, Jane Gail, Joe Welsh.
Walt Disney/Buena Vista (1954). Color/scope, 127 mins.

The definitive version of the tale and undoubtedly the finest cinematic adaptation of any of Jules Verne's works. Professor Aronnax (Paul Lukas) and his aide Conseil (Peter Lorre), along with harpoonist Ned Land (Kirk Douglas), are searching the oceans for a legendary sea beast that has reportedly been attacking warships in the Atlantic. The beast surfaces and rams Aronnax's ship, knocking the threesome overboard. They are rescued by men in strange undersea garb and brought aboard the monster, which turns out to be the futuristic submarine *Nautilus*.

Built, designed, and operated by brilliant Captain Nemo (James Mason), the sub is an atomic-powered craft built in the vague design of an aquatic creature to fool aboveworlders. Nemo's mission in life is to rid the world of warmongers, and so he patrols the seas, sinking warships. His own family, it seems, perished because of the folly of such militaristic types. "They are the assassins," he states, "the dealers in death. I am the avenger."

During a healthy sea battle with one of the warships, the *Nautilus* sustains damage that forces her to retreat. Pausing to repair the craft, Nemo and the men are attacked by a giant squid. It is Ned Land who rescues the captain. Convinced that his three guests are men of honor, he tells the professor of the island laboratory where he conducts his secret experiments. He also tells the professor that if he could be convinced that all nations would live peacefully with one another, he would gladly turn over the secret of atomic energy to them. Aronnax is overjoyed. Humanity is now at a scientific turning point, thanks to the captain.

Ned, meanwhile, begins dropping a

series of notes-in-bottles off the side of the ship, pinpointing the location of the island. When Nemo surfaces in his home port, he is fired upon by a fleet of warships that clearly have gotten Ned's message. Aronnax's dreams of progress are shattered. The warships grow nearer. Nemo rushes ashore and booby-traps his lab. Returning to the *Nautilus*, he is mortally wounded. After Ned, Conseil, and the professor are cast adrift in a lifeboat, Nemo takes his ship to the ocean floor. His island blows up in an atomic explosion to end all screen detonations. Seconds later, the *Nautilus*, too, commits mechanical suicide.

Wonderful acting, excellent scripting, and eye-boggling special effects make this a perfect cinematic undertaking.

PRODUCER: Walt Disney. DIRECTOR: Richard Fleischer. SCREENPLAY: Earl Fenton. ART DIRECTOR: John Meehan. CINEMATOGRAPHY: Franz Planer. SPECIAL EFFECTS: John Hench, Josh Meadors, and Ub Iwerks. MATTE PAINTINGS: Peter Ellenshaw. SPECIAL EFFECTS CINEMATOGRAPHY: Ralph Hammeras. UNDERWATER CINEMATOGRAPHY: Till Gabbani. MUSIC: Paul Smith.

Supply and Demand

"The bodies we use in our dissection for lecture purposes were not perfect enough for him, he said. He wanted us to supply him with other bodies, and we were not to be too particular as to where and how we got them."

Edward Van Sloan to Mae Clarke in *Frankenstein*

SUPPORTING PLAYERS: Robert Wilke, Percy Helton, Fred Graham, Ted Cooper, Ted de Corsia.

TWILIGHT PEOPLE, THE
Dimension (1972). Color, 84 mins.

A crazy scientist on a South Pacific island passes the time by creating a race of part-animal, part-human beings —his own version of the master race. Present and accounted for are a panther-man, an ape-man, a bat-man, a wolf-man, and an antelope-man. When his wife begins to get a bit disgusted with the results of his labor, he turns her into a tree-woman. No sense of humor whatsoever.

PRODUCERS: John Ashley, Eddie Romero. SCREENPLAY: Jerome Small, Eddie Romero. OPTICAL EFFECTS: Richard Abelardo. MUSIC: Ariston Avelino, Tito Arevalo.

CAST: John Ashley, Pat Woodell, Jan Merlin, Pam Grier, Charles Macauley, Ken Metcalfe, Tony Gonsalvez.

TWONKY, THE
UA (1953). B/w, 72 mins.

Terry (Hans Conreid) feels like burning every issue of *TV Guide* in sight when his new TV set is possessed by an alien life-force from the future. The creature wishes only to serve Terry. Terry only wishes the creature to turn itself off and go away. The TV begins to run the household, doing the housework, walking, talking. Terry plots to do it in. The TV acts to defend itself. The FCC ignores the stand-off. Based on a story by HENRY KUTTNER, this updated version changes the object of unreal animation from a large radio-record playing console to a TV set. Futurism at work.

PRODUCER AND DIRECTOR: Arch Oboler. SCREENPLAY: Obler. MUSIC: Jack Meakin.

SUPPORTING PLAYERS: Janet Warren, Al Jarvis, Ed Max.

2001: A SPACE ODYSSEY
MGM (1968). Super Panavision and Metrocolor, 141 mins.

Depending on which school of criticism one ascribes to, this film is either the "ultimate trip" or the "ultimate bore." In truth, it's probably a bit of both. Based on ARTHUR C. CLARKE's tidy little tale "The Sentinel," this, the *Quo Vadis* of space films, traces the effects of alien intelligence on human development.

Unseen aliens first land on Earth during prehistoric times, when a titanic monolith appears in the midst of a tribe of ape-men, taking them to a higher plane of thought. When modern scientists begin trying to link the appear-

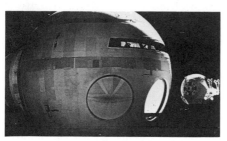

2001: A Space Odyssey

ances of these structures throughout history to a specific intelligence, they reach a conclusion that whatever is giving humanity a helping hand is centered on or near the planet Jupiter.

Astronauts David Bowman (Keir Dullea) and Frank Poole (Gary Lockwood) are sent with three other astronauts to check this theory out. All functions aboard their vessel, *Discovery 1,* are controlled by omniscient computer HAL (the voice of Douglas Rain). The astronauts are less than pleased when HAL decides to sabotage the flight, first killing the three astronauts frozen in a state of suspended animation and then murdering Poole while that astronaut attempts to make a repair on the ship's outer hull.

Bowman dismantles HAL. The ship is then sucked into some sort of time/space tunnel. Bowman meets the life-giving alien force head-on in a phantasmagoric display of sight and sound. The monolith appears. Bowman watches himself age and die. He emerges from traditional death as an embryonic space-child.

PRODUCER AND DIRECTOR: Stanley Kubrick. SCREENPLAY: Kubrick, Arthur C. Clarke. MUSIC: excerpts from the works of Richard Strauss, Ligeti, Aram Khachaturian, and Johann Strauss. MAKEUP: Stuart Freeborn. PRODUCTION DESIGN: Tony Masters, Harry Lange, Ernest Archer. ART DIRECTOR: John Hoelsi. SPECIAL EFFECTS: Stanley Kubrick, Wally Veevers, Douglas Trumbull, Con Pederson, Tom Howard. ASSISTANT SPECIAL EFFECTS: Colin Cantwell, Fred Martin, David Osborne, Bryan Loftus, Bruce Logan, John Malick.

UFO
UA (1956). B/w with color footage, 92 mins.

A monotoned Tom Powers narrates this "in-depth" look at the "real" world of unidentified flying objects. "Actual" footage of flying saucers is unspooled, with some shots so poorly photographed it's difficult to find the UFO in the frame. Only in the 1950s.

EXECUTIVE PRODUCER: Ivan Tors. PRODUCER: Clarence Green. SCREENPLAY: Francis Martin. CINEMATOGRAPHY: Howard Anderson, Ed Fitzgerald, Bert Spielvogel. MUSIC: Ernest Gold.

ULTIMATE WARRIOR, THE
WB (1974). Color, 92 mins.

A nuclear holocaust erupts at the end of the 20th century, leaving the world in a desolated state. In the year 2003, a group of survivors in the heart of New York City is given protection by a mercenary soldier (Yul Brynner). After a series of hectic gang wars, the gaggle of would-be heroes decides that it's time to leave the worm-infested Big Apple in search of greener pastures. The only problem? In a world ravaged by flood, famine, and disease, greener pastures are hard to find.

PRODUCERS: Fred Weintraub, Paul Heller. DIRECTOR AND SCREENWRITER: Robert Clouse. SPECIAL EFFECTS: Gene Riggs. ART DIRECTOR: Walter Simonds.

SUPPORTING PLAYERS: Max von Sydow, Joanna Miles, William Smith, Richard Kelton.

UNDERSEA KINGDOM
Republic (1936). B/w serial, 12 chapters (25 reels).

Some sort of classic. In the lost undersea continent of Atlantis, a power struggle ensues between the white-robed followers of Sharad (William Farnum) and the Black Robe Guards, followers of the evil Unga Khan

(Monte Blue). Khan, having mastered the atom, has developed a nasty disintegrating machine that is aimed at abovewater North America. Khan, it would seem, wants to rule the world in a bad way.

The earthquakes caused by Khan's dry runs come to the attention of Professor Norton (C. Montague Shaw), who immediately reasons that the source of the unrest is coming from the ocean floor and, logically enough, from the legendary world of Atlantis. Inventing a counter-earthquake ray himself, the plucky scientist zooms to the bottom of the ocean in a rocket-powered sub, accompanied by Crash Corrigan (Crash Corrigan), a local athlete; newswoman Diana Compton (Lois Wilde); two sailors, Briny and Salty (Smiley Burnette and Frankie Marvin); and his son, Billy (Lee Van Atta).

Reaching Atlantis, the party finds the going anything but festive. Some are captured by robot "Volkites," others by the benign White Robes. Professor Norton is tossed into a transformation cabin and becomes a slave of Khan. Sharad is killed by the Black Robes when Khan activates the dreaded "projector machine" (it shoots projectiles, natch). With Atlantis crumbling, Khan plans to launch himself and his followers to the abovewater world in a fortress-turned-rocketship. Crash, however, rescues just about everyone and, reaching the surface first, alerts the navy to Khan's plans. Khan's rocket surfaces and the navy shells it to smithereens. Better living through science.

PRODUCER: Nat Levine. DIRECTORS: Breezy Eason, Joseph Kane. SCREENPLAY: J. Rathmell, Maurice Geraghty, and Oliver Drake, from a story by Rathmell and Tracy Night. CINEMATOGRAPHY: William Nobles, Edgar Lyons. MUSIC: Harry Grey.

SUPPORTING PLAYERS: Booth Howard as Ditmar, Lon Chaney, Jr., as Hakur, Jack Mulhall as Lt. Andrews, David Horsley as the navy sentry, Lane Chandler as Darius.

UNDERWATER CITY
Columbia (1962). Filmed in Eastman color and Fantascope, released initially in b/w, re-released in color; 78 mins.

A fairly excruciating excursion into soggy space. With the threat of nuclear holocaust hanging over the scientific community's heads, a group of visionaries, led by Dr. Monica Powers (Julie Adams) and Bob Gage (William Lundigan), constructs an underwater suburb designed as the ultimate fallout shelter. Eventually undersea tremors do it in.

The production was plagued by front-office warfare throughout, and it shows. Per the instructions of the studio, all the "underwater" shots were filmed "dry" on a sound stage, through a fish tank. Making matters worse, the film was initially released in black and white (much to the surprise of the producer), which turned most of the underwater scenes a murky gray.

PRODUCER: Alex Gordon. DIRECTOR: Frank McDonald. SCREENPLAY: Owen Harris. ART DIRECTOR: Don Ament. MUSIC: Ronald Stein. SPECIAL EFFECTS: Howard Lydecker, Howard A. Anderson.

SUPPORTING PLAYERS: Roy Roberts, Paul Dubov, Chet Douglas.

UNEARTHLY, THE
Republic (1957). B/w, 73 mins.

A well-intentioned madman attempts to perfect a glandular operation that will give immortality to the patient. Unfortunately, thus far the operation has proven anything but successful . . . unleashing a brood of ugly failures on the world at large.

PRODUCER AND DIRECTOR: Brooke L. Peters. SCREENPLAY: Geoffrey Dennis and Jane Mann, from a story by Mann. ART DIRECTOR: Dan Hall. MUSIC: Henry Vars, Michael Terr.

CAST: John Carradine, Allison Hayes, Myron Healey, Tor Johnson.

UNEARTHLY STRANGER, THE
AIP (1964). B/w, 72 mins.

A man's marriage is tossed neatly on the rocks when he discovers that his wife is really an alien. His uneasy mind is quieted somewhat when she suddenly dies.

PRODUCER: Albert Fennell. DIRECTOR: John Krish. SCREENPLAY: Rex Carlton. MUSIC: Edward Williams.

CAST: John Neville, Phillip Stone, Gabriella Licudi as the alien.

UNIDENTIFIED FLYING ODDBALL
Walt Disney/Buena Vista (1979). Technicolor, 93 mins.

Originally titled *A Spaceman in King Arthur's Court,* this comedy-adventure is a futuristic version of the Mark Twain classic *A Connecticut Yankee in King Arthur's Court.* NASA ace inventor Tom Trimble (Dennis Dugan) and his look-alike robot are inadvertently hurled into space in a shuttle craft and, zipping into a time warp, land on Earth in Merrie Olde England. Touching down during the reign of King Arthur (Kenneth More), Trimble and his robot pal are pursued by evil Sir Modred (Jim Dale) and Merlin (Ron Moody), who see him as a threat to their plan to take over the kingdom. Lovely Alisande (Sheila White), however, knows Tom's heart is true. Together they prove his honesty, and with a little help from such NASA inventions as a flying chair, a long-range ray gun, and a fireproof space suit, Tom saves King Arthur's throne from the pressure of evil pants.

PRODUCER: Ron Miller. DIRECTOR: Russ Mayberry. SCREENPLAY: Don Tait. CINEMATOGRAPHY: Paul Beeson. ART DIRECTOR: Albert Witherick. SPECIAL EFFECTS: Cliff Culley. MUSIC: Ron Goodwin.

SUPPORTING PLAYERS: John Le Mesurier as Sir Gawain, Rodney Bewes as Clarence, Robert Beatty as Senator Milburn, Cyril Shaps as Zimmerman.

Walt Disney Prod.

Unidentified Flying Oddball

UNKNOWN TERROR, THE
20th Cent.-Fox (1957). B/w, 77 mins.

A deranged scientist uses the legendary Cave of Death in the Caribbean jungle as a dodge for his latest insane experiment: the development of a supersudsy, lethal fungus. His plan? To overrun the world with what looks like soap bubbles. Will the good scientists be able to stop him? If they can't —dynamite.

PRODUCER: Robert Stabler. DIRECTOR: Charles Marquis Warren. SCREENPLAY: Kenneth Higgins. ART DIRECTOR: James W. Sullivan. CINEMATOGRAPHY: Joseph Biroc. MUSIC: Raoul Kraushaar.

CAST: John Howard, Mala Powers, May Wynn, Charles Gray.

UNKNOWN PURPLE, THE
Truart (1923). B/w silent feature, 6,950 ft.

A scientist imprisoned for a crime he didn't commit is finally paroled. Bitter because of his jailbird days, he returns to his lab and uses a purple-light invention to render himself invisible. Unseen by the human eye, he then goes about planning revenge on his crooked partner and his wicked wife.

PRODUCER AND DIRECTOR: Roland West. SCREENPLAY: West, Paul Schofield. CINEMATOGRAPHY: Oliver T. Marsh.

CAST: Henry B. Walthall, Johnny Arthur, Dorothy Phillips, Alice Lake, Frankie Lee.

UNKNOWN WORLD
Lippert (1950). B/w, 74 mins.

Professor Morley (Victor Kilian) leads an expedition of scientists to the center of the Earth in a drilling vessel known as the *Cyclotram.* Seeking the ultimate fallout shelter for humanity in case of atomic attack, they come across a series of gigantic caverns that form an Olympian, albeit boring, subterranean world. Although the substrata ecosystem seems perfect at first, further tests show that the atmosphere causes sterility, thus making it a less-than-ideal postholocaust paradise.

PRODUCERS: Jack Rabin, Irving Block. DIRECTOR AND EDITOR: Terrel O. Morse. SCREENPLAY: Millard Kaufman. SPECIAL EFFECTS: Irving Block, Jack Rabin, Willis Cook. MUSIC: Ernest Gold.

SUPPORTING PLAYERS: Bruce Kellogg, Marilyn Nash, Otto Waldis, George Baxter.

V

VALLEY OF THE DRAGONS
Also known as PREHISTORIC VALLEY.
Columbia (1961). B/w, 79 mins.

A low-budget adaptation of JULES VERNE's *Off on a Comet* that owes more to "Ally Oop" than it does to the legendary author. When a comet sweeps precariously close to Earth, several turn-of-the-century citizens are tossed onto its surface. Once on the heavenly body, they run into a prehistoric tribe of humans and a lot of stock dinosaur footage from the original film version of *One Million B.C.*

PRODUCER: Byron Roberts. DIRECTOR AND SCREENWRITER: Edward Bernds. MUSIC: Ruby Raskin. SPECIAL EFFECTS: Dick Albain.

CAST: Cesare Danova, Sean McClory, Gregg Martell.

VALLEY OF THE EAGLES
Independent Sovereign Films (G.B., 1951); b/w, 86 mins. Lippert (U.S., 1952); b/w, 82 mins.

An invention capable of deriving power from sound is stolen, leading heroes into a strange valley where villains train eagles to dispatch nosy heroes.

PRODUCERS: Nat A. Bronsten, George Willoughby. DIRECTOR AND SCREENWRITER: Terence Young, from a story by Paul Tabori and N. A. Bronsten. ART DIRECTOR: J. Edder Wills. CINEMATOGRAPHY: Harry Waxman. MUSIC: Nino Rota.

CAST: Jack Warner, Nadia Gray, Anthony Dawson, Christopher Lee.

VALLEY OF THE ZOMBIES
Republic (1946). B/w, 56 mins.

A scientist with a lust for life returns from the dead and stays alive by draining the blood of a fellow scientist. He is killed for the second time at the film's conclusion, leaving puzzled audiences to wonder where the rest of the valley's zombies have been hiding for the preceding 55½ minutes.

DIRECTOR: Philip Ford. SCREENPLAY: Dorrell and Stuart McGowan, from a story by Royal K. Cole and Sherman L. Lowe. ART DIRECTOR: Hilyard Brown. MAKEUP: Bob Mark. CINEMATOGRAPHY: Reggie Lanning. SPECIAL EFFECTS: Howard and Theodore Lydecker. MUSIC: Richard Cherwin.

CAST: Robert Livingston, Adrian Booth, Ian Keith, Earle Hodings, Wilton Graff.

VANISHING SHADOW, THE
Universal (1934). B/w serial, 12 chapters.

Stanley Stanfield (Onslow Stevens) is understandably annoyed when a group of corrupt politicians drives his father to an early grave via a smear campaign. With the help of nicely-demented Professor Carl Van Dorn (James Durkin), Stanley embarks on a vendetta that includes the use of a vanishing belt, a destroying ray, and a wonderfully beak-nosed robot. The leader of the crooks, Ward Barnett (Walter Miller), suspects Stanley of hatching some sort of weird scheme and promptly has the avenging angel framed for a murder. Undaunted, Stanley and the professor come up with even more sf wonders, and soon Barnett and cronies Kent (Eddie Cobb), Dorgan (Richard Cramer), and Denny (Sidney Bracey) are on the run. Caught somewhere in the middle of all this is Stanley's sweetheart, Gloria (Ada Ince), who also happens to be nasty Mr. Barnett's offspring. And you thought you had troubles.

DIRECTOR: Louis Friedlander. SCREENPLAY: Het Manheim, Basil Dickey, and George Morgan, from a story by Ella O'Neill. ART DIRECTOR: Thomas F. O'Neill. CINEMATOGRAPHY: Richard Fryer.

SUPPORTING PLAYERS: Tom London, Monte Montague, William Steele.

VARAN THE UNBELIEVABLE
Toho (Japan, 1958); b/w, 87 mins. Crown International (U.S., 1962); b/w, 70 mins.

Hot on the heels of scientific-goof-caused monster Godzilla comes . . . Varan, a large, ugly critter, justifiably temperamental after having been awakened prematurely from a millennium-long sleep. The prehistoric beast comes alive when a salt-water lake is desalinized. Varan promptly takes a walk across some of Japan's more populated areas.

PRODUCER: Tomoyuki Tanaka. PRODUCER (ENGLISH VERSION): Jerry A. Baerwitz. DIRECTOR: Inoshiro Honda. SCREENPLAY: Shinichi Sekizawa, Sid Harris. CINEMATOGRAPHY: H. Koizumi, Jack Marquette. SPECIAL EFFECTS: Eiji Tsuburaya, Howard Anderson. MUSIC: Akira Ifukube.

CAST: Myron Healy, Tsuruko Kobayashi, Kozo Nomura, Koreya Senda.

VILLAGE OF THE DAMNED
MGM (1960). B/w, 77 mins.

An eerie chiller that stands as a low-key classic of the genre. Based on JOHN WYNDHAM's brilliant novel *The Midwich Cuckoos,* the film deals with an invasion of space seedlings. After an entire British village is rendered unconscious by a space mist, the military enters the picture. As British mobile units approach the town, the citizens slowly awaken. In the ensuing weeks, 12 women find themselves pregnant. Several are unmarried and, of those, some claim to be virgins. The 12 children who are born all bear the same physical characteristics (fair hair and fair skin) and personality traits (a total lack of emotion, an aloof manner). Physicist Gordon Zellaby (George Sanders) and wife Anthea (Barbara Shelley) find themselves the parents of the "leader" of the children, David (Martin Stephens).

As the children get older it becomes evident that they possess superior intellectual and telepathic prowess. They avoid the other children of the town, band together, and when gathered, unleash their psi abilities with lethal force. Zellaby concludes that the children were sired by the cosmic cloud and are alien in nature—space half-breeds. The children become aware of the scientist's suspicions and, rather than destroy him, respect him for his deduc-

MGM

Village of the Damned

tive powers and take him into their fold. Although intellectually honored, Zellaby sees the potential menace represented by the brood.

On occasion, the children have used their unusual powers to kill and destroy. In a well-planned maneuver, Zellaby begins to concentrate on refining his own mental skills. Carrying a bomb into a small schoolhouse, he gathers all the children with him for a routine "lesson." The children are suspicious. They unleash a series of devastating mental probes in his direction. He successfully wards off their telepathic feelers by envisioning a brick wall. As their mental talons rip the bricks, one by one, from the imagined wall, the bomb ticks away. Zellaby and the children perish in the film's explosive climax.

An intelligent, literate, and well-directed example of speculative fiction on the screen.

PRODUCER: Ronald Kinnoch. DIRECTOR: Wolf Rilla. SCREENPLAY: Rilla, Sterling Silliphant, George Barclay. MUSIC: Ron Goodwin. SPECIAL EFFECTS: Tom Howard.

SUPPORTING PLAYERS: Michael Gwynne, John Phillips, Richard Vernon.

VILLAGE OF THE GIANTS
Embassy (1965). Color, 80 mins.

An epic idea with a pigmy-sized script.

A scientific genius discovers a spongy substance that makes anyone who eats it grow to gigantic proportions. It falls into the hands of a half-dozen rebellious teenagers who eat the stuff "for kicks." They grow and take over the town. Mike (Tommy Kirk) and pint-sized companion Genius (Ronny Howard) attempt to slow down the giants. The giants, led by Fred (Beau Bridges), are cut down to size in the finale with a hastily concocted antidote. Before the final shrinkage, however, several twist parties are held featuring The Beau Brummels, Freddy Cannon, and Mike Clifford, and actors such as Johnny Crawford (as Horsey) and Joy Harmon (as Merrie) get to shake their individual booties next to 25-foot mutant ducks.

PRODUCER AND DIRECTOR: Bert I. Gordon. SCREENPLAY: Alan Caillou, based on an adaptation by Gordon of *Food of the Gods*, by H. G. WELLS. ART DIRECTOR: Franz Bachelin. CINEMATOGRAPHY: Paul C. Vogel. SPECIAL EFFECTS: Bert and Flora Gordon. MUSIC: Jack Nitzche.

SUPPORTING PLAYERS: Timmy Rooney, Tisha Sterling, Joe Turkel.

VIOLET RAY, THE
General (1917). B/w silent featurette, one reel.

Part of the *Grant, Police Reporter* series, this potboiler was highlighted by a ray machine that could blind humans.

DIRECTOR: Robert Ellis. SCREENPLAY: Robert Welles Ritchie.

CAST: George Larkin, Harry Gordon, Robert Ellis.

VISIT TO A SMALL PLANET
Paramount (1960). B/w, 85 mins.

Alien humanoid Kreton (Jerry Lewis) lives up to his name in this slapstick adaptation of Gore Vidal's satirical sf play. Kreton arrives on Earth to study human behavior. His after-school activities, however, cause quite a few problems. He falls in love with the daughter (Joan Blackman) of a right-wing news commentator (Fred Clark) and embarks on a pratfall-laden lifestyle that makes Abbott and Costello seem reserved in comparison. He's telepathic, superhuman, and has an on-again, off-again force field at his disposal.

PRODUCER: Hal Wallis. DIRECTOR:

Norman Taurog. SCREENPLAY: Edmond Beloin, Henry Garson. MUSIC: Leight Harline. MAKEUP: Wally Westmore. SPECIAL EFFECTS: John P. Fulton.

SUPPORTING PLAYERS: Earl Holliman, Gale Gordon, John Williams as Kreton's alien boss.

VOODOO HEARTBEAT
TWI National (1972). Color, 88 mins.

A group of spies chase a missing formula for eternal youth into the deepest wilds of Las Vegas. A fellow downs the formula, not realizing it has been purloined from a voodoo ceremony without written permission from the voodoo-ers. The serum turns him into an ugly vampire-monster. Adding insult to injury, when he is finally killed, he ages into a wizened old cadaver.

PRODUCER: Ray Molina. DIRECTOR AND SCREENWRITER: Charles Nizet.

CAST: Ray Molina, Ray Molina, Jr., Philip Ahn, Ern Dugo, Forrest Duke, Evvy Rhodes.

VOODOO WOMAN
AIP (1957). B/w, 77 mins.

A sexist scientist headquartered in a jungle attempts to change local women into obedient slaves. But old Doctor Butterfingers slips up and creates a clique of monsters instead.

PRODUCER: Alex Gordon. DIRECTOR: Edward L. Cahn. SCREENPLAY: Russell Bender, V. I. Voss. ART DIRECTOR: Frederick E. West. MUSIC: Darrell Calker.

CAST: Marla English, Tom Conway, Touch Connors, Lance Fuller, Paul Blaisdell.

VOYAGE INTO SPACE
AIP (1968). Color, 98 mins.

A haphazardly dubbed Americanization of a Toho (Japan) sf adventure designed for children. A little boy controls the strength of a titanic robot. An evil emperor from space, meanwhile, wants to control titanic planet Earth. The aliens buzz the planet in oval spaceships and the robot bats them into oblivion like a true Reggie Jackson fan.

PRODUCER: Salvatore Billitteri.

VOYAGE TO A PREHISTORIC PLANET

AIP (1965). Color, 78 mins.

An sf melodrama in which everyone looks appropriately embarrassed, this epic is made up of a rather large hunk of footage culled from PLANET OF THE STORMS, a 1962 U.S.S.R. release. In the year 2020, cosmonaut Marcia (Faith Domergue) orbits the planet Venus while two astronauts and a robot journey to the surface. Also on hand to observe the exploration from a distance is the fairly disinterested Professor Hartman (Basil Rathbone, showing obvious disdain for his role in a movie in which the set used in his segments was not even completed on the first day of his shooting schedule). The explorers are attacked by the usual crew of prehistoric beasts and dialogue. They lose their robot and nearly their skins in a volcanic eruption that engulfs the planet. They conclude that the Venusians were really human beings who destroyed their civilization with nuclear warfare.

PRODUCER: George Edwards. DIRECTOR AND SCREENPLAY: John Sebastian. CINEMATOGRAPHY: Vilis Lapenieks. MUSIC: Ronald Stein.

SUPPORTING PLAYERS: Mark Shannon, Christopher Brand, John Bix, Robert Chanta.

VOYAGE TO THE BOTTOM OF THE SEA

20th Cent.-Fox (1961). Color, 105 mins.

Made by Irwin Allen before that producer turned his attention to such disaster-laden efforts as *The Towering Inferno* and *The Poseidon Adventure*, this spectacular thriller recounts the maiden voyage of the atomic-powered submarine *Seaview*. Commanded by Admiral Harriman Nelson (Walter Pidgeon) and staffed by such stiff upper-lips as Capt. Lee Crane (Robert Sterling), Commodore Lucius Emery (Peter Lorre), Miguel Alvarez (Michael Ansara), Chip Romano (Frankie Avalon), and Dr. Susan Hiller (Joan Fontaine), the *Seaview* is chugging along beneath the Antarctic when it is discovered that the ice caps are melting. The Van Allen radiation belts have

20th Cent.-Fox

Voyage to the Bottom of the Sea

burst into flame, and that means hot stuff for planet Earth. Nelson concocts a plan wherein the glass-nosed sub is to launch a Polaris missile into the belt, its detonation causing the flame barrier to tumble upward into the vacuum of space. World leaders think the admiral is not quite playing with a full deck, so the *Seaview* and its crew take matters into their own hands. Pursued by irate warships, submarines, and a giant squid, the *Seaview* reaches the proposed Antarctic launch site, fires the rocket, and saves the day, the movie, and the world.

PRODUCER AND DIRECTOR: Irwin Allen. SCREENPLAY: Allen and Charles Bennett, from a story by Allen. ART DIRECTORS: Jack Martin Smith, Herman A. Blumenthal. CINEMATOGRAPHY: Winton Hoch. SPECIAL EFFECTS: Lyle B. Abbott. MUSIC: Paul Sawtell, Bert Shefter.

SUPPORTING PLAYERS: Barbara Eden, Regis Toomey, Henry Daniell.

VOYAGE TO THE END OF THE UNIVERSE

Czechoslovakia (1963); color, 91 mins. AIP (U.S., 1965); b/w, 65 mins.

Not as harrowing as its title implies, *Voyage* is an sf morality tale with a twist. Apparently edited with an axe for Stateside release, the film was released in Europe as *Ikaria XB-1*. The crew of the spaceship *Icarus*—Anthony Hopkins (Francis Smolen), Nina Kirova (Dana Medricks), Commander Vladimir Abajev (Zdenek Stepanek), Michael (Otto Lack), and McDonald (Radovan Lakavsky)—search the universe for a planet to call home, turning their backs on their world of origin because of its corrupt nature. En route, the ship is engulfed by a mysterious radioactive cloud. The crew members at first experience a mild case of paranoia, then deep slumber. They are awakened by a benign ray transmitted from a nearby planet. The world, apparently, has spotted the ship's plight and decided to save it from destruction. The crew is edified. They have found their final destination: a planet of compassion and kindness. They full-throttle head for their new home—a planet called Earth by its inhabitants.

But Will It Fly?
Imagine a house with a movable picture window and on that window, there's a housefly. That fly is our saucer.
Warner Keillor explaining how his UFOs "flew" on the screen for *Starship Invasions (Alien Encounter)*

PRODUCER: Rudolph Wohl. DIRECTOR: Jindrich Polak. SCREENPLAY: Pavel Juracek, Polak. SPECIAL EFFECTS: Jan Kulls, Mila Nejedly, Jiri Hilupy.

VOYAGE TO THE PLANET OF PREHISTORIC WOMEN
AIP (1968). Color, 78 mins.

Prehistoric in both plot and execution, this experiment in tedium is actually composed of about half the footage to be found in the Soviet film PLANET OF THE STORMS. A group of spacemen land on a planet populated by less-than-futuristic females. They lock horns with their prehistoric peers and match wits with dinosaurs. For most of the movie, it's a pretty even fight. Finally the women use their telepathic powers to drive the astronauts off their world.
PRODUCER: Norman Wells. DIRECTOR AND NARRATOR: Derek Thomas (a pseudonym used by Peter Bogdanovich while in the employ of Roger Corman). SCREENPLAY: Henry Nay. MAKEUP: Mary Jo Wier.
CAST: Mamie Van Doren, Mary Mark, Paige Lee.

VULTURE, THE
G.B. (1966); color, 91 mins. Paramount (U.S., 1967); b/w, 91 mins.

An aged scientist (Akim Tamiroff) attempts to steal a buried treasure through the use of a matter-transference machine. The treasure, buried off the Cornwall seacoast, was stashed along with the bodies of a male witch and his vulture/pet. When the machine's beam zips up the molecules from beneath the sea, it snatches the wrong sets and, slamming them into the body of the scientist, creates a creature with a man's head and arms but a vulture's body, legs, and wings. Shortly after the incident, ravaged bodies begin to show up in strange, high-up places. Hmmm. Some mystery.
PRODUCER, DIRECTOR, AND SCREENWRITER: Lawrence Huntington. ART DIRECTOR: Duncan Sutherland. MAKEUP: Geoffrey Rodway. CINEMATOGRAPHY: Stephen Dade. MUSIC: Eric Spear.
CAST: Robert Hutton, Broderick Crawford, Diane Clare, Monty Landis.

WAR BETWEEN THE PLANETS
Mercury/Southern Cross (Italy, 1965), Fanfare (U.S., 1971). Color, 80 mins.

A planet controlled by an alien electronic brain is headed for Earth on a collision course. Earth's finest spacemen intervene.
PRODUCERS: Joseph Fryd, Antonio Margheriti, Walter Manley. DIRECTOR: Margheriti. SCREENPLAY: Ivan Reiner, Margheriti. CINEMATOGRAPHY: Riccardo Pallottini. MUSIC: Francesco Lavagnino.
CAST: Jack Stuart, Amber Collins, Peter Martell, Archie Savage.

WAR GAME, THE
BBC (G.B., 1965); b/w, 50 mins. Pathé Contemporary (U.S., 1966); b/w, 47 mins.

Originally produced by the BBC but never shown on TV by that network, this chilling pseudodocumentary predicts life in England following an all-out nuclear attack. Reality and prophecy mix as real news footage is intermingled with bogus news reports and staged interviews portraying the fate of the British survivors.

PRODUCER, DIRECTOR, AND SCREENWRITER: Peter Watkins. ART DIRECTORS: Tony Cornell, Anne Davey. MAKEUP: Lilias Munro. CINEMATOGRAPHY: Peter Bartlette.

NARRATION: Michael Aspel, Dick Graham.

WAR GODS OF THE DEEP
AIP (1965). Color/scope, 84 mins.

Allegedly based on EDGAR ALLAN POE'S poem "City in the Sea," this briny adventure has more kinship to *Flipper*. Young Ben Harris (Tab Hunter), a visitor on the Cornish coast, falls in love with American Jill Tregellis (Susan Hart), also visiting the area. While visiting with Jill, her artist friend Harold Tiffin Jones (David Tomlinson), and the latter's chicken, Herbert (Herbert), Ben watches helplessly as the love of his life is kidnapped by a strange fish-man.

Smelling fowl play, as well as seaweed, Ben and Harold (and Herbert, a.k.a. comedy relief) trace the fin prints to a secret passageway in Jill's mansion that leads to a grotto. The grotto crumbles and all three are sucked down into the mysterious undersea city run by the equally mysterious Captain (Vincent Price). The domed city, filled with air provided by massive pumps, houses a few hundred humans. Outside the city swim the gill-men. Price is regarded as a sort of god by the fish folk and they depend on him to quell a soon-to-erupt undersea volcano. Luckily Ben is a famous geologist and seismologist, a recognized expert on earthquake phenomena and volcanos. To make a long story short, Price thinks Jill is the reincarnation of his long-dead wife. Ben thinks Price is crazy. Price is. The city shakes. The volcano explodes. The abovesea citizens (chicken included) make it to the top as the undersea civilization is buried. The Captain follows his lost love topside, makes a slight miscalculation regarding the effects of fresh air on a

seemingly immortal fellow who has lived for nearly a century beneath the briny blue, and crumbles into a heap of ashes.

PRODUCER: Daniel Haller. DIRECTOR: Jacques Tourneur. SCREENPLAY: Charles Bennett, Louis M. Heyward. SPECIAL EFFECTS: Frank George, Les Bowie. UNDERWATER DIRECTOR AND CINEMATOGRAPHER: John Lamb. MUSIC: Stanley Black.

WARNING FROM SPACE
Also known as MYSTERIOUS SATELLITE.
Daiei (Japan, 1956), AIT (U.S., 1963). Color, 87 mins.

Star-shaped creatures from another world visit Earth to warn the scientific world about the dangers of nuclear experimentation. The cyclopean creatures assume human form in order to get their message across and can only be spotted in a crowd by their superhuman powers.

PRODUCER: Masichi Nagata. DIRECTOR: Hoki Shima. SCREENPLAY: Hideo Oguni.

CAST: Toyomi Karita, Kiyoko Hirai, Bontaro Miake.

WAR OF DREAMS
Selig (1915). B/w silent short, three reels.

A scientist invents an explosive that can be detonated by dream waves. Falling asleep, the inventor dreams of the horror that could result from the explosive if it is misused. Upon awakening, he destroys his notes.

DIRECTOR: E. A. Martin. SCREENPLAY: W. E. Wing.

CAST: Edwin Wallock, Lillian Hayward.

WAR OF THE COLOSSAL BEAST
AIP (1958). B/w with a color finale, 68 mins.

If moviegoers thought nuclear-blast survivor Col. Manning had problems in THE AMAZING COLOSSAL MAN, they hadn't reckoned on the mountain of woe concocted for him in this sequel. Transformed into a giant in the first film, the hapless army staffer fell apparently to his death from Boulder Dam. Unfortunately, he survived. His good looks, however, did not. Looking a bit like a badly made clay pot as the result of his fall, the totally deranged giant (Dean Parkin) scares the daylights out of villagers in Mexico. Brought back to Los Angeles by scientists, the colonel escapes but is given a good tongue-lashing by his spunky sister (Sally Fraser). Realizing the error of his ways, Manning reaches out for a high-tension wire and, in the film's only color sequence, french-fries his fingers and, ergo, the rest of his colossal self.

PRODUCER, DIRECTOR, AND SPECIAL EFFECTS CREATOR: Bert I. Gordon. SCREENPLAY: George Worthing Yates, from a story by Gordon. CINEMATOGRAPHY: Jack Marta. MUSIC: Albert Glasser.

SUPPORTING CAST: Russ Bender, Roger Pace, George Becwar.

WAR OF THE PLANETS
Mercury/Southern Cross (1966). Color, running time unknown.

In the 21st century, a horde of Martian light-creatures attempts to invade Earth. Their success is short-lived: they're light but not bright.

PRODUCERS: Joseph Fryd, Anthony Dawson, Walter Manley. DIRECTOR: A. Margheriti. SCREENPLAY: Ivan Reiner, Renato Moretti. MUSIC: Francesco Lavagnino.

CAST: Tony Russell, Franco Nero, Lisa Gastoni, Michel Lemoine.

WAR OF THE SATELLITES
AA (1958). B/w, 66 mins.

A group of conservative aliens kidnaps a horde of Earth scientists and takes over their minds in a forceful attempt to stop Earth from exploring the rest of the galaxy. The scientists are held captive aboard a space station. Breaking free of their mental bonds, they attempt to blow the station, and the aliens, out of existence.

PRODUCER AND DIRECTOR: Roger Corman. SCREENPLAY: Lawrence Louis Goldman. ORIGINAL STORY AND SPECIAL EFFECTS CREATOR: Jack Rabin, Irving Block, Louis DeWitt. MUSIC: Walter Greene. CINEMATOGRAPHY: Floyd Crosby.

CAST: Dick Miller, Susan Cabot, Michael Fox.

WAR OF THE WORLDS
Paramount (1953). Technicolor, 85 mins.

One of the very few sf films made during the 1950s to be taken seriously by the public-at-large, War of the Worlds won an Oscar for its extraordinary special effects. Despite its conventional screenplay, the film managed to capture both the imagination and power of the original, cataclysmic novel.

H. G. WELLS's famous scenario involving a Martian invasion was moved from 1890 London to (then) contemporary California in this George Pal production. After a meteor crashes to Earth near a small California forest community, a group of scientists and locals—including Dr. Clayton Forrester (Gene Barry); Sylvia Van Buren (Ann Robinson); and Sylvia's uncle, Pastor Matthew Collins (Lewis Martin)—investigates the scene. When the crowd departs the scene for a barn dance, a small patrol is left to guard the meteor and its accompanying crater.

Covered by darkness, the meteor comes to life. The "top" unscrews and a large, tendriled orb arises from within. The sentries approach the cyclopean device and are distintegrated by a death ray shot from the "eye." Before long, a full-scale invasion is apparently underway. Forrester realizes the meteor is, in reality, a Martian spaceship. The U.S. Army arrives, led by Gen. Mann (Les Tremayne). He reveals that "meteors" of this type have been falling all over the world. In every case, communication from the crash site areas has been lost.

The army prepares an attack. The Martians arise from the crater in large, hovering death machines. Half of the army forces are slaughtered. Pastor Collins is zapped rather unceremoniously when, trusty Bible in hand, he approaches the Martian ships speaking words of peace and understanding.

Panic breaks out. Clayton and Sylvia, separated from the main force, take refuge in an abandoned farmhouse. They are met by a tentacled Martian telescope. Clayton wrenches off its eyepiece. A small Martian (Charles Gemora) slithers into the room and makes a grab at Sylvia.

Paramount

War of the Worlds

Paramount

War of the Worlds

Clayton turns his trusty flashlight on the Martian's face and the thing scurries off.

The twosome make it back to Los Angeles, where, in a science lab, Clayton and colleagues Dr. Pryor (Bob Cornthwaite), Dr. Bilderbeck (Sandro Gigilo), Professor McPherson (Edgar Barrier), Dr. James (Alex Fraser), and Dr. Duprey (Anne Codee) connect the Martian telescopic eye to a projector and discover that the Martians perceive Earthlings in a very distorted manner.

Meanwhile, the Martians are seeing the country in an equally twisted way, setting cities and citizens by the thousands on fire. The death ships attack Los Angeles. The city panics. Riots break out. Slaughter fills the streets. As the Martians ready for the final kill, their machines sputter to a stop. The Martians topple out dead . . . victims of common Earth germs, harmless to Earthlings who have built up evolutionary immunity but quite lethal to the mighty Martians.

PRODUCER: George Pal. DIRECTOR: Byron Haskin. SCREENPLAY: Barre Lyndon. MUSIC: Leith Stevens. SPECIAL EFFECTS: Gordon Jennings, Wallace Kelly, Jan Domela, Paul Lerpae, Ivyl Burkes, Irmin Roberts. SOUND EFFECTS: Gene Garvin. ASTRONOMICAL ART: Chesley Bonestell. MARTIAN COSTUME: Charles Gemora, from a design by Albert Nozaki. MAKEUP: Wally West-

more. MINIATURES: Marcel (KING KONG) Delgado.

SUPPORTING PLAYERS: Paul Frees as the Radio Announcer, Sir Cedric Hardwicke as the narrator, Ivan Lebedoff as Dr. Gratzman, Jack Kruschen as Salvatore.

WASP WOMAN, THE
AA (1960). B/w, 66 mins.

The head of a cosmetics company attempts to develop a rejuvenating cream using fluid distilled from wasp enzymes. The cream causes her wrinkles to disappear. Unfortunately, it also causes a few stingers to appear. Turned into a wasp-creature after prolonged usage of the beauty aid, the woman goes on a killing spree.

PRODUCER AND DIRECTOR: Roger Corman. SCREENPLAY: Leo Lordon, from a story by Kinta Zertuche. ART DIRECTOR: Daniel Haller. CINEMATOGRAPHY: Harry Newman. MUSIC: Fred Katz.

CAST: Susan Cabot, Fred Eisley, Michael Mark, Frank Wolff.

WAY . . . WAY OUT!
20th Cent.-Fox (1966). Color/scope, 106 mins.

An alleged comedy concerning the repressed libidos of a Russian-American astronaut team (Jerry Lewis and Dick Shawn) and the problems they face when perky Connie Stevens and sultry Anita Ekberg set up shop a crater away on the Moon. Neat, huh?

PRODUCER: Malcolm Stuart. DIRECTOR: Gordon Douglas. SCREENPLAY: William Bowers, Laslo Vadnay. CINEMATOGRAPHY: William H. Clothier. SPECIAL EFFECTS: Lyle B. Abbott, Emil Kosa, Jr., and Howard Lydecker. MUSIC: Lalo Shifrin.

20th Cent.-Fox

Way . . . Way Out!

WEREWOLF, THE
Columbia (1956). B/w, 78 mins.

Two scientists, in search of a cure for radiation poisoning, inject a local citizen (Don Megowan) with a newly discovered serum. The man promptly turns into a werewolf. Happily enough, however, he never again has to worry about radiation poisoning.

PRODUCER: Sam Katzman. DIRECTOR: Fred F. Sears. SCREENPLAY: Robert E. Kent, James B. Gordon. ART DIRECTOR: Paul Palmentola. CINEMATOGRAPHY: Edwin Linden. MUSICAL DIRECTOR: Mischa Bakaleinikoff.

CAST: Steven Ritch, Joyce Holden, Kim Charney, Ken Christy.

WEREWOLF OF LONDON, THE
Universal (1935). B/w, 75 mins.

An exceedingly literate script keeps this sf-horror tale a bona fide thriller from start to finish. Botanist Dr. Glendon (Henry Hull) is attacked by a strange creature while on an expedition in Tibet to gather specimens of the mariphasa lumina lupina . . . a strange flower that blooms only under the rays of the moon.

Returning to London with his samples, he is hounded by the cryptic Dr. Yogami (Warner Oland), who states only that the two have met before, in Tibet. As it turns out, Yogami is the werewolf who attacked Glendon. Survival of the mariphasa is paramount, he states, in that it is the only antidote known for lycanthropy (werewolfism). Mrs. Glendon (Valerie Hobson) is quite annoyed when her husband takes to roaming the streets of London at night. Unbeknownst to her, Glendon is now a werewolf and lusts for blood and human flesh on moonlit evenings. When Yogami attempts to pilfer Glendon's mariphasa blossoms, the botanist kills the thief. Glendon attempts to deal with his fate realistically and tries to have himself entombed in his home. During an attack of lycanthropy, however, he escapes and is killed by the London police.

PRODUCER: Stanley Bergerman. DIRECTOR: Stuart Walker. SCREENPLAY: John Colton, from a story by Robert Harris. MAKEUP: Jack Pierce. CINEMATOGRAPHY: Charles Stumar.

SUPPORTING PLAYERS: Spring Byington, Lester Matthews, Zeffie Tilbury, Ethel Griffies.

WESTWORLD
MGM (1973). Color, 91 mins.

Robots missing a few vital cogs are the stars of this exceedingly literate sf tale of terror. Delos is an amusement park designed for the rich. For the tab of $1,000 a day, a guest can stay in exotic Medievalworld, Romanworld, or Westworld. Populated by robot citizens who look totally human, each world is designed to bring total pleasure to its human guests. Businessmen outdraw gunslingers; certified public accountants make love to the most beautiful "women" in history.

Tourists Peter Martin (Richard Benjamin) and John Blane (James Brolin)

MGM

Westworld

are taking in the sights in Westworld when the robots revolt. Blane is slaughtered by the Gunslinger robot (Yul Brynner). All the human guests are slaughtered. The final showdown pits the very nervous Martin against the very lethal Gunslinger robot.

PRODUCER: Paul Lazarus, Jr. DIRECTOR AND SCREENWRITER: MICHAEL CRICHTON. CINEMATOGRAPHY: Gene Polito. MUSIC: Fred Karlin.

SUPPORTING PLAYERS: Dick Van Patten, Alan Oppenheimer, Majel Barrett, Victoria Shaw.

WHAT'S SO BAD ABOUT FEELING GOOD?
Universal (1968). Color, 94 mins.

A strange virus that causes happiness is spread throughout New York City when an infected toucan takes a tour of the town. Panic breaks out when happy people decide to behave themselves totally. Liquor sales plummet. Wall Street is in a tizzy. Where's unhappiness when you really need it?

PRODUCER AND DIRECTOR: George Seaton. SCREENPLAY: Seaton, Robert Pirosh. CINEMATOGRAPHY: Ernesto Caparros. MUSIC: Frank De Vol.

CAST: Mary Tyler Moore, George Peppard, Dom De Luise, Susan Saint James, Don Stroud, Cleavon Little, Thelma Ritter.

WHEN THE MAN IN THE MOON SEEKS A WIFE
Clarendon (1908). B/w silent short.

The Man in the Moon—in this silent short, quite a human gent, clad in a vanilla-colored suit—comes to planet Earth in a gas balloon, looking for a love.

DIRECTOR: Percy Slow. SCREENPLAY: Langford Reed.

WHEN WORLDS COLLIDE
Paramount (1951). Color, 83 mins.

Based on the book by PHILIP WYLIE and Edwin Balmer, this classic 1950s excursion into cataclysm is light-years ahead of its cinematic contemporaries. Bellus and Zyra are two runaway worlds on a collision course with Earth. Dr. Handron (Larry Keating) calculates that Zyra, which orbits around Bellus, will pass by the Earth, causing floods, earthquakes, and other major calamities. Nineteen days later, Bellus will slam into the Earth . . . completely destroying it. At that time, Bellus will take the Earth's place in orbit around our sun.

Hendron reveals his findings to the world and is regarded as a kook. Dave Randell (Richard Derr) and Tony Drake (Peter Hanson) think otherwise. (The fact that both of them are chasing after Hendron's daughter, Joyce [Barbara Rush] may have something to do with that.)

All seems lost when multimillionaire Sydney Stanton (John Hoyt) enters the scene, agreeing to finance a space ark that will take 40 Earthlings to temperate Zyra to begin civilization anew . . . Stanton being one of the 40, natch.

Construction of the ship is completed just as all hell breaks loose on Earth. New York City is submerged. Sections of Europe are shaken to bits. Just before the ark is about to take off, the construction workers chosen to stay behind riot. The ship takes off just in time, eventually landing safely on the lush world of Zyra.

PRODUCER: George Pal. DIRECTOR: Rudolph Mate. SCREENPLAY: Sydney Boehm. CINEMATOGRAPHY: John F. Seitz, W. Howard Greene. SPECIAL EFFECTS: Gordon Jennings, Harry Barndollar. TECHNICAL ADVISOR: Chesley Bonestell. MUSIC: Leith Stevens.

SUPPORTING PLAYERS: Mary Murphy, Laura Elliot, Stuart Whitman.

WHERE THE BULLETS FLY
Puck Films (G.B., 1966); color, 90 mins. Embassy (U.S., 1967); color, 88 mins.

Alleged spy spoof, with Tom Adams playing a James Bond–type up to his ears in espionage involving a light alloy that will allow planes to be nuclear-powered.

PRODUCER: S. J. H. Ward. DIRECTOR: John Gilling. SCREENPLAY: Michael Pittock. MAKEUP: Aldo Manganaro. CINEMATOGRAPHY: David Holmes. SPECIAL EFFECTS: Pat Moore, Les Bowie Films. MUSIC: Kenny Graham.

SUPPORTING PLAYERS: Michael Ripper, Dawn Addams, Sidney James, Suzan Farmer.

WHO?
AA (1975). Color, 93 mins.

A top American physicist is horribly mangled in an auto accident near the Berlin Wall. He is picked up by the East Germans and is saved in an operation that reconstructs his body cybernetically. Unrecognizable now, the man-machine (Joseph Bova) is hounded by FBI agent Roberts (Elliot Gould), who must determine whether the glittering humanoid is indeed physicist Martino or a dupe, psychologically conditioned by a crack communist espionage agent Azarin (Trevor Howard).

PRODUCER: Barry Levinson. DIRECTOR: Jack Gold. SCREENPLAY: John Gould, from the novel by ALGIS BUDRYS.

SUPPORTING PLAYERS: John Lehne, James Noble, Ed Grover.

WHO DONE IT?
Ealing (G.B., 1956). B/w, 85 mins.

Spies out to steal an atomic weather-controlling machine are foiled by a bumbling amateur detective (Benny Hill).

PRODUCER: Michael Relph. DIRECTOR: Basil Dearden. SCREENPLAY: T. E. B. Clarke. CINEMATOGRAPHY: Otto Heller. MUSIC: Otto Green.

SUPPORTING PLAYERS: Belinda Lee, David Kossoff, Ernest Thesiger, Thorley Walters, George Margo.

WILD IN THE SKY
AIP (1972). Color, 87 mins.

A group of youths capture an air force bomber and head for Cuba. The youths, escaped criminals, discover on board a live H-bomb, which only gives extra "oomph" to their escape plans. They are overpowered by an idealistic youth (Brandon De Wilde), who wants to bomb Fort Knox and cut off the flow of money funding the Vietnam War.

PRODUCERS AND SCREENWRITERS: William T. Naud, Dick Gautier. DIRECTOR: Naud. STORY: Naud, Gautier, Peter Marshall. CINEMATOGRAPHY: Thomas E. Spalding. MUSIC: Jerry Styner.

SUPPORTING PLAYERS: Keenan Wynn, Tim O'Connor, Dick Gautier, Robert Lansing, Larry Hovis, Bernie Koppell, Dub Taylor.

WILD IN THE STREETS
AIP (1968). Color, 97 mins.

In the not-too-distant future, a young rock idol (Christopher Jones) is used to further the career of a popular politician (Hal Holbrook). The pop star has plans of his own, however, and gets the unwitting politico to lower the voting age. Once that's done, the singer doses Congress with LSD and is elected president. Mom (Shelley Winters) is not overjoyed when sonny boy begins putting everyone over the age of 35 in concentration camps. The rock star is in for a shock, however, when he discovers that there is a healthy population of 13-year-olds who consider anyone out of their teens old hat.

PRODUCERS: James H. Nicholson, Samuel Z. Arkoff. DIRECTOR: Barry Shear. SCREENPLAY: Robert Thom. MAKEUP: Fred Williams. CINEMATOGRAPHY: Richard Moore. MUSIC: Les Baxter.

SUPPORTING PLAYERS: Diane Varsi, Ed Begley, Millie Perkins Pamela Mason, Walter Winchell, Richard Pryor, Dick Clark, Army Archerd, Melvin Belli. NARRATOR: Paul Frees.

WILD, WILD PLANET
MGM (1967). Color, 93 mins.

A group of mucho macho astronauts pursues a group of villainous female space criminals in this futuristic cops-and-robbers drama lensed in Italy.

PRODUCERS: Joseph Fryd, Antonio Margheriti (Anthony Dawson). DIRECTOR: Margheriti. SCREENPLAY: Ivan Reiner, Renato Moretti. MUSIC: Francesco Lavagnino.

CAST: Tony Russell, Umberto Raho, Franco Nero.

WITHOUT A SOUL
World (1916). B/w silent featurette, five reels.

A scientist watches helplessly as his only daughter dies. In a daring experiment, he brings her back to life using an electric ray. His ray reactivates only the body, however, and his new, soulless daughter is cruel and selfish. When she dies the second time of heart failure, he gets the message.

PRODUCER AND SCREENWRITER: James Young.

CAST: Clara Kimball Young, Alec B. Frances, Edward M. Kimball.

WIZARD, THE
Fox (1927). B/w silent feature, 5,629 ft.

An unorthodox surgeon attaches a man's head to the body of an ape. Adding insult to injury, he orders the shambling schlepp to go out at night and do in his enemies. Guess who turns on whom by the finale?

DIRECTOR: Richard Rosson. SCREENPLAY: Malcolm Stuart Boylan. CINEMATOGRAPHY: Frank Good.

CAST: Edmund Lowe, Leila Hyams, Oscar Smith, George Kotsonaros as the creature.

WIZARD OF MARS
American General (1964). Color, 81 mins.

The Yellow Brick Road of Oz is transposed to Mars in this sf parody of *The Wizard of Oz*. A rocketship full of Earthlings lands on a decidedly fantasy-oriented planet Mars. Once outside the ship, the crew encounters a civilization of magic Martians.

PRODUCER, DIRECTOR, AND SCREENWRITER: David Hewitt. TECHNICAL ADVISOR: Forrest J. Ackerman.

CAST: John Carradine, Vic McGee, Roger Gentry.

WIZARD OF OZ, THE
Radio Plays (1908). B/w silent short.

An early version of the L. FRANK BAUM fantasy.

PRODUCER: L. Frank Baum.

CAST: Frank Burns, Joseph Schrode, Grace Elder, Romol Remus.

WIZARD OF OZ, THE
Chadwick (1924). B/w silent feature.

Actor Larry Semon adapted the L. FRANK BAUM story in this ambitious effort. Semon himself starred.

PRODUCER-DIRECTOR: Larry Semon. SCREENPLAY: L. Frank Baum, Jr., Leon Lee. CINEMATOGRAPHY: H. F. Koenkamp, Frank Good, Leonard Smith.

CAST: Larry Semon, Dorothy Dann, Mary Carr, Charlie Murray, Oliver Hardy (as the Tin Woodman), Chester Conklin.

WIZARD OF OZ, THE
MGM (1939). Color, 101 mins.

Basically regarded as the finest fantasy ever put on film, *The Wizard of Oz* does contain certain sf overtones. When Dorothy (Judy Garland) is whisked off into Oz by a tornado, she encounters the Bashful Lion (Bert Lahr), the Scarecrow (Ray Bolger), and the Tin Woodman (robot) without a heart (Jack Haley). Once ensconced in the Emerald City of Oz, she meets the rather overpublicized Wizard (Frank Morgan), an ordinary soul who projects an omniscient personality via the aid of a wall filled with scientific gadgetry.

PRODUCER: Mervyn LeRoy. DIRECTOR: Victor Fleming. SCREENPLAY: Noel Langley, Florence Ryerson, Edgar Allen Woolf, based on the story by L. FRANK BAUM. SPECIAL EFFECTS: A. Arnold Gillespie. MUSICAL ADAPTATION: Herbert Stothart. MAKEUP: Mr. Dawn.

SUPPORTING PLAYERS: Billie Burke, Margaret Hamilton.

MGM

The Wizard of Oz

WIZARDS
20th Cent.-Fox (1977). Color, 80 mins. Animated.

Ralph Bakshi's vision of a futuristic society plagued by both atomic warfare and wizardry, *Wizards* is an uneven effort that attempts both to entertain and to instruct.

In a bizarre nightmare world, two brothers are born. Both become wizards, one evil, the other good. Blackwolf, the villain, seeks to expand his kingdom in a very Hitleresque manner, by conquering the peaceful world with an army of nightmarish creatures. Avatar, the good wizard, tries his best to quell the warfare with magic and good deeds. When all else fails, however, he defeats Blackwolf with a well-aimed shot from an ancient firearm—a 20th-century pistol. Says a lot about magic.

PRODUCER, SCREENWRITER, AND DIRECTOR: Ralph Bakshi. SEQUENCE ANIMATION: Irven Spence. BACKGROUND DESIGN: Ian Miller, David Jonas. ANIMATION CAMERA: Ted Bemiller. MUSIC: Andrew Billing.

Good Fences Make Good Neighbors "He tampered in God's domain" Captain Robbins (Harvey Dunn) in *Bride of the Monster*

VOICES: Mark Hamill, Steve Gravers, Bob Holt, Jesse Wells.

WOMAN IN THE MOON
Also known as GIRL IN THE MOON. UFA (Germany, 1929); b/w silent feature, 156 mins. U.S. (1931); b/w silent feature, 97 mins.

Fritz Lang's futuristic film envisioning a trip to the moon featured the screen's first countdown scene. A small group of astronauts makes it to the lunar surface. They discover a surface covered with massive sand dunes, mountainous terrain, and gold-laden caverns.

PRODUCER AND SCREENWRITER: Fritz Lang. SCREENPLAY: Thea von Harbou. SPECIAL EFFECTS: Konstantin Tschetwerikoff. ART DIRECTORS: Emil Hasler, Otto Hunte, Karl Mollbrecht.

CAST: Gerda Marcus, Willy Fritsch, Fritz Rasp.

WOMEN OF THE PREHISTORIC PLANET
Realart (1965). Color, 91 mins.

They don't make them like this anymore. Thank the deity of your choice.

A spaceship lands on a prehistoric planet and encounters giant lizards, acid pools, and unfriendly natives. They also find the wreckage of a previous explorer ship and the native offspring of the original crew members. Many peo-

ple in loincloths swim in many water-filled grottos.

PRODUCER: George Gilbert. DIRECTOR AND SCREENWRITER: Arthur C. Pierce. SPECIAL EFFECTS: Howard A. Anderson.

CAST: Wendell Corey, Keith Larsen, Mary Anders, John Agar, Stuart Margolin.

WONDERFUL CHAIR, THE
Brockliss (1910). B/w silent short, 420 ft.

A burglar is caught and held prisoner by a chair powered by electricity.

WONDERFUL ELECTRO-MAGNET, THE
Edison (1909). B/w silent short, 400 ft.

A scientist invents a magnet that pulls in people.

WONDERFUL FLUID, A
Pathé (France, 1908). B/w silent short, 492 ft.

A growth elixir causes everything to grow in a most unorthodox manner. Plants become as big as trees, women grow beards, etc.

WONDERFUL HAIR REMOVER, THE
Gaumont (G.B., 1910). B/w (tinted) silent short.

A powder causes people's hair to fall out instantaneously.

WONDERFUL MARRYING MIXTURE, THE
Walturdaw (1910). B/w silent short, 540 ft.

An elixir has the power to create marriages on the spot.

WONDERFUL PILLS
Cines (Italy, 1909). B/w silent short.

A cure for laziness is found in a batch of pills.

WONDERFUL RAYS, THE
Savoia (France, 1919). B/w silent short, 2,220 ft.

An electrical invention has the ability to re-create crimes.

WONDERFUL REMEDY, A
Pathé (France, 1909). B/w silent short, 377 ft.

A new scientific lotion changes an ugly face into a beautiful one and a normal visage into that of a baboon.

WONDER WOMAN
General Film Corp. (U.S./Philippines, 1973). Color, 82 mins.

Having nothing to do with the famous comic-strip heroine, this movie is a fairly sleazy exercise in blood and gore. A demented female scientist on a small island performs organ transplants on athletes. Her errors cause a resident batch of monsters to dwell on the island. By the film's finish, they are revolting, both physically and literally. The mad doctor makes her mysterious escape in a puff of smoke.

PRODUCER: Ross Hagen. DIRECTOR: Robert O'Neil. SCREENPLAY: Lou Whitehill. CINEMATOGRAPHY: Ricardo M. David. SPECIAL EFFECTS: Jessie Domingo. MUSIC: Carson Whitsett.

CAST: Nancy Kwan, Ross Hagen, Sid Haig, Shirley Washington.

WORLD BEYOND THE MOON, THE
U.S. (1953). B/w, 65 mins.

Three edited-together episodes from TV's SPACE PATROL series.

CAST: Ed Kemmer, Lynn Osborn.

WORLD OF 1960, THE
Columbia (1939). B/w short, 9 mins.

The world of 1960 is forecast in all its futuristic glory.

PRODUCER AND DIRECTOR: B. K. Blake. CINEMATOGRAPHY: Don Malkames, James Lillis.

NARRATOR: Edgar Barrier.

WORLD, THE FLESH AND THE DEVIL, THE
MGM (1959). B/w, 95 mins.

A worker (Harry Belafonte) is trapped in a mine accident. Coming to the surface, he finds the world apparently deserted after a nuclear war. Journeying to New York City, the black runs across another survivor, a white woman (Inger Stevens). The third side of the triangle emerges when a slightly bigoted white male (Jose Ferrer) stumbles across the pair.

PRODUCER: George Englund. DIRECTOR AND SCREENWRITER: Ronald MacDougall, suggested by the novel *The Purple Cloud*, by M. P. SHIEL. CINEMATOGRAPHY: Harold J. Marzorati. SPECIAL EFFECTS: Lee LeBlanc. MUSIC: Miklos Rozsa.

WORLD WITHOUT END
AA (1955). Color/scope, 80 mins.

Sf sermonizing abounds in this tale of runaway rocketry. On a return trip from the Red Planet, astronauts Borden (Hugh Marlowe), Ellis (Rod Taylor), Jaffie (Christopher Dark), and Galbraithe (Nelson Leigh) make an unscheduled flight into the future when their ship plunges through a time warp. Winding up on Earth in the year 2508, they encounter the remnants of a post-holocaust society. The normal humans, led by Timmich (Everett Glass), live in caves and fight the not-so-normal mutants led, seemingly, by the sound track of KING KONG.

The astronauts build some nifty 20th-century weapons, like bazookas and sidearms, and smear the mutants over at least 43 of the prenuked 48 states. Victory in hand, they settle down to restructuring society by organizing a school, intermarrying with the tribe-girls, and smiling.

PRODUCER: Richard Hermanance. DIRECTOR AND SCREENWRITER: Edward Bernds. SPECIAL EFFECTS: Milt Rice (mechanical only). MINIATURE AND OPTICAL EFFECTS: Jack Rabin, Irving Block. MUSIC: Leith Stevens.

SUPPORTING PLAYERS: Nancy Gates, Booth Coleman, Shawn Smith.

WRESTLING WOMEN VS. THE MURDEROUS ROBOT, THE
Calderon (Mexico, 1969). B/w.

Self-explanatory—a battle between human and inhuman muscles.

DIRECTOR: Rene Cardona.

CAST: Joaquin Cordero, Regina Torne, Hector Lechuga.

X FROM OUTER SPACE, THE
AIP (1967). Color, 89 mins.

A spaceship picks up a protoplasmic space hitchhiker near the moon. Back on Earth, the blob hatches and grows into a gigantic chicken-lizard monster ("Guilala" in Japan"; "Gilala" in the States). Tokyo is once again leveled by a pair of titanic happy feet. Aircraft of futuristic designs are dispatched to do battle.

DIRECTOR: Kazui Nihomatsu. SCREENPLAY: Eibi Montomorochi, Moriyoshi Ishida, and Nihomatsu. MUSIC: Taku Izumi. SPECIAL EFFECTS: Hiroshi Ikeda.

CAST: Peggy Neal, Franz Gruber, Eiji Okada.

X-RAYS
G. A. Smith (G.B., 1897). B/w silent short, 54 ft.

A professor focuses an X-ray machine on two lovers and reveals a pair of skeletons embracing.

DIRECTOR: G. A. Smith.

X-17 TOP SECRET
Spain/Italy (1965). Color/scope.

Two groups of spies vie for secret formulas, including one for a pair of sunglasses that picks up the sun's rays and reflects them into beams of light so intense they can melt steel.

DIRECTOR: Amerigo Anton. CAST: Lang Jeffries, Aurora De Alba, Moa Thia, Angel Jordan.

"X"—THE MAN WITH X-RAY EYES
AIP (1963). Color, 88 mins.

Dr. James Xavier (Ray Milland) wants to probe the mysteries surrounding the functions of the human eye. What are its limitations? What are its capabilities? He develops a serum designed to strengthen the power of the cornea, enabling it to see beyond normal sight. He uses it on test animals with disquieting results. The animals go into shock and die. What is it they see? Xavier begins using the eyedrops on himself, giving him the power of an X-ray machine. His coworker (Harold J. Stone) worries about such dangerous experimentation and, in a struggle with his colleague, accidentally falls from an office window and is killed. Fearing he'll be charged with the murder, Xavier flees. Continuously increasing his dosage, Xavier hits the road, at first making money as a mindreader in a carnival and finally fleeing reality as his drug-induced vision takes him to the center of the universe itself, and madness. At the film's conclusion he is brought face to face with infinity, unable to shut his eyes to avoid the vision. Echoing in his ears are the words, "If thine eye offend thee, pluck it out!"

PRODUCER AND DIRECTOR: Roger Corman. SCREENPLAY: Robert Dillon and Ray Russell, from a story by Russell. ART DIRECTOR: Daniel Haller. MAKEUP: Ted Coodley. CINEMATOGRAPHY: Floyd Crosby. MUSIC: Les Baxter.

SUPPORTING PLAYERS: Dina Van Der Vlis, John Hoyt, Don Rickles, Dick Miller, John Dierkes.

X, THE UNKNOWN
Hammer (G.B., 1956); b/w, 86 mins. WB (U.S., 1957); b/w, 80 mins.

Well done. Radioactive mud imbued with an intelligent life-force makes its way from the Earth's core to the surface of the planet in Scotland. It seeks to nourish itself on radioactive material and heads for a government installation. The more radioactivity it consumes, the larger it grows. Hapless humans who stray too close to it are dissolved by its radioactive powers.

PRODUCER: Anthony Hinds. DIRECTOR: Leslie Norman. SCREENPLAY: Jimmy Sangster. CINEMATOGRAPHY: Gerald Gibbs. SPECIAL EFFECTS: Jack Curtis, Bowie Macurtte, Ltd. MUSIC: James Bernard.

CAST: Dean Jagger, Edward Chapman, Leo McKern, Anthony Newley, Michael Ripper, Edward Judd, Ian MacNaughton, Mariane Brauns.

YEARS TO COME
Pathé (1922). B/w silent short, one reel.

In the future, women rule the world.

PRODUCER: Hal Roach.

CAST: Snub Pollard, Marie Mosquini.

YOG—MONSTER FROM SPACE
Toho (Japan, 1970); AIP (U.S., 1971). Color/scope, 1971.

An unmanned probe targeted at Jupiter is taken over by a strange and invisible alien life-force. The intelligence, if you want to stretch the point, pilots the ship to a tiny island south of Japan. It begins to mutate local creatures into giants and then take over their bodies. Ultrasonic sound causes the monsterish alien life-force to join the theater's audience in slumber.

PRODUCERS: Tomoyuki Tanaka, Fumio Tanaka. DIRECTOR: Inoshiro Honda. SCREENPLAY: Ei Ogawa. CINEMATOGRAPHY: Yasuichi Sunokura. SPECIAL EFFECTS: Sadamesa Arikawa. MUSIC: Akira Ifukube.

CAST: Akira Kubo, Kenji Sahara, Koshi Tsuchiya.

American International Pictures

Yog—Monster from Space

YONGARY—MONSTER FROM THE DEEP
Kuk Dong/Toei (S. Korea/Japan, 1967); color, 100 mins. AIT (U.S., 1967); color, 79 mins.

Scientists try to stop a gasoline-drinking guzzler from the deep.

DIRECTOR: Kiduck Kim. SCREENPLAY: Yungsung Suh. CINEMATOGRAPHY: K. Nakagawa, I. Byon.

CAST: Yungil Oh, Chungim Nam, Soonjai Lee, Moon Kang.

YOUNG FRANKENSTEIN
20th Cent.-Fox (1974). B/w, 108 mins.

A simply wonderful parody of those classic Universal films of yesteryear, lovingly constructed and supremely executed. Dr. Frederick Frankenstein (Gene Wilder), an American science professor, decides to return to his grandpop's castle and continue the latter's research concerning life and death. Assisting him in his work are hunchback Igor (Marty Feldman) (who has an ambidextrous hump) and Inga (Terry Garr). Housekeeper Frau Blucher (Cloris Leachman) scowls, remembering the good old days with the original Baron. A monster (Peter Boyle) is made and, again, given a subnormal brain. The monster bolts from the lab, eventually winding up in the house of a blind hermit (Gene Hackman). The hermit, Harold, tries to teach the monster good manners, but to no avail.

Finally the creature is captured and sedated by Frankenstein. The creature is rehabilitated and turned into a song-and-dance man. After a particularly moving version of "Putting on the Ritz," both the doctor and the monster are booed off the stage at a convention of prominent scientists. The monster is crushed. He kidnaps Frederick's fiancée, Elizabeth (Madeline Kahn), who is so taken with this good-looking hunk of a man that she marries him. Frankenstein ends up with Inga, and Igor still has his hump to pal around with.

PRODUCER: Michael Gruskoff. DIRECTOR: Mel Brooks. SCREENPLAY: Gene Wilder and Brooks. MAKEUP: William Tuttle.

YOU ONLY LIVE TWICE
UA (1967). Color/scope, 116 mins.

International group of bad chaps, S.P.E.C.T.R.E., gives James Bond (Sean Connery) something to think about this time out. They plan to start an international confrontation that will erupt into World War III. Their plan:

Young Frankenstein

put a huge S.P.E.C.T.R.E. spacecraft into orbit that will swallow, first, a smaller U.S. space capsule and, then, an equally diminutive Russian one.

PRODUCERS: Albert R. Broccoli, Harry Saltzman. DIRECTOR: Lewis Gilbert. SCREENPLAY: ROALD DAHL. PRODUCTION DESIGN: Ken Adam. MAKEUP: Basil Newall, Paul Rabiger. SPECIAL EFFECTS: John Stears. CINEMATOGRAPHY: Freddie Young. MUSIC: John Barry.

SUPPORTING PLAYERS: Donald Pleasance, Tetsuro Tamba, Karin Dor, Desmond Llewelyn, Robert Hutton, Bernard Lee as "M," Lois Maxwell as Moneypenny.

Z

ZAAT
Horizon (1973), color, 100 mins.

A deservedly obscure tale of finned fury. A marine biologist (Marshall Grauer) goes off the deep end and turns himself into an underwater monster (Wade Popwell). Since misery loves company, he also lets loose a small army of mutant fish and sends them off on search-and-destroy missions in local swimming holes. If this wasn't enough of an insult to peace lovers around the world, the monster-man purposely pollutes the ocean. By the end of the film, audiences suspect he works for a major oil company.

PRODUCER AND DIRECTOR: Dan Barton. STORY: Lee Larew, Ron Kivett. MAKEUP: Kivett. CINEMATOGRAPHY: Jack McGowan. MUSIC: Jami Defrates, Barry Hodgin.

SUPPORTING PLAYERS: Dave Dickerson, Sanna Ringhaver, Paul Galloway.

ZAMBO
Bhavani (India, 1937). B/w, 157 mins.

A well-meaning scientist turns his favorite gorilla into a man. The human ape proceeds to do the best imitation of an EDGAR RICE BURROUGHS character in India. Unfortunately, Tarzan he ain't.

PRODUCER, DIRECTOR, AND SCREENWRITER: M. Bhavani. CINEMATOGRAPHY: R. M. Master. MUSIC: Pandit Bedriprasad.

CAST: S. B. Nayampally, Sarla, Indira Wadker, Mehru the gorilla.

ZARDOZ
20th Cent.-Fox (1974). Color, 105 mins.

In the year 2293, life on Earth is slightly less than ideal, with 90 percent of the world overrun by the Brutals and the Exterminators. The Brutals are lowly humans, short on brain power but long on stamina. And they need all the stamina they can muster, being constantly pursued by the gun-crazed Exterminators, masked warriors who worship the great god Zardoz. Zardoz itself is not one's traditional idea of a deity: a gigantic stone "head" that hovers above the ground, spewing guns and ammunition out of its mouth.

The remainder of Earth is declared the Vortex, an almost mystical commune made up of descendants of the previous decades' most brilliant scientists and intellectuals. The community is composed of three subtly-named groups of individuals: the Eternals, the Renegades, and the Apathetics. A quick scan of their labels will reveal their personality traits.

When Exterminator Zed (Sean Connery) hitches an unexpected ride within the great god Zardoz, he discovers it to be a fraud—a flying machine operated by one of the Eternals. Crash-landing within the Vortex, Zed gives the bland inhabitants a taste of life that shatters their sensibilities.

PRODUCER, DIRECTOR, AND SCREEN-PLAY: John Boorman. MUSIC: David Munrow. SPECIAL EFFECTS: Jerry Johnston. CINEMATOGRAPHY: Geoffrey Unsworth.

SUPPORTING PLAYERS: Charlotte Rampling, Sarah Kestleman, Sally Anne Newton, John Alderton.

ZEPPELIN ATTACK ON NEW YORK
Mutual (1917). B/w silent featurette, 660 ft.

The German kaiser's fleet of zeppelins invades the skies over New York and attempts to do the city in.

ZERO IN THE UNIVERSE
Film-Makers (1966). B/w, 85 mins.

A disembodied life-force has the ability to take on any shape and size at will, causing much confusion to the humanoids it comes in contact with.

PRODUCER: Jock Livingston. DIRECTOR: George Moorse. SCREENPLAY: Livingston, Moorse. CINEMATOGRAPHY: Gerard Vandengerg. MUSIC: Donald Cherry.

CAST: Jock Livingston, George Moorse, Pam Badyk, George Bartenieff.

ZETA ONE
Tigon (G.B., 1969); Edward Montoro Enterprises (U.S., 1973). Color, 82 mins.

A group of secret agents do battle with an alien superwoman.

EXECUTIVE PRODUCER: Tony Tenser. DIRECTOR: Michael Cort. SCREENPLAY: Cort, Christopher Neame. ART DIRECTOR: Martin Gascoigne. MUSIC: Johnny Hawksworth.

CAST: Robin Hawdon, Yutte Stensgaard, Dawn Addams.

ZOMBIES OF THE STRATO-SPHERE
Republic (1952). B/w serial, 12 chapters (24 reels), 384 mins. total running time.

Judd Holdren returned as the bullet-helmeted, rocket-belt-wearing Commando Cody in this sf potboiler. The zombies, three Martian meanies in leotards named Marex, Roth, and Narab (Lane Bradford, Craig Kelly, and Leonard Nimoy), attempt to overthrow the peaceful governments of the world by

The Museum of Modern Art/Film Stills Archives

Zombies of the Stratosphere

employing a demented Earth scientist and his robot henchman. The Martians plan to construct a bomb that will blast Earth out of its orbit. Commando Cody plans to blast the Martians out of their leotards. Three guesses who succeeds.

DIRECTOR: Fred C. Brannon. SCREENPLAY: Ronald Davidson. MUSIC: Stanley Wilson. SPECIAL EFFECTS: Howard and Theodore Lydecker.

SUPPORTING PLAYERS: Aline Towne, Wilson Wood, Johnny Crawford, Dale Van Sickle.

Republic

Zombies of the Stratosphere

ZONTAR: THE THING FROM VENUS
AIT (1968). Color, 80 mins.

A nasty bat-creature is guided to Earth by nasty humans attempting to conquer the world. Once here, the monster shows its peer group of nasties that it has a mind of its own . . . and that mind is powerful enough to enslave the wills of local Earthlings. The creature believes that *it* should rule the world, and not the puny Earth crooks. Some logic, huh?

PRODUCER AND DIRECTOR: Larry Buchanan. SCREENPLAY: Buchanan, H. Taylor. CINEMATOGRAPHY: Robert B. Alcott.

CAST: John Agar, Susan Bjurman, Patricia DeLaney, Warren Hammack.

Z.P.G. (ZERO POPULATION GROWTH)
Sagittarius (G.B., 1971); Paramount (U.S., 1972). Color, 97 mins.

Future shock meets future schlock in this dire message-film. In the not-too-distant future, humanity pays for its ecological follies of the present. Cities are ringed with poisonous clouds of smog. Citizens are forced to wear protective suits and breathing apparatus. Synthetic food is rationed. Overpopulation leads to a four-year waiting list for a jaunt in a museum. Flying machines shaped like eggs patrol the streets, droning government-approved news items.

With conditions this awful, the government bans all childbirth. If a couple wants a child, the government will sell them a surrogate one, programmed to behave normally. Those couples that actually bring their own children into the world are put to death in extermination domes. Despite the horror surrounding them, one pair of idealists (Oliver Reed and Geraldine Chaplin) decides, what the heck, why not have a kid. Sounds logical.

PRODUCER: Thomas F. Madigan. DIRECTOR: Michael Campus. SCREENPLAY: Max Erlich, Frank DeFelitta. SPECIAL EFFECTS: Derek Meddings. PRODUCTION DESIGN: Tony Masters. ART DIRECTORS: Harry Lange, Peter Hojmark. CINEMATOGRAPHY: Michael Reed. MUSIC: Jonathan Hodge.

SUPPORTING PLAYERS: Diane Cilento, Don Gordon, David Markham, Sheila Reid.

ZZ OPERATION REMBRANDT
Agata/CAPI/Planet (Spain/Italy/W. Germany, 1967). Color, 98 mins.

Two competing groups of spies battle over the possession of lethal machines used to direct cosmic rays in a destructive manner.

DIRECTOR: Giancarlo Romitelli. SCREENPLAY: Romitelli, Ennio de Concini, and Robert Veller, from a story by Romitelli. ART DIRECTION: Adolfo Cofino. CINEMATOGRAPHY: Guglielmo Mancori. MUSIC: Aldo Piga.

CAST: Lang Jeffries, Mitsuko, Laura Valensuelo, Carlo Hinterman.

Con Ed Lives
I believe that electricity is life!
Lionel Atwill in *The Man-Made Monster*

TELEVISION

ADVENTURES OF FU MANCHU, THE

Syndicated weekly series (1956). B/w, 30-min. episodes.

Dr. Fu Manchu, a well-respected Chinese physician located in London, adopts young Lia Elthram (Laurette Luez), a Caucasian girl. Shortly thereafter, Fu's wife and son are killed accidentally by Britisher Dr. Jack Petri (Clark Howat) during the Boxer Rebellion. Understandably upset, Fu (Glenn Gordon) goes crazy.

Returning to Tibet, he establishes an organization dedicated to evil . . . S.U.B.T.L.Y. His mission: world domination. His nemesis, Nayland Smith (Lester Stevens) of Scotland Yard, manages to thwart his every move.

Based on the characters created by Sax Rohmer.

ALIENS ARE COMING, THE

NBC-TV telefilm (1980). Color, 120-min. airtime.

Now here's a real clever plot wrinkle concocted by producer Quinn Martin. Aliens are invading the Earth!!! The disembodied bad guys land in the Nevada desert to begin their colonization of Earth. Their first mission is to gather data by inhabiting the bodies of selected human hosts. Construction worker Russ Garner (Max Gail) becomes the first all-American alien hard hat. Scientist Scott Dryden (Tom Mason) is hoping the aliens are friendly, but then again, he's always been an optimist.

SUPPORTING PLAYERS: Caroline Mc-Williams as Sue Garner, Matthew Laborteaux as Tommy Garner, Melinda Fee as O'Brien, Fawne Harriman as Joyce Cummings, Eric Braeden as Nero, Ron Masak as Herve Nelson, Laurence Haddon as Fowler.

DIRECTOR: Harvey Hart. TELEPLAY: Robert Lenski.

AMAZING SPIDER-MAN, THE

Later known as THE NEW ADVENTURES OF SPIDER-MAN

CBS-TV limited series (1977–78). Color, 60-min. episodes following a 120-min. pilot.

Based on the Marvel comic book character. A young newspaperman (Nicholas Hammond), bitten by a radioactive spider, gains incredible spiderlike powers. He can crawl up the sides of buildings and, using scientific know-how, hurl spider-web nets at people. Becoming the most misunderstood crime-fighter ever, he emerges as Spider-Man: a fellow chased by both sides of the law.

A Charles Fries production. EXECUTIVE PRODUCER: Charles Fries. PRODUCER: Lee Siegel, Ron Satlof, Bob Janes.

SUPPORTING PLAYERS: Robert F. Simon, Michael Pataki.

AMAZING THREE, THE

Syndicated weekly animated series (1967). Color, 30-min. episodes.

Three aliens come to Earth in the 21st century. Their mission is to try to figure out whether or not they should blow up the planet. They take the guises of a horse, a dog, and a duck for their stay and are befriended by Earth kid Kenny. Together they fight evil and the strains of low-budget animation quality.

CBS-TV

The Amazing Spider-Man

AMERICA: 2100
ABC-TV animated special (1979). Color, 30 mins. airtime.

Two small-town comics (the voices of Jon Cutler and Mark King) are sent into a state of suspended animation in a hotel room, awakening some 120 years later. They are catered to by a perky woman of the future (Karen Valentine) and her German robot Max (Sid Caesar).

A Paramount/Arim production. EXECUTIVE PRODUCERS: Austin and Irma Kalish. PRODUCER: Gary Menteer. DIRECTOR: Joel Zwick. TELEPLAY: Mark Rothman, Lowell Ganze. CAMERA: Merideth Nicholson. ART DIRECTOR: John Vallone. MUSIC: Jonathan Tunick.

SUPPORTING VOICES: Gregory Miller, David Pearse, Tiffany Delaney.

AQUARIANS, THE
NBC-TV telefilm (1970). Color, 90 mins. airtime.

In the not-too-distant future, much of the scientific research regarding the world's oceans is done from undersea complexes. In one such nuclear-powered structure, the Deep Lab, a group of scientists and explorers attempts to gauge just how much pollution will be caused by nerve gas leaking from a sunken freighter.

A Universal film. PRODUCER: Ivan Tors. DIRECTOR: Don McDougall. DIRECTOR OF UNDERWATER SEQUENCES: Ricou Browning. SCREENPLAY: Leslie Stevens and Winston Miller, from a story by Ivan Tors and Alan Caillou. ART DIRECTOR: Gene Harris. CINEMATOGRAPHY: Clifford Polan. MUSIC: Lalo Schifrin.

CAST: Ricardo Montalban, Jose Ferrer, Kate Woodville, Leslie Nielsen, Curt Lowens.

ARK II
CBS-TV weekly series (1976). Color, 30 min. episodes.

Hundreds of years from now, the world is ravaged by a nuclear war. A group of young people—Jonah (Terry Lester), Ruth (Jean Marie Hon), and Samuel (José Flores)—tries to reestablish civilization. They roam the countryside in their *Ark II* and *Ark Roamer* vehicles.

A Filmation Associates production. PRODUCER: Richard Rosenbloom. Created by Martin Roth. DIRECTOR OF PHOTOGRAPHY: Robert F. Sparks.

ASTRO-BOY
Syndicated weekly animated series (1963). Color, 30-min. episodes.

A Nipponese import set in the 21st century. Earth scientist Dr. Boynton, still grief-stricken after the death of his own son, creates robotic-chip-off-the-old-block Astro Boy. The superheroic lad is then called upon to defend Earth from various outer-space villains, monsters, and evildoers.

ATOM SQUAD
NBC-TV daily series (1953). B/w, 15-min. episodes.

Tense tales of the Atom Squad served up on a daily basis. Squad leader Steve Elliot (Bob Hastings) and his loyal patriotic peers (Bob Courtleigh and Bram Nossem) are grim and determined in their New York City base of operations. Their job: to protect America's atomic secrets from the ever-popular forces of Evil.

AVENGERS, THE
Associated British Television (G.B., 1961–68) and ABC-TV (U.S., 1966–69) weekly series, now syndicated. Color, 50/60 (G.B./U.S.)-min. episodes.

One of the biggest cult shows of the 1960s, *The Avengers* was a hit in Great Britain for several years before seeing the light of day Stateside. The show also had the distinction of changing its format four times in seven years. The first version, (1961–62), which evolved from a series titled *Police Surgeon* (1960–61), starred Ian Hendry as Dr. David Keel. When Keel's wife is accidentally killed by a drug ring, he vows revenge. En route to justice, he meets up with mysterious, albeit dapper, crime-fighter Steed (Patrick Macnee). Steed at this time had no government affiliation and, apparently, no first name. Together they fight crime.

The second round of the show (1962–65), gave Steed a first name (John) and a sponsor, the British Government Ministry Agency. Steed and new partner Mrs. Catherine Gale (Honor Blackman) fought crime week after week until, in 1965, Mrs. Emma Peel (Diana Rigg) showed up. At this point *The Avengers* also showed up in the States, and the adventures took an sf turn in a big way. Robots, evil scientists, and germ-warfare boosters all put in their bid for infamy.

Mrs. Peel stuck around until 1968, when her long-lost husband was found in the Amazon jungle after a marathon plane crash. Steed then joined forces with Tara King (Linda Thorson) for a quick go at nastiness lasting until May 1969.

SUPPORTING PLAYERS: Patrick Newell as Mother, Julie Stevens as Venus Smith, Warren Mitchell as Ambassador Valdimer Brodney.

BATMAN
ABC-TV weekly series (1966–68) Color, 30-min. episodes.

William Dozier's high camp, low IQ version of the famous caped crusader of comic-bookdom. Batman/Bruce Wayne (Adam West) and Robin/Dick Grayson (Burt Ward) use muscle and scientific machinery to fight off the exaggerated evil concocted by such villains as the Penguin (Burgess Meredith), Lola La-

sagne (Ethel Merman), the Joker (Cesar Romero), the Riddler (Frank Gorshin, succeeded by John Astin), the Archer (Art Carney), the Catwoman (Julie Newmar, succeeded by Lee Ann Meriweather and, finally, Eartha Kitt), Lady Penelope Peasoup (Glynis Johns), Lord Marmaduke Ffogg (Rudy Vallee), the Black Widow (Tallulah Bankhead), Egghead (Vincent Price), the Sandman (Michael Rennie), Mr. Freeze (George Sanders), the Mad Hatter (David Wayne), the Minstrel (Van Johnson), Clock King (Walter Slezak), King Tut (Victor Buono), Minerva (Zsa Zsa Gabor), and Bookworm and the Devil (Roddy McDowall and Joan Crawford).

SUPPORTING PLAYERS: Yvonne Craig as Batgirl; Alan Napier as Alfred, the Wayne butler; Neil Hamilton as Commissioner Gordon; Stafford Repp as Chief O'Hara; Madge Blake as Aunt Harriet.

BATTLE OF THE PLANETS
Syndicated weekly animated series (1979). Color, 30-min. episodes.

Exceedingly violent Japanese fare featuring weekly battles between goodguy G-Force agents (superheroes all) and alien invaders from the planet Spectra. Spectra's forces are led by zany Zolta (the voice of Key Luke), who manufactures destructive robots to level the Earth. G-Force leader 7-Zark-7 and loyal barking partner 1-Rover-1 fight back aboard the spaceship *The Flying Phoenix,* a vessel that can turn into a giant bird. *The Phoenix*'s mission? Get the drop on Zolta.

Released by Gallerie International Films. PRODUCER AND DIRECTOR: David Hanson.

VOICES: Alan Young, Casey Kasem, Janet Waldo, Ronnie Schell, Alan Dinehart.

BATTLESTAR GALACTICA
ABC-TV weekly series (1978–1979; 1980). Color, 60-min. episodes following 180-min. pilot.

Spurred on by the phenomenal celluloid success of STAR WARS, ABC and Universal Studios conspired to create a TV answer to epic space films. Originally titled *Star Worlds, Battlestar Galactica* was probably one of the most

ABC-TV

Battlestar Galactica

expensive and highly touted disasters in network history. With a one-season budget of over $40 million, the show excelled in special effects but floundered in terms of scripting.

In a faraway galaxy, a colony of 12 humanoid-populated planets is ambushed and systematically destroyed by a robot race known as the Cylons. The entire human population of the dozen planets, as well as most of their defense armada, is obliterated. A few ships escape the slaughter, however, the most notable being the lone remaining battlestar, the *Galactica*. The giant battleship leads a rag-tag fleet of 220 space vehicles of all shapes and sizes in a search for the almost mythical 13th planet of the colony . . . Earth. Hoping to flee the forces of the Cylon Empire, the humans seek another home and another chance at survival. The Cylons, however, rotten to their nuts and bolts, pursue relentlessly.

Commander Adama (Lorne Greene), determined to complete a successful mission, is aided by son Apollo (Richard Hatch), hot-shot pilot Starbuck (Dirk Benedict), and a crew of some of the colony's finest flyers.

EXECUTIVE PRODUCER: Glen A. Larson. SUPERVISING PRODUCER: Leslie Stevens. PRODUCER AND SPECIAL EFFECTS CREATOR: John Dykstra. COSTUMES: Jean-Pierre Dorléac. DIRECTOR OF PHOTOGRAPHY: Ben Colman. ART

DIRECTION: John E. Chilberg. MUSIC: Stu Phillips, Glen A. Larson.

SUPPORTING PLAYERS: Herb Jefferson, Jr., as Boomer, Maren Jensen as Athena, Noah Hathaway as Boxey, Terry Carter as Col. Tigh.

BETWEEN TIME AND TIMBUKTRA
PBS-TV (New Line Cinema) telefilm (1972). Color, 90 mins. airtime.

A potpourri of the work of Kurt Vonnegut, Jr. Stony Stevenson (William Hickey) wins a jingle-writing contest for space food. His prize is to be blasted into space through a time-space warp that allows him to experience simultaneously history past, present, and future. Among the people he meets on his experience are Diana Moon Gompers, Handicapper General of Future Earth (all people are made equal through handicapping of their bodies— a ballet dancer wears 100-pound sandbags, etc.); and Bokonon, a flowerpower guru who leads his pacifists into the hands of the military; where they are promptly led to death. Back on present-day Earth, Mission Control commentators Bob and Ray provide narration.

PRODUCER: Daxid Loxton. DIRECTOR: Fred Barzyk. TELEPLAY: David O'Dell, based on the short stories of Kurt Vonnegut, Jr. SPECIAL EFFECTS: David Atwood. MUSIC: John Q. Adams.

SUPPORTING PLAYERS: William Hickey, Bob Elliott, Ray Goulding, Kevin McCarthy, Dortha Duckworth, Hurd Hatfield, Benay Venuta.

BEYOND WESTWORLD
CBS-TV weekly series (1980). Color, 60-min. episodes.

Based on the premise concocted in MICHAEL CRICHTON's film WESTWORLD film, this series features robots gone nutty. Robot creator Simon Quaid (James Wainwright) is angry that the Delos amusement park has used his creations as oversized toys, so he turns his robots against humanity and tries to set up a robot kingdom beneath the sea. (You can't argue logic.) Out to stop him is Delos security agent John Moore (Jim McMullen), who, week after week, battles bolts.

Filmed at MGM. PRODUCER, CRE-

ATOR, AND ORIGINAL-EPISODE SCREEN-WRITER: Lou Shaw.

BIONIC WOMAN, THE
ABC-TV (1976–77) and NBC-TV (1978) weekly series. Color, 60 mins. airtime per episode.

With the success of THE SIX MILLION DOLLAR MAN, ABC figured they could scrounge up a few spare parts and create *The Bionic Woman*. And it came to pass that, verily, during the *Man's* 1974–75 season, bionic Steve Austin (Lee Majors) returned home to Ojai, California, to woo and make hubba-hubba with high-school sweetheart Jamie Sommers (Lindsay Wagner). Alas, his wooing in the episode (titled "The Bionic Woman") was brought to an untimely end when, during a life-saving operation performed on injured Jamie, her body rejects the bionic parts designed for her.

The network brass saw the ratings and said, "It is good. Bring her back . . . alive." And thus, in 1975–76, did Jamie reappear on *The Six Million Dollar Man* in "The Return of the Bionic Woman." The bionic operation did not kill her, it just gave her a bad case of amnesia. Steve, finding Jamie, returns her to Ojai for a cure. And thus, in 1976, was *The Bionic Woman* born. An Ojai schoolteacher really working for the Office of Scientific Investigation, Jamie takes her orders from Steve's boss, Oscar Goldman (Richard Anderson). When the going got tough during her second season, the network heads looked down upon her and said, "Give this child another gimmick." And thus was the Bionic Dog introduced to the show. Verily, the show proved a Bionic Dud and was scrapped.

EXECUTIVE PRODUCER: Harve Bennett. CREATOR AND PRODUCER: Kenneth Johnson. MUSIC SUPERVISION: Hal Mooney.

BIRDMAN
NBC-TV weekly animated series (1967–68). Color, 30-min. episodes.

Ray Randall (the voice of Keith Andes) is saved from a fiery death by the Egyptian sun god Ra and given superpowers. He then joins forces with the Galaxy Trio–Vapor Man (Don Messick), Galaxy Girl (Virginia Eiler), and Meteor Man (Ted Cassidy)–to fight intergalactic evil.

A Hanna-Barbera production.

BRAVE NEW WORLD
NBC-TV miniseries (filmed in 1978, not telecast). Color, two 120-min. episodes.

An exercise in frustration. Two years in the making, producer Jacqueline Babbin's epic version of ALDOUS HUXLEY'S BRAVE NEW WORLD was unceremoniously yanked by NBC-TV as being too "intellectual" and was reslated for broadcast in 1979 by nervous new NBC chief Fred Silverman. Two weeks before airtime in 1979, it was again yanked and rescheduled by NBC for 1980, as rumors circulated that drastic cutting would reduce the project from a two-part, four-hour drama to a one-part, three-hour opus. Babbin, meanwhile, helplessly watching her product be buried, promptly joined ABC-TV as executive in charge of miniseries.

The plot of the TV show mirrors that of the novel, although all flashbacks have been rearranged into a chronologically correct sequence. In the year 600 AF (After Ford), humans are bred artificially on assembly lines, a person's IQ is dictated by the government, and mood-altering drugs are mandatory. Into this world comes John Savage (Kristofer Tabori), an outcast human being mistakenly born into a human womb because of a slight miscalculation on the part of head baby-manufacturer Thomas Grahambell (Keir Dullea) and his jilted sweetheart, Linda (Julie Cobb). John is brought into civilization and causes an uproar. Joining in the rebellion is social misfit

NBC-TV

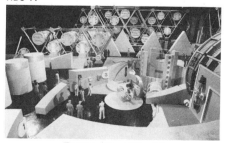

Brave New World

Bernard Marx (Bud Cort), a fellow mixed up by a chemical imbalance that occurred during his assembly-line birth. Further complicating matters are a love interest between Savage and model citizen Lenina Disney (Marcia Strassman) and the meddling of New World leader Mustapha Mond (Ron O'Neal).

PRODUCER: Jacqueline Babbin. SCREENPLAY: Robert E. Thompson, from the novel by Aldous Huxley. PRODUCTION DESIGN: Tom H. John. DIRECTOR OF PHOTOGRAPHY: Harry Wolf. DIRECTOR: Burt Brinkerhoff.

BUCK ROGERS
NBC-TV telefilm (1979). Technicolor, 120 mins. airtime.

Filmed in 1978 as a proposed pilot for a series, released theatrically in March 1979 and, finally, airing on TV in the fall of 1979 (in modified form) as the celluloid introduction for a weekly show (see following entry), *Buck Rogers* is a campy update of the old PHILIP F. NOWLAN comic-strip adventure. Astronaut Buck (Gil Gerard) is sent into a state of suspended animation in his space capsule at the end of the 20th century. Waking up in the 25th century, he rubs elbows with Wilma Deering (Erin Gray), Dr. Huer (Tim O'Connor), and loyal robot Twikki (Felix Silla, with the voice of Mel Blanc). Defending the new Earth capitol of New Chicago against the weaponry of Princess Ardala (Pamela Hensley) and Kane (Henry Silva), he is accepted as a 25th-century hero and the star of a weekly TV show.

A Universal film. EXECUTIVE PRODUCER: Glen A. Larson. DIRECTOR: Daniel Haller. SCREENPLAY: Larson. ART DIRECTOR: Paul Peters. COSTUMES: Jean-Pierre Dorléac. SPECIAL EFFECTS: Bud Ewing, Jack Faggard. MUSIC: Stu Phillips.

BUCK ROGERS
NBC-TV weekly series (1979–   ). Color, 60-min. episodes.

In this continuation of the telefilm, Buck (Gil Gerard) wisecracks his way through a number of star wars as he defends New Chicago from intergalactic evil. Lending support are Dr. Huer (Tim O'Connor), Wilma Deering (Erin Gray), and Twikki (Felix Silla, with the voice of Mel Blanc).

EXECUTIVE PRODUCER: Glen A. Larson. ART DIRECTION: Paul Peters. SPECIAL EFFECTS: Bud Ewing, Jack Faggard. MUSIC: Stu Phillips.

BUCK ROGERS IN THE 25TH CENTURY
ABC-TV weekly series (1950–51). B/w, 30-min. episodes.

In Pittsburgh, Pennsylvania, in 1919, young U.S. Air Force pilot Buck Rogers (Ken Dibbs) takes a job as a mine surveyor. While strolling through an abandoned mine, the supports give way. Buck is trapped in a small pocket of the cave. Worse yet, a strange gas seeps through the debris and knocks him out. A shift in the Earth brings in fresh air and, for Buck, consciousness. Emerging from the cave, he finds himself in the year 2439. Complicating matters even more is that he has emerged from the mine not in Pittsburgh, but in the new capital of America, Niagara, New York.

Running across Lt. Wilma Deering (Lou Prentis), Buck is led to the laboratory of Dr. Huer (Harry Sothern), who is quite impressed with Buck's epic nap. In the ensuing weeks, Buck and his newfound friends fight tyranny wherever they can find it.

PRODUCER AND DIRECTOR: Babette Henry. WRITER: Gene Wycoff. Based on the comic strip written by PHILIP F. NOWLAN.

NBC-TV

Buck Rogers

Take That, Darth Vader

Anybody could play Darth Vader. Vader is basically just a big guy behind a costume. The character shows no emotion, no nothing!

Lou Ferrigno, star of *The Incredible Hulk*

SUPPORTING PLAYERS: Harry Kingston, Sanford Bickart, Robert Pastene.

CAPTAIN AMERICA

CBS-TV telefilm (1979). Color, 120 mins. airtime.

A witless adaptation of the comic-book hero legend. Steve Rogers (Reb Brown) swallows a healthy dose of FLAG, a serum that turns him into Captain America, when bad guys capture the city of Phoenix and hold it for ransom via some strong-arm tactics provided by the presence of a neutron bomb. They want $1 billion in gold. The Captain intervenes for two hours. A speedy payoff would have been a lot easier to swallow.

DIRECTOR: Rod Holcomb.

SUPPORTING PLAYERS: Len Berman, Heather Menzies.

CAPTAIN NICE

NBC-TV weekly series (1967). Color, 30-min. episodes.

Buck Henry's clever but ignored parody of superherodom. In Big Town, U.S.A., scientist Carter Nash (William Daniels) discovers Super Juice, an elixir that transforms him into flying fool Captain Nice. Week after week, Captain Nice saves Big Town from all-around nastiness (you know, such threatening things as atomic-powered caterpillars). Carter's mother (Alice Ghostley) doesn't like her son's moonlighting. Police Sgt. Candy Kane (Ann Prentiss) would like a crack at the Captain. What's a superhero to do?

SUPPORTING PLAYERS: William Zuck-ert as Police Chief Segal, Liam Dunn as Mayor Finny, Byron Fougler as Mr. Nash.

CAPTAIN SCARLET AND THE MYSTERONS

ITC-TV syndicated weekly series (G.B., 1967). Color, 30-min. episodes.

An ambitious kid-vid outing created by Gerry and Sylvia (THUNDERBIRDS; UFO; SPACE: 1999) Anderson and starring a fleet of their Supermarionation citizens (marionettes synched to the soundtrack via computer controls). In the year 2068, an expedition to Mars by the alien Mysterons bumps into a similar mission by the international Earth law-enforcement organization Spectrum. The Mysterons feel that they have been attacked by Earth and launch a counter-assault. Before you know it, there's a war of the wooden worlds going on. Leading the fight for Spectrum is Capt. Scarlet (the voice of Francis Matthews), an Earth agent originally killed and brought back to life by Mysteron scientists in an attempt to create a human spy. Their plan backfires, however, and Scarlet returns to Earth still flying his true colors, but now possessing amazing insights into the workings of the Mysteron mind. Uh-huh.

EXECUTIVE PRODUCERS AND CREATORS: Gerry and Sylvia Anderson. PRODUCER: Reg Hill. SPECIAL EFFECTS: Derek Meddings. MUSIC: Barry Gray.

VOICES: Donald Gray as Col. White, Paul Maxwell as Capt. Grey, Ed Bishop as Capt. Blue, Jeremy Wilkins as Capt. Ochre, Janna Hill as Symphony Angel, Sylvia Anderson as Melody Angel, Gary Files as Capt. Magenta.

CAPTAIN VIDEO AND HIS VIDEO RANGERS

DuMont Network weekly series (1949–56). B/w, 30-min. episodes.

The first of the sf video adventures, Captain Video was one of the most popular TV events of the early 1950s. Beginning in 1949 as *Captain Video and His Video Rangers,* the show mutated into *The Secret Files of Captain Video* from 1953 to 1956 and then, with the advent of a more-sophisticated medium (which would not tolerate low-budget adventures), wound up in 1956 as *Captain Video's Cartoons.*

The show was set on the planet Earth in the year 2254. Golden Rule–spouting Captain Video (played in 1949 by Richard Coogan, and thereafter by Al Hodge) was dubbed "an electronic wizard, master of time and space and guardian of the safety of the world." He was also a natty dresser. Video was a man of mind as well as muscle, inventing such nifty devices as the Cosmic Vibrator (a machine that could puree a fellow to death) and the Opticon Scillometer (a grandiose extension of X-ray specs). He intended those inventions to be used for the betterment of humankind. Evil Dr. Pauli (Hal Conklin), however, always seemed to want to snatch the aforementioned scientific wonders for the betterment of Dr. Pauli. Week after week, Video and his 15-year-old Video Ranger sidekick (Don Hastings) would thwart Pauli's schemes for world domination. They were aided by Dr. Tobor (hint: spell it backwards) and Carter (Dave Ballard and Nat Polen, respectively) on their numerous trips in space aboard the good ship *Galaxy*.

When the good Captain's spacefaring days were over, he hosted his own kiddie show, which featured such personalities as "Betty Boop" and "Popeye" on the monitor screen located in the chest of his loyal robot.

CAPTAIN Z-RO
Syndicated series (1955). B/w, 15-min. episodes.

Dapper Capt. Z-Ro (Roy Steffins), pilot of the rocket ship ZX-99 and inventor of a time-portal machine, passes his time meddling in other people's affairs throughout time and space. Singling out a single day of crisis in a person's life, he sends his young assistant, Jet (Bobby Trumbull), back into time and guides him into a pattern of actions that will avert the threatened calamity.

CHALLENGE, THE
ABC-TV telefilm (1970). Color, 90-min. episodes.

Not wanting to risk an all-out nuclear blowout, two warring superpowers decide to fight World War III on a toe-to-toe, intimate level. Each group picks one man to represent it: Jacob Gallery

(Darren McGavin) and Yuro (Mako). They are placed on a deserted Pacific island and asked to fight each other to the death. The winner of the battle saves his side from cataclysm. The loser . . . now that's another story.

A 20th Cent.-Fox production. PRODUCERS: Jay Cipes, Ed Palmer. DIRECTOR: Allen Smithee. SCREENPLAY: Marc Norman. CINEMATOGRAPHY: Jack Nicklaus. SPECIAL EFFECTS: Lyle B. Abbott. MUSIC: Harry Geller.

SUPPORTING PLAYERS: Broderick Crawford as General Meyers, James Whitmore as Overman, Skip Homeier as Lyman George.

CITY BENEATH THE SEA
NBC-TV telefilm (1970). Color, 120 mins. airtime.

A pilot film that never excited network programmers and instead saw theatrical release in Europe. *City Beneath the Sea* takes place in the year 2050 and centers on the activities of the citizens of Pacifica, an undersea colony. When a meteor heads for Earth on a collision course it's predicted that the impact will wipe Pacifica off the map. Understandably upset over this prospect, scientists within the city try to figure out a way to avoid cataclysm. Adding to the fun are personal rivalries, gigantic undersea monsters, and an experimental race of aquamen created by undersea scientists.

A 20th Cent.-Fox production. PRODUCER AND DIRECTOR: Irwin Allen. SCREENPLAY: John Meredyth Lucas. ART DIRECTION: Roger E. Maus, Stan Jolley. CINEMATOGRAPHY: Kenneth Peach. SPECIAL EFFECTS: Lyle B. Abbott, Art Cruickshank. MUSIC: Richard LaSalle.

CAST: Stuart Whitman, Robert Wagner, Rosemary Forsyth, Richard Basehart, Joseph Cotten, James Darren, Whit Bissell.

CLIFFHANGERS
NBC-TV weekly series (1979). Color, 60-min. episodes.

A lackluster attempt to emulate the serials of the 1930s and 1940s, *Cliffhangers* was three shows in one: "Stop Susan Williams" (a *Perils of Pauline* update), "The Curse of Dracula" (contemporary fangs à go-go), and "The

Secret Empire" (a rip-off of the old Gene Autry sf Western serial, THE PHANTOM EMPIRE). *The Secret Empire* starred Geoffrey Scott as an 1880s marshal who stumbles onto a futuristic city beneath the Earth. The underground nasties are involved in aboveground thievery and it's hard for the lawman to convince concerned citizens that the recent rash of robberies have been carried out by a crew of superscientific humanoids in leotards and togas.

A Universal production. EXECUTIVE PRODUCER: Ken Johnson. PRODUCER: Richard Milton. DIRECTOR AND SCREENWRITER: Johnson. CAMERA: Howard Schwartz. MUSIC: Joe Harnell.

SUPPORTING PLAYERS: Carlene Watkins, Tiger Williams, Pamela Brull, Diane Markoff.

CLONE MASTER
NBC-TV telefilm (1978). Color, 120 mins. airtime.

A pilot for a proposed series that never quite made it. Scientist Simon Shane (Art Hindle) is a cloning genius, coming up with 13 identical adult replicas of himself. Had the script sold, *Clone Master*'s producer planned to spotlight the adventure of a different clone each week. Featured in the show was Ralph Bellamy as Shane's boss.

PRODUCER: Mel Ferber. WRITER: John D. F. Black.

NBC-TV

Clone Master

COLD NIGHT'S DEATH, A
ABC-TV telefilm (1973). Color, 90 mins. airtime.

When a scientist dies at an Arctic research lab, two quarrelsome scientists are sent to take his place. Once they get there, however, they forget all their personality problems. The research-lab monkeys are now conducting experiments of their own and guess who the guinea pigs are? It's enough to drive a scientist bananas.

A Spelling-Goldberg production. DIRECTOR: Jerrold Freedman.

CAST: Robert Culp, Eli Wallach, Michael C. Gwynne.

COMMANDO CODY
NBC-TV weekly series (1955). B/w, 30-min. episodes.

Commando Cody, the movie-serial "Sky Marshal of the Universe," landed with a thud on the video airwaves in 1955, lasting but four months on the air. Judd Holdren re-created his movie character of Cody. Cody was assisted in his fight against dastardliness by assistants Joan Albright (Aline Towne) and Ted Richards (William Schallert). Leading the cheerleading squad for the bad guys was Greg Grey as Retik, the evil alien master of the moon. Along for the ride were Peter Brocco as Dr. Varney and Craig Kelly as henchman Henderson. Not exactly a highpoint in video programming.

COURAGEOUS CAT
Syndicated cartoon series (1961). Color, five-min. episodes.

A semiparody of the superscientific comic-book masked heroes, this series of cartoons pitted Courageous Cat and Minute Mouse against such evil fellows as Rodney Rodent, Professor Shaggy Dog, and Professor Noodle Stroodle. Disney had nothing to worry about.

CRAIG KENNEDY, CRIMINOLOGIST
Syndicated weekly series (1952). B/w, 30-min. episodes.

Scientific sleuthing was the method master criminologist Craig Kennedy (Donald Woods) used to solve gangland crimes in this short-lived series.

CYBORG BIG "X"
Syndicated weekly animated series (1965). Color, 30-min. episodes.

Arika is a cyborg with the brain of a human and the body of a robot. Week after week he fights evil using a magnetic pen—proving that, even in the world of sf, the pen is mightier than the sword.

DARKER SIDE OF TERROR, THE
CBS-TV telefilm (1979). Color, 120 mins. airtime.

Just cloning around again. Ray Milland portrays an elderly chemistry whiz who's hard at work creating a clone of his assistant, a square-jawed fellow played by Robert Forster. Understand-

CBS-TV

The Darker Side of Terror

ably annoyed when a colleague (David Sheiner) cops his papers and wins the department chairmanship, scientist Forster decides to speed up the cloning experiment on his own in order to win fame a bit sooner. He blows it and his full-grown cellmate emerges slightly deranged. This clone's a killer, folks. Proving the point, he does a quick Boris Karloff shuffle through the college community, coming up with a brutal solution to the population explosion. Worse yet, the clone has his eyes (and boy, are they weird) on his dad's wife, played by Adrienne Barbeau. Forster, realizing he's created a test-tube terror, resorts to the tried-and-true method of setting his lab, his creation, and himself on fire during the finale. Traditionalist.

A Shaner/Ramrus production in association with Bob Banner Associates. PRODUCERS: John Shaner, Al Ramrus. DIRECTOR: Gus Trikonis. SCREENPLAY: Shaner and Ramrus. CINEMATOGRAPHY: Don Morgan. SPECIAL EFFECTS: Richard Albane. ART DIRECTOR: Bill Sandell. MUSIC: Paul Chihara.

SUPPORTING PLAYERS: John Lehne, Denise Du Barry, Jack De Mave, Ann Sweeney, Heather Hobbs, Eddie Quillan.

DEADLY DREAM, THE
ABC-TV telefilm (1971). Color, 90 mins. airtime.

A genetics expert (Lloyd Bridges) has discovered a way to manipulate hereditary factors in a manner that would create a superintelligent strain of humans. There are some, however, who consider this line of experimentation immoral. The scientist is plagued by a series of dreams wherein he is stalked, cornered, and condemned to death by a strange tribunal. The dreams are real.

A Universal production. PRODUCER: Stan Shpetner. DIRECTOR: Alf Kjellin. SCREENPLAY: Barry Oringer. CINEMATOGRAPHY: Jack Marta.

Me²

I think that somewhere along the line, Captain Kirk and I melded. It may have been only the technical necessity: the thrust of doing a television show every week is such that you can't hide behind too many disguises. Much of what was Captain Kirk is me. I don't know about the other way around.

William Shatner

SUPPORTING PLAYERS: Janet Leigh, Leif Erickson, Carl Betz, Don Stroud, Richard Jaeckel.

DR. WHO
Time-Life/BBC weekly/daily series (1963–   ; syndicated). B/w (1963–68) and color (from 1968), 30-min. episodes.

The longest-running sf series in the history of TV, *Dr. Who* has been Great Britain's biggest ratings winner for over 15 years. Dr. Who is one of the Time Lords of the Planet Gallifrey . . . a planet adept at travel through time and space. After thousands of years of zip-

Dr. Who

ping through the centuries in their T.A.R.D.I.S. (Time and Relative Distance in Space) machines, devices that look suspiciously like British phone booths, the citizens of Gallifrey decide to call it quits, relax, and time-travel no more. Stealing a T.A.R.D.I.S. for time travel, Dr. Who is caught and exiled to Earth's solar system, where he uses his powers to defend Good against Evil. He has his hands full, too, fighting off alien Daleks, killer viruses, robots, Cybermen, and Mechanoids.

Since debuting in Great Britain in 1963, Dr. Who has changed stars several times. Rather than ignore the change, the producers of the show explain that the Time Lords are capable of regenerating their bodies as the original shapes get too old to function properly. And thus, Dr. Who has assumed the guise (in order) of actors William Hartnell, Patrick Troughton, Jon Pertwee, and Tom Baker.

PRODUCER: Graham Williams. CREATOR: TERRY NATION. VISUAL EFFECTS: Mat Irvine. SOUND EFFECTS: Dick Mills.

SUPPORTING PLAYERS: Elisabeth Sladen, Ian Marter, Louise Jameson, Roger Delgado, Katy Manning, Caroline John, Nicholas Courtney.

DODO—THE KID FROM OUTER SPACE

Syndicated weekly animated series (1967). Color, 30-min. episodes.

From the atomic planet Hena Hydo comes Dodo and his pet, Campy. Arriving on Earth, they aid Professor Fingers in his various projects geared toward the betterment of humanity.

EARTH II

ABC-TV telefilm (1971). Color, 120 mins. airtime.

In the near future, an orbiting space station becomes an independent country. The peaceful goings-on down below on planet Earth are disrupted somewhat by the presence of an orbiting bomb. Guess who's in the general vicinity to take a bit of heroic action?

An MGM production. DIRECTOR: Tom Gries. SCREENPLAY: William Read Woodfield, Alan Balter. ART DIRECTORS: George W. Davis, Edward Carfagno. CINEMATOGRAPHY: Michel Hugo. SPECIAL EFFECTS: J. McMillan Johnson, Robert Ryder, Art Cruickshank, Howard Anderson, Jr. MUSIC: Lalo Shifrin.

CAST: Gary Lockwood, Tony Franciosa, Mariette Hartley, Gary Merrill, Hari Rhodes, Lew Ayres.

EIGHTH MAN, THE

Syndicated weekly animated series (1965). Color, 30 mins. airtime per episode.

In the 21st century, the forces of Good are still dancing toe to toe with the forces of Evil. In Metro City, the home of the Metro International squad of crime fighters, agent Peter Brady is killed while attempting to put the lid on Saucer Lip, an all-around rotten guy. Professor Genius (it pays to advertise) distills Brady's life-force and slips it into robot-creation Tobor—the Eighth Man. A crime fighter to end all crime fighters is born—er—plugged in.

EVIL TOUCH, THE

Syndicated weekly series (1973). Color, 30 mins. airtime per episode.

Host Anthony Quayle guided his audiences on a kamikaze trip into the world of fantasy and sf in this low-budget series. Week after week, guest stars would be trapped in a seemingly endless script, pitting their acting talents against waves of ennui. Nearly out for the count during the show's single season were Darren McGavin as a doctor haunted by the original owner of a heart he has just transplanted, Carol Lynley as a calculating murderer, and Richard Lupino as a doctor who plans to steal from the dead. Anthony Quayle always looked as if he was in front of the camera only because his paycheck had not arrived as yet.

FANTASTIC FOUR, THE
ABC-TV weekly animated series (1967–70). Color, 30-min. episodes.

Based on the Marvel comic book characters, this Saturday morning show recounted the exploits of four scientists: Reed Richards (the voice of Gerald Mohr), Sue Richards (Jo Ann Pflug), Johnny Storm (Jack Flounders), and Ben Grimm (Paul Frees). The quartet are on board an exploratory space rocket that zips through a strange radioactive belt that is skirting the Earth. Strange things happen to their human forms as a result. Reed has the ability to stretch like taffy and renames himself Mr. Fantastic. Sue, his wife, acquires the ability to fade, fade, fade away, thus becoming Invisible Girl. Johnny becomes the too-hot-to-handle Human Torch. Ben becomes super-monstrous and superstrong, ergo his new moniker, the Thing.

A Hanna-Barbera production.

FANTASTIC FOUR, THE
NBC-TV weekly animated series (1978–   ). Color, 30-min. episodes.

A new version of the Marvel comics adventure format, featuring the exploits of Dr. Reed Richards (Mr. Fantastic), Sue Storm (the Invisible Girl), Ben Grimm (the Thing), and Charlie the Robot.

A DePatie-Freland production. Adapted and written by Stan Lee and Roy Thomas. STORYBOARDS: Jack Kirby.

FANTASTIC JOURNEY
NBC-TV telefilm (1977). Color, 90 mins. airtime.

This confused pilot film for the equally confusing series-to-come (see the following entry) managed to dredge up several dozen sf-film clichés and then simply abandon them as the story progressed. A group of scientists led by Dr. Fred Walters (Carl Franklin) and marine biologist Paul Jordan (Scott Thomas) and including in its ranks Paul's son, Scott (Ike Eisenmann), Ben Wallace (Leif Erickson), and Eve Costigan (Susan Howard), is shipwrecked in the Bermuda Triangle and cast ashore on an unknown island. There they meet Indian Varian (Jared Martin), a fellow who is really a man from the 23rd century and whose craft has also rammed into the Triangle.

He explains that the island the survivors have found is really a land "vortex": a place that exists simultaneously in different times and dimensions. If one moves eastward on the island, one can travel into the past, present, and future. While heading east, the modern-day humans are attacked by 16th-century pirates. No sooner do they get out of that mess than they run into the nasty people of Atlantium, a futuristic city containing the survivors of the lost continent of Atlantis.

A Bruce Lansbury production, in association with Columbia Pictures. PRODUCER: Leonard Katzman. DIRECTOR: Andrew V. McLaglen. TELEPLAY: Merwin Gerard, Michael Michaelian, Kathryn Michaelian Powers.

FANTASTIC JOURNEY
NBC-TV weekly series (1977). Color, 60 mins. airtime per episode.

Picking up where the pilot film left off, NBC tried to toss everything but the kitchen sink into this sf stew. Upon viewing the pilot film, in which the survivors on the Bermuda Triangle island-vortex journeyed only into the past, the network brass decided that the past was dull and only the future should be explored. Three characters from the original film were also scrapped. At that point, producer Bruce Lansbury had to rework totally his story concept, deep-six half of his characters, chop off 25 percent of the pilot film, and

NBC-TV

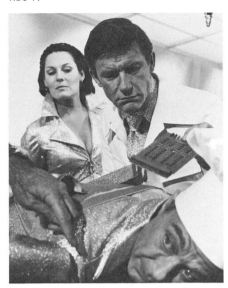

Fantastic Journey

add an extra 24 minutes explaining that, in the future, the only place his stragglers would be heading was to-morrowland. It's no wonder that the subsequent series was scatterbrained.

New regulars Liana (Katie Saylor), a magical Atlantean, and Jonathan Willoway (Roddy McDowall), a larcenous scientist with a heart of gold, were added in the second and third episodes. The show was cancelled after 10 showings.

A Bruce Lansbury production, in association with Columbia Pictures Television. PRODUCER: Leonard Katzman. STORY CONSULTANTS: Calfin Clements, Jr.; D. C. FONTANA.

FANTASTIC VOYAGE
ABC-TV weekly animated series (1968–70). Color, 30-min. episodes.

There oughtta be a law. Loosely based on the film of the same name, this Saturday morning kid-vid show took its viewers into the world of law enforcement as embodied by a secret U.S. organization called the Combined Miniature Defense Force. The Force fights nastiness by shrinking key agents to microscopic size and sending them off into battle in a teeny-weenie plane called the *Voyager*. Main peewee agents are Commander Jonathan Kid,

biologist Eric Stone, all-around scientific whiz Cosby Birdwell, and resident mystic the Guru. Voices were provided by Marvin Miller, Jane Webb, and Ted Knight. Music by Gordon Zahler.

FAR OUT SPACE NUTS, THE
CBS-TV weekly series (1975–76). Color, 30-min. episodes.

Slapstick NASA crewmen Junior (Bob Denver) and Barney (Chuck McCann) are loading food onto a moon rocket when they accidentally launch it. Ha! Ha! They are lost in space forever. Ha! Ha! Ha! Helping them rebound from weird planet to weird planet are alien pal Lantana (Eve Bruce); her pet, the Honk (Patty Maloney); and her robot, Crakor (Stan Jenson). If it's any consolation to genre buffs, 30 years ago the same plot would have been treated as a melodrama.

PRODUCERS: Sid and Marty Krofft, in association with Al Schwartz. ASSOCIATE PRODUCER: Mary Jo Blue. ART DIRECTOR: Herman Zimmerman.

FIREBALL XL-5
ITC-TV (syndicated) weekly series (G.B., 1961). B/w, 30-min. episodes.

A Supermarionation series starring puppets. In the 21st century, World Space Patrol pilot Steve Zodiac takes his ship *Fireball XL-5* to different planets in order to save them from evil. Headquartered in Space City, he is aided by copilot Venus, Commander Zero, Lt. 90, Robert the Robot, and Professor Matic. His biggest enemies are Mr. and Mrs. Superspy (it pays to advertise) and the Brigs Brothers.

EXECUTIVE PRODUCER: Gerry Anderson. Created by Gerry and Sylvia Anderson. MUSIC: Barry Gray. DIRECTOR OF PHOTOGRAPHY: John Read. ART DIRECTOR: Reg Hill. SPECIAL EFFECTS: Derek Meddings.

VOICES: Paul Maxwell, Sylvia Anderson, David Graham, John Bluthal, Gerry Anderson.

FIRE IN THE SKY, A
NBC-TV telefilm (1978). Color, 120 mins.

When AIP announced plans to release METEOR in late 1978 or early 1979, one of the first TV vehicles to cash in on the disaster-from-space ploy was *A Fire in the Sky,* a scaled-down version of *Meteor*'s main premise.

In this tale, a fiery comet, hurtling through space, is on a collision course with Earth. Jason Voight (Richard Crenna) and fellow-astronomer Jennifer Dreiser (Joanna Miles) figure out that the invader from space is going to totally wipe out Phoenix, Arizona, in eight days. The trouble is, no one believes them. The governor of the state (Nicholas Coster) is just too mellow to fall for the ploy. Newspaper publisher David Allen (David Dukes) is too busy making hubba-hubba with perky reporter Carole Wasco (Maggie Wellman) to even think about any other sort of hot stuff. His estranged wife, TV station owner Sharon Allen (Elizabeth Ashley), breaks the story. The president of the United States (Andrew Duggan) wants to break Arizona's governor. The evacuation proceeds a wee bit too late. Voight gives his truck to a bunch of stranded Indians, remaining behind with a few others. He gets a bird's eye-view of the comet's hit on Phoenix; unfortunately, it's from beneath the comet. Voight is demolished. Phoenix is demolished. The governor is demolished even before Phoenix, crashing his plane in a panicky getaway. Sharon and David find true love under the debris and AIP doesn't release *Meteor* for another year anyhow.

A Bill Driskill production, in association with Columbia Pictures Television. PRODUCER: Hugh Benson. DIRECTOR: Jerry Jameson. SCREENPLAY: Dennis Nemic and Michael Blankfort, from a story by Paul Gallico.

FLASH GORDON
Syndicated weekly series (1953). B/w, 30-min. episodes.

Giving new meaning to the word "cheap" was this short-lived version of the Alex Raymond comic strip. Flash Gordon (Steve Holland), citizen of 21st-century Earth, fought evil on a weekly basis with Dale Arden (Irene Champlin) and Dr. Alexis Zarkov (Joseph Nash).

FLASH GORDON
NBC-TV weekly animated series (1979–   ). Color, 30-min. episodes.

In the distant future, Flash Gordon, Dale Arden, and Dr. Zarkov battle Ming the Merciless on the planet Mongo. Based on Alex Raymond's comic-strip character, this series is a prelude to a proposed two-hour, animated, made-for-TV movie.

A Filmation production. EXECUTIVE PRODUCERS: Lou Scheimer, Norm Prescott. PRODUCER: Don Christiensen. WRITER (TWO-HOUR TELEPLAY): Sam Peeples.

FRANKENSTEIN JR. AND THE IMPOSSIBLES
CBS-TV weekly animated series (1966–68). Color, 30-min. episodes.

Frankenstein, Jr., is a 30-foot robot (the voice of Ted Cassidy). The Impossibles are a group of strange-looking folks named Multi Man (Don Messick), Fluid Man (Paul Frees), and Coil Man (Hal Smith). They are U.S. government agents disguised as members of a rock band. The beat goes on.

A Hanna-Barbera production. SUPPORTING VOICES: Dick Beals as Buzz, John Stephenson as Father.

FRANKENSTEIN: THE TRUE STORY
NBC-TV telefilm (1973). Color, two 120-min. episodes.

Not exactly the "true" story in the literary sense of the word, this epic dramatization of the MARY W. SHELLEY novel uses the main premise of the legend as a springboard for some monstrous goings-on, both good and slightly goofy. Appalled by the brutal life around him, Dr. Victor Frankenstein (Leonard Whiting) creates a new "Adam" from the parts of deceased humans. The striking young creature (Michael Sarrazin) is brought to "life" in the traditional mad-lab manner, with the able assistance of Dr. Henry Clerval (David McCallum). Hopes for a faithful adaptation of the book are high when Frankenstein smiles down upon his creation and states, "*You* shall teach *us* how to live."

The monster, of course, is wrapped none too tightly in the head area and goes on his rampage according to schedule. Belittling the dignity of the tale a bit, however, is the addition of new character Dr. Polidori (James Mason), a dapper old coot who decides to create a mate for the monster in a most haphazard manner.

A Universal production. PRODUCER: Hunt Stromberg, Jr. DIRECTOR: Jack Smight. SCREENPLAY: Christopher Isherwood, Don Barchardy. MUSIC: Gil Melle. CINEMATOGRAPHY: Arthur Ibbeston.

SUPPORTING PLAYERS: Jane Seymour as Agatha, Nicola Paget as Elizabeth, Michael Wilding as Sir Richard Fanshawe.

FUTURE COP
ABC-TV telefilm (1976). Color, 90 mins. airtime.

The pilot for a short-lived series (see following entry). Cop Joe Cleaver (Ernest Borgnine) and partner Bill Bundy (John Amos) are assigned a rookie partner John Haven (Michael Shannon) who is, in reality, an android.

EXECUTIVE PRODUCER: Tony Williams. DIRECTOR: Jud Taylor.

FUTURE COP
ABC-TV weekly series (1976). Color, 60-min. episodes.

One of three attempts to launch a show featuring a robot cop. Michael Shannon starred as the rookie android, Ernest Borgnine as his tough partner. John Amos played mediating Officer Bundy.

ABC-TV

Future Cop

Zone Defense

Once I couldn't mention Hitler's gas ovens because a gas company sponsored the show. I simply got tired of battling. I'm not writing anything controversial in the new series. Now that we're petulant aging men,

it no longer behooves us to bite the hand that feeds us.

Rod Serling, creator of *The Twilight Zone*

EXECUTIVE PRODUCERS: Anthony Wilson, Gary Damsker. PRODUCER: Everett Chambers. CREATORS: Anthony Wilson, Allen Epstein.

GALACTICA 1980
ABC-TV weekly mini-series (1980). Color, three 60 min. episodes, and weekly series (1980).

A hastily concocted, kiddie-oriented sequel to the departed megabuck *Battlestar Galactica* series, *Galactica 1980* started off as a 90-minute telefilm, which was subsequently expanded to a three-part mini-series. Provided an early-evening time slot, the show did so well with the small fry that it was given a green light by the network for a weekly format.

Set approximately 30 years after the action of the first series, *1980* finds the crew of the *Galactica* (led by a bearded Commander Adama, still played by Lorne Greene) still being pursued by the Cylons (plenty of stock footage from the original show). Wonder of wonders, the aliens discover their pre-ordained new home planet Earth. But wait! Earth of 1980 is no match technologically for the might of the Cylons. With the *Galactica* and its sister spaceships luring the Cylons away from the defenseless planet, two young crew members—Captain Troy (Boxey grown up, played by Kent McCord) and Lt. Dillon (Barry Van Dyke)—are sent to Earth to help advance the cause of science. They are aided by Earthling Jamie (Robyn Douglass) and thwarted by a third *Galactica* crew member who hops, skips, and jumps through Earth history in an attempt to boost the power base of such evil historical groups as the Nazis.

EXECUTIVE PRODUCER: Glen Larson. SUPERVISING PRODUCER: David O'Connell.

GEMINI MAN, THE
NBC-TV telefilm (1975). Color.

When NBC's INVISIBLE MAN series folded in 1975, the network quickly remodeled the story line and came up with this pilot film (see following entry). Ben Murphy was the scientist who could remain invisible for a limited amount of time. Problem was that even when visible, it was hard for him to make his presence felt.

A Universal production. PRODUCERS: Harve Bennett, Leslie Stevens. DIRECTOR: Allan Levi.

SUPPORTING PLAYERS: Katherine Crawford, Richard Dysart, Dana Elcar.

GEMINI MAN, THE
NBC-TV weekly series (1976). Color, 60-min. episodes.

A mercifully short-lived Invisible Man rip-off produced by Harve Bennett of THE SIX MILLION DOLLAR MAN fame. Researcher Sam Casey (Ben Murphy) is caught in a nuclear explosion. His body's cellular structure comes unhinged a wee bit as a result. Girl friend/colleague Dr. Abby Lawrence (Katherine Crawford) and boss Leonard Driscoll (William Sylvester) are quite amazed to find out that Sam can make himself invisible for 15 minutes a day by using a small wristwatch device he has developed. He becomes the government's most important, albeit boring, secret weapon. This one lasted half a season.

GENESIS II
CBS-TV telefilm (1973). Color, 90 mins. airtime.

Following the demise of STAR TREK, producer Gene Roddenberry attempted to return to video sf with *Genesis II*, a well-intentioned pilot film for a series never picked up by the network. A 20th-century scientist (Alex Cord) is involved with cryogenic experimentation when a malfunction puts him into a prolonged state of suspended animation. Awakening in the year 2133, he finds a brave new world that's not so brave and has a brand of newness that makes one long for the good old "bad" days. It's mutants vs. humans, with our hero caught in the middle.

PRODUCER AND SCREENWRITER: Gene Roddenberry. DIRECTOR: John Llewellyn Moxey. ART DIRECTOR: Hilyard Brown. CINEMATOGRAPHY: Gerald Perry Finnerman.

SUPPORTING PLAYERS: Ted Cassidy, Mariette Hartley, Percy Rodrigues, Lynn Marta, Harvey Jason.

GET SMART!
NBC-TV (1965–69) and CBS-TV (1969–70) weekly series, now syndicated. Color, 30-min. episodes.

Codeveloped by Buck Henry and Mel Brooks, *Get Smart!* was an epic of its satirical genre. A spoof of the James Bond/MAN FROM U.N.C.L.E. school of thought, the show centers around the blunders made by intrepid but inept CONTROL secret agent Maxwell Smart (Don Adams), a.k.a. Agent 86, and sultry Agent 99 (Barbara Feldon). CONTROL is a grandiose organization led by Thaddeus, a.k.a. the Chief (Ed Platt), and populated by such characters as Hymie the Robot (Dick Gautier); supermacho Larrabee (Robert Karvelas); master of disguise (sort of) Agent 44 (Victor French); Dr. Steele (Ellen Weston), head of the CONTROL Lab, which is, in turn, located in an old burlesque theater; Charlie Watkins (Angelique), a beautiful blond who is really a man; and Fang, the wonder dog (a.k.a. Agent K-13).

Fighting the forces of goodness and niceness is evil organization KAOS. KAOS loves to be loathsome and, to insure that quality, is populated by such heavies as Conrad Siegfried (Bernie Kopel), the head of KAOS, and aide Starker (King Moody). Week after week, KAOS fights CONTROL, with Smart usually getting in the way.

GIGANTOR
Syndicated weekly animated series (1966). Color, 30-min. episodes.

From Japan came 21st-century robot Gigantor. Fighting crime week after week with 12-year-old master Jimmy

Sparks, Gigantor helps overworked police inspector Blooper get his man and/or creature.

GIRL FROM U.N.C.L.E., THE

NBC-TV weekly series (1966–67). Color, 60-min. episodes.

A spin-off from the popular MAN FROM U.N.C.L.E. series, but with none of the original's sense of humor and flair, this brief show offered Stefanie Powers as United Network Command for Law and Enforcement agent April Dancer and Noel Harrison as stalwart Mark Slate. Week after week, they are sent into gadgetry-laden adventures by Mr. Waverly (Leo G. Carroll), the head of the establishment.

An MGM-Arena production. EXECUTIVE PRODUCER: Norman Felton.

GODZILLA POWER HOUR, THE

NBC-TV weekly animated series (1978–   ). Color, 60- and 30-min. episodes.

Fire-breathing lizard-mutant Godzilla becomes a hero in this animated series. Along with nephew Godzooky and Captain Majors of the spaceship *Calico*, the big fella defends Earth on a weekly basis.

A Hanna-Barbera production. DESIGN: Dave Stevens.

HAUSER'S MEMORY

NBC-TV telefilm (1970). Technicolor, 120 mins. airtime.

A well-respected European scientist, physicist Hauser, is dying. As his body lapses into coma, the United States panics over the vast wealth of scientific knowledge and secrets that will disappear with the consciousness of Hauser. They devise a daring plan to rescue the crucial secrets from the withering brain. In a radical operation, they extract a fluid from Hauser's brain that contains much of his memory. The CIA plans to inject the fluid into a willing human

guinea pig and thus keep Hauser's memory alive.

But who will become the memory's new owner? The CIA picks a condemned criminal. The U.S. scientific community picks an elderly fellow whose body may not take the strain. Seeking to end the standoff, a dedicated young scientist, Hillel Mondoro (David McCallum) injects Hauser's brain fluid into his system. The liberal young Jew finds himself possessed by the emotions and thoughts of Hauser, an ex-Nazi who spurned the Nazis when he saw the atrocities they performed with the use of his medical ideas. He was captured by the SS, declared a traitor by the party, and nearly killed.

With Hauser gaining more and more control with every waking hour that passes, Hillel sees fit to leave his pregnant wife, Karen (Susan Strasberg), and journey behind the Iron Curtain and into the heart of Germany in search of Hauser's long-lost son, his wife, and the SS man who turned him in. A memorable Jekyll and Hyde drama ensues.

PRODUCER: Jack Laird. DIRECTOR: Boris Sagal. SCREENPLAY: Adrian Spies, from the novel by CURT SIODMAK. CINEMATOGRAPHY: Petrus Schloemp. ART DIRECTOR: Ellen Schmidt. MAKEUP: Bud Westmore. MUSIC: Billy Byers.

SUPPORTING PLAYERS: Lili Palmer as Anna Hauser, Robert Webber as Dorsey, Leslie Nielsen as Slaughter, Helmut Kautner as Kramer, Peter Ehrlich as Kucera.

THE HERCULOIDS

CBS-TV weekly animated series (1967–69). Color, 30-min. episodes.

In the future, on a far-off planet of Utopian design, a group of superstrong, futuristic animals, The Herculoids, band together to protect their home and their leader, Zandor (the voice of Mike Road), from intergalactic gangsters. In for the hand-to-tendril combat are Tarra (Virginia Gregg), Iggo the living rock (Mike Road), Gleep the blob (Don Messick), Gloop the blob (Messick), Dorno the 10-legged rhino (Teddy Eccles), and Zok the dragon (Mike Road).

HOLMES AND YO-YO
ABC-TV weekly series (1976). Color, 30-min. episodes.

Get Smart! producer Leonard Stern turned to nuts-and-bolts burlesque in this alleged comedy. Richard B. Shull starred as dimwit cop Alexander Holmes and John Shuck appeared as equally-ditzed robot partner Gregory "Yo-Yo" Yoyonovich. The show did pioneer one new sf-genre concept, despite its flaws: it was the first show ever to have a robot named Yoyonovich. Take that, FORBIDDEN PLANET!

IMMORTAL, THE
ABC-TV telefilm (1970). Color, 90 mins. airtime.

This ABC Movie of the Week served as a pilot film for a short-lived series of the same name (see the following entry). After an accident, test driver Ben Richards (Christopher George) discovers that he has a totally unique blood type—a type that makes him immune to all disease and actually allows him eternal youth. Everything looks rosy for Ben's future until word of his strange condition reaches the ears of aging multimillionaire Jordan Braddock (Barry Sullivan). Braddock is determined to capture Richards and imprison him in his mansion. The object of the kidnapping scheme is to give the millionaire his own private fountain of youth, with constant transfusions from Ben restoring youth to the senior citizen. Ben doesn't exactly endorse the scheme and begins a seemingly endless run for his life.

A Paramount Films production. PRODUCER: Lou Morheim. DIRECTOR: Joseph Sargeant. SCREENPLAY: Robert Specht, based on the novel *The Immortals*, by JAMES GUNN. CINEMATOGRAPHY: Howard Schwartz. MUSIC: Dominic Frontiere.

SUPPORTING PLAYERS: Jessica Walter as Janet Braddock, Carol Lynley as Sylvia Cartwright, Ralph Bellamy as Dr. Pearce.

IMMORTAL, THE
ABC-TV weekly series (1970). Color, 60-min. episodes.

Ben Richards (Christopher George) has a blood type that can act as a fountain of youth to various oldsters via blood transfusions. Since Ben does not want to spend the rest of his life as the flesh-and-blood equivalent of a Stop 'n' Shop snack bar, he takes it on the hoof. His running lasted but one season.

A Paramount production. Based on the novel *The Immortals*, by JAMES GUNN.

INCREDIBLE HULK, THE
CBS-TV telefilm (1977). Color, 120 mins. airtime.

Based on the Marvel Comics character, this pilot film for a subsequent series (see the following entry) was intelligently scripted and deftly directed. Dr. David Bruce Banner (Bill Bixby) is experimenting with gamma radiation when he accidentally subjects himself to a massive overdose. As a result, whenever the handsome young scientist undergoes intense emotional strain, he finds himself metamorphosing into a

CBS-TV

The Incredible Hulk

seven-foot-tall green hulk of a human (Lou Ferrigno). Fellow-scientist Dr. Elaina Marks (Susan Sullivan) attempts to cure Banner, but a lab accident leads to her death, Banner's supposed death, and an accusation of murder against the green creature. Banner is doomed to roam the countryside under a variety of aliases while trying to come up with a cure.

A Universal production. PRODUCER, WRITER, AND DIRECTOR: Kenneth Johnson.

INCREDIBLE HULK, THE
CBS-TV weekly series (1977–   ). Color, 60-min. episodes.

Dr. David Bruce Banner (Bill Bixby) can change into a hulking green creature (Lou Ferrigno) whenever emotionally overwrought. Roaming through the world looking for a cure, he is pursued by a relentless newspaperman (Jack Colvin) who believes the green creature to be a murderer.

Based on the Marvel Comics character. EXECUTIVE PRODUCER: Kenneth Johnson. PRODUCERS: Johnson, Nick Corea, James O. Parriott, Chuck Bowman.

INVADERS, THE
ABC-TV weekly series (1967–68). Color, 60-min. episodes.

Roy Thinnes starred in this series as David Vincent, a flying-saucer-plagued first cousin of *The Fugitive*, yet another misunderstood character created by *Invaders* producer Quinn Martin. The premise of this show was actually quite interesting. Vincent has seen the vanguard of an alien invasion of Earth, the humanoid aliens slipping effortlessly into the population. They resemble Earthlings in every detail but one . . . mutated pinky fingers. David tries to warn his fellow citizens but is dismissed as a madman. The aliens, trying to find a nice new home since their old one is slowly dying, would like to see David dead. David would like to see the aliens dead. The populace at large would like to see David put away in a padded cell.

Week after week, David fights a one-man counterattack against the alien invaders. When that plot premise grew tedious, producer Martin introduced during the second season an organization known as the Believers, a group of alien-watching oldsters who pay David for his legwork. Kent Smith, head of the Believers, became a regular (as Edgar Scoville) during the second year.

EXECUTIVE PRODUCER: Quinn Martin. PRODUCER: Alan Armer. CREATOR: Larry Cohen. MUSIC: Dominic Frontiere.

INVISIBLE MAN, THE
Syndicated weekly series (G.B., 1958). B/w, 30-min. episodes.

Scientist Peter Brady is working on experiments dealing with the refraction of light when an accident occurs in his lab, rendering him invisible. Initially imprisoned by the British government as a threat to the country's security, Brady later reaches an understanding with the Ministry and becomes an invisible spy. He conducts his missions while simultaneously attempting to find an antidote for his condition.

CAST: Lisa Daniely as Diane Brady, Deborah Walting as Sally Brady, Ernest Clark as Sir Charles, and an anonymous actor as the Invisible Man.

PRODUCER: Ralph Smart. Based on the novel by H. G. WELLS.

INVISIBLE MAN, THE
NBC-TV telefilm (1975). Color, 90 mins. airtime.

Daniel Weston (David McCallum) is a scientist working on a machine that can render solid matter invisible in this pilot for an NBC series (see the following entry). He uses the machine on himself and, logically, turns himself invisible. Using the machine a second time, he finds that he cannot make the return trip back to visibility. Worse yet, every government and military establishment in the world wants to get its hands on his machine. He destroys his work and wanders about the land invisible until he can approach an old friend for an antidote. His wife (Melinda Fee) just can't see what all the fuss is about.

A Universal production. Based on the novel by H. G. WELLS. DIRECTOR: Robert M. Lewis.

SUPPORTING PLAYERS: Henry Darrow, Jackie Cooper.

INVISIBLE MAN, THE
NBC-TV weekly series (1975). Color, 60-min. episodes.

Daniel Weston (David McCallum) is employed by the KLAE Corporation to investigate the possibilities of matter transference. Using a new laserbeam technique, Weston develops a serum that renders him invisible. Although his wife, Kate (Melinda Fee), doesn't see the advantage of such a serum, Daniel's boss, Walter Carlson (Craig Stevens), sure does. KLAE is a research center that handles many government contracts. Carlson envi-

---

Spooky Stuff
The way the studio wants to show it, a character won't be able to walk by a graveyard; he'll have to be chased. They're trying to turn it into *Mannix* with a shroud!
    Rod Serling, on his short-lived *Night Gallery* series

---

sions Weston as the perfect U.S. undercover man. The U.S. agrees, and so, before you can say "H. G. Wells," there's invisible espionage afoot.

IT'S ABOUT TIME
CBS-TV weekly series (1966–67). Color, 30-min. episodes.

One of CBS's epic losers, this tale of time travel was overhauled twice during its single season on the air. In the first format, astronauts Frank (Frank Aletter) and Hector (Jack Mullaney) plunge into the Earth's atmosphere at a speed that sends them hurtling back to prehistoric times. They are befriended (sort of) by a host of cave people, including Gronk (Joe E. Ross), Shad (Imogene Coca), Mlor (Mary Grace), Breer (Pat Cardi), and the Cave Boss and his aide (Cliff Norton and Mike Mazurki).

When this format stiffed, plot numero two was hastily concocted. Repairing their rocket with the help of the Cave Family, the astronauts are ready to try to zip back to present-day Los Angeles. The Cave Boss, meanwhile, sees the Cave Family as having

aided evil spirits and orders them put to death. Gronk and his brood stow away on the rocket and—guess what—land in L.A. with the astronauts. The remaining shows centered around their assimilating into L.A. culture (no problem, there) and Mac and Hector's attempts to keep their presence a secret from NASA.

SUPPORTING PLAYERS: Kathleen Freeman as Mrs. Boss, Jan Arvan as Dr. Hamilton, and Alan De Witt as General Taylor.

JASON OF STAR COMMAND
CBS-TV weekly series (1978–). Color, episodes of varying length shown during the *Tarzan and the Super 7* Saturday-morning show.

A spin-off from SPACE ACADEMY. A secret operation of the Asteroid Academy, Star Command is a law-enforcement agency championed by agent Jason (Craig Littler). Fighting for niceness throughout the galaxy, Jason is aided by Dr. Parsafoot (Charlie Dell), Nicole (Susan O'Hanlon), and valiant Commander Canarvin (James Doohan). The object of their attention, for the most part, is evil Dragos (Sid Haig), commander of the Dragon ship. Toss in a couple of Star Command–controlled robots, Peepo and Wiki, and you have a mini-STAR WARS action series.

EXECUTIVE PRODUCERS: Lou Scheimer and Norm Prescott for Filmation. PRODUCER AND DIRECTOR: Arthur Nadel. ART DIRECTOR: Bill McAllister. SPECIAL EFFECTS: Gordon Graff, Bruce Behan. STOP-MOTION ANIMATION: Jim Aupperle, Stephen Czerkas.

JETSONS, THE
ABC-TV (1962–64), CBS-TV (1965–66), NBC-TV (1966–67), CBS-TV (1969–70), and NBC-TV (1971–75) weekly animated series. Color. 30-min. episodes.

A Hanna-Barbera animated look at

the typical family of the futuristic 21st century: George Jetson (the voice of George O'Hanlon), Jane Jetson (Penny Singleton), Judy Jetson (Janet Waldo), and Elroy Jetson (Daws Butler). Also partaking in the futurism is George's boss, Mr. Spacely (Mel Blanc); Astro the dog (Don Messick); and robot maid Rosie (Jane van der Pyl).

Hanna-Barbera

The Jetsons

JOHNNY CYPHER IN DIMENSION ZERO
Syndicated series animated cartoons (1967). Color, six-min. episodes.

Johnny Cypher discovers the world of Dimension Zero while experimenting in his lab. Developing the power to travel through time and space, he begins a crime-fighting career.

JOHNNY JUPITER
DuMont Network weekly series (1953–54). B/w, 30-min. episodes.

Vintage kid-vid, *Johnny Jupiter* went through two formats before disappearing from the tube. In the first series, Ernest P. Duckweather, clerk and resident inventor of the Frisbee general store, accidentally discovers interplanetary television and makes contact with the planet Jupiter and puppets Johnny Jupiter, B-12, Reject the Robot, Katherine, and Dynamo.

In the second series, Duckweather,

now a mild-mannered janitor at a TV station, accidentally invents interplanetary television after-hours and again makes contact with planet Jupiter.

SUPPORTING PLAYERS: Vaughn Taylor and Cliff Hall as Mr. Frisbee, Wright King as Duckweather.

JOHNNY SOKKO AND HIS FLYING ROBOT
Syndicated weekly animated series (1968). Color, 30-min. episodes.

In the 21st century, crime fighting is carried out by the secret organization known only as UNICORN. Among its top agents are Johnny Sokko (Agent U-7); his giant robot, Marne; U-3; U-6; and the Commander.

JOSIE AND THE PUSSYCATS IN OUTER SPACE
CBS-TV weekly animated series (1972–74). Color, 30-min. episodes.

This spin-off from the animated *Josie and the Pussycats* kid-vidder (1970–72) sees the all-girl rock band posing in a NASA rocket when it is accidentally launched. They become spacey crime-fighters in the reaches of deep space.

VOICES: Janet Waldo as Josie, Jackie Joseph as Melody, Barbara Pariot as Valerie, Jerry Dexter as Alan, Sherry Alberoni as Alexander Sebastian, Don Messick as Bleep.

JOURNEY TO THE CENTER OF THE EARTH
ABC-TV weekly animated series (1967–69). Color, 30-min. episodes.

Spinning off from the JULES VERNE tale, this animated adventure once again takes Professor Oliver Lindenbrooke to the center of the Earth, accompanied by student Alec, duck Gertrude, guide Lars, and niece Cindy. Unbeknownst to the party, however, they are being trailed by evil Count Saccnusson and servant Tor. Saccnusson's ancestor, Arnie, discovered the Earth's core, and now the count wants to claim it for himself. He sets off an explosion meant to kill the professor and his pals but only succeeds in trapping them all at the core. Menaced by prehistoric beasts and strange critters, they struggle to find a way back to the Earth's surface.

VOICES: Ted Knight, Pat Harrington, Jane Webb. MUSIC: Gordon Zahler.

KILLDOZER
ABC-TV telefilm (1974). Color, 90 mins. airtime.

An asteroid slams into the Earth near a remote Pacific island, unleashing a hostile alien force. Stranded on the island are a team of construction workers who are out to build a World War II landing strip on a tight deadline. The alien presence takes over a King Kong–sized bulldozer and a hideous game of cat and mouse ensues wherein the helpless construction workers assume rodent roles in the headlight-eyes of the carnivorous killdozer.

A Universal production. PRODUCER: Herbert F. Solow. DIRECTOR: Jerry London. TELEPLAY: THEODORE STURGEON and Ed Mackillop, from the novella by Sturgeon.

CAST: Clint Walker, Carl Betz, Neville Brand, James Wainwright, Robert Ulrich.

KING KONG
ABC-TV weekly animated series (1966–69). Color, 30-min. episodes.

King Kong and his pals Professor Bond and Bobby Bond battle the forces of Evil, led by Dr. Who. Also on board the half-hour adventure is U.S. agent Tom of T.H.U.M.B. (Tiny Humans Underground Military Bureau) and his Oriental assistant, Swinging Jack.

KOLCHAK: THE NIGHT STALKER
ABC-TV weekly series (1974). Color, 60-min. episodes.

An interesting little show that was virtually destroyed by its network, *Kolchak: The Night Stalker* took the popular down-and-out newspaper reporter from his post as made-for-TV movie star and thrust him into a weekly series. The premise for the show is simple: Kolchak (Darren McGavin) is a brash, old-time newspaper reporter with the habit of getting involved with larger-than-life (or death) stories. He finds the evidence the police overlook, reaches a conclusion that usually deals with the supernatural, brings the creatures-in-question to justice, and then has his work tossed out the window as being either a pipe dream or too hot for the public to handle. Although during his single season on the tube Kolchak usually confronted his editor, Tony Vincenzo (Simon Oakland), with stories of a supernatural nature, he also had close encounters with aliens ("U.F.O."), an invisible force that consumed raw energy ("The Energy Eater"), aquamen ("The Sentry"), and rampaging robots ("Mr. R.I.N.G.").

EXECUTIVE PRODUCER: Darren McGavin. PRODUCERS: Paul Playton, Cy Chermak. CREATOR: Jeff Rice. STORY CONSULTANT: David Chase. MUSIC: Gil Melle.

SUPPORTING PLAYERS: Jack Grinnage as Ron Updyke, Ruth McDevitt as Emily Cowles.

KROFFTS SUPERSHOW, THE
ABC-TV weekly series (1976). Color, 90-min. episodes.

The *Quo Vadis* of Saturday morning kid-vidders, this ambitious effort was composed of several live adventure/comedy formats helmed by Sid and Marty Krofft. Included in this massive dose of sf super-heroics were the following segments:

"Dr. Shrinker": Villainous Dr. Shrinker (Jay Robinson) shrinks children for fun. Featuring Billy Barty as Hugo and Susan Lawrence, Ted Eccles, and Jeff McCay as the shrinkees. PRODUCER AND DIRECTOR: Jack Regas.

"Wonderbug": A Volkswagen possesses superpowers. Featuring David Levy as Barry, Carol Ann Sefflinger as Susan, John Anthony Bailey as C.C. PRODUCER AND DIRECTOR: Al Schwartz.

"Electrawoman": Reporters Lori and Mara become superheroines Electrawoman and Dynagirl, offering to their preteen male viewers both superhuman feats of strength and supertight leotards. Featuring Deirdre Hall as Electrawoman, Judy Strangis as Dynagirl, Norman Alden as Frank Hefflin. PRODUCER AND DIRECTOR: Walter Miller.

LAND OF THE GIANTS
ABC-TV weekly series (1968–70). Color, 60-min. episodes.

An ordinary spaceflight turns into a modern reworking of *Gulliver's Travels* in this futuristic fantasy. Space pilots Steve Burton (Gary Conway) and Dan Erickson (Don Marshall) are taking a shipful of passengers to London when their spacecraft is enveloped by a strange mist. Losing control of the vessel, the two men watch helplessly as they crash in strange jungle terrain. Emerging from the disabled vessel, they find themselves in an alien land, surrounded by human giants. Week after week, they battle for survival, the ultrasmall vs. the supertall.
PRODUCER AND CREATOR: Irwin Allen. MUSIC: Johnny Williams. SPECIAL EFFECTS: Lyle B. Abbott and Art Cruickshank, with Emil Kosa, Jr. MAKEUP: Ben Nye. DIRECTOR OF PHOTOGRAPHY: Howard Schwartz.

SUPPORTING PLAYERS: Kurt Kasznar as Fitzhugh, Heather Young as Betty Hamilton, Don Matheson as Mark Wilson, Deanna Lund as Valerie Scott, Stefan Arngrin as Barry Lockridge.

LAND OF THE LOST
NBC-TV weekly series (1974–77). Color, 30-min. episodes.

For the first two seasons, this opulently packaged kid-vidder offered the spectacular adventures of the Marshall family in a prehistoric world. Forest Ranger Rick (Spencer Mulligan) and children Will (Wesley Eure) and Holly (Kathy Coleman) are cruising down a river when they suddenly plunge down a waterfall, turning up in a prehistoric world populated by stop-motion animated dinosaurs, cave people, and aliens. The third season saw actor Mulligan quitting the show and, perforce, being tossed back into his own time. Simultaneously, Uncle Jack (Ron Harper), searching for his lost brother and kids, is tossed into the prehistoric prison, thus taking up the adult-oriented slack.
PRODUCERS AND CREATORS: Sid and Marty Krofft. PRODUCER: John Kubichan. STOP-MOTION ANIMATION DIRECTOR: Gene Warren. MUSIC: Larry Neiman, Jack Tiller.

SUPPORTING PLAYERS: Phillip Paley as Chake the monkey boy, Sharon Baird as Sa the monkey girl, Scott Fullerton as Ta, Walter Edminston as Enik the Sleestak, Van Snowden (with the voice of Marvin Miller) as Zarn the light-creature.

L.A. 2017
NBC-TV special presentation (1970). Color, 90 mins. airtime.

An episode of TV's *Name of the Game,* this futuristic scenario took the form of a dream. Newspaperman Gene Barry envisions what Los Angeles will be like in the future, when pollution causes the human population to live beneath the planet's surface.
PRODUCER: Dean Hargrove. DIRECTOR: Steven Spielberg. TELEPLAY: PHILIP WYLIE.

SUPPORTING PLAYERS: Edmund O'Brien, Barry Sullivan, Paul Stewart, Louise Latham.

LAST CHILD, THE
ABC-TV telefilm (1971). Color, 90 mins. airtime.

In the not-too-distant future, when the government forbids couples to have more than one child, one couple (Janet Margolin and Michael Cole) fights to save the life of their as-yet-unborn second child. Population Control Enforcement Section employee Ed Asner is out to trap the couple. A liberal senator, played by Van Heflin, is out to abolish the child-hating law.

A Paramount production. PRODUCER: Aaron Spelling. DIRECTOR: John L. Moxey. SCREENPLAY: Peter S. Fischer. CINEMATOGRAPHY: Arch Dalzell. MUSIC: Laurence Rosenthal.

SUPPORTING PLAYERS: Harry Guardino, Kent Smith.

LAST DINOSAUR, THE
ABC-TV telefilm (1977). Color, 120 mins. airtime.

Masten Thrust (Richard Boone)

leads a scientific party to a prehistoric land beneath the polar ice caps. When a Tyrannosaurus Rex attacks his party, big-game hunter Thrust vows to track it down and kill it before returning topside.

PRODUCERS: Arthur J. Rankin, Jules Bass. DIRECTORS: Alex Grasshoff, Tom Kotani. SCREENPLAY: William Overgard. SPECIAL EFFECTS: Kaziro Sagawa. MUSIC: Maury Laws.

SUPPORTING PLAYERS: Joan Van Ark, Steven Keats, Luther Rackley.

LATHE OF HEAVEN, THE
PBS (WNET) miniseries (1980). Color, 120-mins. airtime.

This ambitious, witty adaptation of URSULA K. LE GUIN's novel of the same name is a pilot for a proposed speculative-fiction series on public TV due to debut in 1981–82. Set at the end of the 20th century, *Lathe* tells the story of

PBS

The Lathe of Heaven

George Orr (Bruce Davison), a man plagued by terrifying dreams—terrifying insofar as his dreams actually come true, changing reality when he awakens. In a world where the polar ice caps have melted as a direct result of pollution, Orr sees his horribly effective dreams as another burden for the Earth to bear.

Orr begins therapy with a psychia-

trist, Dr. Haber (Kevin Conway). Rather than cure Orr, Haber tries to exploit his power, forcing the boy to dream up new realities free of war, disease, and overpopulation. Unfortunately, the dreamlike panaceas start a domino effect, and Orr is continuously forced to dream and dream again in an attempt to create a totally Utopian world . . . a world that always seems to elude his grasp.

Produced by WNET's Television Laboratory. COPRODUCERS AND CODIRECTORS: David Loxton, Fred Barzyk. SCRIPT CONSULTANT: Ursula K. Le Guin.

SUPPORTING PLAYERS: Margaret Avery, Nikki Flacks.

LEGENDS OF THE SUPERHEROES
NBC-TV special presentation (1979). Color, two 60-min. episodes.

Divided into two chapters, "The Challenge" and "The Celebrity Roast," this Superheroes satire was produced strictly for the subteen crowd. Groups of superheroes and supervillains battle it out in contests during the first week and insult each other at a celebrity "roast" in the second. (The roast is hosted by an embarrassed Ed McMahon.) Featured in both shows were Charlie Callas as Sinistro, Frank Gorshin as the Riddler, Garret Craig as Captain Marvel, Jeff Altman as Weather Wizard, Adam West and Burt Ward as Batman and Robin, Howard Morris as Dr. Sivana, Gabe Dell as Mordu, William Schallert as Retired Man (formerly, the Scarlet Cyclone), A'Leshia Brvard as Giganta, Danuta as the Black Canary, Rod Haase as the Flash, Mickey Morton as Solomon Grundy, Bill Nuckols as Hawkman, and Barbara Joyce as the Huntress.

Martians Chronicled

Tell everyone it's a good show. It's good. It's certainly better than *The Illustrated Man*. That film was dead on arrival!

Ray Bradbury, on NBC's
The Martian Chronicles

PRODUCER: Bill Carruthers. DIRECTORS: Chris Carley, Carruthers. TELE-

PLAY: Mike Marmor, Peter Gallay. ART DIRECTORS: Ed Flesh, Roger Speakman. COSTUME DESIGN: Warden Neil. SPECIAL EFFECTS: Image West, Ltd. MUSIC: Fred Werner.

LOGAN'S RUN

CBS-TV telefilm (1977). Color, 90 mins. airtime.

A pilot film for what was then intended as a series called *Logan's World* (see the following entry), this film essentially rehashed the plot of the feature film of the same name. Doomed to death at the age of 30, Logan (Gregory Harrison) and Jessica (Heather Menzies) hoof it from the futuristic Domed City and head for Sanctuary, a legendary place of good vibes. Out to stop Logan is Sandman Francis (Randy Powell), who is promised a good life in the post-30 world by the Domed City's Elder if he can cut down Logan and Jessica.

Logan and Jessica, meanwhile, are imprisoned by lonely robots Draco and Siri (Keene Curtis and Lina Raymond), who live alone in Mountain City and need a couple of masters to serve. The humans are saved by the thinking person's robot, Rem (Donald Moffat). Together, the trio hunts for Sanctuary.

An MGM production. EXECUTIVE PRODUCERS: Ivan Goff, Ben Roberts. PRODUCER: Leonard Katzman. DIREC-

CBS-TV

Logan's Run

TOR: Robert Day. TELEPLAY: WILLIAM F. NOLAN, Saul David, Leonard Katzman, based on the novel by Nolan and George C. Johnson. PRODUCTION DESIGNER: Mort Rabinowitz.

SUPPORTING PLAYERS: Ron Jahek as Riles, J. Gary Dontzig as Akers, Anthony de Longis as Ketchum.

LOGAN'S RUN

CBS-TV weekly series (1977–78). Color, 60-min. episodes.

Logan didn't run as much as stumble in this spiritless reworking of the equally cliché-ridden film. Futuristic citizens Logan (Gregory Harrison) and Jessica (Heather Menzies), along with dour robot-pal Rem (Donald Moffat), flee the pursuing Sandmen, led by Francis (Randy Powell). Logan and Jessica are fleeing the domed city in search of Sanctuary. They're both over 30, you see, and in the Domed City that means death. On TV, that can often mean tedium. Lasted 13 episodes.

An MGM production. EXECUTIVE PRODUCERS: Ivan Goff, Ben Roberts. PRODUCER: Leonard Katzman. STORY EDITOR: D. C. FONTANA. Based on the novel by WILLIAM F. NOLAN and George C. Johnson. PRODUCTION DESIGNER: Mort Rabinowitz.

LOST IN SPACE

CBS-TV weekly series (1965–68). Originally b/w, later in color, 60-min. episodes.

The ultimate kid-vid show, *Lost in Space* proved itself a prime-time hit, much to the delight to the young at heart and to the dismay of serious genre buffs. Based on the comic book *The Space Family Robinson,* this Irwin Allen series mixed sophomoric dialogue and plot lines with some interesting special effects and a cliff-hanging weekly twist that left viewers (and very often, cast members) in a state of stupefaction.

The Robinson family (Guy Williams as Professor John Robinson, Billy Mumy as son Will, June Lockhart as wife Maureen, Marta Kristen as older daughter Judy, and Angela Cartwright as younger daughter Penny) are traveling through space aboard the good ship *Jupiter Two* looking for a new

CBS-TV

Lost in Space

world to colonize. Along for the ride are copilot Don West (Mark Goddard), a loyal family robot (the voice of Don May) and evil-as-all-get-out Dr. Zachary Smith (Jonathan Harris).

Because of Smith's villainy, the Robinsons become hopelessly lost in space. Week after week, the family tries both to find their way home to Earth and to cope with various alien guest-stars that pop up from planet to planet. Smith, meanwhile, constantly connives either to abandon the family and make it back to Earth solo (via any means) or to become emperor of some small, jewel-laden planet.

EXECUTIVE PRODUCER AND CREATOR: Irwin Allen. STORY CONSULTANT: Anthony Wilson. SPECIAL EFFECTS: Lyle B. Abbott, Howard Lydecker. MAKEUP: Ben Nye. MUSIC: John Williams.

LOST SAUCER, THE
ABC-TV weekly series (1975–76). Color, 30-min. episodes.

Fi and Fum (Ruth Buzzi and Jim Nabors), two androids, land their saucer on Earth. They invite Jerry (Jarrod Johnson) and his baby-sitter, Alice (Alice Playten), aboard and take off for a planet-by-planet trip through the far reaches of slapstick space.

PRODUCERS: Sid and Marty Krofft. SPECIAL EFFECTS: Gordon Fraff.

LOVE WAR, THE
ABC-TV telefilm (1970). Color, 90 mins. airtime.

Two warring planets, Argon and Zinan, decide to settle their differences by fighting an interplanetary war by proxy. Picking one alien team from each civilization, the planets' leaders send the creatures to Earth in human form to settle their differences. It's a fight to the death, with the winning alien team's home world declared the victor in the war. Complications arise when Argonian warrior Kyle (Lloyd Bridges) falls head over tendrils in love with Earthling Sandy (Angie Dickinson). The complications get even more complicated when equally smitten Sandy turns out to be a Zinan spy. Love hurts.

A Paramount production. PRODUCER: Aaron Spelling. DIRECTOR: George McCowan. SCREENPLAY: Guerdon Trueblood, David Kidd. CINEMATOGRAPHY: Paul Uhl. MUSIC: Dominic Frontiere.

SUPPORTING PLAYERS: Harry Basch as Bal, Dan Travanty as Tod, Bill McClean as Reed, Allen Jaffe as Hort.

MAN FROM ATLANTIS, THE
NBC-TV telefilm (1977). Color, 120 mins. airtime.

A fairly interesting gimmick was concocted for this pilot film designed to usher in a subsequent series (see the following entry). Mark Harris (Patrick Duffy) is the last surviving resident of Atlantis. Surfacing off the coast of California, the webbed-fingered aquaman is saved from a landlubber's death by the quick thinking of Dr. Elizabeth Merrill (Belinda Montgomery) and C. W. (Alan Fudge). Mark is an emotional child and, new to the abovewater world, runs the risk of being taken advantage of by various unscrupulous governmental employees. He is saved by his two friends from the Foundation of Oceanic Research. Just in time, too, for Dr. Merrill, C. W., and Mark must join forces to save the world from the evil schemes concocted by villainous but lovable Mr. Schubert (Victor Buono).

EXECUTIVE PRODUCER: Herbert F. Solo for Solo Productions. PRODUCER: Robert H. Justman. DIRECTOR: Lee H. Katzin. SCREENPLAY: Mayo Simon. SPECIAL EFFECTS: Tom Fisher. PHOTOGRAPHIC EFFECTS: Gene Warren. MAKEUP: Don Cash, Jr. ART DIRECTOR: J. Smith Poplin. MUSIC: Fred Karlin.

NBC-TV

The Man from Atlantis

MAN FROM ATLANTIS, THE
NBC-TV weekly series (1977). Color, 60-min. episodes.

After getting off to a promising start, *The Man from Atlantis* quietly drifted to the bottom of the ratings quagmire. During spring of the 1977 miniseason, the show stuck fairly close to its initial premise. Atlantean Mark Harris (Patrick Duffy) week after week joined forces to battle evil with his aboveworld friends Dr. Merrill (Belinda Montgomery) and C. W. (Alan Fudge). Quite often, this evil was conjured up by rotund rascal Mr. Schubert (Victor Buono). Returning for the fall of 1977, the series underwent drastic alteration, with most of the charm of the Harris character deep-sixed in favor of less-subtle superhero qualities. Harris became the Amazing Spider-

man less the feety pajamas and a ratings casualty before the end of the year.

A Solo production. EXECUTIVE PRODUCER: Herbert F. Solow. PRODUCER: Robert H. Justman. PHOTOGRAPHIC EFFECTS: Gene Warren. MUSIC: Fred Karlin.

MAN FROM 1997, THE
ABC-TV (1957). B/w, 60-min. episodes.

First telecast as an episode of *King's Row*. A man from the future journeys to the present, bringing with him one of his contemporary history books, which will, of course, seem to forecast the future for present-day citizens.

CAST: James Garner, Gloria Talbot, Charles Ruggles.

MAN FROM U.N.C.L.E., THE
NBC-TV weekly series (1964–68). Color, 60-min. episodes.

Arising out of moviedom's fascination with James Bond, Agent 007, came this, probably the ultimate tongue-in-cheek cloak-and-dagger series. Filled with gadgetry, monomaniacally mad geniuses, and outrageous puns, *The Man from U.N.C.L.E.* took swashbuckling to its furthest degree of derangement. In New York's tiny Del Florias

MGM-TV

The Man from U.N.C.L.E.

tailor shop is housed the underground headquarters of U.N.C.L.E., the United Network Command for Law and Enforcement. Week after week, this international spy organization worked for the forces of Good and against the attempts of Evil, usually represented by enemy agents of T.H.R.U.S.H., to take over the world. U.N.C.L.E.'s main men are Napoleon Solo (Robert Vaughn), a suave and orthodoxly dashing agent, and Illya Kuryakin (David McCallum), a taciturn Russian who became the unexpected sex symbol of the show. Cheering the duo on is the head of U.N.C.L.E., Alexander Waverly (Leo Carroll), and a bevy of agent-beauties.

An MGM-Arena production. EXECUTIVE PRODUCER: Norman Felton. ART DIRECTORS: George W. Davis, Merrill Pye, others. CAMERA: Fred Koenekamp, others. MUSIC: Morton Stevens, Jerry Goldsmith, Lalo Schifrin, Leith Stevens.

MAN WHO WANTED TO LIVE FOREVER, THE
ABC-TV telefilm (1970). Color, 90 mins. airtime.

Doctors Enid Bingham (Sandy Dennis) and McCarter Purvis (Stuart Whitman) are pleased as punch to be hired by a prestigious private Canadian surgical-research center—that is, until they figure out what boss T. M. Trask (Burl Ives) is up to. The old duffer would like to live forever. To live forever, he needs new parts. And to get new parts he needs human donors . . . of both the voluntary and unsuspecting types.

A Palomar Pictures production. PRODUCER: Terry Dene. DIRECTOR: John Trent. SCREENPLAY: Henry Denker. CINEMATOGRAPHY: Marc Champion. MAKEUP: Ken Brooke.

SUPPORTING PLAYERS: Jack Creley as Dr. George Simmons, Ron Hartman as Dr. John Emmett.

MARINE BOY
Syndicated weekly animated series (1966). Color, 30-min. episodes.

In the 21st century, Ocean Patrol agent Marine Boy patrols the underwater channels of Earth, guarding against all possible submerged subversives. Aided by Splasher, his pet dolphin, and by Professor Fumble, the aquakid takes his orders from Dr. Mariner, his dad and, conveniently enough, the head of the Ocean Patrol. Made in Japan.

MARTIAN CHRONICLES, THE
NBC-TV miniseries (1980). Color, three 120-min. episodes.

Based on RAY BRADBURY's classic of the 1950s, *The Martian Chronicles* is a series of vignettes dealing with humanity's colonization of Mars and the response of the Martians to that effort. It was originally scheduled to kick off NBC's fall 1979 season but was yanked rather unceremoniously some two weeks before airtime.

NBC-TV

The Martian Chronicles

EXECUTIVE PRODUCER: Charles Fries, Dick Berg. PRODUCERS: Andrew Donally, Milton Subotsky. DIRECTOR: Michael Anderson. TELEPLAY: RICHARD MATHESON, based on the novel by Ray Bradbury. DIRECTOR OF PHOTOGRAPHY: Ted Moore. ART DIRECTOR: Ashton Gorton. COSTUMES: Cynthia Tingey. SPECIAL EFFECTS: John Stears. MUSIC: Stanley Myers. ELECTRONIC MUSIC: Richard Harvey. MAKEUP: George Frost.

CAST: Rock Hudson as Col. John Wilder, Gayle Hunnicutt as Ruth Wilder, Bernie Casey as Spender, Nicholas Hammond as Black, Maggie Wright as Ylla, Terence Longdon as the Wise Martian, Roddy McDowall as Father Stone, Darren McGavin as Parkhill, Maria Schell as Anna Lustig, Fritz Weaver as Father Peregrine, James Faulkner as Mr. K., Derek Lamden as the Sandship Martian.

MEN INTO SPACE

CBS-TV weekly series (1959). B/w, 30-min. episodes.

A pseudo-science-fact account of the U.S. government's attempts to launch mankind into the farthest reaches of space. William Lundigan starred as Col. Edward McCauley, Joyce Taylor as his wife. Corey Allen played Lt. Johnny Baker, and Kem Dibbs portrayed Captain Harvey Sparkman.

MUSIC: David Rose.

MR. TERRIFIC

CBS-TV weekly series (1967). Color, 60-min. episodes.

Back in the late 1960s the big question in network circles was, Who will triumph in the ratings war, *Mr. Terrific* or *Captain Nice?*—two almost identical superhero takeoffs that differed from each other only in execution. Execution seems to be a key word in describing *Mr. Terrific,* a video character who definitely did not live up to his name.

The show begins in Washington, D.C. A U.S. government researcher has discovered a superpower pill while working on a cure for the common cold. The pill works on animals but makes strong men sick to their tumtums when swallowed. A search for the perfect subject is conducted. Nebbish Stanley Beemish (Stephen Strimpell) is finally discovered, given the pill, and . . . ta-da . . . becomes Mr. Terrific. Stanley becomes a government agent and tries to cope with his super powers.

SUPPORTING PLAYERS: Dick Gautier as Hal, John McGiver as Barton J. Reed, Paul Smith as Hanley Trent.

MORK AND MINDY

ABC-TV weekly series (1978–   ). Color, 30-min. episodes.

Sort of a TV hybrid of Gore Vidal's *Visit to a Small Planet.* Alien Mork (Robin Williams), from the planet Ork, arrives on Earth to observe human

Mork and Mindy

society. He immediately becomes involved with pretty, perky Mindy (Pam Dawber), the only human to realize that Mork is from . . . out there . . . and the possessor of slapstick superpowers. Not overly thrilled over Mork's arrival are Mindy's dad, Frederick McConnell (Conrad Janis), and indulgent Grandmother, Cora Hudson (Elizabeth Kerr). No matter. By the series' second season, the latter two characters were written out of the show's format anyhow.

EXECUTIVE PRODUCERS: Garry K. Marshall, Tony Marshall. PRODUCERS: Bruce Johnson, Dale McRaven. Created by Garry Marshall.

MUNSTERS, THE

CBS-TV weekly series (1964–66). B/w, 30-min. episodes.

At 1313 Mockingbird Lane lives the Munster family, a close-knit brood guaranteed to attract attention at any quick-check shopping mart. Herman (Fred Gwynne) is the Frankenstein monster, a fellow put together surgically from the spare parts of others and brought to life with lightning. Lily (Yvonne DeCarlo) is a dead ringer (pardon the expression) for Vampira. Ten-year-old Eddie Munster is a werewolf. Grandpa Munster (Al Lewis) is a 378-year-old mad vampire-scientist. Their poor, unfortunate niece, Marilyn (Beverly Owen, later Pat Priest) is normal.

SUPPORTING PLAYERS: Butch Patrick as Eddie; John Carradine as Herman's funeral parlor owner/employer, Mr. Gateman; Chet Stratton as Clyde

Thorton; Paul Lynde as family physician Dr. Dudley.

MY FAVORITE MARTIANS
CBS-TV weekly series (1963–66). Color, 30-min. episodes.

Los Angeles *Sun* reporter Tim O'Hara (Bill Bixby) witnesses the crash-landing of a UFO. Rushing to the crash site, he finds and befriends the flying saucer's pilot, Martian Martin (Ray Walston), a professor of anthropology from the Red Planet whose special field of study is primitive Earth people. Martin adopts the Earth identity of Tim's uncle, Martin O'Hara, while struggling to repair his damaged spacecraft.

SUPPORTING PLAYERS: Pamela Britton as Tim's landlady, Lorelei Brown; Alan Hewitt as Detective Bill Brennan; J. Pat O'Malley as Los Angeles *Sun* editor Mr. Burns.

MY FAVORITE MARTIANS
CBS-TV weekly animated series (1973–75). Color, 30-min. episodes.

A cartoon version of the popular prime-time show, this plot line called for Tim O'Hara to discover a disabled flying saucer with three passengers onboard: Martian Martin, his nephew Andy, and their dog, Oakie Doakie. Take it from there.

A Filmation production.

VOICES: Jonathan Harris, Edward Morris, Jane Webb, Lane Scheimer.

MY LIVING DOLL
CBS-TV weekly series (1964–65). 30-min. episodes.

Dr. Carl Miller (Henry Beckman), head of Air Force Project 709, constructs the ultimate robot—a buxom, ravishing lass named Rhoda (Julie Newmar). Rating a "10" or "11" on the hubba-hubba scale, innocent Rhoda is given to psychiatrist Dr. Bob McDonald (Bob Cummings) for a quick personality-implant. The doc is to coach the innocent droid on the *do*'s and *don't*'s of human-ness. Not knowing Rhoda is a robot (she's top-secret stuff, folks), Bob's sister, Irene, suspects her brother of hanky-panky-clanky. While Irene (Doris Dowling) simmers, love-smitten playboy-neighbor Peter

Robinson (Jack Mullaney) burns with passion. Rhoda's circuitry remains intact . . . for one season, anyhow.

NEW ADVENTURES OF BATMAN AND ROBIN, THE
CBS-TV weekly animated series (1976). Color, 30-min. episodes.

Animated version of Batman and Robin (voices of Adam West and Burt Ward) and their fight against evildoers, the Joker, the Riddler, the Penguin, etc.

Chicken World

The show is *too* good! There are no jiggles, no car chases, and no idiotic lines. Everyone connected with the show was taken by surprise at this last cancellation. It's a strange production for TV: engrossing, engaging, thought-provoking. And it's a funny show, although NBC forbids us to use the evil word "satire."

> Jacqueline Babbin, producer of the NBC miniseries *Brave New World:* postponed for a period exceeding two years

---

PRODUCERS: Filmation Associates. PRODUCERS Don Christensen. ANIMATION DIRECTORS: Rudy Larriva, Lou Zukor, Gwen Wetzler. MUSIC AND SOUND EFFECTS: Horta-Mahana.

NEW ADVENTURES OF SUPERMAN, THE
CBS-TV weekly animated series (1966–77). Color, 30-min. episodes.

Radio's Man of Steel, Bud Collyer, re-created his roles of the voices of Superman and Clark Kent in this animated version of the comic-book hero's world of super adventure. Joan Alexander played Lois Lane; Jackson Beck was the narrator.

NEW AVENGERS, THE

CBS-TV weekly series (1978–79). Color, 60-min. episodes.

A fairly schizoid sequel to the original AVENGERS series, *The New Avengers* made its debut Stateside after running for two solid seasons in Europe and Canada. This time out, John Steed (Patrick Macnee) is joined by two superagent sidekicks, Purdey (Joanna Lumley) and stolid Gambit (Gareth Hunt), in his battle against international evil. A wide assortment of demented scientists, inventors, and out-and-out gangsters made appearances during the show's single U.S. season, as the show swung precariously from humor to abject *angst*.

PRODUCERS: Albert Fennell, Brian Clemens. DIRECTORS: Desmond Davis, Ernest Day, Graeme Clifford, James Hill, Brian Clemens. WRITERS: Brian Clemens, Terence Feeley, Dennis Spooner, Ray Austin. DIRECTOR OF PHOTOGRAPHY: Mike Reed. ART DIRECTOR: Robert Bell. MUSIC: Laurie Johnson.

NEW, ORIGINAL WONDER WOMAN, THE

ABC-TV telefilm (1975). Color, 90 mins. airtime.

After trying unsuccessfully to update the vintage comic-book heroine, ABC tried a second time to bring her to the tube, this time as a period piece. Set during World War II, this film saw Wonder Woman/Diana Prince (Lynda Carter), a super-Amazon from Paradise Isle, fighting off Axis-power nasties. In for the good, clean fun were Maj. Steve Trevor (Lyle Waggoner) and Gen. Blankenship (John Randolph). Divided between high camp and low action, this new version generated enough power to warrant a subsequent miniseries that eventually blossomed into a full-season offering.

A Warner Brothers presentation. PRODUCER: Douglas S. Cramer. DIRECTOR: Leonard Horn. SCREENPLAY: Stanley Ralph Ross, based on the comic-book character created by Charles Moulton.

SUPPORTING PLAYERS: Cloris Leachman, Red Buttons, Stella Stevens, Eric Braeden, Kenneth Mars, Fannie Flagg, Severn Darden.

NIGHT SLAVES

ABC-TV telefilm (1970). Color, 90 mins. airtime.

Clay Howard (James Franciscus) and Marj Howard (Lee Grant) are young and in love and in trouble. Passing through a small town, they become stranded in a place filled with decent folks who become zombies at night. Under the cover of darkness, the hypnotized townfolk disappear from their homes. Clay, a lucky fellow with a metal plate in his head, is immune to the mass hypnosis. It turns out the whole city is in the power of an alien intelligence. The humans go out to make repairs on the damaged extraterrestrial craft at night and then, in the morning, forget all about it. Wouldn't you?

A Bing Crosby (Warner Brothers) production. PRODUCER: Everett Chambers. DIRECTOR: Ted Post. SCREENPLAY: Chambers and Robert Specht, from a novel by Jerry Sohl. CINEMATOGRAPHY: Robert Hauser. MUSIC: Bernard Segall.

SUPPORTING PLAYERS: Scott Marlowe as Matthew Russell, Andrew Prine as Fess Beany, Tisha Sterling as Naillil, Leslie Nielsen as Sheriff Henshaw.

NIGHT STALKER, THE

ABC-TV telefilm (1972). Color, 90 mins. airtime.

In this, the pilot for the later *Kolchak: The Night Stalker* series, reporter Kolchak (Darren McGavin) is aided by Carol Lynley in a battle against a modern-day vampire (Barry Atwater).

ABC-TV

The Night Stalker

SUPPORTING PLAYERS: Simon Oakland, Ralph Meeker, Claude Akins, Charles McGraw, Kent Smith, Elisha Cook, Jr.

PRODUCER: Dan Curtis. DIRECTOR: John Llewellyn Moxey. SCREENPLAY: RICHARD MATHESON. MAKEUP: Jerry Dash. CINEMATOGRAPHY: Michel Hugo. MUSIC: Robert Cobert. Based on a novel by Jeff Rice.

NIGHT STRANGLER, THE

ABC-TV telefilm (1973). Color, 90 mins. airtime.

Reporter Kolchak (Darren McGavin) discovers the existence of a seemingly ageless alchemist (Richard Anderson) who lives beneath the city of Seattle and retains his youth by piping the blood of innocent women into his veins . . . after first strangling them senseless, of course.

SUPPORTING PLAYERS: Jo Ann Pflug, Simon Oakland, Scott Brady, Wally Cox, Margaret Hamilton, John Carradine, Nina Wayne.

PRODUCER AND DIRECTOR: Dan Curtis. SCREENPLAY: RICHARD MATHESON. MAKEUP: William Tuttle. CINEMATOGRAPHY: Robert Hauser. SPECIAL EFFECTS: Ira Anderson. MUSIC: Robert Cobert.

NIGHT THAT PANICKED AMERICA, THE

ABC-TV telefilm (1975). Color, 90 mins. airtime.

A pseudodocumentary that re-creates Orson Welles's 1938 radio broadcast of H. G. WELLS's *The War of the Worlds*, this made-for-TV movie combines a realistic portrayal of 1930s radio plays with hackneyed drama. As the broadcast leaves the New York radio station and enters the homes of thousands of listeners, various stereotypes react in various off-the-wall ways. Not what you'd call gripping.

CAST: Vic Morrow, Cliff De Young, Michael Constantine, Meredith Baxter.

DIRECTOR: Joseph Sargeant. TELEPLAY: Nicholas Meyer (later to pen the film TIME AFTER TIME) and Anthony Wilson, based, in part, on the original radio broadcast written by Howard Koch.

OUTER LIMITS, THE

ABC-TV weekly series (1963–65). B/w, 60-min. episodes.

Without a doubt the finest sf anthology series ever to make it to the air, *The Outer Limits* was a series misunderstood by the network brass, misrepresented by the network publicity machine, and, ultimately, mishandled by network programmers. Created by noted screenplay writer/producer Leslie Stevens, *The Outer Limits* attempted to treat sf seriously on the small screen. Well-known writer/producer Joseph Stefano was given the reins by Stevens and allowed total creative freedom in shaping the show. Stefano immediately contacted some of the most promising young writers in TV and told them to have a go at it. The resulting first season contained some of the most thought-provoking teleplays ever attempted in the genre. The traditional alien space "monster" was represented as a three-dimensional creation, different from humans in appearance, but not in logic. Mad scientists gave way to obsessed humanitarians. Invading aliens turned out to be one step removed from Earthly soldiers. In short, sf clichés were replaced by representations that came very close to reality.

The show immediately attracted top-name guest stars (Cliff Robertson, Robert Culp, David McCallum, Martin Landau, Warren Oates, Sam Wanamaker, Nick Adams, Ralph Meeker) and veteran directors (Byron Haskin, Gerd Oswald). ABC, however, not happy with the show's "intellectualism," deep-sixed it. Stefano was dismissed as producer and Ben Brady was brought in for the second season. Although still better-than-average, the second year of *The Outer Limits* never quite equaled the experimental daring of the first. The show was cancelled at season's end.

EXECUTIVE PRODUCER: Leslie Stevens.

Daystar Prod.

The Outer Limits

PRODUCERS: Joseph Stefano, Ben Brady. CREATOR: Leslie Stevens. STORY CONSULTANT: Lou Morheim. DIRECTOR OF PHOTOGRAPHY: Conrad Hall, John Nickolaus, Kenneth Peace. SPECIAL EFFECTS: Projects Unlimited, Ray Mercer Co. MAKEUP: Fred Phillips, John Chambers. MUSIC: Dominic Frontiere, Harry Lubin.

PARTRIDGE FAMILY: 2200 A.D., THE
CBS-TV weekly animated series (1974–75). Color, 30-min. episodes.

Based on the ABC-TV prime-time comedy series, this animated kiddie show took the singing Partridge clan into the year 2200, in which, aided by manager Reuben Kinkade, they perform while planet-hopping.

VOICES: Sherry Alberoni, Danny Bonaduce, Suzanne Crough, Susan Dey, Brian Foster, Joan Gerber, Dave Madden, Chuck McLennan.

PEOPLE, THE
ABC-TV telefilm (1971). Color, 90 mins. airtime.

Based on stories from *Pilgrimage: The Book of The People,* by ZENNA HENDERSON, *The People* involves the adventures of a schoolteacher (Kim Darby) who discovers a commune of folks in a hidden valley that seems to combine the best attributes of *The Waltons* with those found on MY FA-

VORITE MARTIAN. They levitate. They read minds. They're somewhat more than jus' plain folks. It turns out that they're the remainder of the alien race that colonized Earth years ago. They've become marooned on the planet and now try to hide their presence. The aliens are peace-loving folk, ya see, and they don't want to be exploited for their powers by a warmongering society.

EXECUTIVE PRODUCER: Francis Ford Coppola, for American Zoetrope. PRODUCER: Gerald I. Isenberg. DIRECTOR: John Korty. SCREENPLAY: James M. Miller. CINEMATOGRAPHY: Edward Rosson. MUSIC: Carmen Coppola.

SUPPORTING PLAYERS: William Shatner, Dan O'Herlihy, Diane Varsi, Laurie Walters.

PLANET EARTH
ABC-TV telefilm (1974). Color, 90 mins. airtime.

A sequel to GENESIS II, *Planet Earth* marked yet another attempt by STAR TREK producer Gene Roddenberry to launch a network series. Set in the 22nd century, this futuristic drama spotlighted the efforts of 20th-century man John Saxon (replacing Alex Cord from GENESIS) and a batch of futuristic friends in locating a missing scientist in an area populated by hostile Amazon warriors. The Amazon women, led by Diana Muldaur, are less than impressed with Saxon's efforts until he rescues them from a group of ugly mutants.

EXECUTIVE PRODUCER: Gene Roddenberry. PRODUCER: Robert Justman. SCREENPLAY: Roddenberry and Juanita Bartlett, from a story by Roddenberry. DIRECTOR: Marc Daniels.

SUPPORTING PLAYERS: Janet Margolin, Ted Cassidy, Christopher Cary, Jo De Winter, Sally Kemp, Majel Barrett, Rai Tasco.

PLANET OF THE APES
CBS-TV weekly series (1974). Color, 60-min. episodes.

Based on both the PIERRE BOULLE novel and the Arthur P. Jacobs series of successful feature films, this series was so inept it lasted only three months on the air.

A U.S. Air Force capsule passes through a time barrier, sending it hurtling from 1988 to 3085. Plummeting to the Earth, the capsule smashes into a jungle-laden terrain. One of the three astronauts on board perishes in the crash. The two surviving spacemen, Alan Virdon (Ron Harper) and Peter Burke (James Naughton), are captured by talking apes. The apes are afraid that the presence of civilized humans might lead the human slaves of future Earth into a revolt. Intelligent ape Galen (Roddy McDowall) wants to communicate with the humans. Evil Veska (Woodrow Parfrey) wants them dead. Defending the two humans, Galen accidentally sends Veska to that big Evolutionary Chain in the sky. Going bananas, Galen flees into the jungle, taking Alan and Pete with them. The trio, branded as fugitives, are chased by Zaius (Booth Colman) and Urko (Mark Lenard).

POWER WITHIN, THE
ABC-TV telefilm (1979). Color, 90 mins. airtime.

A somewhat less-than-electrifying film concerning Chris Darrow (Art Hindle), a young man whose mother was exposed to radiation, which he has stored up internally. Hit by a lightning bolt, he becomes so energy-laden that he can shoot electricity at metal objects just by pointing his fingers. Alarmed at these shocking developments, Chris runs to his dad, Gen. Darrow (Edward Binns), who, in turn, contacts a physician (Susan Howard). The doctor tells Chris that periodically he has to recharge himself and gives the lad a special wristwatch that lets him know when he's due for a new set of plugs. Meanwhile, three villains (Eric Braeden, David Hedison, and Richard Sargent) try to make off with a suspended-animation device Gen. Darrow has been toying with. Before you know it, there's a wattage war going on in the general's lab.

A 20th Cent.-Fox production. EXECUTIVE PRODUCERS: Aaron Spelling, Douglas S. Cramer. PRODUCER: Alan S. Godfrey. DIRECTOR: John Llewellyn Moxey. SCREENPLAY: Edward J. Lakso. CINEMATOGRAPHY: Emil Oster. MUSIC: John Addison.

SUPPORTING PLAYERS: Joe Rassulo, John Dennis, Karen Lamm.

PRISONER, THE
ITC/CBS-TV (G.B./U.S. weekly series (1968), now syndicated. Color, 60 mins. per episode.

A British government employee, agent No. 6 (Patrick McGoohan), resigns his post and determines to make a go of it as a normal, unfettered citizen. Returning home, he begins pulling vacation folders together and packing for a trip when gas is piped into his apartment. Awakening in a strange cottage, he finds himself in a strange place called the Village, an eerie, Kafka-esque community. It could be anywhere. There are no entrances and no exits. A three-dimensional limbo, the Village is also bugged with various microphones and TV monitors. Every movement of every one of its citizens is observed. No. 6 is brought into the lair of No. 2 (Guy Doleman) for interrogation. "A lot of people are curious about what lies behind your resignation," No. 6 is told. "They want to know why you suddenly left."

When No. 6 later has a second audience with No. 2, he finds that there is a new face beneath the number (this time it's actor George Baker). Because the Village is ruled by No. 1, No. 2 is expendable. There is a parade of No. 2's throughout the series as the Prisoner, a stranger in an even stranger land, drifts from allegory to allegory in a never-ending attempt to escape from an all-seeing society.

PRODUCER: David Tomblin. CREATOR: Patrick McGoohan. DIRECTOR OF PHOTOGRAPHY: Brandon Stafford. MUSIC: Ron Grainier.

SUPPORTING PLAYER: Angelo Muscat as the Butler.

PROJECT UFO
NBC-TV weekly series (1977–78). Color, 60-min. episodes.

Enjoyably straight-faced excursions into absurdity of the UFO kind, this Jack Webb production brought *Dragnet* sensibilities to a CLOSE ENCOUNTERS OF THE THIRD KIND–obsessed viewing audience. The dramas concern UFO sightings reported to the air force by citizens both honest and *e*-vil. Project Blue Book investigators Maj. Jake Gatlin (William Jordan) and Sgt. Harry Fitz (Caskey Swaim) are sent out to

NBC-TV

Project: UFO

investigate each story, which is told (and visually re-created) according to the witness's observations. In the second year, Gatlin was replaced by Capt. Ben Ryan (Edward Winter). Unfortunately, the UFO sightings remained the same. Allegedly based on actual Project Blue Book reports, the UFO portions of the show were visually interesting but, suspensewise, bland.

EXECUTIVE PRODUCER: Jack Webb. PRODUCER: Col. William T. Coleman, U.S.A.F., retired. SPECIAL EFFECTS: Don Weede, Wally Gentleman. MINIATURES: Brick Price.

QUARK
NBC-TV weekly series (1977). Color, 30-min. episodes.

A comedy series that failed to take off. United Galaxy Sanitation Patroller Adam Quark (Richard Benjamin) scours the skies in search of intergalactic Baggies to pick up and dispose of. Onboard for the fun are twins Betty 1 and Betty 2 (Tricia and Cyb Barnstable), who argue over which one is the clone; Jean/Gene (Tim Thomerson), a transmute with both male and female chromosomes who swings from mucho-macho to mincing; Ficus (Richard Kelton), a superlogical first officer who is "more vegetable than animal"; Andy (Bobby Porter), an android built

from spare parts; and (in the pilot episode), Dr. O. B. Mudd (Douglas Fowley). Lending support to Quark's endless quest is space station Perma One's head (Alan Caillou), a fellow who lives up to his name with a 36 hat-size, and Dr. Otto Palindrome (Conrad Janis), Quark's technical boss, who wouldn't mind seeing his employee lost in space. For animal lovers there is Ergo, the U.G.S.P. spaceship's resident blob. *Quark* made its debut as a pilot in the spring of 1977 and wound up as a midseason replacement in the 1977–78 NBC fiasco.

PRODUCER: Buck Henry. DIRECTOR (PILOT EPISODE): Peter H. Hunt. TELEPLAY (PILOT EPISODE): Buck Henry. EXECUTIVE PRODUCERS FOR COLUMBIA

NBC-TV

Quark

PICTURES TELEVISION (SERIES): David Gerber and Mace Neufeld. PRODUCER (SERIES): Bruce Johnson.

QUESTOR TAPES, THE
NBC-TV telefilm (1974). Color, 120 mins. airtime.

A simply wonderful little made-for-TV movie, intended as a pilot for a proposed series by Gene (STAR TREK) Roddenberry. Questor (Robert Foxworth) is an android who has been faultily programmed. The tapes pertaining to his origin, mission, creator, and capacity for human emotion have been erased. The movie centers on his search for the meaning of his existence. Accompanied by a human engineer (Mike Farrell as Jerry Robinson), Questor embarks on an odyssey that eventually produces astounding results. Questor is the last in a series of self-perpetuating robot guardians of the human race that were dropped off on Earth thousands of years back by an unnamed alien source. Throughout human history, these androids have gently shoved the human race along the right paths—a concept that some humans are not ready to swallow, much to Questor's dismay . . . and danger.

PRODUCER: Howie Horowitz. DIRECTOR: Richard A. Colla. SCREENPLAY: Gene Roddenberry and Gene L. Coon, from a story by Roddenberry.

SUPPORTING PLAYERS: John Vernon, Lew Ayres, Dana Wynter, James Shigeta, Majel Barrett, Walter Koenig, Alan Caillou.

CBS-TV

The Return of Captain Nemo

RETURN OF CAPTAIN NEMO, THE

CBS-TV miniseries (1978). Color, three 60-min. episodes.

Irwin Allen's answer to JULES VERNE makes one never want to think of the initial question. Set in contemporary times, this miniseries begins with two U.S. Navy scuba divers, Tom Branklin (Tom Hallick) and Jim Porter (Burr DeBenning), discovering the original *Nautilus* wedged under a shelf of coral in the far reaches of the Pacific. Entering the ancient sub, they awaken Captain Nemo (Jose Ferrer) from a state of suspended animation.

Meanwhile, Professor Waldo Cunningham (Burgess Meredith), master of the futuristic sub *Raven* and the possessor of an army of robots, declares war on Washington. Unless $1 billion in gold is paid to the old prof, he'll destroy the city.

Nemo goes to work for the U.S. government and, with his two young friends in tow, disables the *Raven*, thus preventing Cunningham's plan from working. Afterward, he and his friends search for Atlantis. Nemo's search is interrupted by the government. They ask him to dive some 36,000 feet into the Mindanao Trench to make sure that the radioactive wastes buried down there are okie-dokee. (Modern navy subs can't attempt the plunge but the

wonderful *Nautilus* can, of course.) Two scientists, Cook (Mel Ferrer) and Kate (Linda Day George), join Nemo for the dive. Unfortunately, Cook is in the employ of Cunningham and tries to destroy the ship. He doesn't succeed and winds up getting caught. Cunningham closes in for the kill in his own sub but attacks and destroys a bogus *Nautilus* created by Nemo for just such occasions.

Meanwhile, (tired yet?), Nemo arrives at Atlantis and meets King Tibor (Horst Buchholz), a nice fellow who turns not so nice when Cunningham and his crew invade Atlantis and threaten to destroy the ancient kingdom unless Nemo gives up the secrets of the *Nautilus*'s nuclear reactor and laser-beam system. Nemo doesn't. Cunningham doesn't. Atlantis proves that history can repeat itself quite often in prime time.

PRODUCER: Irwin Allen. TELEPLAY: William Keyes. DIRECTOR: Alex March.

ROCKET ROBIN HOOD

Syndicated weekly animated series (1967). Color, 30-min. episodes.

In 3000 A.D., Rocket Robin Hood and his band of Merry Men are interplanetary defenders of justice who travel from planet to planet aboard *New Sherwood Forest*, a floating, solar-powered asteroid.

ROCKY JONES, SPACE RANGER

NBC-TV weekly series (1954–55). B/w, 30-min. episodes.

In the 21st century, Space Ranger pilot Rocky Jones (Richard Crane) has his hands full protecting the planets of the United Solar System from space bad guys. Aiding him are Winky (Scott Beckett), Vena Ray (Sally Mansfield), and Professor Newton (Maurice Cass). Week after week, the good ship *Orbit Jet* scans the skies in the name of niceness.

Scout's Honor

Galactica is my first opportunity to play an upbeat character with a sense of humor and who enjoys life. He'll cheat, but he's never malicious or out to hurt anybody.

Dirk Benedict, *Battlestar Galactica's* Starbuck

PRODUCER: Roland Reed. DIRECTORS: Hollingsworth Morse, William Beaudine, others. TELEPLAYS: Warren Wilson, Clark Hittleman, others.

Roland Reed Prod.

Rocky Jones, Space Ranger

ROD BROWN OF THE ROCKET RANGERS

CBS-TV weekly series ((1953–54). B/w, 30-min. episodes.

"CBS Television presents *Rod Brown of the Rocket Rangers.* Surging with the power of the atom, gleaming like great silver bullets, the mighty Rocket Rangers spaceships stand by for blast-off. Up, up, rockets blazing with white-hot fury, the manmade meteors ride through the atmosphere, breaking the gravity barrier, pushing up and out, faster and faster—and then, outer space and high adventure for the Rocket Rangers!"

That introduction heralded the coming of Ranger Rod Brown (Cliff Robertson) and Wilbur Wormser (Jack Weston) in their weekly battle against interplanetary evil set on 22nd century Earth. Along for the ride were Commander Swift (John Boruff) and Ranger Cheerleader Shirley Standlee. Rod's rocket was the *Beta*. His headquarters: Omega Base. His TV fame: short-lived.

ROD SERLING'S NIGHT GALLERY

NBC-TV weekly series (1970–72). Color, 60-min. (1970–71) and 30-min. (1972) episodes.

ROD SERLING'S last bout with TV proved unfortunate for all concerned. *Night Gallery,* an anthology series that, more often than not, centered on the occult, used the gimmick of having Serling the host introduce a spooky portrait to his TV audience. The portrait would then become part of a story told to the viewers. Unfortunately, Serling's duties on the show were restricted fairly much to hosting. Signing away all creative control, Serling spent much of the show's three seasons wincing. Several of his scripts were turned down and the direction provided by producer Jack Laird hovered between the ridiculous and the absurd. Comic-bookish vignettes and shaggy-dog stories lasting only five minutes often turned up when they should have been turned out.

On several occasions, *Night Gallery* delved into sf, most notably in the episodes "The Little Black Bag," wherein a wino discovers a 21st-century doctor's black bag; "The Nature of the Enemy," which featured an astronaut investigating a disappearance on the moon; and "Tell David," the tale of a girl who is given a glimpse of the future.

PRODUCER: Jack Laird. CREATOR: Rod Serling. MAKEUP: Bud Westmore, John Chambers. MUSIC: Gil Melle.

ROGER RAMJET

Syndicated animated cartoon series (1965). Color, 5-min. episodes.

Scientist Roger Ramjet invents a pill that, when swallowed, gives him the power of over 20 A-bombs . . . for 20 seconds. He learns to fight crime very quickly.

SALVAGE
ABC-TV telefilm (1979). Color, 120 mins. airtime.

A two-hour pilot film for a proposed series (see the following entry), *Salvage* is a low-key sf adventure littered with liberal doses of high-flying comedy. Visionary junk dealer Harry Broderick (Andy Griffith) comes up with an idea that could make him a fortune. He figures he can make a trip to the moon, collect all the scientific litter left there by U.S. astronauts, and then resell it to the government. The only hitch in his plan is that in order to make the trip, he has to design and build (and pilot) his own spaceship.

Enlisting the aid of ex-astronaut Skip Carmichael (Joel Higgins) and demolition expert Melanie Slozar (Trish Stewart), and helped by the back-work of Mack and Fred (J. Jay Saunders and Raleigh Bond), Harry finishes the rocket (the *Vulture*). The three principals blast off for the moon under the watchful eye of FBI agent Jack Klinger (Richard Jaeckel) and find the return trip a bit bumpier than expected.

A Columbia Pictures/Bennett-Katleman production. EXECUTIVE PRODUCERS: Harve Bennett, Harris Katleman. PRODUCERS: Norman S. Powell, Mike Lloyd Ross. DIRECTOR: Lee Philips. SCREENPLAY: Ross. CINEMATOGRAPHY: Fred Koenekamp. ART DIRECTOR: Ross Bellah. SPECIAL EFFECTS: Wayne Edgar. MUSIC: Walter Scharf.

SALVAGE I
ABC-TV weekly series (1979). Color, 60-min. episodes.

The further adventures of junk dealer Harry Broderick (Andy Griffith) and his assistants, Melanie Slozar (Trish Stewart), Skip Carmichael (Joel Higgins), and Mack (J. Jay Saunders). With the mighty spaceship *Vulture* now at their disposal, Harry and his crew take on fairly bizarre search-and-

salvage missions. During their single season they became involved in iceberg towing and an attempt to save *Skylab*, adopt a killer robot, search for rare spider monkeys on the remote island of Bantu Larova, and exorcise a haunted house of its alien "ghost." The FBI's Jack Klinger (Richard Jaeckel) is always around.

EXECUTIVE PRODUCERS: Harve Bennett, Harris Katleman. SUPERVISING PRODUCER: Mike Lloyd Ross. PRODUCER: Ralph Sariego. CREATOR: Ross. CAMERA: Gerald P. Finnerman. ART DIRECTOR: Robert Purcell. SPECIAL EFFECTS: Marcel Bercourtre. MUSIC: Walter Scharf.

SCIENCE FICTION THEATRE
NBC-TV weekly series (1955–56). B/w, 30-min. episodes.

The great-granddaddy of all sf anthology shows, *Science Fiction Theatre* lasted but one season. Host-narrator Truman Bradley opened each episode explaining the scientific idea or principle that the following show would be centered around. Episodes included "The Dark Side" (the ultimate telescopic camera), "The Sound of Murder" (a scientist is unjustly accused of murder), and "Gravity Zero" (a scientific team attempts to discover a way to break the laws of gravity). Guest stars included Skip Homeier, Howard Duff, and Gene Lockhart.

SEALAB 2020
NBC-TV weekly animated series (1972–73). Color, 30-min. episodes.

Hanna-Barbera's cartoon series depicting the struggles of a scientific community housed within *Sealab 2020*: the world's first underwater community.

VOICES: John Stephenson as Captain Murphy, Ross Martin as Dr. Paul Williams, Jerry Dexter as Hal, Ann Jillian as Gail, Ron Pinckard as Ed, Josh Albee as Bobby.

SECOND HUNDRED YEARS, THE
ABC-TV weekly series (1967–68). Color, 30-min. episodes.

Sixty-seven-year-old Edwin Carpenter (Arthur O'Connell) is called to Washington by Col. Garroway (Frank Maxwell). Edwin's father, Luke (Monte Markham), buried and frozen in an

Alaskan avalanche in 1900, has been found . . . alive. Though chronologically 100 years old, the mountain man is, physically and mentally, the same 33-year-old fellow he was at the turn of the century. A top-secret government find, Luke is placed in Edwin's protective custody. He is brought home to suburbia, where he meets his grandson, Ken (Monte Markham) . . . his exact double. Stories portray the eldest Carpenter's attempts to cope with 1967-style living and the mixups caused by the twin effects of grandpa and grandson. Ken's girl friend, Erica (Kay Reynolds), and his boss, Mr. Tolliver (Dan Beddow), are perplexed.

SHADOW ON THE LAND
ABC-TV telefilm (1968). Color, 120 mins. airtime.

A pilot for an unsold series, *Shadow on the Land* was an interesting excursion into the *1984* idiom. In the near future, the U.S. is turned into a dictatorship run by a Hitleresque character. Out to restore democracy is a small but determined group of underground freedom-fighters.

PRODUCER: Matthew Rapf for Screen Gems. DIRECTOR: Richard C. Sarafian. SCREENPLAY: Nedrick Young, from an idea by Sidney Sheldon. CINEMATOGRAPHY: Fred Koenekamp. MUSIC: Sol Kaplan.

CAST: Jackie Cooper, John Forsythe, Carol Lynley, Janice Rule, Gene Hackman, Myron Healey.

SHAZAM/ISIS HOUR, THE
CBS-TV weekly series (1975–76). Color, 60-min. episodes.

During the past five years or so, Saturday morning programmers have seen fit to juggle various bits and fragments of shows together to pull in extra ratings. Thus it is possible to catch both *Shazam* and *Isis* as independent Saturday-morning offerings, depending on what part of the country you are glued to your tube in.

Shazam is basically a reworking of the adventures of Captain Marvel. Billy Batson (Michael Gray) and his older companion, Mr. Mentor (Les Tremayne), battle crime. Billy has the power to turn himself into mighty superhero Captain Marvel (Jackson Bost-

wick in the half-hour *Shazam* show, John Davey in the *Shazam/Isis* stew) whenever he utters "Shazam!"

In *Isis*, a beautiful schoolteacher is also a beautiful super crime-fighter, Isis (JoAnna Cameron). SUPPORTING PLAYERS: Brian Culter as Rick Mason, Ronalda Douglas as Rennie, Joanna Pang as Cindy Lee. Created by Marc Richards.

SIX MILLION DOLLAR MAN, THE
ABC-TV telefilm (1973). Color, 90 mins. airtime.

Based on MARTIN CAIDIN's novel *Cyborg*, this made-for-TV film introduced to TV audiences test pilot Steve Austin (Lee Majors), a fellow who, after a plane crash, emerges as a cyborg . . . half-man, half-robot. The pilot for the TV series (see the following entry).

A Silverton Production/Universal Studios. EXECUTIVE PRODUCER: Harve Bennett.

SIX MILLION DOLLAR MAN, THE
ABC-TV weekly series (1973–77). Color, 60-min. episodes.

Test pilot Steve Austin (Lee Majors) is pulled barely alive from the wreckage of his jet. His life is saved when a team of doctor-scientists replace the mangled portions of his body with bionic components. In effect, he becomes a cyborg—a human robot. His bionic legs allow him to trot at an average of 60

ABC-TV

The Six Million Dollar Man

miles per hour. His bionic arm gives him superhuman strength and his manmade eye gives him telescopic vision. The only hitch? Steve's operation cost $6 million. In order to pay back the secret government agency that footed the aforementioned tab, Steve becomes a superagent. His actions are guided by pal/agent Oscar Goldman (Richard Anderson). The show eventually spawned a second series, THE BIONIC WOMAN, as well as leading to the introduction of the Bionic Boy (Vincent Van Patten) and the Bionic Dog.

EXECUTIVE PRODUCER: Harve Bennett. Based on the novel *Cyborg*, by MICHAEL CAIDIN. MUSIC: Oliver Nelson. PRODUCERS: Lionel Siegal, Kenneth Johnson.

SPACE ACADEMY
CBS-TV weekly series (1977–80). 30-min. episodes.

A Saturday morning kid-vidder noteworthy because of its exceptionally fine special-effects work. The Academy is an asteroid-based school for cadets. One such group (Pamelyn Ferdin, Rick Carrott, Ty Henderson, Maggie Cooper, Eric Green, and Brian Tochi) are taught the ropes by seemingly immortal Commander Gampu (Jonathan Harris). Week after week, Gampu and robot Peepo teach the cadets the meaning of life as well as how to avoid getting stepped on by alien monster-giants.

A Filmation production. EXECUTIVE PRODUCERS: Lou Scheimer and Norm Prescott. DIRECTOR OF PHOTOGRAPHY: Alric Edens. MINIATURES: Robert A. Maine, Chuck Comiskey, Paul Huston. ART DIRECTORS: Ray Beal, William McAllister. SPECIAL EFFECTS: John Frazier. COSTUMES: Bill Campbell. MUSIC: Yvette Blais, Jeff Michael.

SPACE ANGEL
Syndicated series of cartoons (1964). Color, 5-min. episodes.

Scott McCloud is an Interplanetary Space Force agent with a very deep voice. He protects the galaxy from bad guys with high, whiny voices.

SPACE GHOST
CBS-TV weekly animated series (1966–68). Color, 30-min. episodes.

This Hanna-Barbera production fol-lowed the exploits of rugged space-crime-fighter Space Ghost (the voice of Gary Owens) and his teenage wards, Jan and Jayce (the voices of Ginny Tyler and Tim Matthieson). MUSIC: Hoyt Curtin.

SPACE GHOST/FRANKENSTEIN JR.
NBC-TV weekly animated series (1976). Color, 30-min. episodes.

A trio of cartoon adventures. Two adventures per week offer the adventures of Space Ghost (the voice of Gary Owens), an intergalactic crime-fighter. Able to turn invisible with the aid of his off-the-wall belt, Space Ghost takes off for space aided by teenage wards Jayce and Jan (the voices of Tim Matthieson and Ginny Tyler) and space monkey Blipp. Also on hand is Frankenstein Jr. (the voice of Ted Cassidy), who apparently has lost his own show and now must shamble around as a sloppy second-sidekick. Aiding Frankie is boy scientist Buzz (the voice of Dick Beals) and Buzz's dad (the voice of John Stephenson).

A Hanna-Barbera production. MUSIC: Hoyt Curtin.

SPACE GIANTS
Syndicated weekly series (1968). Color, 30-min. episodes.

A live-action adventure from Japan that pitted 50-foot robot Goldar against a horde of marauding alien monsters.

SPACE KIDDETTES
NBC-TV weekly animated series (1966–67). Color, 30-min. episodes.

A Hanna-Barbera cartoon series spot-lighting the efforts of the Space Kiddettes to route outer-space evil.

VOICES: Chris Allen as Scooter, Lucille Bliss as Snoopy, Don Messick as Countdown, Janet Waldo as Jenny, Daws Butler as Captain Skyhook.

SPACE: 1999
ITC (syndicated) weekly series (G.B., 1975–77). Color, 60-min. episodes.

Gerry and Sylvia Anderson, producers of a fleet of Supermarionation sf shows starring puppets (*Thunderbirds, Captain Scarlet and the Mysterons,* etc.) designed *Space: 1999* as a live-action space opera made in Great Britain but geared toward an American audience. When every major U.S. network refused the project, they presented it to ITC and the show was produced and syndicated throughout the world, reaching far more viewers in this fashion than it would have as an U.S. network offering.

The much-ballyhooed show was talked of in terms of its innovative special effects (masterminded by Brian Johnson), its futuristic costuming (courtesy of Rudi Gernreich) and its top-flight cast (headed by Barbara Bain, Martin Landau, and Barry Morse). Once the initial sparkle of the publicity wore off, however, viewers were faced with a show featuring two-dimensional characters, stilted dialogue, and, more often than not, hackneyed plots. Although none of the above constitutes a terminal sickness in TV terms, making things a bit more dire was the fact that the show took itself ever so seriously.

By the second season, changes were in the offing. Sylvia Anderson was out. Fred Freiberger was in as producer. New, juvenile-oriented characters and plot ideas were introduced. However, the show never saw the year 2000, being cancelled after its second season.

The plot structure of the show was fairly simple. Moonbase Alpha, home of Commander John Koenig (Martin Landau), Dr. Helen Russell (Barbara Bain), and scientist Victor Bergman (Barry Morse), is a futuristic complex located on the moon. In the first episode, the moon is blasted out of its orbit by an ill-timed explosion of nuclear waste stored on the satellite's surface. For the rest of the show's tenure, the moon, and hence moonbase Alpha, bounced

ITC

Space: 1999

billiard-ball-like through space, meeting and greeting new alien friends and foes week after week.

The second season saw the moonbase keep a-rollin' but found Bergman missing in action. Replacing him in terms of starring power was metamorph alien Maya (Catherine Schell). A former resident of the planet Psychon, Maya could change her shape at will—a neat trick in anyone's book.

CREATORS: Gerry and Sylvia Anderson. PRODUCERS: Sylvia Anderson, Fred Freiberger. EXECUTIVE PRODUCER: Gerry Anderson. PRODUCTION DESIGN: Keith Wilson. SPECIAL EFFECTS: Brian Johnson. MUSIC: Barry Gray, Derek Wadsworth.

Beam Me Past 'em, Scotty

With *Star Trek,* I saw a chance to say a lot of politically and sociologically relevant things without the NBC censors ever catching on.

Gene Roddenberry, creator
of *Star Trek*

SUPPORTING PLAYERS: Tony Anholt as Tony Verdeschi, Nick Tate as Alan Carter.

SPACE PATROL
ABC-TV weekly series (1950–56). B/w, 30-min. episodes.

"High adventure in the wild, vast regions of space. Missions of daring in the name of interplanetary justice. Travel into the future with Buzz Corey . . . commander-in-chief of the . . . Spaaace Patrollll."

And thus began, for six long years, the slapdash saga of stolid space cadet Buzz Corey (Ed Kermer), commander-in-chief of the Space Patrol. In the 21st century, it's up to Buzz to protect the United Planets (Earth, Mars, Mercury, Jupiter, and Venus) against crime with the aid of Cadet Happy (Lyn Osborn), Dr. Von Meter (Rudolph Anders), Tonga (Nina Bara), and pretty Carol Garlyle (Virginia Anders), the daughter of the secretary-general of the United Planets. Aboard the good ship *X-R-Z,* Buzz and his crew buzzed baddies repeatedly.

PRODUCER: Mike Moser. ASSOCIATE PRODUCER: Bela Kovacs. DIRECTORS:

Mike Moser, Helen Moser, Lou Spence, Dick Darley. WRITERS: Norman Jolly, Lou Houston, Mike Moser.

SPIDER-MAN

ABC-TV weekly animated series (1967–69). Color, 30-min. episodes.

Based on the Marvel Comics creation. Peter Parker is bitten by a radioactive spider. When the venom mixes with his own blood, he becomes Spiderman, a being with the climbing abilities of a creepy-crawler.

VOICES: Bernard Cowan as Peter Parker/Spider-man (Paul Sols in later episodes), Paul Kligman as J. Jonah Jameson, Peg Dixon as Betty Brandt.

STARLOST, THE

Syndicated weekly series (1973). Color, 60-min. episodes.

HARLAN ELLISON came up with the idea for this series, which evolved into an epic misadventure. In the year 2790, Devon (Keir Dullea), Rachel (Gay Rowna), and Garth (Robin Ward) try to save the remains of Earth life aboard a drifting spacecraft, with the help of their computer Mulander One Sixty-five (William Osler).

STAR MAIDENS

Also known as SPACE MAIDENS Teleworld (syndicated) weekly series (G.B./W. Germany, 1977). Color, 30-min. episodes.

Filmed in Great Britain in 1975. Two men escape from the planet Medusa, a not-so-hot world where men are treated as slaves by women. They steal a spacecraft and crash-land on present-day Earth. In pursuit of the slaves are two women pilots keen on recapturing them.

PRODUCER: James Gatward. DIRECTORS: Gatward, Wolfgang Storch, Freddie Francis, Hans Heinrich. WRITERS: Eric Paice, John Lucarottie, Ian Stuart Black, Otto Strang.

CAST: Pierre Brice as Adam, Gareth Thomas as Shem, Christine Kruger as Octavia, Judy Geeson as Fulvia, Lisa Harrow as Liz, Christian Quadflieg as Rudi, Derek Farr as Professor Evens, Ronald Hines as Inspector Stanley.

STARSTRUCK

CBS-TV special presentation (1979). Color, 30 mins. airtime.

A pilot for a deservedly unsold comedy series, this project recounts life in a 23rd-century space motel. Ben McCallister (Beeson Carroll) runs a motel "halfway between Earth and Pluto." Aided by robot cook and butler Mrs. Bridges and Hudson, McCallister copes with a disco that goes STAR WARS; a singer, Amber Larue (Lynne Lipton), who can't sing; and an enterprising chiseler (Roy Brocksmith) who wants to franchise an apple-pie concession, since Ben has the only apples in the Universe. A close encounter all right.

A Herbert B. Leonard production. DIRECTOR: Al Viola. SCREENPLAY AND ORIGINAL IDEA: Arthur Kopit. CAMERA: Craig Greene. ART DIRECTION: Kirk Axtell. MUSIC: Alan Arper.

SUPPORTING PLAYERS: Guy Raymond, Meegan King, Tania Myren, Elvia Allman, Kevin Brando, Robin Strand, Joe Silver.

STAR TREK

NBC-TV weekly series (1966–69). Color, 60-min. episodes.

The most popular TV show in the world, *Star Trek* has now assumed an almost religious status with many of its diehard fans. *Star Trek* began in the early 1960s as a pipedream of writer/producer Gene Roddenberry. While producing a TV show titled *The Lieutenant,* Roddenberry was having difficulties getting topical themes past the network censors and thought sf an ideal format for editorializing. Taking one of his favorite literary heroes, Captain Horatio Hornblower, and giving him a slightly futuristic twist, he came up with Captain Pike, the commander of the U.S.S. *Enterprise.*

After a lot of bargaining, Roddenberry finally got the go-ahead from NBC for a pilot. Headquartered at Paramount Pictures, Roddenberry produced the first *Trek* episode, titled "The Cage." The networks viewed it and liked it . . . with reservations. They told Roddenberry that it was a tad intellectual and that certain elements of the show had to be toned down or trimmed out. There were too many women aboard the ship, for instance. A

Paramount

Star Trek

50–50 ratio could give children the impression that there was "fooling around" (Roddenberry's words) going on in space. Also, the fellow with the funny ears, that Spock guy, had to go.

Roddenberry took this criticism in stride. Adding to his worries, however, was the reluctance of actor Jeff Hunter to continue in his role as Pike. Hunter demurred when it came to shooting a second pilot, and so Captain James T. Kirk (William Shatner) was born. A second pilot, "Where No Man Has Gone Before," was filmed, and the show was picked up by NBC.

The show's format was simple: in the future, Federation ship *The Enterprise* seeks out and explores new worlds, helping local citizens wherever possible; on board the ship is a crew of some of the finest spacefarers in the Federation. Once the pilot was accepted (and original regulars Paul Fix, Lloyd Haynes, and Andrea Dromm jettisoned), the key crew of the *Enterprise* evolved into Kirk, Spock (Leonard Nimoy as a stoic, logical Vulcan alien), Dr. Leonard "Bones" McCoy (DeForest Kelley), Engineering Officer Scotty (James Doohan), Nurse Chapel (Majel Barret), Helmsman Sulu (George Takai), Ensign Chekov (Walter Koenig), and Communications Officer Uhuru (Nichelle Nichols).

The show was an immediate hit with the youth audience. Unfortunately, ratingswise it didn't appear to NBC that

Star Trek was pulling its weight (in those days ratings demographic were unheard-of, and so the network was unaware of what audience they were reaching). The show was almost scuttled at the end of its first season. It was officially cancelled at the end of its second, but a massive letter-writing campaign (millions of pieces of mail were received by befuddled executives) saved the show for a third and final season. (This latter "miracle," by the way, is a phenomenon unequaled in the history of network TV.) In all fairness, it must be pointed out that NBC did everything to hinder the show's popularity, albeit unknowingly, by moving its time slot repeatedly and miscalculating the series' projected audience.

The show went into syndication and by 1971 was reaching more viewers via reruns than it had in first run. A cult was born, and by the mid-1970s, *Star Trek* conventions were commonplace all over the world, with eager fans buying *Trek* books, blueprints, models, weapons, uniforms, posters, photos, trading cards, comics, photonovels, Vulcan ears, pendants, watches, medallions, film clips, frame blow-ups, magazines, and medical kits. The popularity of the show mushroomed to the point where Paramount, finally realizing what a gold mine it had in its files, gave the official go-ahead for STAR TREK—THE MOTION PICTURE, a classy class reunion released in 1979.

CREATOR: Gene Roddenberry. PRODUCERS: Roddenberry, Gene L. Coon, John M. Lucas, and Fred Freiberger. SPECIAL EFFECTS: Howard Anderson Co., Film Effects of Hollywood, Inc., Westheimer Co., and Jim Rugg. MAKEUP: Fred Phillips. MUSIC: Alexander Courage, Gerald Fried. DIRECTOR OF PHOTOGRAPHY: Ernest Haller. STORY CONSULTANTS: Steven Carabatsos, D. C. FONTANA.

STAR TREK
NBC-TV animated weekly series (1973–74). Color, 30-min. episodes.

Filmation Associates' cartoon adaptation of the original TV series proved interesting Saturday-morning fare for the wee folk, although its limited anima-

Paramount

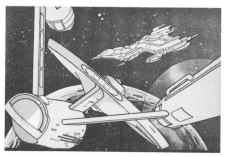

Star Trek (animated)

tion process provided some tough sledding for the older viewers. The live-action series' main characters provided their cartoon counterparts with the appropriate voices and many of the first series' writers returned to the fold to pen a few half-hour installments.

Produced by Filmation Associates. PRODUCERS: Lou Scheimer, Norm Prescott. DIRECTOR: Hal Sutherland. Based on the TV series created by Gene Roddenberry. STORY EDITOR AND ASSOCIATE PRODUCER: D. C. FONTANA.

VOICES: William Shatner, Leonard Nimoy, DeForest Kelley, James Doohan, Nichelle Nichols.

STINGRAY
ITC (syndicated) weekly series (G.B., 1962–63). Color, 30-min. episodes.

Gerry and Sylvia Anderson's *sixth* Supermarionation series that brought puppetry into sf's turf, and the first British series ever to be filmed in color. Troy Tempest (the voice of Don Mason) journeys from 21st-century Marineville in his sub the *Stingray* in a never-ending fight for underwater right conducted by the World Aquanaut Security Patrol.

EXECUTIVE PRODUCER: Gerry Anderson. CREATORS: Gerry and Sylvia Anderson. SPECIAL EFFECTS: Derek Meddings. MUSIC: Barry Gray.

VOICES: Lois Maxwell as Atlanta, Ray Barrett as Sam Shore, Robert Easton as Phones and X-20.

STRANGE CASE OF DR. JEKYLL AND MR. HYDE, THE
ABC-TV telefilm (1968). Videotaped in color, two 90-min. episodes.

In an effort to separate good from evil, Dr. Jekyll (Jack Palance) comes up with an omniscient alter-ego evil Mr. Hyde. Well-intentioned literacy and unintentional hilarity mark the rest of his wretched life.

PRODUCER: Dan Curtis. DIRECTOR: Charles Jarrot. TELEPLAY: Ian McCleelan Hunter, from the novelette by Robert Louis Stevenson. ART DIRECTOR: Trevor Williams. MAKEUP: Nicki Balch. MR. HYDE'S MAKEUP: Dick Smith. SPECIAL EFFECTS: Karl Moellhausen. MUSIC: Robert Cobert.

SUPPORTING PLAYERS: Denholm Elliott, Billie Whitelaw, Tessie O'Shea, Torin Thatcher, Oscar Homolka, Leo Genn, Duncan Lamont.

STRANGE NEW WORLD
ABC-TV telefilm (1975). Color, 120 mins. airtime.

Sf gets the Republic-serial treatment in this slaphappy space adventure, a sort of bastard son of Gene Roddenberry's GENESIS II and PLANET EARTH. Three 20th-century citizens (John Saxon, Kathleen Miller, and Keene Curtis), astronauts all, are sent into a state of suspended animation for nearly two centuries. Awakening abruptly, the trio stumbles onto Eterna, a nasty Utopian society with even nastier secrets. Before moving on, the astronauts destroy Eterna.

Next the trio enters a dense (in more ways than one) forestland community in which the Hunters fight the Zookeepers (hint: rifle nuts vs. ecologists). Before leaving the forest, the astronauts destroy quite a bit of both sides, eventually bringing the warring factions together.

At the film's end, the threesome wanders off to search for their "loved ones," presumably other astronauts still stuck in suspended animation in underground chambers or the back seats of Chevy Impalas or something.

A Warner Brothers production. PRODUCER: Robert Larson. DIRECTOR: Robert Butler. SCREENPLAY: Walon Green, Ronald F. Graham, Al Ramrus.

SUPPORTING PLAYERS: Martine Beswick, Gerrit Graham, James Olson.

STRANGER, THE
ABC-TV telefilm (1972). Color, 120 mins. airtime.

A variation of the doppelganger theme pioneered in the movie JOURNEY

TO THE FAR SIDE OF THE SUN, this film served as a pilot for an unsold Bing Crosby Productions series. An astronaut finds himself stranded on a world on the opposite side of Earth's sun. The government is totalitarian and the astronaut (Glenn Corbett) is a freedom-loving kind of guy.

PRODUCERS: Alan Armer, Gerald Sanford. DIRECTOR: Lee H. Katzin. SCREENPLAY: Sanford. ART DIRECTOR: Paul Sylos. CINEMATOGRAPHY: Kent C. Smith. MUSIC: Richard Markowitz.

SUPPORTING PLAYERS: Cameron Mitchell, Lew Ayres, Sharon Acker, Dean Jagger, Tim O'Connor.

STRANGER WITHIN, THE

ABC-TV telefilm (1974). Color, 90 mins. airtime.

An Earth woman (Barbara Eden) gives birth to an all-American alien boy.

A Lorimer production. DIRECTOR: Lee Phillips. SCREENPLAY: RICHARD MATHESON.

SUPPORTING PLAYERS: George Grizzard, Joyce Van Patten.

SUPERCAR

ITC (syndicated) weekly series (G.B., 1962–64). 30-min. episodes.

Mike Mercury (the voice of Paul Maxwell) pilots his Supercar (it flies, dives, and rides) for the benefit of his puppet peers. Filmed in Supermarionation.

EXECUTIVE PRODUCER: Gerry Anderson. CREATORS: Gerry and Sylvia Anderson. SPECIAL EFFECTS: Reg Hill. MUSIC: Barry Gray.

VOICES: David Graham, John Bluthal, Sylvia Anderson.

SUPERFRIENDS

ABC-TV weekly animated series (1976). Color, 60-min. episodes.

Animated adventures of superheroes Superman (voice of Danny Dark), Batman (Olan Soule), Robin (Casey Kasem), Wonderwoman (Shannon Farnon), Aquaman (Norman Alden), and Wondergod (Frank Welker), who fight crime with the help of teenagers Wendy and Marvin (Sherri Alberroni and Frank Welker).

A Hanna-Barbera production. MUSIC: Hoyt Curtin, Paul DeKorte.

SUPERMAN (THE ADVENTURES OF SUPERMAN)

Syndicated weekly series (1953–57). B/w and color, 30-min. episodes.

On the planet Krypton, scientist Jor-el (Robert Rockwell) warns Leader Rozan (Herbert Rawlinson) that their world is about to explode and that measures should be taken for mass evacuation. Jor-el is dismissed by the Kryptonians as a fool. Journeying home, he joins with wife Lara (Aline Towne) in planning a means of escape for their tiny son, Kal-el. The boy is sent to Earth in a rocket ship. The rocket makes it off Krypton just as the planet explodes. The vessel lands in a field near Smallville, where it is discovered by Eben and Sarah Kent (Tom Fadden and Frances Morris).

Finding the small boy within, they adopt him and name him Clark Kent (Joel Nestler). While still a youth, Clark discovers that he is the possessor of superpowers, a condition caused by his alien status. Assuming a meek, mild-mannered identity, the boy hides his physical strength. When he reaches manhood, he migrates to the big city of Metropolis, where, donning a red, blue and yellow uniform, he becomes Superman, a fellow who fights for "truth, justice and the American Way."

Clark/Superman (George Reeves) gets a job on the *Daily Planet* as a reporter. He works alongside cub reporter Jimmy Olson (Jack Larson), snoopy reporter Lois Lane (Phyllis Coates, later replaced by Noel Neill),

Lippert

Superman (The Adventures of Superman)

and crusty Editor-in-Chief Perry White (John Hamilton). When the going gets really rough, Clark and Superman work hand-in-hand with Police Inspector Henderson (Robert Shayne).

Phasers on Stunned

People shouldn't tune in expecting outer space because they're going to get inner space. You're not going to see Lorne Greene on the screen in a cape. What we tried to do is put a book onto the screen.

Author Ursula K. Le Guin, on *The Lathe of Heaven*

One of the longest running sf-oriented shows ever, *Superman* mixed mirth and mayhem with a good-natured quality that was irresistible. A good deal of the show's inherent charm was generated by George Reeves as the Man of Steel. A soft-spoken, wry, and yet totally heroic character, he melded the two natures of Kent and Superman into one supremely affable portrayal. The show proved so popular that its producers, in a show of daring, filmed the final three seasons in color. Following the show's cancellation in 1957, star Reeves allegedly grew despondent. Shortly thereafter, he committed suicide.

PRODUCERS: Robert Maxwell and Bernard Luber (first season), Whitney Ellsworth. CREATORS: Jerry Siegal and Joe Shuster, for D.C. Comics. DIRECTORS OF PHOTOGRAPHY: Harold Stine, Harold Wellman, Joseph Biroc. SPECIAL EFFECTS: Thol (Si) Simonson. MAKEUP: Harry Thomas, Gus Norin.

SUPER SIX, THE
NBC-TV weekly animated series (1966–69). Color, 30-min. episodes.

Tales of futuristic crime fighters the Super Six.

SUPERTRAIN
NBC-TV telefilm (1979). Color, 120 mins. airtime.

The pilot film for the series (see the following entry) that proved to be the biggest bomb to go off since Hiroshima. The star of the series proved to be the Supertrain, a futuristic, atomic-powered vehicle that featured a disco, an underwater pool, an outdoor-game area, and oodles of luxurious cabin space. The train was derailed quite quickly, however, by a story line incapable of supporting itself. A Hollywood agent (Steve Lawrence), in debt some $40,000 to a bookie, is the target of a hit instigated by the aforementioned bookie. Good-old-boy Don Meredith, as a neglected husband of a Hollywood bombshell, helps his dapper pal escape death at the hands of killer Don Stroud. Keenan Wynn portrayed the owner of the train. Edward Andrews, Harrison Page, Patrick Collins, and Michael Delano were the super-crew.

A Dan Curtis production. EXECUTIVE PRODUCER AND DIRECTOR: Dan Curtis. PRODUCER: Anthony Spinner. SCREENPLAY: Earl W. Wallace.

SUPPORTING PLAYERS: Char Fontane, Deborah Benson, Ron Masak, Vicki Lawrence, George Hamilton, Fred Williamson, Robert Alda, Nita Talbot, Charlie Brill.

SUPERTRAIN
NBC-TV weekly series (1979). Color, 60-min. episodes.

Never, ever picking up the momentum needed for success, *Supertrain* floundered for half a season, changing time slots and producers with marked regularity, before being scrapped. The atomic-powered Supertrain was impressive enough, but the plot lines were anything but super.

A Dan Curtis production. PRODUCER: Rod Amateau. SUPERVISING PRODUCER: Bob Stambler.

NBC-TV

Supertrain

CAST: Edward Andrews, Robert Alda, Patrick Collins, Nita Talbot.

TALES OF THE UNEXPECTED
Syndicated weekly series (1979). Color, 30-min. episodes.

A colorful anthology of ROALD DAHL's best known stories of fantasy and sf-suspense, featuring such stories as "Neck," "Taste," "Skin," "Edward the Conqueror," "Royal Jelly," "Way up to Heaven," "The Man from the South," "William and Mary," "Lamb to the Slaughter," "The Landlady" and "Dip in the Pool."

A Survival Anglia, Ltd., production. PRODUCER: Sir John Woolf. HOST: Roald Dahl.

GUEST CAST: Joan Collins, Joseph Cotten, Jose Ferrer, Susan George, Sir John Gielgud, Alec Guinness, Julie Harris, Wendy Hiller, Derek Jacobi, Katy Jurado, Siobbhan McKenna, Michael Ontkean, Elaine Stritch, and Jack Weston.

TALES OF TOMORROW
ABC-TV weekly series (1951–56). B/w, 30-min. episodes.

An early speculative-fiction anthology series that presented some truly fine adaptations of sf classics such as *20,000 Leagues Under the Sea,* as well as original teleplays. Less known than SCIENCE FICTION THEATER, *Tales of Tomorrow* was far more ambitious. Featured during its long run were such actors as Thomas Mitchell, as Captain Nemo in *Leagues;* Paul Tripp, as the inventor of a time machine in "Ahead of His Time"; and Susan Holloran, as a young girl who befriends an alien playmate in "Discovered Heart."

TELECOMICS, THE
NBC-TV (1950–51) and CBS-TV (1951) weekly animated series. B/w, 15-min. episodes.

The first made-for-TV cartoon series featured one sf segment, *Space Barton.*

"Space" is, in reality, pilot Horace Barton, Jr., who wants to be both the world's best pilot and the world's first astronaut.

THUNDERBIRDS
ITC (syndicated) weekly series (G.B., 1964–66). Color, 60- and 30-min. episodes.

On a remote Pacific Island, International Rescue, an organization dedicated to helping people out of tight jams, tinkers away at new and wonderful scientific gadgetry. Among their best inventions are *Thunderbird 3* (a spacecraft operable both on Earth and in space) and *Thunderbird 5* (an orbiting space station). Filmed in Supermarionation, the show starred puppets.

EXECUTIVE PRODUCER: Gerry Anderson. CREATORS: Gerry and Sylvia Anderson. ASSOCIATE PRODUCER: Reg Hill. SPECIAL EFFECTS: Derek Meddings. MUSIC: Barry Gray.

VOICES: Peter Dyneley as Jeff Tracy, Shane Rimmer as Scott Tracy, David Holliday as Virgil Tracy, Matt Zimmerman as Alan Tracy, David Graham as Gordon Tracy, Ray Barret as John Tracy, Sylvia Anderson as Lady Penelope Creighton-Ward, David Graham as Professor Brains.

TIME MACHINE, THE
NBC-TV telefilm (1978). Color, 120 mins. airtime.

The big question here is, why? An unabashed copy of George Pal's wonderful 1960 adaptation of the H. G. WELLS tale, this telefilm lacked style, substance, and wit. In this outing, the time traveler (John Beck) is building his time machine for a scientific institution that is about to cut off funding. Attempting to test his machine before the big bucks run out, he shoots himself into a Salem witch-burning (guess who's the burnee?) and a Western shootout before journeying into the future, where the Eloi and the Morlocks battle for supremacy. Whit Bissell, a survivor of the first film, looks fairly embarrassed about the entire affair.

A Sunn Classic picture. DIRECTOR: Henning Schallerup.

TIME TRAIN
CBS-TV weekly series (1979). Color, 60-min. episodes.

Vincent Price and Coral Brown starred as the owners and operators of a special express train that took selected "travelers" to a time when their lives were altered by circumstances beyond their control. This time out, the passengers are given a chance to relive their lives and undo those events.

An Ivan Goff and Ben Roberts production. CREATORS: Goff, Roberts. PRODUCER: Leonard B. Kaufman.

TIME TRAVELERS, THE
ABC-TV telefilm (1975). Color, 90 mins. airtime.

A group of scientists leaps back through time and attempts to stop the great Chicago fire. A pilot for an unsold sf series.

PRODUCER: Irwin Allen. DIRECTOR: Alex Singer. SCREENPLAY: Rod Serling.

CAST: Richard Basehart, Trish Stewart, Sam Groom, Tom Hallick.

TIME TUNNEL, THE
ABC-TV weekly series (1966). Color, 60-min. episodes.

A group of scientists invents a time-portal device that can send someone tumbling either forward or backward through time. The only catch is that the portal can never bring them back to their point of departure. Bad news. When scientist Tony Newman (James Darren) dives through the tunnel, pal Dr. Doug Phillips (Robert Colbert) jumps in after him. This scientific buddy-system transcends the laws of time and space as the twosome winds up meddling in D-Day, the Chicago Fire, the War of 1812, the plot to assassinate President Lincoln, the *Odyssey*, and the future world of 1978. Lt. Gen. Haywood Kirk (Whit Bissell) is dumbfounded. So were members of the viewing audience. The show was cancelled after one season. Back to the old drawing board.

EXECUTIVE PRODUCER AND CREATOR: Irwin Allen. DIRECTOR OF PHOTOGRAPHY: Winton Hoch. SPECIAL EFFECTS: Lyle B. Abbott. MAKEUP: Ben Nye. MUSIC: John Williams.

SUPPORTING PLAYERS: Wesley Lau as Sgt. Jiggs, John Zaremba as Dr. Swain.

TOM CORBETT, SPACE CADET
NBC-TV thrice-weekly (1950–56). B/w, 15- and 30-min. episodes.

In the year 2350 A.D. in Space Academy, U.S.A., a group of young cadets are trained to be Solar Guards, protectors of the Earth, Mars, Venus, and Jupiter (a.k.a. the Solar Alliance). Among the crème de la crème of cadetdom are Tom Corbett (Frankie Thomas), Roger Manning (Jan Merlin), and T. J. Fissell (Jack Grimes). Rounding out the spacey school are such characters as Astron, the Venusian (Al Markhim), teachers Betty and Gloria (Beryl Berney and Martina Brash), Dr. Joan Dale (Patricia Ferris, later to be replaced by Margaret Garland), Space Academy commander Arkwright (Carter Blake), and Capt. Larry Strong (Michael Harvey). By the time Tom blasts off in his ship, the *Polaris*, he is well schooled in the art of space finesse.

PRODUCER: Mort Abrams. ASSOCIATE PRODUCER: Muriel Buckridge. DIRECTORS: George Goul, Ralph Ward. WRITERS: ALFRED BESTER, Jack Weinstock, William Gilbert, Dick Jessup, others.

TOMORROW MAN, THE
Mega-Media (syndicated) special presentation (Canada, 1980). Color, 60 mins. airtime.

A Canadian pilot film for a proposed series, *Through the Eyes of Tomorrow*. *The Tomorrow Man* takes place sometime in the future, somewhere in North America, in the terrifying world of a maximum-security prison. Tom Weston (Stephen Markle) is a political prisoner of the New Regime and is being held without knowing what the charge is. For ten years, Weston survives the torture of a technological nightmare ruled

Mega Media/Norfolk

The Tomorrow Man

by the Warden (Don Francks) and his robot drones. The Warden is a fellow whose knowledge of the future drives him to bait Weston with countless ways to escape, only to confront him in the end with the ultimately shocking fate that might await all future citizens.

A Mega-Media production of a Stephen Zoller/Tibor Takacs film. DI-RECTOR: Tibor Takacs. TELEPLAY: Stephen Zoller and Peter Chapman, from a story by Zoller. PRODUCER: William MacAdam. DIRECTOR OF PHOTOGRAPHY: Alar Kivilo. ART DIRECTOR: Mark Frawcynski. MUSIC: Neville Miller, The Q-T's.

SUPPORTING PLAYERS: David Clement, Gail Dahms, Stan Wilson, Michelle Chicoine.

TWILIGHT ZONE, THE

CBS-TV weekly series (1959–64). B/w, 30-min and 60-min. (fourth season only) episodes.

Winner of three Emmys, *The Twilight Zone* was one of the most expertly crafted and well-written anthology shows on TV. Created by ROD SERLING, one of the fair-haired boys of TV's fabulous 1950s (penning such critically acclaimed TV dramas as *Patterns, Requiem for a Heavyweight,* and *The Comedian*), the show was a brilliant excursion into the many twilight areas of fantasy. CBS entered into the proposition warily, trusting Serling but not the subject matter. Although critically acclaimed, the show never lived up to the network's expectations in terms of mass appeal. During the show's fourth season, CBS briefly expanded the show to an hour. When this format flopped, the show was yanked off the air. Serling assumed it had been cancelled. He was subsequently informed to get back to work and crank out half-hour episodes once more. He did so. The show was cancelled. Serling couldn't figure out why.

What made *The Twilight Zone* so interesting was its fine mixture of sf and fantasy. Serling, a prolific writer himself, also relied on some of the industry's heavyweights to provide additional clout. Aside from Serling, most of the *Zone*'s episodes were written by RICH-ARD MATHESON and CHARLES BEAUMONT. Among some of the more notable sf offerings shown during the show's long run were "To Serve Man," an adaptation by Matheson of DAMON KNIGHT's tale of alien visitation; "Will the Real Martian Please Stand Up?"; "People Are Alike All Over"; "Elegy"; "Death Star"; and "The Invaders," the classic teleplay in which Agnes Moorhead is menaced by a tiny spaceship in her home. She crushes the vessel at the play's conclusion, and it is then that the viewer notices the American flag on the ship's hull.

Following the demise of *The Twilight Zone,* Serling turned to screenwriting (PLANET OF THE APES) and TV series work (ROD SERLING'S NIGHT GALLERY) before opting for teaching. He died in 1975.

A Cayuga production. PRODUCERS: Rod Serling, Buck Houghton. CREATOR: Serling. MAKEUP: William Tuttle. MUSIC: Bernard Herrmann, Jerry Goldsmith.

UFO

ITC (syndicated) weekly series (G.B., 1972). Color, 60-min. episodes.

Gerry and Sylvia Anderson's first live-action series concerned the efforts of S.H.A.D.O. (Supreme Headquarters, Alien Defense Organization) to protect the Earth from potential alien invasions. Located in both England (beneath a movie studio)and on the moon, S.H.A.D.O. HQ was overseen by Ed Straker (Ed Bishop). Straker was given help by Col. Freeman (George Sewell), Col. Foster (Michael Billington), Col. Lake (Wanda Ventham), Lt. Ellis (Gabrielle Drake), and SID, the orbiting Space Intruder Detector.

CREATORS: Gerry and Sylvia Anderson, with Reg Hill. PRODUCER: Hill. EXECUTIVE PRODUCER: Gerry Anderson. STORY EDITOR: Tony Barwick. DIRECTOR OF PHOTOGRAPHY: Brendon Stafford. SPECIAL EFFECTS: Derek Meddings. MUSIC: Barry Gray.

SUPPORTING PLAYERS: Grant Taylor, Vladek Sheybal, Keith Alexander, Peter Gordeno, Harry Baird.

UFO INCIDENT
NBC-TV telefilm (1975). Color, 90 mins. airtime.

Based on Betty and Barney Hill's book *Interrupted Journey*, this movie was an allegedly factual account of two Earthlings who are captured by a group of grounded extraterrestrials. Taking the humans aboard their ship, the aliens examine the couple and then, hypnotizing them into a state of forgetfulness, let them go. The Hills (Estelle Parsons and James Earl Jones) begin having flashbacks during dreams and eventually seek professional help. Through hypnosis and psychotherapy, a story emerges that astounds UFO believers and amuses skeptics.

DIRECTOR: Richard A. Colla.

SUPPORTING PLAYERS: Bernard Hughes, Beeson Carroll.

ULTIMATE IMPOSTER, THE
CBS-TV telefilm (1979). Color, 120 mins. airtime.

Into the voidoid zone. An American spy (Joseph Hacker) is caught by the Chinese behind their borders. His memory is destroyed by diabolical Oriental chemicals, a state of affairs immediately noticeable to girl friend/fellow spy Erin Gray when she meets her beau upon his return Stateside. Tests show that the spy cannot even spell *d-o-g-g-i-e*, which is upsetting to his espionage boss (Keith Andes). Smart spy/doctor Macon McCalman suggests that Hacker's blank slate would be ideal for the Alpha Computer Project.

What Alpha Computer Project? Well, with wires attached to his head, the memoryless spy can be programmed by a master computer and taught everything from Mandarin Chinese to advanced disco dancing. Unfortunately, his memory gives out after 72 hours. His boss figures that the time limit is OK. His spy will just have to work fast. The espionage team teaches the fellow everything there is to know about a certain race-car driver in order to infiltrate a spy ring that is holding captive a Russian sea captain (the kind filled with secret info). Out on assignment, the hapless lad realizes that no one has taught him how to drive a car, so he has to shinny up a telephone pole and connect his brain long-distance to the computer via Ma Bell. He gets the Russian fellow out in just under 72 hours and returns to the U.S. a hero, albeit a dumb one.

A Universal Production. EXECUTIVE PRODUCER: Lionel E. Siegel. DIRECTOR: Paul Stanley. SCREENPLAY: Siegel based on "The Capricorn Man" by William Zacha. CINEMATOGRAPHY: Vincent Martinelli. MUSIC: Dana Kaproff.

SUPPORTING PLAYERS: John van Dreelen, Bobby Riggs.

ULTRA MAN
Syndicated weekly animated series (1967). Color, 30-min. episodes.

Created by Toho Films greatest special-effects master, Eiji Tsuburaya, this cartoon series took place in 21st-century Japan. Two UFOs collide over Earth. One saucer crashes harmlessly into the sea. The other, however, smashes into a Scientific Patrol Headquarters exploratory ship and kills its pilot, Iota. The alien driver, a being from the Nebula M-78 in the 40th galaxy, brings Iota back to life and gives him a special capsule. Whenever Iota finds himself in trouble, he is to use the capsule and become Ultra Man, a super crime-fighter.

VALLEY OF THE DINOSAURS
CBS-TV weekly animated series (1974). Color, 30-min. episodes.

A 20th-century family, boating down the Amazon River, is caught in a strange whirlpool, carried through a decidedly eerie cave, and transported into a prehistoric world. They meet and befriend a cave family, and together the two families fight for survival using both scientific savvy and brute strength. John Butler, a science instructor, wife

Kim, daughter Katie, son Greg, and pet dog Digger find that they have a lot in common with prehistoric people Gorak, wife Gera, daughter Tana, son Lock, and pet stegosaurus Glomb.

More Powerful Than, etc.

Supertrain was my first futuristic project. I loved it. I was really allowed to go no-holds-barred. I could go as far as I wanted in terms of design. If I made a mistake . . . who'd notice?

Ned Parsons, designer of NBC's *Supertrain*

VOICES: Melanie Baker, Shannon Farnon, Joan Gardner, Kathy Gori, Alan Oppenheimer, Andrew Parks, Mike Road.

VOYAGE TO THE BOTTOM OF THE SEA

ABC-TV weekly series (1964–68). B/w and color, 60-min. episodes.

Irwin Allen's series, based on the hit film, featured the crew of the futuristic submarine *Seaview* in a never-ending battle against alien monsters, Earthly madmen, and undersea monsters.

CREATOR AND EXECUTIVE PRODUCER: Irwin Allen. STORY CONSULTANT: Sidney Marshall. DIRECTOR OF PHOTOGRAPHY: Carl Guthrie. SPECIAL EFFECTS: Lyle B. Abbott. MAKEUP: Ben Nye.

CAST: Richard Basehart as Admiral Nelson, David Hedison as Captain Lee Crane, Bob Dowdell as Chip Morton, Terry Becker as Sharkey, Del Monroe as Kowalski.

ABC-TV

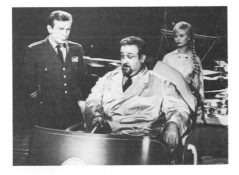

Voyage to the Bottom of the Sea

WHERE HAVE ALL THE PEOPLE GONE?

NBC-TV telefilm (1974). Color, 90 mins. airtime.

While on a camping trip, an all-American family explores a cave. As they wend their way through the twisting corridors inside, they feel a sudden Earth tremor and see a distant flash of light. Emerging from the cave, they find that their camper won't start. Hiking to the nearest town, they discover a slew of abandoned cars and trucks and what looks like a thousand or so bodies . . . or at least clothing with some sandy stuff inside that could be bodies. Dad and the two kids embark on a dangerous journey to find out the fate of mom, still at home in Malibu, California. Trekking across the state, they discover that a solar flare has occurred (the flash of light) and has fused the ignitions of all cars. Appearing simultaneously was a new and deadly virus that turns people into sand. By the time they get home, they find that mom, too, has opted for the nickname Sandy. And so, northward they go, toward a better life and, hopefully, a new batch of relatives with firmer bodies.

A Jozak/Alpine/Metromedia production. PRODUCER: Jerry Isenberg. DIRECTOR: John I. Moxey. SCREENPLAY: Lewis John Carlino and Sandor Stern, from a story by Carlino.

CAST: Peter Graves, Verna Bloom, Ken Sanson, George O'Hanlon, Jr., Kathleen Quinlan, Michael-James Wixted.

WONDER WOMAN

ABC-TV telefilm (1974). Color, 90 mins. airtime.

ABC's original pilot film for a proposed super-heroine TV series proved to be anything but wonder-inducing, either in terms of ratings or execution. Based on the D.C. Comics character, the film traces the efforts of Diana Prince (Cathy Lee Crosby) in her never-ending fight against evil. In the pilot episode she was pitted against a fellow named, literally, Mr. Evil (Ricardo Montalban). So much for subtlety. Diana is, in reality, Paradise Isle's best known super-Amazon, Wonder Woman. She does her best. The script doesn't.

A Warner Brothers TV production. PRODUCER: John Stephens. DIRECTOR: Vincent McEveety. SCREENPLAY: John D. F. Black.

SUPPORTING PLAYERS: Kaz Garas, Andrew Prine, Anita Ford, Jordan Rhodes.

WONDER WOMAN
ABC-TV and CBS-TV weekly series (1976–79). Color, 60-min. episodes.

A story with a history almost as wacky as its comic-book adventure style. Originally planned as a series, but abandoned by William (BATMAN) Dozier, *Wonder Woman* was first brought to the tube as a 1974 telefilm (see the preceding entry) produced by John G. Stephens. It stiffed. A second telefilm, produced by Douglas Cramer, was aired a year later; this version starred Lynda Carter and stuck more closely to comic-book lines. A limited series was ordered by ABC, with two episodes airing in the 1975–76 season and 11 in the 1976–77 season. Sick of this treatment, the producers jumped to CBS-TV for two seasons of regular programming. Retitled *The New Adventures of Wonder Woman*, the show ran first-run until May 1979. Briefly, the episodes concerned the crime-fighting abilities of super-Amazon Wonder

ABC-TV

Wonder Woman

Woman/Diana Prince (Lynda Carter).

PRODUCERS: Douglas S. Cramer, Bruce Lansbury.

SUPPORTING PLAYERS: Lyle Waggoner as Maj. Steve Trevor, Beatrice Colen as Etta Candy, Richard Estham as Gen. Blankenship.

WORLD OF THE GIANTS, THE
Syndicated weekly series (1961). 30-min. episodes.

Mel Hunter and Bill Winters (Marshall Thompson and Arthur Franz) are two dedicated American counterspies who agree to have themselves shrunk to six inches in height, the better to infiltrate foreign espionage groups.

AUTHORS

ABBOTT, EDWIN A(BBOTT)
(1838–1926)

A British clergyman, schoolmaster, and biographer, Edwin A. Abbott is best known for his nongenre work: *Francis Bacon* (1885), *A Shakespearian Grammar* (1870), and *The Anglican Career of Newman* (1892). His sole excursion into sf occurred in 1884, with the publication of *Flatland: A Romance of Many Dimensions*. Published in London with illustrations by the author (under the pseudonym A. Square), the book concerns the adventures of Mr. Square in Flatland, a world of two dimensions. After offering the reader a guided tour of two-dimensionality, the author proceeds to other worlds of other dimensions. The book was published in Boston one year later, bearing the author's true name.

ABE, KOBO
(1924–   )

A popular Japanese writer known for his existential novels, Kobo Abe has occasionally strayed into the realm of sf, most notably with the publication (1959) of his novel *Inter Ice-Age 4*. Set in the not-too-distant future, the work portrays a world rapidly sinking beneath tidal seas caused by melting ice caps. Humanity is forced to alter biologically its newborn in order to survive the new, watery world.

A later novel, *The Box Man* (1973), featured a protagonist who lives in an ambulatory cardboard box. The possessor of a degree in medicine, Abe is best known for his nongenre work, including *The Woman in the Dunes* (1960) and *The Ruined Map* (trans. 1969).

ACKERMAN, FORREST J(AMES)
(1916–   )

America's number one sf fan, Forrest J. Ackerman, is best-known to millions of young-at-heart readers as the ever-punning editor of the magazine *Famous Monsters of Filmland* (first issued 1958). Before turning his attention to monster movies, however, Ackerman had already established himself as a prime mover in sf fandom. During the 1930s, he worked on several fanzines, including *The Time Traveler* and *Science Fiction Digest*. In 1934 he served as one of the founding members of the Los Angeles Science Fantasy Society.

The self-proclaimed coiner of the term "sci-fi," Ackerman was presented a Hugo award in 1953 as "Number One Fan Personality." An editor of anthologies, a literary agent (with such clients as A. E. VAN VOGT), and a genre devotee, Ackerman has amassed one of the largest collections of genre memorabilia in the world. He has filled two entire homes in the Los Angeles area with his collection, and one day hopes to raise enough funds to incorporate the various roomfuls of books, photos, posters, and movie props into one unified museum. The editor of the "Perry Rhodan" series of books in the States, Ackerman's best-known bound anthologies include *The Best from Famous Monsters of Filmland* (1964), *Son of Famous Monsters of Filmland* (1964), *Famous Monsters of Filmland Strike*

Back (1965), *The Frankenstein Monster* (1969), and *Best Science Fiction of 1973.*

ADAMSKI, GEORGE
(1891–   )

Polish-born George Adamski rose to prominence during the great UFO flap of the early 1950s. It was Adamski who claimed to have talked with Venusians in his controversial book *Flying Saucers Have Landed* (1953). Although some critics objected to his literary career as sheer hokum, Adamski persisted, much to the delight of ufologists everywhere. Other high-flying works include *Inside the Space Ships* (1956), *Flying Saucers Farewell* (1961), and *Behind the Flying Saucer Mystery* (1967).

ADLARD, MARK
(1932–   )

Born Peter Marcus Adlard, British novelist Mark Adlard was educated at Trinity College, Cambridge, and spent over two decades as a manager in the steel industry. Discovering the sf genre in the 1960s, he found a way to incorporate much of his knowledge of the business world into stories of the future. His best known works are the three books that comprise the "Tcity" trilogy: *Interface* (G.B., 1971), *Volteface* (G.B., 1972) and *Multiface* (G.B., 1975). All three books deal with the life-styles of workers and management in the future.

ALDISS, BRIAN W(ILSON)
(1925–   )

The past president (1960–64) of the British Science Fiction Assn., Brian Aldiss is one of Great Britain's most popular sf writers. Born in Norfolk, he was raised in private schools before serving in the British Army in Burma during World War II. In peacetime, Aldiss spent a number of years in bookselling before turning his hand to writing. His first sf short story, "Criminal Record," was published in 1954 in *Science Fantasy.* A prolific writer, Aldiss penned a few dozen more short stories (which were duly anthologized) during the remainder of that decade, emerging in 1958 with his first novel, *Non-Stop,* a tale of starships.

During the 1960s, Aldiss expanded his novelistic style, aligning himself

Brian W. Aldiss

with the relevance-in-sf preached by advocates of the so-called New Wave. Story collections such as *Barefoot in the Head* (G.B., 1969), in which all of Europe is dosed with a hallucinogenic gas, and novels such as *Cryptozoic!* (1967), detailing a new wrinkle on time travel, placed him in the vanguard of the new movement in progressive sf.

The year 1973 saw the publication of *Billion Year Spree,* an ambitious history of the sf genre. Other works published during the 1970s include *Frankenstein Unbound* (G.B., 1973), *Hell's Cartographers* with HARRY HARRISON (G.B., 1975) and *The Malacia Tapestry* (G.B., 1976). The winner of Hugo awards in 1959 and 1962, Aldiss has also been honored (1968) as Britain's most popular sf writer by the British Science Fiction Assn., been presented (1977) with the first James Blish Award for sf criticism, the Australian Ditmar Award for excellence (1970), and a Nebula (1965).

Currently working on an sf "history of Stapledonian proportions," Aldiss is the possessor of a self-proclaimed "fertile mind that is an enemy of endeavor."

Some of his better-known short stories can be found in such anthologies as *Space, Time and Nathaniel* (G.B., 1957), *Airs of Earth* (G.B., 1963), *A Brian Aldiss Omnibus* (G.B., 1969), and *The Book of Brian Aldiss* (1972).

AMIS, KINGSLEY
(1922–   )

British writer and critic Kingsley Amis gave sf a somewhat more respectable status with the masses when, in 1960, he published *New Maps of Hell,* a serious analysis of the genre culled from lectures he had given the previous year at Princeton.

Born and educated in London, Amis served in the British Army during World War II. Following his stint in the service, Amis quickly established himself as a popular writer via such social comedies as *Lucky Jim* (G.B., 1954), *That Certain Feeling* (1955), and *Take a Girl like You* (1960).

Following the publication of *New Maps of Hell*, Amis devoted much of his time to the genre, compiling (with Robert Conquest) the *Spectrum* series of sf anthologies, a highly touted series that ran from 1961 to 1966 and offered five volumes of literature and criticism. His novel *The Alteration* (1976) won the 1977 John W. Campbell Memorial Award for Best Novel.

Photo courtesy of G. P. Putnam's Sons

Poul Anderson

ANDERSON, POUL
(1926–   )

Pennsylvania-born Poul Anderson published his first short story ("Tomorrow's Children," with F. N. Waldrop) in 1947, one year before he received a degree in physics from the University of Minnesota. A long-time genre fan (a member of the Minneapolis Fantasy Society), Anderson was slow in getting his career off the ground. It was not until 1951 that he began producing in quantity, placing 10 stories that year. His first novel, *Vault of the Ages*, geared toward youngsters, was published in 1952. It was in 1953, however, that Poul Anderson really began establishing himself as an author to be reckoned with, writing 19 short stories and publishing the magazine versions of three novels.

Since that time he has written nearly 40 novels and countless short stories. Among his best-known works: *Three Hearts and Three Lions* (1953), in which a World War II soldier is transported into a Nordic world of sword-and-sorcery; *Brain Wave* (1954), in which, after passing through a force field that inhibits neurological growth, humanity for the first time in its history experiences an overwhelming increase in intelligence; *Tau Zero* (1970), a hard-science novel detailing the adventures of a shipful of spacefarers traveling at sublight speed; *The High Crusade* (1960), chronicling how a

group of knights defeats an alien invasion in the 1200s, steals the spaceship, and establishes a kingdom in space, which is discovered years later; and the "Time Patrol" series, including *The Guardians of Time* (1960) and *The Corridors of Time* (1965).

An incredibly prolific author who mixes hard science with swashbuckling, humor, and a healthy dose of mythological wonder, some of Anderson's best short stories can be found in *The Worlds of Poul Anderson* (1974), *Homebrew* (1976), and *The Best of Poul Anderson* (1976). Other works of merit include *No World of Their Own* (1955), *Un-Man and Other Novellas* (1962), *Shield* (1963), *Time and Stars* (1964), *The Trouble Twisters* (1964), *A Midsummer Tempest* (1974), and *The Earth Book of Stormgate* (1978).

Anderson has won five Hugo awards for short fiction (1961, 1964, 1969, 1972, 1973), two Nebulas (1971, 1972), and has served (1971–72) as president of the Science Fiction Writers of America.

ANTHONY, PIERS
(1934–   )

Born in England, Piers Anthony Dillingham Jacob emigrated to the United States, becoming an American citizen in 1958. After writing technical releases for a U.S. communications company, Anthony became an English teacher and, eventually, a full-time sf writer. Beginning to write short stories in 1963, he quickly became known as a wordsmith who had the ability to breathe new life into standard plot lines. Among his better known novels (his first, *Chthon*, was published in 1967) are *Macroscope* (1969), in which an invention leads four humans into a totally alien terrain where all is unity; *Prostho Plus* (1971), in which aliens kidnap an Earth dentist; *Omnivore* (1968), about three human explorers who investigate a strange planet populated by fungoid life-forms, and its sequels, *Orn* (1971) and *Ox* (1976); and the "Battle Circle" trilogy—*Sos the Rope* (1968), *Var the Stick* (1973), and *Neq the Sword* (1975)—all of which take place in a postholocaust world where science battles barbarism (a volume containing all three, *The Battle Circle*, was published in 1977).

ANVIL, CHRISTOPHER

Pseudonym of American writer Harry C. Crosby, Jr. (year of birth unknown). Anvil's work, in general, is sf of a comic nature. First appearing in 1956 within the pages of *Astounding* with "The Prisoner," Anvil soon expanded his following with the popular "Pandora" series of stories, which ran (1956–61) in *Astounding* and *Analog* and included "Pandora's Planet" and "Pandora's Envoy." *The Day the Machines Stopped*, published in 1964, is a jingoistic look at the worldwide chaos resulting from the Russians literally short-circuiting the entire Earth . . . permanently cutting off electrical impulses. *Warlord's World* (1975) is a slaphappy look at space opera.

ARNOLD, EDWIN L(ESTER)
(1857–1935)

The son of Britain's Sir Edwin Arnold, whose *Light of Asia* popularized Buddhism in Victorian England, Edwin L. Arnold is best-remembered for his novel *Gulliver of Mars* (G.B., 1905), a work that mixed fantasy and science in tracing the adventures of modern-day Lt. Gulliver Jones on Mars. Jones takes a quick trip via flying carpet to the Red Planet, where he encounters very Asian antics involving kidnapped princesses and harried princes. Other works include *The Wonderful Adventures of Phra the Phoenician* (1890) and *Lepidus the Centurion: A Roman of Today* (1901).

ASIMOV, ISAAC
(1920–   )

Isaac Asimov has produced more words in his lifetime than the average printing-press, with over 200 titles to his credit. Born in the U.S.S.R., the prolific Mr. A emigrated to the U.S. with his family in 1923. He became a U.S. citizen at the age of eight and, by the age of ten, was an avid sf fan. Reading the sf publications on display in his father's candy store, young Isaac entertained notions of becoming a professional writer, eventually joining the sf-fan organization the Futurians while a teenager.

Intellectually advanced for his age, Asimov left high school at the age of 16 and obtained a degree in chemistry from Columbia University at the age of 19. At the age of 21, he was the possessor of a master's, and by 28, a Ph.D. From 1949 to 1958, he served as associate professor of biochemistry at the Boston University School of Medicine. He resigned his post to write full time.

Asimov's writing career began in 1939, when he published "Marooned off Vesta" in AS. Within 12 months he was one of legendary editor JOHN W. CAMPBELL's favorite new faces at *ASF*. Campbell guided and advised the neophyte writer, and shortly after entering *ASF*'s fold, Asimov produced his first short stories concerning robots, "Strange Playfellow" (1940) and "Liar!" (1941), the latter introducing Asimov's famous Three Laws of Robotics. The year 1941 also saw the publication of what is considered Asimov's finest story, "Nightfall."

Following World War II, Asimov emerged as both well-respected short-story writer and a novelist. His first novel, *Pebble in the Sky* (1950), was quickly followed by the short-story collection *I, Robot* (1950), the novel *The Stars Like Dust* (1951), and the epic *Foundation* (1951). The latter work was the first installment of his much-heralded "Foundation" trilogy, the

Isaac Asimov

others being *Foundation and Empire* (1952) and *Second Foundation* (1953).

A writer who did much to advance the cause of science in sf, Asimov continued his amazing output throughout the 1960s, dabbling in juvenile novels under the pseudonym of Paul French. As French, he penned six "Lucky Starr" novels, beginning in 1952 and ending in 1958. The 1960s and 1970s saw the author divide his time between science fiction and science fact, offering such factual titles as *The Intelligent Man's Guide to Science* (1960), *View from a Height* (1963), *Asimov's Biographical Encyclopedia of Science and Technology* (1964), *The Human Brain* (1964), *An Easy Introduction to the Slide Rule* (1966), *The Neutrino* (1966), *Asimov's Guide to the Bible* (1968 and 1969), *Where Do We Go from Here?* (1971), *Jupiter, the Largest Planet* (1973), *Science Past, Science Future* (1975), and *Opus 200* (1979).

While most of his sf output of the past two decades has been composed of anthologies of short fiction both new and old, his few excursions into the novel realm have been well worth waiting for. *Fantastic Voyage* (1966) was an enjoyable adaptation of a movie script of the same name, and *The Gods Themselves* (1972) won both a Hugo and a Nebula award. His short-story collection *The Bicentennial Man* (1976) was a critically acclaimed potpourri of Asimov past and present.

Long regarded as one of the most popular authors in the genre, it has only been of late that Asimov has re-ceived adequate recognition from his peers and fans alike. In 1966 he was presented a Hugo for the "Foundation" trilogy, which was named the Best All-Time Series; in 1963 he was given a Hugo for Distinguished Contributions to the Field; and in 1972 he was awarded both a Hugo and a Nebula for *The Gods Themselves*.

AVALLONE, MICHAEL
(1924–   )

An American writer best known for his novelizations of TV and movie scripts, Michael Avallone has written under dozens of pseudonyms (including Ed Noon, Edwina Noone, Priscilla Dalton, Mark Dane, Steve Michaels, and Sidney Stuart). He is best known for his novelizations of THE MAN FROM U.N.C.L.E. stories such as *The Thousand Coffins Affair* (1965), THE GIRL FROM U.N.C.L.E. stories such as *The Birds of a Feather Affair* (1966), and for *The Blazing Affair* (1966) and BENEATH THE PLANET OF THE APES (1970).

BAILY, HILARY
(1936–   )

British-born Hilary Baily is best known as an anthologist and short-story writer. Educated at Cambridge, she began writing in the early 1960s, shortly after her marriage to sf author MICHAEL MOORCOCK (they were divorced in 1978). She served as cocompiler (with Charles Platt) of the *New Worlds 7* (1974) anthology and has since assumed full responsibility for the *New Worlds* series.

BALL, BRIAN
(1932–   )

British author of juvenile fiction. Among his more popular works: *Sundog* (G.B., 1965), *Timepiece* (G.B., 1968), *Timepit* (G.B., 1971), *The Probability Man* (1972), and *Night of the Robots* (G.B., 1972).

BALLARD, J(AMES) G(RAHAM)
(1930–   )

One of the true black sheep of the genre, J. G. Ballard is a master crafts- man of disasters both big and small. Possessing an uncanny knack for pin- pointing the source point of mental and physical disintegration, Ballard has penned a number of awesome novels both in and out of the sf genre. Born in Shanghai, Ballard spent some of his boyhood years imprisoned in a Japa- nese prisoner-of-war camp. Arriving in Great Britain in 1946, he studied medi- cine at Cambridge before opting for a career in literature. His first writing jobs consisted of cranking out advertis- ing copy and polishing movie scripts.

Moving into sf while serving in the Royal Air Force in Canada, Ballard garnered his first sf byline in 1956, with the story "Prima Belladonna," published in *Science Fantasy*. He soon became a regular contributor to Britain's *New World* magazine, and his extraordinary style swept him up in the New Wave movement.

His apocalyptic views jolted audi- ences in the 1960s via such novels as *The Wind from Nowhere* (1962), wherein the Earth is assaulted by never-ending gales, and *The Drowned World* (1962), which pictured the planet being pummeled by unrelenting oceans. His fascination for disaster con- tinued in books such as *The Burning World* (1964), *The Crystal World* (G.B., 1966), and *The Atrocity Exhi- bition* (1970). In the latter work, a collection of related stories, Ballard de- parted from traditional sf imagery, opt- ing toward more everyday, mainstream horrors. He continued this trend in novels such as *Crash* (G.B., 1973; auto wrecks), *Concrete Island* (G.B., 1974; a man is marooned in a forgotten area of a metropolis), and *High-Rise* (G.B., 1975; stranded in a high-rise, tenants resort to barbarism, rape, and plunder).

His best short stories can be found in *Passport to Eternity* (1963), *The Impossible Man* (1966), and *Vermilion Sands* (G.B., 1973).

BARJAVEL, RENÉ
(1911–   )

A popular French novelist and screenwriter, Barjavel is a regular con- tributor to the French publication *An- ticipations*. Among his best known works are *The Ice People* (France, 1968), a novel concerning two ancient humans thawed from an icy state only to find a postholocaust Earth stretched out before them; *Ashes to Ashes* (France, 1943), a tale depicting the effects of the loss of electricity on the world; and *The Strong Man* (France, 1946), a story detailing the hopeless attempts of a self-created su- perman to bring happiness to the world.

BATES, HARRY
(1900–   )

American-born writer and editor Harry Bates is probably best known for penning "Farewell to the Master" (1940; printed in *ASF*), the story that inspired the 1951 film THE DAY THE EARTH STOOD STILL. Bates also edited *ASF* from 1930 until 1933 and *Strange Tales* from 1931 until 1932, and, with Desmond W. Hall, assumed the pseudo- nym Anthony Gilmore in penning the popular "Hawk Carse" series of stories for *ASF*.

BAUM, L(YMAN) FRANK
(1856–1919)

Born in Chittenango, New York, American writer L. Frank Baum is best known for his "WIZARD OF OZ" series of juvenile offerings. He also penned the sf children's-book *The Master Key: An Electrical Fairy Tale* (1901). Among his best known books: *The Marvelous Land of Oz* (1904), *Ozma of Oz* (1907), *The Road to Oz* (1909), *Sky Island* (1912), *Tik-Tok of Oz* (1914), and *The Tin Woodsman of Oz* (1918). Baum also wrote under the pseudonyms Hugh Fitzgerald, Suzanne Metcalf, Schuyler Staunton, Floyd Akers, and Edith Van Dyne.

BAXTER, JOHN
(1939–   )

Australian writer and editor John Baxter did much to advance the cause of Australian sf with the publication of the anthologies *The Pacific Book of Australian Science Fiction* (Australia, 1968) and *The Second Pacific Book of Australian Science Fiction* (Australia, 1971), both of which he edited. As an sf writer, he is best known for his novel

The Off-Worlders (1966), a tale depicting an agricultural society that survives by banning the study of science. More recently, he has taken to non-fiction writing, penning *Science Fiction in the Cinema* (1970) and (with Thomas A. Atkins) *The Fire Came By* (G.B., 1976), the latter a collection of science-fact pieces.

BAYLEY, J. BARRINGTON

British sf writer J. Barrington Bayley began his career in the early 1950s, penning a host of short stories under both his own name and several pseudonyms, including P. F. Woods, Alan Aumbry, and John Diamond. As Michael Barrington he cowrote the popu-

---

Train of Thought

I'm an idea writer. Everything of mine is permeated with my love of ideas—both big and small. It doesn't matter what it is as long as it grabs me and fascinates me. And, then, I'll run out and do something about it.
Ray Bradbury

---

lar "Peace on Earth" with MICHAEL MOORCOCK. His best known novels include *Star Virus* (1970), *The Annihilation Factor* (1972), *Empire of Two Worlds* (1972), *The Fall of Chronopolis* (1974), and *The Soul of the Robot* (1974).

BEAUMONT, CHARLES
(1929–67)

Pseudonym used by American writer Charles Nutt. Best known as a screenwriter, scripting nearly one-third of the popular TWILIGHT ZONE TV series, as well as such films as THE SEVEN FACES OF DR. LAO, Beaumont was also a prolific short-story writer who mixed elements of fantasy and sf with the macabre. His best short stories can be found in *Shadow Play* (1957), *Hunger* (1957), and *Yonder* (1958). He died in 1967 after a prolonged illness.

BELL, ERIC TEMPLE
(1883–1960)

Born in Aberdeen, Scotland, Eric Temple Bell moved to the U.S. when barely out of his teens. In 1927 he became professor of mathematics at the

California Institute of Technology, a post he held until he retired in 1953. During the early part of the century, Bell became well known for his books on mathematics and science fact. Such works as *Algebraic Arithmetic* (1927), *The Search for Truth* (1934), *Men of Mathematics* (1937), *The Development of Mathematics* (1940), and *Mathematics, Servant of Science* (1952) helped popularize the subject of math among lay people.

His works written under the pseudonym John Taine, however, earned Bell the most fame. Taine was a daring sf writer for his day, delving into such topics as evolution, cyclical universes, and genetics when most of his peers were still staging elaborate space battles in print. Some of Taine's best known novels include *The Purple Sapphire* (1924), *The Iron Star* (1930), *Before the Dawn* (1934), *The Time Stream* (1946), *The Cosmic Geoids and One Other* (1949), *Seeds of Life* (1951), and *The Crystal Horde* (1952).

A one-time president of the Mathematics Association of America, Bell also wrote under the name of James Temple.

BENFORD, GREGORY
(1941–   )

Alabama-born Gregory Benford is an sf writer whose greatest strength is his scientific accuracy. An associate professor in physics, Benford graduated from the University of Oklahoma in 1963, garnering a Ph.D. in 1967 from the University of California. His interest in sf dates back to childhood, when, as the son of a U.S. Army officer whose travels took the Benford family throughout Europe and Japan, he began editing an sf fanzine.

In 1965 he won a writing contest held in *F&SF*, and he has been writing ever since. In 1974 he won a Nebula, with GORDON EKLUND, for the short story "If the Stars Are Gods" (later expanded to novel length). His novel *Deeper than the Darkness* (1970) was also revised and reissued as *The Stars in Shroud* (1978). The book stands as a thought-provoking tale of alien contact, with hostile aliens invading Earth via a psychic plague. *In the Ocean of Night* (1977), Benford's best-known novel, is an amazing treatment of the "first contact" theme in which an astronaut, sent into space to destroy what is believed to be a comet, rebels when he discovers the space body to be a derelict spaceship from an ancient society.

BERRY, BRYAN
(1930–55)

One of Great Britain's most active pulp writers in the early 1950s, Bryan Berry died at a very early age, leaving behind a host of short stories buried beneath pseudonyms known only to the author. Novels written under his real name include *And the Stars Remain* (1952), *Dread Visitor* (1952), *Born in Captivity* (1952), *From What Far Star?* (1953), and *The Venom Seekers* (1953). Possibly his best known works, penned under the name Rolf Garner, comprise his "Venus" trilogy, a body of work that portrays the remainder of the human race attempting to rekindle civilization on Venus after Earth has been destroyed. The titles in the "Venus" series are *The Resurgent Dust* (1953), *The Immortals* (1953), and *The Indestructible* (1954).

BESTER, ALFRED
(1913–   )

Born in New York City, Alfred Bester embarked on a career in sf literature relatively late in his professional life. After graduating from the University of Pennsylvania with a degree in science and fine arts, Bester was attending law school when he decided to enter a short story into a contest being conducted in 1939 at *Thrilling Wonder Stories*. The story, "The Broken Axiom," won the competition and was printed. At that point he began writing regularly, his short stories appearing in many sf pulps, his dialogue showing up in such comic books as *Superman* and *Captain Marvel*. After writing almost exclusively for radio melodramas in the late 1940s, Bester returned to sf in a big way during the 1950s, producing two of his best-known novels, *The Demolished Man* (1953) and *The Stars My Destination* (1956). The former book is a murder mystery in which telepathy is a key factor; in the latter novel (which the author confesses was

inspired by *The Count of Monte Cristo*), yet another excursion into a future society where justice is slightly out of whack, hero Gully Foyle is transformed from dolt to superavenger in his quest for revenge.

Bester's output dwindled to a trickle during the 1960s, his primary concern being his duties as literary editor for *Holiday* magazine. He returned to the fold in 1974 with *The Computer Connection*. Other works include *Starburst* (1958) and *The Dark Side of the Earth* (1964), two short-story collections. In 1953 his *Demolished Man* won the first Hugo awarded to a novel. While certainly not a prolific writer, much of Bester's output in the 1950s is considered unparalleled in the genre.

BIERCE, AMBROSE
(1842–1914?)

Best known as a master of fantasy and horror, Ambrose Bierce often wrote works that touched on sf themes. An American journalist who mixed satire and cynicism with pathos and pain, Bierce made a large impression on the American public through such works as *The Cynic's Word Book* (1906; later to become famous as *The Devil's Dictionary*) and through his genuinely eerie portrayals of post–Civil War life, inspired by his years as a soldier during that conflict. He disappeared in Mexico in 1914, leaving behind dozens of short stories and titles such as *Tales of Soldiers and Civilians* (1891), *Can Such Things Be?* (1893), *Fantastic Fables* (1899), *A Son of the Gods and a Horseman in the Sky* (1907), *Black Beetles in Amber* (1892), and *Shapes of Clay* (1903). At times, Bierce wrote both prose and poetry under the pseudonyms of Dod Grile, William Herman, and J. Milton Sloluck.

BIGGLE, LLOYD, JR.
(1923–   )

Since American author Lloyd Biggle, Jr., holds a Ph.D. in musicology, it's no wonder that much of his sf output concerns the arts. His first short story, "Gypped" (1956; *Galaxy*), deals with a musical theme. His first novel, *The Angry Espers* (1961), established yet a second Biggle pattern: that of mixing mystery-novel axioms with sf sensibilities. He has written four works concerning the futuristic detective work of Jan Darzek: *All the Colors of Darkness* (1963), *Watchers of the Dark* (1964), *This Darkening Universe* (1975), and *Silence Is Deadly* (1977). *The Still, Small Voice of Trumpets* (1968) combines elements of both his major styles; *The Metallic Muse* (1972), his best-known collection of sf short stories, prominently displays Biggle's multifaceted interests.

BINDER, EANDO

The pseudonym used by two brothers, Earl Andrew Binder (1904–   ) and Otto Oscar Binder (1911–75), Eando Binder is best known for the creation of robot Adam Link. Beginning its run in *AS* in 1939, the "Link" series of stories, which were "narrated" by humanistic robot Adam Link himself, ran until 1942. (Link would later appear on TV in an *Outer Limits* adaptation and turn into a comic strip in the early 1960s via Warren Publications' *Creepy* comic magazine).

Earl and Otto, writing as Eando, also offered "The First Martian," a short story published in *AS* in 1932. Although the two brothers worked together only a decade or so (also using the names Dean D. O'Brien and John Coleridge), Otto continued using the name Eando throughout his career, supplementing his income during his lean years by writing scripts for the *Captain Marvel* and *Superman* comics. Much of Eando Binder's work was reissued in the 1960s in paperback anthologies. Some of the Binder brothers' best-known titles include *Anton York, Immortal* (1965), *Adam Link, Robot* (1965), *Martian Martyrs* (as John Coleridge; c. 1940), *The New Life* (as John Coleridge; c. 1940), *Lords of Creation* (1949), and *The Avengers Battle the Earth-Wrecker* (1967).

BISHOP, MICHAEL
(1945–   )

One of the hottest young authors to come into prominence during the 1970s, Michael Bishop published his first short story in *Galaxy* in 1970. Titled "Piñon Fall," it signaled the beginning of a career marked by intelligence, imagination, and a blatant disregard for traditionalism. *A Funeral for the Eyes of Fire* (1975), his first novel, is a subtle twist on the alien-encounter theme, with an alien culture being examined by the increasingly empathetic eyes of two human protagonists. *And Strange at Ecbatan the Trees* (1976; later retitled *Beneath the Shattered Moons*), concerns futuristic spying in a society of genetically engineered castes. *A Little Knowledge* (1977), which takes place in the domed future city of Atlanta, introduces an alien into a strict Christian government. *Stolen Faces* (1977) is a twist on the marooned-colony motif. Bishop has been nominated for four Hugos and five Nebulas for his short fiction.

BIXBY, JEROME
(1923–   )

American writer, editor, and screenplay writer Jerome Bixby's first encounter with the arts was as a concert pianist. Turning to writing in the 1940s, he has since penned over 1,000 stories using both his own name and such fictitious monikers as Jay B. Drexel, Harry Neal, and Alger Rome. He edited *Planet Stories* in 1950–51 before working in a lesser capacity at *Galaxy* and *Startling Stories*. His best-known sf screenplay is probably IT! THE TERROR FROM BEYOND SPACE (which, two decades later, inadvertently gave birth to ALIEN), although FANTASTIC VOYAGE was based on a story he co-authored. His best-known collection of sf stories can be found in *Space by the Tale* (1964).

BLADE, ALEXANDER

Probably the most popular pseudonym in the history of sf, Alexander Blade was one of the house names used by the Ziff-Davis publishing group. Originally the personal alter-ego of David Vern, it was later picked up and used by Howard Browne, Edmond Hamilton, Heinrich Hauser, Herb Livingston, David Wright O'Brien, Robert Silverberg, Don Wilcox, and Leroy Yerxa, to name a few. Some of Blade's "best" stories include "Dr. Loudon's Armageddon" (1941; by Louis H. Sampliner), "Is This the Night?" (1945; by Leroy Yerxa), "The Alien Dies at Dawn" (1956; by Randall Garrett and Robert Silverberg), "Brainstorm" (1948; by Roger P. Graham), "The Cosmic Kings" and "Battle for the Stars" (1956; by Edmond Hamilton), and "The Android Kill" (1957; by Robert Silverberg). Blade's work was primarily found in *Fantastic Adventures, Imaginative Tales, Other Worlds, Space Travel,* and *AS.*

BLISH, JAMES (BENJAMIN)
(1921–75)

One of sf's more intellectual authors, American writer James Blish was the possessor of a multifaceted literary style that took him everywhere from theology (1958's *A Case of Conscience* featured a Jesuit biologist encountering aliens with no concept of sin) to space opera (the last years of Blish's life found him penning short stories based on STAR TREK TV episodes).

Discovering sf while a teenager in New York, Blish joined the Futurians, a fan organization which boasted such members as DAMON KNIGHT, FRED POHL, and C. M. KORNBLUTH. After graduating from Rutgers in 1942 with a degree in microbiology, he served in the army during World War II as a medical lab technician. First published in 1940 ("Emergency Refueling" in *Super Science Stories*), Blish abandoned his postwar plans of becoming a zoologist to concentrate on writing full time. He was most fertile in the 1950s, producing his famous futuristic "Okie" stories, in which the futuristic descendants of the Great Depression's Okies leave their home planet (via flying cities) to search the universe for employment, much in the same way as their ancient relatives had fled the Dust Bowl. The stories were eventually culled into four novels —*Earthman, Come Home* (1955), *They Shall Have Stars* (1956), *The Triumph of Time* (1958), and *A Life for the Stars* (1962)—before being sandwiched into one popular volume, *Cities in Flight* (1970).

On the more philosophical side are the three novels comprising what Blish referred to as his "After Such Knowledge" trilogy: a series of books that asks the question, Is the search for knowledge actually evil? The books in the trilogy are *Doctor Mirabilis* (1964), *A Case of Conscience* (1958), and the

combined thrust of the novel *Black Easter* (1968) and the novella *The Day After Judgement* (1970). Moving to England during the last years of his life, Blish poured much of his energies into the writing and editing of the *Star Trek* series of books (from 1967 until his death in 1975), a task that, he explained, not only paid the rent, but brought him in close contact with the newest breed of young sf fans, the Trekkies—the latter by-product a decided delight to the veteran writer.

A Hugo-winner, Blish was the guest of honor at the 18th World Science Fiction Convention, in 1960. His death was attributed to cancer.

BLOCH, ROBERT
(1917–   )

Chicago-born Robert Bloch is the closest thing to a bogeyman in American literature. Known primarily as a writer of the macabre and the just plain scary—it was Bloch who wrote *Psycho* (1959) and *The Scarf* (1949)—he won a 1959 Hugo for his short story "The Hell-Bound Train." A fan and protégé of H. P. LOVECRAFT, Bloch began his prolific career in 1934, when, at the age of 17, he sold the story "Lilies" to *Marvel Tales.* The writer of over 1,000 short stories and a dozen or so novels, Bloch is also a well-respected screenplay writer, penning many of the popular E. C. Horror Comic film adaptations, including *The House That Dripped Blood* and *Tales from the Crypt.*

BOUCHER, ANTHONY
(1911–68)

The pseudonym of American writer and editor William Anthony Parker White, Boucher was best known as a sf writer with a wry sense of humor. Beginning his career as a writer and anthologist of detective fiction, Boucher was first published in the genre during the early 1940s, the bulk of his work appearing in *ASF.* In 1949, with J. F. McComas, he cofounded *The Magazine of Fantasy and Science Fiction* and, shortly thereafter, began the long-running series *The Best from Fantasy and Science Fiction.* A book reviewer for such publications as the New York *Herald-Tribune,* the New York *Times,* and the San Francisco *Chronicle,* Boucher is best known as a writer for his two collections of short stories, *Far and Away* (1955) and *The Compleat Werewolf* (1969).

BOULLE, PIERRE
(1912–   )

French writer Pierre Boulle is best known for his epic novel *The Bridge over the River Kwai* (1952). Born in Avignon, Boulle was profoundly influenced by his years in Malaysia both as a rubber planter and, later, with the Free French mission in World War II. He was subsequently captured and interred in Indochina while fighting with a guerrilla army. He later escaped. Boulle's feelings on captivity and warfare eventually found their way into his best known sf offering, *Planet of the Apes* (1963). Other genre titles include *Time Out of Mind and Other Stories* (1966), *Garden on the Moon* (1965), and *Games of the Mind* (1971).

BOVA, BEN(JAMIN WILLIAM)
(1932–   )

When JOHN CAMPBELL, the editor's editor, died in 1971, the task of filling his legendary shoes at *Analog* (formerly *ASF*) fell to sf writer Ben Bova. As editor at *Analog,* Bova won five successive Hugos (1973–77). Leaving *Analog* in 1978, he became fiction editor of the ambitious, albeit ambiguous, *Omni* before assuming editor-in-chief status in 1979.

With a background in journalism (a degree in same from Philadelphia's Temple University), and a solid background in science research, Bova is best known for his novels rather than his short fiction. His first book, a juvenile entitled *The Star Conquerors,* was published in 1959. Since that time, he has amassed quite a large fan following via such works as *Millennium* (1976), which deals with the futuristic status of the Cold War; *The Multiple Man* (1976), an sf mystery featuring four identical presidents of the United States, three of whom have been murdered . . . Is the remaining one the real thing?; *The Weathermakers* (1967), a tale of climate control; and *The Starcrossed* (1975), an alleged

comedy starring the futuristic version of Bova's close friend HARLAN ELLISON.

Other Bova titles include *Star Watchman* (1964), *As on a Darkling Plain* (1972), *The Winds of Altair* (1973), and the juvenile "Exile" series: *Exiled from Earth* (1971), *Flight of Exiles* (1972), and *End of Exile* (1975).

BOYD, JOHN
(1919–   )

Born in Georgia of British lineage, Boyd Braffield Upchurch, who writes under the name John Boyd, did not enter the realm of sf until nearly the age of 50. Working for a photographic company based in Los Angeles, Boyd was thrown into an emotional upheaval during the Watts race riots of the 1960s. His first sf novel, *The Last Starship from Earth* (1968), is an exercise in dystopianism, profiling a world where one's position in life is dictated by a scientifically controlled government ruled by unscrupulous leaders. A complex, philosophical tale, *Starship* was an immediate critical sensation. Subsequent novels include *The Pollinators of Eden* (1969), *The Rakehells of Heaven* (1969), and *Sex and the High Command* (1970), all of which deal with sexual mores; *The Andromeda Gun* (1974), a spacey Western; and *Barnard's Planet* (1975).

BRACKETT, LEIGH
(1915–78)

A multifaceted talent, Leigh Brackett was just as famous in Hollywood for her screenplay work as she was around the world for her sf stories. The wife of sf author EDMOND HAMILTON, Brackett first entered the sf field in 1940, with the story "The Martian Quest" for *ASF*. Her best-known genre work involved epic, space-swashbuckling adventures, including those experienced by her classic creation, all-around hero Eric John Stark. The "Stark" stories originally appeared in the 1940s and 1950s, with the bulk of Brackett's pulp swashbuckling being amassed, in later years, in such volumes as *The Sword of Rhiannon* (1953), *The Secret of Sinharat* (1964), and *People of the Talisman* (1964).

After a long hiatus, Brackett returned to sword-infested sf in the 1970s

Leigh Brackett

Ray Bradbury

with *The Ginger Star* (1974), *The Hounds of Skaith* (1974), and *The Reavers of Skaith* (1976). Later, all three volumes appeared under the single umbrella title of *The Book of Skaith* (1976).

Well-respected for her wide-screen work (her credits include *The Long Goodbye*, *The Big Sleep*, and *Rio Bravo*), Brackett was working on the script to the STAR WARS sequel, THE EMPIRE STRIKES BACK, when she died.

BRADBURY, RAY
(1920–　　)

Every young boy has longed, at one time or another, to dwell in Ray Bradbury's wondrous sf fantascapes. And in essence, the magic of Ray Bradbury is the magic that lives, albeit fleetingly, in the imagination of every child. Bradbury's poetic, eternally youthful imagery, as best represented in such works as *Dark Carnival* (1947) and *Dandelion Wine* (1957), has long been a source of contention in the sf field. Recognized and hailed as a brilliant sf writer by critics outside the genre, Bradbury has been accused of being a fantasy writer only dabbling in sf imagery by some of his harsher genre detractors. Indeed, his bona fide sf works are few, consisting mainly of *The Martian Chronicles* (1950), *Fahrenheit 451* (1953), *R Is for Rocket* (1966), and *S Is for Space* (1966). For the

most part, Bradbury excels in swirling, evocative tales that border on the magical.

Born in Waukegan, Illinois, Bradbury and his family moved to Los Angeles during the Depression. In L.A., Bradbury immediately became interested in fantasy and sf fandom, falling in with the likes of young fan FORREST ACKERMAN, filmmaker-to-be Ray Harryhausen, and would-be writer HENRY KUTTNER. In 1939 he began publishing his own fanzine, *Futuria Fantasia*, which featured the work of young Kuttner and of ROBERT HEINLEIN. After selling his first story, "Pendulum" (co-authored by Henry Hass), in 1941 to *Super Science Stories*, Bradbury embarked on a dazzling career that would mix elements of fantasy and sf with sheer poetry.

Many of the stories Bradbury wrote during the 1940s dealt with various aspects of the colonization of Mars. These were, of course, later collected into the single volume *The Martian Chronicles* (1950), a controversial work of epic proportions tracing humanity's efforts to recolonize Mars and re-create an uplifting mirror-image of the once-peaceful Earth, now on its way to destruction because of pettiness. *Fahrenheit 451*, based on a *Galaxy* short story called "The Fireman," portrayed a futuristic world in which the printed word was forbidden, all books being burned upon discovery.

Of late, Bradbury has turned his attention mainly to the stage (mounting productions of *The Martian Chronicles* and *The World of Ray Bradbury*) and poetry (*Where Robot Mice and Robot Men Run Round in Robot Towns* [1977], *Old Ahab's Friend, and Friend to Noah, Speaks His Piece* [1971]). A frequent guest on talk shows, he has hosted several science shows on network TV and is currently interested in writing the scripts for several screen adaptations of his works.

Among Bradbury's best-loved books are *The Illustrated Man* (1951), *Golden Apples of the Sun* (1953), *The October Country* (1955), *Dandelion Wine* (1957), *Something Wicked This Way Comes* (1962), *I Sing the Body Electric* (1969), and *The Wonderful Ice Cream Suit and Other Plays* (1972).

BRADLEY, MARION ZIMMER
(1915–   )

Born in Albany, New York, Marion Zimmer Bradley began reading sf while still a teenager. Her first stories, published in 1953 and 1954 by *Vortex 2* and *F&SF*, were called "Keyhole," "Women Only," and "Centaurus Changeling." Her main claim to fame, however, rests on her sword-and-sorcery "Darkover" series, in which the human population of the world of Darkover fights total takeover by the evil Galactic Empire. Her "Darkover" books include *The Sword of Aldones* (1962), *The Planet Savers* (1962), *The Bloody Sun* (1964), *Star of Danger* (1965), *Winds of Darkover* (1970), *The World Wreckers* (1971), *Darkover Landfall* (1972), *The Spell Sword* (1974), *The Heritage of Hastur* (1975), *The Shattered Chain* (1976), and *The Forbidden Tower* (1977).

BROWN, FREDERIC
(1906–72)

No one in his or her right mind could ever call the sf produced by American writer Frederic Brown "predictable." Best known as a detective writer, Brown's sf was meticulously plotted and, more often than not, hilarious.

During the 1940s, his sf output consisted mainly of short-to-microscopic short stories with shaggy-dog endings that kept readers glued to the pages.

His first novel in the genre, *What Mad Universe* (1949), was an accurate portent of lunacy to come, offering a multileveled alternate-universe invasion plot. Two heroes, an editor of an sf pulp magazine on Earth and his double out *there* in an alternate universe, stave off an alien invasion. *Martians Go Home* (1955) continued the strangeness, as a group of Martians arrive on Earth and simply poke fun at Earth customs much to the annoyance of Earth residents, who try to rid themselves of the green pests with "heavy water, holy water and Flit."

On a more serious level, Brown offered *The Lights in the Sky Are Stars* (1953), capturing the wonder of a new era in the field of 21st-century space travel, and *The Mind Thing* (1961), a tale spotlighting a marooned alien who must get home no matter what the price in terms of human life.

Brown's best short fiction can be found in *The Best of Frederic Brown* (1977), a collection highlighted by "Arena," his classic tale of alien conflict.

BROWN, ROSEL GEORGE
(1926–67)

With a degree in ancient Greek, Rosel George Brown promised to be one of sf's most literate writers. Although her career was cut short at the age of 41, she did manage to introduce a few interesting literary twists into the sf genre. Her first short story, "From an Unseen Censor," appeared in 1958 in *Galaxy*, and her subsequent short stories were collected in the volume *A Handful of Time* (1963). *Sybil Sue Blue* (1966) detailed the rough-and-tumble exploits of a futuristic woman cop, as did *The Waters of Centaurus* (1970). In 1966 she collaborated with KEITH LAUMER on the sprawling tale *Earthblood*.

BRUNNER, JOHN
(1934–   )

John Kilian Houston Brunner wrote and sold his first novel at the age of 17. Born in Oxfordshire and captivated at an early age by the work of H. G.

WELLS, Brunner leaped into sf in the 1950s with the same tenacity as he entered the political arena during that decade, when he became a staunch foe of nuclear power. Making his American debut in 1953 with "Thou Good and Faithful" (using the pseudonym John Loxmith) in *ASF*, Brunner immediately began forming his style-to-come. Intellectual without being pompous, psychological without being cliché-ridden, and generally pessimistic, Brunner's brand of fiction was immediately embraced by the soon-to-be New Wave school of thought, and by the 1960s he was recognized as one of Great Britain's most prolific and most respected sf authors, writing under both his own name and those of K. Houston Brunner, John Loxmith, Trevor Staines, and Keith Woodcott.

Pessimism Is Good for You

Literature will have a great role to play in the reversal of today's more depressing trends, if such a thing is indeed possible. As a science-fiction writer, I feel compelled to point out exactly where I think society is heading. Like most science-fiction writers, I'm a pessimist in my head and an optimist in my heart. If I wasn't, I couldn't go on writing my imaginary tales.

John Brunner

Some of Brunner's better known works include *The Whole Man* (1964), a psychological profile of a deformed telepath; *Out of My Mind* (1967), a collection of short stories; *Stand on Zanzibar* (1968), a novel about over-population; *The Jagged Orbit* (1969), a "what if?" scenario in which the military complex joins forces with organized crime; *From This Day Forward* (1972), an anthology; *The Sheep Look Up* (1972), a futurescape in which pollution brings outright horror; and *The Shockwave Rider* (1975), a dystopian view of the communications field.

BUDRYS, ALGIS
(1931–   )
Prussian-born Algirdas Jonas Budrys moved to the U.S. at the age of five and formerly entered the sf literary world

at the age of 21 with "The High Purpose" (1952; *ASF*). Holding down a nine-to five job (at Galaxy Publications), he continued writing throughout the 1950s, earning himself a reputation as a short-story writer to be reckoned with. His best stories are featured in such collections as *The Unexpected Dimension* (1960) and *Budrys' Inferno* (1963).

During his career he has also contributed several thought-provoking novels to the genre. *Who?* (1958) was the tale of a Western scientist horribly disfigured in a lab accident overseas. Reconstructed bionically, the scientist returns to the States only to be suspected of being an imposter because of his robotic looks. The book was later made into a film starring Elliot Gould and Joseph Bova. *Rogue Moon* (1960), probably the best known of Budrys' longer works, concerns an alien structure discovered on the moon and the impact it has on the lives of those who attempt to penetrate its secrets. *The Amsirs and the Iron Thorn* (1967) is a tale featuring synthetic life-forms, and *Michaelman* (1977) profiles an ordinary TV reporter of the not-too-distant future who, in reality, shapes the world through the aide of his supercomputer, Domino.

During his career, Budrys has also written under the names of David C. Hodgkins, Ivan Janvier, Paul Janvier, Robert Marner, Alger Rome (in collaboration with JEROME BIXBY), William Scarff, John Sentry, and Albert Stroud.

BULMER, KENNETH
(1921–   )
London-born Henry Kenneth Bulmer was an avid fan of sf before breaking into the field professionally following World War II. His sf adventures first started appearing in print in 1952, and in his three decades as a professional, he has written dozens of books using both his own name and the pseudonyms Alan Burt Akers, Tully Zetford, Nelson Sherwood, Karl Maras, Kenneth Jones (in collaboration with John Newman), Philip Kent, and Chesman Scot.

Some of his better known titles include *The Stars Are Ours* (1953), *City Under the Sea* (1957), *The Changeling*

Worlds (1958), *The Million Year Hunt* (1964), *To Outrun Doomsday* (1967), and *On the Symb-Socket Circuit* (1972).

As Alan Burt Akers, he is well known for his "Scorpio," "Antares" and "Kregan" titles, including *Transit to Scorpio* (1972), *The Suns of Scorpio* (1973), *Warriors of Scorpio* (1973), *Swordships of Scorpio* (1973), *Prince of Scorpio* (1974), *Secret Scorpio* (1977), *Man Hounds of Antares* (1974), *Arena of Antares* (1974), *Fliers of Antares* (1975), *Bladesmen of Antares* (1975), *Armada of Antares* (1976), *The Tides of Kregan* (1977), *Krozair of Kregan* (1977), *Savage Scorpio* (1978), *Captive Scorpio* (1978), *Golden Scorpio* (1978).

BURGESS, ANTHONY
(1917–   )

British writer John Anthony Burgess Wilson is best known for his efforts in mainstream fiction. An English teacher who conducted classes both in England and in Malaysia, he began writing full-time in 1969. His best known works in the sf field are *A Clockwork Orange* (1962), a horrific look into a future in which the world at large is held in check by roving bands of juvenile delinquents; *The Wanting Seed* (1962), a futuristic nightmare involving curbing overpopulation; and *1985* (1978), a factual, fictitious sequel (of sorts) to the GEORGE ORWELL book.

BURKE, JOHN
(1922–   )

John Frederick Burke, a British public-relations executive turned writer, is best known abroad for his novelizations of horror and sf screenplays, as well as for his anthologies of Hammer Film scripts/short stories. Born in Rye, Sussex, Burke became active in sf fandom in the 1930s, first being published in *New Worlds* (1953) with the short story "Chessboard." He immediately embarked on a prolific career as a novelist. *Dark Gateway* and *The Echoing Worlds* were both published abroad in 1953, with *The Twilight of Reason, Hotel Cosmos,* and *Pattern of Shadows* seeing release a year later.

During the 1960s, the bulk of his work was film-connected. His best-known British titles are *Dr. Terror's House of Horrors* (1965; based on the film of the same name), *Moon Zero Two* (1969; based on the film of the same name), *The Hammer Horror Omnibus* (1966; based on various films), and *The Second Hammer Horror Omnibus* (1967; based on various films).

BURROUGHS, EDGAR RICE
(1875–1950)

Best known for the classic "Tarzan" series (beginning with *Tarzan of the Apes* [1914]), Edgar Rice Burroughs tried a number of careers before settling on fiction writing. Educated at Michigan Military Academy, Burroughs tried his hand at cavalry duty, shop-keeping, gold mining, and law enforcement before publishing (1912) his first story, "Under the Moons of Mars," in *All-Story Magazine*. This was the first of the author's epic sf-adventure tales concerning Barsoom (Mars). Although the original story was published under the name of Norman Bean, soon Burroughs would be using his own name while penning a seemingly inexhaustible supply of space swashbucklers. Most of the Mars books concerned Earthman John Carter (or a close relative) and his adventures on the marvelous planet. The first book of the series, a revamped version of "Under the Moons of Mars," appeared in 1917 as *A Princess of Mars*. Other titles followed: *The Gods of Mars* (1918), *The Warlords of Mars* (1919), *Thuvia, Maid of Mars* (1920), *The Chessmen of Mars* (1922), *The Master Mind of Mars* (1928), *A Fighting Man of Mars* (1931), *Swords of Mars* (1936), *Synthetic Men of Mars* (1940), *Llana of Gathol* (1948), and *John Carter of Mars* (1964) (the latter two volumes being collections of stories originally penned for *AS*).

Burroughs' second popular series of sf books detailed life in the underground world of Pellucidar: *At the Earth's Core* (1922), *Pellucidar* (1923), *Tanar of Pellucidar* (1930), *Tarzan at the Earth's Core* (1930), *Back to the Stone Age* (1936), *Land of Terror* (1944), and *Savage Pellucidar* (1963).

Yet another series related the adventures of Earthman Carson Napier on the planet Venus: *Pirates of Venus* (1934), *Lost on Venus* (1934), *Carson of Venus* (1939), and *Escape from Venus* (1946).

Three Burroughs novellas (originally published in 1918)—"The Land That Time Forgot," "The People That Time Forgot," and "Out of Time's Abyss"—also proved popular enough to warrant a reprise in a single volume titled *The Land That Time Forgot* (1924).

At the time of his death, Burroughs was the head of a multimillion-dollar publishing estate; buoyed by the popularity of the Tarzan books and myriad spinoffs (films, comic books, merchandise). In the 1960s, well after his death, Burroughs-mania swept the country, with not only Tarzan seeing the light of day once more, but all of ERB's novels returning to print. In addition, during the past decade film versions (popular but cheesy) of *At the Earth's Core, The Land That Time Forgot,* and *The People That Time Forgot* (1976, 1975, and 1977) have appeared.

CAIDIN, MARTIN
(1927–   )

Best known for his books on aviation, Martin Caidin is a writer, pilot, and aerospace expert whose sf work is marked by technical accuracy. His first published sf surfaced in 1956—the novel *The Long Night*. His subsequent genre novels brought him both critical and financial success. *Marooned* (1964), a tale of a group of astronauts stranded in space, was filmed in 1969. His cyborg tales—*Cyborg* (1972), *Operation Nuke* (1973), *High Crystal* (1974), and *Cyborg IV* (1975)—inspired the popular SIX MILLION DOLLAR MAN and BIONIC WOMAN TV series. Other works include *No Man's World* (1967), *The God Machine* (1968), *The Mendelov Conspiracy* (1969), and

Destination Mars (1972). He has written over 40 books on aviation.

CAMPBELL, JOHN W., JR.
(1910–71)

Next to HUGO GERNSBACK, John Wood Campbell, Jr., did more to shape the substance of 20th-century sf than any other man. An editor, a writer, a guiding influence on up-and-coming writers—Cambell, as editor of *ASF*, introduced such writers as ROBERT HEINLEIN, ISAAC ASIMOV, LESTER DEL REY, A. E. VAN VOGT, CLIFFORD SIMAK, JACK WILLIAMSON, and THEODORE STURGEON into the genre, giving them helpful tips on style as they developed their skills. (It was Campbell, for instance, who helped Asimov formulate his famous Three Laws of Robotics.)

Campbell was born in New Jersey. Educated at the Massachusetts Institute of Technology and Duke University (a degree in physics), Campbell was a long-time devotee of sf (especially of writer E.E. "DOC" SMITH) and sold his first stories while still in his teens. By the time Campbell was in his early 20s, he was considered "Doc" Smith's chief rival in penning superscience space adventures. After concentrating during the early 1930s in getting his stories placed in *AS*, Campbell switched allegiance in 1934, submitting the bulk of his material to *ASF*, both under his own name and under the pen name Don A. Stuart (based on his wife's maiden name, Donna Stuart). During that decade, he offered both science fiction and science fact outings. In the former category, Don A. Stuart turned in the classic story "Who Goes There?" a wonderful tale of alien invasion later filmed as the horrific THE THING (1951); in the latter category, he did a series of articles on the planets.

In 1937 he became editor of *ASF*, a post he held until his death. During the 1940s, with Campbell acting as an editorial magnet, a number of new authors began their prolific careers under his tutelage, and, the so-called Golden Age of sf was at hand.

By the 1950s, Campbell had some heavy competition in the field caused by the popularity of competitors *Galaxy, F&SF*, and other, smaller pulps. Campbell then began concentrating on holding the fort as opposed to stimulating his writers, and as a result few new faces were launched at *ASF* in the 1950s. In 1960, when *ASF* became *Analog Science Fact/Science Fiction*, Campbell, too, changed, becoming mesmerized by psi tales and parapsychological studies and trends and championing former sf writer L. RON HUBBARD's Dianetics movement. Nevertheless, *Analog* remained a popular forum for fiction, winning a Hugo award as best magazine eight times during Campbell's reign (1953, 1955–57, 1961–62, 1964–65).

Campbell's death brought an end to a three-decade chapter of sf. Two literary awards were created in his honor. Campbell's best short stories can be found in the anthologies *Who Goes There?* (1948), *The Moon Is Hell* (1950), and *The Best of John W. Campbell* (1973).

ČAPEK, KAREL
(1890–1938)

Czech philosopher, novelist, and playwright Karel Capek introduced the world to the word *robot* in 1921, in the play *R.U.R.* (Rossum's Universal Robots). In Capek's play, however, the robots were not the traditional metalmen popularly thought of as filling the bill, but rather, chemically constructed humanoid androids—servants. The word *robot* itself, in the Czech language, means "compulsory labor" and, in Polish, "worker." In *R.U.R.*, the robots, overworked by their harsh human overseers, in a last bit of desperation rebel, setting the stage for countless plays, films, and stories to come.

Other examples of Capek's genre work include *War with the Newts* (1936; trans. 1937) in which the amphibian creatures of the title attempt to leap from a subservient state of existence to one of equal footing with their human masters; *An Atomic Fantasy* (1924; trans. 1925), a novel detailing the development of the ultimate explosive; *The Absolute at Large* (1922; trans. 1927), a satire concerning a scientist who invents a method of extracting free power from atomic energy; and *The Makropoulos Secret* (1925; trans. 1927), a story of longevity.

CARR, TERRY
(1937–   )

Oregon-born Carr became one of sfdom's prime movers during the 1960s, when he acted as editor (1964–71) of Ace Books' sf line. It was Carr who was responsible for the "Ace Specials" series. After leaving Ace, he continued to edit on a freelance basis, compiling and editing the popular *Universe* paperback anthologies.

As a writer, he won two Hugos for his fan work, as well as critical praise for both his short fiction ("Ozymandias," 1972) and his novels (*Cirque*, 1977). His best short fiction can be found in the collection *The Light at the End of the Universe* (1976).

CARTER, ANGELA
(1940–   )

Mainstream British writer Angela Carter's approach to sf can best be described as bizarre. In *Heroes and Villains* (1969), the law-enforcers and the lawless battle it out in the future, with the young female protagonist taking up with the latter band because their life looks ever-so-much-more exciting. *War of Dreams* (1972), *The Passion of New Eve* (1977), and the anthology *Fireworks* (1974) blend abstract sf imagery with almost surrealistic eroticism.

CARTER, LIN(WOOD VROOMAN)
(1930–   )

American writer and editor Lin Carter is best known for his sword-and-sorcery novels and short stories, which carry on the ROBERT E. HOWARD tradition (some going so far as to continue some of the adventures of Howard's classic character Conan the Barbarian). While most of Carter's output can be termed fantasy (such as his "World's End" and "Thongar" books), some are sf in the EDGAR RICE BURROUGHS tradition. His *Jandor of Callisto* (1972), *Black Legion of Callisto* (1972), *Sky Pirates of Callisto* (1973), *Mad Emperors of Callisto* (1975), *Mind Wizards of Callisto* (1975), *Lankar of Callisto* (1975), and *Ylana of Callisto* (1977) pit hero Jandor against dangerous odds on the moon of Jupiter in very John Carteresque (Rice's famous character) fashion (Carter himself gueststars in *Lankar*).

In *Under the Green Star* (1972), *When the Green Star Calls* (1973), *By the Light of the Green Star* (1974), *As the Green Star Rises* (1975), and *In the Green Star's Glow* (1976), Carter conjures up spacey swashbuckling for his Earthly hero, who "wills" himself into the land of the Green Star.

As both a freelance editor and a consultant for Ballantine Books in the early 1970s, Carter is regarded as a champion of sf/fantasy.

CHALKER, JACK L(AURENCE)
(1944–   )

Originally a nonfiction and questionable-fiction writer, with titles such as *An Informal Biography of Scrooge McDuck* (1974), *The New H. P. Lovecraft Bibliography* (1961), and *Index to the Science-Fantasy Publishers* (1966) to his credit, Chalker was well known as the one-man army behind Mirage Press before entering the world of commercial fiction. Even in commercial terms, however, Chalker's work must be regarded as being inventive to the point of orthodox weirdness. *A Jungle of Stars* (1974), his first novel, tells the tale of two opposing superbeings out to control the universe; unfortunately, they're both villains. *Midnight at the Well of Souls* (1977) presents the plight of a spaceshipful of passengers sucked into an artificial "well" constructed by a long-dead alien race and populated by 1,560 alien-filled hexagons.

CHANDLER, A. BERTRAM
(1912–   )

A seagoing officer in Great Britain's merchant navy, Arthur Bertram Chandler began writing sf in the 1940s as a means of relaxation while aboard ship. His first piece of fiction, "This Means War," was a JOHN CAMPBELL, JR., discovery that appeared in *ASF* in 1944. Turning to novel-writing in the late-1950s, Chandler emerged with a series set on the very edge of the Milky Way: the "Rim Worlds" books. Included in this expansive list are *The Rim of Space* (1961), *Contraband from Otherspace* (1967), *The Road to the Rim* (1967), *False Fatherland* (1968), *Catch the Star Winds* (1969), *To Prime the Pump* (1971), *The Hard Way Up*

(1972), and *The Broken Cycle* (1975). The protagonist of the Rim series is a space captain whose career mirrors Chandler's Merchant Navy experiences, to a degree. Chandler retired in 1975 and currently resides in Australia.

CHERRYH, C. J.
(1942–   )

American writer Carolyn Janice Cherry, who writes under the name C. J. Cherryh, specializes in detailed sf-fantasy. In her first novel, *Gate of Ivrel* (1976), an intergalactic sorceress/ law-enforcement agent teams up with a barbarian to defeat an evil wizard. The book earned her the 1977 John W. Campbell Award for most promising new writer. *Brothers of Earth* (1976) portrays the inner turmoil experienced by two humans on a humanoid-alien planet. *Hunter of Worlds* (1977) profiles the alien Iduve culture, with which the protagonist must come to grips after being captured and imprisoned by the Iduve captain of an immense spacecraft.

CHRISTOPHER, JOHN
(1922–   )

John Christopher is the name that British writer Christopher Sam Joud found fame with during the 1950s in the sf genre. After leaving the British Army following World War II, Christopher was first published in 1949 in *ASF* with "Christmas Story." Soon Christopher turned his sights to cataclysmic themes in the novel format. Among his best known in that postdisaster motif are *The Death of Grass* (1956; later retitled *No Blade of Grass* and subsequently filmed under that title), a story depicting the disaster befalling Great Britain when all grasslike plants die; *The Long Winter* (1962), a novel forecasting a new Ice Age; *The Ragged Edge* (1965), an earthquake-laden tale; *Cloud on Silver* (1964), a story spotlighting an islandful of mutants; and *Pendulum* (1968), a grim story depicting the hazards of day-to-day survival following the collapse of civilization as we know it. The alien-invasion motif got a nice turnabout in the claustrophobic *The Possessors* (1965), in which a ski resort, isolated from the world by a blizzard, is invaded by life-forms; and things-in-the-attic scenarios got a shot in the arm via the chilling *The Little People* (1967).

During the late 1960s, Christopher turned his attention to juvenile fiction, coming up with such titles as *The White Mountains* (1967), *The City of Gold and Lead* (1967), *and The Pool of Fire* (1968; a boy battles the Tripod aliens). Like his adult fiction, most of his juvenile tales are fairly cataclysmic.

CLARKE, ARTHUR C(HARLES) (1917–)

Arthur C. Clarke, in some circles, is synonymous with the word "god." At any rate, he is certainly one of the true geniuses to dwell in the sf field. Author, inventor, and scientist, Britisher Clarke was born in Minehead, Somerset, and moved to London at the age of 19 to take a job as a civil-service auditor. A long-time sf fan as well as an astronomy buff, Clarke began submitting science-fact articles to *Tales of Wonder* magazine and short stories to the amateur publications of the British Science Fiction Assn. during his formative years.

During World War II, he served as a technical officer with the Royal Air Force and in peacetime, took his B.Sc. in physics and math at Kings College, London. During the mid-1940s, he wrote technical articles for science-fact magazines and actually forecast the coming of the communications satellites in a 1945 edition of *Wireless World* magazine. Clarke's nonfiction piece "Extra-Terrestrial Relays" (1945), describing three satellites orbiting 22,000 miles from the Earth on a plane parallel to the equator, each relaying radio and TV signals all over the world, was greeted with skepticism at the time. However, the project was later almost duplicated by the U.S. National Aeronautics and Space Administration's Early Bird satellite system, and he was later awarded the Franklin Institute's Gold Medal for his astounding prediction.

His first professional sf story, "Loophole" (1946), appeared in *ASF*. His short-story output increased for the remainder of the decade, with most of his narratives pinned on a solid scientific

Photo courtesy of Harcourt Brace Jovanovich

Arthur C. Clarke

basis, often dealing with the positive aspects of space travel.

During the early 1950s Clarke turned his attention to novel-writing, his first efforts appearing in 1951: *Prelude to Space* and *The Sands of Mars*. His 1953 anthology *Expedition to Earth* featured the short story "The Sentinel," the work that would eventually inspire Stanley Kubrick's epic 2001: A SPACE ODYSSEY —a film for which Clarke would write the script and the novelization, and receive worldwide acclaim.

His output never flagged during the 1950s and 1960s, although it has lagged appreciably during the 1970s. In 1956 he relocated to Ceylon (now Sri Lanka), where to this day he pens his sf and science-fact tales surrounded by a tropical paradise. Among Clarke's most noteworthy titles are *Childhood's End* (1953), a 1960s cult novel that deals with the beneficially disruptive appearance of a race of aliens who force Earth into a Utopian state in preparation for an evolutionary leap; *Against the Fall of Night* (1953, rewritten in 1956 as *The City and the Stars*), a story centered on the lifestyle of the last Utopian city on Earth, Diaspar, and the secret it holds concerning the nature of the human race; *Rendezvous with Rama* (1973), a tale that takes place on a titanic spacecraft (the story won the Hugo, Nebula, John W. Campbell, Jr., Memorial, British Science Fiction, and Jupiter awards); and *Imperial Earth* (1975), a story of interplanetary relations at a time when Earth has colonized most of the solar system.

Other popular Clarke titles include the anthologies *Reach for Tomorrow* (1956), *The Other Side of the Sky* (1958), *The Nine Billion Names of God* (1967), *The Wind from the Sun* (1972), as well as *Dolphin Island* (1963) and *The Fountains of Paradise* (1978).

CLEMENT, HAL
(1922–   )

Hal Clement is the professional name used by science teacher (educated in astronomy and chemistry) and part-time writer Harry Clement Stubbs. His first story in the genre, "Proof," was published in 1942 in *ACF* and, for the remainder of the decade, he proved a mainstay of that magazine. His novels, always entertaining, often are brilliant exercises in factual science as well as full of imaginative twists and turns. *Needle* (1950) and its sequel, *Through the Eye of the Needle* (1978), are well-plotted sf mysteries. *Mission of Gravity* (1954) deals with a human rescue mission to the planet Mesklin, where gravity ranges on the planet's surface from 3 g's to 700 g's. *Close to Critical*

Hal Clement

(1964) and *Star Light* (1971) are two semisequels to the popular *Mission* adventure. *Iceworld* (1953) mixes narcotics with a frozen world, and *Space Lash* (1969) offers a glimpse at the short fiction of the talented Mr. C.

COBLENTZ, STANTON A(RTHUR)
(1896–   )

American poet and author Stanton Arthur Coblentz began his sf career in 1928 with a satirical look at Utopian life in "The Sunken World" (*AS*). His excursions into the genre since that time have been marked by a singularly jocular attitude toward traditional plot lines and a complete disdain for clichés. In *Hidden World* (appearing as "In Caverns Below" in 1937; novelized in 1957), he takes on underground worlds, with warring subterranean powers Wu and Zu battling it out quite half-wittedly. In *Under the Triple Suns, Lord of Tranercia* (1966), and *The Moon People* (1964), he jabs at space science, dictatorships, and racism.

COMPTON, D(AVID) G(UY)
(1930–   )

British radio playwright and novelist D. G. Compton's works are not so much sf as contemporary exercises in fiction set in the not-too-distant future. Dealing mainly with characterization and socio-ecological themes, as opposed to hard science, he has managed to produce a healthy number of genre novels. Among the best known are *The Quality of Mercy* (G.B., 1965), a tale of overpopulation; *Farewell, Earth's Bliss* (G.B., 1966), a novel concerning the convict-colonists of Mars; *Synthajoy* (G.B., 1968), a nightmarish look at psychotherapy as orchestrated by machines; and *The Unsleeping Eye* (1974; originally titled *The Continuous Katherine Mortenhoe*), in which a woman whose cure for terminal disease is shown on national TV becomes the victim of the ultimate exercise in voyeurism.

CONKLIN, GROFF
(1904–68)

Editor, anthologist, and literary reviewer Groff Conklin was one of the most famous anthologists in modern sf. His first effort, *The Best of Science*

Fiction, was one of the earliest collections of short sf fiction ever published, reaching bookstores in 1946. It is also one of the best ever, offering a smorgasbord of sf literature to a public perhaps not overly familiar with the genre. He edited over 40 eclectic collections of sf and fantasy, the last titles being published in the year of his death.

COOPER, EDMUND
(1926–   )

Also a teacher, merchant seaman, and sf reviewer British writer Edmund Cooper entered the sf-fantasy genre in 1951 with a short story, "The Unicorn." He has been writing ever since, offering heroic space operas that border on juvenile fiction. Under the pseudonym Richard Avery, he penned a series of novels under the umbrella title "The Expendables"—*The Deathworms of Kratos* (1975), *The Rings of Tantalus* (1975), *The War Games of Zelos* (1975), *and The Venom of Argus* (1976)—as well as thought-provoking exercises in adult sf themes. *Deadly Image* (1958) gives a new twist to the old android idea; *All Fool's Day* (G.B., 1966) presents a world wherein all the sane citizens have committed suicide; and *The Overman Culture* (G.B., 1973) portrays a computer's attempt to repopulate with human citizens a postholocaust world. His best short fiction can be found in *Tomorrow's Gift* (1958), *The Square Root of Tomorrow* (G.B., 1971) and *News from Elsewhere* (G.B., 1968).

COULSON, JUANITA (RUTH)
(1933–   )

A former schoolteacher and longtime

Hooked

In 1950, I was sick with bronchitis, which is my usual winter sport. I started reading a lot of current science-fiction magazines and I came across Edmond Hamilton's *Star Kings.* I put the magazine down. That's what I wanted to do. Fantastic! Great! I had never read anything like this before. I wanted it! It was like a drug. I couldn't keep my hands off science fiction.

Anne McCaffrey

---

sf fan, American Coulson and her husband, Robert, won a Hugo in 1965 for their fanzine *Yandro.* She has since turned to professional writing, penning *Crisis on Cheiron* (1967), *The Singing Stones* (1968), *War of the Wizards* (G.B., 1970), and *Space Trap* (1976).

COWPER, RICHARD
(1926–   )

Richard Cowper is the pseudonym of longtime schoolteacher John Middleton Murry, Jr., who did not enter the sf field until 1967, with the novel *Breakthrough,* an innovative tale of ESP. Equally impressive were *Phoenix* (G.B., 1968) and *Kuldesak* (G.B., 1972)—a postholocaust novel in which mankind, after 1,000 years in subterranean exile, finally makes its way back to the surface. *The Twilight of Briareus* (G.B., 1974) reveals the mutated fate of mankind after effects of a supernova bombards the planet Earth with cosmic radiation. *Clone* (G.B., 1972) is a comic adventure concerning the paranormal abilities of a clone, and *Time out of Mind* (1973) is a tale of telepathy caused by drugs. Also noteworthy is a short-story collection *The Custodians* (1976).

CRICHTON, MICHAEL
(1942–   )

A quadruple-threat man, American M.D., novelist, screenplay writer, and film director Michael Crichton began his prolific career in the late 1960s penning detective novels under the name of John Lange. His best-known sf works include *The Andromeda Strain* (1969), a novel (and later a film) concerning an invasion of Earth by disease-carrying spores from space; *The Terminal Man* (1972), a Frankensteinesque tale of a computer controlled human; and WESTWORLD (1973), a movie script dealing with a futuristic playground populated by humanistic robots that eventually go berserk and, of course, turn on their human guests. WESTWORLD later spawned the movie FUTUREWORLD and the TV show BEYOND WESTWORLD.

CUMMINGS, RAY(MOND KING)
(1887–1957)

One of the true pioneers of modern sf, Ray Cummings actually began his career before HUGO GERNSBACK ever stumbled upon the genre. One of the American writer's best-known stories, "The Girl in the Golden Atom," and its sequel, "People of the Golden Atom," were actually published before the first sf magazine came into existence, appearing in *All-Story Weekly* in 1919 and 1920. The tales involve a scientist who shrinks himself and winds up in a microscopic world—a theme Cummings would return to periodically throughout his prolific career in such books as *Beyond the Stars* (1942), *The Princes of the Atom* (1950), *Beyond the Vanishing Point* (1958), and *Explorers Into Infinity* (1965).

Cummings eventually found a place in the sf pulps via Gernsback in the early editions of *AS*. But times changed, and unfortunately Cummings' style didn't. Eventually he fell from grace in the sf community, although his work did enjoy a brief bit of nostalgia-induced popularity during the 1960s.

Notable Cummings titles include *The Man Who Mastered Time* (1929), *A Brand New World* (1964), *The Insect Invasion* (1967), and *The Man on the Meteor* (1952).

DAHL, ROALD
(1916–   )

Primarily known as a writer of the macabre, Welsh-born Dahl has strayed into the realm of sf on occasion, as is evidenced in his two best-known anthologies, *Someone like You* (1953) and *Kiss, Kiss* (1960). In the 1960s he hosted and sometimes scripted the short-lived CBS-TV series WAY OUT and in 1979, hosted the syndicated and more successful anthology series TALES OF THE UNEXPECTED. The latter show featured an adaptation of his chilling sf tale "Royal Jelly" (written in 1960), in which a youngster is changed into a jellylike creature after being fed in infancy a diet of honey.

DAVIDSON, AVRAM
(1923–   )

New York-born writer, editor, anthologist, and wit Davidson saw action with both the U.S. Navy during World War II and with the Israeli Army in the 1948–49 Arab-Israeli War before embarking on a career as a writer in the 1950s. His first story, "My Boy Friend's Name Is Jello" appeared in *F&SF* in 1954, introducing the world to an author with a slightly unorthodox view of sf. He won a Hugo for short fiction in 1958 (for "Or All the Seas with Oysters") and became editor of *F&SF* in 1962, holding the position for two years before turning to novel writing. *Mutiny in Space* (1964) was a stirring space opera, as were the subsequent *Rork!* (1965), *The Enemy of My Enemy* (1966), and one of the most amazing parallel-world adventures ever, *Masters of the Maze* (1965). *Clash of Star-Kings* (1966), despite its title, proved to be an extraordinary alien-warfare tale set in a sleepy Mexican town. During the 1970s, Davidson has moved more toward fantasy, *The Island Under the Earth* (1969) and *Peregrine: Primus* (1971) being the most obvious examples.

His best short stories can be found in *Or All the Seas with Oysters* (1962) and *Strange Seas and Shores* (1971).

DE CAMP, L(YON) SPRAGUE
(1907–   )

Best known for his swashbuckling sf fantasy, L. Sprague De Camp planned to become an aeronautical engineer before opting for writing. Educated at the California Institute of Technology and the Stevens Institute of Technology, De Camp first turned to the typewriter to compile a book dealing with the patenting of inventions.

He was subsequently encouraged in sf writing by JOHN W. CAMPBELL, and many of De Camp's earliest excursions into the genre appeared in *ASF* and *Unknown*. He was most prolific in sf prior to 1950, with some of his best-known short pieces being about Johnny Black, the thinking bear ("The Command," 1936; "The Incorrigible," 1939; "The Exalted," 1940; "The Emancipated," 1940).

During his early writing years, De

Camp's interest in history surfaced in what is probably his best-known novel, *Lest Darkness Fall* (1941), in which a time-traveler attempts to stave off the fall of the Roman Empire.

During the 1940s and 1950s, De Camp began straying from sf into fantasy territory, with his last real sf series being the "Viagens Interplanetarias" stories—tales that take place in a future in which Brazil is a world power—and his Gavagan's Bar tales (written with Fletcher Pratt). In the mid-1950s, the author became heavily involved in the sword-and-sorcery genre, offering several "Conan" titles. Of late he has dwelled mainly in the swashbuckling-fantasy area of fiction.

Among his best known sf novels are *Rogue Queen* (1951), *The Search for Zei* (1962), and *The Hand of Zei* (1963).

DELANEY, SAMUEL R(AY)
(1942–   )

Samuel R. Delaney burst into the sf spotlight in 1962, when at the age of 20 his first novel, *The Jewels of Aptor*, was published. In quick succession, he then offered the "Tomoromon" trilogy, *Captives of the Flame* (1963), *The Towers of Toron* (1964), *and City of a Thousand Suns* (1965). A black American born and raised in New York, Delaney impressed his readership immediately with a style that combined elements of mythos, modern-day sociology, and adventure within a quest motif. The above-mentioned trilogy was offered in a single volume in 1970 as *The Fall of the Towers;* as a unit, it reaffirmed Delaney's importance in the genre, offering a penetrating insight into the decay and fall of a futuristic culture.

The Ballad of Beta 2 (1965) portrays the efforts of a futuristic anthropologist to solve a seemingly nonsensical folk song concocted years before by a spacefaring Earth culture. *Empire Star* and *Babel-17* (1966) dabbled in both sociology and linguistics; *Babel-17* won a Nebula for best novel. *The Einstein Intersection* (1967), a complex tale in which an alien race attempts to figure out humanity by reconstructing the species' myths, won a second Nebula. A third Nebula was garnered for his short story of that year "Aye, and Gomorrah . . ." and a fourth in 1969 for the novelette "Time Considered as a Helix of Semi-Precious Stones," a work that also won a Hugo (1970).

His later novels, *Nova* (1968), *Dhalgren* (1975), and *Triton* (1976), were also well received; they dealt with, respectively, family rivalry, a futuristic youth culture, and future sexuality.

DEL REY, LESTER
(1915–   )

The real name of American writer and editor Lester Del Rey may or may not be Ramon Felipe San Juan Mario Silvio Enrico Smith Heathcourt-Brace Sierra y Alvarez del Rey y de los Uerdes. Anyhow, his friends call him Lester. Del Rey began writing in the late 1930s, his first published piece, "The Faithful," appearing in *ASF* in 1938. His early work swayed from the emotional to the nerve-shattering, two of his most famous efforts of that time period being the robot love-story "Helen O'Loy" (1938) and *Nerves* (published first in 1942, novelized in 1956), a tense story recounting the events leading up to and following a nuclear-power-plant accident.

Del Rey proved a prolific writer during the 1940s and 1950s, with many of his titles being swashbuckling juvenile novels along the lines of *Marooned on Mars* (1952), *Rocket Jockey* (1952), *Attack from Atlantis* (1953), *Battle on Mercury* (1953), and *Rockets to Nowhere* (1954). Since his output was so amazing, he often resorted to using such pseudonyms as Erik van Lhin and Philip St. John for his juve titles. Still, Del Rey managed to keep his hand in adult fiction as well, offering *The Eleventh Commandment* (1962), featuring the world ruled by the Catholic church; *Pstalemate* (1971), an ESP thriller; and *Police Your Planet* (1956), dealing with futuristic cops and robbers.

Lester, a noted editor and book reviewer during the 1950s and 1960s, and his wife, Judy L. Del Rey, moved their base of operations to Ballantine Books in 1977, when the Del Rey Books imprint was inaugurated. Lester Del Rey's best short fiction can be found in *And Some Were Human* (1948) and *The Best of Lester Del Rey* (1978).

DENT, LESTER
(1905–59)

American author Lester Dent is best known to adventure fans as Kenneth Robeson, the author who wrote 165 out of the 181 novels that appeared in *Doc Savage Magazine*. It was Dent who imbued Doc Savage, the Man of Bronze, with most of his stalwart characteristics. During the 1960s, many of the "Doc Savage" novels reappeared in paperback form, and in the early 1970s, a movie version of the fictitious hero's exploits was filmed by George Pal.

DERLETH, AUGUST WILLIAM
(1909–71)

The patron saint of H. P. LOVECRAFT fans, August Derleth was born in Sauk City, Wisconsin, and while still a student began corresponding with his literary idol, macabre fantasy-sf writer H. P. Lovecraft. Although a prolific writer in the detective genre and a noted editor of anthologies dealing both with sf (*The Other Side of the Moon*, 1949) and fantasy (*Sleep No More*, 1944), he is best known as the guiding light behind Arkham House, a publishing company dedicated to printing the complete works of Lovecraft. Not only did Derleth see to it that all of the master craftsman's works were reissued, but he actually completed several of Lovecraft's unfinished manuscripts. It was largely because of Derleth's efforts that Lovecraft enjoyed a resurgence in popularity during the 1960s.

DICK, PHILIP K(ENDRED)
(1928–   )

California resident Philip K. Dick is one of the most respected writers in the genre today. In a career that spans nearly three decades (his first work, "Beyond Lies the Wub," was published in 1952), Dick has won a John W. Campbell Memorial Award (1974's *Flow My Tears, the Policeman Said*), a Hugo (1962's post–World War II Axis-victory novel, *The Man in the High Castle*), and the praise of his peers.

Dick has the uncanny ability to take the complex and reduce it to understandable terminology, usually placing an unassuming protagonist in a strange situation that is not quite what it appears to be. *Eye in the Sky* (1957) tosses a crew of characters into an existence that is dictated by the minds of the neurotics in the crew. *Time Out of Joint's* (1959) hero lives in a peaceful sham concocted by a war-torn society that wishes to make use of his powers of precognition. *Dr. Futurity's* (1960) main character is a normal physician kidnapped out of his own time period, and *Do Androids Dream of Electric Sheep?* (1968) is a chilling account of a postholocaust world in which a citizen's best friend is either his animal pet or his android.

Dick often toys with his readers, leading them down one small road that, unexpectedly, branches off into a larger, more thought-provoking one. His latest work, *A Scanner Darkly* (1977) is an excellent example of his fiction, depicting the distorting effects hallucinogens have on the human personality. His short stories can be found in such volumes as *A Handful of Darkness* (1955), *The Variable Man* (1956), and *The Book of Philip K. Dick* (1973).

DICKSON, GORDON R(UPERT)
(1923–   )

Born in Alberta, Canada, and moving to the U.S. at the age of 13, Gordon Dickson began his literary career shortly after graduating from the University of Minnesota with a B.A. in English. Dickson is both a prolific and a versatile writer, dabbling in everything from hard sf to brilliant satire. His work is earmarked with healthy doses of humor and light, breezy characterizations.

In the early 1950s, he collaborated on the "Hoka" series with POUL ANDERSON. His first "solo" novels appeared in 1956: *Alien from Arcturus* and *Mankind on the Run*. He is perhaps best known for his "Dorsai" series of future histories—*Necromancer* (1962), *Soldier, Ask Not* (1967), *Tactics of Mistake* (1971), and *Dorsai!* (1976)—all books dealing with the planet Dorsai and its human inhabitants, most notably Donal Graeme, a superfellow created by forced evolution.

On the lighter side, *The Dragon and the George* (1976) transports a 20th-century college professor into a world in which his mind takes up residence in the body of a clumsy dragon, and *Gremlins Go Home* (1974) is an amusing juvenile entry coauthored by BEN BOVA.

Dickson won a Nebula award for "Call Him Lord" (1966) and the August Derleth Award of the British Fantasy Society for *The Dragon and the George*.

His short stories can be found in a number of volumes, including *Danger—Human* (1970) and *Ancient, My Enemy* (1974).

DISCH, THOMAS M(ICHAEL)
(1940–   )

One of the beacons of the 1960s New Wave movement, Minnesota-born and New York-raised, Disch worked in an ad agency before entering the sf genre in 1962 with *Fantastic*'s "The Double-Timer." Starting off quite conventionally but gradually moving into more-uncharted areas of fiction, Disch became associated with the British New Wave movement because of his involvement with hell-raising author MICHAEL MOORCOCK's *New Worlds* publications.

Disch's first novel, *The Genocides* (1965), is a unique tale of alien involvement with Earth; *Mankind Under the Leash* (1965) portrays a set-up in which humans are aliens' best friends, in the pet-master sense; and *Echo Round His Bones* (1967) is a standard sf tale involving matter transmission.

In 1968 Disch's career began to soar, with the publication of *Camp Concentration*, a terrifying tale of near-future concentration-camp experiments conducted on political prisoners involving the use of Pallidine, a drug that heightens the intelligence to the point of death.

Since that point, Disch has sustained both critical and popular interest with such titles as *334* (1972), a collection of stories about a futuristic Manhattan; and *Fun with Your New Head*, a bizarre collection of short stories published in 1968.

DOYLE, ARTHUR CONAN
(1859–1930)

Born in Edinburgh and trained as a medical doctor at Edinburgh University, Arthur Conan Doyle turned to writing in 1887 in order to supplement a meager income earned by practicing medicine. His first book, *A Study in Scarlet* (1887), introduced the legendary character Sherlock Holmes to the British reading public.

Throughout his career, he touched upon sf in varied forms, with his best-known genre works being *The Lost World* (1912), *The Poison Belt* (1913), and *The Land of Mist* (1926). All three titles deal with the adventures of the explorer Professor Challenger. In the first tale, the professor encounters a dinosaur-laden lost area of South America; in the second, a sequel, Challenger battles to save the Earth from a poisonous atmosphere; in the third, Challenger encounters the subject of mysticism. Challenger's shorter adventures are collected in *The Professor Challenger Stories* (G.B., 1952), while two of Doyle's best known non-Challenger genre tales, "The Horror of the Heights" and "The Great Keinplatz Experiment," are collected in *The Conan Doyle Stories* (G.B., 1929).

E

EKLUND, GORDON
(1945–   )

Gordon Eklund, who was born in Seattle and moved to San Francisco during the counter-culture revolution of the 1960s, has produced a brand of sf that is both traditionalist and contemporary. His first novel, *The Eclipse of Dawn* (1971), was followed by *A Trace of Dreams* (1972) and *Beyond the Resurrection* (1973).

His *All Times Possible* (1974) was a "What if?" look at U.S. history in which the political activists succeed in changing the shape of the country . . . in dozens of different ways in dozens of different alternative universes. Other Eklund books are *The Inheritors of Earth* (with POUL ANDERSON; 1974), *The Grayspace Beast* (1976's story of a space-chase into the den of the aforementioned beastie), *Falling Toward Forever* (1975), and *Dance of the Apoca-*

lypse (1976's tale of two friends trying to reawaken a dying world).

ELLISON, HARLAN J(AY)
(1934–   )

Once upon a time, somewhere along the line, someone dubbed Harlan Ellison "science fiction's angry young man." Although no longer as young as the firebrand of the 1950s and 1960s, Ellison is still fairly feisty. It wasn't exactly that Ellison was belligerent in his sf style—it was that he was an original. Surrounded by a genre mainly occupied with allegorical space-operas and alien worlds, Ellison, armed only with a typewriter, cut through the decoration and went straight for the jugular with his fiction. His style was (and is) terse and to the point; today's social realities figure strongly into his futurescapes, and his characters are often tomorrow's mirrors of present-day denizens.

Born and raised in Ohio, he was bounced out of Ohio State University for showing contempt for his creative-writing teacher. Emigrating to New York, he became a prolific short-story writer while barely out of his teens. His first sf sale, "Glowworm," appeared in *Infinity Science Fiction* in 1956. In the next three years, he would sell over 150 short fictions and essays. Following a stint in the army, he moved to Los Angeles and came into his own during the 1960s. (His first sf novel, *The Man with Nine Lives*, appeared in 1960, as did his first collection, *A Touch of Infinity*.) During the decade he wrote some of his best-known and most influential works, including " 'Repent, Harlequin!' Said the Ticktockman" (1965; winner of both the Nebula and Hugo in 1966), "I Have No Mouth and I Must Scream" (1967; a Hugo winner in 1968), "The Beast That Shouted Love at the Heart of the World" (1968; a 1969 Hugo winner), and "A BOY AND HIS DOG" (1969's Nebula-winning novelette, later made into a motion picture).

Ellison also proved himself an able TV scriptwriter, with his best genre work being the Hugo-winning STAR TREK episode "The City on the Edge of Forever" and the OUTER LIMITS script "Demon with the Glass Hand," which garnered Ellison the Writers' Guild of America award for the outstanding script of 1964.

His output during the 1970s, although reduced in quantity, did not lose its luster in terms of quality. "The Deathbird" (1973) won a Hugo for best novelette; 1975's "Adrift Just off the Islets of Langerhans, Latitude 38° 54′ N, Longitude 77° 00′ 13″ W" snared a Hugo; 1973's "The Whimper of Whipped Dogs" won an Edgar award from the Mystery Writers of America; 1977's short story "Jeffty Is Five" took a Nebula and a Hugo; and the script for the 1976 film of *A Boy and His Dog* copped a Hugo.

An influential writer, Ellison also has proved a guiding light as an editor, encouraging other writers to strike out in unorthodox paths via such anthologies as *Dangerous Visions* (1967), *Again, Dangerous Visions* (1972), and *The Last Dangerous Visions* (1978). The first collection won Ellison a Hugo as an editor. Well known and well loved (despite his somewhat less than low-key personality), Ellison is one of speculative fiction's unique talents.

ELWOOD, ROGER
(1933–   )

One of the U.S.'s premier sf anthologists, Roger Elwood has advanced the genre a great deal, selling over 80 sf collections between the years 1970 and 1976. Among his best-known anthologies: *And Walk Now Gently Through the Fire* (1972), *Frontiers I: Tomorrow's Alternatives* (1973), *Frontiers II: The New Mind* (1973), *The Graduated Robot* (1973), *The Berserkers* (1974), *The Learning Maze* (1974), and *Dystopian Visions* (1975).

ENGLAND, GEORGE ALLAN
(1877–1936)

The son of a U.S. Army officer, Harvard-graduate author and treasure-hunter England was the closest thing to a swashbuckling literary rival EDGAR RICE BURROUGHS ever saw in the early part of this century. Among his more popular fictions were "The Elixir of Hate" (1911's tale of immortality), "Beyond White Seas" (a serial that appeared in 1909–10, concerning a lost civilization), "The Empire of the Air" (a 1914 story about an invasion from another dimension), "June 6, 2016," (1916; the title refers to the date of women's futuristic emancipation), and *The Flying Legion* (1920's massive tale of an attempt at world enslavement).

His "Darkness and Dawn" trilogy was reissued in the 1960s in five volumes: *Darkness and Dawn* (1964), *Beyond the Great Oblivion* (1965), *The People of the Abyss* (1966), *Out of the Abyss* (1967), and *Afterglow* (1967).

He died, mysteriously, on a treasure hunt.

FAIRMAN, PAUL W.
(1916–77)

Paul Fairman's first sf work, "No Teeth for the Tiger," appeared in 1950, and for the rest of the decade he became a mainstay in *AS*, with most of those stories collected in *The Forgetful Robot* (1968).

He served as editor of *AS* from 1956 to 1958 and later launched a rival magazine, *Dream World*, which lasted only three issues in 1957. Using various Ziff-Davis house names (E. K. Jarvis, Paul Lohrman, Ivar Jorgensen), he produced two of his best-known works, "Deadly City" (as Jorgensen; 1953) and "The Cosmic Frame" (1953). These stories served as the basis for the 1950s sf films TARGET EARTH! and INVASION OF THE SAUCER MEN (later remade as *The Invasion of the Eye Creatures*). Among his best-known novels are *City Under the Sea* (1963; based on *Voyage to the Bottom of Sea*) and *The World Grabbers* (1964; based on an episode of TV's ONE STEP BEYOND).

FARMER, PHILIP JOSÉ
(1919–   )

Up until the time Philip José Farmer burst upon the sf scene in 1952, sf as a literary genre possessed a fairly adolescent (and unrealistic) view of sex. Scantily clad females often graced the covers of pulp magazines and books, but within the covers women were strictly for saving (or, in the case of Amazons, for fighting)—extensions of the hero's idealistic valor.

American writer Farmer won a Hugo for the best new writer of the year (1953) for "The Lovers" (published as a novel in 1961), which appeared in *Startling Stories*. It dealt with the physical love affair between a human male and a parasitic alien life-form that took the form of a female. The frankness of its sexual attitude and the realism of its characters astounded both critics and fans alike.

Farmer continued to pen interesting tales along sexual, emotional lines, including "A Woman a Day" (1953) and "Rastignac the Devil" (1954). Drawing a bead on theologians after dealing with sexual mores, he began his famous "Father Carmody" series in *F&SF*, dealing with a spacefaring holyman and his planetary philosophy. His first novel, *The Green Odyssey*, appeared in 1957; it was followed by such popular longer works as *The Gate of Time* (1966's tale of a parallel universe), *The Wind Whales of Ishmael* (a 1971 update of *Moby Dick* projected into the future), *The Other Log of Phileas Fogg* (1973's JULES VERNE futurescape), and *Flesh* (1960's story of a futuristic matriarchy).

His trilogy made up of *The Maker of Universes* (1965), *The Gates of Creation* (1966), and *A Private Cosmos* (1968) attained popularity as portraits of a manmade world where reality and myth exist side by side. This pocket-universe motif later was used successfully in *Behind the Walls of Terra* (1970) and *The Lavalite World* (1977).

In 1968 Farmer won a second Hugo for the short story "Riders of the Purple Wage" (1967), and in 1972, a third for the novel *To Your Scattered Bodies Go* (1971)—the first book in his "Riverworld" series, which includes *The Fabulous Riverboat* (1971) and *The Dark Design* (1977). The series takes place on a planet where the dead of the Earth have been resurrected along a seemingly infinite river.

FERMAN, EDWARD L(EWIS)
(1937–)

One of the best known sf editors around, Edward Lewis Ferman took over the reins of *F&SF* in 1966, prodding that publication into a new stage of ultrarespectability and garnering it Hugo awards as best magazine in the years 1969, 1970, 1971, and 1972. The editor of *The Best from Fantasy and Science Fiction* anthologies from 1966 on, he has also compiled a number of unrelated collections, including *Final Stage* (1974) and *Arena: Sports Science Fiction* (1976).

FINNEY, CHARLES G(RANDISON)
(1905–)

One of the masters of the fantasy genre, who has greatly influenced the styles of such sf writers as RAY BRADBURY and CHARLES BEAUMONT, Charles G. Finney largely has been overlooked by the American book-buying public. In 1935 the Arizona-based writer and newspaperman penned the truly amazing *The Circus of Dr. Lao*, a tale involving the sudden presence of a magical Chinese circus-master in a provincial Arizona community and the lessons he teaches through the use of mythological creatures-come-alive. His other works include *The Unholy City* (1937), *The Old China Hands* (1961), and *The Magician out of Manchuria* (1976).

FINNEY, JACK
(1911–)

Jack Finney is the penname of American writer Walter Braden Finney, a mainstream writer who began dabbling in sf in 1951 in the pages of *Collier's* magazine (many of the same stories later were reprinted in *F&SF*). Finney's best-known work is the 1955

Act Naturally

Basically, writing is an unnatural act. You spend most of the time in a room with the door closed, totally alone, except for the people you've created in your stories. In fact, you probably spend at least one third of your waking life in this unnatural environment. It's a wonder that any of us are fit for social intercourse.

Jerry Pournelle

---

novel *The Body Snatchers*, which, one year later, became the classic creepy film INVASION OF THE BODY SNATCHERS. His sf short-story work can be found in such collections as *The Third Level* (1956) and *I Love Galesburg in the Springtime* (1963). His later novels are not that well known. They include *The Woodrow Wilson Dime* (1968), a book taking a romantic triangle into a parallel world, and *Time and Again* (1970), an sf-fantasy that features a hero who journeys back into the New York City of 1880 and finds a woman he loves.

FONTANA, D(OROTHY) C.
(?–)

D. C. Fontana is an American sf buff who is primarily recognized for her talents in the area of TV. Story editor for STAR TREK, LOGAN'S RUN, the STAR TREK animated series, and FANTASTIC JOURNEY, she also wrote the novel *The Questor Tapes* (1974), a book based upon the made-for-TV film of the same name produced by GENE RODDENBERRY and written by Roddenberry and Gene L. Coon.

FOSTER, ALAN DEAN
(1946–)

Raised in Los Angeles, Alan Dean Foster is a young American sf exponent who can justifiably be called a "pop" sf writer. First published in 1971, he is best known for his works based on

Photo courtesy of Del Rey Books

Alan Dean Foster

either TV shows or feature films. His best known "novelizations" include *Dark Star* (1974), *Star Trek Log One* (1974), *Star Trek Log Two* (1974), *Star Trek Log Three* (1975), *Star Trek Log Four* (1975), *Star Trek Log Five* (1975), *Star Trek Log Six* (1976), *Star Trek Log Seven* (1976), *Star Trek Log Eight* (1976), *Star Trek Log Nine* (1977), *Alien* (1979), and *The Black Hole* (1979).

Among his original space operas are *Orphan Star* (1977), *Bloodhype* (1973), and *Ice Rigger* (1974).

GALLUN, RAYMOND Z(INKE)
(1911–   )

Born and educated in Wisconsin, veteran sf writer Raymond Z. Gallun published his first sf story at the age of 18—"The Space Dwellers" (1929; *Science Wonder Stories*). The bulk of his work, however, appeared in *AS* and *ASF* before World War II; his most notable stories include the trilogy comprising "Old Faithful" (1934), "Son of Old Faithful" (1935), and "Child of the Stars" (1936)—all concerning a self-sacrificing Martian and his descendants. His first novel, *People Minus X* (1957), was about human duplication. *The Planet Strappers* (1961) was sheer space opera, concentrating on the exploits of a rocketful of astronauts exploring space for the first time. After a long dry spell that lasted well into the 1970s, Gallun returned with *The Eden Cycle* (1974), a book that concerned itself with immortality.

GARRETT, RANDALL
(1927–   )

American writer Randall Garrett was one of the most prolific story-churners at the Ziff-Davis publishing house during the 1950s and 1960s, producing an avalanche of stories for *AS* and *Fantastic* using both his own moniker and those of David Gordon, Walter Bupp,

William Atheling, Jr., as well as a host of in-house pseudonyms.

His best-known short stories deal with the futuristic doings of detective-magician Lord Darcy, including "The Eyes Have It" (1964), "A Case of Identity" (1964), A Matter of Gravity" (1974), and "The Ipswich Phial" (1976)—all of which appeared in *ASF*.

A longtime short-story collaborator with such peers as ROBERT SILVERBERG, LIN CARTER, and AVRAM DAVIDSON, Garrett also collaborated on many novels: *Shrouded Planet* (1958) and *Dawning Light* (1959) were written with Silverberg, and *Pagan Passions* (1960), *Brain Twister* (1962), *The Impossibles* (1963), and *Supermind* (1963) were written with Larry Harris. His solo works include *Too Many Magicians* (1967) and *Unwise Child* (1962).

GERNSBACK, HUGO
(1883–1967)

Commonly referred to as the "Father of Science Fiction," Luxembourg-born writer and editor Gernsback is generally credited with coining the term "science fiction" ("scientifiction" in some legends). A self-taught scientist and experimenter, Gernsback emigrated to the United States in 1904 in an effort to peddle a battery he had just developed. Four years later, he launched *Modern Electrics* (which later mutated into *Electrical Experimenter*). It was in this publication that he published much of his own fiction, including "Ralph 124C 41+" (a superhuman vs. a Martian meanie) and a series of "Baron Munchhausen" stories.

With many of his readers responding positively to this "new" type of fiction, Gernsback started *Science and Invention* (1920), which featured even more sf work. It was in April 1926, however, that he began the first real sf publication: *Amazing Stories*. The magazine was a hit. Unfortunately, its publishing company folded after a year. Gernsback, not to be deterred by finances, began his own company and produced *Air Wonder Stories* and *Science Wonder Stories* (later to meld as simply *Wonder Stories*), as well as *Science Wonder Quarterly* and *Scientific Detective Quarterly*.

Relying heavily on the reprinted

works of JULES VERNE and H. G. WELLS, Gernsback also nurtured such writers as E. E. "DOC" SMITH, JACK WILLIAMSON, RAY CUMMINGS, EDMOND HAMILTON, and MURRAY LEINSTER. In the 1930s, his publishing empire declined and practically disappeared thereafter, with Gernsback drifting into comic books (*Superworld Comics* in 1939) and a few pulps that lasted into the 1950s. The *Hugo* awards are named in his honor.

GERROLD, DAVID
(1944–   )

Born and raised in Los Angeles, David Gerrold is best known in fandom for his contributions to the STAR TREK TV realm—most notably, his script for *The Trouble with Tribbles* (1967) and his book *The World of Star Trek* (1973). His novels include *Space Skimmer* (1967), *When Harlie Was One* (1972), *The Man Who Folded Himself* (1973), and *Deathbeast* (1978).

GOULART, RON(ALD JOSEPH)
(1933–   )

Former advertising copywriter Ron Goulart first introduced his topsy-turvy concept of sf writing in 1952, with the publication in *F&SF* of "Letters to the Editor." In most of his short stories and novels, Goulart mixes mayhem with masterful plotting.

The Sword Swallower (1968) spotlights the sleuthing done by a detective from the Barnum planetary system. *Wildsmith* (1972) involves slightly out-of-whack robots. *After Things Fell Apart* (1970) portrays a futurescape in which an underground lesbian organization takes great pains to eliminate the male species. *The Hellhound Project* (1975) was an ultimate-weapon adventure.

Goulart's wild and wooly Barnum system gave birth to such novels as *Flux* (1974), *Spacehawk, Inc.* (1974), *A Whiff of Madness* (1976), and the short-story collection *The Chameleon Corps and Other Shape Changers* (1972).

Of late he has authored a series of novels based on the shapely Warren Publications character Vampirella. With Gil Kane, he also launched (1977) the comic strip *Star Hawks*.

GUNN, JAMES E(DWIN)
(1923–   )

Sf writer and critic James Gunn was born in Kansas City in 1923. His interest in sf led, after World War II, to his writing at Northwestern University an M.A. thesis on the genre (sections of the scholarly work were later reprinted in *Dynamic Science Fiction,* in 1953 and 1954). First published in 1949 with a story "Communications," in *Startling Stories,* Gunn frequently used the pseudonym Edwin James during his fledgling years.

By the mid-1950s, Gunn was an acknowledged master of the sf short story. At that point, he tackled novels, his first being *The Fortress World* (1955), which pitted its futuristic hero against a militaristic religion.

During the 1960s, his novels caught on with the sf readership. Some of the best known are as follows. *The Joy Makers* (1961): a futuristic tale concerning a hedonistic society in which pleasure-seeking eventually becomes too much for its human populace. *The Immortals* (1962): the basis for the late 1960s TV series, THE IMMORTAL, this novel told of the plight of a group of humans whose blood type guarantees agelessness and hence becomes a valuable commodity to the world at large. *The Listeners* (1972): a close encounter of the verbose kind occurs when a radio antenna picks up the entire history of an alien culture from a deep-space message; the knowledge, in turn, profoundly affects human culture.

Most of Gunn's work concerns the relationship between man and the state of technology. His best short stories can be read in *Station in Space* (1958) and *Happiness and Immortality* (1975).

HAGGARD, H(ENRY) RIDER
(1856–1925)

During the late 19th century, when "science" was still a mystery to the general public, H. Rider Haggard mixed pseudoscience with mysticism and adventure to concoct a series of popular fictions. Although today most of his work would not be considered sf in the strictest sense, at the time of their writing it was quite acceptable.

A civil servant and lawyer, Haggard spent six years in the colonial service in South Africa . . . a sojourn that in later years would provide much inspiration for his fiction writing.

Undoubtedly Haggard's most popular fantasy-sf character was Ayesha, the immortal white queen of the lost civilization in *She* (1887). Both Ayesha and the book's hero, Allan Quatermain, turned into regular Haggard characters, with the immortal lass turning up in *Ayesha, the Return of She* (1905), *She and Allan* (1921), and *Wisdom's Daughter* (1923).

Intrepid Allan, on his own, starred in a series of fictions that included *Allan and the Holy Flower* (1915) and *Allan and the Ice Gods* (1927), the latter featuring drug-induced time travel.

Haggard introduced the theme of "lost worlds" in such books as *When the World Shook* (1919), a tale of Atlantis; *The People of the Mist* (1894); and *Heart of the World* (1895).

Haggard was knighted in 1912.

HALDEMAN, JOE W(ILLIAM)
(1943–   )

Joe Haldeman's first sf novel, *The Forever War* (1974), won both a Hugo and a Nebula for the young author. That in itself is some indication of the power of Haldeman's taut prose. A Vietnam veteran whose grim experiences overseas greatly affected his work, Haldeman manages to combine all the lunacy and the horror of combat life, on both a grandiose and a personal level, with swift sf plotting. The effects are, in a word, flabbergasting.

Starting his career in sf in 1969 with *Galaxy's* "Out of Phase," Haldeman (who has a degree in physics and astronomy) soon emerged as one of the genre's brightest young talents, penning a host of intricate and moving short stories; four of which served as the basis for *The Forever War*.

Mindbridge (1976) is a complex yet totally readable novel that includes alien races, psi power, and matter

Photo by Gay Haldeman

Joe Haldeman

transmission in its helter-skelter plot. *All My Sins Remembered* (1977), yet another novel culled from previously written stories, traces the adventures of Otto McGavin, undercover agent for TB II and someone who has to change shape for each assignment. *Planet of Judgment* (1977) is an interesting entry in the *Star Trek* series.

Study War No More (1977) is an anthology put together by Haldeman and featuring the works of various writers in offering sf alternatives to warfare.

Haldeman won a second Hugo in 1977 for his short story "Tricentennial."

HAMILTON, EDMOND M(OORE)
(1904–77)

One of the acknowledged masters of the "space opera," Edmond Hamilton penned works in the early years of modern sf that did much to influence the writing style of authors-to-come. A science student turned sf writer, Hamilton was first published in 1926's *Weird Tales* with the short story "The Monster-God of Mamurth." Within ten years, he had published over 70 pieces of fiction, many of them of novelette length, and many of them for *Air Wonder Stories* and *AS*.

His best known creation is, undoubtedly, valiant Capt. Future, mainstay of the quarterly *Captain Future* magazine (1940–50). Four times a year, futuristic hero Curt Newton fought galactic villainy with the aid of Grag the robot, Otho the android, and immortal brain-in-a-box Simon Wright, a former pal of Curt's dad. Eventually the Capt. Future stories were released in book form and included such titles as *Danger Planet* (1968), *Outlaw World* (1969), *Quest Beyond the Stars* (1969), *The Comet Kings* (1969), *Calling Captain Future* (1969), and *The Magician of Mars* (1969).

Yet another stalwart sort concocted by Hamilton was Morgan Change, the "Starwolf," who starred in such novels as *The Weapon from Beyond* (1967), *The Closed Worlds* (1968), and *The World of the Starwolves* (1968). Other slam-bang Hamilton books include *The Star Kings* (1949) and *The Haunted Stars* (1960).

Hamilton married LEIGH BRACKETT in 1946, and they were inseparable until his death in 1977. Leigh Brackett died one year later.

HARRISON, HARRY
(1925–　　)

Harry Harrison is the possessor of an extraordinary sense of humor and a profound penchant for nail-biting suspense. Put both qualities onto the printed page and one has a formula for fiction that is practically irresistible. Probably his most famous, or infamous, character is Slippery Jim DiGriz, interstellar crook turned lawman, also known as the "Stainless Steel Rat." The star of such novels as *The Stainless Steel Rat* (1961), *The Stainless Steel Rat's Revenge* (1970), and *The Stainless Steel Rat Saves the World* (1972), DiGriz, like Harrison himself, mixes mayhem with monkeyshines on a regular basis.

American-born Harrison began his career as a comic-book artist before being published in 1951 in *Worlds Beyond* with the story "Rock Diver." After dabbling in editing while living in the New York area, Harrison introduced his DiGriz character to JOHN W. CAMPBELL, JR., at *ASF* and then embarked on a series of around-the-world moves that would take him (and his family) from New York to Mexico, through half of Europe and finally, to Ireland, where he still resides.

In between bouts with the moving van, Harrison managed to conjure up amazing visions in a series of novels that, again, slipped easily from high adventure to high camp. In a humorous vein, *Bill, the Galactic Hero* (1965) was an affectionate send-up of stock sf; *Star Smashers of the Galaxy Rangers* (1973) was the ultimate space-opera satire, and *The Technicolor Time Machine* (1967) recounted the tale of a *real* sf time-travel film.

On the serious side, *Make Room! Make Room!* (1966) painted a not-too-rosy picture of an overpopulated and underfed future (later translated to film as SOYLENT GREEN, in 1973); *Captive Universe* (1969) was a straight space-ark tale, and *Skyfall* (1976) was a pre-Skylab tale of debris-from-above.

Some of his best short stories can be found in *War with the Robots* (1962), *Two Tales and Eight Tomorrows* (G.B., 1965), and *The Best of Harry Harrison* (1976).

HEINLEIN ROBERT A(NSON)
(1907–　　)

The source of constant controversy, Robert Heinlein may be the quintessential sf writer. Period. Popular from the first, alternately praised and condemned for his literary philosophies (often termed fascistic, militaristic and chauvinistic) and admired by his peers, both young and old, Heinlein has managed to sidestep trends and literary fads, producing popular sf from 1939 to the present.

Born in Missouri and educated at the University of Missouri and the U.S. Naval Academy, Annapolis, he mixed a longstanding interest in sf literature with a curiosity about science fact (most notably physics, a subject he studied briefly at UCLA) as he embarked on a literary career. His first story, "Lifeline," appeared in *ASF* in 1939. His early work is nothing short of superb, a collection of stories that are still considered classics in the field: "The Roads Must Roll" (1940) is a futuristic story of moving roadways and their maintenance; "Blowups Happen" (1940) portrays the dangers of atomic energy; "Solution Unsatisfactory" (1941) shows the futility of the nuclear arms race; and "By His Bootstraps" (1941) gave time travel a new wrinkle. These tales, which appeared in *ASF*, showed Heinlein as a master craftsman of futurescapes and were later collected in book form, along with his other early works, in *The Man Who Sold the Moon* (1950), *The Green Hills of Earth* (1951), and *Revolt in 2100* (1953).

Not of all of Heinlein's work in the 1940s concerned itself with future histories, however, and some of his better known "straight" excursions into sf include "Waldo" (1942), the oft-republished tale of a crippled inventor housed in a satellite, and "And He Built a Crooked House" (1941), the story of an architect whose strange design for a house takes him and his structure into another dimension.

In the late 1940s, Heinlein entered yet another area of sf he would soon master, that of the juvenile novel. After coming up with *Rocket Ship Galileo* (1947)—space soldiers vs. Nazis headquartered on the moon . . . later to serve as the basis for the 1950 film DESTINATION MOON—Heinlein offered a host of children's sf adventures, including *Space Cadet* (1948), *Red Planet* (1949), *Between Planets* (1951), *The Rolling Stones* (1952), *Starman Jones* (1953), *The Star Beast* (1954), *Tunnel in the Sky* (1956), *Citizen of the Galaxy* (1957), and *Have Spacesuit—Will Travel* (1958).

Although concentrating on juveniles during the 1950s, Heinlein managed to pen such "adult" fare as *The Puppet Masters* (1951's classic tale of alien invasion), *Double Star* (1956's Hugo-winning novel of an actor who impersonates a spacefaring politico), *The Door into Summer* (a 1957 time-travel story) and most importantly, *Starship Troopers* (1959), a Hugo award-winning novel that astounded and/or revolted some of Heinlein's fans. An openly militaristic tale, it earned Heinlein the title fascist in some fan circles.

Stranger in a Strange Land (1961) is probably Heinlein's most popular (and atypical) work, a Hugo-winning story of a young Martian Messiah.

In terms of controversy, the best was yet to come. *Farnham's Freehold* (1965) had futuristic black masters chomping on their white lackeys. *The Moon Is a Harsh Mistress* (1966 Hugo winner) envisioned the futuristic Earth being assaulted by a penal colony on the moon; the colonists, like their American counterparts in 1776, are the good guys. *I Will Fear No Evil* (1971) was a strange tale of sexual mores in which the ancient hero's brain is transplanted into the body of his secretary. Although Heinlein's latest works have been fairly philosophical (to the point of being a tad preachy), he has never lost the respect of his peers or his popularity in fan circles.

In 1974 he received a Nebula award as a "Grand Master" of the genre.

His shorter works can be found in *The Worlds of Robert Heinlein* (1966), *The Past Through Tomorrow* (1967), and *The Best of Robert Heinlein* (1973).

HENDERSON, ZENNA
(1917–   )

American schoolteacher Zenna Henderson is best known for her "People" stories in *F&SF*. The series began in 1952 with the short work "Ararat," telling the tale of a group of humanoid aliens, the possessors of incredible telepathic powers, who are marooned on Earth. Identical in appearance with the common Earthling, they endeavor to keep their presence a secret. This series later gave birth to an ABC-TV movie of the same name. The "People" stories can be found in the collections *Pilgrimage: The Book of the People* (1961) and *The People: No Different Flesh* (G.B., 1961). First published in 1951 with "Come On, Wagon," Henderson is still penning imaginative short fiction today. Some of her best can be found in *The Anything Box* (1965) and *Holding Wonder* (1971).

HERBERT, FRANK
(1920–   )

In 1965 Frank Herbert brought forth a novel that would become one of the all-time success stories of sf literature: *Dune*. Embraced by genre readers as well as counter-culture citizens of the 1960s, *Dune* is an epic adventure set on the sandy, swirling world of Arrakis. Described in meticulous detail, Arrakis is truly the "star" of the novel; replete

Frank Herbert

with titanic sandworms, mysterious spice traders, and desperately valiant Fremen. Adding extra mystical clout to the book is the presence of hero Paul Atrides, a fictitious character loosely based on Mohammed.

For Herbert, *Dune* was the first commercial success of a career that, up until that point, had been enormously promising. The Washington-born journalist-editor-turned-sf-writer worked during the 1950s in the genre (his first work, "Looking for Something?" appearing in *Startling Stories* in 1952; his first novel, *The Dragon in the Sea*, in 1956) but did not achieve real popularity until the early 1960s, with the publication of the short fictions "Dune World" (1963) and "The Prophet of Dune" (1965) in *ASF*.

The novel *Dune* won both a Nebula and a Hugo and set the stage for the sequels *Dune Messiah* (1969) and *Children of Dune* (1976).

A complex, intellectually-stimulating writer, Herbert manages to mix intense characterization with meticulous plotting and ambitious themes. Some of his other well known novels include *The Eyes of Heisenberg* (1966; about genetic engineering), *The Green Brain* (1966; mutant insects become corporate giants), *Destination Void* (1966; cyborg power), *The Heaven Makers* (1968), *The Santaroga Barrier* (1968), *Whipping Star* (1970), *The God Makers* (1972), *The Hellstrom Hive* (1973's tale of humans raised on insect-

like principles), and *The Dosadi Experiment* (1977's novel of alien cultures and psi experimentation).

His short fiction can be found in *The Book of Frank Herbert* (1973) and *The Best of Frank Herbert* (1975).

HERZOG, ARTHUR
(1928–   )

American writer and teacher Arthur Herzog is an sf writer whose tongue-in-cheek manner has great appeal for mainstream readers. After starting off quite seriously enough with *The Swarm* (1974) and *Earthsound* (1975)—works concerning an invasion of North America by killer bees and a single seismologist's attempts to warn New England of a coming earthquake—Herzog soon lapsed into a semislapstick style with such novels as *IQ 8E* (1978; genetic dumbbells), *Make Us Happy* (1979; futuristic, hedonistic idiots), and *Glad to Be Here* (1979's sequel to *Happy*, featuring characters Bil and Alce, Dian Toffler and Ralf Nadir . . . funny, huh?). Herzog is also the author of *Orca,* the story of a nasty killer whale.

HOLLY, J. HUNTER
(1932–   )

Michigan-born Joan Carol Holly assumed the sexually ambiguous pseudonym J. Hunter Holly in 1959 with the publication of her first sf novel, *Encounter*. A psychologist, J. Hunter managed to weave numerous psychological twists into her premier work. Other novels were to follow, including *The Green Planet* (1960), *The Time Twisters* (1964), *The Dark Planet* (1962), *The Dark Enemy* (1965), *The Flying Eyes* (1962) and *The Gray Aliens*. In 1967, her *Man from U.N.C.L.E.* novelization, *The Assassination Affair,* was published as the 10th entry to that long-running series of novels based on the TV series.

An illness from 1966 to 1970 caused Holly to let up on her writing chores. Happily enough, however, she has recently returned to the typewriter, producing novels such as *Keeper* (1976) and short fictions such as "The Gift of Nothing" (1973) and "PSI Clone" (1977).

HOWARD ROBERT E(RVIN)
(1906–36)

In his relatively short life, Texas-born-and-raised Robert E. Howard managed to take the "sword and sorcery" concept and virtually establish it as a mainstay in sf. His characters Conan the Barbarian, Alburic, and Bran Mak Morn virtually defined the genre. Conan was later put into book form during the 1950s by Gnome Press, spawning an entirely new legion of fans. In the 1960s and 1970s they were, once again, regrouped and republished, with L. SPRAGUE DE CAMP and LIN CARTER picking up Howard's fallen sword and continuing the series. Two comic books, *Conan the Barbarian* and *The Savage Sword of Conan,* have proved popular items with bloodthirsty youngsters.

Howard killed himself at the age of 30 upon learning of his mother's fatal illness.

HOYLE, FRED
(1915–)

A distinguished British scientist/astronomer, Sir Fred Hoyle did not enter the sf genre until after he had achieved fame as a writer of science fact. In 1957 his first novel was published in Great Britain. Entitled *The Black Cloud,* it featured a hero who was (oddly enough) an astronomer who discovers and attempts to communicate with a strange space cloud coming between the sun and the Earth. His second work, *Ossian's Ride* (1959), portrayed a group of scientist/politicos.

Most of Hoyle's subsequent works have been collaborative efforts. With John Elliot, he penned *A for Andromeda* (1962) and *Andromeda Breakthrough* (1964), two novels tracing a man vs. machine conflict as a gigantic computer based in the Andromeda area flexes its powerful muscles.

With son Geoffrey he has written *Fifth Planet* (1963), *Rockets in Ursa Major* (1969), *Seven Steps to the Sun* (1970), *The Molecule Men and the Monster from Loch Ness* (1971), *The Inferno* (1973), *Into Deepest Space* (1974), and *The Incandescent Ones* (1977).

Hoyle's best-known solo novel is probably *October the First Is Too Late* (1966), in which different parts of the world become unstuck in time, leaving some geographical areas in the present, and others simultaneously in the distant past and the far future.

HUBBARD, L(AFAYETTE) RON
(1911–)

Before becoming the founder of the Church of Scientology and the quintessential huckster for the Dianetics movement, L. Ron Hubbard was a respected sf and fantasy author, and a quite prolific one at that.

First appearing in *ASF* in 1938 with the short story "The Dangerous Dimension," he embarked on a career that mixed action with *angst*. Among his best-known longer works are *Final Blackout* (1948), the story of a postwar British dictatorship; and *Fear and Typewriter in the Sky* (1951), two stories in one book, one dealing with paranoia, the other with a fellow who suddenly becomes the protagonist in an sf story being written by a friend. *The Kingslayer* (1949) and *Return to Tomorrow* (1954) are two fairly savage space operas, and *Ole Doc Methuselah* (1970) is a collection of related short fictions originally published in *ASF* from 1947 until 1970.

During his short-lived writing career, he used several pseudonyms, Kurt von Rachen and René Lafayette among them.

HULL, E(DNA) MAYNE
(1905–75)

Canadian-born, American-bred E. Mayne Hull gained her greatest sf fame during the 1940s, with the appearance of her "Arthur Blord" series of short stories. Blord was a different type of sf hero, a planet-hopping business entrepreneur with a nose for adventure. His tall tales were later collected in book form, *Planets for Sale* (1954). Hull married sf writer A. E. VAN VOGT in 1939 and collaborated with him—most notably on *The Winged Man* (1966) and the short-story volume *Out of the Unknown* (1948)—until her death.

HUXLEY, ALDOUS
(1894–1963)

A brilliant novelist, British-born Aldous Huxley dabbled only occasionally in the sf genre, although his best-known work is undoubtedly *Brave New World*

(1932), the dystopian novel to end all dystopian novels. The grandson of Darwinist thinker T. H. Huxley, and the brother of zoologist Julian Huxley, Aldous Leonard Huxley attended Eton, leaving prematurely because of eye problems. Later educated at Balliol College, Oxford, he initially began his career in letters via journalism. Some of his finest fiction was penned during the 1920s (e.g., *Point Counter Point* in 1928, *Those Barren Leaves* in 1925), and he quickly gained a reputation of a keen, if somewhat cynical, observer of social mores.

In 1932, however, he took many of his readers by surprise with the appearance of *Brave New World,* his most ambitious work up to that time. Set in the distant future, A.F. (After Ford), the novel portrays a hedonistic society in which social castes are artificially created and educated; entertainment is provided by casual sex and "feelies," and tranquility is guaranteed by the drug soma. When a "savage" human actually born of a woman's womb is introduced into the machinelike society, several sociological cogs begin to come loose.

What set *Brave New World* head and shoulders above its genre counterparts was its unyielding sense of literacy and social satire, as well as its inventiveness. Huxley left Europe shortly after the publication of his novel and settled in California in the mid-1930s. There, he began experimenting with hallucinogenic drugs and studying modern mysticism.

He continued to dabble in sf concepts throughout his career. *After Many a Summer Dies the Swan* (1939) concerned practical immortality, and *Time Must Have a Stop* (1944) actually featured a main character who dies halfway through the book; his narrative, however, continues from the afterlife.

Ape and Essence (1948) is another dystopian futurescape, set in the postatomic world of 2108. In a world ravaged by fallout and bacteriological horror, only New Zealand has remained untouched. When a New Zealand explorer visits the postholocaust land of America, he finds the entire country gripped by a savage strain of devil worship.

In *Brave New World Revisited* (1958), a nonfiction work almost as bizarre as the original novel, Huxley compares his "predictions" of the 1930s with the "realities" of the 1950s. *Island* (1962) showed Huxley as the, perhaps, patron saint of the soon-to-be counterculture, describing a utopian society created by beneficial drug intake.

Homework
Scientific accuracy isn't necessary for good science fiction, but scientific *inaccuracy* kills it. You can write a good science-fiction story without any science, but a writer who blathers about *any* subject without knowledge of it is going to create ugly fiction.

Joe W. Haldeman

BRAVE NEW WORLD has been filmed for television but, as yet, has not been shown.

JONES, NEIL R(ONALD)
(1909–   )

A New York State unemployment-insurance claims investigator by day, an sf pulp writer by night, Neil R. Jones began his professional career at the age of 21 with the story "The Death's Head Meteor," which appeared (1930) in *Air Wonder Stories.* (Trivia buffs take note: it marked the first time the word "astronaut" appeared in an sf story.) Of his dozens of enjoyable (albeit forgettable) short fictions during the next three decades, his most famous works concerned Professor Jameson, an Earth scientist who is found in a state of suspended animation in a satellite orbiting a long-destroyed Earth. His discoverers, the alien Zoromes; fast-traveling aliens in robot bodies outfit the Earthling with a metal housing, and he's off for some two decades worth of adventures.

Many of the short stories were published in book form under the titles *The Planet of the Double Sun, The Sunless World, Space War* and *Twin Worlds* (1967) and *Doomsday on Ajiat* (1968).

JONES, RAYMOND F.
(1915–)

A solid pulp-writer, Raymond F. Jones took a fancy to sf while a lad living in Salt Lake City. By the 1940s, he was a regular contributor to *ASF*. His best known novels are *Renaissance* (1951), a parallel-worlds adventure; *The Alien* (1951), which is about the discovery of an alien artifact; *The Secret People* (1956), a tale of mutants; *The Cybernetic Brains* (1962), in which human brains meet circuitry; *The Non-Statistical Man* (1964), a collection of short fiction; *Syn* (1969); and *The River and the Dream* (1977).

A prolific author of juvenile sf novels, Jones also penned a minor classic of the genre, *This Island Earth* (1952), a nice alien-invasion work that later (1956) was made into an sf film.

KEYES, DANIEL
(1927–)

Brooklyn-born Daniel Keyes's career in sf is really centered upon one exceptional work: the Hugo award-winning novella "Flowers for Algernon," published in *F&SF* in 1959. The story recounts the life and times of Charlie Gordon, a mentally retarded fellow whose IQ is 68. Charlie and a lab-mouse counterpart, Algernon, are experimented upon by a group of scientists, and their IQs develop to genius level. Charlie becomes a whole man. Unfortunately, his summit is short-lived; the IQ boost proves temporary, and he must feel himself terrifyingly lapse back into idiocy.

In 1966 Keyes expanded the story to novel length (winning a Nebula), di-luting the impact somewhat. A movie version of the story, CHARLY, won an Academy Award for actor Cliff Robertson.

Prior to *Algernon*, Keyes served (1951) as associate editor of *Marvel Science Fiction*.

KNEALE, NIGEL (THOMAS)
(1922–)

In British sf circles, Nigel Kneale is known as the father of Quatermass. A versatile talent who has written everything from children's books to screen adaptations of John Osborne plays, Kneale addicted an entire nation of TV viewers to their tubes in the 1950s with the BBC-TV serials *The Quatermass Experiment* (1953), *Quatermass II* (1955), and *Quatermass and the Pit* (1958). Each six-part TV serial attracted a phenomenal audience, as thousands of viewers watched dedicated scientist Quatermass ward off various space beasties.

In 1953 it was space ooze; in 1955, substrata nasties; and in 1958, ancient Martians. These plays were later adapted for the screen in *The Creeping Unknown, Enemy from Space,* and *Five Million Years to Earth.* Quatermass was revived in 1979 for *The Quatermass Conclusion* on Thames television. Set slightly in the future, this series portrayed a now elderly and jaded Quatermass stumbling over an alien-takeover plot.

Kneale is also well known, largely in Great Britain, for his TV adaptation of GEORGE ORWELL'S *1984* (in 1954) and his future-satire *The Year of the Sex Olympics* (1969). Both telecasts caused a great deal of controversy.

KNIGHT, DAMON
(1922–)

Sf writer, editor, and teacher Damon Knight is one of the few genre authors to win a Hugo for his criticism. In 1956 his magazine critiques were bound in the volume *In Search of Wonder* and garnered immediate acclaim. Quite an odd set of circumstances—but, then again, in the world of Damon Knight, oddities seem commonplace.

Possessing a literary knack for the

quirky and amusing, yet thought-provoking sf, Knight first became involved with the genre while still a New York teenager. He joined the Futurians, a fan organization populated by the likes of FRED POHL, C. M. KORNBLUTH, and JAMES BLISH. He sold his first story in 1941 ("Resilience" in *Stirring Stories*) and never looked back. Some of his better known short works (revered for their bizarre endings) include "Not with a Bang" (1949's end-of-the-world story to end all end-of-the-world stories), "To Serve Man" (1950; the piece of alien literature mentioned in the title turns out to be a cookbook), and "Masks" (1968's psychological profile of a cyborg).

Knight's well-received novels include *Hell's Pavement* (1955), a dystopian view of the future; and *Mind Switch* (1965), in which a man and an alien accomplish what the title implies. As an editor, Knight ran *Worlds Beyond* in 1950 and *If* from the fall of 1958 to the spring of 1959. In 1966, Knight created the *Orbit* collection, one of the most successful anthology series ever.

Knight is best known for his exciting short stories, some of the best of which can be found in *Far Out* (1961), *In Deep* (1963), and *Turning On* (1966). Some of his outstanding anthologies include *A Century of Science Fiction* (1962), *First Flight* (1963), and *Tomorrow × 4* (1964).

KOMATSU, SAKYO
(1931–   )

Japanese journalist-turned-novelist Sakyo Komatsu caused an uproar in his native land with the publication of *Nippon Chimbotsu* in 1973. Translated in 1976 as *The Submersion of Japan*, the book tells, quite matter-of-factly, of a series of events that causes the island landmass to slide into the surrounding sea. The book sold over 4 million copies in Japan and was successfully filmed in 1973. The movie was later reedited, dubbed, and generally butchered by Roger Corman and released in the U.S. as *Tidal Wave*.

KOONTZ, DEAN R(AY)
(1945–   )

Pennsylvania-born Dean Koontz is an ex-schoolteacher who opted for a career in sf in 1969, after starting out as a part-time writer in 1967. His first published work, "Soft Come the Dragons," appeared in *F&SF* in 1967, and his first novel, *Star Quest*, in 1968. His novel *Demon Seed* (1973) served as the basis for the film of the same name. Among his other novels are *Fear That Man* (1969), *The Fall of the Dream Machine* (1969), *Dark of the Woods* (1970), *The Anti-Man* (1970), *Beastchild* (1970), *Time Thieves* (1972), and *The Vision* (1977).

KORNBLUTH, C(YRIL) M.
(1923–58)

One of the most underrated masters of the sf short story, Cyril Kornbluth mixed bitter irony with fast-paced plotting for a quick one-two literary punch. His best-known short story, "The Marching Morons" (1951), forecast a world wherein the population at large was made up of idiots and the intelligentsia was a minority group that had to concoct "treats" to keep the masses happy (in retrospect, it seems C. M. was a prognosticator as well as a writer).

As a youth, C. M. belonged to the New York–based Futurians fan club. He began writing professionally in the days before World War II using both his own name and such monikers as Cecil Corwin, S. D. Gottesman, and Kenneth Falconer. Following the war, he began using his own name on most of his work. His short-story output was nothing less than amazing, with many of his offerings being deemed classics by his peers.

"The Little Black Box" (1950) tells of the consequences felt in the present when a futuristic medical bag shows up in an alleyway. "The Cosmic Charge Account" (1956) gives the power of creation to a little old lady. "Shark Ship" (1958) deals with overpopulation.

Kornbluth is probably best known for his sardonic sf novels coauthored with FRED POHL. *The Space Merchants* (1953) offered a futuristic world run by ad agencies. *Search the Sky* (1954) and *Gladiator-at-Law* (1955) were two thrillers set in equally-absurd surroundings.

In 1973 he won a posthumous Hugo
for the Kornbluth-Pohl tale "The Meeting." His short fictions can be found in
The Marching Morons (1959) and *Best
SF Stories of Cyril Kornbluth* (1968).

KUTTNER, HENRY
(1919–58)

Born in Los Angeles, Henry Kuttner
proved an unstoppable short-story
writer during the 1940s. Starting as a
worker at a West Coast literary agency,
Kuttner first became interested in writing because of H. P. LOVECRAFT, an
author whom he admired and corre-
sponded with as a youth. Kuttner's first
published work. "The Graveyard Rats,"
appeared in 1936 in *Weird Tales*.
Within a year, he moved to the sf
genre, offering a series of stories about
futuristic moviemaker Tony Quade in
Thrilling Wonder Stories.

During that time period, Lovecraft
suggested that Kuttner collaborate with
female writer C. L. MOORE. He did so,
and they often used the pen names
Lawrence O'Donnell, Keith Hammond,
Lewis Padgett, and others. Kuttner and
Moore married in 1940 and remained
together until his death.

Some of Kuttner's better-known short
stories (many coauthored by Moore)
are "The Time Trap" (1938), "Dr. Cyclops" (1940; based on the film), "The
Twonky" (as Padgett; 1942; later made
into a film), "Mimsy Were the Boro-
goves" (as Padgett; 1943) and the
"Hogben" series of hillbilly-alien stories:
"Exit the Professor" (1947), "Pile of
Trouble" (1948), "See You Later"
(1949), and "Cold War" (1949). His
work appeared in *Thrilling Wonder
Stories, Marvel Science Stories, AS,* and
Startling Stories. Many of his best short
works can be found in the collections
A Gnome There Was (as Padgett; 1950),
Robots Have No Tails (1951; again as
Padgett), *Bypass to Otherness* (1961),
Return to Otherness (1962), and *The
Best of Henry Kuttner* (1975).

His novels include *Fury* (as Lawrence O'Donnell; 1950), *Well of the
Worlds* (as Padgett; 1952), *Valley of
the Flame* (as Keith Hammond; 1964),
and *Earth's Last Citadel* (with C. L.
Moore; 1964).

LAFFERTY, R(ALPH) A(LOYSIUS)
(1914–   )

R. A. Lafferty became an sf writer
after being an electrician for over 35
years. The Iowa-born author has penned
over 100 short stories since making his
debut in 1960 with "Day of the Gla-
cier," and one, "Eurema's Dam," won a
Hugo in 1973.

Among his novels are *Past Master*
(1968), set in a future utopia where a
group of citizens resurrects Sir Thomas
More to help them out; *The Reefs of
Earth* (1968), *Space Chantey* (1968);
Nine Hundred Grandmothers (1970);
*Arrive at Easterwine, The Devil Is
Dead,* and *The Flame Is Green* (all in
1971); *Strange Doings* (1972); *Not to
Mention Camels* (1976); and *Archi-
pelago* (1977).

LAUMER, KEITH
(1925–   )

New York–born Keith Laumer has
devoted almost as many years to various government services as he has to
writing. After serving in the army in
1943–45, he joined the air force (1953–
56) before opting for a career in the
U.S. Foreign Service. He rejoined the
Air Force in 1960. In the interim, he
began writing sf, incorporating both
his combat and diplomatic experiences
as well as a healthy dose of humor.

One recurring character in his longer
fictions is Jaime Retief, an interstellar
diplomat. His adventures can be found
in *Envoy to New Worlds* (short stories;
1963), *Galactic Diplomat* (short
stories; 1964), *Retief's War* (1966),
Retief and the Warlords (1968), *Retief: Ambassador to Space* (short
stories; 1969), *Retief of the CDT*
(short stories; 1971), *Retief's Ransom*
(1971), and *Retief: Emissary to the
Stars* (1975).

Yet another Laumer series is a parallel-worlds chain consisting of *Worlds
of the Imperium* (1962), *The Other*

Side of Time (1965), and *Assignment in Nowhere* (1968). His humorous "Lafayette O'Leary" chronicles include *Time Bender* (1966), *The World Shuffler* (1970), and *The Shape Changer* (1972).

Other titles include *A Trace of Memory* (1963); *The Great Time Machine Hoax* (1964); *The Invaders* and *Enemies from Beyond* (both in 1967; based on THE INVADERS TV show); *Galactic Odyssey* (1967), The *Star Treasure* (1971), and *The Infinite Cage* (1972). Other short stories can be found in such collections as *The Big Show* (1972) and *The Best of Keith Laumer* (1977).

LEE, TANITH
(1947–　)
British writer Tanith Lee began her career writing juvenile fantasies such as *The Dragon Hoard* (1971) and *Animal Castle* (1972). Before long, however, she was concentrating on adult fictions, mixing sf settings with sword-and-sorcery plotting and quest imagery. Among her best known novels: *Companions on the Road* (1975), *The Winter Players* (G.B., 1976), *East of Midnight* (G.B., 1977), *Don't Bite the Sun* (1976), and *Drinking Sapphire Wine* (1977).

LE GUIN, URSULA K(ROEBER)
(1929–　)
One of the finest writers ever to grace the pages of an sf publication, Ursula Le Guin has, in her relatively short career in the genre, been awarded four Hugos and three Nebulas. Born in California, Le Guin read sf as a youngster, although she did not actually offer any sf of her own until the 1962 short story "April in Paris."

In 1966 she published the first of her "Hainish" books, a series of novels taking place on or about the planet Hain. A planet populated by humanoids in a humanoid-laden galaxy, Hain and its adventures give present-day sf readers a chance to envision a large chunk of future history beginning some four centuries from now and spanning (over the course of five books) some 2,000 years. The first novel, *Rocannon's World* (1966), drew immediate praise and was quickly followed by *Planet of Exile* (1966), and *City of Illusions* (1967).

Le Guin's biggest impact to date occurred in 1969, however, with the publication of *The Left Hand of Darkness,* an inspired work dealing with the androgynous life-styles of the planet Gethen ("Winter"). The next two Hainish tales, novellas, appeared in 1971 and 1972: "Vaster Than Empires and More Slow" and "The Word for World Is Forest."

The Lathe of Heaven (1971) is a humorous and ingenious tale of a hapless fellow of the future, George Orr, who has the power to alter reality—past, present, and future—through his dreams. *The Dispossessed* (1974) returns to the Hainish realm to look at two neighboring worlds that are poles apart politically.

Le Guin has authored juvenile fiction as well as adult novels, her best known juves being the "Earthsea" trilogy: *A Wizard of Earthsea* (1968), *The Tombs of Atuan* (1971), and *The Farthest Shore* (1972). In 1980 PBS-TV adapted her LATHE OF HEAVEN to a TV format, with Le Guin supervising scripting. She is currently working on a historical novel.

LEIBER, FRITZ (REUTER)
(1910–　)
A master craftsman of the fantasy tale, Fritz Leiber quickly established himself in that genre with his creation of the characters Fafhrd and the Gray Mouser, who first appeared in *Unknown* in 1939.

The son of stage and screen actor Fritz Reuter Leiber, Leiber, Jr., studied psychology and physiology at the University of Chicago before studying theology and eventually opting for a career on the stage. By the late 1930s, however, he had begun to devote all his time and interests to writing, initially in the fantasy genre but soon drifting into sf as well.

He won a Hugo and a Nebula for his 1967 story "Gonna Roll the Bones." "Ill Met in Lankhmar" (1970) won both awards in 1971, and "Catch That Zeppelin" (1975) won the pair, again, in 1975. His best-known short stories include "Conjure Wife" (1943; novelized in 1953) and "Coming Attraction" (1951). His best-known novels include *Gather, Darkness!* (1950), a tale of a religious dictatorship; *The Big Time* (1958), a Hugo winner depicting the history of a futuristic way-station; *The Wanderer* (1964), yet another Hugo winner concerning a drifting planet coming too close to Earth's moon; and *A Spectre Is Haunting Texas* (1969). His short stories can be found in *The Mind Spider and Other Stories* (1961), *A Pail of Air* (1964), and *The Book of Fritz Leiber* (1974).

Some of his fantasy-oriented awards include a Lovecraft and an August Derleth award for "Belsen Express" (1975), a 1975 Gandalf Award, and the 1976 Life Achievement Lovecraft Award.

LEINSTER, MURRAY
(1896–1975)

Murray Leinster is the pen name used by American author William Fitzgerald, who, in all probability was the sf writer active the longest. His career began in 1919 with the story "The Runaway Skyscraper" (*Argosy*) and was still going strong at the time of his death. Leinster continued writing short stories and novelettes throughout his career. Among the seemingly endless list: "The Mad Planet" (1920), in which the world is attacked by giant insects; the "Masters of Darkness" series (1929–30); the "Bud Gregory" quartet of stories; "First Contact" (1945); "If You Was a Moklin"; and the Hugo award-winning "Exploration Team" (1956).

Many of his longer works were expanded versions of previously published short stories. Among his more interesting offerings: *Out of This World* (1958's "Bud Gregory" compilation), *The Last Space Ship* (1949), *Space Captain* (1966), *Space Gypsies* (1967), *Colonial Survey* (1956), *The Forgotten Planet* (1954), *War with the Gizmos* (1958), *Creatures of the Abyss* (1961), *The Duplicators* (1964), *Land of the Giants* (1968; based on the TV show), and *Time Tunnel* (1967; based on the TV show).

Many of his short stories can be found in *Sidewise in Time* (1950), *The Aliens* (1960), *Twists in Time* (1960), and *Get off My World* (1966).

LEM, STANISLAW
(1921–   )

Currently the center of a strong and dedicated literary cult, Polish sf writer Lem is Eastern Europe's most famous genre writer. He intended originally to become a medical man, but his career was cut short by the Nazi occupation of Poland. A versatile as well as prolific writer, Lem entered the sf genre in the late 1940s, and since that time has penned dozens of short fictions and novels on every topic under (or above) the sun.

His best-known work Stateside, *Solaris* (1961; trans. 1971), is a psychological tale involving the communication between a single human and a planet-sized entity.

The Astronauts (1951) is a work concerning space exploration, and *The Magellan Nebula* (1955) and *Guest in Space* (1952) also revolve around space exploration and futuristic societies. *Memoirs Found in a Bathtub* (1971) is a send-up of utopias. *The Invincible* (1963) pits a titanic spaceship full of explorers against a society of machines. *The Cyberiad* (1965) relates robotic adventures caused by crazy inventors Trurl and Klapaucius. *The Futurological Congress* (1971) is a novel of terrorism and drug weaponry. *A Perfect Vacuum* (1979) is a wonderful collection of satires on various schools of literary criticism and fads.

LEVIN, IRA
(1929–   )

American author Levin is known to mainstream readers as the originator of the New York–based deviltry found in *Rosemary's Baby*. Also out of his fertile imagination, however, came a few sf thrillers. *This Perfect Day* (1970) was a machine-laden dystopian novel. *The Stepford Wives* (1972), the source of the movie of the same name, presented the perfect solution to a boring marriage, with antsy husbands replacing their beautiful wives with beautiful, but less independent, robots. *The Boys from Brazil* (1976), also the source of a movie, had the world quaking at the thought of dem clones, dem clones, dem Hitler clones.

LEWIS, C(LIVE) S(TAPLES)
(1898–1963)

Theologian, critic, and author C. S. Lewis was born in Belfast and educated in England. A professor of medieval and Renaissance English at Cambridge, Lewis wrote numerous books on the Christian religion and a dozen or so fantasy titles, both juvenile and adult-oriented. Two of his most famous, in both categories, were *The Lion, the Witch and the Wardrobe* (1950) and *The Screwtape Letters* (1943), the latter offering a batch of instructive notes from the devil to his son.

Lewis's sf output was confined, primarily, to three fables: *Out of the Silent Planet* (1938), *Perelandra* (1943), and *That Hideous Strength* (1945). Constituting a Christian allegory, the three books concern the adventure of philologist Ransom, a character loosely based on Lewis's close friend J. R. R. Tolkien.

In *Out of the Silent Planet*, Ransom is kidnapped by mad scientist Weston, who sends the man of letters to Mars as a supposed human sacrifice that will earn Weston the friendship of the Martians forever. The Martians, Ransom discovers, are spiritual folk led by the kindly Oyarsa. Oyarsa sends Ransom homeward-bound with words of peace. In *Perelandra,* Ransom watches a space-age version of the fable of Adam and Eve reenacted on the water-world Venus. In *Strength,* Ransom battles a spiritually corrupt scientist, Horace Jules (a cruel caricature of H. G. WELLS and his humanistic beliefs), bringing into the skirmish magic and religion.

Apparently, at the time of his death, Lewis had been planning a fourth book concerning Ransom, *The Dark Tower.*

LONG, FRANK BELKNAP
(1903–   )

First published in 1924, American author Frank Belknap Long began his career in the fantasy genre, emulating the works of H. P. LOVECRAFT. The journalist-turned-talespinner later strayed into the sf-serial area, penning countless adventures for such magazines as *Weird Tales* and *Thrilling Wonder Stories*. Many of his early sf works have been published in book form along with later original novels. Among his spacier titles are *John Carstairs: Space Detective* (1949), *Space Station No. 1* (1957), *Women from Another Planet* (1960), *Mars Is My Destination* (1962), *It Was the Day of the Robot* (1963), *The Martian Visitors* (1964), *This Strange Tomorrow* (1966), *Survival World* (1971), *Let Earth Be Conquered* (1966), *Journey into Darkness* (1967), *And Others Shall Be Born* (1968), and *The Three Faces of Time* (1969).

LOVECRAFT, H(OWARD) P(HILLIPS)
(1890–1937)

One of the masters of 20th-century fantasy, Howard Phillips Lovecraft was a reclusive resident of Providence, Rhode Island, who found a creative outlet in tales of horror and unworldly mythology. He created his own legions of gods and devils in the "Cthulhu Mythos." Still, from time to time, he dabbled with plot lines that could be considered "straight" sf as opposed to far-flung fantasy. "The Colour out of Space" (*AS;* 1927) tells of an alien substance being deposited on Earth, via a meteor crash, with horrific results. "Herbert West—Reanimator," "The Shadow Out of Time," and "At the Mountains of Madness" were printed in *ASF* in 1936. "Madness" concerns an Antarctic expedition from Miskatonic University (Lovecraft's beloved fictitious place of higher education, found in equally mythical Arkham) that discovers a group of frozen alien entities. The aliens thaw and then there's a hot time among the ice caps. "Shadow" concerns the dreams of a scholar who envisions himself in an ancient civilization that predates humanity, only to discover that his dreams are getting to look suspiciously more and more like reality.

Most of Lovecraft's short fictions were revived in book form later on by Arkham House. Among the best-known titles are *The Case of Charles Dexter Ward* (1951), *The Dunwich Horror and Others* (1963), *The Colour out of Space* (1964), *At the Mountains of Madness and Other Novels* (1964), and *The Horror in the Museum and Other Revisions* (1970).

LOWNDES, ROBERT (AUGUSTINE) W(ARD)
(1916–   )

Connecticut-born Robert W. Lowndes found himself enmeshed in sf literature via the Futurians, that legendary fan organization headquartered in New York City during the 1930s and 1940s. Primarily known as an editor in the genre, Lowndes ran *Future Fiction* and *Science Fiction Quarterly* during the 1940s until they folded, and resumed his chores during their brief revival ten years later. He then moved on to other Columbia publications, such as *Dynamic Science Fiction* and *Science Fiction Stories*. He continued editing the Columbia sf line until the company went under in 1960. At that point, he moved to Health Knowledge, Inc., where he created such publications as *The Magazine of Horror, Startling Mystery Stories,* and *Famous Science Fiction* for their stable. That company met its mulchy maker in 1970.

Most of Lowndes's short fictions were either collaborative efforts penned under various pseudonyms or else solo projects written under assumed names. His novels include *The Duplicated Man* (written with JAMES BLISH; 1959), *The Puzzle Planet* (1961), and *Believers' World* (1961).

MCCAFFREY, ANNE
(1926–   )

Anna Inez McCaffrey, born in Cambridge, Massachusetts, began her sf career at the age of 26 with "Freedom of the Race," published in *Science Fiction Plus*. Although her earlier work was somewhat conventional, she quickly moved into the humanistic vein of sf-fantasy that proved her forte. Her most popular books comprise the "Dragon-riders of Pern" series: *Dragonflight* (1968), *Dragonquest* (1971), and *The White Dragon* (1978). The books concern the exploits of the war-

Anne McCaffrey

riors of Pern and their loyal dragon-beasts in symbiotic attempts to save the planet from deadly space fibers.

A juvenile subseries, *Dragonsong* (1976) and *Dragonsinger* (1977) have also proved very popular. McCaffrey began her novelizing with the most misunderstood book in the world, *Restoree* (1967), a satire on male-dominated space operas that proved so subtle that many of her male peers (and readers) did not catch on.

The Ship Who Sang (1969) is a touching story of a deformed young girl whose brain is placed in the guidance system of a spaceship. *Decision at Doona* (1969) finds two advanced planets colonizing an alien world, with each assuming that the other's colony is a long-overlooked alien race. *Dinosaur Planet* (1978) is the beginning of yet another projected series, this one concerning the leaping-lizard–inhabited planet of Ireta and the humans who are stranded there.

McCaffrey won a 1968 Hugo award for the novella "Weyr Search" and a Nebula the same year for "Dragonrider."

MCINTYRE, VONDA
(1948–   )

Young American writer Vonda N. McIntyre studied sf writing at the Clarion Writers' Workshop in the early 1970s and won the Clarion Award for her novella "Of Mist, and Grass, and Sand." The work later brought her national fame and a Nebula award in 1973. A second Nebula was awarded the author in 1979 for her extended version of the same story, *Dreamsnake* (1978). *The Exile Waiting* (1975) is a postholocaust story detailing the life of a young female telepath.

MCKENNA, RICHARD M(ILTON) (1913–64)

Known in mainstream circles for his epic novel *The Sand Pebbles* (1962), Richard M. McKenna was an unassuming author who dabbled in sf because he genuinely enjoyed it and reasoned that the pressures of competition would be less in a genre fraught with space opera. Born in Idaho, he served in the navy for nearly two decades before donning his civvies and picking up a pen.

His first published genre work, "Casey Agonistes," was a 1958 classic. Other short stories include "The Fish-dollar Affair" (1958), "Hunter Come Home" (1963), "Fiddler's Green" (1967), and "The Secret Place (1966)." The last-named story was awarded a posthumous Nebula.

MAINE, CHARLES ERIC (1921–)

Charles Eric Maine is the pseudonym used by British author David McIlwain in his sf efforts. He did not begin his literary career until the days following World War II. His first novel, *Spaceways* (1953), proved an auspicious debut. Based on his own radio play, the novel later became one of the first sf films of the 1950s not to be loaded down with bug-eyed monsters and maidens in leotards.

His finest genre novel is generally considered to be THE MIND OF MR. SOAMES (1961; filmed in 1969), the story of a man who remains in coma until the age of 30. Awakening, he must be slowly educated out of his infant mental state.

Other well-known works include *High Vacuum* (G.B., 1958), a description of the first moon landing; *World Without Men* (1958), about the last man alive in a matriarchy; *The Tide Went Out* (G.B., 1959), in which H-bomb tests shrink the seas; *The Darkest of Nights* (G.B., 1962), in which modern society is undone by disease; and *B.E.A.S.T.* (G.B., 1966), which relates how evolutionary experiments go bonkers in the Biological Evolutionary Animal Simulation Test.

A Matter of Vision

A really good sf story is more than just entertainment. When you're finished with it, it should leave concepts in your brain that make you wonder about "what might happen *if* . . ." It gives you a view of your life, of the society you're part of, that's totally unique; suggesting what possible alternatives there are, what other types of life there might be. It gives you what astronomers call "the view from a distant star." Science fiction gives you a glimpse of the world from the *outside*.

Fred Pohl

MALZBERG, BARRY N. (1939–)

Barry N. Malzberg began writing sf in 1968; he quit writing it in 1976, saying that he was not happy. And so it goes. Using the pseudonym K. M. O'Donnell, he attained notoriety in 1968 with the novella "Final War," a bitter tale about never-ending future follies. As O'Donnell, Malzberg was published in book form in the titles *Final War and Other Fantasies* (1969), *In the Pocket* (1971), *The Empty People* (1969), *Universe Day* (1971), *Dwellers of the Deep* (1970) and *Gather in the Hall of the Planets* (1971).

Under his own name, Malzberg penned a number of intriguing, *angst*-ridden stories populated with existentially alienated heroes and villains alike. *The Falling Astronauts* (1971), *Revelations* (1972), and *Beyond Apollo* (1972) all feature intellectually tortured astronauts as protagonists. *The Day of the Burning* (1974) has aliens giving Earth 12 hours to come up with a good move to stave off its destruction. *The Destruction of the Temple* (1974) offers a cinematic re-creation of the most realistic kind of the J. F. Kennedy assassination. *Herovit's World* (1973) spotlights a confused sf writer's bout with reality. *The Gamesman* (1975) is a dismal look at organized sex play. *Scop* (1976) offers a time-traveler attempting to save the life of the Kennedys.

Other novels are *The Last Transac-*

tion (1977), *Phase IV* (1973), *On a Planet Alien* (1974), *The Sodom and Gomorrah Business* (1974), *Conversasations* (1974), *In the Enclosure* (1973), and *Guernica Night* (1975).

Malzberg won the 1973 John W. Campbell Award for *Beyond Apollo*.

MARGULIES, LEO
(1900–75)

Born in Brooklyn and educated at Columbia University, longtime sf editor Leo Margulies entered the sf field in the 1930s and spent the next 40 years editorially immersed in the genre. Over the years, he served as editor for such publications as *Thrilling Wonder Stories, Captain Future, Startling Stories, Fantastic Universe, Satellite Science Fiction,* and a host of detective magazines.

He later turned to planning countless sf book anthologies. Among his better known entries: *Three Times Infinity* (1958), *Three from Out There* (1959), *Get Out of My Sky* (1960), *The Unexpected* (1961), and *The Ghoul Keepers* (1961). With Oscar J. Friend, he assembled *From Off This World* (1949), *My Best Science Fiction Story* (1949), *The Giant Anthology of Science Fiction* (1954), and *Race to the Stars* (1958).

MATHESON, RICHARD (BURTON)
(1926–   )

An amazingly creative and versatile writer, Richard Matheson is regarded as a triple-threat man: a top-notch screenwriter, science-fiction storyteller, and fantasy author. Born in New Jersey and educated at the University of Missouri (in journalism), he entered the sf field in 1950 with the *F&SF* story "Born of Man and Woman," a first-person account of what it's like being a mutant offspring.

His first sf novel followed shortly thereafter: *I Am Legend* (1954), the story of the lone human survivor of a ruined world now plagued by virus-spawned vampires. (The book was later filmed as THE LAST MAN ON EARTH and THE OMEGA MAN, two cinematic stiffs.) Matheson's second novel in the genre, *The Shrinking Man* (1956), earned him a stint as the screenwriter for the movie version, THE INCREDIBLE SHRINK-ING MAN. The film's success moved him

into screenwriting on a permanent basis.

Among his sf-fantasy screenplays: *Master of the World* (1961; based on JULES VERNE's *Robur the Conqueror* and *Master of the World*), *Tales of Terror* (1962; E. A. POE adaptations), *Burn, Witch, Burn* (1962; based on FRITZ LEIBER's *Conjure Wife*), *The Legend of Hell House* (1973; psi power), and *Somewhere in Time* (1980).

His TV scripts include "And When the Sky Was Opened" (TWILIGHT ZONE; 1959), "Third from the Sun" (TZ; 1960), "A World of His Own" (TZ; 1960), "Nick of Time" (TZ; 1960), "The Invaders" (TZ; 1961), "Once upon a Time" (TZ; 1961), "Little Girl Lost" (TZ; 1962), "Young Man's Fancy" (TZ; 1962), "The Return of Andrew Bentley" (*Thriller;* 1962); "Mute" (TZ; 1963), "Death Ship" (TZ; 1963), "Steel" (TZ; 1963), "Nightmare at 20,000 Feet" (TZ; 1963), "Night Call" (TZ; 1964), "Spur of the Moment" (TZ; 1964), "Time Flight" (*Bob Hope's Chrysler Theater;* 1966), "The Enemy Within" (STAR TREK; 1966), *Duel* (1971), *The Night Strangler* (1973), *Dying Room Only* (1973), *The Stranger Within* (1974), and *The Martian Chronicles* (1980).

His short fictions can be found in *Born of Man and Woman* (1954), *The Shores of Space* (1957), and *Shock, Shock II,* and *Shock III* (1957, 1964, and 1966, respectively).

MERRIL, JUDITH
(1923–   )

Josephine Judith Zissman began writing sf in 1948, when the genre was still very much a man's world. Billing herself Judith Merril, she refused to adopt an asexual pen name (the better to be published with, my dear) and her first story, "That Only a Mother," ran in ASF. A member of the New York–based Futurians, Merril quickly began writing short stories in earnest, occasionally under the pen name Rose Sharon. Some of her stories can be found in *Out of Bounds* (1960), *Daughters of Earth* (G.B., 1968), *Survival Ship* (1974), and *The Best of Judith Merril* (1976).

In the early 1950s, she began collaborating with writer C. M. KORNBLUTH, writing two novels under the name of Cyril Judd: *Gunner Cade* and *Outpost Mars* (1952). Her own novels include *Shadow on the Hearth* (1950), a description of a nuclear attack on New York and the aftermath as experienced by a young mother and her children, and *The Tomorrow People* (1960), an East-West confrontation over the possession of Mars.

A well-respected editor, she began the annual series *SF: The Year's Greatest Science-Fiction and Fantasy* in 1956 and has compiled such anthologies as *Beyond Human Ken* (1952), *The Best of the Best* (1967), and *England Swings SF* (1968).

She currently lives in Toronto, Canada.

MERRITT, A(BRAHAM)
(1884–1943)

The acknowledged master of purple prose in sf, American sf-fantasy author A. Merritt began his literary career as a means of supplementing his income as a working journalist. His first published work, "Through the Dragon Glass" appeared in *All Story Magazine* in 1917. Not an exceedingly prolific writer, A. Merritt would greatly influence the field nonetheless, offering lavish descriptions of equally exotic locales. Although most of his "science fiction" had little or nothing to do with science (fantastic gadgetry and settings were often explained away in pseudoscientific gobbledygook), he nevertheless impressed young readers with such novels as *The Moon Pool* (1919), *The Ship of Ishtar* (1926), *Seven Footprints to Satan* (1928), *The Face in the Abyss* (1931), *The Dwellers in the Mirage* (1932), *Creep, Shadow, Creep!* (1934), *Burn, Witch, Burn* (1933), and *The Metal Monster* (1946).

Merritt excelled in describing unimaginable geographic locales. *The Moon Pool* portrayed the exotic remnants of the Lemurian civilization in an undersea world caused when the moon tore itself loose from Earth in ancient times. *The Metal Monster* combines extraterrestrial machinery/intelligence with the romantic mystery of the Himalayas. *The Face in the Abyss* is that of the Snake Mother, the last one of her kind, a being from a world long gone.

Merritt served as associate editor of *American Weekly* until 1937, when he assumed editorship. He held the post until his death.

MERWIN, SAM(UEL) JR.
(1910–   )

Starting out as an sf writer (first work: "The Scourge Below" in *Thrilling Wonder Stories,* 1939), Sam Merwin came into his own nearly a decade later as an editor with a strong vision concerning the responsibilities of an sf pulp to its readership. In 1945 he became editor of *Thrilling Wonder Stories* and *Startling Stories* at Standard Magazines. While there, he inaugurated an imaginative letters column that offered readers a serious forum to discuss their ideas, likes, and dislikes. While at Standard, he also launched *Fantastic Story Magazine* and *Wonder Story Annual.*

Leaving his post in 1951, he returned to writing with a passion, offering such volumes as *The House of Many Worlds* (1951), *Killer to Come* (1953), *The White Widows* (1953), and *Three Faces of Time* (1955). During the 1950s he also edited *Fantastic Universe* and *Satellite Science Fiction* (1956) and served as assistant editor of *Galaxy* and of *Beyond* (1953–54).

MILLER, WALTER M(ICHAEL), JR.
(1922–   )

After leaving the air force following World War II, Walter M. Miller embarked on an sf-writing career that would produce very little actual work but countless accolades for the few gems published. His first story, "Secret of the Death Dome," appeared in *AS* in 1951. During the 1950s, he wrote short fiction fairly regularly, the most recognizable piece being the Hugo award-winning novelette "The Darfsteller," the story of an unemployed futuristic actor who rigs a computer-controlled, life-size puppet theater to allow him to take the place of one of the wooden performers.

His best known novel is *A Canticle for Leibowitz* (1960), a 1961 Hugo winner. One of the few sf novels ever to delve into religion, *Canticle* tells a sprawling tale of a futuristic Earth dominated by the Order of Leibowitz, a religious order named after a famous

20th-century scientist. The Church becomes the guardian of technological secrets from the Old Age (prenuclear) and debates what to do with them.

Miller's short fiction can be found in the volumes *Conditionally Human* (1962) and *The View from the Stars* (1964).

MOORCOCK, MICHAEL
(1939–   )

London-born and -bred, Michael Moorcock became one of Great Britain's most controversial sf writers during the 1960s, when his name became synonymous with the genre term "New Wave." He began his career while still a teenager engrossed with fantasy literature. He edited *Tarzan Adventures* in 1956–58, writing a series of fantasy adventures later to be dubbed the "Sojan" stories.

He turned to sf during the early 1960s, contributing to *SF Adventures* and *Science Fantasy.* His first major work, published in 1962 and 1963 in *SF,* later appeared in novelized form as *The Sundered Worlds* (1965). In 1964 he became the editor of *New Worlds* magazine (a post he held until the magazine's demise in 1971). Moorcock openly encouraged experimental fiction in the genre and, as such, was one of the guiding lights in the New Wave movement, giving headway to such writers as NORMAN SPINRAD, THOMAS M. DISCH, and J. G. BALLARD.

Oddly enough, Moorcock's main preoccupation as a writer has been with mind-boggling sword-and-sorcery epics. Among his "straight" sf novels are *City of the Beast* (1965), *The Lord of the Spiders* (1965) and *The Masters of the Pit* (1965), three Edgar Rice Burroughs-esque adventures. *Breakfast in the Ruins* (1972) and *Behold the Man* (1969) are two thought-provoking books concerning the character Karl Glogauer's trips through the world, past and future. In the former book, Glogauer attempts to wend his way through the modern/futuristic world successfully. In the second title, he travels back through time to take the place of Christ.

Another popular Moorcock series are the books concerning futuristic globetrotter Jerry Cornelius, the eternal James Bond rake of sf; books in this series include *The Final Programme* (1968), *A Cure For Cancer* (1971), *The English Assassin* (1972), and *The Condition of Muzak* (1977).

Moorcock won a Nebula in 1967 for the novella version of "Behold the Man." He was married to sf writer Hilary Bailey from 1962 to 1978.

MOORE, C(ATHERINE) L(UCILLE)
(1911–   )

A creator of thoroughly delightful sf of the high-adventure caliber, C. L. Moore broke into the sf world wielding a two-fisted adventure yarn ("Shambleau," in *Weird Tales,* 1933) and an asexual pen name that would allow her to contribute frequently to the then male-oriented realm of sf. Her initial story led to a series of sequels featuring the character Northwest Smith.

In 1934 she introduced to the genre two-fisted heroine Jirel of Joiry in *Weird Tales* (collected in book form as *Jirel of Joiry,* 1969). A regular contributor to *Weird Tales* and *ASF* during the 1930s, she married writer HENRY KUTTNER in 1940 and began writing collaborative efforts using a series of pen names. On her own, however, she continued to produce amazingly thought-provoking yet fast-paced fictions, including "No Woman Born" (1944) and "Vintage Season" (as Kenneth O'Donnell; 1946).

Following Kuttner's death, she turned to TV writing. Her best short fiction can be found in *No Boundaries* (with Kuttner; 1955); *Shambleau and Others* (1953), *Northwest of Earth* (1954), and *The Best of C. L. Moore* (1976).

MOSKOWITZ, SAM(UEL)
(1920–   )

Sf editor and historian Sam Moskowitz's involvement with the genre dates back to his youth in the New York City area, when he was one of the guiding lights in the national sf fandom movement of the 1930s. His first "major" work of sf appeared in 1954: *The Immortal Storm,* a book about the fan movement. Later works included *Explorers of the Infinite* (1963) and *Seekers of Tomorrow* (1966), two tomes concerned with sf writing up to the year 1940 (*Explorers*) and from

1940 to the present (*Seekers*). *Science Fiction by Gaslight* (1968) is an anthology of tales written prior to 1911. *Under the Moons of Mars: A History of the Scientific Romance in the Munsey Magazine* (1970) presents exactly what its title suggests, albeit for a rather select cadre of interested readers. *Strange Horizons* (1976) is a collection of short sf fiction demonstrating sf's reaction to such themes as religion, racism, etc.

During the 1960s, Moskowitz conducted interviews with sf authors at the behest of *AS*. He has served as editor/compiler for dozens of anthologies, including *Editor's Choice in Science Fiction* (1954), *Doorway into Time* (1966), *Masterpieces of Science Fiction* (1967), *Microscopic God and Other Stories* (1968), *When Women Rule* (1972), and *Horrors in Hiding* (1973).

NATION, TERRY
(1930–   )

British screenplay-writer Terry Nation captured an entire generation of the young and the young at heart during the 1960s, when he offered DR. WHO to BBC-TV in Great Britain. Currently in syndication all over the world, *Dr. Who* comprises whimsical tales of a time-traveling alien "doc" who hops, skips, and jumps through time and space while fending off alien foes. In recent years, Nation has offered British TV audiences *The Survivors* (1975)—weekly dilemmas in a postholocaust world—and *Blake's Seven* (1978)—in which a group of political prisoners sent to a prison planet immediately set about planning their escape; eventually they make the rounds throughout the galaxy in a computer-controlled rocket.

NIVEN, LARRY
(1938–   )

Born and raised in California, Laurence van Cott Niven has won a myriad of awards during his short genre career.

Photo by Michael Vilain

Larry Niven

The story "Neutron Star" won him his first Hugo (1967). *Ringworld* (1970) won both a Hugo and a Nebula. "Inconstant Moon" won a 1972 Hugo, "The Hole Man" a 1974 Hugo, and "The Borderland of Sol" a 1976 Hugo.

The possessor of a B.A. in mathematics from Washburn University, in Kansas, Niven sold his first sf story in 1964: "The Coldest Place," which appeared in *If*. Shortly thereafter, Niven became a recognizable byline in sf stories via his literate, complex tales of space travel, alien encounters, and telepathy.

Much of his work deals with future history and falls into his "Tales of Known Space" series. Some of the better known titles of that sequence include *World of Ptavvs* (1966), *Protector* (1967), *A Gift from Earth* (1968), *Neutron Star L* (short stories; 1968), *The Shape of Space* (short stories; 1969), *Ringworld* (1970), and *All the Myriad Ways* (short stories; 1971).

With writer JERRY POURNELLE, Niven has also penned such popular books as *The Mote in God's Eye* (1974), *Inferno* (1976), and *Lucifer's Hammer* (1977).

NOLAN, WILLIAM F(RANCIS)
(1928–   )

American writer William F. Nolan is best known as the coauthor of *Logan's Run* (with George Clayton Johnson; 1967), a flower-power-laden tale of utopia gone wrong wherein all oldsters over the age of 29 are put to death. Arising from the ranks of fandom, Nolan published his first sf story, "The Joy of Living," in *If* in 1954. His first book, *Impact 20*, was a collection of his shorter works. Other books include *Logan's World* (1977) and *Space for Hire* (1971). He has edited a number of anthologies, including *Man Against Tomorrow* (1965), *The Pseudo-People* (1965), and *A Sea of Space* (1970).

NORMAN, JOHN
(1931–   )

John Norman is the pen name of American writer John Frederick Lange, Jr., an exponent of the lusty literary land of sword-and-sorcery. A philosophy teacher turned adventure-writer, Norman is best known for his series of novels concerning the planet Gor, a world directly opposite Earth in the orbit around the sun and hence always unseen from this planet. When Earthling Tarl Cabot finds himself on the primitive planet, he finds he must fend for himself à la the best of the EDGAR RICE BURROUGHS heroes. The first in the series, *Tarnsman of Gor*, was published in 1963. The series continues ever onward today.

NORTON, ANDRÉ
(1912–   )

One of the finest juvenile writers in sf. Born in Cleveland, Ohio, Alice Mary Norton was a librarian for two decades before emerging as a full-time sf-fantasy author. Using both her best-known pseudonym (suitably nonfemale for the male-dominated sf community of the 1940s) and the additional pen name Andrew North, she began mixing sf adventure with fantasy overtones, creating swashbuckling space operas for the small fry.

Her first sf piece, "The People of the Crater," appeared in 1947 in *Fantasy Books*. Among her best known titles are *The Beast Master* (1959), *Lord of Thunder* (1962), *Sargasso of Space* (1955), *Plague Ship* (1956), and *Voodoo Planet* (1959)—all within her "Strange Planet" motif.

Also popular are *The Time Traders* (1958), *Catseye* (1961), *The Eye of the Monster* (1962), and the "Witch World" series.

Her short fiction can be found in such collections as *High Sorcery* (1970) and *The Book of André Norton* (1974).

NOURSE, ALAN E(DWARD)
(1928–   )

A physician with an eye for the future, Alan E. Nourse has written a series of taut juvenile narratives that combine sf skill with science-fact savvy. Born in Iowa and educated at Pennsylvania Medical School, Nourse penned his first sf novel, *Trouble on Titan*, in 1954. A solid space opera, *Titan* was the forerunner of such other possible-space adventures as *Rocket to Limbo* (1957) and *Raiders from the Rings* (1962). Many of Nourse's novels take into account his medical training, including *A Man Obsessed* (1955; brain surgery), *Star Surgeon* (1960), *The Mercy Men* (1968), and *Rx for Tomorrow* (short stories; 1971).

NOWLAN, PHILIP FRANCIS
(1888–1940)

American writer Philip Francis Nowlan dabbled just a bit in sf in the early part of this century and wound up creating one of the classic sf heroes of all time . . . Buck Rogers. His first story (published in *AS*), "Armageddon 2419" (1928), tells of a former World War I air ace trapped in a mine accident and sent into a state of suspended animation. Reawakening, the sleeper, Anthony Rogers, finds himself in the 25th century. The character immediately appealed to readers. A sequel, "The Airlords of Han," appeared in 1929. (Both stories were released in 1962 in book form as *Armageddon 2419 A.D.*).

A comic-strip version of Buck, a product of the combined talents of Nowlan and Dick Calkins, appeared in 1929 and ran until 1967. Nowlan worked practically exclusively on the comic strip until his death, forsaking a straight literary career. At the time of his death, however, he was planning a new series of space adventures for *ASF*.

He lived to see the first BUCK ROGERS serial filmed in 1939. In the late 1970s, his character became a popular TV personality.

ORWELL, GEORGE
(1903–50)

George Orwell is the pen name used by British writer Eric Arthur Blair during a long literary career that consisted mainly of journalistic essays and criticism. Born in India, Orwell moved to England in 1907, when his father, a civil servant, ended his foreign tour of duty. He was educated at Eton and later went to Burma as part of the Indian Imperial Police. He sailed back to England in 1928, beginning his career as a literary editor for the *Tribune* a few years later.

His best-known sf novel is *Nineteen Eighty-four* (1949), a dystopian novel to end all dystopian scenarios. In the not-too-distant future, a dictatorship led by the omniscient Big Brother leads humanity into an existence fraught with servitude and despair. *Animal Farm* (1945) is a satire on Soviet communism, using a single farm and its animal inhabitants as the embodiment of a socialist state perverted by totalitarianism. *Animal Farm* was made into a film in 1955, and *Nineteen Eighty-four* reached the screen (as *1984*) the same year.

PANSHIN, ALEXEI
(1940–   )

American sf author, critic, and historian Alexei Panshin wrote his first sf story in 1963: 'Down to the Worlds of Men," which appeared in *If*. Off to a promising start, Panshin won a Nebula for his 1968 novel *Rite of Passage* (a multileveled tale of space flight highlighted by the adventures of a young-girl narrator aboard the rocket fleeing from a postholocaust Earth) and a Hugo in 1967 for his writings and work in fandom.

Panshin is also well known for his "Anthony Villiers" space-opera trilogy: *Star Well* (1968), *The Thurb Revolution* (1968), and *Masque World* (1969). Among his critical writings, *Heinlein in Dimension* (1968) is considered his finest work and, indeed, one of the best literary analyses ever to come out of the genre.

POE, EDGAR ALLAN
(1809–49)

The acknowledged master of short fictions dealing with the macabre and mystery, Edgar Allan Poe also did much to advance the cause of the sf tale. The Boston-born Poe's oft-chronicled life was, of course, one punctuated by despair, sickness, and bouts with alcoholism. While critics debate how much of the author's brooding literary skill arose from his sometimes-wretched existence, his exercises in sf seem fairly inexplicable.

"Hans Pfall—A Tale" (1835) describes a trip to the moon accomplished by a balloonist. "The Facts in the Case of M. Valdemar" (1845), "Mesmeric Revelation" (1844), and "A Tale of the Ragged Mountains" (1844) all deal with hypnotism. "The Man That Was Used Up" (1839) is about a man who is part-human and part-machine. "MS. Found in a Bottle" (1833) and *The Narrative of A. Gordon Pym* (1837) tell of expeditions into uncharted, lost realms. "Mellonta Tauta" (1849) is a portrait of a less-than-thrilling future society.

It is commonly acknowledged that Poe, in his very early stories, influenced some of the works to come from JULES VERNE and H. G. WELLS, among others.

POHL, FREDERIK
(1919–   )

One of the giants of sf, writer, editor and, recently, historian, Fred Pohl is the possessor of a keen wit and a knack for meticulous plotting. Born in New York City, he first entered the world of sf via fandom, most notably through the legendary organization the Futurians. His first published piece was

Photo by Jay K. Klein

Frederik Pohl

actually an sf poem, "Elegy to a Dead Planet: Luna," which appeared in *AS* in 1937.

During 1940–41, he edited *Astonishing Stories* and *Super Science Stories*. During this period, he bought many tales from his fellow Futurians, from himself (under a few pseudonyms), and from a combination of the above. Much of his early work consisted of collaborative efforts with his Futurian peers. From 1953 until 1959, he edited *Star Science Fiction Stories*, and from 1962 to 1969 he edited both *Galaxy* and *If*. Leaving the magazine field, he moved to Bantam Books in the late 1970s as sf editor. He currently is an editorial consultant for that company.

During his fruitful career, Pohl has dabbled in just about every strain of sf imaginable, from satire to space opera to psychological drama. His collaborative novels with C. M. KORNBLUTH are classics: *The Space Merchants* (1953) is an advertising-age portrait of a futuristic dystopia; *Search the Sky* (1954) recounts humanity's attempts to rediscover Earth centuries from now; *Gladiator-at-Law* (1955) takes the old battle-to-the-death concept and transforms it into a business credo; *Wolfbane* (1959) is an account of a helter-skelter battle against evil human rulers and equally as magnanimous robot-soldiers. Pohl and Kornbluth won a Hugo in 1973 for their story "The Meeting."

Some of Pohl's better-known solo novels include *Slave Ship* (1957), *Drunkards Walk* (1960), *A Plague of Pythons* (1965), *Man Plus* (1976's Nebula award-winner about the rede-

sign of the first astronaut slated for a Mars landing), and *Gateway* (1977's epic novel about adventure in space).

He has collaborated often with sf writer JACK WILLIAMSON to produce a long list of books, among them the juvenile adventures *Undersea Quest* (1954), *Undersea Fleet* (1955), and *Undersea City* (1958). Pohl's editorial hand at *If* won the magazine three Hugos for best magazine in 1966, 1967, and 1968. His best-known stories can be found in *Alternating Currents* (1956), *Day Million* (1970), *The Gold at the Starbow's End* (1972), and *The Early Pohl* (1976).

POURNELLE, JERRY
(1933–   )

Jerry Pournelle's first thoughts of science involved his 15-year stint in the U.S. space program. Breaking into sf in the 1970s, Pournelle espoused a slightly right-wing philosophy, with much of his fiction dealing with militaristic settings. His first story, "Peace with Honor," appeared in 1971. His best-known solo novels include *West of Honor* (1976), *The Mercenary* (1977), and *A Spaceship for the King* (1973).

With LARRY NIVEN, he has authored *The Mote in God's Eye* (1974), *Inferno* (1976), and *Lucifer's Hammer* (1977). His short fiction can be found in *High Justice*. He won the John W. Campbell Memorial Award for the best new writer of 1973.

PRATT, FLETCHER
(1897–1956)

Fletcher Pratt obviously believed that the concept of the Renaissance man was not a dead one. During his lifetime he was an sf writer, a reporter, a boxer, a critic, and a historian. His first published story was the "Octopus Cycle" (1928), in *AS*. Striking up a friendly relationship with editor HUGO GERNSBACK, Pratt took it upon himself to translate dozens of foreign genre tales for Gernsback's various sf publications. When not editing and translating, Pratt also penned quite a few tales, including "City of the Living Dead" (1930), with Laurence Manning. He is best known for his fantasy collaborations with L. SPRAGUE DE CAMP, including *The Incomplete Enchanter*

(1942), *The Castle of Iron* (1950), and *Wall of Serpents* (1960). His solo work includes *The Well of the Unicorn* (1948), *The Undying Fire* (1953), and *Double Jeopardy* (1952).

PRIEST, CHRISTOPHER
(1943–   )

A relatively new face on the sf scene, Christopher Priest began publishing stories while working as an accountant in Great Britain. His first work, "The Run," appeared in 1966 in *Impulse* magazine.

Self-Help

A lot of people ask me, "Just how do you write a science fiction story?" Well, first, you sit down in front of a typewriter. Then, you put a clean sheet of paper in the typewriter. You begin to type. The words that appear on the paper sometimes become a story.

Fred Pohl

His best-known novels are *Indoctrinaire* (G.B., 1970); *Fugue for a Darkening Island* (G.B., 1972), a book about a near-future England bearing the brunt of an influx of displaced Africans; *Inverted World* (G.B., 1974), winner of the 1975 British Science Fiction Award; *The Space Machine* (G.B., 1976), the 1977 Ditmar award-winning novel based on missing plot constructions culled from H. G. WELLS's *The War of the Worlds* and *The Time Machine* and starring Wells; and *A Dream of Wessex* (G.B., 1977), published in the U.S. as *The Perfect Lover*.

RACKHAM, JOHN
(1916–76)

John Rackham is the pen name used by British writer John Thomas Phillifent for a host of sf and fantasy work. A former Royal Navy man and an engineer for the British Electrical Board,

he began penning sf in the 1950s, some of his most prominent titles being *Space Puppet* (1954), *Jupiter Equilateral* (1954), and *Master Weed* (1954). *Touch of Evil* (1963) was a reprise of Rackham's "Chappie Jones" stories originally written for *Science Fantasy*. Toward the latter part of his career, he divided his time between penning space operas and writing novels based on the popular TV series THE MAN FROM U.N.C.L.E. Among the space fantasies were *We, the Venusians* (1965), *The Double Invaders* (1967), *Alien Sea* (1968), and *The Proxima Project* (1968). His TV spy-thrillers include *The Mad Scientist Affair* (1966), *The Corfu Affair* (1967), and *The Power Cube Affair* (1968).

RAND, AYN
(1905–   )

Russian-born American novelist, playwright, and screenwriter Ayn Rand was a popular writer with American youth during the 1950s, espousing a literary philosophy that can charitably be termed right-wing. Best known for her mainstream fiction (e.g., *The Fountainhead*, 1943), she has occasionally dabbled within the genre to make her own philosophical points. *Anthem* (1938) takes place in a future postholocaust dystopia in which all individualism has been lost and the rights of the state are all-important. The protagonist discovers how to "look out for number one" and flees into a nearby forest with his heroine/flame. *Atlas Shrugged* (1957) spotlights the efforts of a group of people to ignore America's socialistic leanings. They flee to the mountains and watch the U.S.A. crumble under the weight of its liberal policies, vowing to return only when the government can be rebuilt along more objectivist lines.

REYNOLDS, MACK
(1917–   )

Mack Reynolds (the professional name used by Dallas McCord Reynolds) is obsessed with the future. The California-born writer, editor, world traveler, and socialist first was published in 1950 with *Fantastic Adventures'* "Isolationist." Very soon he was penning futuristic novels that showed a great deal of the shape of things to come couched in detective and/or thriller terminology. Some of his best-known works include *The Case of the Little Green Men* (1951), an sf detective novel; *The Earth War* (1963), a forecast of warfare to come; *Time Gladiator* (1966), which tells of a futuristic professor of Etruscan history entering the gladiatorial ring; and the series of futuristic novels dealing with Section G of the United Planets Organization: *Planetary Agent X* (1965), *Amazon Planet* (1967). *Dawnman Planet* (1966), *The Rival Rigelians* (1967), *Code Duello* (1968), and *Section G: United Planets* (1967). His short works can be found in *The Best of Mack Reynolds* (1976).

ROBINSON, SPIDER
(1948–   )

A new face in sf, Robinson is an sf critic and writer. In 1974 he was one of two neophytes awarded the John W. Campbell Memorial Award for best new writer. His first sf story (1973), "The Guy with the Eyes," served as the basis for a later collection of short stories, *Callahan's Crosstime Saloon* (1977). *Telempath* (1976) is a postholocaust tale featuring a hero out to destroy the man who actually began the final war. In 1975, Spider married Jeanne Corrigan, with whom he had collaborated on several works of late. In 1977 he won a Hugo for his novella "By Any Other Name," and in 1978 the twosome won a Hugo award for their 1977 Nebula-award-winning work "Stardance," which was expanded to novel form in 1979.

RODDENBERRY, GENE
(1926–   )

The fertile mind of writer/producer/screenwriter/director Gene Roddenberry has spawned one of the most awesome sociological phenomena to hit the youth culture in the 20th century . . . the STAR TREK TV show. At present *Star Trek* is the object of adulation by millions—a source of an almost religious experience for "trekkies" worldwide. Back in the 1960s, when Roddenberry first came up with the idea for the show, he believed he was merely creating an sf outlet for social criticism. Little did he know that soon

Gene Roddenberry

his modest space opera would become a best-selling media monster.

Roddenberry began his writing career while serving as an airline pilot after World War II. Following a traumatic crash, he emigrated to Los Angeles, where he took a post on the Los Angeles Police Department. During that time, he became advisor to the TV show *Dragnet*, eventually submitting scripts. Upon quitting the police force, he became a TV screenwriter, eventually rising to the rank of head writer on the popular Western series *Have Gun, Will Travel*.

In 1963, he produced the NBC-TV show *The Lieutenant*. Simultaneously, he penned a pilot for a proposed sf series based on his childhood hero, Captain Horatio Hornblower. The show, of course, was *Star Trek*. It ran from 1966 until 1969, but reached its zenith in popularity only while in syndication during the 1970s. Roddenberry contributed several pilots to TV during the 1970s, including GENESIS II, PLANET EARTH, THE QUESTOR TAPES, STRANGE NEW WORLD, and *Spectre*. Unfortunately, none of the shows went into series. In 1979, *Star Trek—The Motion Picture* was released, with Roddenberry's novelization published simultaneously.

RUSS, JOANNA
(1937–   )

New York-born writer and teacher Joanna Russ is most concerned with the more humanistic aspects of sf writing. Her stories are *people* stories deal-

Joanna Russ

ing with the reactions of ordinary men and women caught in extraordinary circumstances. Her first story, "Nor Custom Stale," appeared in *F&SF* in 1959.

Her first novel, *Picnic on Paradise*, published in 1968, is a strange tale concerning a group of tourists on the planet Paradise who are caught in the middle of a sudden corporate war; heroine Alyx must guide them to safety. *And Chaos Died* (1970) is about psi powers. In *The Female Man* (1975), a triumph of feminist fiction, the four protagonists—Janet, Jeannine, Joanna, and Alice—explore the various futuristic fates of women in the world. *We Who Are About To* (1977) is solid space opera.

In 1972 Joanna Russ won the Nebula award for best short story, "When It Changed."

RUSSELL, ERIC FRANK
(1905–78)

A longtime exponent of the genre, Eric Frank Russell began penning sf stories in the years prior to World War II. Influenced by the sf fan movement in Great Britain, he published his first story in 1937, "The Saga of Pelican West." He was soon regularly appearing in JOHN W. CAMPBELL's *ASF*, his career interrupted only by the war.

His first novel, *Sinister Barrier* (1943), which created quite a stir in fan circles, portrayed humans as being slaves in their everyday actions of alien globes called Vltons. The novel was based on an idea of Charles Fort. His

other novels include *Dreadful Sanctuary* (G.B., 1951); *Sentinels from Space* (1954); and *Men, Martians and Marchines* (1955), a unified collection of three long stories.

In 1955, Russell was awarded a Hugo for his story "Allamagoosa," one of the dozens of top-notch short fictions produced during his career. The full list includes "Symbiotica" (1941; one of his "Jay Score" series), "Hobbyist" (1947), "Dear Devil" (1950), "I Am Nothing" (1952), and "Diabologic" (1955). His short stories can be found in such collections as *Deep Space* (1954), *Far Stars* (1960), *Dark Tides* (1962), and *Somewhere a Voice* (1962, 1965).

SABERHAGEN, FRED
(1930–   )

A one-time editor of the *Encyclopedia Britannica*, Chicago-born Fred Saberhagen is best known for his half-crazed "Berserker" stories, tales of conflict between humans and large and lethal war machines. The stories were collected in the volume *Berserker* (1967), and spun off into the novels *Brother Berserker* (1969) and *Berserker's Planet* (1975).

Saberhagen published his first sf piece in 1961, in *Galaxy:* "Volume PAA-PYX." Since that time, he has offered such novels as *The Golden People* (1964), a psi and space-warfare tale; *The Water of Thought* (1965); *The Broken Lands* (1968) and *The Black Mountains* (1971), both about a mutant civilization of the future, and *Changeling Earth* (1973), a futuristic tale in which magic takes the place of science in society.

The Book of Saberhagen (1975) is a collection of some of his shorter works.

SAMALMAN, ALEXANDER
(1904–56)

Alexander Samalman was coached by writer/editor Frank Harris in the field of editing. Soon Samalman was an sf editor to be reckoned with. Working for Standard Magazines for over three decades, he edited, at different points during his career, *Thrilling Wonder Stories, Startling Stories,* and *Fantastic Story Magazine.* Coming into prominence in the early 1950s, he edited all three magazines in their last days. Within a year of his editorship, all the magazines had disappeared from the newsstands.

SERLING, ROD
(1924–75)

One of American TV's guiding lights, producer/screenwriter/playwright Rod Serling created the memorable TWI-LIGHT ZONE series, a long-running show that spotlighted creativity in the fields of writing, acting, and direction. Becoming a freelance writer following World War II, Serling contributed scripts to local radio and, subsequently, TV presentations. During the 1950s, his career soared and he became one of the fair-haired boys of the tube via such TV plays as *Patterns, Requiem for a Heavyweight,* and *The Comedian.*

In 1959 he offered the *Twilight Zone,* a weekly 30-minute anthology series that offered thought-provoking excursions into sf and fantasy. The show was the recipient of several Emmys and much misinterpretation on the part of

Rod Serling

the CBS network. The organization knew it had a critically acclaimed series but couldn't figure out why. After changing its time period and format a few times, the network let the show slide after five seasons. Serling tried once more with a whimsical series, NIGHT GALLERY (1972)—a show over which he had no control and which soon drifted into comic-book absurdity and hence oblivion.

Before his untimely death, Serling penned several genre screenplays, including *Seven Days in May* and the first draft of PLANET OF THE APES. He adapted a number of *Twilight Zone* scripts into book form under the titles *Stories from the Twilight Zone* (1960), *More Stories from the Twilight Zone* (1961), and *New Stories from the Twilight Zone* (1962). He edited such anthologies as *Witches, Warlocks and Werewolves* (1963), and *The Season to Be Wary* (1967).

SHAW, BOB
(1931–   )

Belfast-born Robert Shaw began writing short sf in the 1950s (his first work, "Aspect," appeared in a 1954 issue of *Nebula Science Fiction*) but did not attempt a novel until 1967, with *Nightwalk,* an eerie tale of a blind man sent to a planet of exile who constructs a device that allows him to "see" empathetically through the eyes of aliens and animals. *The Two-Timers* (1968) portrays a protagonist's search through an alternate universe for the double of his murdered wife. *Other Days, Other Eyes* (1972) tells of the discovery of "slow glass," a substance that retards light rays. *Ground Zero Man's* (1971) hero discovers a way to blow up all the Earth's nuclear weapons. *Orbitsville* (1975) tells of the discovery of an enigmatic alien artifact in space, and *A Wreath of Stars* (1976) portrays a strange planet *within* the planet Earth.

In 1966, Shaws "Light of Other Days" was nominated for a Nebula. Other works include *The Palace of Eternity* (1969), *The Shadow of Heaven* (1969), and *Medusa's Children* (1977). His short fiction can be found in *Tomorrow Lies in Ambush* (1973) and *Kaleidoscope* (1976).

SHECKLEY, ROBERT
(1928–   )

Robert Sheckley is a master of a brand of sf that is almost absurdist in nature. Tightly woven plots are littered with well-intentioned but exceedingly exasperated characters who are as vulnerable as they are heroic.

Best known for his short stories, the New York-born writer was first published in 1952 in *Imagination* with the short story "The Examination." Most of his first books were excellent collections of his equally outstanding short fiction. *Untouched by Human Hands* (1954), the first such collection, featured the best of his early work, including "The Monsters" and "The Seventh Victim." Subsequent collections include the titles *Citizen in Space* (1955), *Pilgrimage to Earth* (1958), *Notions Unlimited* (1960), *Store of Infinity* (1960), *Shards of Space* (1962), *The People Trap* (1968), and *Can You Feel Anything When I Do This?* (1971).

A master of the short sf story, Sheckley has also penned some truly remarkable novels. Perhaps the best known is the novelization of "The Seventh Victim," called *The Tenth Victim* (1966), a chilling tale of a futuristic lottery system in which humans both hunt and are hunted by their peers. Other novels include *Immortality Delivered* (1958), a story in which a long-dead accident victim is revived 150 years later; *The Status Civilization* (1960), a sociological send-up taking place on a prison planet; and *Crompton Divided* (1978), a wondrous journey into futuristic psychobabble in which our hero is a chap who has been literally divided into three separate people—now he'd like to stage a one-man family reunion, and the going is tough.

In 1979, Sheckley became fiction editor of *Omni* magazine.

SHELLEY, MARY WOLLSTONECRAFT
(1797–1851)

Wife of the British poet Percy Bysshe Shelley and daughter of feminist Mary Wollstonecraft and philosopher William Godwin, Mary Wollstonecraft Shelley penned the prototypical mad-scientist novel, *Frankenstein: or, The Modern Prometheus* (1818), which raised goose-bumps on thousands of unsuspecting readers and raised the status of the sf novel several leagues. The by-now classic tale portrayed the horrific results of experiments by Swiss scientist Frankenstein in creating artificial life. The "creation," a tormented innocent, is gradually driven to murder. When the creature slaughters Frankenstein's fiancée and brother, the maker turns on the monster and tracks him halfway across the globe.

A second sf work by Shelley, *The Last Man* (1826), takes place in the year 2073, when the human population has been wiped out by a global plague.

SHIEL M(ATTHEW) P(HIPPS)
(1865–1947)

An Irish author born in the West Indies and educated in London, Matthew Phipps Shiel was an inventive if somewhat racist writer who penned a number of works in the sf genre. *The Yellow Danger* (G.B., 1898) was essentially a jazzed-up Yellow Peril tale in which Great Britain is pitted against the Chinese in a war to end all wars. The British, of course, win the battle, nearly exterminating the Chinese. *The Purple Cloud* (1901) portrays a world laid waste by poisonous gas; the lone male survivor passes his free time by destroying everything in his path. *The Young Men Are Coming* (1937) is an exercise in Nietzschean philosophy in which a superman concept is expounded upon and science triumphs over religion. Other novels include *The Lord of the Sea* (1901) and *The Dragon* (1913). *The Purple Cloud* later served as the inspiration for the 1959 film THE WORLD, THE FLESH AND THE DEVIL.

SILVERBERG, ROBERT
(1936–   )

In less than two decades Robert Silverberg has written over 70 sf books (nearly 30 being novels), contributed over 200 uncollected short stories to the genre, and written dozens of related sf pieces. In 1956 he won a Hugo award as most promising new author. Another Hugo was awarded him for his novella "Nightwings" (1968), and Nebulas were given for *Time of Changes* (1971), "Passengers" (1968), "Good News from the Vatican," (1970) and "Born with the Dead" (1974). "The

Feast of St. Dionysus" (1972) won a Jupiter award, and *Nightwings* (1976) copped France's Prix Apollo award. In the mid-1970s he announced his retirement from the genre. In 1978, however, he announced his return with an epic fantasy novel, *Lord Valentine's Castle*. He chalked up his retirement to overwork and resentment over the fact that he had never written that "breakthrough book," despite his critical acclaim and popularity.

Born in New York and educated at Columbia University, Silverberg entered the field in 1954 with the short story "Gorgon Planet." His fiction showed a strong sense of imagination and vigor and was immediately accepted by the sf readership. Although his first novel, *Revolt on Alpha C* (1955), was clearly youth-oriented, he quickly moved to the adult genre.

Some of his best-known novels include *Recalled to Life* (1967), a frightening tale involving restored corpses; *To Open the Sky* (1967), a portrait of a trendy futuristic world; *Nightwings* (1969), in which one man survives an alien attack that levels all of Earth; *Up the Line* (1969), a twisted tale of time travel; *A Time of Changes* (1971), in which an alien experiments with Earth drugs; *Tower of Glass* (1970), a futuristic twist on the Tower of Babel; *The Second Trip* (1972), a study of an artificial being created by the combining of a criminal's body and a telepathic girl's mind; and *Dying Inside* (1972), a fascinating account of a telepath slowly losing his abilities.

Among his best short-story collections are *Next Stop the Stars* (1962), *Needle in a Timestack* (1966), *Dimension Thirteen* (1969), *Born with the Dead* (1974), *The Best of Robert Silverberg* (1976).

SIMAK, CLIFFORD D(ONALD)
(1904–   )

Born and raised in Wisconsin, Clifford D. Simak initially embarked on a career in journalism before turning to fiction. After studying journalism at the University of Wisconsin, he soon was working for local newspapers. He ventured into sf in 1931 with "World of the Red Sun," for *Wonder Stories*. He then stepped back from the genre, not really reentering until 1938, when he deluged *ASF* (under JOHN W. CAMPBELL's watchful eye) with such epic stories as "Rim of the Deep" (1940), "Reunion on Ganymede" (1938), "Hunch" (1943), and the incredibly popular "City" series, which began in 1944 with the publication of "City" and "Huddling Place." The "City" stories, as well as their sequels, portray a near-futuristic Earth in which intelligent dogs and robots are left to run abandoned cities. (The stories eventually were collected in *City*, 1952.)

Simak's reputation, at that point, was cemented. He wrote tales of simple folks surrounded by complex situations. In 1959 he won a Hugo for the novelette "The Big Front Yard," a whimsical tale whose hero finds his front yard transported to another planet. *Way Station* (1964), which picked up a Hugo for best novel, recounts the exploits of the human tender of an alien way-station.

Among his best-known books are *Empire* (1951), *Ring Around the Sun* (1953), *They Walked like Men* (1962), *Time Is the Simplest Thing* (1961), *Why Call Them Back from Heaven* (1967), *The Werewolf Principle* (1967), and *Cemetery World* (1973). Some of his best short stories can be found in *Strangers in the Universe* (1956), *The Worlds of Clifford Simak* (1960), *Worlds Without Flesh* (1964), and *The Best of Clifford D. Simak* (1975).

SIODMAK, CURT
(1902–   )

German-born Curt (originally spelled Kurt) Siodmak is best known as the author of the classic novel *Donovan's Brain* (1943), a tale in which the disembodied brain of a dead businessman is kept alive by a doctor who gradually falls under the brain's telepathic powers.

Siodmak began his writing career in Germany as a screenplay writer. His earliest works include F.P.I. DOES NOT REPLY (his 1932 movie script was based on his 1930 novel) and THE TUNNEL (1933). With the coming of the Nazi Party, Siodmak emigrated to the U.S., where he quickly established himself as a top-notch horror and sf screenwriter, offering such popular films as THE IN-

VISIBLE MAN RETURNS (1939), THE INVISIBLE WOMAN (1941), *Son of Dracula* (1942), FRANKENSTEIN MEETS THE WOLFMAN (1943), I WALKED WITH A ZOMBIE (1943), HOUSE OF FRANKENSTEIN (1944), THE LADY AND THE MONSTER (1944; based on his novel *Donovan's Brain*), THE BEAST WITH FIVE FINGERS (1953), and THE CREATURE WITH THE ATOM BRAIN (1955).

His novels include *Skyport* (1959), *Hauser's Memory* (1970; a semisequel to *Donovan's Brain*, with a similar theme), *The Third Ear* (1971), and *City in the Sky* (1974).

Siodmak has also directed several films, including *Bride of the Gorilla* (1951) and THE MAGNETIC MONSTER (1953).

SMITH, CORDWAINER
(1913–66)

Sf's most mysterious figure, the pseudonym Cordwainer Smith belonged to the secretive writer Paul Myron Anthony Linebarger, a professor specializing in Asiatic studies at Johns Hopkins University. A master of spacey fantasy, "Smith" contributed his first short story to the genre in *Fantasy Book*, "Scanners Live in Vain" (1950).

Most of Smith's work concerns the state of humanity some 10,000 years hence, when the planets are ruled by an Instrumentality of Lords and Ladies. Simultaneously, a group of underpeople—animals biologically altered into half-human slaves—stages a gradual rebellion. Smith's short stories can be found in the collections *You Will Never Be the Same* (1963), *Space Lords* (1965), *Under Old Earth* (1970), and *Stardreamer* (1971).

His novels include *The Planet Buyer* (1964), *Guest of Three Worlds* (1966), and *The Underpeople* (1968).

SMITH E(DWARD) E(LMER) ("DOC")
(1890–1965)

American writer, chemist, bus conductor, and lumberjack "Doc" Smith is affectionately remembered as the "Father of the Space Opera." Born in Wisconsin, Smith began work on his first serial (a novel, actually) in 1914, finishing it in 1920. *The Skylark of Space* (as it was published in novel form in

1946) was an epic space opera featuring a hero/scientist fighting spacey evil in a series of shoot-'em-up situations. Unfortunately, in 1920 there was no outlet for such a sprawling sf scenario. The work waited eight years to be published, eventually appearing in *AS*.

A second novel, *The Spacehounds of IPC* (1931), was less spacey and hence less popular with Doc Smith's fans. (*Spacehounds* was released in book form in 1947.) Two years later, Doc sped across the galaxy once more with *Triplanetary* (book form, 1948), the novel that originated the "Lensman" series. Most of the "Lensman" books concern the exploits of Kim Kinnison and his flame, Clarissa MacDougall, who, in a future in which the good Arisians fight with the evil Eddorians, are the Adam and Eve of a new race of Arisians who are destined finally to defeat the Eddorians. Books in this series include *First Lensman* (1950), *Galactic Patrol* (1950), *Gray Lensman* (1951), *Second-Stage Lensman* (1953), *Children of the Lens* (1954), and *The Vortex Blaster* (1960).

Smith's "Skylark" series includes *Skylark Three* (1948), *Skylark of Valeron* (1949), and *Skylark DuQuesne* (1967). Other Smith titles include *Subspace Explorers* (1965), *The Galaxy Primes* (1965), and *The Best of E. E. "Doc" Smith* (1975).

SPINRAD, NORMAN (RICHARD)
(1940–   )

A New York–born literary-agent-turned-writer, Norman Spinrad first came into prominence during the mid-to-late 1960s, as a mainstay of the New Wave movement. His controversial and unorthodox approach to the genre, replete with rampant violence and overt sex scenes, won him instant popularity. After three novels, *The Solarians* (1966), *Agent of Chaos* (1967), and *The Men in the Jungle* (1967), he reached his stride with *Bug Jack Barron* (1969), a novel that was alternately praised to the heavens and condemned to the hot joint below because of its profanity, etc. The story of futuristic TV figure Jack Barron, the novel painted a vivid, albeit tainted, picture of a dystopian, hyped-up U.S.A. to come.

Other novels include *Riding the Torch* (1978), which won a Jupiter award in 1975 as best novella of the year, and *The Iron Dream* (1972). His short fiction can be found in *No Direction Home* (1975) and *The Last Hurrah of the Golden Horde* (1970).

STAPLEDON (WILLIAM) OLAF
(1886–1950)

A British doctor of philosophy who often lectured at Liverpool University, William Olaf Stapledon wrote sprawling, imaginative sf tales that can only be termed mind-boggling. Most Stapledonian fiction resembled Cecil B. De Mille space scenarios. Although they were always thought-provoking (at times, profound), meticulously plotted, and energetically written, for some odd reason his books are seldom read today.

A pacifist and a socialist, Stapledon embarked on his intellectualistic sf career with *Last and First Men* (1930), a book that tells the history of humanity from creation to the point, some 2,000 million years to come, when the last human dies, on Neptune. On a smaller, yet not less impressive scale, *Odd John* (1935) recounts the exploits of an intellectual and physical mutant who is, quite literally, a superman to end all supermen.

Stapledon returned to future histories with *Star Maker* (1937), a narrative that recounts the complete history of the universe, and all its denizens therein. *Sirius*, Stapledon's 1944 followup book, again took the author to a less grandiose setting, though an equally imaginative one; it tells of a dog gifted with advanced intelligence.

Other novels included *Last Men in London* (1932), *The Flames* (1947; a tale of aliens originally from the sun), *Death into Life* (1946), *Darkness and the Light* (1944), and *Old Man and New World* (1944). *A Man Divided* (1950) is a novel with autobiographical overtones.

STURGEON, THEODORE
(1918–   )

A remarkably gifted writer just as at home in the fantasy genre as in sf, Theodore Sturgeon has contributed countless short stories to the genre, as well as quite a few novels of note. Born in New York as Edward Hamilton Waldo (Sturgeon is his stepfather's surname), Sturgeon puttered about in trapeze artistry, bulldozer driving, and hotel work before turning to writing as a full-time occupation.

His first sf story, "Ether Breather," appeared in JOHN W. CAMPBELL's *ASF* in 1939. Sturgeon soon became one of the driving forces behind Campbell's publication, contributing such stories to the magazine as "It," a tale concerning a life-form that gathers around a human skeleton and gives it a sense of life. Later stories of a frightening and/or controversial nature include "Baby Is Three" (1952); "The World Well Lost," (1953), a story of alien homosexuals; "Claustrophile" (1956), which is about the adolescence of an alien being; and "Slow Sculpture" (1970), a Hugo and Nebula award-winner.

He is best known for his classic novel of 1953, *More Than Human*, a wonderfully written adventure yarn advancing the idea of "homo *gestalt*"—a human entity composed of many individual parts, in this case of many beings somewhat less than whole physically. It won the International Fantasy Award of 1954.

Other novels include *The Dreaming Jewels* (1950), the story of a runaway who joins the circus only to find that he is somewhat more than human; *The Cosmic Rape* (1958), in which an alien presence invades the Earth and inadvertently betters the species; *Venus Plus X* (1960), a novel concerning a utopian society composed of voluntarily produced hermaphrodites; and *Voyage to the Bottom of the Sea* (1961), a novelization of the impressive film.

His short stories can be found in

Mr. Clean
I don't use dope. I don't drink. I'm not into religion. I'm not interested in est. I'm a very pragmatic dude. For me, the act of creating, the act of building a dream, is the most exciting thing I could possibly do. Writing, for me, is a holy chore.
Harlan Ellison

Sturgeon in Orbit (1964), *Beyond* (1960), and *Sturgeon's West* (1973's collection of Western stories), as well as in the early volumes *Without Sorcery* (1954), *E. Pluribus Unicorn* (1953), *Caviar* (1955), and *A Way Home* (1955).

J

TEMPLE, WILLIAM F(REDERICK) (1914–   )

British author William F. Temple once shared an apartment with young ARTHUR C. CLARKE. Later on, he would share a similar career, giving up his work on the London Stock Exchange for the world of sf. His best-known work, "Four Sided Triangle" (*AS*, 1939; novelization, 1949), concerns an eternal romantic triangle that is given a fourth side when one of the two smitten male scientists artificially duplicates the woman in question; unfortunately, the duplicate woman loves the same man as the prototype. Other novels include *The Automated Goliath* (1962), *Battle on Venus* (1963), *Shoot at the Moon* (1966), and *The Fleshpots of Sansato* (1968).

His juvenile titles include *Martin Magnus, Planet Rover* (1954), *Martin Magnus on Venus* (1955) and *Martin Magnus on Mars* (1956).

TIPTREE, JAMES, JR. (1915–   )

Long thought to be a reclusive male writer, James Tiptree, Jr., was revealed, in 1977, to be the alter ego of psychologist Alice B. Sheldon. Born in Chicago, Tiptree—or Sheldon, if you please —spent much of her youth in India and Africa and later traveled in the service of the American government. Tiptree's first sf effort, "Birth of a Salesman," was published in a 1968 issue of *ASF*. "The Milk of Paradise" caused quite a stir when published in the collection *Again, Dangerous Visions* (ed. by HAR-LAN ELLISON) the same year. In 1973

Tiptree won a Nebula for "Love Is the Plan, the Plan Is Death," a second Nebula in 1976 for "Houston, Houston, Do You Read?" (a story that also garnered a Jupiter and shared a Hugo for best novella), and a Hugo in 1974 for the novella "The Girl Who Was Plugged In" (1973).

Her short stories can be found in *Ten Thousand Light-Years from Home* (1973) and *Warm Worlds and Otherwise* (1975). Her first novel, *Up the Walls of the World* (1978) is a multileveled space adventure.

TREMAINE, F(REDERICK) ORLIN (1899–1956)

American sf editor and publisher, F. Orlin Tremaine entered the world of publishing shortly after his graduation from Valparaiso University. He became editor of *ASF* in October 1933, bringing out some 50 issues and making the magazine the leader in the field. Leaving *ASF* in 1937, he assumed editorial control of many other of *ASF*'s parent corporation's (Street and Smith) magazines.

In 1940 he founded his own publishing company and launched the short-lived *Comet Stories*. He retired from sf in the late 1940s but continued to work in the publishing business.

TUBB, E(DWIN) C(HARLES) (1919–   )

A British writer and editor famous for his enjoyable space operas, long-time sf fan E. C. Tubb began writing in the 1950s (his first story, "No Short Cuts," was published in *New Worlds* in 1951) and, by 1956, was editor of *Authentic Science Fiction*. Writing under both his own name and more than 50 pseudonyms, he has penned an amazing number of short stories and novels.

His first novels were all pseudonymous. *Saturn Patrol* (1951) was by King Lang, *Planetfall* (1951) by Gill Hunt, *Argentis* (1952) by Brian Shaw, and *Alien Universe* (1952) by Volested Gridban. Under his own name, he offered such works as *The Space Born* (1956), a book that takes place on a massive starship; *Moon Base* (1964), a solid space-opera; *Death Is a Dream* (1967), a tale taking three 20th-century humans into a dire future after a bout with suspended animation; and *Escape from Space* (1969).

Also popular are his "Dumarist" books, a series of 17 novels featuring spacefaring Earl Dumarist, a futuristic fellow trying to find his home planet, Earth. The series began in 1967 with the *Winds of Gath* and is still popular today.

VANCE, JACK
(1920–   )

Born in San Francisco and educated at the University of California, John Holbrook Vance has studied mining engineering, physics, and journalism, worked on construction sites, and played in numerous local jazz bands. He turned to sf writing in 1945, with the publication of "The World Thinker" in *Thrilling Wonder Stories*. He is known as a prolific novel writer and has won two Hugos, for *The Dragon Masters* (1963) and "The Last Castle" (1967), which also netted him a Nebula. Among his best-known novels are *The Space Pirate* (1953), *Big Planet* (1957) and *The Languages of Pao* (1958).

He has also penned a number of interconnected books in series formats. One trilogy is composed of *The Star King* (1964), *The Killing Machine* (1964), and *The Palace of Love* (1967). His "Durdane" trilogy consists of *The Anome* (1971), *The Brave Free Men* (1972), and *The Asutra* (1973). Futuristic hero Adam Reith is featured in *Servants of the Wankh* (1969), *The Dirdir* (1969), and *The Pnume* (1970).

Some of his early short stories can be found in the collection *The Dying Earth* (1950).

VAN VOGT, A(LFRED) E(LTON)
(1912–   )

Alfred Elton van Vogt is a writer obsessed with formulas. He looks for the best possible way to structure a novel

or a story and then religiously adheres to the pattern. His best-known book, a classic of the genre, is *Slan* (1946), the tale of telepathic mutant Jommy Cross and his fight for freedom.

Canadian Van Vogt first entered the sf field as an expectant writer-to-be mesmerized by JOHN W. CAMPBELL'S creative *ASF*. His first story, "Black Destroyer," was published in 1939. During the next decade, he would write nearly 40 sf stories, most of them highly complex and intellectual space operas.

Among van Vogt's best-known novels are *The World of Null-A* (1948) and its sequel, *The Pawns of Null-A* (1956). The two books take place in the year 2560 A.D., when the majority of the population is trained in Null-A, the science of General Semantics. Enter hero Gilbert Gosseyn with some very existential questions, and there's trouble, right there in Null-A city.

The Voyage of the Space Beagle (1950) recounts the exploits of a survey spaceship. *The Weapon Makers* (1946) and *The Weapon Shops of Isher* (1951) profile the adventures of immortal Robert Hedrock, the creator of the Weapons Shops themselves. Other notable works of van Vogt's include *The House That Stood Still* (1950), *The Mind Cage* (1958), *Children of Tomorrow* (1970), and *Darkness on Diamondia* (1972).

His short works can be found in *Planets for Sale,* written with his wife, E. MAYNE HULL; (1954), *The Far-Out Worlds of A. E. van Vogt,* and *The Best of A. E. van Vogt* (1968 and 1970).

VARLEY, JOHN H(ERBERT)
(1947–   )

A new writer on the American sf scene, Nebula award-winner (1979) John Varley is best known for his strange novel *The Ophiuchi Hotline* (1977). Taking place during a time when humanity is doomed to roam the stars, the story centers on geneticist Lilo, who is condemned to die for her experiments. By cloning herself, however, she seeks to avoid her fate. *The Persistence of Vision* (1978) continued Varley's career in an imaginative vein.

VERNE, JULES
(1828–1905)

Considered by many to be the "Father of Science Fiction," Jules Gabriel Verne was born in Nantes, a seaport town—a fact that greatly affected the color of his later literary works. He began his literary career in 1851 with "A Voyage in a Balloon." Obsessed with machinery and the wonders of the industrial age, Verne soon introduced amazing gadgetry in his works. *Five Weeks in a Balloon* (1863) was a glorification of the hot-air balloon. *Journey to the Center of the Earth* (1864) was a lost-world epic. *From the Earth to the Moon* and *Round the Moon* (1865 and 1870) were tales of spaceflight, with the Baltimore Gun Club firing its rocketship from a large cannon.

Verne's fascination with the work of E. A. POE surfaced in *The Ice Sphinx* (1897), a semisequel to Poe's *Arthur Gordon Pym*. The *Steam House* (1880) was a tale of steam-driven inventions . . . including an automated elephant. *20,000 Leagues Under the Sea* (1870) introduced the daring submarine commander Capt. Nemo to the world. The Captain proved so popular that he reappeared in *The Mysterious Island* (1875). *Hector Servadac, or Off on a Comet* (1877) tore a chunk off the Earth and placed it on a passing comet, carrying the hapless Earthling on said chunk deep into space. *The Clipper of the Clouds* (1886) featured the airborne counterpart of inventor Nemo in Robur, the master of a 100-foot-long propeller-driven airship. Robur, a little spaced-out, returned years later in *Master of the World* (1904). *Propeller Island* (1895) placed intrigue on a superfloating city. *For the Flag* (1896) featured a mad scientist out to sink ships via guided missiles.

Starting off on a rather idealistic tone, Verne finished his literary career writing in pessimistic, pensive prose. Many of Verne's best sf novels practically define the fine art of inventions, and most of his inventors, even the maddest ones, have the good of the world at heart at the outset.

VONNEGUT, KURT, JR.
(1922–   )

Smile when you call him an sf writer.

Author Kurt Vonnegut really hates to be lumped into the sf genre, although much of his work seems to stray in that direction. The brilliantly satirical style of Vonnegut is, perhaps, best known via *Slaughterhouse Five* (1969), whose main character, Billy Pilgrim, comes unstuck in time and makes his way from the bombing of Dresden during World War II to safety in outer space.

Vonnegut himself witnessed the Dresden holocaust from his position as a prisoner of war in that town. Born in Indianapolis and educated at Cornell University and the University of Chicago, Vonnegut turned to writing in the early 1950s, offering pieces for *Collier's* and *Galaxy*. Soon he was writing novels. *Player Piano* (1952) depicts a dystopian U.S. in the near future. *The Sirens of Titan* (1959) presents Earth history as the plaything of the alien Tralfamadorians. *Cat's Cradle* (1963) displays the ultimate weapon, "icenine," a substance that can crystallize all the water on planet Earth. *Breakfast of Champions* (1973) recounts the woeful existence of a recurring Vonnegut character, sf writer Kilgore Trout (ol' Kilgore, dismissed in *Breakfast*, unexpectedly turns up as a convict in 1979's *Jailbird* . . . and so it goes).

Vonnegut's style is deceptively simple in structure, yet complex in ideology. He has a tendency to pinpoint the foibles of the world and stress them with a shrug of the shoulders.

Other Vonnegut books include *God Bless You, Mr. Rosewater* (1965), *Mother Night* (1961), *Slapstick* (1976), *Welcome to the Monkey House* (1968), and *Wampeters, Foma and Granfalloons* (1974).

WATSON, IAN
(1943–   )

A British writer and teacher with an interest in language, philosophy, and the future, Ian Watson mixes intellectualism with imagination, producing ofttimes heady results. His first foray into the genre took place in 1969, with the publication of "Roof Garden Under Saturn," in *New Worlds*. Since that time, he has written quite a few short stories and novels.

The Embedding (1973) is a book obsessed with linguistics. Aliens, an anthropologist, and members of a remote Brazilian tribe all somehow combine their knowledge in a story that searches for the ultimate root language. *The Jonah Kit* (1975) describes the findings of a spacefaring, manmade whale; earth, it seems, is a mere echo of reality. Hmmmm.

The Martian Inca (1977) takes a crew of a returning Russian Mars probe and strands them in the jungles of Bolivia, surrounded by curious Incas. Other books include *Alien Embassy* (1977), *Orgasmachine* (France; 1976), *The Miracle Visitors* (1978), and the juvenile book *Japan: A Cat's Eye View* (1969).

WEINBAUM, STANLEY G(RAUMAN) (1900–35)

The alien's best friend, Stanley Weinbaum, took the juvenile image of the bug-eyed alien and gave it intelligence and more importantly, dignity and a sense of compassion. An American who started off in mainstream fiction, Weinbaum's first submission to the sf pulps, "A Martian Odyssey," printed in *Wonder Stories* in 1934, caused an instant sensation in terms of both editorial considerations and reader response. In it, an Earthman encounters a Martian creature, Tweel, who becomes a faithful companion and eventually a well-loved friend.

Weinbaum was an instant hit, with further stories appearing every month in either *Wonder* or *ASF*. Other stories include "The Lotus Eaters," "The Man Moon," "Flight on Titan," "Parasite Planet," "The Worlds of If," "The Ideal," and "The Point of View" (all but the last story being published in 1935, "Point of View" appearing in 1936).

Weinbaum died suddenly in 1935, just as his career had begun to soar. His work has been collected in such anthologies as *Dawn of Flame and Other Stories* (1936), *A Martian Odyssey and Others* (1949), and *The Best of Stanley G. Weinbaum* (1974). His posthumously published novels are *The New Adam* (1939), *The Dark Other* (1950), and *The Black Flame* (1948).

WELLMAN, MANLEY WADE (1903–   )

Born in West Africa and educated in the U.S., Manley Wade Wellman came into prominence during the pulp-magazine heyday. Best known for his fantasy work, Wellman has also produced some "straight" sf tales. His first sf effort, "When Planets Crashed," appeared in *Wonder Stories Quarterly* in 1931. One of his most enjoyable pulp series was that consisting of a number of stories about John the Minstrel, an Appalachian witchcraft-fighter armed with a silver-stringed guitar who turned up in the 1960s in *F&SF*.

Among his best-known sf books are *The Beasts from Beyond* (1950; an alternate-world adventure), *The Devil's Planet* (1951; Martian intrigue), *Twice in Time* (1957; a backward leap into Renaissance Italy); *Giants from Eternity* (1959), *Island in the Sky* (1961), and *Sherlock Holmes' War of the Worlds* (1975). Coauthored by his son Wade Wellman, the latter book places the famous fictional detective in the middle of the H. G. WELLS story of alien invasion.

His short fiction can be found in *Who Fears the Devil?* (1963) and *Worse Things Waiting* (1973).

WELLS, H(ERBERT) G(EORGE) (1866–1946)

The son of a gardener-turned-shopkeeper and a house servant, Herbert George Wells was, as a youth, a dreamer and a lover of science. Born in Bromley, on the outskirts of London, he was encouraged to enter the tailoring trade. A scholarship, however, took him from the Midhurst Grammar school to the Normal School of Science in London, where he studied under Darwinist biologist Thomas Henry Huxley. Wells attempted teaching but ill health drove him to writing. By 1893 he was freelancing, offering such early tales as "The Man of the Year Million" and "The Advent of the Flying Man."

H. G. Wells

He soon turned to longer works, coming up with some of the classics of the genre. *The Time Machine* (1895) took a British inventor far into the future for a fairly ominous look at where the foibles of humans could lead civilization. *The Island of Dr. Moreau* (1896) presented a detailed portrait of man-of-science Moreau, a chap who, on a deserted island, is attempting to create surgically a new race of humans from jungle animals.

The Invisible Man (1897) tells of the discovery of a serum for invisibility and the dire ramifications it has for its hapless inventor. *The War of the Worlds* (1898) gives the scenario for what is perhaps the ultimate alien-invasion book. In *When the Sleeper Wakes* (1899), the hero dozes into a dystopian future in which he finds himself revered as a long-lost messiah; the book ends on a most disturbing note as the hero commits suicide in a dog-fight high above a futuristic city.

The First Men in the Moon (1901) took readers and several Englishmen below the surface of the moon and into the land of the Selenites, courtesy of Professor Cavor's gravity-defying substance, cavorite. *The Food of the Gods and How It Came to Earth* (1904) mixed socialism with science, as the creation of growth-inducing "boom-food" creates a separate Earth civilization of giants. *A Modern Utopia* (1905)—politics disguised as sf—displays perfection in a parallel Earth. In *In the Days of the Comet* (1906), humanity finds world peace because of a gas emitted into the atmosphere from a passing comet's tail.

The War in the Air (1908) is a grim prediction of massive aerial combat. *The World Set Free* (1914) forecasts atomic war. *Men like Gods* (1923) involves yet another trip into a utopian atmosphere. *Mr. Blettsworthy on Rampole Island* (1928) recounts the imaginary problems encountered by day-dreaming Blettsworthy and a tribe of uncivilized natives. *The Work, Wealth and Happiness of Mankind* (1931) is an impressive two-volume speculative history of the human race.

The Shape of Things to Come (1933) forecasts the future of the Earth. *The Croquet Player* (1936) portrays a sportsman haunted by visions of his prehistoric past. *Star-Begotten* (1938) has humanity bettering itself via the interference of "happy rays" from Mars. *The Camford Visitation* (1937) features a disembodied voice quite upsetting the routine of a college campus life-style. *The Holy Terror* (1939) portrays a world overcome by fascism.

By the end of his career, Wells was recognized as a British institution and, as such, was not taken all that seriously. His later works betray a tendency to ramble, often into passage upon passage of socialistic sermonizing, and they were sparse in terms of action. Still, Wells remains probably the strongest influence in the shaping of sf.

Throughout the period of time in which he contributed his finest novels, he continued to offer thought-provoking and tightly woven short stories, including "The Empire of the Ants" (1905); "The Land Ironclads" (1903), a tale that predicted the invention of the armored tank; and "The Man Who Could Work Miracles" (1898). His short stories can be found in *The Complete Short Stories of H. G. Wells* (1927).

During his last years, Wells became very interested in the possibilities that motion pictures offered to storytelling. Wells himself scripted THINGS TO COME

(1935), based on *The Shape of Things to Come*); and *The Man Who Could Work Miracles,* a delightful farce lensed in 1935.

Some of Wells's most interesting works of nonfiction are *The Outline of History* (1920), *Where the World Is Going: Guesses and Forecasts of the World Ahead* (1928), *The Science of Life* (with Julian Huxley; 1930); *The Fate of Homo Sapiens* (1939), and *The New World Order* (1939). A revealing work about the master craftsman is *Experiment in Autobiography* (1934).

WHITE, TED
(1938–   )

American writer and editor Ted White first came into prominence as an sf fan extraordinaire by winning a Hugo in 1968 as the best fan writer. His first short story, a collaborative effort with MARION ZIMMER BRADLEY, "Phoenix," appeared in *AS* in 1963. His novels include *Invasion from 2500* (with TERRY CARR under the pseudonym Norman Edwards; 1964), *Lost in Space* (based on the TV series, a collaborative effort with Dave van Arnam under the pseudonym Ron Archer; 1967), *The Android Avenger* (1965), *Phoenix Prime* (1966), *The Sorceress of Qar* (1966), *The Secret of the Marauder Satellite* (1967), *The Spawn of the Death Machine* (1968), and *Furies Possessed* (1970).

He was assistant editor of *F&SF* from 1963 to 1968. In 1969, he became editor of *AS* and of *Fantastic.* In 1979 he assumed the editorship of *Heavy Metal,* an sf comic-strip magazine.

WILHELM, KATE
(1928–   )

One of the finest storytellers ever to grace the genre, Kate Wilhelm was first published in 1956, with the story "The Pint Size Genie," which appeared in *Fantastic.* She is best known for her short stories, some of the finest of which can be found in the collections *Andover and the Android* (1966), *The Mile-Long Spaceship* (1963), *The Downstairs Room and Other Speculative Fiction* (1968), and *The Infinity Box* (1975). In 1968 she won a Nebula for the story "The Planners."

Her novel *Where Late the Sweet Birds Sang* (1976), which won both a Hugo and a Nebula, offers a tale taking place in a community of clones. Other novels include *The Clone* (1965), *Abyss* (1971), *The Killing Thing* (1967), *The Clewiston Test* (1976), and *Fault Lines* (1977).

WILLIAMSON, JACK
(1908–   )

A master of the space opera, Arizona-born John Steward Williamson traveled with his family at a very early age, via covered wagon, to the state of New Mexico. While growing up on a homestead, he became obsessed with literature. He began writing early, and his first sf story appeared shortly after his 20th birthday: "The Metal Man," published in *AS* in 1928. Williamson soon became a familiar byline in the publication, offering an endless sea of space serials. Following World War II, he returned to school, taking a Ph.D. in English at the University of Colorado and becoming an English professor specializing in sf.

Some of his best-known books are derived from his earlier sf pulp serials. These include *The Legion of Space* (1947), *The Cometeers* (1950), and *The Legion of Time* (1952). Other novels include *Dome Around America* (1955); *Seetee Shock* (1950) and *Seetee Ship* (1951), two books of antimatter exploits written under the pseudonym Will Stewart; *Darker Than You Think* (1948), a science versus lycanthropy story; *Dragon's Island* (1951), *Star Bridge* (with JAMES GUNN, 1955), and *The Moon Children.* He has often collaborated with FRED POHL, coming up with such titles as *The Reefs of Space* (1964), *Starchild* (1965), and *Rogue Star* (1969). His short fiction can be found in *The Pandora Effect* (1969) and *People Machines* (1971).

WOLLHEIM, DONALD A(LLEN)
(1914–   )

An sf fan in the 1930s, New Yorker Donald A. Wollheim later transplanted his fannish enthusiasm for the genre into his professional life, becoming one of sfdom's most important editors and anthologists. As a writer, he first entered the professional field in 1934, with *Wonder Stories*' "The Man from

Ariel." Not for another decade, however, did he publish short fiction regularly, with most of his novels appearing in the 1950s and 1960s, including the juvenile "Mike Mars" series. In 1941 he assumed editorship of *Stirring Science Stories* and *Cosmic Stories*, two pulps that were not long for this (or any other) world.

After World War II, he moved on to Avon Books, where he edited the *Avon Fantasy Reader* and the *Avon Science Fiction Reader*, among other titles. He moved to Ace Books in 1952, and for two decades served as Ace's sf editor. In 1972 he started Daw Books.

Among his best-known anthologies are *The Pocket Book of Science Fiction* (1943; one of the first paperback collections ever), *Portable Novels of Science* (1945), *Flight into Space* (1950), *The End of the World* (1956), *Men on the Moon* (1958), *More Adventures on Other Planets* (1963), and *Operation: Phantasy* (1967).

WRIGHT, FARNSWORTH
(1888–1940)

American editor of *Weird Tales* who helmed that magazine from 1924 until his death in 1940. Some of his early protégés were RAY CUMMINGS, David H. Keller, and MURRAY LEINSTER.

WRIGHT, S(YDNEY) FOWLER
(1874–1965)

A prolific British writer of mysteries, the editor of *Poetry* magazine, and a biographer of Sir Walter Scott, S. Fowler Wright also treaded on sf literary ground. His sf novels include *The World Below* (1924), *The Amphibians* (1929), *Deluge* (1928), *The Island of Captain Sparrow* (1928), *Dawn* (1929), *The Secret of the Screen* (1933; an sf mystery), *The War of 1938* (1935), *The Adventure of Whyndham Smith* (1938), and *Spiders' War* (1954).

WYLIE, PHILIP
(1902–71)

A well-respected American mainstream author before he entered the sf field, Philip Wylie became one of the U.S.'s most outrageous and/or hated literary figures in the land with his chauvinistic tomes *The Savage Gentleman* (1932) and *Generation of Vipers*

(a 1942 attack on "Momism"). He entered the sf genre in 1930 with the novel *Gladiator,* a "superhuman" tale that served as the basis of the *Superman* cartoon strip. *When Worlds Collide* (written with Edwin Balmer in 1932 and filmed in 1951) told of the end of the world as we know it, but in *After Worlds Collide* (again with Balmer; 1934), the tale is given a happy ending. *The Disappearance* (1951) separates the two sexes and sends each into its own separate world, with astonishing results. *Tomorrow!* (1964) and *Triumph* (1963) are two "look out for nuclear warfare" novels. *The End of the Dream* (1972) is an ecological-disaster scenario.

Wylie also penned the screenplay for THE ISLAND OF LOST SOULS (1932) and the ecological-disaster episode L.A. 2017 for the NBC-TV series *The Name of the Game.*

WYNDHAM, JOHN
(1903–69)

John Wyndham is the work name often used by British writer John Wyndham Parkes Lucas Beynon Harris. Born in Warwickshire and educated at Bedales School, Wyndham tried everything from farming to advertising before opting for a career as a writer during the 1930s. His first sf story, "Worlds to Barter," appeared in a 1931 issue of *Wonder Stories,* and his earliest novels, *The Secret People* and *Stowaway to Mars,* in 1935 and 1937. It was not until the 1950s, however, that he emerged as a novelist to be reckoned with worldwide.

The Day of the Triffids (1951) is a gripping account of an invasion of Earth by mobile, man-sized plants. Following a meteor storm, the population of Earth is blinded. Enter the spacefaring plants, who intend to take over the planet, killing the blinded citizenry one by one.

The Kraken Wakes (1953) describes the efforts of a group of extraterrestrials hidden beneath the sea to melt the polar ice caps and flood the Earth. *The Chrysalids* (1955) is a postcataclysm tale. *The Midwich Cuckoos* (1957) describes, with chilling detail, the effects of a small group of mutant children with terrifying mental prowess on a small British town. *The Outward Urge* (1959) comprises a series of short stories about the spacefaring Troon family. *Chocky* (1968) is a spooky story of a boy in mental link with an alien child.

Other Wyndham books include *The Trouble with Lichen* (1960), *Sleepers of Mars* (1973), *Wanderers of Time* (1973), *The Seeds of Time* (1956), and *The Best of John Wyndham* (1973).

ZELAZNY, ROGER
(1937–   )

First published in the early 1960s, American author Roger Zelazny leaped into the limelight in 1965, winning two Nebulas for his stories "He Who Shapes" and "The Doors of His Face, the Lamps of His Mouth." He quickly established himself as a prolific novel writer, offering both intellectual and two-fisted-action tales. In the first category, *Lord of Light* (1967's Hugo winner) takes Hindu culture and religion and places it on an alien world. In the latter category, 1969's *Damnation Al-*

ley is a sprawling survival-tale set in a postnuke Earth populated by nasty mutants.

The Dream Master (1966) offers a terrifying glimpse of dream analysis taken to the ultimate level. *Creatures of Light and Darkness* (1969) mixes mythology with fantasy. The "Amber" series takes place on the planet Amber, a world ruled by squabbling siblings; the series includes *Nine Princes in Amber* (1970), *The Guns of Avalon* (1972), *Sign of the Unicorn* (1975), and *The Hand of Oberon* (1976).

General Confusion
Our nation, our world, desperately needs more generalists. It's a matter of human survival, I think. We need people who are busy building overviews. People who say, "The king is naked!"

Frank Herbert

Doorways in the Sand (1976) is a send-up of the space-opera motif, with aliens getting involved in a blackmail plot. His short fiction can be found in *Four for Tomorrow* (1967) and *The Doors of His Face, The Lamps of His Mouth, and Other Stories* (1971). In addition to winning a Hugo for *Lord of Light*, Zelazny won a best-novel award for 1965's *And Call Me Conrad*.

AWARDS
MAGAZINES
THEMES

OSCARS IN SPACE

Although plentiful and popular for many years, sf films have not garnered all that many Academy Awards. The following is a list of spacey Oscars awarded to out-of-this-world motion pictures.

SPECIAL EFFECTS
1950: *Destination Moon*, Eagle-Lion.
1951: *When Worlds Collide*, Paramount.
1953: *The War of the Worlds*, Paramount.
1954: *20,000 Leagues Under the Sea*, Walt Disney Studios.
1960: *The Time Machine*, Galaxy Films/MGM.

SPECIAL VISUAL EFFECTS
1965: John Stears for *Thunderball*, UA.
1966: Art Cruickshank for *Fantastic Voyage*, 20th Cent.-Fox.
1968: Stanley Kubrick for *2001: A Space Odyssey*, Polaris Productions/ MGM.
1969: Robbie Robertson for *Marooned*, Columbia.

SOUND EFFECTS
1964: Norman Westfall for *Goldfinger*, Eon Productions/UA.

VISUAL EFFECTS/SPECIAL ACHIEVEMENT AWARD
1976: Carlo Rambaldi, Glen Robinson, and Frank Van Der Veer for *King Kong*, De Laurentiis/Paramount.
1976: Lyle B. Abbott, Glen Robinson, and Matthew Yuricich for *Logan's Run*, Saul David/MGM.
1978: Colin Chilvers for *Superman*.

SOUND EFFECTS/SPECIAL ACHIEVEMENT AWARD
1977: Benjamin Burtt for *Star Wars'* alien and robot voices, 20th Cent.-Fox.
1977: Frank Warner for *Close Encounters of the Third Kind's* editing, Columbia.

VISUAL EFFECTS

1977: Roy Arbogast, Douglas Trumbull, Matthew Yuricich, Gregory Jein, and Richard Yuricich for *Close Encounters of the Third Kind*, Columbia.

1977: John Stears, John Dykstra, Richard Edlund, Grant McCune, and Robert Blalack for *Star Wars*, 20th Cent.-Fox.

BEST ACTOR

1931: Fredric March for *Dr. Jekyll and Mr. Hyde*, Paramount.

CINEMATOGRAPHY

1977: Vilmos Zsigmond for *Close Encounters of the Third Kind*, Columbia.

ART DIRECTION/SET DECORATION

1966: Jack Martin Smith, Dale Hennessy, Walter M. Scott, and Stuart Reiss for *Fantastic Voyage*, 20th Cent.-Fox.

1977: John Barry, Norman Reynolds, Leslie Dilley, and Roger Christian for *Star Wars*, 20th Cent.-Fox.

SOUND

1977: Don MacDougall, Ray West, Bob Minkler, and Derek Ball for *Star Wars*, 20th Cent.-Fox.

FILM EDITING

1977: Paul Hirsch, Marcia Lucas, and Richard Chew for *Star Wars*, 20th Cent.-Fox.

BEST ORIGINAL SCORE

1977: John Williams for *Star Wars*, 20th Cent.-Fox.

COSTUME DESIGN

1977: John Mollo for *Star Wars*, 20th Cent.-Fox.

HONORARY AWARDS

1964: William Tuttle for his unusual makeup for *The Seven Faces of Dr. Lao*, MGM.

1968: John Chambers for his makeup for *Planet of the Apes*, 20th Cent.-Fox.

SF AWARDS

Hugo. Jupiter. Nebula. Although they may sound like far-off plane-toids or spacey locales, they're just a few of the more famous sf Awards given annually. Here's a quick reference guide to some of science fictiondom's key acknowledgments of merit.

BRITISH SCIENCE FICTION AWARD

Sponsored by the British Science Fiction Association (BSFA), this award was first given in 1966, the recipient being JOHN BRUNNER. Since 1970, the award has been given to books as opposed to individual writers. The method of voting has varied over the years, using both polls of British fandom and the opinions voiced by an elite cadre of judges. The BSFA presentation is a scroll.

DITMAR

An annual award given in Australia at the Australian National Science Fiction Convention, the Ditmar first appeared in 1969. It is awarded to the best Australian fiction of the year, best global fiction, and best Australian fanzine.

HUGO

The "Oscar" of literature, "Hugo" (dubbed for HUGO GERNSBACK) is the slang term used to denote the annual Science Fiction Achievement Award. A fan award, the Hugo is presented solely on the results of polls conducted among attendees of that year's World Convention (the Con is open to anyone who wishes to attend). It was first presented in 1953, at the Cleveland World Con. It was discontinued in 1954 but reinstated in 1955 and it has been an annual event ever since. Today the categories include best novel, best novella, best novelette, best short story, best dramatic presentation, best editor, best artist, best fan-zine, and various special nominations. The Hugo itself is a statuette of incredibly sleek design.

INTERNATIONAL FANTASY AWARD

A short-lived award given in Great Britain for the best sf or fantasy work of the year from 1951 until 1957. The choices were made by a small group of writer/judges.

JOHN W. CAMPBELL AWARD

A recently inaugurated award in honor of the late JOHN W. CAMPBELL, JR., and given to the best new sf writer of the year. The choice is made by sf fans and presented at the annual World Con. It was first given in 1972.

JOHN W. CAMPBELL MEMORIAL AWARD

An annual award given to the best novel of the year, this Memorial statuette was first awarded in 1973, on the basis of a poll conducted among a small group of sf writers (most of whom reside in Great Britain). The award itself is a metal Möbius strip.

JUPITER

Begun in 1973 by the Instructors of Science Fiction in Higher Education (centered at the University of Maine), this annual event singles out the best sf in novel, novella, novelette, and short-story form. They are administered by Dr. Marshall B. Tymm of the English Department at Eastern Michigan University, Ypsilanti, Michigan. The awards themselves take the form of scrolls.

NEBULA

Established in 1966 by the Science Fiction Writers of America, the Nebulas are writing awards given to authors by their peers. Only members of SFWA may nominate and vote. The award is given for best novel, novella, novellette, and short story. In addition, there is a Grand Master trophy for outstanding achievement. Nebulas are awarded annually every April and the winning short fiction is published annually in a collection by Harper & Row.

PRIX APOLLO

First given in France in 1971, this annual literary award is presented to the best sf novel of the year published in that country. Dubbed to commemorate Apollo XI, the Prix Apollo is awarded according to the opinion of a handful of literary critics and writers.

PRIX JULES VERNE

Originally given in the years 1927–33 to novels written in the same adventuresome spirit as that of JULES VERNE, the Prix Jules Verne was largely a ploy by the French publisher Hachette to obtain new fiction for its periodical *Lectures pour tous*. Discontinued in 1933, the awards were once again presented on an annual basis beginning in 1957. The French publishers Hachette and Gallimard were responsible for this resurrection.

THE SCIENCE FICTION FILM AWARDS

Presented yearly by the California-based Academy of Science Fiction, Fantasy and Horror Films (an organization begun in 1972), the SF Film Awards are given according to judgments made by committees composed of one-third fans, one-third professionals in the various fields, and one-third academics. According to the Academy's founder, Dr. Donald Reed, the SF Film Awards are designed to "do for SF, fantasy and horror films what the Oscar has done for general films."

HUGO AWARDS

NOVELS

1953: Alfred BESTER, *The Demolished Man*
1955: Mark CLIFTON and Frank RILEY, *They'd Rather Be Right*
1956: Robert A. HEINLEIN, *Double Star*
1958: Fritz LEIBER, *The Big Time*
1959: James BLISH, *A Case of Conscience*
1960: Robert A. HEINLEIN, *Starship Troopers*
1961: Walter M. MILLER, Jr., *A Canticle for Leibowitz*
1962: Robert A. HEINLEIN, *Stranger in a Strange Land*
1963: Philip K. DICK, *The Man in the High Castle*
1964: Clifford D. SIMAK, *Way Station*
1965: Fritz LEIBER, *The Wanderer*
1966: Roger ZELAZNY, *. . . And Call Me Conrad*, and Frank HER-
BERT, *Dune* (tie)
1967: Robert A. HEINLEIN, *The Moon Is a Harsh Mistress*
1968: Roger ZELAZNY, *Lord of Light*
1969: John BRUNNER, *Stand on Zanzibar*
1970: Ursula K. LE GUIN, *The Left Hand of Darkness*
1971: Larry NIVEN, *Ringworld*
1972: Philip José FARMER, *To Your Scattered Bodies Go*
1973: Isaac ASIMOV, *The Gods Themselves*
1974: Arthur C. CLARKE, *Rendezvous with Rama*
1975: Ursula K. LE GUIN, *The Dispossessed*
1976: Joe HALDEMAN, *The Forever War*
1977: Kate WILHELM, *Where Late the Sweet Birds Sang*
1978: Frederik POHL, *Gateway*
1979: Vonda McINTYRE, *Dreamsnake*

SHORT FICTION

1955
Novelette: Walter M. MILLER, Jr., "The Darfsteller"
Short Story: Eric Frank RUSSELL, "Allamagoosa"

1956
Novelette: Murray LEINSTER, "Exploration Team"
Short Story: Arthur C. CLARKE, "The Star"

1958
Short Story: Avram DAVIDSON, "Or All the Seas with Oysters"

1959
Novelette: Clifford D. SIMAK, "The Big Front Yard"
Short Story: Robert BLOCH, "The Hell-Bound Train"

1960
Short Fiction: Daniel KEYES, "Flowers for Algernon"

1961
Short Story: Poul ANDERSON, "The Longest Voyage"

1962
Short Fiction: Brian W. ALDISS, the "Hothouse" series

1963
Short Fiction: Jack VANCE, "The Dragon Masters"

1964
Short Story: Poul ANDERSON, "No Truce with Kings"

1965
Short Fiction: Gordon R. DICKSON, "Soldier, Ask Not"

1966
Short Fiction: Harlan ELLISON, " 'Repent, Harlequin!' said the Tick-tockman"

1967
Novelette: Jack VANCE, "The Last Castle"
Short Story: Larry NIVEN, "The Neutron Star"

1968
Novella: Anne MCCAFFREY, "Weyr Search," and Philip José FARMER, "Riders of the Purple Wage" (tie)
Novelette: Fritz LEIBER, "Gonna Roll the Bones"
Short Story: Harlan ELLISON, "I Have No Mouth and I Must Scream"

1969
Novella: Robert SILVERBERG, "Nightwings"
Novelette: Poul ANDERSON, "The Sharing of Flesh"
Short Story: Harlan ELLISON, "The Beast That Shouted Love at the Heart of the World"

1970
Novella: Fritz LEIBER, "Ship of Shadows"
Short Story: Samuel R. DELANY, "Time Considered as a Helix of Semi-Precious Stones"

1971
Novella: Fritz LEIBER, "Ill Met in Lankhmar"
Short Story: Theodore STURGEON, "Slow Sculpture"

1972
Novella: Poul ANDERSON, "The Queen of Air and Darkness"
Short Story: Larry NIVEN, "Inconstant Moon"

1973
Novella: Ursula K. LE GUIN, "The Word for World Is Forest"
Novelette: Poul ANDERSON, "Goat Song"
Short Story: R. A. LAFFERTY, "Eurema's Dam," and Frederik POHL
    and C. M. KORNBLUTH, "The Meeting" (tie)

1974
Novella: James TIPTREE, Jr., "The Girl Who Was Plugged In"
Novelette: Harlan ELLISON, "Deathbird"
Short Story: Larry NIVEN, "The Hole Man."

1975
Novella: George R. R. MARTIN, "A Song for Lya"
Novelette: Harlan ELLISON, "Adrift Just Off the Islets of Langerhans,
    Latitude 38°54′ N, Longitude 77° 00′ 13″ W"
Short Story: Larry NIVEN, "The Hole Man"

1976
Novella: Roger ZELAZNY, "Home Is the Hangman"
Novelette: Larry NIVEN, "The Borderland of Sol"
Short Story: Fritz LEIBER, "Catch That Zeppelin"

1977
Novella: Spider ROBINSON, "By Any Other Name," and James TIP-
    TREE, Jr., "Houston, Houston, Do You Read?" (tie)
Novelette: Isaac ASIMOV, "The Bicentennial Man"
Short Story: Joe HALDEMAN, "Tricentennial"

1978
Novella: Spider and Jeanne ROBINSON, "Stardance"
Novelette: Joan VINGE, "Eyes of Mmber"
Short Story: Harlan ELLISON, "Jeffty Is Five"

1979
Novella: John VARLEY, "The Persistence of Vision"
Novelette: Poul ANDERSON, "Hunter's Moon"
Short Story: C. J. CHERRYH, "Cassandra"
New Writer: Stephen DONALDSON
The Gandalf Book-Length Fantasy Award: Anne McCAFFREY, *White
    Dragon*
The Gandalf Grand Master: Ursula K. LE GUIN
Best Dramatic Presentation: Superman (the movie)

NEBULA AWARDS

NOVELS

1965: Frank HERBERT, *Dune*
1966: Daniel KEYES, *Flowers for Algernon,* and Samuel R. DELANY, *Babel-17* (tie)
1967: Samuel R. DELANY, *The Einstein Intersection*
1968: Alexei PANSHIN, *Rite of Passage*
1969: Ursula K. LE GUIN, *The Left Hand of Darkness*
1970: Larry NIVEN, *Ringworld*
1971: Robert SILVERBERG, *A Time of Changes*
1972: Isaac ASIMOV, *The Gods Themselves*
1973: Arthur C. CLARKE, *Rendezvous with Rama*
1974: Ursula K. LE GUIN, *The Dispossessed*
1975: Joe HALDEMAN, *The Forever War*
1976: Frederik POHL, *Man Plus*
1977: Frederik POHL, *Gateway*
1978: Vonda MCINTYRE, *Dreamsnake*

NOVELLAS

1965: Brian W. ALDISS, "The Saliva Tree," and Roger ZELAZNY, "He Who Shapes" (tie)
1966: Jack VANCE, "The Last Castle"
1967: Michael MOORCOCK, "Behold the Man"
1968: Ann MCCAFFREY, "Dragonrider"
1969: Harlan ELLISON, "A Boy and His Dog"
1970: Fritz LEIBER, "Ill Met in Lankhmar"
1971: Katherine MACLEAN, "The Missing Man"
1972: Arthur C. CLARKE, "A Meeting with Medusa"
1973: Gene WOLFE, "The Death of Dr. Island"
1974: Robert SILVERBERG, "Born with the Dead"
1975: Rogert ZELAZNY, "Home Is the Hangman"
1976: James TIPTREE, Jr., "Houston, Houston, Do You Read?"
1977: Spider and Jeanne ROBINSON, "Stardance"
1978: John VARLEY, "The Persistence of Vision"

NOVELETTES

1965: Roger ZELAZNY, "The Doors of His Face, the Lamps of His Mouth"

1966: Gordon R. DICKSON, "Call Him Lord"

1967: Fritz LEIBER, "Gonna Roll the Bones"

1968: Richard WILSON, "Mother to the World"

1969: Samuel R. DELANY, "Time Considered as a Helix of Semi-Precious Stones"

1970: Theodore STURGEON, "Slow Sculpture"

1971: Poul ANDERSON, "The Queen of Air and Darkness"

1972: Poul ANDERSON, "Goat Song"

1973: Vonda MCINTYRE, "Of Mist, and Grass, and Sand"

1974: Gregory BENFORD and Gordon EKLUND, "If the Stars Are Gods"

1975: Tom REAMY, "San Diego Lightfoot Sue"

1976: Isaac ASIMOV, "The Bicentennial Man"

1977: Raccoona SHELDON (James TIPTREE, Jr.), "The Screwfly Solution"

1978: Charles R. GRANT, "A Glow of Candles, a Unicorn's Eye"

SHORT STORIES

1965: Harlan ELLISON, " 'Repent, Harlequin!' said the Ticktockman"

1966: Richard MCKENNA, "The Secret Place"

1967: Samuel R. DELANY, "Aye, and Gomorrah . . ."

1968: Kate WILHELM, "The Planners"

1969: Robert SILVERBERG, "Passengers"

1970: no award

1971: Robert SILVERBERG, "Good News from the Vatican"

1972: Joanna RUSS, "When It Changed"

1973: James TIPTREE, Jr., "Love Is the Plan, the Plan Is Death"

1974: Ursula K. LE GUIN, "The Day Before the Revolution"

1975: Fritz LEIBER, "Catch That Zeppelin"

1976: Charles L. GRANT, "A Crowd of Shadows"

1977: Harlan ELLISON, "Jeffty Is Five"

1978: Edward BRYANT, "Stone"

DRAMATIC PRESENTATION

1973: *Soylent Green*

1974: *Sleeper*

1975: *Young Frankenstein*

1976: no award

1977: no Nebula, but a Special Award to *Star Wars*

1978: no award

GRAND MASTER NEBULA

L. Sprague DE CAMP

SPECIAL RECOGNITION

Jerry SIEGEL and Joe SCHUSTER

THE SF ZINES:
A QUICK GUIDE

What's the oldest sf magazine in existence? What was the first ever published? The following is an alphabetical listing of some of the most famous (and infamous) sf magazines ever to land on the newsstands.

AIR WONDER STORIES (July, 1929–May, 1930) Edited by HUGO GERNS-BACK, this sf pulp later merged with *Science Wonder Stories*. Result: *Wonder Stories*.

ALGOL (1963–   ) Begun as a fanzine in 1963, *Algol* is a magazine about sf. Under the editorship of Andy Porter, it has surpassed itself in terms of quality in both content and appearance. It won a Hugo in 1974 as one of the best fanzines of that year.

ALIEN WORLDS (1966) Edited by Charles Partington and Harry Nadler, this British sf digest lasted but one issue.

ALL-STORY WEEKLY Beginning as a monthly (*All-Story*) in 1905 and becoming a weekly pulp publication March 7, 1914, ASW presented sf and fantasy tales with regularity until its merger with *Argosy Weekly* in 1920. It's best known for running EDGAR RICE BURROUGHS' "John Carter of Mars" series.

AMAZING SCIENCE STORIES (1951) A British pulp that lasted only two issues.

AMAZING STORIES (1926–   ) Founded by HUGO GERNSBACK in April 1926, AS declared itself "the magazine of scientifiction" and inspired scores of sf genre magazines in years to come. Still in existence (barely), the magazine has, through the years, undergone numerous upheavals, some of which resulted in title changes. In March 1958, it was dubbed *Amazing Science Fiction*. Two months later, it was called *Amazing Science Fiction Stories*. In October 1960, it once more became simply *Amazing Stories*.

AMERICAN FICTION (1944–46) A British pocketbook publication edited by Benson Herbert and Walter Gillings, *American Fiction* specialized in the macabre, with frequent excursions into sf.

AMERICAN SCIENCE FICTION MAGAZINE (1952–55) An Australian pulp magazine, published monthly, that specialized in reprints.

A. MERRITT'S FANTASY MAGAZINE (1949–50) Edited by Mary Gnaedinger, this short-lived pulp specialized in sf-fantasy tales.

ARGOSY (1882–43) Best known in contemporary times as a men's adventure magazine, the original *Argosy* was a pulp adventure magazine that offered epic sf-fantasy with marked regularity. Beginning in 1882 as *The Golden Argosy*, it became *The Argosy* in 1888 before mutating into *Argosy Weekly* in 1917, *Argosy All Story Weekly* in 1920, *Argosy Weekly* in 1929, and *Argosy* (a monthly) in 1941. In 1943 it became a men's magazine and the emphasis on sf disappeared.

ARIEL (1976–   ) An oversized paperback publication specializing in graphically illustrated sf-fantasy, *Ariel: The Book of Fantasy* is published on an irregular basis.

ARKHAM SAMPLER (1948–49) A short-lived U.S. magazine dedicated to the work of H.P. LOVECRAFT and his disciples.

ASTONISHING STORIES (1940–43) A U.S. pulp publication that, though it lasted only 16 issues, offered a host of fine stories penned by such young authors as ALFRED BESTER, HENRY KUTTNER, and C. M. KORNBLUTH. This was largely because of the fact that one of its young editors was FRED POHL, who had a habit of using his friends in the book whenever possible.

ASTOUNDING SCIENCE-FICTION/ANALOG (1930–   ) The winner of numerous Hugo awards, *ASF* (later to be known as *Analog*) was begun in January 1930 at the behest of magazine publisher William Clayton. Original editor HARRY BATES dubbed the publication *Astounding Stories of Super-Science*. Its title later amended to simply *Astounding Science-Fiction*, the magazine became the premier publication in the field under the editorship of JOHN W. CAMPBELL, JR. (1937–71). Under Campbell's direction, the magazine flourished during the 1930s and 1940s, but lost some of its luster in the 1960s. The magazine mutated into *Analog Science Fact and Science Fiction* in 1960. BEN BOVA assumed editorship of the magazine in 1971, before leaving in 1978 to become fiction editor of *Omni* magazine.

AUTHENTIC SCIENCE FICTION (1951–57) A British magazine devoted to the genre.

AVON FANTASY READER (1947–52) A digest-sized American effort edited by DONALD A. WOLLHEIM.

AVON SCIENCE FICTION AND FANTASY READER (1953) Lasting two issues, this short-lived publication was published by Avon Books and edited by Sol Cohen.

AVON SCIENCE FICTION READER (1951–52) A digest lasting but three issues. Published by Avon Books, edited by DONALD A. WOLLHEIM.

BEST SCIENCE FICTION (1964) A brief excursion into reprintdom which lasted only two issues.

BEYOND FANTASY FICTION (1953–55) Published by Galaxy Publishing and edited by Horace Gold, this was a companion magazine to *Galaxy Science Fiction.*

BEYOND INFINITY (1967) Edited by Doug Stapleton, this sf-fantasy review lasted one issue.

BLUE BOOK MAGAZINE (1905–52) Originally a pulp fiction magazine (beginning as *Monthly Story Magazine* in 1905, then *Monthly Story Blue Book Magazine* in 1906, and *The Blue Book Magazine* in 1907), *Blue Book Magazine* specialized in sf-fantasy efforts. It became *Blue Book* in 1952 and ceased publishing sf.

CAPTAIN FUTURE (1940–44) An American pulp that lasted 17 issues. Edited by LEO MARGULIES and Mort Weisinger for one year and Oscar J. Friend for three, it was a space-opera zine devoted to the adventures of Curt Newton, a.k.a. Capt. Future.

CAPTAIN HAZZARD (1938) Space swashbuckling that buckled after one issue. Capt. Hazzard was sort of a poor man's Doc Savage.

CAPTAIN ZERO (1949–50) An American publication that lasted three issues. Captain Zero was a fellow who could turn invisible at night, thanks to a nuclear mishap. Most readers couldn't see the point.

COLLIER'S (1888–57) Long-staying American magazine that on occasion offered top-notch sf, including works by H. G. WELLS and RAY BRADBURY. Best known as *Collier's Weekly,* a title it held from 1904 until 1953.

COMET STORIES (1940–41) An American sf effort edited by Orlin Tremaine, it lasted only 18 months and boasted a juvenile editorial slant.

COSMIC SCIENCE STORIES (1950) British pulp magazine that lasted only one issue.

COSMIC STORIES (1941) Lasting three issues, this early sf magazine was edited by DONALD A. WOLLHEIM and featured short fiction by ISAAC ASIMOV, C. M. KORNBLUTH, and other members of the New York–based Futurians.

COSMOS SCIENCE FICTION AND FANTASY MAGAZINE (1953–54) A digest sf-publication that lasted four issues, edited by L. B. Cole. The *Cosmos* title was resurrected in 1977 for a bimonthly publication edited by David G. Hartwell.

DELAP'S FANTASY AND SCIENCE FICTION REVIEW (1975–   ) Edited by Richard Delap, this monthly publication is an exercise in literary criticism, reviewing new fantasy and sf titles as well as offering a complete listing of the month's new books.

DOC SAVAGE MAGAZINE (1933–49) Epic tales of sf-inspired adventure dominated this pulp magazine (which appeared regularly as both a quarterly and a monthly during its long life). Hero Clark Savage, the Man of Bronze, fought villainy with style.

DOCTOR DEATH (1935) Named for its main character, *Doctor Death* magazine recounted the exploits of a villain who was out to destroy the world with science and magic. This New York–based publication lasted three issues.

DREAM WORLD (1957) Edited by PAUL W. FAIRMAN, this American publication lasted three issues and told "stories of incredible power."

DUSTY AYRES AND HIS BATTLE BIRDS (1934–35) Making it for 12 big issues was this juvenile magazine detailing the adventures of Dusty Ayres and his airship brigade. The magazine was edited by Rogers Terrill.

DYNAMIC SCIENCE FICTION (1952–54) An American pulp effort edited by R. W. LOWNDES. It lasted six issues.

DYNAMIC SCIENCE STORIES (1939) Alive for two issues was this American pulp magazine edited by Robert O. Erisman. It was intended to be the sister publication of *Marvel Science Stories*.

ETERNITY SCIENCE FICTION (1972–74) An attempt to present an oversized sf magazine on a regular basis led to four issues of *ESF* appearing on a sporadic basis from editors Stephen Gregg and Scott Edelstein.

FAMOUS FANTASTIC MYSTERIES (1939–53) Basically a publication devoted to reprints, *FFM* lasted some 81 issues under the editorial gaze of Mary Gnaedinger.

FAMOUS SCIENCE FICTION (1966–69) A digest-sized periodical published in the U.S., this reprint magazine lasted nine issues and was edited by R. W. LOWNDES.

FANCIFUL TALES OF TIME AND SPACE (1936) A one-issue American digest-magazine edited by DONALD A. WOLLHEIM and featuring a mixture of sf and the macabre.

FANTASTIC (1952–   ) A long-lived digest-sized magazine, *Fantastic* began as one of the Ziff-Davis publications in 1952, switching ownership in 1965 when the title was bought by Ultimate Publishing. Its editors have included Howard Browne, PAUL W. FAIRMAN, and TED WHITE.

FANTASTIC ADVENTURES (1939–53) The sister publication of *AS*, this Ziff-Davis periodical began as an oversized publication, winding up as a digest-size pulp. Its editors included Ray Palmer, Howard Browne, and William Hamling. In 1953 it merged with *Fantastic*.

FANTASTIC NOVELS (1940–41; 1948–51) A U.S. pulp magazine dedicated to reprinting well-known sf-fantasy tales, this sister publication of *Famous Fantastic Mysteries* lasted five issues in the early 1940s and was revived in the latter part of that decade for 20 more issues. It was edited both times by Mary Gnaedinger.

FANTASTIC SCIENCE FICTION (1952) A juvenile magazine lasting only two issues and edited by Walter Gibson.

FANTASTIC STORY QUARTERLY (1950–55) A reprint publication emanating from the U.S., this pulp lasted 23 issues, beginning as *FS Quarterly* and changing, after four issues, to *Fantastic Story Magazine*. SAM MERWIN, JR., was the original editor.

FANTASTIC UNIVERSE (1953–60) Published by LEO MARGULIES' King-Size Publications, *Fantastic Universe* mixed sf and fantasy, often with exciting results. Editors included SAM MERWIN, JR., Beatrice Jones, Leo Margulies, and Hans Stefan Santesson.

FANTASY BOOK (1947–1951) Lasting eight issues, this irregularly published American periodical was edited by William Crawford under the pseudonym Garrett Ford.

FANTASY FICTION (1950) Lasting two issues, this U.S. digest-size magazine changed its title after its premier tome, becoming *Fantasy Stories* for its second and final appearance. It was edited by Curtis Mitchell.

FANTASY MAGAZINE (1953) Edited by LESTER DEL REY for three of its four issues, this short-lived periodical emanating from the U.S. changed its name to *Fantasy Fiction* after its first issue. HARRY HARRISON edited the last issue, under the pseudonym Cameron Hall.

FUTURE FICTION (1939–43; 1950–60) After offering 17 issues in its first publishing lifetime, *Future Fiction* disappeared for seven years, then offered another 48 issues beginning in 1950. It was originally intended as a sister publication of *Science Fiction,* under the editorship of Charles D. Hornig. R. W. LOWNDES took over the editorship in 1941 and again assumed those duties in 1950. In its first incarnation, it was known as *Future Fiction, Future Combined with Science Fiction* (thus gobbling up its sister magazine), *Future Fantasy and Science Fiction,* and *Science Fiction Stories.* Second time around it was also called *Future Combined with Science Fiction Stories, Future Science Fiction Stories,* and *Future Science Fiction.*

FUTURE SCIENCE FICTION (1953–55; 1967) An Australian digest-sized publication that offered six issues in its first incarnation, two in its second.

FUTURISTIC SCIENCE STORIES (1950–54) A British series of paperback-zines edited by John S. Manning.

FUTURISTIC STORIES (1946–47) A British sf pulp that offered two issues.

GALAXY SCIENCE FICTION (1950–   ) One of the high points of the sf magazine world of the 1950s, the original *Galaxy,* under the editorial guidance of H. G. Gold, offered dozens of classic sf stories and shared the first Hugo award ever given for best magazine (1953). Gold left in 1961 and was replaced, in turn, by FRED POHL, Ejler Jakobsson, James Baen, and J. J. Pierce. During the past few years, the magazine has been published very sporadically and a number of times has been put up on the auction block. At this point, *Galaxy*'s future is insecure at best.

GALAXY SCIENCE FICTION NOVELS (1950–61) A companion piece to *Galaxy,* this sporadically published series reprinted the magazine's most outstanding works.

GALILEO (1978–   ) An exciting oversized format produced in Boston and edited by Charles C. Ryan. Quality fiction and intelligent editorial slanting abound.

GAMMA (1963–65) An American digest-sized magazine lasting five issues and edited by Charles Fritch.

G-8 AND HiS BATTLE ACES (1933–41) An American pulp magazine of the adventuresome, albeit juvenile, variety. Edited by Rogers Terrill and, subsequently, by Aldern H. Norton.

GREAT SCIENCE FICTION (1965–71) Published by the Ultimate Publishing Company, this U.S. digest was composed entirely of reprints. It subsequently became known as *Science Fiction Greats*.

IF (1952–74) An American digest-sized publication, *If* won three Hugos under the editorial hand of FRED POHL (1966, 1967, 1968). Always a bit unfocused, the publication began under the rule of editor PAUL W. FAIRMAN. Fairman, in turn, was succeeded by James Quin, DAMON KNIGHT, H. L. Gold, Pohl, Ejler Jakobsson, and James Baen. In 1967 it was combined with *Worlds of Tomorrow* and rechristened *Worlds of If*.

IMAGINATION (1950–58) An American digest-sized publication that began its existence as *Imagination Stories of Science and Fantasy* before mutating, in 1955, to *Imagination Science Fiction*.

IMAGINATIVE TALES (1954–58) American magazine that started out as the sister publication of *Imagination*. Its last three issues were published under the title *Space Travel*.

INFINITY SCIENCE FICTION (1955–58) An American sf digest that was edited by Larry Shaw and lasted some 20 issues. Although not one of the most popular of genre magazines, it did offer a number of high-quality stories.

INTERNATIONAL SCIENCE FICTION (1967–68) This magazine boasted an interesting premise but garnered little interest on the part of readers. Dedicated to printing the best of global sf, *ISF* lasted two issues. FRED POHL served as editor.

ISAAC ASIMOV'S SCIENCE FICTION MAGAZINE (1977–   ) With ISAAC ASIMOV listed as "Editorial Director," this U.S. digest-sized magazine is a successful attempt to capitalize on the doctor's good name in the genre, offering regular sf by the genre's best-known authors, as well as commentary by Asimov.

MAGAZINE OF FANTASY AND SCIENCE FICTION, THE (1949–   ) One of the oldest genre magazines in existence, *F&SF* was first published in the fall of 1949 as *The Magazine of Fantasy*. Offering imaginative fiction from some of the genre's most respected writers, the publication won Hugos as the best magazine in 1958, 1959, 1960, 1963, 1969, 1970, 1971, and 1972. EDWARD L. FERMAN is the current editor.

MARVEL SCIENCE STORIES (1938–41; 1950–52) Originating in 1938, this American pulp became *Marvel Tales* in 1939. In 1940 its name mutated into *Marvel Stories* before it disappeared until 1950 when *Marvel Science Stories* resurfaced as a digest-sized publication. It was rechristened *Marvel Science Fiction* for its final three issues.

MARVEL TALES (1934–35) Edited by William L. Crawford, this semi-professional publication lasted five issues.

METAL HURLANT/HEAVY METAL (1975–   ) Begun in 1975 in France by Bernard Farkas, Jean-Pierre Dionnet, Jean Giraud, and Philippe Druillet, this oversized sf-comic magazine made its way Stateside as *Heavy Metal* in 1977. Published by 21st Century Publications, *Heavy Metal* is one of the most popular genre magazines in the country. In 1979 TED WHITE assumed the editorship.

MIRACLE SCIENCE AND FANTASY STORIES (1931) Edited by Douglas M. Dold, this U.S. pulp publication lasted two issues.

MOST THRILLING SCIENCE FICTION EVER TOLD, THE (1966–75) A U.S. reprint magazine that offered old stories from *AS* and *Fantastic*. Also known as *Thrilling Science Fiction Stories*.

MYSTERIOUS TRAVELER MAGAZINE (1951–52) Lasting four issues, this American digest-sized publication boasted sf mysteries in its pages until 1952 when, with its fifth issue, it became a straight mystery zine.

MYSTERIOUS WU FANG (1935–36) A short-lived (seven issues) American pulp ripoff of the Fu Manchu school of adventuresome thought, this magazine offered pseudoscience nastiness.

NEW WORLDS (1946–78) Great Britain's longest-running sf magazine, *New Worlds* has had a checkered career, showing up, at various times, as a pulp, a digest-sized magazine, an oversized publication, and a series of paperbacks. In 1946–47 it was edited by E. J. Carnell and appeared on the stands as a standard pulp. In 1949, after two years of dormancy, it reappeared as a digest. In 1964 MICHAEL MOORCOCK assumed editorial duties and *NW* took on paperback size. In 1969 Charles Platt took over Moorcock's position. Although it ceased regular publication in 1970, *NW* has reappeared over the years as a series of paperback books and as an irregularly published periodical.

ORBIT SCIENCE FICTION (1953–54) An American digest-sized publication that churned out five issues and had Jules Saltman as editor.

ORIGINAL SCIENCE FICTION STORIES (1953–60) A U.S. digest-sized periodical edited by R. W. LOWNDES.

OTHER WORLDS (1949–57) An American digest-sized periodical created and edited by Ray Palmer during a time when Palmer served as editor for both *AS* and *Fantastic Adventures*.

OUT OF THIS WORLD ADVENTURES (1950) Editor DONALD A. WOLLHEIM helmed two issues of this pulp magazine, which combined genre fiction with comic-book stories in full color.

PERRY RHODAN (1961–   ) The most popular genre magazine in West Germany, *Perry Rhodan*, created by Walter Ernsting and Karl-Herbert Scheer, features tales of the magazine's spacefaring namesake. In 1979 it began incorporating sections of *Future Life* magazine in its format— the latter being an American futurism publication edited by Robin Snelson and Ed Naha.

PLANET STORIES (1939–55) Dedicated to offering "strange adventures on other worlds," this mainstay sf pulp was edited, over the years, by Malcolm Reiss, Wilber Peacock, Chester Whitehorn, Paul Payne, JEROME BIXBY, and Jack O'Sullivan.

POPULAR SCIENCE FICTION (1953–55) An Australian digest of sf that lasted six issues in the early 1950s. It was revived for two issues in 1967.

ROCKET STORIES (1953) Three mighty issues of this well-intentioned, digest-sized periodical appeared in 1953. It was edited by Wade Kempfert.

SATELLITE SCIENCE FICTION (1956–59) Appearing, at various times, as a digest and an oversized publication, *Satellite* attempted to offer a complete novel every issue. It was edited by SAM MERWIN, JR., and Cylvia Kleinman.

SATURN: THE MAGAZINE OF SCIENCE FICTION (1957–58) Published and edited by Robert C. Sproul, this American digest-sized periodical offered a spacey title and little else.

SCIENCE AND INVENTION (1908–29) Founded by HUGO GERNSBACK, *Science and Invention* started off as *Modern Electrics* and, then, *Electrical Experimenter*, before assuming *S&I* status in 1920. It ceased publication because of bankruptcy.

SCIENCE FANTASY (1950–67) A British digest-sized magazine that became a paperback-zine in 1964, *Science Fantasy* mutated into *Impulse* and *SF Impulse* before disappearing. Its editors included Walter Gillings, John Carnel, Kyril Bonfiglioli, HARRY HARRISON, and Keith Roberts.

SCIENCE FICTION (1939–41) A dozen issues of this U.S. pulp appeared before the title merged with *Future Fiction* in 1941, becoming *Future Combined with Science Fiction.*

SCIENCE FICTION ADVENTURES (1952–54; 1956–58; 1958). The title of three separate magazines. One publication, edited by LESTER DEL REY lasted nine issues and was published by Science Fiction Publications. The second magazine, edited by Larry Shaw, lasted 12 issues. The third publication, emanating from Great Britain, lasted five issues and used reprints from Shaw's U.S. magazine as well as original British entries chosen by British editor John Carnel.

SCIENCE FICTION CLASSICS (1967–75) Also known as *Science Fiction Adventure Classics*, this U.S. digest offered a variety of sf reprints.

SCIENCE FICTION DIGEST (1954) Two issues of this digest-sized magazine edited by Chester Whitehorn appeared on newsstands in 1954.

SCIENCE FICTION LIBRARY (1960) A short-lived paperback magazine published by G. G. Sawn in London. It lasted three issues.

SCIENCE FICTION MONTHLY (1955–57) An Australian sf digest lasted some 18 issues in the mid-1950s. Published by Atlas Publications, it offered fine reprints from American magazines. Also the title of a British magazine that appeared in 1974 on a monthly basis.

SCIENCE FICTION PLUS (1953) A U.S. magazine lasting some seven issues. Published by HUGO GERNSBACK, it was edited by SAM MOSKOWITZ.

SCIENCE FICTION QUARTERLY (1940–43; 1951–58) An American pulp effort that saw two lifetimes. *SFQ* first appeared in the 1940s and offered a complete novel every issue; it lasted ten issues. In its second life, the zine published 28 issues under the editorial eye of R. W. LOWNDES.

SCIENCE STORIES (1953–54) An American digest, this periodical lasted four issues and was edited by Ray Palmer and Bea Mahaffey.

SCIENCE WONDER STORIES (1929–30) HUGO GERNSBACK edited this oversized magazine for a dozen issues, until its demise.

SCIENTIFIC DETECTIVE MONTHLY (1930) Twelve months were not in the cards for this 10-issue extravaganza edited by HUGO GERNSBACK.

SCOOPS (1934) A British juvenile magazine offering "stories of the wonder-world of tomorrow" and edited by Haydn Dimmock.

SF DIGEST (1976) One issue of this British magazine edited by Julie Davis appeared in the mid-1970s, although it was intended to be a quarterly.

SKY WORLDS—CLASSICS IN SCIENCE FICTION (1971) A one-issue effort reprinting tales from the old *Marvel Science Stories*.

SPACE ADVENTURES CLASSICS (1970–1971) American digest consisting of reprints.

SPACE FACT AND FICTION (1954) British pulp periodical geared toward children.

SPACE SCIENCE FICTION (1952–53) An American digest-zine edited by LESTER DEL REY and lasting eight issues. Also, *Space Science Fiction Magazine:* a second digest-zine, edited by Lyle Kenyon Engel and offering two issues.

SPACE STORIES (1952–53) A U.S. pulp that offered five issues under the editorship of Sam Mines.

SPACEWAY (1953–55; 1969–70) An American digest that offered 12 issues before its demise. In 1969–70 it was resurrected for four more issues.

STARTLING STORIES (1939–55) A mainstay pulp periodical, *Startling* combined sf with surprise and offered a complete novel each issue, as well as short fiction. Offering 99 issues in its lifetime, the magazine's editors included Mort Weisinger, Oscar Friend, SAM MERWIN, JR., Sam Mines, and ALEXANDER SAMALMAN. It was intended to be the companion publication of *Thrilling Wonder Stories*.

STIRRING SCIENCE STORIES (1941–42) A brief appearance at the newsstands by this magazine edited by DONALD A. WOLLHEIM occurred in the early 1940s. The publication ran four issues before sinking into the sf sea.

STRAND MAGAZINE (1891–50) A British mainstream publication that, over the years, introduced readers to the works of H. G. WELLS and ARTHUR CONAN DOYLE.

STRANGE ADVENTURES (1946–47) A British pulp periodical that, in its two issues, offered kids stories that were "queer, uncanny and super natural (sic)."

STRANGE STORIES (1939–41) A U.S. pulp effort edited by LEO MARGULIES, SS was a sister publication of *Startling Stories* and *Thrilling Wonder Stories*. It offered 13 issues before dying a strange death.

STRANGE TALES (1931–33) Publishing being stranger than fiction, this companion to *ASF* lasted seven issues before folding. HARRY BATES was editor.

SUPER SCIENCE FICTION (1956–59) An American digest-zine edited by W. W. Scott, this forgettable publication lasted 18 issues.

SUPER SCIENCE STORIES (1940–43; 1949–51) Originally edited by FREDERIK POHL, this magazine lasted 16 issues in its first life and 15 in its second, under the editorial hand of Ejler Jakobsson.

TALES OF TOMORROW (1950–54) British pocketbook-zine published on an irregular basis for 11 issues by John Spencer Publishing of London.

TALES OF WONDER (1937–42) A British pulp periodical, *Tales of Wonder* offered 16 issues before folding. Walter Gillings was the editor.

THRILLING WONDER STORIES (1936–55) *Thrilling Wonder Stories* was the logical extension of HUGO GERNSBACK's *Wonder Stories* publication and lasted 111 issues under the editorship of Mort Weisinger, Oscar Friend, SAM MERWIN, JR., Samuel Mines, and ALEXANDER SAMALMAN. It offered some true classics of the genre over the years but came to the end of the line when, during the decline of the pulps in the 1950s, it was forced to merge with *Startling Stories*.

TOPS IN SCIENCE FICTION (1953) A U.S. magazine that bottomed out after two issues, *Tops* was edited by Jack O'Sullivan (#1) and Malcolm Reiss (#2). It consisted solely of reprints.

TREASURY OF GREAT SCIENCE FICTION STORIES (1964–71) An eight-issue pulp published by Popular Library in the States, this publication consisted of reprints from *Startling Stories* and *Thrilling Wonder Stories*.

UNCANNY STORIES (1941) Uncanny was the fact that this American pulp offered but one issue under the editorial grimace of R. O. Erisman.

UNCANNY TALES (1940–43) A Canadian pulp periodical that produced 21 issues before its demise. It was edited by Lyle Kenyon Engel and mixed reprints with original fiction. Also: a U.S. pulp with the identical title appeared in the U.S. in 1938–40. Edited by R. O. Erisman, it combined sf with sex.

UNKNOWN (1939–43) An American pulp edited by JOHN W. CAMPBELL, JR., *Unknown* was the fantasy companion-piece to *ASF*.

VARGO STATTEN SCIENCE FICTION MAGAZINE (1954–56) A British periodical edited by Vargo Statten (John Russell Fearn) and geared toward the juvenile market.

VENTURE SCIENCE FICTION (1957–70) An American digest, this publication was intended to be the sister periodical to *F&SF*. It lasted 16 issues as both a bimonthly and a quarterly before its demise.

VERTEX (1973–75) An American magazine edited by Donald J. Pfeil, *Vertex* mixed science fact with sf. It published 16 bimonthly issues in its short life-span.

VISION OF TOMORROW (1969–70) A British magazine edited by Philip Harbottle, *Vision* offered good intentions and good fiction for 12 issues.

VOID SCIENCE AND FANTASY (1975–   ) An Australian digest mixing sf with outer-worldliness and edited by Paul Collins.

VORTEX SCIENCE FICTION/VORTEX (1977–   ) *Vortex* is a British magazine begun in 1977 and edited by Keith Seddon. *Vortex Science Fiction* lasted but two issues, in 1953; it was an American digest edited by Chester Whitehorn.

WEIRD TALES (1924–54) If it weren't for bankruptcy, *Weird Tales* would probably still be around today celebrating close to its 55th year of publishing. As it was, a retirement at the age of 30 wasn't all that unrespectable. Founded in 1923 by J. C. Henneberger, the magazine mixed sf with Lovecraftian adventure for years. Its editors included Edwin Baird, Otis Adelbert Kline, FARNSWORTH WRIGHT, and Dorothy McIlwraith.

WEIRD WORLD (1955) A British pulp periodical that offered two issues.

WONDERS OF THE SPACEWAYS (1950–54) A British paperback magazine edited by John Spencer that geared itself toward youthful readers. It lasted 10 issues.

WONDER STORIES (1930–36) A combination of HUGO GERNSBACK's *Air Wonder Stories* and *Science Wonder Stories, Wonder Stories* produced 66 issues before being sold to another publishing house and being redubbed *Thrilling Wonder Stories*.

WORLDS BEYOND (1950–51) An American digest publication edited by DAMON KNIGHT, this magazine was composed of both reprints and original fiction. It lasted only three issues before it went beyond the grasp of newsstands.

WORLDS OF FANTASY (1950–54) A British pocketbook-zine published by John Spencer of London, *Worlds of Fantasy* gave the world 14 out-of-whack issues before disappearing. The title was revived Stateside in 1968–71 for a U.S. digest magazine edited by LESTER DEL REY and, later, Ejler Jakobsson.

WORLDS OF TOMORROW (1963–67; 1970–71) Two lives had this U.S. digest-zine. In the first incarnation, the bimonthly zine went through 23 issues as edited by FRED POHL. Three issues appeared a few years later, edited by Ejler Jakobsson.

THEME AND THEME AGAIN

Throughout the history of sf, several key concepts in terms of plot lines have developed, recurring with marked regularity. Herewith is a Rosetta Stone of sf literature's main categories.

ALIENS Aliens usually appear in stories concerning close encounters with the human race; they are either of a hostile or a benign kind. Examples: *The War of the Worlds,* by H. G. WELLS; "First Contact," by MURRAY LEINSTER; "Who Goes There?" by JOHN W. CAMPBELL, JR. (as Don A. Stuart).

ALTERNATE WORLDS A meticulously constructed theme in which a character or characters journey to an Earth-world whose characteristics points out how society *might* have been on a mirror-image planet or a parallel world. Examples: *House of Many Worlds,* by SAM MERWIN, JR., "Sidewise in Time," by MURRAY LEINSTER; *Eye in the Sky,* by PHILIP K. DICK.

DISASTER A plot line in which expecting the worst proves prophetic indeed. Examples: *When Worlds Collide,* by Balmer and WYLIE; *No Blade of Grass,* by JOHN CHRISTOPHER; *The Drowned World,* by J. G. BALLARD.

ENVIRONMENT Often allegorical, environmental tales take place on future Earth or on different planets, usually portraying societies influenced by environmental quirks taken to their most radical ends. Examples: "Nightfall," by ISAAC ASIMOV; *Dune,* by FRANK HERBERT; the "Dragon" series, by ANNE MCCAFFREY.

FUTURE WORLDS A glimpse into a logically constructed future. Examples: *Last and First Men,* by OLAF STAPLEDON; *The Foundation Trilogy,* by ISAAC ASIMOV.

MACHINES Robots, computers, and various gizmos pop up both to help and harry their inventors in this area of sf thought. Examples: *I, Robot,* by ISAAC ASIMOV; "The Roads Must Roll," by ROBERT HEINLEIN; *Colossus,* by D. F. JONES; *R.U.R.,* by KARL CAPEK.

RELIGION Humanity's beliefs and reasons for beliefs get a workout with marked regularity in the genre. Examples: *Tau Zero*, by POUL ANDERSON; *A Canticle for Leibowitz*, by WALTER M. MILLER, JR.; "Adam and No Eve," by ALFRED BESTER.

SOCIETY/TOMORROW'S SOCIETIES Utopias, dystopias, and various social arrangements are profiled in this attempt to show how humans are either progressing or regressing. Examples: *Nineteen Eighty-four*, by GEORGE ORWELL; *Brave New World*, by ALDOUS HUXLEY; *The Space Merchants*, by F. POHL and C. M. KORNBLUTH; *Fahrenheit 451*, by RAY BRADBURY, "The Country of the Blind" by H. G. WELLS.

SCIENCE Technology of all areas, both beneficial and gone-bonkers, is the star of this train of thought. Mad scientists and mad labs also figure heavily in vintage examples in this category. Examples: *Frankenstein*, by MARY W. SHELLEY; *The Island of Dr. Moreau*, by H. G. WELLS; *Dr. Jekyll and Mr. Hyde*, by ROBERT LOUIS STEVENSON.

SUPERMEN/SUPERPOWERS Superhuman species and superhuman abilities are the main factors involved in this theme. Examples: *Odd John*, by OLAF STAPLEDON; *More Than Human*, by THEODORE STURGEON; *The Immortals*, by JAMES GUNN; *After Many a Summer Dies the Swan*, by ALDOUS HUXLEY.

TRAVELING BEYOND Trips into new worlds, both real and surreal, have long proved to be a favorite pastime of sf heroes. Examples: *The Time Machine*, by H. G. WELLS; *Journey to the Center of the Earth*, by JULES VERNE; *2001: A Space Odyssey*, by ARTHUR C. CLARKE; *At the Earth's Core*, by EDGAR RICE BURROUGHS.

WAR The savage nature of life is portrayed in this combative category. Examples: *The War in the Air*, by H. G. WELLS; *The Men in the Jungle*, by NORMAN SPINRAD; *Final Blackout*, by L. RON HUBBARD.